Texts in Cor

Volume 23

Computation Counts

An Introduction to Analytic Concepts in Computer Science

Volume 10
Foundations of Logic and Theory of Computation
Amílcar Sernadas and Cristina Sernadas

Volume 11
Invariants: A Generative Approach to Programming
Daniel Zingaro

Volume 12
The Mathematics of the Models of Reference
Francesco Berto, Gabriele Rossi and Jacopo Tagliabue

Volume 13
Picturing Programs
Stephen Bloch

Volume 14
JAVA: Just in Time
John Latham

Volume 15
Design and Analysis of Purely Functional Programs
Christian Rinderknecht

Volume 16
Implementing Programming Languages. An Introduction to Compilers and Interpreters
Aarne Ranta, with an appendix coauthored by Markus Forsberg

Volume 17
Acts of the Programme *Semantics and Syntax*. Isaac Newton Institute for the Mathematical
Sciences, January to July 2012.
Arnold Beckmann and Benedikt Löwe, eds.

Volume 18
What Is a Computer and What Can It Do?   An Algorithms-Oriented Introduction to the
Theory of Computation
Thomas C. O'Connell

Volume 19
Computational Logic. Volume 1: Classical Deductive Computing with Classical Logic
Luis M. Augusto

Volume 20
An Introduction to Ontology Engineering
C. Maria Keet

Volume 21
A Mathematical Primer on Computability
Amílcar Sernadas, Cristina Sernadas, João Rasga and Jaime Ramos

Volume 22
Languages, Machines, and Classical Computation
Luis M. Augusto

Volume 23
Computation Counts: An Introduction to Analytic Concepts in Computer Science
Paul E. Dunne

Texts in Computing Series Editor
Ian Mackie   mackie@lix.polytechnique.f

Computation Counts

An Introduction to Analytic Concepts in Computer Science

Paul E. Dunne

ISBN 978-1-84890-310-4

College Publications
Scientific Director: Dov Gabbay
Managing Director: Jane Spurr

http://www.collegepublications.co.uk

Cover produced by Laraine Welch

For

Natalie

and

Jade, Cindy, Josh & Jeremy

Contents

Contents   vii

List of Tables   xv

List of Figures   xvii

List of Algorithms   xix

Preface   xxi

1   Introduction   1
   1.1   Overview and Supporting Motivation   1
   1.2   Background Assumed   4
   1.3   Projects   5
   1.4   Endnote   6
   1.5   On Indices   6

2   The basic computational object
   The idea of Number   7
   2.1   The importance of Number   7
   2.2   Types of number and their use 16
         Representations for $p \in \mathbb{Q}$ 18
   2.3   Beyond Rationality: the class of Real numbers 21
   2.4   Polynomial forms and roots 24
   2.5   Operations involving Polynomials 29
         Polynomial Addition and Scalar Multiplication 30
         Polynomial Multiplication 30
         Polynomial Division 33
         Factorization and Roots 37
         Special cases: closed form solutions 43

2.6   A brief note on Multivariate Polynomials   45
2.7   Summary   47
2.8   Projects   48
2.9   Endnotes   49

3   Creating order
    Vectors and Matrices   **57**
3.1   Imposing structure on collections of objects   57
3.2 n-vectors vs. n-tuples   59
3.3   Operations involving vectors   62
3.4   Vector spaces: Dimension & Independence   76
3.5   A first look at Matrix Algebra   83
3.6   Linear (and non-linear) Transformations   90
      Linear Transformations   92
      Affine Transformations   97
      A Brief Note on Projection and Perspective   99
3.7   Application to Computer Graphics and Animation   99
3.8   Summary 109
3.9   Projects 110
3.10 Endnotes 111

4   The world in motion
    A Basic Introduction to Calculus   **117**
4.1   The origins of Differential Calculus 117
4.2   Functions, Lines and Derivatives 123
4.3   Standard differentiation rules 136
4.4   Turning Points and the Second Derivative Test 139
      Some Examples of Using the Second Derivative Test . 142
4.5   Differential Calculus and Optimization 144
4.6   Digging out roots using Derivatives 152
      Classifying root finding methods 154
      Halley's Method for Finding Roots 155
      Laguerre's Method for Polynomial Roots 156
      Example Comparison of the Two Methods – Polynomial Roots 157
      Summary of Root Finding Techniques 160
4.7   Dealing with several variables 161
      3 or more variables 168
      2 variable optimization example – Management Avarice 169
4.8   Summary of Differential Calculus in CS 173

4.9   Overview of Integral Calculus 174
4.10 Standard integration rules 180
4.11 Summary 184
4.12 Projects 185
4.13 Endnotes 186

5   An unorthodox view of number
     Complex Numbers   **191**
     5.1   Introductory Comments 191
     5.2   Historical origins: "awkward polynomials" 194
     5.3   Basic properties and operations 198
           Complex Addition and Scalar Multiplication 199
           Complex Multiplication 199
           Complex Division 200
     5.4   A multiplicity of forms 202
           Matrix Form 202
           Argand diagrams 202
           Polar Coordinates 203
           Exponent (Euler) form 205
           Summary of different schemes 207
     5.5   Complex Numbers and powers 208
     5.6   Primitive roots of Unity 211
     5.7   Summary of Complex Power Operations 214
     5.8   A selection of computational uses 214
           Laguerre's Method Redux 214
           Quaternions 216
           Properties of typical structures 221
           The Discrete Fourier Transform and its use 224
                Important Computational Properties of the DFT 228
                Inverse Transform 228
                The Convolution Property 230
                DFT and Image Compression 231
                DFT and Large number Arithmetic. 233
                The Cooley-Tukey Fast DFT Algorithm 241
           Music through chaos 246
                Fractals, Computer Art and $\mathbb{C}$ 247
                From $\mathbb{C}$ to Fractal Sets 249
                Voss' $1/f$-music Algorithm 252
     5.9   Summary 254

5.10 Projects 257
5.11 Endnotes 258

6 Computing as experiment
Statistics and Data Analysis   **263**
6.1 Probability theory v. statistics: differences 263
6.2 Classical scientific experimental method 268
6.3 It's not about "machines": artefact & algorithm 271
6.4 Basic statistical concepts 274
    Population and distribution 274
    Random variables 278
    Expectation, mode & median 281
        Expected Value of a random variable 281
    Independence & Conditional Probability 284
        Independent events 286
        Dependent Events 286
    Variance & standard deviation 287
        Probability distributions as "area under a curve" 287
6.5 Adjustment to "Pure" Standard Deviation 294
6.6 The Normal and some discrete distributions 298
        The Normal Distribution $\mathcal{N}(\mu, \sigma^2)$ 298
        The Binomial Distribution 299
        The Geometric Distribution 300
        The Poisson Distribution 301
        Summary of Discrete Probability Distributions 302
6.7 Moments and their application 303
6.8 Confidence and hypothesis testing 306
        Comparing two samples – Welch's Test 312
6.9 Statistical fallacies and misuse 314
        Bigger is not the same as better: large vs. small 314
        Post hoc ergo propter hoc and Causality fallacies . . . 316
        Outlier effects 317
        Reading too much into results: overgeneralizing . . . 318
        Proving the Null Hypothesis 319
6.10 Selected example cases 319
        Constant Factors in Quicksort Implementations 320
        Exam strategy and the Geometric Distribution 322
        Web-page "Hits" 324
        Poisson with Small Data sets 327

          Exam standards Comparison 328
    6.11 Statistics & CS – Summary 330
    6.12 Finding a fit: Interpolation and Extrapolation 331
          Underlying aims of interpolation 331
          Overview 332
              Regression and Residuals 334
          Least Squares approaches 335
              Derivation of Least Squares Approximation 337
          Fitting a line: Linear Regression 339
          Selected Non-linear models 344
          Fitting a curve: Polynomial Interpolation 350
              Quadratic Regression 353
          How good a fit is it? 355
              Pearson's Correlation Coefficient 358
              Spearman's Rank Correlation 360
    6.13 Example Regression & Correlation Cases 364
          Binary Tree Depths 364
          Zipf's Law in Text Analysis 366
    6.14 Summary 370
    6.15 Projects 371
    6.16 Endnotes 372

7   **Matrices revisited**
    Introduction to Spectral Methods   **373**
    7.1   Operations on $n \times n$-matrices 374
    7.2   Inverse Matrices and the Determinant 374
          Computing det **A** 376
              Example 3×3 determinant 378
              Matrix Inverse 379
              Triangular Matrices 380
          The determinant as a sum of permutations 381
    7.3   Matrix Rank and the relationship to singularity 382
              Elementary row operations 384
    7.4   Introduction to Spectral Analysis 387
          The concept of eigenvalue & eigenvector 388
              The determinant as polynomial 391
          Properties of eigenvalues 393
          The Perron-Frobenius Theorem 398
    7.5   Computing Eigenvalues and Eigenvectors 402

Overview of the Power Method 403
The Rayleigh Quotient 406
Finding other eigenvalues and eigenvectors 407
Inverse Power Method 407
Deflation 409
Special Case: Symmetric Matrices 413
Summary 415
7.6   Applications of spectral methods in Computing 416
The Google Page Rank Algorithm 416
The web as a large graph 419
Dead-ends & Dangling Pages 429
Summary 434
Matrices and their Singular Value Decomposition 435
Underlying form of Singular Value Decomposition . . 435
Image Compression through SVD 438
Summary 441
Computational Argument 442
Spectral methods to check instability 449
Conditions that guarantee "good behaviour" 449
Summary – Spectral methods and Argument 450
7.7   Summary – Matrix and Spectral Methods in CS 450
7.8   Projects 452
7.9   Endnotes 453

8   Epilogue   **457**
8.1   Introductory Remarks 457
8.2   Significance and Prospects 458
Numbers & Polynomials 460
Vectors, Matrices and Graphics 462
Calculus & Computer Science 463
Complex Analysis and its Importance in CS 465
Statistical Methods: Computing **is** Empirical 466
Matrices, Spectral Methods and CS 468
8.3   Lacunae 469
8.4   Conclusion – Some Personal Observations 471

Bibliography   **475**

List of Symbols   **495**

Main Index   **497**

Index of Names   **503**

List of Tables

2.1   Number Representation Schemes – Small Values   10
2.2   Number Representation Schemes – Large Values   10
2.3   Some Examples of Polynomials   25
2.4   Roots of $q_3(x) \in \mathbb{R}[X]$ and its discriminant   45
2.5   Roman Fractional Number Schemes   51

3.1   Vector Space Examples   78
3.2   Bases of Finite Vector Spaces   79
3.3   A Clowder of 2-D Graphics Effects   100

4.1   Some Examples of Functions   124
4.2   Selected Plots of Functions in Table 4.1   125
4.3   Line Functions getting "closer" to the line touching $(1, 12)$ 131
4.4   8 Simple Rules for Finding a First Derivative   137
4.5   Halley's Method applied to $f(x) = \sin x + 2x \cos x$ with $x_0 = 3.5$ 156
4.6   Halley's Method applied to $p_5(x)$ with $x_0 = 1$ 158
4.7   Laguerre's Method applied to $p_5(x)$ with $x_0 = 1$ 158
4.8   Halley's Method applied to $p_5(x)$ with $x_0 = 1000.0$ 159
4.9   Laguerre's Method applied to $p_5(x)$ with $x_0 = 1000.0$ 160
4.10 8 Not so Simple Rules for Finding an Anti-derivative   181

6.1   Statistical Measures   296
6.2   Characteristics of Discrete Probability Distributions   302
6.3   Experimental Outcomes for Quicksort Comparisons   321
6.4   Daily Web page Access Per Week over Six Months   325
6.5   Recent Web page Access in past Fortnight   326
6.6   Revised Page Access I   326
6.7   Revised Page Access II   326
6.8   Example Data–Observation Pairs   332

6.9   Four possible fits for Table 6.8 333
6.10 Substitution by $\log_e$ in Table 6.8 346
6.11 Comparison of Linear and Geometric Regression for Table 6.8 . . 347
6.12 Example of Tied Ranking Data 362
6.13 Resolving X_N and Y_N Tied Ranking 363
6.14 Average Depth 364
6.15 Letter Frequencies in Text 366
6.16 Letter Ranking from Table 6.15 367
6.17 Word Ranking 368

7.1   Single dead-ends in the 6 page web 433
7.2   Six shades of Grey(scale) – Image Compression through SVD . . . 441
7.3   Six shades of Colour – Image Compression through SVD 455

List of Figures

2.1   Number as Object and Encoding 16
2.2   Drawing a line of length u/v: $0 < u \leq v$ and $u \in \mathbb{N}$, $v \in \mathbb{N}$. . . . 53
2.3   Drawing a square with area equal to 2 53

3.1   1 (a), 2 (b) and 3-dimensional (c) Coordinate axes. 58
3.2   Basic vector operations 64
3.3   Vector addition from standard position 65
3.4   2 and 3-vector length 66
3.5   Trigonometric interpretation of Vector Length 68
3.6   Geometric interpretation of Vector Dot Product 70
3.7   Geometric interpretation of Vector Cross Product 72
3.8   Left and Right Handed Coordinate Axes 73
3.9   The Right Hand Rule 74
3.10 Combining dot and cross product 75
3.11 Moving a shape in 2 dimensions 97
3.12 Five Different Shearing Effects 101
3.13 Another view of X (A) and Y (B) Shears 103
3.14 Rotation about $< 0, 0 >$ and arbitrary point 106
3.15 Rotation of (u, v) by $\theta°$ counterclockwise about $(0, 0)$. 107
3.16 Rotation of cube about about a line 108
3.17 Traversing the edges of a unit cube. 115

4.1   A "difficult" measurement problem 121
4.2   Arrow direction from Figure 4.1 as "touching lines" 126
4.3   The line between two points 128
4.4   Example Maximization Problem 129
4.5   Approximating the line touching $(1, 12)$ on $9 - x^2 + 4x$ 129
4.6   More detailed view of line from Figure 4.5 130
4.7   Replacing the line to $(1, 12)$ using the line from $(1.5, 11.5)$. 130

4.8   Increase–max–decrease & Decrease–min–increase touching lines.   141
4.9   The function $z = -(3x^2 + 2y^2 + xy)$ between $-2 \leq x, y \leq 2$ . .   162
4.10 Area Computation Problem   175
4.11 Upper and Lower Estimates for Area Problem   176
4.12 Improved Upper and Lower Estimates for Area Problem   176
4.13 3-dimensional volume by rotating $f(x)$ 183

5.1   Polar Coordinates   204
5.2   Polar vs Argand Form   204
5.3   The Karatsuba Multiplication Algorithm   236
5.4   The Mandelbrot Set, $\mathcal{M}$ 251
5.5   Untitled piece produced by Voss' $1/f$-method   254
5.6   Variant of Figure 5.5   261
5.7   Voss $1/f$ algorithm using 3 dice   261

6.1   Outcomes for Fair Coin (20 throws)   288
6.2   Outcomes for Fair Coin (100 throws)   289
6.3   Counting number of standard deviations   293
6.4   The Normal Distribution $\mathcal{N}(0, 0.4)$ 310
6.5   The 95% confidence region (2-tailed) for $\mathcal{N}(0, 0.4)$ 311
6.6   The Poisson process with $\lambda = 3$ 311
6.7   Plot of data in Table 6.8   333
6.8   The line function found by Least Squares for Table 6.8   342
6.9   Correlation Behaviour in Scatter Plots   357
6.10 Average Depth – BST   365
6.11 Best Fit estimate for BST Data in Table 6.14.   365
6.12 Letter Rank v. Frequency   368
6.13 Word Rank v. Frequency   369
6.14 Best-fit line for Figure 6.12   369

7.1   A world of six web pages   420
7.2   Inflating a page's importance   422
7.3   Dead-ends in the 6 page web world   429
7.4   Greyscale Uncompressed Image   439
7.5   A very basic Argument Framework   445
7.6   Possible instantiation of the framework in Figure 7.5   446

List of Algorithms

2.1 Find decimal representation of m 16

2.2 Find decimal expansion of $p = u/v$ 20

2.3 Polynomial Division 37

4.1 Halley's Method for finding roots of $f(x)$ 156

4.2 Laguerre's Method for finding roots of polynomials $p(x)$ . . . 157

5.1 The fast DFT Method: DFT$(\mathbf{x}, n, \omega)$ 245

5.2 Fast inverse DFT method: IDFT$(\mathbf{y}, n, \omega)$ 245

5.3 Approximation of Mandelbrot Set, $\mathcal{M}$, in Complex Plane . . . 250

6.1 Polynomial Interpolation from (X_n, Y_n) 350

7.1 Building an approximation to a dominant eigenvector. 404

Preface

Saepe humanos actus aut provocant aut mitigant amplius exempla quam verba.
("Often the minds of people are inspired, as much as their emotions are calmed,
more by examples than by words.")

Historia calamitatum
PETER ABELARD (1079-1142)

The noted Belgian artist, René Magritte, in one of his most famous works comments on the distinction between appearance and reality. The painting in question depicts a traditional wooden pipe: the sheen and reflection of light from the varnished surface carefully crafted, so also the subtle curve of the mouthpiece and gold band connecting stem and bowl. The whole is shown floating against a background described, in the words of one critic, as having the colour and texture of warm *café au lait*. Magritte, in the body of the painting itself, then offers what may be read as a warning or reminder: the legend presented in a cursive script *"Ceci n'est pas une pipe"*. The viewer, momentarily disconcerted by such an apparent contradiction, eventually recognizes the soundness of the artist's claim guided to this awareness by the work's title: *"La Trahison des Images"*.[1] That a painting *depicts* a smoking accessory does not mean that its beholder is able to *use* the displayed object as such: *"Indeed, this is **not** a pipe – it's a **painting** of one"*.

These opening sentences, perhaps, appear to be a somewhat eccentric digression unrelated to the core substance of the text itself. After all, what could possibly connect the theme of a major 20th century work of art with the presentation of, among other topics, Linear Algebra, Calculus, Complex Numbers and so on? The answer, as I have little doubt many have found in the course of presenting such techniques to audiences of Computer Science students, lies in that single word "appear".

---

[1]The Treachery of Images.

A module dealing with the rudiments of Linear Algebra, say, is one which is likely to be found within the programme of study offered by most Departments of Mathematics. Linear Algebra, in this sense, is therefore *ipso facto* "a Maths course". If we turn to developments in Computer Science, we find a long-established tradition of modelling structures by graphs and networks and thence a natural view of these objects as *matrices*. An interpretation which by exploiting the rich and powerful theory of Matrix Algebra in its deeper elements (e.g. spectral analysis) has led to significant advances being achieved in *computational* settings: web search engines, machine learning, computer graphics, etc. An appreciation of some of these fields would, one hopes, form aspects covered within a typical Computer Science programme: it is in the foundations required on which realistically to build such appreciation that a difficulty emerges. Continuing with the example of Linear Algebra, as a branch of *Mathematics* its presentation to neophytes will emphasize core mathematical concerns: precision of language, terminology and notation; derivation of results by sound and correct deductive reasoning; care and patient attention to detail and analysis. It may, of course, be the case that the force of a particular nuance is helpfully conveyed by recourse to an illustrative application, but what is important is more the understanding of ideas as *Mathematics* and less so the capability creatively to apply these. In Computer Science, and Science and Engineering disciplines generally, the need to instil an awareness of *how* techniques are *used* in *relevant* contexts leads to a situation in which the illustrative application is no longer simply an occasional pedagogical aid to understanding: it becomes the central, core, rationale for their study.

It is this dichotomy in presentation approaches, between study as formal *mathematical* theories and *use* in practice as applied to computational settings that provides the motivation for the style and focus of this book. The intention is to provide a basic awareness of the elements underpinning divers analytic concepts in sufficient depth to present a range of *computational* areas and issues in which these have been applied. Indeed, not only simply applied, but applied with considerable success so that an understanding of *how* these should be deployed in given scenarios is an essential computational skill.

Of course, in order to make clear the nature and use of different methods in a computational setting some knowledge of the techniques in themselves is needed: one cannot hope to demonstrate how matrix-vector products are used to animate shapes on graphical displays to audiences familiar with neither matrices nor vectors. Those embarking on the study of Computer Science to degree level typically have a wide variety of background knowledge: from individuals very well-equipped to pursue mathematics as a specialism to significant numbers who have only minimal (and then, often, achieved some years past) preparation. One has become only too familiar after over thirty years experience working with Computer Science students that this range of preparedness is, often, reflected in an equally wide range of response. There may be a very small number who view the formal elements of Computer Science, such as Logic, Computational Complexity Theory, Semantics etc., enthusiatically and with great interest. On the other side one finds attitudes that range from polite disdain ("It's very interesting but I don't see what its relevance is") through to suspicion bordering on resentment ("Why do I have to study this? It's got nothing to do with CS") to a resigned near refusal to engage ("I can't do Maths and I've never been able to do Maths"). All of which brings matters back to "Appearances". That one opens a discussion on the importance of calculus to CS by way of a discourse on the subtleties of continuity, behaviour of limits, and differentiability is to create an impression (appearance!) that one is presenting a mathematics course so that the significance of differential calculus as, for example, an extremely powerful tool in optimization will be lost: "he's using strange signs and Greek letters: looks like a maths course; he said '*proof*' it *is* a maths course".

There are various tricks one has adopted in the past in order to stress the point that a use of particular signs, symbols and alphabets does not (necessarily) proclaim content to be "mathematical" in nature. Amongst such tricks one tries to design module descriptions in such a way that the word "mathematics" and its variants is zealously shunned in favour of vague substitutes ("formal", "foundational" etc.): this approach, eventually, fails to convince students that a module is presenting CS not Mathematics. On other occasions the word "Mathematics" is scrupulously avoided within lectures: this also fails to achieve the end sought. Finally, one realizes that the most effective means of demonstrating why formal methodologies are of importance to CS is to present the *minimum* of foundational support and couple this with (ideally) copious examples of practical use.

I feel it is important to clarify, possibly even to correct, some impressions that may have been created from what has been written above. So while some length has been expended on the view that a detailed scrutiny of formalism as would be *necessary* for *mathematical needs* could be counterproductive in the context of communicating how specific methods are used, this is by no means dismissing the validity or importance of the former, or for that matter, as expressing any opinion whatsoever on its merits. It is simply to observe that particular bodies of knowledge (e.g. Linear Algebra) are important to many different specialisms (Mathematics, CS, Chemistry, etc.) and that the goals of one discipline differ radically from the goals of others. As such, different emphases come into play depending on the interests of the target audience. It is not a question of one style being "better" than another: they are just different.

Secondly, the observation on how formal techniques are perceived as mathematics and the (in my personal experience) reaction engendered, is precisely that: an observation. It is *not* a criticism of student views still less of those who have expended painstaking efforts in ensuring students are prepared for the rigours of degree level study.

One might speculate endlessly unable to arrive at any enlightening conclusion as to where and why what one might term a "latent hostility/suspicion/fear" towards mathematical ideas and thinking arises. One might ask whether other spheres of intellectual activity face similar problems (e.g. Foreign Languages, Literature, Music) and so one's perception is the result of being focused on a single discipline relevant to CS rather than just an instance of a more general academic malaise (or, perhaps more charitably, *ennui*). Certainly the status of Mathematics is not helped by the infantile conflation of "Mathematics" and "arithmetic" that features rather too often within popular entertainment: as if the facility to recite the seven-times table by rote heralded its declaimer as a potential Fields medallist any more than slavish adherence to the precepts in Gower, Fowler or similar guides, are a portent of a future Nobel Literature laureate.

In the Introduction which follows I will expand in greater depth on the specific areas and topics that will be addressed over the remainder of this book. To those who have perused the table of contents there may be appear to be a significant lacuna. An impression that will be reinforced following the overview within Chapter 1. This concerns the topics, often loosely grouped together under the umbrella heading Discrete Methods: Propositional Logic, Set Theory, Combinatorics, Relational and Boolean algebra, Probability Theory, etc. There is no discussion of these and their absence is quite deliberate. There are several reasons for this. Firstly, the themes covered under this heading have, for over forty years, been recognised as core material within first-year Computer Science programmes. One consequence of this is that there are a large number of excellent, carefully written and targetted textbooks specifically dealing with "Discrete Methods for Computer Scientists". Yet another, even assuming the threshold of excellence set by existing works was attained, cannot be viewed as an essential addition to first-year reading lists. In contrast, it can hardly be claimed that, in comparison with "Discrete Methods", there is a wealth of *relevant* studies addressing "Analytic Concepts". As one looks at the increasing focus within modern CS programmes on ideas such as Data Science, Machine

Learning, Computational Game Theory, and Optimization Theory, and the importance of experimental methods in CS it is clear that the basic supporting tools for their study rely very heavily on the technologies that are the central focus of this book.

Although the presence of an "Analytic Concepts" module is not guaranteed to form part of every CS programme, it does not seem too much of an exaggeration to claim that an introductory level presentation will become a required part of CS programmes. In scientific studies such as Chemistry this has long been the case and one can find many examples of courses and supporting texts with titles such as "Linear Algebra for Chemists" being offered. One cannot, however, simply offer as a guiding textbook something written with first-year Chemists in mind, or first-year Physicists, Biologists, Electrical Engineers etc. Why not? Because the motivating applications will be in the context of Chemistry: in principle one could demonstrate the use of spectral techniques to Computer Scientists by discussing the Estrada Index and its application to analyzing molecular structures; in practice one is likely to achieve more success in this regard by discussing the mechanics of Google's Web Search approach.

To conclude I can appreciate that, having scanned the schedule of topics, a reader may already be forming the impression "This looks like a Maths book". As ably demonstrated by Magritte's image appearances deceive: this is not a "Maths book".

Acknowledgements

This book has its origins in the module "Analytic Techniques for Computer Science" that was introduced within the first year of programmes offered by the Department of Computer Science at the University of Liverpool in 2018. The module itself was added as part of a radical overhaul of undergraduate provision in CS, the design of which was initiated in early 2016. A number of staff in the department were heavily involved in the discussion, evolution and eventual delivery of this.

It is a pleasure to thank all of those who engaged with enthusiasm, creativity, and energy in this exercise.

In particular, Prof. Katie Atkinson who initiated the process shortly after taking over the rôle of Head of Department; Prof. Boris Konev who oversaw its progress and development, as well as undertaking the Herculean task of steering the proposal through the byzantine administrative obstacles which university "quality control" mechanisms consider appropriate to place in the path of creative activity.[2]

Thanks are also due to my colleagues who contributed to this working group: Drs. Floriana Grasso, David Jackson, Russ Martin, Terry Payne and Valentina Tamma.

Initiatives of this scale place a considerable burden on Student Office support staff, and here again, it is a pleasure to take the opportunity to acknowledge the important contribution of Ms. Bethan Birch, Ms. Judith Birtall, Ms. Lindsay Chadwick and Ms. Jan Harding not only in liaising with the academic team but also in ensuring that students (both current and prospective) were kept fully appraised.

A number of invaluable suggestions were provided by reviewers of the proposed structure and the effort expended by both external commentators (Profs. Omer Rana and Anthony Hunter) and internal assessors (Drs. Pascal Salaun and John Satherley) in considering almost one thousand pages of documentation are greatly appreciated.[3] Finally, in respect of individuals who were instrumental in seeing that the new structure was able to begin in September 2017, it would be remiss to fail to mention the rôle played by Prof. Liz Sheffield, who, unprecedented in my 35 year experience at the University of Liverpool brought admirable qualities of competence, efficiency and insight to her senior managerial duties in the Faculty.

I think it is important to acknowledge the contributions of those named in the paragraphs above, since without their efforts the module on which this book is based would, in all likelihood, not exist. There are, however, other, perhaps less obvious aspects. Thus students arriving in the department for the 2017-18 session were the first cohort to follow the new programme structure. An important factor in whether this was received positively throughout the academic year is, of course, the delivery of content. On starting teaching "Analytic Techniques for Computer Science" at the end of January 2018, it quickly became clear just how well students had been prepared from the start of the session. This is in no small part down to the efforts of Prof. Frank Wolter, Mr. Keith Dures, and Dr. John Fearnley in presenting particular specialisms, as well as,

---

[2]I do not consider these terms to be unreasonable: amongst other moving the goalposts actions imposed were a complete change around in programme development processes at the end of discussion: the new paperwork involved, of course, completely incompatible with its predecessor.

[3]It is said that the writer André Gide, presented with a draft of Marcel Proust's *Á la recherche du temps perdu* to review for publication, finding the length off-putting skimmed its contents and rejected the manuscript on the basis of some minor grammatical infelicities. It is gratifying to note the rather more dedicated approach of these four reviewers.

again, Dr. Floriana Grasso and Prof. Boris Konev. The latter's "Foundations of Computer Science" module being an early example of the creative writing of specifications mentioned earlier.

A number of colleagues and students provided valuable feedback regarding the first draft of the text and their comments have been much appreciated. I wish particularly to acknowledge the suggestions of Prof. Paul Spirakis which have considerably improved Chapter 6 from its original drafting. Important and valuable insights were obtained from the thorough and careful reading provided by Mr. Dave Shield as well as the observations and corrections offered by Ms. Doha Moamina, a first-year student who not only tolerated the barbarisms committed on the English language during my lectures but also provided a useful student-level view of the initial text of this volume.

There is one final group of individuals to whom I wish to express my deep gratitude. Without delving into background details, I wish to offer my sincere thanks to all the staff working at the Walton Centre in Liverpool for their dedication and help. In particular, first Dr Woijcech Pietkiewicz, and subsequently Dr. Sundus Alusi; to these should be added Drs. Sarah Jarvis and Heather Walton: their alertness and professionalism were instrumental in ensuring that an obscure issue was not only identified but also, if not eradicated, at least contained.

Chapter 1

Introduction

There is nothing quite so terrifying as the results of education

I am a cat
NATSUME SŌSEKI (1867-1916)

1.1 Overview and Supporting Motivation

This chapter gives an overview of the topics dealt with subsequently together with a preliminary rationale for their inclusion. It is worth noting, as was hinted at in the Preface earlier, that Computer Science is not unique in using a basic grounding in fields such as Linear Algebra, Calculus, Complex Number Theory etc. in order to support understanding of specific applications. If anything, compared to the long standing treatments in Physics, Chemistry, Biology and Medicine, the awareness that such matter to Computer Science has come about relatively recently. In part this is explained through the actual applications having themselves been comparatively recent achievements. For example the links between spectral analysis and web searching, Complex Number Theory and algorithmic composition and so on. In setting Computer Science applications in context, it may be worthwhile, briefly to review some of the uses of analytic concepts within traditional sciences.

Starting with Physics an extensive variety of analytic methods are used. Vector algebra in the modelling of mechanical systems; calculus as an essential tool in studying motion (under both Newtonian and relativistic models) as well as orbits (planetary in addition to sub-atomic). A full treatment of problems in dynamics (e.g. harmonic analysis, wave motion) will involve understanding of

Ordinary Differential Equations. The breadth of mathematical ideas essential
for even a cursory appreciation of Physics has been a factor in its study and
advance for over three centuries, e.g. considering the contributions of such
figures as Isaac Newton in the 17th century, James Clerk Maxwell in the 19th,
through to the major 20th century contributors such as Erwin Schrödinger,
Werner Heisenberg, Paul Dirac, and, of course, Albert Einstein. The intimate
association of the supporting formalisms needed seriously to advance the state
of knowledge in Physics and the subtle move towards a research methodology
that was to become much more mathematical in form almost to the extent of
superceding what had been the classical experimental approach, is the source
of the famous quotation attributed to the great German mathematician David
Hilbert: *"Ach die Physik! Die ist ja für die Physiker viel zu schwer!"*.[1]

In Chemistry, Linear Algebra, sometimes in quite advanced treatments,
is widely used. The central motivation arose by viewing molecular structures as graphs and thence analyzing properties of the matrix defined from
this graph. A classical combinatorial treatment arising from this convention
is that of Pólya's Theory of Counting whereby one important application is
to the enumeration of distinct compounds, see e.g. Pólya [189], Pólya and
Read [190]. The use of advanced linear algebra methods may be found in
areas such as quantum chemistry, e.g. Goldstein and Levey [104], and the formulation of spectral measures via the eigenvalues of a matrix structure, e.g.
the Estrada Index, whose properties were studied over a series of papers by
Estrada [79, 80, 81].

Turning to Biological Sciences one significant area of study is that of models of Population Growth. Here, in addition to stochastic treatments, one finds
models relying on an understanding of differential calculus and spectral methods, e.g. Cushing [52], Tilman *et al.* [234]. Population growth models are also
of importance in studies of how diseases spread, see e.g. Allen *et al.* [8].

In all of these, the importance of experimental methodology means that an
awareness of statistical techniques is essential.

In Computer Science fields such as Machine Learning, Data Science, Advanced Graphics, Optimization, and Computational Game Theory have re-

---

[1]A typical rather free translation is *"Physics is too hard for Physicists"*. This, I feel, somewhat misses the point being raised by Hilbert, rendering the observation an unfair comment
on the limitations of practicioners (Physicists) instead of an accurate insight into the direction
in which the subject (Physics) itself was headed. Physics as a discipline does seem to attract
a number of unflattering observations. Hilbert's is relatively benign compared to the thoughts
expressed by the character Viktor Shtrum, the physicist who is central to a (suppressed) novel
by the Soviet writer Vasily Grossman: "There is a terrible similarity between the principles of
Fascism and those of contemporary physics" [109, Part 1, Chap. 19].

sulted in a significant expansion of the range of specialized formal techniques required in order for a basic appreciation of these areas to be possible. We present a number of such areas over the remainder of this text following the outline summarized below.

Chapter 2 presents the fundamental idea of number. We discuss its importance and summarize the historical development of number representation schemes. We then examine the notion, reflected in most standard programming languages, of differing types of number, where and how these arise and the limitations apparent from the most basic such types. Developing this, we introduce the concept of polynomial form and their roots.

Chapter 3 takes as its starting point the observation that the models advanced in the preceding chapter are unordered and unstructured. There is, however, a need for ordered forms such as the notions of vector and tuple. The latter is discussed with respect to how the object tuple differs from that of vector our main aim, however, is to examine operations on vectors and measures defined on them. The concept of vector space is presented together with their properties. In recognition of the part played by 2 and 3-dimensional vectors in the context of Computer Graphics, we examine how animation effects can be encoded in terms of simple matrix-vector products and the central idea of Linear Transformation.

Chapter 4 considers the importance of Calculus in Computer Science. We examine the concept of function presenting some important examples: polynomial, trigonometric, exponential and logarithmic functions. We consider the motivating origins behind Calculus, showing how the notion of first derivative is formed in a geometric sense and thence to its relevance in understanding the behaviour of functions. These ideas allow a demonstration of how solutions to basic optimization cases can be obtained. We examine how ideas from differential calculus lead to algorithms for approximating the roots of different functions. Our review of methodologies within differential calculus continues with some basic methods for dealing with functions that are dependent on several variables, our previous analyses having dealt with single argument instances. The chapter concludes with a short overview of integral calculus and its origins as a solution approach to area measurement questions.

Chapter 5 returns to an issue arising, but unresolved, at the end of Chapter 2: the existence of polynomial forms without roots belonging to the number types considered. We present the rudiments of Complex Numbers as a means of addressing this issue, arguing that the notational device used is no different, in principle, from established notational conventions. We examine operations on and properties of Complex numbers together with the variety of equivalent representation forms. In discussing applications fields within Computer Science we review how the idea of Complex algebra can be interpreted as a starting model for quaternions and the important use of the latter technology in modern advanced graphics. In addition we summarize how Complex Analysis was applied in developing a rich technical theory of average-case analysis. We also examine ideas involved in Fourier Transforms. In conclusion we consider how the concept of fractal sets has been exploited in the specialized AI field of computational creativity, in particular its use in Algorithmic Composition.

Chapter 6 promotes the argument for Computer Science as an experimental discipline in which the classical scientific experimental methodologies are relevant. We distinguish "Computer Science as the study of artefacts" from "Computer Science as the study of process" and the attendant scenarios wherein this distinction is important. As an experimental discipline the relevance of statistical techniques is clear, and we present the basic elements used in statistics, distinguishing the rationale of Statistics from that of Probability Theory. This chapter concludes with a very elementary review of techniques for analyzing data points, in particular the notion of interpolation. We present some standard approaches for finding best-fit lines and polynomials within given data sets as well as discussing techniques, e.g. correlation coefficients for assessing the accuracy of the results.

Chapter 7 continues the treatment of Linear Algebra initiated in Chapter 3. Here the notions of determinant, singularity and inverse are examined. The central aim of this Chapter, however, is to give an introduction to the topic of Spectral Analysis. The importance of this subject in Computer Science is illustrated with examples from Web Search, Image Compression and Computational Argument.

Chapter 8 offers some concluding remarks and highlights further contexts in which the techniques presented earlier may be encountered and used.

We stress that, in general, we shall eschew formal technical exposition of proofs. Our focus is on methods (for example, an *algorithmic* treatment of determinant computation) and on applications within CS (hence illustrating *why* the determinant of a matrix may be an object which it is useful to be able to compute).

1.2   Background Assumed

In general it is assumed that readers are familiar, or at least comfortable, with basic arithmetic operations ($+, -, \times, \div$, powers of numbers), set notation and operations such as membership ($\in$), union ($\cup$), and intersection ($\cap$). Similarly some awareness of the notion of modular arithmetic at least to the level of counting in binary etc., while not essential would certainly be of assistance. Some ease with algebraic manipulations as may be involved in multiplying out expressions such as $(x + y)(u + v)$ would also be helpful, although concepts such as the Binomial Theorem and its application in expanding expressions such as $(x + y)^n$ are not required. Further assumed are familiarity with coordinate schemes, e.g. the (x, y)-Cartesian axes, basic trigonometric functions and their behaviour (sin, cos and tan) and the notions of logarithms and bases. Some awareness of the process of graphing or plotting functions is also assumed. Most of these ideas one assumes will have been encountered either at school level or within an introductory Discrete Topics module within the first-year (fresher year) of a Computer Science Bachelor's degree programme.

1.3 Projects

It is, I believe, customary in works such as the present one to offer at the conclusion of each technical chapter long screeds of "exercises" in order to drill into the reader the exact matters that have been the topic of the previous pages' content. Customary it may well be: helpful it is not. There is little useful purpose served in aiding appreciation of polynomial expressions in asking readers to test their grasp of concepts by factoring examples, by extracting roots, by listing degrees and coefficient sets etc etc etc *ad nauseam*. Not only is such legerdemain unlikely to arise in practice but also where such prowess is called for any sensible individual will seek the assistance of tools already designed and tested.

The above paragraph, however, is not to deny the importance of experience in actual use as a help to understanding. This, I feel, is more likely to be achieved not through variation-on-a-theme repetition but rather through trying to use the techniques in realistic contexts.

I have added what are dubbed **Projects**: rather larger scale implementation style tasks involving development of a software solution. In my view understanding the subtleties of, say polynomial division, is more readily achieved having attempted to implement an algorithm which given two polynomial expressions as input proceeds to report their quotient and remainder, than would be accomplished by the destruction of acres of forest sacrificed to produce paper on which to hack though two or three "small" examples "by hand".

1.4   Endnote

1. In a number of chapters there will be a short section of further commentary at the conclusion. These provide some further details on specific points that would, were they to be included in the main text, be rather too disruptive to the main argument. Readers uninterested in such points of elucidation may omit with no loss of technical insight.

1.5   On Indices

As well as the undoubtedly, vastly inadequate, main index, a List of Symbols and an Index of Names, are given. The former (should) indicate the first place in the text where a particular notation is introduced and the latter, while aiming to be exhaustive may suffer from omissions. Such of these as are present are solely the result of author incompetence rather than an intention to slight.

Chapter 2

The basic computational object
The idea of Number

Numbers, however, will account for a great proportion of unbalanced
and suffering humanity.

At Swim-Two-Birds
FLANN O'BRIEN (1911–1966)

2.1 The importance of Number

Number is pervasive. The concept of numbers and their manipulation domi-
nates all spheres of endeavour, every action, every facet of ordinary life. We
count; we measure; we calculate. Everyday we pose questions such as "How
much will this cost?", "Are you sure that's the correct change?", "Do I have
enough petrol left?", "What's the speed limit on this road?", "How long will
this take?", "How old are they?". Students obsess over "marks", managers
over "costs" and "resources", customers over "value", politicians over "poll
standings" and governments over "revenue and balances". We browse titles on
bookshelves only to find *Catch-22*, *Fahrenheit 451*, *The House of the Seven
Gables*, *The Four Horsemen of the Apocalypse* and *Butterfield 8*. In cinemas
we are offered *Deux ou trois choses je sais de qu'elle*, *3 Colours: Blue*, *Five
Easy Pieces*, *The Seven Samurai*, *14 Hours*, and, as if the gallimaufry of whole
values were insufficient, $8\frac{1}{2}$ and $9\frac{1}{2}$ *Weeks*. The theatre brings *6 Characters
in Search of an Author*, *The Servant of Two Masters* and *The 3 Sisters*. The
opera-house presents *Two Widows*, *The Love for Three Oranges* and, on par-

ticularly bleak evenings, *4 Saints in 3 Acts*. Even the concert-hall may find us confronted with, in addition to numbered works (symphonies, concerti, etc) the prospect of "listening" to $4'$ $33''$ or performances of Schmidt's *Das Buch mit Sieben Siegeln*[1] or Stockhausen's *Aus den sieben Tagen*.[2]

These phenomena are neither recent nor occasioned through the now ubiquitous availability of computational devices: whether electronic calculator, smart phone, tablet or laptop/notebook computer. The potential for number to dominate and obsess thought processes is commented upon in the concluding passages of Flann O'Brien's 1939 comic novel quoted from above. The great Austrian composer, Anton Bruckner (1824–96), no stranger to debilitating psychological ailments, was for much of his life afflicted with the obsessive-compulsive disorder known as numeromania sufferers from which feel compelled constantly to count and enumerate what seem trivial minutiae to on-lookers: leaves on trees, raindrops on windows, etc. Bruckner was at least able partially to sublimate his obsession in the magisterial architecture of his symphonic works:[3] not all are as fortunate.

In total we find the abstraction of number, counting and measurement to be deeply embedded, subconsciously colouring all manner of activity. It is, of course, not the only such abstraction: one other important instance is that of language. The evolution of spoken language and the subsequent enrichment to notions of *written* expression forms one hugely significant watershed in societal and cultural development. The awareness of number and the concomitant emergence of effective representation methods marks another. Language provides the power to *describe* the world around us and to pass on by oral and written tradition our knowledge of this world. Number and the associated manipulation processes offers the potential not only to describe but also to change, adapt and plan. If this seems like an exaggeration, one need only consider the range of real issues which language *alone* is powerless to manage: determining the *length* of time governing seasonally dependent activities, e.g. planting and gathering crops, awareness of animal migration patterns with respect to hunting; planning *how much* of a crop is surplus to requirements and, indeed, what

---

[1]Franz Schmidt's intense setting of the Book of Revelation is badly neglected. Although a number of excellent recordings have been made, actual performances are extremely rare (bordering on non-existent). Possibly concert promoters are, mistakenly, under the impression that Schmidt's interpretation of Revn 8:1 is over literal.

[2]Although the unorthodox demands of this work make the chances of finding scheduled performances rather small.

[3]Whereas typically a composer's symphonic oeuvre is numbered from 1, Bruckner's includes, in addition to the standard 1 through 9, not only a Symphony No. 0 (WAB 100 in D minor, *"Die Nullte"*) but also a Symphony No. 00 (WAB 99 in F minor, "Study Symphony").

defines such requirements in terms of typical daily *amounts* used; similarly, estimating reliably *how much space* should be allocated to storing such surplus. As social groups moved from extended family units through to loose communities (villages, towns etc.) through to concepts of state and national bloc intricate questions concerning economic balance arose involving allocation of resources among competing interests. For example, defence against external threats whether environmental such as flood and extreme climactic conditions or from other communities; infrastructure (roads, communal facilities, housing) and welfare concerns such as provision for children, older members, etc. It is against such backgrounds that the fundamental computational question emerges: "How do I *count* and *measure* this object?". The object may be a population size, an area of land and matters of its division into sub-plots, an incentive to undertake unpleasant tasks (work, pay taxes, military service, etc), an equitable division of rights and responsibilities.[4]

We cannot address questions of the nature presented in the last paragraph without *computational* means. Such means must operate on some basic elemental structure: that structure is *Number*. Would that it were so simple! We need one further step before the concept of number can begin to approach its full potential. We have been presenting the idea of number as an abstraction, an entity that we manipulate in calculating some desired quantity: we cannot manipulate abstractions, e.g. try to conduct a census whereby a population size is reported as an abstract object. We need to be able to *record* outcomes and, in satisfying such needs, we must use some effective *representation* scheme. In the remainder of this opening section we examine this question of representation.

In an extremely loose sense we can divide the most widely-used historical number representation schemes into two classes: "tally" or "unary" styles; and "positional" schemes relative to some *base*. Under the former we find methods such as marks made on an available medium, e.g. notches cut into a stick of wood. We also have, apparently more subtle approaches such as the systems adopted in classical Greek forms or structures such as Roman numerals as presented in Table 2.1 and Table 2.2.

Note: The characters for 6 (digamma, F), 90 (koppa) and 900 (san) became obsolete and do not feature in the standard 24 character Greek alphabet.

The tally, Greek and Roman systems quickly become unwieldly.

---

[4]It is not claimed, of course, that the results of calculation would, necessarily be observed: should *calculation* suggest that a fair tax levy is for all adults to contribute 10% of earnings, this is very far from guaranteeing that such a fiscal policy will be adopted or, even in the event of it being so, that all individuals will act in accordance with its stipulations.

Table 2.1: Number Representation Schemes – Small Values

Tally	Greek	Roman	Modern	Tally	Greek	Roman	Modern
I	α	I	1	卌 卌	ι	X	10
II	β	II	2		κ	XX	20
III	γ	III	3		λ	XXX	30
IIII	δ	IV	4		μ	XL	40
卌	ε	V	5		ν	L	50
卌 I	F	VI	6		ξ	LX	60
卌 II	ζ	VII	7		o	LXX	70
卌 III	η	VI	8		π	LXXX	80
卌 IIII	θ	IX	9		"koppa"	XC	90

Table 2.2: Number Representation Schemes – Large Values

Greek	Roman	Modern	Greek	Roman	Modern
ρ	C	100	$\overset{\alpha}{M}$	$\overline{X}$	10000
σ	CC	200	$\overset{\beta}{M}$	$\overline{XX}$	20000
φ	D	500	$\overset{\varepsilon}{M}$	$\overline{L}$	50000
${}^{\iota}A$	M	1000	$\overset{\iota}{M}$	$\overline{C}$	100000
${}^{\iota}E$	$\overline{V}$	5000	$\overset{\rho}{M}$	$\overline{M}$	1000000

The tally system may be interpreted as a pure unary method: a single mark being used and the strike-through convention e.g. ~~group~~, to collect like size groups together for visual convenience. On the surface the Greek and Roman methods seem more flexible and to be using, an albeit primitive, positional form similar to modern style. While it is true that, in common with modern usage, the Greek convention is able to represent numbers between 1 and 9999 using as few characters as contemporary systems, the manner in which it does so is *not* positional: the numbers 532 and 235 (modern) correspond to (Greek) $\varphi\lambda\beta$ and $\sigma\lambda\varepsilon$ respectively. The significance of the symbol 5 in the two latter-day usages is that the *position* (of 5) distinguishes the quantities $5 \cdot 10^2$ and $5 \cdot 10^0$. In the older form two *distinct* symbols (φ and ε) are used. In contemporary notation the same symbol (i.e. 5) has two distinct interpretations (as 5 and as $5 \cdot 10^2$) depending on the *position* at which it occurs.

For very large quantities this method requires quite involved notational contortions: e.g. the use of $\overset{w}{\mathrm{M}}$ to prescribe multiplication of the value in w by $10,000$.[5]

We find similar, arguably worse, complications with the mechanism of Roman numerals: although limited to a basic set of seven characters, large values necessitate using systems such as the *vinculum*, whereby a bar is written over a number to express "multiply by 1000".[6]

The Roman and Greek systems offer a range of methods for describing large numerical values and systems such as these are just about adequate as a means with which to represent quantities. But to compute with? Consider the outcome of the Roman numeral calculations MDCXXXVIII $\div$ CCLXXIII and CDXL $\div$ V. The former calculation reports VI whereas the latter reports LXXXVIII. In contemporary notation we have $1638 \div 273 = 6$ and $440 \div 5 = 88$. We can, immediately, identify one issue with these outcomes: the first calculation replaces an expression involving 18 symbols with a result using only 2. The second, however, replaces 5 symbols with an outcome having 8. Overall there appears to be little connection between the input length and the output. For contemporary styles we can very roughly estimate how large the output value will be: in the corresponding computations a "number in the thousands" is divided by a "number in the hundreds": we expect an outcome of "some number of units". Similarly the second example has "a number in the hundreds" divided by a "number of units": we expect an answer to be "some number of tens". Both expectations are satisfied in the representation found.

In 1202 Leonardo of Pisa[7] published the *Liber Abaci*, a work in which the Indo–Arabic *decimal positional* system with an *explicit* symbol for the value zero was presented.[8] As has been observed by Bailey and Borwein [18], full acceptance of this system in Europe took almost six centuries. One can identify two causes for this hiatus: accountants and religious zealotry. With respect to

---

[5]The value M, in addition to being the point at which the alphabetic approaches of Table 2.1 begin to be problematic has some significance as the historian Herodotus' estimate of the size of the Persian forces at the battle of Marathon (490BC): the suggestion being given the exhaustion of basic letter schemes after the value 9999 that these forces were uncountable. The Greek word $\mu\nu\rho\iota\omicron\iota$ used gives the source of the English word "myriad".

[6]The *vinculum* was just one of the notational devices adopted by Roman arithmeticians. Perhaps less well-known, but equally contorted, is the *apostrophus* whereby values are composed using CIƆ to indicate multiplying by higher and higher powers of 10, e.g. IƆ is 500, CIƆ describes 1000 and CCCIƆƆƆ represents 100,000. More involved expressions are possible: 10,515 being CCIƆƆIƆXV. Here CCIƆƆ is 10,000; IƆ is 500 and XV the number 15: all of which are added to give the result.

[7]Also, possibly better, known as Fibonacci.

[8]Strictly speaking *re*-presented, see Endnote 2.

the former: manipulating figures in Roman numerals was a highly-skilled task, and those adept in this skill were in great demand. Even figures such as the essayist Montaigne (1533–1592) had no qualms about admitting their inability to grasp arithmetical skills.[9] European universities of the time varied widely in their depth of study of arithmetical technique.[10]

So why should accountants feel hostile to a system that will make their tasks easier? Precisely because it *will* make things easier. A system in which a child can accomplish in a matter of minutes computations that had hitherto taken skilled practicioners several months is a threat to the standing of the profession.

And religious zeal? Despite its disseminators both Arab scholars such as the 10th century al-Khowarizmi[11] and European advocates rightly attributing the discovery to sources on the Indian sub-continent, suspicion remained that "decimals with zero" represented some form of Islamic propaganda meriting suppression by the recognized authorities.[12]

The two aspects – **positional notation** and **explicit representation** of *zero* – have rightly been emphasized by Bailey and Borwein [18], as being of huge significance in developing effective computational methods.

Once we have "positional notation in decimal" accepted it is a short step to "positional notation" in *other bases*: 2 (binary) 8 (octal) and 16 (hexadecimal).[13]

We have been seeing this term "positional notation" rather a lot, seemingly assuming an intuitive sense of its meaning. We now offer a more precise formulation: what *exactly* do we mean by "positional notation with respect to some *base*"?

Let us start taking the notion of a symbol for zero/nought/nothing as a given with the concrete example of *decimal*. We have *ten symbols*:

$$\{0, 1, 2, 3, 4, 5, 6, 7, 8, 9\}.$$

When we write some *sequence* of these in *order* from left to right this sequence describes (represents) a *numerical quantity*. Furthermore, if the first (i.e. left-

---

[9] cf. *Essays, Book II, Ch. 17; 652*

[10] Ifrah [125, p. 577] quotes the advice given to a wealthy merchant about where his son should study: *"If you only want him to be able to cope with addition and subtraction, then any French or German university will do. But if you are intent on your son going on to multiplication and division – assuming that he has sufficient gifts – then you will have to send him to Italy.".*

[11] Whose achievement is recognized in the English word *algorithm*.

[12] Ifrah [125, pp. 588-9] discusses the association with occult practices still permeating language via the word "cipher" (a secret message) and its derivation from the Arabic *"zephir"* (or zero).

[13] Some further examples are mentioned in Endnote 3.

most) symbol in the sequence is *not* the symbol 0, then the sequence describes a *unique* such quantity. Which quantity? That obtained by *adding* the outcome of *multiplying digits* by increasing *powers of 10* moving from right to left. The initial power of 10, i.e. the one by which the *rightmost* digit is multiplied, being 10^0: in other words the value 1.

Here is a small example. The *sequence* 2565 describes the *number* resulting from the computation:

$$5 \; + \; 60 \; + \; 500 \; + \; 2000$$

Or, equivalently,

$$5 \cdot 10^0 \; + \; 6 \cdot 10^1 \; + \; 5 \cdot 10^2 \; + \; 2 \cdot 10^3$$

Looking more closely at this example we can note two points. Firstly although the quantity is **written** with the individual digits presented from left to right (i.e. 2 then 5 then 6 then 5) it is **evaluated** moving from rightmost digit to leftmost: 5 is *added to* 60; the result is added to 500 and, finally the total is added to 2000.

The second point of importance is the two different views of the digit 5: these are disambiguated by considering the *place* (position) within the sequence of each occurrence: reading right to left, the first (*least significant*) place is that describing the number of units ($5 \cdot 10^0$); the next occurrence of the digit 5 gives the number of hundreds ($5 \cdot 10^2$).

In general, suppose our sequence contains k digits for some value of k at least 1, these being

$$d_{k-1} \; d_{k-2} \; d_{k-3} \; \cdots \; d_3 \; d_2 \; d_1 \; d_0$$

Following our "add the results of multiplying the digit d_r by 10^r" method shows that this sequence corresponds to the *number*

$$d_0 + d_1 \cdot 10 + d_2 \cdot 100 + d_3 \cdot 1000 + \; \cdots \; + d_r \cdot 10^r + \; \cdots \; + d_{k-1} \cdot 10^{k-1}$$

Or, in shorter form,

$$\sum_{r=0}^{k-1} d_r \cdot 10^r$$

The reason for the rider "the first, i.e. leftmost, symbol in the sequence is *not* the symbol 0" as a prerequisite for uniqueness of interpretation should now be clear: suppose the symbols d_{k-1} through to d_t all equal 0 and that d_{t-1} is one of the digits $\{1, 2, 3, 4, 5, 6, 7, 8, 9\}$. Then we find that the number described by

$$d_{k-1}d_{k-2}\cdots d_{t+1}d_td_{t-1}d_{t-2}\cdots d_2d_1d_0$$

is, for each value of n between k and t, *exactly the same* as that described by

$$d_{n-1}d_{n-2}\cdots d_{t+1}d_td_{t-1}d_{t-2}\cdots d_2d_1d_0$$

And this value is

$$\sum_{r=0}^{n-1} d_r 10^r \;=\; \sum_{r=0}^{t-1} d_r 10^r \;+\; \sum_{r=t}^{n-1} 0 \cdot 10^r \;=\; \sum_{r=0}^{t-1} d_r 10^r$$

The ten distinct digits prescribed within the decimal system and the mapping from sequences of digits to numerical quantities is reasonably familiar from everyday experience. As all Computer Scientists are aware, we are not restricted to ten symbols. This is where the concept of number base arises. Another term for "decimal representation" is that it uses *base* ten. Hence, sequences of symbols chosen from ten available translate to the numerical value expressed by "summing symbol values multiplied by an appropriate power of ten".

It is often the case in Computer Science settings that "base 8" (octal) or "base 2" (binary) are used. We follow very much the same processes here as were used in describing decimal forms: for decimal the defining value (base) is 10; for octal it will be 8; for binary 2.

In these two instances we no longer need the full set of ten digits used before. Octal symbols will be $\{0, 1, 2, 3, 4, 5, 6, 7\}$ and binary $\{0, 1\}$. How do we now interpret the *numerical value* of a sequence of *octal* symbols?

We adopt the convention that $(\cdots)_{base}$ describes the fact that the symbols within $\cdots$ are to be interpreted as values in the given *base*. In this way $(2565)_8$ defines a *different* numerical quantity than $(2565)_{10}$.

Considering the example 2565 but now reading the individual symbols as *octal* values the corresponding numerical quantity is found as the outcome of the calculation

$$5 \cdot 8^0 \;+\; 6 \cdot 8^1 \;+\; 5 \cdot 8^2 \;+\; 2 \cdot 8^3$$

That is,

$$5 \;+\; 6 \cdot 8 \;+\; 5 \cdot 64 \;+\; 2 \cdot 512$$

Recall that in *decimal* this sequence of four symbols described the quantity:

$$5 \cdot 10^0 \;+\; 6 \cdot 10^1 \;+\; 5 \cdot 10^2 \;+\; 2 \cdot 10^3$$

Elementary arithmetic easily shows that the **decimal encoding** of $(2565)_8$ turns out to be

$$(2565)_8 \; = \; (5 + 48 + 320 + 1024) \; = \; (1397)_{10}$$

With a little more work we find that,

$$(2565)_{10} \; = \; 5 \cdot 8^0 \; + \; 0 \cdot 8^1 + 0 \cdot 8^2 + 5 \cdot 8^3$$

so that, just as $(2565)_8 = (1397)_{10}$ so too $(2565)_{10} = (5005)_8$.

In binary, we now use powers of *two* and the symbols $\{0, 1\}$ with the outcome

$$\begin{aligned} (2565)_{10} & = (1010000000101)_2 \\ & = 2^{11} + 2^9 + 2^2 + 2^0 \\ & = (2048)_{10} + (512)_{10} + (4)_{10} + 1 \end{aligned}$$

We are, of course, not limited to bases containing at most 10 symbols. Again another common form in Computer Science is *hexadecimal* or base 16. In this, for convenience of notation the decimal symbol set is extended using six new symbols $\{A, B, C, D, E, F\}$. These defining the *numerical* values $\{10, 11, 12, 13, 14, 15\}$. What is the numerical value of 2565 when the symbols are treated as *hexadecimal*, i.e. the corresponding decimal form of $(2565)_{16}$? It is simply

$$5 + 6 \cdot 16 + 5 \cdot 256 + 2 \cdot 4096 \; = \; 5 \cdot 16^0 + 6 \cdot 16^1 + 5 \cdot 16^2 + 2 \cdot 16^3 \; = \; (9573)_{10}$$

Similarly, $(2565)_{10}$ turns out to be $(A05)_{16}$, i.e. $5 + 0 \cdot 16 + 10 \cdot 256$

We have considered, in the above development, the process by which a *representation* of some quantity expressed in a specific number base is translated to recover the actual quantity itself. What about the reverse process? That is, suppose we have some quantity, m say, and we wish to form for a given base the sequence of symbols, $\rho(m)$ with the property that $(\rho(m))_{base} = m$.

Again we start with the concrete example of decimal. For a given $m \geq 0$ there is a unique value, r, with $0 \leq r \leq 9$ with the property that $(m - r)$ is an *exact multiple* of 10. In writing m in decimal we let d_0 be this value r. In standard programming language terminology d_0 is the *remainder* resulting when m is divided by 10. Now we can apply a related process to find the remaining digits. First subtract d_0 from m. The result will be an exact multiple of 10 so we can *divide* the quantity $(m - d_0)$ by 10 without any left-over. And now we apply exactly the same process to $(m - d_0)/10$ to obtain d_1. Writing this in pseudo-code we get the method in Algorithm 2.1.

Algorithm 2.1. Find decimal representation of m

1: $k := 0$;
2: **while** $m > 0$ **do**
3:     $d_k := m \bmod 10$ {d_k is the *remainder* after dividing m by 10}
4:     $m := (m - d_k)/10$ {10 divides $m - d_k$ without remainder.}
5:     $k := k + 1$ {Find next digit (going right to left)}
6: **end while**

If, instead of decimal we wish to use octal or binary or hexadecimal or, indeed, *any* fixed base, b say, then all that is needed is to replace every occurrence of the number 10 in Algorithm 2.1 with b, i.e. l. 3 and l. 4 become

$$d_k := m \bmod b \ ; \ m := (m - d_k)/b$$

Overall we have the distinction illustrated in Figure 2.1.[14]

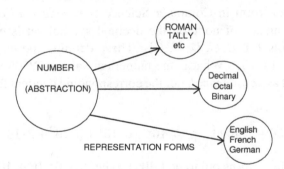

Figure 2.1: Number as Object and Encoding

2.2   Types of number and their use

Consider the questions below:

a. How many people live in this town?

b. How many children do they have?

c. How has the population of this city changed in the last year?

---

[14]This distinction between numerical quantity and *representation* of that quantity is, very informally, elaborated in Endnote 4.

d. Why do I only receive two-thirds of what he's paid?

The answers not only concern numerical quantities but also *different types* of numerical quantity. For example, possible responses could be,

A. 100 or 1406 or 25, 821 etc.

B. 0 or 1 or 14.

C. "It's *decreased* by 1832" or "It's the same" or "It's *increased* by 496".

The quantities referred to in (A) to provide answers to question (a) are simple *counting* values: 1, 2, 3, ... 4617, etc. These form the set of *Natural* numbers denoted by the symbol $\mathbb{N}$.

In answering (b) we need to allow for the possibility of *zero*. We do not, however, require anything further in the way of new concepts. The answer may with allowances for prodigious feats of procreation, be drawn from 0 *or* any of the Natural numbers. The numbers comprising the Natural numbers augmented by the value 0 form the set of *Whole* numbers denoted by the symbol $\mathbb{W}$.[15]

The response to (c) recognizes that, relative to some initial quantity, e.g. an answer to question (a), a value may

- have increased (had a *Natural* number *added*);

- or be unchanged (so that this, and the first possibility, are captured as having had a *Whole* number *added*)

- or have decreased (had a *Natural* number *subtracted*).

Thinking of the third possibility in terms of "had a *Natural* number *subtracted*", would, however, necessitate distinct operations to describe the outcomes.

We can express *all three* possibilities in terms of the change to the original value as "has had an *integer* added". This view gives our third category of Numbers: the integers denoted $\mathbb{Z}$.

Instead of thinking of a *decrease* in population size as *size* − 157 it is now read as *size* + (−157). The *integers* are formed by the *Whole* numbers augmented by "*negative* values" applied to *Natural* numbers. In other words,

$$\mathbb{Z} \; = \; \mathbb{W} \cup \{ \, -p \, : \, p \text{ is a Natural number}\}$$

---

[15]Some authors treat 0 as a Natural number. In our subsequent discussion we explicitly distinguish $\mathbb{N}$ (counting numbers starting at 1) from $\mathbb{W}$ ($\mathbb{N}$ with the value 0 added to this collection).

Or more concisely, $\mathbb{Z} = \mathbb{W} \cup \{ -p : p \in \mathbb{N} \}$.

The notion encapsulated within question (d) deals with a comparison of two quantities. Suppose that Bill, in receipt of £5400 per month is the over-renumerated individual of whom Alice complains since she only receives "two-thirds of what he is given". How much is Alice paid? Monthly she receives "two-thirds of £5400", i.e. £3600. The *ratio* of Alice's salary to Bill's is $\frac{3600}{5400}$ which, in its simplest form, is $\frac{2}{3}$. This gives another class of numerical quantities: the *Rational* numbers (denoted $\mathbb{Q}$) formed as those quantities given by the *ratio* of some integer, p, with some *Natural* number q. That is,

$$ \mathbb{Q} = \left\{ \frac{p}{q} : p \in \mathbb{Z} \text{ and } q \in \mathbb{N} \right\} $$

To summarize we have:

$\mathbb{N}$ Counting numbers starting from 1.

$\mathbb{W}$ $\mathbb{N}$ with 0 added.

$\mathbb{Z}$ *integers*: *Positive* (> 0) counting numbers, i.e. $\mathbb{N}$;
0;
Negative (< 0) counting numbers.

$\mathbb{Q}$ *Rational*: values expressible as the *ratio* of an
integer ($\mathbb{Z}$) to a
Natural number ($\mathbb{N}$).

The integers and Rationals provide a very rich source suitable for addressing most computational issues that arise in real cases: analyzing census data, configuring payroll and accounts systems, ranking of a Web page by a Web search engine, and so on. There is an argument[16] that, in fact, no further classes of number are needed for *any* computational setting. Before discussing the range of numbers outside the formal arena of Rationals, we very briefly return to the issue of representation as it concerns describing fractional quantities.[17]

Representations for $p \in \mathbb{Q}$

We saw at the end of Section 2.1 not only how number bases (10, 8, 2, 16 etc.) can be used as a method of interpreting a sequence of digits as a numerical value but also how to *construct* a suitable sequence in order to *represent* such

---

[16]See Endnote 5

[17]For discussion of the historical development of modern notation in this setting see Endnote 6.

a value. The numerical values we considered, however, were *Natural* numbers.[18] What can we do with Rational numbers such as 3/4, 1/5, 4/7 etc? It
turns out we can adopt a very similar approach, although there are some subtle
complications that may arise. When describing $p \in \mathbb{W}$ the choice of number
base will mainly affect the length of the encoded form. This length, however,
will always be *finite*. Turning to representations for $q \in \mathbb{Q}$, we may have representations which require *infinitely many* symbols for some choice of base but
which are finite length when *another base* is used.

As previously, before looking at this complication in more depth, we start
with decimal representation. Let us suppose we have a value $q \in \mathbb{Q}$ and that,
furthermore, $0 < q < 1$.[19]

Here one such choice is the value $q = 3/4$. We know, already, that this can
also be written as $q = 0.75$. How did we arrive at this expression?

In the expression 0.75 to recover the value q we must use

$$7 \cdot 10^{-1} + 5 \cdot 10^{-2} = \frac{7}{10} + \frac{5}{100}$$

When treating Whole numbers, the member p of $\mathbb{W}$ to which a sequence
of decimal digits, $d_{t-1}d_{t-2} \cdots d_2 d_1 d_0$ mapped was found as a result of the
calculation,

$$p = \sum_{k=0}^{t-1} d_k \cdot 10^k$$

The powers of 10 are all Whole numbers. In looking at the fractional part of
q we now need to consider powers which are successively smaller and smaller
negative integers.

Just as we previously recovered $p \in \mathbb{W}$ by adding a sequence of Whole
numbers obtained by *multiplying* digits (going from right to left) using increasing powers of 10, now in recovering q we process the sequence representing
it going from *left to right* forming the Rational value obtained by *dividing* the
corresponding digit value using increasing powers of 10: first the rightmost
digit is divided by 10, then the second rightmost digit divided by 100 (10^2)
and so on. Having formed all of the Rational quantities that are described we

---

[18]Having chosen explicity to include a symbol denoting zero, the extension from $\mathbb{N}$ to $\mathbb{W}$
poses no great challenge.

[19]If $q \geq 1$, we can use our standard approach to represent the *integer* part of q, and focus
attention on describing the *fractional* part, $frac(q)$ being $q - int(q)$ and $int(q)$, its integer
part, the unique Whole number r for which $r \leq q$ and $r > q - 1$. Should $q < 0$ we can focus
attention on representing $-q$ which will exceed 0.

then just add all of the outcomes. In total suppose we have

$$0.d_1 d_2 d_3 \cdots d_k$$

and wish to know which Rational value, q, is being described. Then this value is

$$q = \sum_{t=1}^{k} \frac{d_t}{10^t}$$

What if we wish to go in the other direction? i.e. given $q \in \mathbb{Q}$, with $0 < q < 1$ how do we find a sequence

$$r_1 r_2 r_3 \cdots r_t$$

for which

$$q = \sum_{k=1}^{t} \frac{r_k}{10^k} \ ?$$

We saw how, using Algorithm 2.1, this can be done for any $m \in \mathbb{N}$. Looking at related processes for $q \in \mathbb{Q}$ with $0 < q < 1$ we know that since q is a *positive Rational* it must be the case that $p = u/v$ for *Natural* numbers u and v with $u < v$, e.g. in our example $u = 3$ and $v = 4$. In order to obtain the decimal expansion, $0.r_1 r_2 \cdots r_k \cdots$ we can use Algorithm 2.2.

Algorithm 2.2. Find decimal expansion of $p = u/v$

1: $k := 1$;
2: **repeat**
3:    $r_k := (10u) \mathrm{div}\ v$ {r_k is the *integer division* of $10u$ by v}
4:    $u := (10u \bmod v)$ {Now looking for expansion of $(10u - r_k v)/v \in \mathbb{Q}$}
5:    $k := k + 1$ {Find next digit (going right to left)}
6: **until** $u = 0$

Applying Algorithm 2.2 to our example $q = 3/4$.

1. $u = 3;\ v = 4$;

2. $r_1 := \lfloor 30/4 \rfloor = 7$;

3. $u := 30 \bmod 4 = 2$;

4. $r_2 := \lfloor 20/4 \rfloor = 5$;

5. $u := 20 \bmod 4 = 0$;

In Algorithm 2.1 in order to compute the representation of $m \in \mathbb{N}$ for a base, b, other than 10 it sufficed to change the occurrences of 10 (in ll. 3–4) to occurrences of b. Exactly the same changes in Algorithm 2.2, i.e. replacing l. 3 by $r_k := (bu)\mathrm{div}\, v$ and l. 4 with $u := (bu \bmod v)$ now give the expansion of q as $0.r_1 r_2 \cdots r_k$ in base b.

For example, the expansion of $3/4$ in octal is found to be: $(3/4)_8 = 0.6$, in hexadecimal we get $(3/4)_{16} = 0.C$.

It was mentioned that one possible issue that can arise with the process of describing $q \in \mathbb{Q}$ $(0 < q < 1)$ as an expansion, $0.r_1 r_2 \cdots r_k$ in some base b, is that the choice of base may lead to this sequence having infinite length. In terms of what happens in Algorithm 2.2, this means that the condition in l. 6, required for the "**repeat**$\cdots$**until**" to finish, never becomes **true**.

Familiar examples are the repeating decimals, e.g.

$$(1/3)_{10} = 0.333333 \cdots \quad ; \quad (1/9)_{10} = 0.111111 \cdots$$

and more subtle patterns $(1/7)_{10} = 0.142857142857 \cdots$.

If a different base is used it may be finite.

2.3 Beyond Rationality: the class of Real numbers

The number types we have seen in the previous section – $\mathbb{N}$, $\mathbb{W}$, $\mathbb{Z}$ and $\mathbb{Q}$ – have one property in common. First notice that, as is easily seen, "every Natural number is a Whole number" and "every Whole number is an integer" and "every integer is a Rational number": more tersely $\mathbb{N} \subset \mathbb{W} \subset \mathbb{Z} \subset \mathbb{Q}$. Now consider any $q \in \mathbb{Q}$ so that, by virtue of the fact that $q \in \mathbb{Q}$, we find $u \in \mathbb{Z}$ and $v \in \mathbb{N}$ for which $q = u/v$. Irrespective of how large u and v may be, irrespective of the number base we are using, we can find *finite* length sequences of symbols $\rho(u)$ and $\rho(v)$ for which the *numerical value*, q, is completely described through the relation $\rho(u)/\rho(v)$.

There is, however, a class of number, that standard programming languages attempt to describe by variables types dubbed **float** or **double**, for which this finite representation property *cannot be guaranteed*.

In order to introduce this class we start with a, perhaps rather artificial, application setting.

Problem 1. *Using only a 1m length rule, how should we form a **square** region whose **area** is **exactly** $2m^2$?*

Of course, the obvious solution is just draw a line, of some length, L say, with the property $L^2 = 2$.

We only know about Rational numbers. Now, we cannot choose $L \in \mathbb{N}$: either the area (L^2) will be too small ($L = 1$) or too big ($L \geq 2$). We could try and find values, u and v in $\mathbb{N}$, for which $(u/v)^2 = 2$ and then draw a line of length $L = u/v$. We cannot, however, use this approach: *not* because we are unable to mark out a line of length q for members $q \in \mathbb{Q}$[20] but because *no such Rational number exists*, i.e. no $q \in \mathbb{Q}$, has the property that $q^2 = 2$.[21]

In capturing quantities such as those with behaviour similar to L, i.e. for which $L^2 = 2$ we need to go beyond merely Rational numbers: we need **Real** numbers, these being denoted $\mathbb{R}$.[22]

Let us look at some consequences of being unable to describe the quantity L with the property $L^2 = 2$ as a Rational number.

IR1. The value L, with $L^2 = 2$ cannot be written in a *finite* representation of the form $(x)_b.(y)_b$ with $x \in \mathbb{W}$, $y \in \mathbb{W}$ for *any* choice of number base $b \in \mathbb{N}$. [Here we slightly abuse the "." notation to distinguish integer (x) and fractional (y) parts of the representation.]

IR2. *If* we wish to describe the quantity L with $L^2 = 2$ in a concise style, then some novel convention must be introduced.

Given the fact, discussed at the conclusion of Section 2.2, above that there are (already) *Rational* values, q, for which $(q)_{10}$ is not a finite length (and, despite this, the decimal system continues to hold sway), it may seem that the issue raised by the first point is unimportant. The point raised in (IR1), however, is with respect to *every* choice of number base. In fact, the set of (positive) Rational numbers can also be characterized in the following way:

Property 1. *The number q with $0 < q < 1$ is a Rational number if and only if there is a choice of base b and a finite collection $< p_1, \ p_2, \ \ldots, \ p_n >$ of Natural numbers for which*

$$q \ = \ \sum_{k=1}^{n} \frac{p_k}{b^k}$$

---

[20] See Endnote 7 for one method of drawing a line of length $q = u/v$ for a given $q \in \mathbb{Q}$.

[21] A formal proof of this is, usually, attributed to the Greek mathematician Pythagoras, *ca.* 570BC–*ca.* 495BC (or to be rather more pedantic to an unknown member of the School of Pythagoras, some authorities, e.g. von Fritz [245], attributing this discovery to Hippasus of Metapontum). The argument used is one of the watershed achievements of ancient Mathematics and is still that favoured today in demonstrating this claim.

[22] We can, of course, solve the measurement problem without *explicitly* mentioning the concept of $\mathbb{R}$, see Endnote 8.

Turning to the issue arising from (IR2), an extensive class of "Real but not Rational" numbers can be described via the following approach. Firstly consider the property of L with which we opened our discussion: $L^2 = 2$. Ideally we wish to capture L *directly*, that is independently of how some expression involving L (i.e. L^2) behaves. The standard approach would be to write $L = \sqrt{2}$, however, it is useful to look in more depth at what the convention "$\sqrt{\cdots}$" is describing. So far (e.g. in describing both Whole number and fractional representations with respect to some base) we have been using the concept of raising a given *Natural* number to a *power*, $k \in \mathbb{Z}$, e.g. 10^2, 16^{-1}. The property of L for which $L^2 = 2$ can be seen as resulting from using powers which are *Rational* numbers: $L = 2^{1/2}$. The binary operation of "raising to a power" given x, y both in $\mathbb{Z}$ is defined as the result of computing x^y. If, however, $x \geq 0$ we do not need to restrict to only $\mathbb{Z}$:[23] we can choose $x \in \mathbb{Q}$ or more generally, $x \in \mathbb{R}$ and $y \in \mathbb{Q}$ (similarly, more generally, $y \in \mathbb{R}$).

We note, in passing, that x^y for $x \in \mathbb{R}$, $y \in \mathbb{R}$, $x \geq 0$ behaves as we might expect: returning to $L = 2^{1/2}$, this does, indeed, meet our requirement that $L^2 = 2$:

$$(2^{1/2})^2 \;=\; 2^{1/2} \cdot 2^{1/2} \;=\; 2^{\frac{1}{2}+\frac{1}{2}} \;=\; 2^1 \;=\; 2$$

In general, putting to one side the vacuous case of $y = 0$ whenever $x \geq 0$ and $y \in \mathbb{R}$ we find that

$$(x^y)^{\frac{1}{y}} \;=\; \left(x^{\frac{1}{y}}\right)^y \;=\; x^{\frac{y}{y}} \;=\; x^1 \;=\; x$$

The class of numbers given by evaluating x^y satisfying the constraints stipulated often turn out not to be Rational. Just as it can be shown that $2^{1/2} \notin \mathbb{Q}$, so too we can find infinitely many instances for which $x^y \notin \mathbb{Q}$ for $x \in \mathbb{N}$ and $y \in \mathbb{Q}$. Such *Irrational* numbers, as we may dub the set of all members of $\mathbb{R}$ incapable of being expressed in the form p/q constitute for now our final collection of number classes. In summary, for these

$$\mathbb{N} \subset \mathbb{W} \subset \mathbb{Z} \subset \mathbb{Q} \subset \mathbb{R}.$$

In the next section we examine how the collection $\mathbb{R}$ may be refined further and in a manner that leads directly to the questions discussed in Chapter 5.

---

[23] As will be seen in Chapter 5, the qualification $x \geq 0$ is important if we wish to compute x^y for arbitrary $y \in \mathbb{Q}$.

2.4 Polynomial forms and roots

In the previous section we introduced the notion of irrational number via a quantity, x, for which $x^2 = 2$. If we rearrange $x^2 = 2$ this is satisfied by those value(s) x such that

$$x^2 - 2 = 0$$

Consider a, superficially, similar problem: that of constructing a *cube* whose volume is exactly $20m^3$. Again we seek a quantity x that this time must have the property $x^3 = 20$, or in the style of the rearrangement just given, that satisfies the identity

$$x^3 - 20 = 0$$

There is, of course, no reason why we need to be restricted to *single* terms in x. Just as the area and volume problems lead to solutions described in the forms $x^2 - 2$ and $x^3 - 20$ we may, in more complicated arenas, find that the quantities sought are given by expressions such as

$$x^4 - 2x^3 + x^2 + x + 15$$
$$x^5 - x^3 + x - 1$$
$$x^2 + 4x + 4$$
$$\cdots$$

Expressions such as these are called *polynomials in (the variable)* x. Such expressions are characterized by two attributes:

A1. The *largest* power of x that appears.

A2. The values by which distinct powers of x (including $x^0 = 1$) are multiplied.

The attribute (A1) is called the *degree* of the polynomial, denoted $\deg(p)$ and the values qualifying the character of (A2) are referred to as the *coefficients*.

More formally, if $\mathbb{T}$ is some arbitrary number type on which operations $+$ and $\cdot$ (addition and product) are defined, and $\mathbb{T}$ satisfies

P1. Given any x and y in $\mathbb{T}$, $x + y \in \mathbb{T}$.

P2. $x \cdot y \in \mathbb{T}$

e.g. all of the number types we have seen so far with the standard arithmetic interpretations of $+$ and $\cdot$.[24] A *polynomial of degree* n ($n \in \mathbb{W}$) in x is specified
by an *ordered* collection of $n+1$ values from $\mathbb{T}$,

$$\underline{c} \;=\; < c_0,\, c_1,\, c_2,\, \ldots,\, c_k,\, \ldots,\, c_n > \quad (c_n \neq 0)$$

Using $p_{n,\underline{c}}(x) \in \mathbb{T}[X]$ to denote a typical polynomial of degree n in x with
coefficients $\underline{c}$ from $\mathbb{T}$ (often abbreviating this to $p_n(x)$ or even just $p(x)$ where
the issues of exact degree and coefficients are not immediately important),
$p_{n,\underline{c}}(x)$ describes a specific set of computations performed on the variable x.
Namely, that $p_{n,\underline{c}}(x)$ is the outcome of evaluating (for a given input x) the
expression

$$\sum_{k=0}^{n} c_k x^k$$

Table 2.3 gives some simple examples of polynomials in x.

Table 2.3: Some Examples of Polynomials

	$p(x)$	Degree	Coefficients $(< c_0, \ldots, c_n >)$	$\mathbb{T}$
a.	$x^2 - 2$	2	$< -2, 0, 1 >$	$\mathbb{Z}$
b.	$x^3 - 20$	3	$< -20, 0, 0, 1 >$	$\mathbb{Z}$
c.	$x^5 - x^4 + x^3 - x^2 + x - 1$	5	$< -1, 1, -1, 1, -1, 1 >$	$\mathbb{Z}$
d.	$0.5x^3 + 7x^2 - (1/7)x + 89$	3	$< 89, 1/7, 7, 0.5 >$	$\mathbb{Q}$
e.	$x^3 + x^2 + x$	3	$< 0, 1, 1, 1 >$	$\mathbb{W}$
f.	$(2^{1/3})x + 10^{0.5}$	1	$< 10^{0.5}, 2^{1/3} >$	$\mathbb{R}$
g.	5	0	$< 5 >$	$\mathbb{N}$

Looking at the seven examples in Table 2.3 we can note a few points of
interest. Firstly the degree of $p(x)$ can be any *Whole* number, including, as
evidenced in case (g), the value 0. There is exactly one term of the form $c_k x^k$
for each of the powers k between 0 and the polynomial degree. By convention,
when $c_k = 0$ we do not explicitly represent the term $c_k x^k$ in writing out the
polynomial. As is seen in examples (b), (c) and (e) we deal with a *collection*
of coefficients not a *set*: c may be the same for several distinct powers of x in
$p(x)$. As one final point we note the convention for describing the coefficients

---

[24]We can, of course, choose $\mathbb{T}$ other than these forms. Some examples will be seen in
Chapter 3, however, we mention at this point instances such as $\mathbb{T} = \{0, 1, 2, \ldots, k-1\}$ for
some $k \in \mathbb{N}$ and $k \geq 2$ with $\{+, \cdot\}$ described by arithmetic **modulo** k.

of $p_k(x)$: although we write $< c_9, c_1, \ldots, c_k >$ in the formal specification of these for a degree k polynomial, often (especially for small k) the polynomial would be explicitly written out with this order reversed, e.g. we would write the degree 2 (or *quadratic*) whose coefficients are $< 1, 5, 3 >$ as $3x^2 + 5x + 1$.

In these examples, the underlying types from which coefficients are drawn range from $\mathbb{N}$ in case (g), $\mathbb{W}$ in case (e), through to $\mathbb{Z}$ (cases (a) through (c)), $\mathbb{Q}$ (d) and even $\mathbb{R}$ (f). Our focus, however, will be primarily on $\mathbb{Q}[X]$ and, to a lesser extent, $\mathbb{R}[X]$.

Why should limiting to $\mathbb{Q}[X]$ be, potentially, useful? The answer to this question is found in the concept of the *roots* of a polynomial. Our length quantities, $2^{0.5}$ and $20^{1/3}$ for the area and volume problems, have a specific relationship of interest with respect to the polynomials ($x^2 - 2$ and $x^3 - 20$) from which they originate: evaluating $p_2(x) = x^2 - 2$ with $x = 2^{0.5}$ gives the outcome 0 (in more concise terms, $p_2(2^{0.5}) = 0$); evaluating $p_3(x) = x^3 - 20$ with $x = 20^{1/3}$, and again $p_3(20^{1/3}) = 0$.

What if it were the case that *every* Real number could be so described? That is to say if Assertion 1 below were to hold?

Assertion 1. *For every $\alpha \in \mathbb{R}$ there is some $n \in \mathbb{W}$ and collection of $n + 1$ Rational values $\underline{c} =< c_0, c_1, \ldots, c_n >$ for which $p_{n,\underline{c}}(\alpha) = 0$.*

One immediate consequence, of great relevance to computational concerns, is that we could give a *finite* description to *any* Real number, thereby, at least in principle, obviating or at worst alleviating the limitations arising from the finite nature of digital computer architectures. Why would this be the case? Because we would be able to *describe*[25] any Real number simply by a finite collection of Rational numbers: the degree of the encoding polynomial (from $\mathbb{W}$); its coefficients (from $\mathbb{Q}$) and *the position in a decreasing ordering of the Real numbers for which this polynomial is* 0. So for example $2^{0.5}$ which we have seen to be irrational is described by $< 1, 2, 1, 0, -2 >$: "$2^{0.5}$ is the largest (1) Real value such that the degree 2 polynomial whose coefficients are $< 1, 0, -2 >$ will be 0". Similarly, $20^{1/3}$ is $< 1, 3, 1, 0, 0, -20 >$: "$20^{1/3}$ is the largest Real value for which the degree 3 polynomial having coefficients $< 1, 0, 0, -20 >$ is 0".

This idea of associating with $p(x)$ "an ordered collection of the Real values, α for which $p(\alpha) = 0$" is appealing and merits further investigation.

Let us begin by getting rid of some verbiage that clutters up our informal introduction in the last few paragraphs. In particular we do not want constantly

---

[25]"Describe", of course, does not necessarily entail the description is computationally useful.

to repeat phrases such as "collection of Real values for which the degree n polynomial having coefficients $\underline{c}$ is 0". We call such values the *roots* of the polynomial $p_{n,\underline{c}}(x)$.

Let $p_n(x) \in \mathbb{T}[X]$ be a polynomial. Any value α for which $p_n(\alpha) = 0$ is said to be a *root* of $p_n(x)$. Those $\alpha \in \mathbb{R}$ satisfying $p_n(\alpha) = 0$ are referred to as the *Real* roots of $p_n(x)$.

We now state without proof some useful properties of polynomials and their associated polynomial roots.

Fact 1. *Let $p_n(x)$ be a polynomial of degree n from $\mathbb{R}[X]$.*[26]

R1. There is a collection $R(p) =< r_1, r_2, \ldots, r_n >$ of n values for which $p_n(r_k) = 0$ for each $1 \leq k \leq n$. In other words, every polynomial of degree n has n roots.

R2. Let $< r_1, r_2, \ldots, r_m > (m \leq n)$ be the Real roots of p_n in the formulation from R1. We may order these using

$$r_1 \leq r_2 \leq r_3 \leq \cdots r_k \leq r_{k+1} \leq r_m$$

It may be noticed that there are some questions suggested by our formulation of Fact 1. For example:

Q1. Why do we say "n values" in (R1) and not "n *Real* values"?

Q2. The ordering relation in (R2) is "$\leq$" rather than "$<$", does this mean that the (Real) roots may not be distinct?

In response to (Q1), as we shall see in much greater depth in Chapter 5, it is *not guaranteed* to be the case that a given degree n polynomial has n *Real* roots. So while all such polynomials do, indeed, have n roots, some of these may not accurately be described as Real.

The issue raised in (Q2) may seem a little strange: if some roots are the same in what meaningful sense does a degree n polynomial have "n roots"? In regarding identical incidents of the same value as separate roots, we are motivated more by convenience than semantic accuracy. A number of general techniques and consequences are more easily presented under the convention polynomials of degree n have n roots since this avoids the tedium of having to qualify general statements in order to respect only distinct roots. The notion

---

[26]The statement of this result also holds for $\mathbb{Q}[X]$. We simply give the most general form recalling that $\mathbb{Q} \subset \mathbb{R}$.

by which the view that polynomials of degree n have n roots may be justified is that of *multiplicity*.

Suppose we take the polynomial of degree 3 (or *cubic* as these are sometimes called) below

$$p_3(x) = x^3 - 3x^2 + 3x - 1$$

This is equivalent to multiplying out the expression

$$(x - 1)(x - 1)(x - 1) = (x - 1)^3$$

Now it is clear that 1 is a root of $p_3(x)$. There are, however, **no** other *distinct* roots. Looking at the structure of $(x-1)(x-1)(x-1)$ we view the root $x = 1$ as occuring *three* times or, in the usual terminology, the root $x = 1$ of $p_3(x)$ *has multiplicity* 3. Here is another example, a degree 6 polynomial,

$$p_6(x) = x^6 + 4x^5 - 10x^4 - 40x^3 + 45x^2 + 108x - 108$$

As with our example $p_3(x)$ being the result of expanding $(x - 1)^3$, this time $p_6(x)$ results by expanding

$$(x - 1)(x - 2)^2(x + 3)^3$$

In this case we have roots 1 with *multiplicity* 1; 2 with *multiplicity* 2; and -3 with *multiplicity* 3. If we sum the multiplicities with which each *distinct* root occurs we obtain $1 + 2 + 3 = 6$: the degree of $p_6(x)$.

In the most general form we have Property 2

Property 2. *If $p_n(x)$ is any polynomial in x of degree n having k **distinct** roots*

$$\{r_1, r_2, \ldots, r_k\}$$

with root r_i having multiplicity $\mu(r_i) \geq 1$, then

$$\sum_{i=1}^{k} \mu(r_i) = n$$

It is the result of Property 2 that provides the justification for our statement polynomials of degree n have n roots. Notice that the statement refers to the collection of roots of $p_n(x)$ as a whole: no differentiation between Real and other roots is made.

So what of the issue that led to the discussion of roots of polynomials and, in particular, the proposal postulated in Assertion 1? Is it, indeed, the case that *every* $x \in \mathbb{R}$ can be given as the root of *some* polynomial, $p(x)$, the coefficients of which are all chosen from $\mathbb{Q}$? Unfortunately, as undoubtedly the reader will already have surmised, this is *not* the case. In fact there are many commonly arising Real numbers having the property that they *cannot* be defined through the roots of a polynomial with only Rational coefficients.[27] This behaviour gives a further refinement of $\mathbb{R}$ into the *algebraic* and non-algebraic (or *transcendental*) numbers:

A. $z \in \mathbb{R}$ is an *algebraic number* if there is a polynomial, $p(x)$, all of whose coefficients are from $\mathbb{Q}$ and for which $p(z) = 0$.

B. $z \in \mathbb{R}$ is a *transcendental number* if every polynomial $p(x)$ having coefficients from $\mathbb{Q}$ is such that $p(z) \neq 0$.

One of the best-known instances of a transcendental Real number is the value π describing the ratio between the *circumference* (C) of a circle and its *diameter* (d), i.e. the well-known formula $C = \pi d$.

2.5 Operations involving Polynomials

In the next chapter we shall see that the structures defined by the class of degree n polynomials from $\mathbb{R}[X]$ can be treated as a particular instance of a much more general form. Before moving onto this view, however, it may be useful to look at algorithmic (i.e. computational) operations that typical polynomials may raise.

In the list of interrelated problems below we consider arbitrary polynomials $p_n(x)$ and $q_m(x)$ in $\mathbb{T}[X]$.

P1. Addition of $p_n(x)$ and $q_m(x)$ and scalar multiplication by $\alpha \in \mathbb{T}$.

P2. Forming the degree $n + m$ polynomial $p_n(x) \cdot q_m(x)$.

P3. Constructing the polynomial $p_n(x)/q_m(x)$.

P4. *Factoring* $p_n(x)$, that is constructing polynomials $f_k(x)$, $g_{n-k}(x)$ for which $p_n(x) = f_k(x) \cdot g_{n-k}(x)$.

P5. Determining the roots of $p_n(x)$, i.e. the collection $R(p_n(x))$, or its Real roots, or even just one of its Real roots.

---

[27]Unlike the arguments that demonstrate $2^{1/2} \notin \mathbb{Q}$ those required to show some $z \in \mathbb{R}$ is not the root of any polynomial with Rational coefficients are highly non-trivial. Famous examples are the work of Lindemann [156, 157] and Gordan [107].,

Polynomial Addition and Scalar Multiplication

Letting $p_{n,\underline{c}}(x)$ and $q_{m,\underline{d}}(x)$ be polynomials in $\mathbb{T}[X]$ (we assume that $n \geq m$) and $\alpha \in \mathbb{T}$. The polynomial, $t_{n,\underline{h}}(x) \in \mathbb{T}[X]$ resulting by adding $p_{n,\underline{c}}(x)$ and $q_{m,\underline{d}}(x)$ has coefficients $\underline{h} =< h_0, h_1, \ldots, h_n >$ given by

$$
h_i = \begin{cases} c_i + d_i & \text{if} \quad 0 \leq i \leq m \\ c_i & \text{if} \quad m+1 \leq i \leq n \end{cases}
$$

Notice that we do not require $p(x)$ and $q(x)$ to have the same degree. Effectively in defining $p_n(x) + q_m(x)$ when $n > m$, $q(x)$ is treated as a "degenerate" degree n polynomial with coefficients $d_i = 0$ whenever $i > m$.

The operation of scalar multiplication which plays an important rôle in the structures considered in the next Chapter involves a constant $\alpha \in \mathbb{T}$ and polynomial $p_{n,\underline{c}} \in \mathbb{T}[X]$. The outcome of $\alpha \cdot p_{n,\underline{c}}$ is the degree n polynomial $t_{n,\underline{h}}(x)$ whose coefficients are given through $h_i = \alpha c_i$.[28]

Polynomial Multiplication

We present a general description of what is understood by "the polynomial $t(x)$ resulting by multiplying two polynomials $p(x)$ and $q(x)$". The problem is of considerable interest from a Computer Science perspective, since fast algorithmic solutions influence effective multiplication methods. The latter are of importance where the size of integer values involved requires the arithmetic outcomes to be emulated in software rather than using hardware methods. Such contexts are a standard feature of analyzing data from modern large-scale scientific experiments. A number of programming languages provide support for such large-scale arithmetic obviating the need for users to code basic arithmetic processes, e.g. the classes `BigDecimal` and `BigInteger` in JAVA.[29]

Let $p_{n,\underline{c}}(x)$ and $q_{m,\underline{d}}(x)$ be polynomials in x with respective degrees n and m and coefficients $\underline{c} =< c_0, \ldots, c_n >$, $\underline{d} =< d_0, \ldots, d_m >$. Without any loss of generality, let us also assume that $n \geq m$, i.e. that the degree of $p_n(x)$ is at least as large as the degree of $q_m(x)$. At a high-level the polynomial $t(x)$ formed by multiplying these is described by

$$
t(x) = \left(\sum_{i=0}^{n} c_i x^i \right) \cdot \left(\sum_{j=0}^{m} d_j x^j \right)
$$

---

[28] Notice that the special case $\alpha = 0$ gives a constant polynomial, i.e. $t(x) = 0 \cdot p_{n,\underline{c}}(x) = 0$.

[29] https://docs.oracle.com/javase/7/docs/api/java/math/BigInteger.html;
https://docs.oracle.com/javase/7/docs/api/java/math/BigDecimal.html.

Now it is not too hard to see that $t(x)$ will be a degree $n + m$ polynomial: the highest power of x in $p(x)$ is x^n and that in $q(x)$, x^m. In algebraically multiplying out the expression just presented we will have *exactly one* term $(c_n \cdot d_m)x^{n+m}$. There will be no terms $b_k x^k$ with $k \geq n + m + 1$ in the result because in order for these to be present would need some term $c_l x^l$ from $p_n(x)$ to be multiplied by some term $d_r x^r$ from $q_m(x)$ *and* $l + r \geq n + m + 1$. In other words that $l \geq n + m + 1 - r$ and, since $r \leq m$, this would imply $l \geq n + 1$: a status inconsistent with $p_n(x)$ being degree n.

In total, in determining the outcome of multiplying the two we have to find the coefficient of x^k in $t(x)$ for each choice of k between 0 and $n + m$. Consider the term $c_i x^i$ from $p_n(x)$. If k is such that $0 \leq k - i \leq m$ then fixing $j = k - i$ will lead to $(c_i d_{k-i})x^i x^{k-i}$ contributing to the coefficient of x^k in $t(x)$. Of course there may be several choices of i from $p(x)$ and several choices of j from $q(x)$ which lead to $i + j = k$ so that *all* of these have to be considered in finalizing the coefficient, h_k of x^k in $t(x)$. This gives us,

Input: $p_{\underline{c},n}(x)$ and $q_{\underline{d},m}(x)$ $(n \geq m)$
Output: $t_{\underline{h},n+m}(x)$
The coefficient, h_k of $t(x)$ is given by

$$h_k = \sum_{i,j \,|\, i+j=k} c_i \cdot d_j$$

Small Example
Suppose

$$p(x) = x^3 + 2x^2 - x - 3 \;;\; q(x) = x^2 + 2x - 1$$

so that

$$\begin{aligned} < c_0, c_1, c_2, c_3 > &= < -3, -1, 2, 1 > \\ < d_0, d_1, d_2 > &= < -1, 2, 1 > \end{aligned}$$

Then $t(x) = p(x) \cdot q(x)$ has degree 5 with

$$\begin{aligned} h_0 &= c_0 d_0 = (-3) \cdot (-1) & &= 3 \\ h_1 &= c_0 d_1 + c_1 d_0 = (-3) \cdot 2 + (-1) \cdot (-1) & &= -5 \\ h_2 &= c_0 d_2 + c_1 d_1 + c_2 d_0 = (-3) \cdot (1) + (-1) \cdot (2) + (2) \cdot (-1) & &= -7 \\ h_3 &= c_1 d_2 + c_2 d_1 + c_3 d_0 = (-1) \cdot (1) + (2) \cdot (2) + (1) \cdot (-1) & &= 2 \\ h_4 &= c_2 d_2 + c_3 d_1 = (2) \cdot (1) + (1) \cdot (2) & &= 4 \\ h_5 &= c_3 d_2 = (1) \cdot (1) & &= 1 \end{aligned}$$

Hence,

$$t_5(x) = x^5 + 4x^4 + 2x^3 - 7x^2 - 5x + 3$$

It is worth noting the link between finding the values of coefficients from the result of multiplying $p_n(x)$ and $q_m(x)$ and that of constructing the outcome of multiplying large integer values. So we have seen that the polynomial expression $p_n(x)$ represents

$$\sum_{i=0}^{n} c_i x^i$$

Earlier we considered the representation of numerical quantities from $\mathbb{W}$ with respect to a given base, b. Suppose we limit $\mathbb{T}$ (recall this is the collection from which we draw coefficient values) to the finite subset of $\mathbb{W}$ formed by

$$\{0,\ 1,\ 2,\ \ldots,\ r,\ \ldots\ b-1\}$$

interpreting $\{+, \cdot\}$ as arithmetic modulo b.

Now consider polynomials $p_n(x)$ and $q_n(x)$ whose coefficients are formed from this set. If we look at evaluating $p_n(b) \cdot q_n(b)$, that is with x set to the value b, then this is,

$$\left(\sum_{k=0}^{n} c_k b^k \right) \cdot \left(\sum_{k=0}^{n} d_k b^k \right)$$

And this is,

$$\sum_{r=0}^{2n} \sum_{i,j \mid i+j=r} (c_i d_j) b^r$$

So that the symbolic encoding of the polynomial multiplication, when we replaced the variable x by the specific value, b, of the base, gives us the result of computing the product of the two integers represented. The pattern formed by the combinations of coefficients has been explored in many algorithms for performing this calculation in an efficient manner. Some of these methods we will discuss in a later chapter.

The next three applications are very closely related. We discuss some basic approaches, however, practical computational methods rely on techniques and ideas introduced later in this volume specifically Chapters 4 and 5. In consequence we will return to root finding methods later.

We will for the moment concentrate on polynomials in $\mathbb{Q}[X]$.

Polynomial Division

The arithmetic process of dividing $x \in \mathbb{N}$ by $y \in \mathbb{N}$ with x and y represented in some number base is a standard and well-defined computational process. Not only can we formulate precisely what is meant by dividing a polynomial $p_n(x) \in \mathbb{Q}[X]$ by a non-zero polynomial $q_m(x) \in \mathbb{Q}[X]$ but we may also describe computational approaches to performing this process. Such methods are an important sub-procedure in describing techniques for *Polynomial Factorization* as we shall see in the next subsection.

In the case of standard arithmetic the result of $x \div y$ ($x \in \mathbb{N}$, $y \in \mathbb{N}$) is given through values $q \in \mathbb{N}$ and $r \in \mathbb{W}$ for which

$$x = q \cdot y + r$$

(q being called the *quotient* and $r < y$ the *remainder*), so too given $f_n(x) \in \mathbb{Q}[X]$ and $g_m(x) \in \mathbb{Q}[X]$ (and assuming that $m \leq n$) the outcome $f_n(x) \div g_m(x)$ is given through two *polynomials* $q(x)$ and $r(x)$ the degree of r being less than m and satisfying

$$f_n(x) = g_m(x) \cdot q(x) + r(x)$$

In keeping with the terminology of standard arithmetic $q(x)$ is called the quotient and $r(x)$ the remainder.

Constructing q and r can be accomplished by a process very similar to the traditional primary (junior) school method of "long division".[30]

We describe the mechanics of polynomial long division and present an elementary algorithmic description. We note, in passing, that special cases of $q(x)$, in particular *binomials* $(x - r)$ are often more efficiently dealt with by methods such as Ruffini's Rule.[31]

Let $f_n(x) \in \mathbb{Q}[X]$, $g_m(x) \in \mathbb{Q}[X]$ with $m \leq n$.

$$f_n(x) = \sum_{k=0}^{n} c_k x^k \quad ; \quad g_m(x) = \sum_{k=0}^{m} d_k x^k$$

To start as in normal long division form a table as illustrated below

---

[30]One is assuming, at the risk of exposing a generational abyss, that this method *is* still a standard feature of primary school arithmetic, the prevalence of electronic calculators not having entirely eradicated basic arithmetic proficiencies from syllabi.

[31]Dating from 1804, the article by Cajori [41] offers a careful comparison of the independent derivations of the method from Horner [123], to whom the technique is often wrongly attributed, and Ruffini.

$$\sum_{k=0}^{m} d_k x^k \quad \overline{\left) \sum_{k=0}^{n} c_k x^k \right.}$$

In order to decide what should be placed "above the bar" we divide the highest degree term (the term $c_n x^n$) of $f_n(x)$ by the highest degree term of $g_m(x)$ (the term $d_m x^m$).

Writing h_{nm} for c_n / d_m, this results in,

$$\sum_{k=0}^{m} d_k x^k \quad \left) \overline{\begin{array}{c} h_{nm} x^{n-m} \\ \sum_{k=0}^{n} c_k x^k \end{array}} \right.$$

Now multiply the divisor (g_m) by the term just obtained and write this expression in the next row,

$$\sum_{k=0}^{m} d_k x^k \quad \left) \overline{\begin{array}{c} h_{nm} x^{n-m} \\ \sum_{k=0}^{n} c_k x^k \end{array}} \right.$$
$$-$$
$$c_n x^n + h_{nm} x^{n-m} \sum_{k=0}^{m-1} d_k x^k$$

The outcome of the subtraction is then written underneath where we use $d_t = 0$ when $m + 1 \leq t \leq n$

$$\sum_{k=0}^{m} d_m x^m \quad \left) \overline{\begin{array}{c} h_{nm} x^{n-m} \\ \sum_{k=0}^{n} c_k x^k \end{array}} \right.$$
$$-$$
$$c_n x^n + h_{nm} x^{n-m} \sum_{k=0}^{m-1} d_k x^k$$
$$\overline{}$$
$$\mathbf{0} + \sum_{t=m}^{n-1} c_t x^t + \sum_{t=0}^{m-1} (c_t - h_{nm} d_t) x^t$$

Now we have eliminated the term in x^n from $f_n(x)$ the divisor $g_m(x)$ being unchanged. To obtain the next term to add above the bar we just repeat the process, now working with dividing $d_m x^m$ the lead term of $g_m(x)$ into $(c_{n-1} - h_{nm} d_{n-1})x^{n-1}$ or if $m < n - 1$ $d_m x^m$ into $c_{n-1} x^{n-1}$.

This continues until the degree of the lead term into which $d_m x^m$ is divided is less than m or the subtraction results in 0.

The quotient term is then simply the expression that has resulted over the bar while the remainder term is that left when the process completes. Either 0 or the degree less than m polynomial.

As an example consider dividing $2x^3 + x^2 + x + 3$ by $x^2 + 4x + 4$

$$x^2 + 4x + 4 \quad \overline{\smash{)}2x^3 + x^2 + x + 3}$$

Dividing $2x^3$ by x^2 gives $2x$

$$\begin{array}{r} 2x \\ x^2 + 4x + 4 \quad \overline{\smash{)}2x^3 + x^2 + x + 3} \end{array}$$

Multiplying $x^2 + 4x + 4$ by $2x$ and writing in the term to subtract, i.e.

$$\begin{array}{r} 2x \\ x^2 + 4x + 4 \quad \overline{\smash{)}2x^3 + x^2 + x + 3} \\ - \\ 2x^3 + 8x^2 + 8x \end{array}$$

Now the result of subtracting the polynomial $2x^3 + 8x^2 + 8x$ from $2x^3 + x^2 + x + 3$ will eliminate the highest degree power $(2x^3 - 2x^3 = 0)$ leading to us now facing computing the outcome of dividing $-7x^2 - 7x + 3$ by $x^2 + 4x + 4$, i.e.

$$\begin{array}{r} 2x \\ x^2 + 4x + 4 \quad \overline{\smash{)}2x^3 + x^2 + x + 3} \\ - \\ 2x^3 + 8x^2 + 8x \\ \hline -7x^2 - 7x + 3 \end{array}$$

The next term is the result of dividing the new lead term $-7x^2$ by x^2.

$$
\begin{array}{r}
2x - 7 \\[4pt]
\hline
\end{array}
$$

$$
x^2 + 4x + 4 \quad)\,2x^3 + x^2 + x + 3
$$

$$
-
$$

$$
2x^3 + 8x^2 + 8x
$$

$$
\hline
$$

$$
-7x^2 - 7x + 3
$$

$$
-
$$

$$
-7x^2 - 28x - 28
$$

$$
\hline
$$

$$
21x + 31
$$

Now the process is completed since

- $21x + 31$ has degree 1 and this is less than the degree of $x^2 + 4x + 4$.

- The quotient term is $2x - 7$.

- The remainder term is $21x + 31$.

In total we see that

$$
2x^3 + x^2 + x + 3 \;=\; (2x - 7) \cdot (x^2 + 4x + 4) \;+\; (21x + 31)
$$

The process is described by the stages in Algorithm 2.3

Algorithm 2.3. Polynomial Division

1: $\{p_{n,\underline{c}}(x)/q_{m,\underline{d}}(x), q(x) \neq 0, m \leq n\}$
2: $dcon := d_{\deg(q)}$;
   {$dcon$ holds the coefficient of the leading term in $q(x)$}
3: $quot := 0$;
4: $remain := p(x)$;
   {**Invariant:** $p(x) = q(x) \cdot quot + remain$}
5: **while** $remain \neq 0$ && $\deg(remain) \geq \deg(q)$ **do**
6:    $rcon := c_{\deg(remain)}$;
      {$rcon$ holds the coefficient of the leading term remaining}
7:    $NextTerm := (rcon/dcon) \cdot x^{\deg(remain)-m}$;
      {The value $rcon/dcon$ in in $\mathbb{Q}$.}
8:    $quot := quot + NextTerm$;
9:    $remain := remain - NextTerm \cdot q(x)$;
      {**Note:** $NextTerm \cdot q(x)$ just multiplies each $d_k x^k$ in $q(x)$ by αx^t}
      {(for some $\alpha \in \mathbb{Z}, t \in \mathbb{W}$)}
10: **end while**
11: **return** $< quot, remain >$;

Factorization and Roots

Informally a non-constant polynomial[32] $p(x) \in \mathbb{Q}[X]$ is said to be *irreducible* if there are no non-constant polynomials $g(x)$ and $h(x)$ in $\mathbb{Q}[X]$ for which $p(x) = g(x) \cdot h(x)$.

Given $p(x)$ the *Factorization Problem* is to find $\alpha \in \mathbb{Q}$ and polynomials

$$< q^{(1)}(x), q^{(2)}(x), \ldots, q^{(r)}(x) >$$

such that

F1. Each $q^{(i)}(x)$ is non-constant and irreducible.

F2. Each $q^{(i)}(x) \in \mathbb{Q}[X]$.

F3. The polynomial $p(x)$ is obtained by,

$$p(x) = \alpha \cdot \left(\prod_{i=1}^{r} q^{(i)}(x) \right)$$

---

[32]If $p(x)$ is non-constant then its degree is at least 1.

For example, $x^3 - 3x^2 + 3x - 1$ is factorized as $(x-1) \cdot (x-1) \cdot (x-1)$. The polynomial

$$2x^4 - 8x^3 + 10x^2 - 16x + 12$$

is

$$2 \cdot (x-1) \cdot (x^2+2) \cdot (x-3)$$

We see an immediate connection between the problems "find the factorization of $p(x)$" and "find the roots of $p(x)$": with

$$p(x) = \alpha \cdot \left(\prod_{i=1}^{r} q^{(i)}(x) \right)$$

the (set of) roots of $p(x)$ are simply

$$R(p(x)) = \bigcup_{i=1}^{r} R(q^{(i)}(x))$$

It is also noted that the multiplicity, $\mu_p(r)$ for $r \in R(p(x))$ is just

$$\sum_{i \, : \, r \in R(q^{(i)})} \mu_{q^{(i)}}(r)$$

For the case of $p(x) \in \mathbb{Q}[X]$ there are some simplifications that can be made.

We can limit consideration to the problem of finding factorizations of $q(x) \in \mathbb{Z}[X]$.

This is because, given $p_{n,\underline{c}}(x) \in \mathbb{Q}[X]$, since $c_k \in \mathbb{Q}$ we can describe c_k in a form

$$c_k = \frac{b_k}{d_k} \qquad b_k \in \mathbb{Z}, \ d_k \in \mathbb{N}$$

Now define

$$\alpha = \prod_{c_k \neq 0} d_k$$

The polynomial $q_{n,\underline{h}}(x) = \alpha p(x)$ has only coefficients in $\mathbb{Z}$ since

$$h_i = (\alpha)c_i = \left(\frac{b_i}{d_i}\right) \cdot \left(\prod_{k=0}^{n} d_k\right) = b_i \cdot \left(\prod_{k \neq i} d_k\right)$$

Furthermore if

$$q(x) = \prod q^{(i)}(x)$$

is a factorization of $q(x) \in \mathbb{Z}[X]$ then

$$p(x) = \left(\frac{1}{\alpha}\right) \prod q^{(i)}(x)$$

is a factorization of $p(x)$ in $\mathbb{Q}[X]$.

For example, suppose $p_3(x) \in \mathbb{Q}[X]$ is

$$\frac{1}{2}x^3 + \frac{2}{3}x^2 - x + \frac{1}{4}$$

then

$$\alpha = 2 \cdot 3 \cdot 1 \cdot 4 = 24$$

and $q_3(x) = 24p_3(x)$ is

$$12x^3 + 16x^2 + 24x + 6 = 2 \cdot (6x^3 + 8x^2 + 12x + 3)$$

[Notice that while we have chosen α to be the result of multiplying *all* of the denominators $< d_0, d_1, \ldots, d_n >$ we could equally have defined it to be the lowest common multiple, i.e. the smallest value g such that $g = y_k d_k$ for some $y_k \in \mathbb{N}$ for each k: in the example $g = lcm(2, 3, 1, 4) = 12$.]

Until the development of special-purpose highly tuned algorithms, see e.g. the surveys Kaltofen [134, 135, 136] a frequently used method was Kronecker's Method (Kronecker [148] although this is a rediscovery of the method presented in Schubert [208]).

From the discussion above we can focus our initial developments on $p(x) \in \mathbb{Z}[X]$.

Let $p_n(x) \in \mathbb{Z}[X]$ be given by

$$p_n(x) = \sum_{k=0}^{n} c_k x^k$$

We can assume that $p_{n,\underline{c}}(x)$ is *primitive*, that is to say

$$\gcd(c_0, c_1, \ldots, c_k, \ldots, c_n) = 1$$

For otherwise, since the greatest common divisor of its coefficients is $\alpha > 1$,

$$p_{n,\underline{c}}(x) = \alpha \cdot q_{n,\underline{d}}(x)$$

with $d_i = c_i/\alpha$ and $d_i \in \mathbb{Z}$ we can focus on $q_{n,\underline{d}}(x)$ rather than $p_{n,\underline{c}}(x)$.

Summary: $p_n(x) \in \mathbb{Z}[X]$ is a primitive polynomial which we wish to factorize as

$$\alpha \cdot \left(\prod_{j=1}^{r} q^{(j)}(x) \right)$$

with $\alpha \in \mathbb{Q}$ and each $q^{(j)}(x) \in \mathbb{Z}[X]$ is irreducible.

Our first observation concerns the effect of roots of $p_n(x)$ on its factorization. We know, of course, by definition, that when r, possibly $r \notin \mathbb{Q}$ is a root of $p_n(x)$ then $p_n(r) = 0$.

What if it is the case that $r \in \mathbb{Q}$ is a root of $p_n(x)$: does this special case allow us any greater freedom? Now, in principle, whenever $r \in \mathbb{Q}$ is a root of $p_n(x) \in \mathbb{Q}[X]$ there is some polynomial $q_{n-1}(x) \in \mathbb{Z}[X]$ such that

$$p_n(x) \;=\; (x - r) \cdot q_{n-1}(x)$$

The factor $(x-r)$ is self-evidently already irreducible, and by writing $r = \alpha/\beta$ we get

$$(x - r) \;=\; \frac{1}{\beta}(\beta \cdot x - \alpha)$$

with $(\beta \cdot x - \alpha) \in \mathbb{Z}[X]$.

Not only in principle, however, but also *in practice*. A polynomial with the properties described always exists and, furthermore from $p_n(x)$ and the factor $(x - r)$ we can recover $q_{n-1}(x)$ as the outcome of the polynomial division $p_n(x)/(x - r)$.

Overall, in constructing the factorization of (the primitive) $p_n(x) \in \mathbb{Z}[X]$ our steps will be:

S1. Find all *Rational* roots $- \{r_1, r_2, \ldots, r_s\}$ of $p_n(x)$.

S2. Factor out all of the terms $(x-r_i)$ from $p(x)$ leaving a degree m $(m < n)$ polynomial, $q(x) \in \mathbb{Z}[X]$.

S3. Noting that $q(x)$ has no further Rational roots, find a factorization of $q(x)$.

Let us look at each of these stages in turn.

First step: finding Rational roots of $p_n(x) \in \mathbb{Z}[X]$.

Recall that,

$$p_n(x) = \sum_{k=0}^{n} c_k x^k$$

Now we can assume that $c_0 \neq 0$ otherwise we can factor out x and that $c_n \neq 0$ (for, again, were this to be the case then $p(x)$ is not a *degree* n polynomial). Suppose that $r = a/b$ *is* a root of $p(x)$ then it must be the case that

$c_0 = a \cdot u$ i.e. a divides c_0 without remainder so that $u \in \mathbb{N}$.
$c_n = b \cdot v$ i.e. b divides c_n without remainder so that $v \in \mathbb{N}$.

This is the *Rational Root Test* which prescribes a necessary condition for $r \in \mathbb{Q}$ to be a root of $p_n(x) \in \mathbb{Z}[X]$.

Now since c_0 and c_n are both in $\mathbb{Z}$ there are a *finite* number of possibilities to consider. For example if $c_0 = 4$ and $c_n = 3$ we have choices for a and b from

$$\{-1, 1, -2, 2, -4, 4\} \times \{-1, 1, -3, 3\}$$

So that *if* there are any Rational roots these *must* come from the set

$$\left\{ 1, \ -1, \ \frac{1}{3}, \ \frac{-1}{3}, \ 2, \ -2, \ \frac{2}{3}, \ \frac{-2}{3}, \ 4, \ -4, \ \frac{4}{3}, \ \frac{-4}{3} \right\}$$

These 12 possibilities can be tested exhaustively to see if any satisfies $p_n(a/b) = 0$.

Second step: factoring out Rational roots.

Suppose we discover that $r \in \mathbb{Q}$ is a root of $p_n(x) \in \mathbb{Z}[X]$. We now find $q_{n-1}(x) \in \mathbb{Q}[X]$ for which

$$p_n(x) = (x - r) \cdot q_{n-1}(x)$$

by computing $p_n(x)/(x-r)$

Third step: Finding remaining factors.
After reducing $p_n(x)$ to $q_m(x)$ by the processes of identifying all[33] of its Rational roots and factoring out related binomials, $(x - r)$ through division, we will be left with a degree m polynomial $q_m(x)$ ($m \leq n$). There are two possibilities for $q_m(x)$.

---

[33]Notice that "all" must account for Rational roots with multiplicity exceeding 1. That is if r is a root with, say $\mu(r) = 2$ then $p(x) = (x-r)q(x)$ but r is also a root of $q(x)$.

Q1. The degree of $q_m(x)$ is at most 3.

Q2. The degree of $q_m(x)$ is at least 4.

The first of these indicates that the factorization process (relative to finding factors $q^{(i)}(x) \in \mathbb{Q}[X]$) is completed: the only possibilities are $q_m(x) \in \mathbb{Q}$ (degree 0); $q_m(x) = (x - a)$ (degree 1); or $q_m(x)$ is a quadratic (degree 2) without Rational roots; similarly that $q_m(x)$ is a cubic (degree 3) without Rational roots.

For the second case it is *possible* that $q_m(x) = f(x) \cdot g(x)$ where $\deg(f) = 2$, It could, also, be the case that $q_m(x)$ is already irreducible. While, just as the Rational root test allowed us to prescribe conditions that factors $(x - r)$ had to satisfy, we can stipulate how such putative quadratic factors, $f(x)$, must relate to $q_m(x)$. Given the nature of these conditions it would also be useful to have a guaranteed way of deciding if $q_m(x) \in \mathbb{Z}[X]$ is already irreducible. Unfortunately while there are methods that offer sufficient conditions[34] no necessary properties have been established.[35]

Although there are methods which allow us to filter out quadratic, then cubic, quartic, etc. polynomial factors from $q_m(x)$ irrespective of how large $\deg(q)$ may be, these raise increasingly onerous computational demands. While suitable for handling small scale (at worst degree 10) polynomials, for polynomials whose degree is of the order of 1000 much more sophisticated techniques must be used. The first practical approach capable of factorizing very high degree polynomials in $\mathbb{Z}[X]$ was discovered by Lenstra, Lenstra and Lovász [153] , in the early 1980s.

To give a flavour of by-hand approaches, we look at how filtering *quadratic* factors from $p(x)$ ($\deg(p) \geq 4$) may be tackled.

Letting $p(x) \in \mathbb{Z}[X]$ have degree at least 4 and no roots in $\mathbb{Q}$. Suppose it were to be the case that $t(x) = ax^2 + bx + c \in \mathbb{Q}[X]$ is a factor of $p(x)$? This would allow us to write

$$p(x) = (ax^2 + bx + c) \cdot q(x)$$

where $\deg(q) = \deg(p) - 2$. We can narrow down the possible values of $< a, b, c >$ in the quadratic $t(x)$ by

---

[34]Probably the best-known of these is that given by the Schönemann–Eisenstein Theorem. [206, 77]

[35]This is for $p(x) \in \mathbb{Z}[X]$, there are such tests available in some choices for coefficient domains.

T1. Choose *three* distinct values of x, e.g. $\alpha_1 = -1$, $\alpha_2 = 0$, $\alpha_3 = 1$.[36]

T2. Find the outcomes $< p(\alpha_1),\ p(\alpha_2),\ p(\alpha_3) >$.

T3. **If** it is the case that $p(x) = (ax^2 + bx + c) \cdot q(x)$ then we must have

$$
\begin{aligned}
p(\alpha_1) &= (a \cdot (\alpha_1)^2 + b \cdot \alpha_1 + c) \cdot q(\alpha_1) \\
p(\alpha_2) &= (a \cdot (\alpha_2)^2 + b \cdot \alpha_2 + c) \cdot q(\alpha_2) \\
p(\alpha_3) &= (a \cdot (\alpha_3)^2 + b \cdot \alpha_3 + c) \cdot q(\alpha_3)
\end{aligned}
$$

From the conditions in (T3) we need to consider each of the distinct ways in which $p(\alpha) = u \cdot w$ (with $u, w \in \mathbb{Z}$). So letting,

$$
C_i = \{\, u\ :\ p(\alpha_i) \div u = w \in \mathbb{Z} \,\} \quad (1 \le i \le 3)
$$

For each of the distinct ways of choosing $u_1 \in C_1$ and $u_2 \in C_2$ and $u_3 \in C_3$ we need to check if there is a choice of coefficients $< a, b, c >$ that satisfies

$$
\begin{aligned}
a \cdot (\alpha_1)^2 + b \cdot \alpha_1 + c &= u_1 \\
a \cdot (\alpha_2)^2 + b \cdot \alpha_2 + c &= u_2 \\
a \cdot (\alpha_3)^2 + b \cdot \alpha_3 + c &= u_3
\end{aligned}
$$

Should it be the case $t(x) = ax^2 + bx + c$ satisfies $t(\alpha_i) = u_i$ for a given choice of $< u_1, u_2, u_3 >$ we need to check that $t(x)$ is a factor of $p(x)$: in other words that $p(x)/t(x)$ has no remainder.

The mixture of *integer* factorization and exhaustive testing is computationally very intensive and, while feasible for hand calculations is unrealistic for program level implementation and practical use.

Special cases: closed form solutions

More sophisticated techniques are needed to handle $p(x) \in \mathbb{R}[X]$. but there are cases of $p(x) \in \mathbb{R}[X]$ for which we can describe all Real roots by explicit calculation using a closed form formula. That is to say, we have a formula, $root(\underline{c})$ which given a collection of coefficients, $\underline{c}$, from $\mathbb{R}$ reports *all* of the (Real) roots of the polynomial $p_{n,\underline{c}}(x) \in \mathbb{R}[X]$.

Low Degree Polynomials – Quadratics, Cubics and Quartics
Consider a typical degree 2 polynomial,

$$
q(x) = ax^2 + bx + c
$$

---

[36]We are free to choose *any* three distinct values.

This has two roots which may be found by calculating

$$\frac{-b + \sqrt{b^2 - 4 \cdot a \cdot c}}{2a} \quad ; \quad \frac{-b - \sqrt{b^2 - 4 \cdot a \cdot c}}{2a}$$

If the *discriminant* (the term $b^2 - 4 \cdot a \cdot c$) is *non-negative* (i.e. at least 0) then both roots are in $\mathbb{R}$.

A degree 3 (cubic) polynomial has the general form,

$$q(x) = ax^3 + bx^2 + cx + d$$

Here we can also describe a closed formula (characterized by the values $< a, b, c, d >$) that describes the roots of $q_3(x) \in \mathbb{R}[X]$. This first appears in the 1545 treatise of Gerolamo Cardano [42].[37] This formula is given below: Let

$$f = \left(\frac{-b^3}{27a^3} + \frac{bc}{6a^2} - \frac{d}{2a} \right)$$

$$g = \left(\frac{c}{3a} - \frac{b^2}{9a^2} \right)$$

Solutions for x of $ax^3 + bx^2 + cx + d$ are,

I. $\quad 2 \cdot \left(f + \sqrt{f^2 + g^3} \right)^{\frac{1}{3}} - \frac{b}{3a}$

II. $\quad 2 \cdot \left(f - \sqrt{f^2 + g^3} \right)^{\frac{1}{3}} - \frac{b}{3a}$

III. $\quad \left(f + \sqrt{f^2 + g^3} \right)^{\frac{1}{3}} + \left(f - \sqrt{f^2 + g^3} \right)^{\frac{1}{3}} - \frac{b}{3a}$

In these expressions $\sqrt{f^2 + g^3}$ (whenever $f^2 + g^3 \geq 0$) contributes both in positive form (cases I and III) and negative form (cases II and III).

We mentioned briefly the notion of discriminant (the term $b^2 - 4ac$) with respect to roots of quadratics. A similar notion[38] can be defined for cubics as

$$\Delta = 18abcd - 4b^3d + b^2c^2\, 4ac^3 - 27a^2d^2$$

The nature of Real roots for $q_3(x) \in \mathbb{R}[X]$ is characterized as in Table 2.4.

---

[37]A volume that has been considered as influential in its domain as Copernicus' 1545 defence of a heliocentric model of planetary motion: *De revolutionibus orbium coelestium.*

[38]The concept of the discriminant of a polynomial is well-defined for arbitrary polynomials. It is, however, particularly useful for quadratic and cubics in allowing the nature of the two (respectively three) roots to be described.

Table 2.4: Roots of $q_3(x) \in \mathbb{R}[X]$ and its discriminant

Δ	Roots
$\Delta > 0$	$q_3(x)$ has **3** distinct Real roots.
$\Delta = 0$	$q_3(x)$ has only Real roots, one of which has multiplicity at least 2.
$\Delta < 0$	$q_3(x)$ has *exactly one* Real root.

The solution for cubics is considerably more intricate than that for quadratics. The solution for *quartics* (degree 4 polynomials) in terms of its convoluted nature is to cubics as the involved nature of the cubic solution is to quadratics. What is (usually accepted[39]) as the first general solution for finding roots of $q_4(x) \in \mathbb{R}[X]$ is the method of Lodovico Ferrari (1522–1565) a protégé of Cardano. Ferrari's technique builds on the general solution to cubics and appeared in Cardano's *Artis Magnae* [42] mentioned earlier. The intricacies involved in the closed form solution for quartics render its inclusion beyond the scope of this text. Beyond quartics it is not possible to go: that there are no general closed form expressions applicable for capturing the roots of $p_k(x) \in \mathbb{R}[X]$ for any $k \geq 5$ is demonstrated by the Abel-Ruffini Theorem. This was an achievement of Paulo Ruffini whose (incomplete) 1799 argument was refined by Niels Abel in 1824. Ayoub [16, §5–7, pp. 265–272, §9, pp. 272–5] offers a careful discussion of work on quintics.

2.6   A brief note on Multivariate Polynomials

The forms we have looked at, $p(x) = \sum c_k x^k$ are defined using a single formal variable (x) so that these describe what are called **univariate** functions. There are a number of applications in which functions involving more than one variable naturally arise. We shall see one such example within Chapter 4. Such objects are usually called **multivariate** functions. With these we have, $n \in \mathbb{N}$ formal variables, $\{x_1, x_2, \ldots, x_n\}$. Retaining the notation $p(x_1, \ldots, x_n)$ for multivariate polynomials, such a function is a sum of **terms**, each term being a function (specifically a **product**) of, possibly different, powers of the x_i. An arbitrary term over $\{x_1, \ldots, x_n\}$ is denoted by $t_k(x_1, x_2, \ldots, x_n)$ In total,

$$p(x_1, x_2, \ldots, x_n) = \sum_k t_k(x_1, x_2, \ldots, x_n)$$

---

[39]See Endnote 9.

Each term being qualified by a collection $\alpha_{\mathbf{i}} = (\alpha_1^{(i)}, \alpha_2^{(i)}, \ldots, \alpha_n^{(i)})$ of values from $\mathbb{W}$ so that, writing in full,

$$p(x_1, x_2, \ldots, x_n) = \sum_k c_k \prod_{i=1}^n x_i^{\alpha_i^{(k)}}$$

(with c_k being a constant linked to the term t_k). For example, using x, y, z, and so on rather than x_1, x_2, etc. the following are examples of multivariate polynomials.

$$2x^2 + y + 3x^2y$$
$$x + y + z$$
$$2x^3y + x^2y^2 + xyzw + 5x^3y^2 + x^2yz^2w^3$$
$$\cdots$$

Notice (in consequence of qualifying powers of x_i within terms being drawn from $\mathbb{W}$ rather than $\mathbb{N}$) we do not have explicitly to include every formal variable, x_i, within each term.

For each concept we introduced with respect to (univariate) polynomials we can offer an analogue with respect to multivariate forms.

The **degree** of the multivariate polynomial $p(x_1, x_2, \ldots, x_n)$ having m terms $\{t_1, \ldots, t_m\}$ is

$$\max_{1 \le k \le m} \left(\sum_{i=1}^n \alpha_i^{(k)} \right)$$

That is to say, the maximum degree of any contributing term: the outcome of summing individual powers of x_i within the term. Of the three examples presented, the first has degree 3 (from the term $3x^2y$), the second degree 1 (all three terms reporting exactly the same degree) and the third example degree 8 ($x^2yz^2w^3$). As can be seen from the second and final examples, we do not require there to be at most one term with a given degree (for the univariate case this is required since the terms of such are just the divers c_kx^k): in the third example we have three terms with degree 4, namely $\{2x^3y, x^2y^2, xyzw\}$.

The (Real) **zeros** of a multivariate polynomial $p(x_1, x_2, \ldots, x_n)$ are those settings $(\beta_1, \beta_2, \ldots, \beta_n)$ under which $p(\beta_1, \beta_2, \ldots, \beta_n) = 0$. The terminology "zero of a polynomial" (in preference to "root") being used here in order to distinguish from the univariate case. The computational problem of finding all zeros of a polynomial is (as we have indicated with root finding) one with an extensive history. In contrast to the concepts we have considered above we have no general result analogous to "every (univariate) polynomial of degree k has k roots". Multivariate polynomials often arise in optimization contexts, a class of problems that we shall see again in Section 4.5.

2.7 Summary

In this Chapter we have argued that the concept of number is a fundamental entity arising throughout everyday activity. We have discussed how in order to exploit number in a computational setting precise and effective *representation* schemes are needed and presented some approaches. We have examined the ideas giving rise to different types of number and considered the differing contexts where these are relevant. This led us to the foundational idea of Real number which starting from the property "not expressible as Rational" led to "expressible as the root of a polynomial (with Rational coefficients)". The algebraic numbers so described do not allow us to capture *every* Real number. So that the Real numbers divide into algebraic (roots of polynomials in $\mathbb{Q}[X]$) numbers and non-algebraic (or transcendental) numbers, such as π.

The structure of polynomial forms will recur throughout this book and there is one issue concerning roots of polynomials that raises a problem whose resolution we must defer till later.

We have focused on polynomial expressions, properties and operations on these principally because, as noted, this structure will occur repeatedly over the course of the next chapters. Thus roots of polynomials are central to one instance of Optimization Problems that we will look at in Chapter 4. We deal with the apparent lacuna between roots and *"Real* roots" in Chapter 5. In Chapter 7 where we examine the notion of Spectral analysis the key conceit in defining "eigenvalues" turns out to be as the roots of a specific polynomial expression. In total our chief interest is, therefore, not so much in the direct application of polynomial forms (for example, as we see in the next Chapter, small matrices may be used) but more in their importance as a supporting player.

In the next Chapter we look to add some sense of order to these ideas.

2.8 Projects

1. An algorithm takes as input **three** parameters: a value $m \in \mathbb{W}$ (or $m \in \mathbb{Q}$ for the more adventurous minded); $b_m \in \mathbb{N}$ and $b_k \in \mathbb{N}$. These are interpreted to be that m is a value described in the base b_m and is to be converted into base b_k. Assuming these conventions implement the methods given in Algorithms 2.1 and Algorithm 2.2. Notice that the input m will have to be validated as a legitimate base b_m form, e.g. if $b_m = 4$ then m cannot contain any of the digits $\{4, 5, 6, 7, 8, 9\}$: numbers expressed in base 4 use only the digits $\{0, 1, 2, 3\}$.

2. Implement a suite of methods for operations on polynomials that include

   a. Evaluating a polynomial, $p(x)$ at a point $x = \alpha \in \mathbb{R}$.

   b. polynomial **addition**.

   c. polynomial **scalar multiplication**.

   d. polynomial **multiplication**

   e. polynomial **division**.

   Use the implementation of polynomial multiplication to provide a facility for multiplying very large integer values.

2.9 Endnotes

1. There is an extensive volume of research on the development of numeric notation within various cultures. Ifrah [125], to the best of my knowledge, remains the definitive historical study although has been critically ill-regarded in some quarters, e.g. Dauben [54, 55]. The works by Smith and Ginsburg [215] and Brooks [33] are less comprehensive but very accessible and clear: some may find the style of presentation (very much a reflection of the time of writing) rather off-putting. An excellent modern perspective is Bailey and Borwein [18] which offers a cogent defence of how significant the impact of positional notations including zero was. Also worth looking at is the article by Chrisomalis [45] which makes several salient observations concerning the importance of numeral representation formalisms beyond the standard view of these as only of relevance to mathematical ideas. Concerning which, in addition to historians the use and perception of differing number representation schemes has proved to be of great interest to, among others, philosophers e.g. Tal [232], educational theorists, see e.g. Lengnink and Schlimm [152], cognitive and neuro-scientists, e.g. Dehaene [58], Wynn [260], Verguts and Fias [241], Kadosh and Walsh [132].

2. Regarding the *Liber Abaci*, although appearing in 1202 there is strong evidence that the decimal system was introduced to European thinkers certainly no later than 999: indeed, as noted in [18], possibly as early as 500 in southern Europe. Towards the end of the 10th century, Gerbert of Aurillac (subsequently elected to the papacy taking the pontifical title Sylvester II) learnt of the system from Islamic scholars while visiting Spain.

3. We have observed the natural continuation from positional form in *decimal* (ten digits) to other number bases. The concept of using other bases had been explored as a means of *angular* measurement: e.g. in Mayan and Babylonian schemes. One also finds notions such as the "long hundred", see Goodare [106]. A detailed and thorough survey of less well-known choices of number base spanning a wide range of cultures may be found in Hammarström [115].

   The idea of "zero" is, however, a very deep and subtle concept: using "something" (a symbol) to describe "nothing" (an absence of quantity).

4. There is a very important distinction between the concept of a *numeri-cal quantity* – let us say x for example – and the *representation* of that quantity within some defined scheme, $\rho(x)$. Here the formalism, ρ may be any of the systems we have discussed: tally, Roman numerals, fi-nite number base, etc. What x "means" as a quantity and its attendant properties are questions that have been of deep interest to Philosophy of Mathematics.

5. Modern digital computers represent all numerical quantities using *finite length* "words". These may typically be 32, 64 (or in high-precision scientific applications 128 or longer) "bits" (binary digits). In order to model non-integer values as would be needed for Rational and indeed Real quantities a number of standards have been developed regarding conventions for interpreting 64, 128 bit words as floating point num-bers. It is unimportant, with respect to our argument, what the spe-cific forms of these standards are. What *is* relevant, however, is the fact that the number of bits used is *finite*. Using n bits one can describe 2^n distinct patterns: these can be interpreted as $\mathbb{W}$ or (in the so-called "1s'-complement" convention), members of $\mathbb{Z}$ or, by splitting the n bits into sections defining numerator and denominator, some finite number of members of $\mathbb{Q}$. In principle, since the collections of numbers formed by $\mathbb{W}$, $\mathbb{Z}$ and $\mathbb{Q}$ are *countable*[40] one side-effect is that, given a large enough word size, we can represent *every* integer, p, that satisfies $-M \leq p \leq M$ for some $M \in \mathbb{N}$. Consequently we can describe every *Rational* number p/q whose numerator p lies between $-M$ and M and whose denomina-tor, q, is a Natural number for which $q \leq M$. We are unable to achieve this breadth of coverage with the *Real* numbers, $\mathbb{R}$: even limiting to $x \in \mathbb{R}$ with $0 \leq x < 1$, the number of distinct possibilities exceeds what can be distinguished using finitely many bits. In very loose terms, there are "more than" 2^n different Real numbers that fall between 0 and 1, irrespective of how large we choose n to be. In total, in the context of digital computer encodings and standard program language types such as **double** and **float**, we can only ever accomplish what might informally be described as an "approximation within the Rationals" to Real values being unable to achieve the *full* range of possibilities.

---

[40]The term *countable* has a very specific technical meaning. We will eschew precise elab-oration being content to note that countable collections have the property that we can put the members of the collection into order so allowing us to refer to a "first", "second", and in general, n'th member.

6. As with the conventions mentioned earlier, Roman arithmeticians had a system for fractions. Reflecting its use in coinage, the Roman system made heavy use of *duodecimal* (base twelve) as its foundation.[41] The basic components of this scheme are presented in Table 2.5 below.

Table 2.5: Roman Fractional Number Schemes

Quantity	Notation	Name
1/12	·	*Uncia* ("Ounce")
2/12 = 1/6	·· or :	*Sextans*
3/12 = 1/4	··· or ∴	*Quadrans*
4/12 = 1/3	···· or : :	*Triens*
5/12	····· or ⫶··	*Quincunx*
6/12 = 1/2	**S**	*Semis*
7/12	**S**·	*Septunx*
8/12 = 2/3	**S**·· or **S**:	*Bes*
9/12 = 3/4	**S**··· or **S**⫶·	*Dodrans* (also *Nonuncium*)
10/12 = 5/6	**S**···· or **S**: :	*Dextans* (also *Decunx*)
11/12	**S**····· or **S**⫶··	*Deunx*
12/12 = 1	**I**	*Aes*

---

[41] A tradition that continued to influence monetary (and, indeed, weights and measures generally) in the U.K. up until 15th February 1971, which saw the introduction of a Decimal Currency system. Now, instead of having to contend with notions such as "Number of florins in a pound" (10), "Number of shillings in a florin" (2), and "Number of pennies in a shilling" (12), it was sufficient to work with "The number of pence in one pound" (100).

Regarding the first appearance (in Europe) of the notational style recognizable today, this is variously credited to the Flemish mathematician Simon Stevinus[42] (1548–1620); the German scientist Bartholomaeus Pitiscus[43] (1561–1613); and the Scots mathematician, developer of logarithms, and (as he considered himself) theologian John Napier.[44]

Stevinus' approach probably seems rather clumsy by comparison with the now standard methods. Suppose we take a value such as 562.8017 as it would appear in contemporary style. The form used in Stevinus' approach would be

The use of the decimal point to separate integer ($p \geq 0$) and fractional ($0 < q < 1$) parts (in our example $p = 562$ and $q = 8017/10000$) dates from Napier. The "full stop/period" symbol is standard in most countries for which English is or had been an official language, e.g. U.K., U.S.A., Canada, etc. but also Japan, Luxembourg, and Thailand. There are, however, a select number of places mainly continental European countries where this is replaced by comma. For example in France and French speaking countries, including parts of Canada, Spain and Spanish speaking[45] countries. It is, also, the case that both forms are recognized where there are multiple official languages, e.g. Canada, South Africa, Switzerland, etc.

7. Figure 2.2 illustrates one construction that can be used to draw a line having a positive Rational length $q \leq 1$. First mark off a distance 1 (on the horizontal axis) and then distances 1 and v (on the vertical axis). Next draw a line connecting v to 1 and *parallel* to this, a line from the point 1 on the vertical axis to the horizontal axis. The distance at which this line cuts the horizontal axis is exactly $1/v$. Repeating the process

---

[42]In *De Tiende* (*The Tenths*) from 1585.

[43]Responsible for the neologism "Trigonometry" in *Trigonometria: sive de solutione triangulorum tractatus brevis et perspicuus* (1595).

[44]cf. *A Plaine Discovery of the Whole Revelation of St. John* (1593) dedicated to James VI (James I of England) with a call that the monarch should "see that justice be done against the enemies of God's church, to reform the universal enormities of his country, and first to begin at his own house, family, and court.". Based on Napier's analysis, the work predicts the end of the world in 1688 (or 1700). Probably the most influential and highly regarded text in Napier's lifetime. As with so many apocalyptic predictions Napier's early demise (1617) preceded the world's.

[45]With Mexico a notable exception.

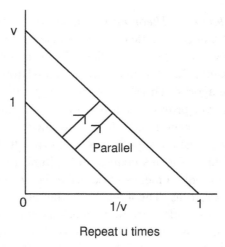

Repeat u times

Figure 2.2: Drawing a line of length u/v: $0 < u \leq v$ and $u \in \mathbb{N}$, $v \in \mathbb{N}$.

(from the point $1/v$ instead of 0) u times will eventually give a line whose total length is u/v.

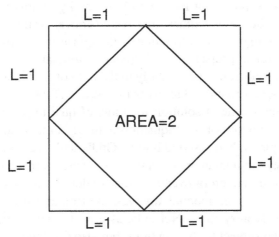

Figure 2.3: Drawing a square with area equal to 2

8. Referring to Figure 2.3, the length of the hypotenuse is $\sqrt{1^2 + 1^2}$, i.e. $\sqrt{2}$, so that the square marked out with the four hypotenuse of right-angled triangles both of whose shorter sides have length 1 will have the required area. In the construction presented above, we use a result well-

known as *Pythagoras' Theorem*: the square of the length of the longest side of a right-angled triangle (its *hypotenuse*) is equal to the sum of the squares of the lengths of the other sides. In his landmark review of scientific development – *The Ascent of Man* – Jakob Bronowski (1908–1974), described Pythagoras' Theorem as "the single most important Mathematical result ever proved". On first inspection this is a startling (and apparently wildly exagerrated) claim. Bronowski's description does not, in my view, overstate the significance of this result. We noted, in our introductory remarks for this chapter the cultural importance of number as providing not only a means to describe the world but also to *change* and *adapt*. Pythagoras' Theorem shows that numbers are more than an abstract game of no relevance to the world around us, but can be related to each other in a manner that allows us to *predict* an outcome: we *know* that if we draw two lines at right-angles to each other, one of length x and the other of length y then the length of the line connecting their ends *will be* $\sqrt{x^2 + y^2}$.

9. Re: "usually accepted". It is claimed in a 1954 text by Ivan Depman[59, p. 24] that one Paolo Valmes had discovered a general solution for quartics in 1486, predating Ferrari's discovery by almost 60 years. Independent evidence of Valmes' discovery (or even Valmes' existence) has yet to be found. This attribution is thought to be motivated by Soviet era anti-clerical propaganda – Depman's study appearing in the immediate post-Stalin era – particularly in the light of Depman's assertion that Valmes' achievement led to his being burned at the stake. The claim to have found a general solution for roots of quartic polynomials having incurred the wrath of the Inquisitor-General Torquemada who (according to Depman) had asserted it to be God's will that solution of quartics remain beyond human understanding. One aspect that casts some doubt on this lurid version of events, is that zealous as the Inquisition in late 15th century Spain undoubtedly was, the Roman variant[46] was equally so in 16th century Italy. Not only, as is well-known, were Copernicus and Galileo subject to its attentions, but also Cardano.

It seems rather unlikely, were there to be any basis for Valmes' alleged fate and the reason given for this, that Cardano would have openly published *Artis Magnae* [42] which contained Ferrari's method for quar-

---

[46]*The Supreme Sacred Congregation of the Roman and Universal Inquisition* to give its full title, formally established in 1542 by Pope Paul III and still active today under the title *"Congregation for the Doctrine of the Faith"*.

tics. Unlike Copernicus' 1543 *De revolutionibus orbium coelestium* (from 1616 until 1837) and Galileo's 1632 *Dialogo sopra i due massimi sistemi del mondo* (1633–1835) the *Artis Magnae* was never formally proscribed by being listed on the *Index Librorum Prohibitorum*. Depman's version was reported (and questioned) by Petr Beckmann [23, p. 80, p. 191]. Beckmann's report is used as a basis for attributing discovery to "Valmes" by some authors who do not trouble to discuss his caveats about authenticity, e.g. Agarwal *et al.* [1, p. 143], Dixon [64, p. 389], Suominen [231, p. 315].[47]

There is no known independent support providing grounds for treating Depman's claims as anything other than fanciful: despite recent clamour, the phenomenon of "Fake News" has been around a very long time and originated with neither BREXIT nor presidential campaigns.

---

[47] It is surprising just how widespread this misconception is, with even tongue-in-cheek articles such as O'Connor and Jacobs [178] which claims to have unearthed Torquemada's correspondence with the Vatican being treated seriously in some quarters.

Chapter 3

Creating order
Vectors and Matrices

Well how was I to know it was going to be so complicated! I thought it was just going to be a straightforward bash on the nut up an alley.

The Missing Page (from BBC Series Hancock's Half Hour, 1960)
RAY GALTON & ALAN SIMPSON

3.1   Imposing structure on collections of objects

Sid James' bemoaning of his inability to fathom the plot ramifications of a pulp detective thriller as quoted above, may strike a chord with those surprised at the intricacies entailed in looking at as basic a notion as Number. The forms discussed in the preceding chapter have, however, a common simplifying feature: in the main these are dealing with single, unstructured entities. We considered individual numbers according to attributes such as rationality; we examined sets of numbers sharing common attributes but did not really go beyond this notion.

Nonetheless there is one obvious everyday context in which it is immediate that such an elements in isolation treatment is wanting: describing locations on a map. Whether this is done through a precise navigational convention (latitude and longitude), or an informal reference to a city locale ("corner of 5th and Main") or by very loose verbal description ("it's the second right after the third set of traffic lights") in all these forms we present not merely a single isolated datum but a *pair* of linked data. And, of course, we are not limited to movement in the plane: in a number of environments the need for a third *co-ordinate* (expressing elevation or height) will arise, or indeed a fourth (notions of time).

In such situations we are no longer expressing an idea through a single numerical object but rather through an *ordered* collection of these. A classical approach to the description of points in higher dimensions is the *Cartesian coordinate* system from Descartes [61]. Within this system we progress from points on the line (x–coordinate only) to points in the plane ((x, y)–coordinate) through to points in space ((x, y, z)–coordinate) and, in principle, yet richer forms. A conventional diagrammatic view is depicted in Figure 3.1.

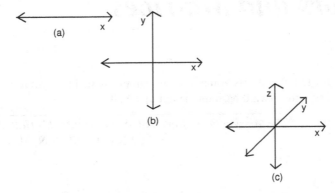

Figure 3.1: 1 (a), 2 (b) and 3-dimensional (c) Coordinate axes.

It is one thing to have a convention (as above) to describe points, however, in this chapter we extend this idea to consider also *lines*, *areas*, *volumes* and higher order forms. We do not, however, require a separate development of each of these: the treatment can be handled by a single, uniform method so that the ideas used to describe manipulation of forms in the 2-dimensional ((x, y)-axis) indicate directly how to implement 3 (and 4 and 5 and, in general, n) dimensional settings.

The treatment of *vectors* and *vector algebra* as these fields are called has enormous significance in (at least) one computational arena: that of Computer Graphics. The programming of animation effects such as scaling, rotation, and movement can be handled through a combination of easily computable operations applied (in a consistent manner) to individual points in 2 (and 3) dimensions. Such methods underpin almost all of the prototype Computer and Arcade Games that began to appear in the late 1970s and early 1980s. Primitive and unsophisticated as such diversions[1] may seem to contemporary audiences these have an extremely important part in the overall growth of popular personal computing. In the late 1970s, home computing was generally the domain of a very small clique of hobbyist users, however (even before the arrival of the world-wide web and effective intercommunication between physically separated machines in the late 1990s) partly as a result of affordable technology but also as a consequence of realizing the scope of possibilities,[2] home computing became much less of a niche interest. Less obviously, but also in the context of Computer Graphics and Image Processing techniques in general, treatments of 3 (and, indeed 4) component forms appear in manipulation of *colour*: one, still widely used, convention being the RGB encoding whereby the colour of a point on (suitably equipped) displays is given as a mixture of Red, Green and Blue values described as numbers lying between 0 and 255.[3]

The concept of n-vector, as such an "ordered collection of n numbers" is dubbed formally, has applications in Computer Science beyond just an aid to graphics and we have, in fact, already encountered one context where such an ordered components view is important: coefficients of bounded degree polynomials from some domain $\mathbb{T}$.

In the next section we consider this idea of ordered collection of numbers, that is to say the concept of n-vector, in greater depth stressing distinctive features by which this differs from the superficially similar notion of n-tuple.

3.2 n-vectors vs. n-tuples

For our formal definition of n-vector we have the following approach.

Description 1. *Letting $\mathbb{T}$ be a number type (e.g. as before, $\mathbb{T} = \mathbb{R}$, $\mathbb{T} = \mathbb{Q}$, etc.), and $n \in \mathbb{N}$, any n-vector, $\mathbf{x}$ over $\mathbb{T}$ is an ordered collection of values $x_i \in \mathbb{T}$, so that*

$$\mathbf{x} = \ <x_1, x_2, \ldots, x_n>$$

We emphasize the following aspects,

---

[1]Typical of such were one player configurations such as "Asteroids", two player "bat-and-puck" arrangements ("tennis"), and moving target games.

[2]The requirement to be able to "program" was overcome through the availability of bespoke software packages to provide bookkeeping (e.g. spreadsheets, simple database support), document production, calculators and, of course, games.

[3]That is to say in 8 bits, so a colour screen can, in principle, display $2^{24} = 16,777,216$ distinct colours. The limitations of human optical powers and display hardware tends to result in not all of these being distinguishable.

V1. The two significant attributes of an *n-vector*, **x**, are its *size* (also called *magnitude* or *length*) and its *direction*. In depicting diagrams of vectors, this direction is indicated by placing an arrow on the line (whose length corresponds to the vector size) showing the vector.

V2. The *components* (the x_i) form a *collection* not (necessarily) a *set*: different *component indices*, x_i and x_j ($i \neq j$), may be the same element from $\mathbb{T}$.

V3. The *ordering* of individual components is significant. For instance, using $\mathbb{T} = \mathbb{W}$ and $n = 3$, the 3-vectors $< 6, 14, 14 >$, $< 14, 6, 14 >$, $< 14, 14, 6 >$ describe 3 *distinct* 3-vectors.

In many Computer Science arenas, most importantly within the design and organization of *databases* but also in aspects of the AI discipline known as *Knowledge Representation*, a mechanism that is superficially very similar to the notion of n-vector arises: that of *n-tuple*. It is useful to dedicate a brief discussion to the question of distinctive features of the two.

Let us start by presenting an informal description of this concept of n-tuple, which we will attempt to do in a very general way.

Description 2. *Let $n \in \mathbb{N}$ and consider n sets of objects*[4]

$$S_1, \ S_2, \ \ldots \ S_n$$

It should be noted that the set S_i may be identical to the set S_j (for $i \neq j$) and that the individual sets may be either infinite, e.g. $S_i = \mathbb{Q}$ or finite, e.g. upper case Roman letters 'A' through 'Z'.

An n-tuple drawn from $\underline{S} = S_1 \times S_2 \times \cdots \times S_n$ is an ordered collection

$$\underline{s} = \ < s_1, \ s_2, \ldots, s_n >$$

for which $s_i \in S_i$ for each $1 \leq i \leq n$.

We can begin by noting some salient points of both similarity and difference arising through the forms given in Description 1 and Description 2.

---

[4]More precisely "object labels/descriptors". Here, as with the concept of number discussed in Chapter 2, we must distinguish between abstract concepts of object in itself, e.g. some Natural number $p \in \mathbb{N}$ and the *representation* of that object for computational purposes, e.g. $(p)_{10}$: the number p expressed in decimal.

VT1. Every n-vector over $\mathbb{T}$ can be viewed as and therefore treated like an n-tuple in which $S_i = \mathbb{T}$ for each $1 \leq i \leq n$.

VT2. We shall consider the components of n-vectors to be *numerical in nature*, and thus giving rise to well-defined notions of adding two n-vectors, scalar multiplication of an n-vector by some $\alpha \in \mathbb{T}$. Indeed, perhaps less obviously, as having some defined concept of multiplying 2 n-vectors and for capturing the size or length of such a vector. In contrast the components of an n-tuple, not being necessarily numeric in form, need not have any defined notions of adding two n-tuples let alone scalar multiplication of an n-tuple (even, should it be relevant, by some $\alpha \in S_i$ when S_i is numeric in form), let alone multiplication of two n-tuples within the same $\underline{S}$. Similarly there is no necessity to have a concept of n-tuple length/size and direction has no natural analogue with respect to n-tuples.

VT3. Noting the separation implied by point VT2 above: while every n-vector is a (specific type of) n-tuple, it is not, in general, the case that we would (or, indeed, could in any useful manner) view an n-tuple as an n-vector.

The formal treatment and manipulation of n-tuple structures finds one of its richest exemplars in the theory of *Relational algebra* which is central to the logical and coherent design of relational databases. Although the organization of structured information via the (for want of a less pretentious term) "relational paradigm" did not figure in the earliest database structures,[5] the Relational Database Model is central to the design and implementation of modern databases. Another important area in which treatments of data presented via n-tuples is the sub-field of Artificial Intelligence concerned with Knowledge Representation.

In total the concerns of relational algebra[6] are less focused on numerical legerdemain and more at a level of abstract interaction. In dealing with vectors in the remainder of this chapter our interest will, primarily, be on the more numerical aspects of manipulation: vector operations and *Matrix-vector* product.

---

[5]See Endnote 1.

[6]This is a subject (perhaps not under this heading) that would, typically, be considered as part of a Discrete Methods for CS introductory course.

3.3 Operations involving vectors

First we offer some notational conventions.

We will use bold font lower-case Roman letters (e.g. **u**, **v**, **x**, **y** etc) to denote an arbitrary n-vector. Unless it is explicitly stated otherwise we will work with *Real* valued vectors, i.e. $\mathbb{T} = \mathbb{R}$. For $k \in \mathbb{N}$, the notation $\mathbb{T}^k$ denotes the *set* of all k-vectors with elements drawn from $\mathbb{T}$.

It is important to distinguish vectors in $\mathbb{T}^k$ and elements in $\mathbb{T}$ and, to this end, we refer to the latter as *scalars* choosing to denote arbritrary scalar values by lower case Greek letters, α, β, γ etc.

Especially in 2 and 3 dimensional contexts (but not exclusively so) it is important to distinguish a vector as (informally) "a line having a *direction*" and "a *point* in n-dimensional space". We use angled brackets $(< \ldots >)$ for the former case and standard parentheses for the latter. Thus

$< x_1, x_2, \ldots, x_n >$ denotes the **vector** $< x_1, \ldots, x_n > \in \mathbb{R}^n$.

$(x_1, x_2, \ldots, x_n)$ denotes the **point** $(x_1, \ldots, x_n)$ in n-dimensional space.

It is useful to have a protocol for comparing different vectors in $\mathbb{T}^n$ and to this end given **x**, **y** $\in \mathbb{T}^n$ we write **x** $\leq$ **y** whenever $x_i \leq y_i$ for *every* component index $1 \leq i \leq n$; we write **x** $<$ **y** if **x** $\leq$ **y** *and* there is (at least) one index for which $x_i < y_i$.   These relations extend in a natural way to provide formulations for **x** $\geq$ **y** and **x** $>$ **y**, as well as **x** $=$ **y** (the component x_i of **x** is equal to the component y_i of **y** for every $1 \leq i \leq n$) and **x** $\neq$ **y** (there is some component for which $x_i \neq y_i$). It should be noted that it is not possible, with this convention, to give a **complete** ordering of the vectors in $\mathbb{T}^n$: we will have n-vectors **x** and **y** for which neither **x** $\leq$ **y** nor **y** $\leq$ **x** are true. This aspect provides one of many differences between the character of vectors over $\mathbb{T}$ and that of $\mathbb{T}$ itself. All of the number types, $\mathbb{T}$, considered in Chapter 2 are what is known as "*totally ordered*": given any α, $\beta \in \mathbb{T}$ exactly one of $\alpha < \beta$, $\alpha > \beta$, or $\alpha = \beta$ holds. In contrast, given **x** and **y** we cannot say that "**x** $<$ **y** or **y** $<$ **x** or **x** $=$ **y**" must be the case.[7]

In a number of domains we identify special vectors with a given structure. Among these we mention the *zero vector*, which we denote **0** the n-vector all of whose components are 0.

Finally, so-called for reasons that will become clearer in Section 3.4 we have the n *standard basis* vectors,[8]

$$E_n = \{\mathbf{e}_1, \ldots, \mathbf{e}_k, \ldots, \mathbf{e}_n\} \subset \mathbb{R}^n$$

---

[7]That is to say, with this particular notion of vector comparison. See, however, Endnote 2.

[8]This idea of standard basis vector is also well-defined for choices of $\mathbb{T}$ other $\mathbb{R}$.

The standard basis vector, $\mathbf{e}_k$ is

$$\mathbf{e}_k \;=\; <\; \underbrace{0,\, 0,\, \ldots,\, 0}_{k-1 \text{ times}},\, 1,\, \underbrace{0,\, 0,\, \ldots,\, 0}_{n-k \text{ times}}\; >$$

Given two numbers p and q in $\mathbb{Q}$ we are familiar from school with the notion of a third number defined through the *arithmetic operations* of *addition* $(p + q)$ and *multiplication* $(p \cdot q)$. In the case of n-vectors one of our motivating ideas is that of creating an ordered structural form by which collections of numerical quantities can be processed in a coherent manner. To this end, therefore, we should look to define analogous notions of **vector** addition and (although here we shall encounter some complications) **vector** multiplication.

The reader may recall that we have, already, met similar issues: in Section 2.5 where we discussed the form of *polynomial* addition and (scalar) multiplication.[9]

These operations provide a convenient starting point for vector processes.

Vector Addition

For

$$\mathbf{x} \;=\; <\, x_1,\, x_2,\, \ldots,\, x_n \,>$$
$$\mathbf{y} \;=\; <\, y_1,\, y_2,\, \ldots,\, y_n \,>$$

both n-vectors from $\mathbb{R}^n$ the result, $\mathbf{z} \in \mathbb{R}^n$ is the n-vector whose component z_i $(1 \le i \le n)$ is given by

$$z_i \;=\; x_i + y_i$$

Thus, $\mathbf{z} = \mathbf{x} + \mathbf{y}$ is the result of *component-wise* addition of elements of $\mathbf{x}$ with $\mathbf{y}$.

Scalar Multiplication

For $\mathbf{x} \in \mathbb{R}^n$ and $\alpha \in \mathbb{R}$ the vector $\mathbf{z}$ resulting from *scalar* multiplication of $\mathbf{x}$ by α, is the n-vector $\mathbf{z} = \alpha \cdot \mathbf{x} \in \mathbb{R}^n$ whose component z_i $(1 \le i \le n)$ is

$$z_i \;=\; \alpha \cdot x_i$$

---

[9]We, of course, also presented the process of multiplication of one polynomial $p(x) \in \mathbb{T}[X]$ by another $q(x) \in \mathbb{T}[X]$.

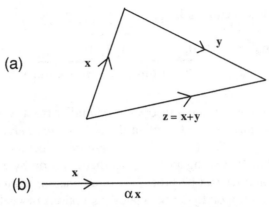

(a)

(b)

Figure 3.2: Basic vector operations

The effect of these processes is depicted in Figure 3.2: Figure 3.2(a) show-ing the outcome of adding vectors $\mathbf{x}$ and $\mathbf{y}$ while Figure 3.2(b) that of scaling $\mathbf{x}$ by α.

It is important to recognize that *position* is *not* an attribute of a vector: two vectors whose size and direction are identical are viewed as the same vector. In a number of applications it is useful to separate such vectors by delineating specific start and end coordinates. Often, in the "standard position" convention this start point will be the origin of the relevant coordinate axes, e.g. $(0,0)$, $(0,0,0)$, etc. In treating vector addition $\mathbf{x} + \mathbf{y}$ geometrically the start point of $\mathbf{y}$ can be taken to be the end point of $\mathbf{x}$. Thus, Figure 3.3(a) illustrates the outcome of adding $\mathbf{v}$ to $\mathbf{u}$ when the latter is in standard position, while Figure 3.3(b) shows the result when $\mathbf{u}$ is added to $\mathbf{v}$ with $\mathbf{v}$ in standard position. As one would expect, the *vectors* $\mathbf{u} + \mathbf{v}$ and $\mathbf{v} + \mathbf{u}$ are *identical*: these have the same length and direction but also in this instance the same *position*. The construction illustrated in Figure 3.3 is an example of the *Parallelogram Law* as shown by Figure 3.3(c).

With one caveat these operations are exactly the same as we saw defined in Section 2.5 for polynomial addition and scalar multiplication. The single distinction concerns the process of addition. The addition of $p_n(x) \in \mathbb{T}[X]$ and $q_m(x) \in \mathbb{T}[X]$ is well-defined even should it be the case that the poly-nomials involved have different degree, i.e. $n \neq m$. The reason being that (assuming, say, $m < n$) we can treat $q(x)$ as a degenerate degree n poynomial whose coefficients, d_k, are 0 for $m < k \leq n$. The operation of vector addition, however, is *only* well-defined if *both* $\mathbf{x}$ and $\mathbf{y}$ have exactly the same number of components: we do not define any idea of adding $\mathbf{x} \in \mathbb{R}^n$ to $\mathbf{y} \in \mathbb{R}^m$ when

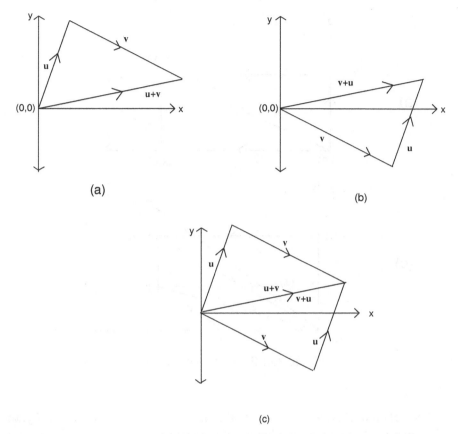

Figure 3.3: Vector addition from standard position

$n \neq m$.

We will come to multiplication shortly but before doing so we have one new (in the sense that we have not met a polynomial analogue) concept: the *size* (or *length*) of an n-vector. In order to motivate the definition consider Figure 3.4.

In Figure 3.4(a) the length of the line joining the origin $(0,0)$ to the point (x, y) is easily found: the 2-vector $< x, y >$ has *length* $\| < x, y > \|$ which is

$$\| < x, y > \| = \sqrt{x^2 + y^2}$$

Notice that (developing this approach)

$$\| < x, 0 > \| = \sqrt{x^2 + 0^2} = x \quad ; \quad \| < 0, y > \| = \sqrt{0^2 + y^2} = y$$

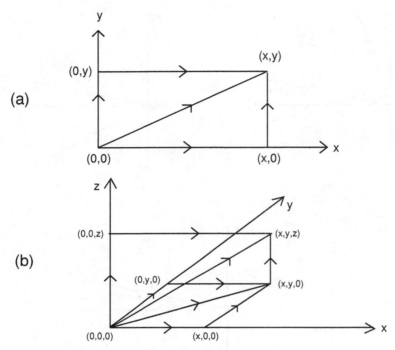

Figure 3.4: 2 and 3-vector length

This, of course, is simply adapting the classical result well-known as Pythagoras' Theorem. What about the length of the vector $< x, y, z >$ as depicted in Figure 3.4(b)? Again we have a right-angled triangle structure formed by the points $\{(0,0,0),\ (x,y,0),\ (x,y,z)\}$. We know how to find the length of the longest side ($< x, y, z >$ in this instance) of a right-angled triangle: the two shorter sides have respective lengths $\|< x, y, 0 >\|$ and $\|< 0, 0, z >\|$.[10]
So that,

$$\|< x, y, z >\| \;=\; \sqrt{\|< x, y, 0 >\|^2 \;+\; \|< 0, 0, z >\|^2}$$

This, however, is simply

$$\sqrt{x^2 + y^2 + z^2}$$

Overall we see a similar pattern to that of the 2-dimensional case: "add the results of squaring the individual components and take the (positive) square

---

[10]The second arising from the fact that we have to move a distance z upwards from the *point* $(x, y, 0)$ to reach the *point* (x, y, z).

root of this sum". Notice this operation does not require individual components
to be non-negative and the square root operation will always be applied to a
non-negative (≥ 0) quantity. This pattern gives our formulation of vector size
for arbitrary $\mathbf{x} \in \mathbb{R}^n$.

For $\mathbf{x} =< x_1, \ldots, x_n >$

$$\|\mathbf{x}\| = \sqrt{\sum_{k=1}^{n} |x_i|^2}$$

The notation $|\cdot|$ indicates *absolute value* (or *modulus*): the quantity $|x|$ is just
x when $x \geq 0$ and $-x$ when $x < 0$: $|x|$ is always *non-negative*.[11]

This form is sometimes referred to as the *Euclidean* length.[12] Although the
concept of "n-dimensional right angled triangles" may seem rather abstruse,
it is worth noting that, in exactly the same way that we justified our length of
$< x, y, z >$ in geometric terms via the (more obvious) length of $< x, y >$
computation, we can apply *exactly* the same process to support the form stated
for $\|\mathbf{x}\|$.

Referring again to Figure 3.2(a) the relationship between $\|\mathbf{x}\|$, $\|\mathbf{y}\|$, and
$\|\mathbf{x} + \mathbf{y}\|$ is easily given a geometric interpretation: travelling in the direction
shown from the start of the vector $\mathbf{x}$ for the distance $\|\mathbf{x}\|$ (i.e. the entire length
of $\mathbf{x}$) and then taking the direction indicated by the vector $\mathbf{y}$ for its length ($\|\mathbf{y}\|$)
defines a vector ($\mathbf{z} = \mathbf{x} + \mathbf{y}$). The three vectors mark out the sides of a triangle
with respective lengths $\|\mathbf{x}\|$, $\|\mathbf{y}\|$ and $\|\mathbf{x} + \mathbf{y}\|$. We can either obtain $\|\mathbf{x} + \mathbf{y}\|$
using the definitions of vector addition and length just presented, i.e. as

$$\|\mathbf{x} + \mathbf{y}\| = \sqrt{\sum_{k=1}^{n} |x_i + y_i|^2}$$

Alternatively we can apply standard school trigonometry so that redrawing
Figure 3.2(a) as Figure 3.5

We now see that

$$\|\mathbf{x} + \mathbf{y}\| = \frac{\|\mathbf{x}\|}{\cos\theta} = \frac{\|\mathbf{y}\|}{\sin\theta}$$

Returning to our observation that vectors are characterized by their direction and size, the concept of vector length just described provides a means of

---

[11]Although in the specific case $\|\mathbf{x}\|$ defined, the use of $|\cdots|$ is unnecessary to ensure we
are summing non-negative quantities, as discussed in Endnote 3 it is useful to include for more
general forms.

[12]The term L_2-metric may also be seen.

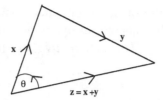

Figure 3.5: Trigonometric interpretation of Vector Length

choosing a representative vector. This is through the process known as *normalization*.[13]

For a (non-zero) vector, $\mathbf{x} \in \mathbb{R}^n$ its **normalization** is the vector, denoted by $\|\mathbf{x}\|_2 \in \mathbb{R}^n$ given through,

$$\|\mathbf{x}\|_2 = \frac{\mathbf{x}}{\|\mathbf{x}\|}$$

Thus, the vector $\|\mathbf{x}\|_2$ is a scalar multiple of $\mathbf{x}$ with the qualifying scalar α being $\alpha = 1/\|\mathbf{x}\|$. Notice the process of normalization preserves the direction of $\mathbf{x}$: $\|\mathbf{x}\| > 0$ so whether an individual component, x_i of $\mathbf{x}$ is ≥ 0 or ≤ 0 the matching component $x_i/\|\mathbf{x}\|$ in $\|\mathbf{x}\|_2$ will also be ≥ 0 or ≤ 0.

What about the concept of multiplication of n-vectors? It may be thought that we have already seen how this *should* be defined: exactly as it was done for multiplying two polynomials. This, however, only represents a style in which vector multiplication *could* be defined. In fact the formal structures, as used in computational settings, for vector product (as this is operation is called when vectors are the objects operated upon) use a quite different approach.

On first inspection proposing an alternative (which, as we will see, has its own technical eccentricities to consider) to a notationally already involved definition (as the interaction of coefficients in defining polynomial multiplication may appear) looks like an act of wilful obfuscation. It is, however, no such thing and the model(s) of vector product which will be presented are not only highly relevant to computational domains such as Computational Geometry but are also central to the treatment of vector algebra in classical Physics models of motion and mechanical modelling.

Nonetheless it is worth considering some of the reasons why the polynomial multiplication form as a model for n-vector product is unsuitable. Here

---

[13]The concept of "normalization" is, like the concept of vector size, not limited to the form we present, technically called the L_2-*norm*. Any of the examples discussed in Endnote 3 can be used as the underlying length measure with which to describe normalization of a given vector.

we can start by observing that the formal structure of polynomial multiplication is determined by the fact the result is driven by a very specific interpretation of what the coefficient vector, $\underline{c}$ for $p_{n,\underline{c}}(x) \in \mathbb{T}[X]$ represents: c_i qualifies the constant multiplying the power of x, x^i. Faced with multiplying $p_{n,\underline{c}}(x)$ and $q_{n,\underline{d}}(x)$ the outcome will not be another degree n polynomial: it will be a polynomial with degree $2n$ because the terms $c_n x^n$ (from p) and $d_n x^n$ (from q) will force a term $c_n d_n x^{2n}$ in the outcome. Polynomial multiplication is capturing an algebraic process: finding the output *coefficients* from the computation $(\sum_{k=0}^{n} c_k x^k) \cdot (\sum_{k=0}^{n} d_k x^k)$. For vector product in which the most significant form – for our immediate purposes – will involve 3-vectors we wish to have not only an algebraic justification but also a *geometric* interpretation. This is what drives the powerful exploitation of vector algebra in classical Physics; this is what also underpins the equally rich usage of vector algebra in *realistic* graphical rendering and display: for example in 3-dimensional motion, shadowing and lighting effects, hidden surface detection. Here binary operations involving two 3-vectors must define another 3-vector or, in some cases for a concept of length a 1-vector i.e. element in $\mathbb{R}$. What has little or no *geometric* sense is "a 6-vector produced as the result of 'multiplying' two 3-vectors": that, however, would be the outcome of interpreting vector product to be polynomial multiplication.

Vector product formation

There are *two* distinct notions of what is generally understood as vector product that arise in computational settings: one such form (the **dot** (or *scalar*) product) can be defined with respect to *any* pair of n-vectors, $\mathbf{x}$ and $\mathbf{y} \in \mathbb{R}^n$, The other form (the **cross** product, sometimes, in recognition of its geometric interpretation, dubbed the *directed area* product) is restricted to 3-vectors.[14]

The Dot Product: definition and properties

The *dot product* of 2 n-vectors $\mathbf{x}$ and $\mathbf{y}$ in $\mathbb{R}^n$ is denoted $\mathbf{x} \cdot \mathbf{y}$ and is a *scalar*. That is $\mathbf{x} \cdot \mathbf{y} \in \mathbb{R}$.[15] The formal (algebraic) definition of $\mathbf{x} \cdot \mathbf{y}$ for n-vectors in $\mathbb{R}^n$ is,

$$\mathbf{x} \cdot \mathbf{y} \;=\; \sum_{k=1}^{n} x_i y_i$$

---

[14]See Endnote 4.
[15]More generally, for $\mathbf{x}$ and $\mathbf{y}$ in $\mathbb{T}^n$, $\mathbf{x} \cdot \mathbf{y} \in \mathbb{T}$.

That is to say, the result of adding the (component-wise) multiplication of elements in **x** and **y**.

This form possibly looks rather odd, however, despite the fact that the dot product produces a scalar value from 2 n-vectors examining its geometric interpretation (which is of great importance to applications in computer graphics) reveals some interesting properties.

Recall Figure 3.5 wherein the length of the vector produced by addition of vectors was examined in terms of trigonometric relations. Now consider the five cases shown in Figure 3.6.[16]

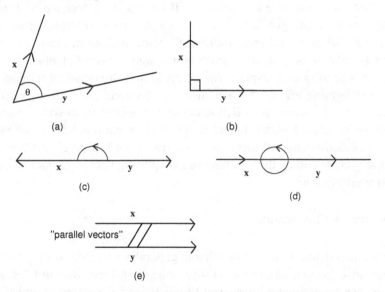

Figure 3.6: Geometric interpretation of Vector Dot Product

In Figure 3.6(a) we have (as in the illustration interpreting length resulting from vector addition) vectors **x** and **y** separated by an angle θ. If we analyze the algebraic definition of **x** · **y** (again via school trigonometry) we find[17]

$$\mathbf{x} \cdot \mathbf{y} \;=\; \|\mathbf{x}\| \, \|\mathbf{y}\| \cos \theta$$

Now this relationship becomes of particular interest for specific angles θ. In Figure 3.6(b), the angle separating **x** from **y** is a right-angle: 90°. But $\cos 90 =$

---

[16]We note that the notion of line is not limited to 2 (or even 3-dimensional) coordinate axes and can be processed as an object in an n-dimensional set up.

[17]Some rather tedious algebraic hacking can be used formally to justify. We do not bother to present this leaving it for, as Muriel Spark reports Miss Jean Brodie's opinion of the Girl Guides, "those who like that kind of thing (that is the kind of thing that they like)".

0 and so this tell us that the dot product of vectors at right angles to each other is 0: such vectors are called *orthogonal*. Continuing to Figure 3.6(c), now x and y lie on the *same straight line* (are *collinear* as such is dubbed) and in opposite directions. What does this tell us about $x \cdot y$? Since the angle separating the two is now $180°$ and $\cos 180 = -1$, in this case $x \cdot y = -\|x\|\,\|y\|$. In Figure 3.6(d), x and y are not only collinear but also have the same direction so that the angle between them is $360°$ (or, equivalently $0°$): $\cos 360 = 1$ and so, in this case, $x \cdot y = \|x\|\,\|y\|$.

Finally we have Figure 3.6(e) in which the two vectors x and y are *parallel*: a property that holds if and only if one is a scalar multiple of the other, that is to say $y = \alpha x$.[18] In this case (for parallel vectors x and y) we have

$$x \cdot y = \alpha x \cdot x = \alpha \|x\|^2$$

It is worth noting that the three cases (c)–(e) are basically identical. Noting the "x and y are parallel if and only if $x = \alpha y$" property: in case (c), $x = \alpha y$ with $\alpha < 0$ capturing the fact that these are in opposite directions; in case (d), however $\alpha > 0$ so that both vectors have the same direction. Before moving on to the (arguably more involved) concept of cross product, it is useful to summarize some helpful aspects and properties of dot products.

DP1. $x \cdot y = y \cdot x$.

DP2. $x \cdot (y + z) = x \cdot y + x \cdot z$

DP3. For non-zero vectors, x and y.

$x \cdot y = 0$ if and only if x and y are *orthogonal*, i.e. form a right-angle.

DP4. If $x \cdot y = x \cdot z$ $(x \neq 0)$ it is **not** (necessarily) the case that $y = z$.

The property exhibited within (DP1) is, technically, known as *commutativity*: this is, of course, a well-known property also held by the standard arithmetic operations addition and multiplication. There are, many binary operations which do not have this property, obvious examples being arithmetic subtraction and division but (as we shall see) there are more subtle cases. Within (DP2) we have the *Distributive Property*: this, informally, relates how addition and multiplication (i.e. product) operations interact. Finally (DP4) indicates

---

[18]Another property whose formal proof we eschew but for which some very informal insight is gained by recalling that position is not a vector attribute so that parallel vectors might be seen (in the standard position starting at the origin) as extending in exactly the same direction and having the same angle with respect to the x-axis.

that the dot product does *not* obey what is called the *cancellation law*: this is in contrast to standard multiplication whereby (for $x \neq 0$) should $xy = xz$ then it follows that $y = z$. We now turn to the other widely used notion of vector product.

The Cross Product (of two 3-vectors) – form and properties.

Suppose that **x** and **y** are vectors in $\mathbb{R}^3$. We have seen how this lends itself to a geometric interpretation by treating such vectors witin the (x, y, z)–Cartesian coordinate system as shown in Figure 3.1(c).

The *cross product* of **x** and **y** is denoted $\mathbf{x} \times \mathbf{y}$ and, informally, corresponds to the 3-vector resulting from a vector perpendicular (or '*normal*') to the "plane marked out by **x** and **y**". Let's look at an illustration to try and clarify what this informal description is saying as presented in Figure 3.7.

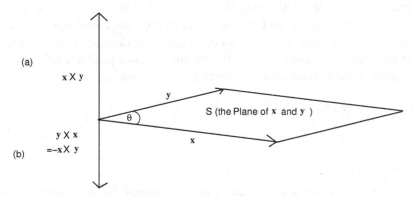

Figure 3.7: Geometric interpretation of Vector Cross Product

Thinking of the lines indicated by **x** and **y** in Figure 3.7, these are at an angle θ to each other, and we can view them as drawn on the same flat surface (i.e. *plane*) as indicated by the area S. With respect to this plane, geometrically the vector directed upwards (indicated by (a) in Figure 3.7) defines $\mathbf{x} \times \mathbf{y}$ while that directed downwards i.e. (b), corresponds to $\mathbf{y} \times \mathbf{x}$ which is exactly the same as $(-1) \cdot \mathbf{x} \times \mathbf{y}$. There are a couple of points which we have to bear in mind, however. Firstly for this geometric interpretation to make sense, it must be *possible* uniquely to define the relevant plane containing **x** and **y**. In Figure 3.7 this is done by forming the parallelogram (S) having **x** and **y** as two of its sides. If, however, the two vectors are *parallel*, a property that we have seen to mean that the vectors lie on the same *line* cf. Figure 3.2(b), then there is not a *uniquely defined* plane (parallelogram if preferred) containing them. In such cases the cross product is **0**, i.e. the 3-vector $< 0, 0, 0 >$.

There is one other geometric complication, awareness of which is crucial to the application of vector algebra in Physics and especially modelling electrical and magnetic fields.[19]

To see this factor, consider Figure 3.8.

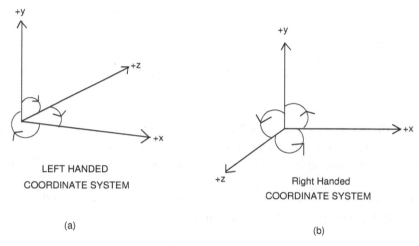

Figure 3.8: Left and Right Handed Coordinate Axes

The importance of which system is relevant is that the direction of the cross product vector differs. In some computer graphics operations (in particular those involving rotation of objects in 3 dimensions) care must be taken to apply the underlying system in a consistent manner. In a right handed coordinate system, the so-called "Right Hand Rule" can be used to determine the direction of **u** × **v** as shown in Figure 3.9: consider gripping a bar with the fingers of the right hand aligned so that these imitate the effect of moving **u** in the direction of **v**. The orientation of the right thumb as either upward (a) or downward (b) gives the direction of **u** × **v**. Three dimensional coordinate systems in which this process applies are called "right handed", those in which it does not are referred to as "left handed".[20]

For the present we give only a useful geometric interpretation for $\|\mathbf{x} \times \mathbf{y}\|$ but will return to the 3-vector outcome later in this chapter when we look at some basic (2×2 and 3×3) **matrix** forms.

---

[19]For example "Fleming's Left Hand Rule" describes the interaction of Electric Current, Magnetic Field, and Force in a manner that differs from "Fleming's Right Hand Rule".

[20]See Endnote 5.

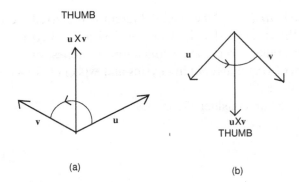

Figure 3.9: The Right Hand Rule

Recall, as shown in Figure 3.7 that, in order for $\mathbf{x} \times \mathbf{y}$ to be non-trivial the vectors $\mathbf{x}$ and $\mathbf{y}$ must define a unique 2-dimensional plane and such is ensured if the angle separating them allows a *parallelogram* with sides $\mathbf{x}$ and $\mathbf{y}$ to be formed.

From classical studies of "*Area Mensuration*" it is known that the *area* of the parallelogram spanned by $\mathbf{x}$ and $\mathbf{y}$ in this environment is exactly

$$\|\mathbf{x}\|\|\mathbf{y}\| \sin \theta$$

This quantity (provided it is interpreted as a **positive** value) turns out to be exactly the same as the *size* of the cross product vector $\mathbf{x} \times \mathbf{y}$. In other words,

$$\|\mathbf{x} \times \mathbf{y}\| = \|\mathbf{x}\|\|\mathbf{y}\||\sin \theta|$$

(Notice that the $|\sin \theta|$ form allows the case $180° < \theta < 360°$ to be handled without problems.)

This relationship between parallelogram area and cross product length provides one reason for the alternative name "directed area product" mentioned earlier.

The geometric view just presented, in addition provides one useful link between dot and cross products. It should be clear that an expression such as $\mathbf{u} \times (\mathbf{v} \cdot \mathbf{w})$ is ill-formed (even if all three vectors are from $\mathbb{R}^3$): $\mathbf{v} \cdot \mathbf{w} \in \mathbb{R}$ (a scalar) and cannot be combined (via $\times$) with $\mathbf{u} \in \mathbb{R}^3$. What about expressions such as $\mathbf{u} \cdot (\mathbf{v} \times \mathbf{w})$ when $\mathbf{u}$, $\mathbf{v}$ and $\mathbf{w}$ are all drawn from $\mathbb{R}^3$? We cannot make the same statement that this combination is ill-defined and in fact the outcome of $\mathbf{u} \cdot (\mathbf{v} \times \mathbf{w})$ in this case will be some value in $\mathbb{R}$. The computation represented in $\mathbf{u} \cdot (\mathbf{v} \times \mathbf{w})$ is called the *scalar triple product*. We conclude this overview of basic vector operations by looking at exactly what this quantity describes.

Consider Figure 3.10.

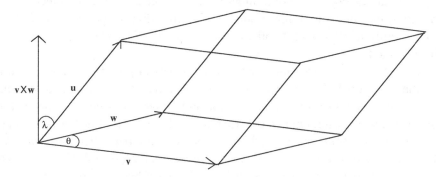

Figure 3.10: Combining dot and cross product

What is the **volume** of the *parallelepiped* whose sides are prescribed by the vectors **u**, **v** and **w**? If it were the case that the angle λ was $0°$ and θ equalled $90°$ we would know this to be $\|\mathbf{u}\| \cdot \|\mathbf{v}\| \cdot \|\mathbf{w}\|$. In order to account for the skew we need to correct this using trigonometric functions, cf. the area of a parallelogram computation from Figure 3.7 which tells that the area of the base is simply

$$\|\mathbf{v} \times \mathbf{w}\| = \|\mathbf{v}\|\|\mathbf{w}\||\sin\theta|$$

The remaining contribution is the length of **u** relative to the normal (i.e. **cross product**) $\mathbf{v} \times \mathbf{w}$ which basic trigonometry gives as $\|\mathbf{u}\||\cos\lambda|$. In total the volume is

$$\|\mathbf{u}\||\cos\lambda| \cdot \|\mathbf{v} \times \mathbf{w}\|$$

Looking back to the geometric interpretation of dot product, we saw earlier that $\mathbf{x} \cdot \mathbf{y} \in \mathbb{R}$ is equal to $\|\mathbf{x}\| \cdot \|\mathbf{y}\| \cos\varphi$ where φ is the angle between the two vectors. So we now know that the volume V needed (combining these relations) is exactly:

$$\begin{aligned} V &= \|\mathbf{u}\||\cos\lambda| \cdot \|\mathbf{v} \times \mathbf{w}\| \\ &= \mathbf{u} \cdot \mathbf{v} \times \mathbf{w} \end{aligned}$$

Thus the scalar triple product allows a non-trivial volume computation to be carried out simply in terms of the dot and cross product. We have seen that the dot product computation is fairly straightforward. The actual computation of the cross product *vector* will be encountered in Section 3.5.

3.4 Vector spaces: Dimension & Independence

We have presented vectors as rather amorphous objects, only developing a concept of structure above that of number from Chapter 2 by dint of collecting and arranging like items together in such a way that divers operations (addition, scalar multiplication, length calculation, products of two types) are (reasonably) defined.

The concept of *vector **space*** provides a means of grouping related vectors together into sets V (which may be finite as well as infinite) in such a way that performing basic operations (i.e. addition and scalar multiplication) on vectors within V always results in a vector that also belongs to V. Furthermore, associated with any vector space, V, there is a Natural number called the *dimension* of V (denoted $\dim V$) for which we may chose a set, B, of $\dim V$ members of V in such a way that *every* vector in V can be described in terms of B.

Recall that $\mathbb{T}$ denotes an arbitrary number type and that $\mathbb{T}$ may be finite. When presenting this notation, in Section 2.4 we required there to be operations $\{+, \cdot\}$ for which given α, β in $\mathbb{T}$ it held that $\alpha + \beta \in \mathbb{T}$ and $\alpha \cdot \beta \in \mathbb{T}$. Before describing the formal structure of vector spaces it is necessary to expand some further assumptions concerning $\mathbb{T}$ all of which are satisfied by the specific cases we have looked at so far.

In total, in order for $(\mathbb{T}, +, \cdot)$ to be usable as a structure from which a vector space may be built we need (in addition to the closure properties $\alpha + \beta \in \mathbb{T}$, $\alpha \cdot \beta \in \mathbb{T}$) for every α, β, and $\gamma \in \mathbb{T}$:

G1. $\alpha + (\beta + \gamma) = (\alpha + \beta) + \gamma$ (+ *is associative*).

G2. $\alpha + \beta = \beta + \alpha$ (+ *is commutative*).

G3. There is an element, denoted 0 in $\mathbb{T}$ for which $\alpha + 0 = \alpha$.

G4. There is an element, denoted $-\alpha \in \mathbb{T}$ such that $\alpha + (-\alpha) = 0$. (Every $\alpha \in \mathbb{T}$ has a *negative*).

G5. $\alpha \cdot (\beta \cdot \gamma) = (\alpha \cdot \beta) \cdot \gamma$ (· *is associative*).

G6. $\alpha \cdot \beta = \beta \cdot \alpha$ (· *is commutative*).

G7. There is an element, denoted 1 (not equal to 0) in $\mathbb{T}$ with $\alpha \cdot 1 = x$

G8. $\alpha \cdot (\beta + \gamma) = \alpha \cdot \beta + \alpha \cdot \gamma$ (· *is distributive over* +).

G9. For every (non-zero) $\alpha \in \mathbb{T}$ there is an element, denoted $\alpha^{-1} \in \mathbb{T}$ such that $\alpha \cdot \alpha^{-1} = 1$. (Every non-zero $\alpha \in \mathbb{T}$ has a multiplicative *inverse*).

The number types $\mathbb{Q}$ and $\mathbb{R}$ discussed in Chapter 2 all satisfy (G1–G9) with respect to standard arithmetic. It is also the case, however, that given $k \in \mathbb{N}$ and considering $\mathbb{Z}_k = \{0, 1, 2. \ldots, k-1\}$ then the form $(\mathbb{Z}_k, +, \cdot)$ when $\{+, \cdot\}$ are standard arithmetic but performed **modulo** k also meets the requirements stipulated by (G1–G9).[21]

Although we will not consider detailed examples, we note that $(\mathbb{T}, +, \cdot)$ in these treatments is not limited to basic number forms (for $\mathbb{T}$) nor standard arithmetic views of $\{+, \cdot\}$. In a number of applications we often find $\mathbb{T}$ not to be simply numerical, e.g. one example (of a non-obvious ring structure) that we have already seen is $(\mathbb{Q}[X], +, \cdot)$: the set of bounded degree polynomials having coefficients from $\mathbb{Q}$. In this case $(+, \cdot)$ are the corresponding operations between polynomials as discussed in Section 2.5.

Vector Space Form

Let $(\mathbb{T}, +, \cdot)$ satisfy the requirements stipulated in (G1)–(G9). For $k \in \mathbb{N}$ the subset V of $\mathbb{T}^k$ is a *vector space* if for every $\alpha \in \mathbb{T}$ and $\mathbf{u}, \mathbf{v} \in V$

VS1. $\alpha \cdot \mathbf{u} \in V$.

VS2. $(\mathbf{u} + \mathbf{v}) \in V$.

We observe given the negative element property that $(\mathbb{T}, +, \cdot)$ must possess, i.e. (G4), for each $\mathbf{v}$ in a vector space V it must be the case that $-\mathbf{v} \in V$: suppose that $\mathbf{v} = < v_1, v_2, \ldots, v_r > \in \mathbb{T}^r$ then $-\mathbf{v} = < -v_1, -v_2, \ldots, -v_r > \in \mathbb{T}^r$ and $-\mathbf{v} = (-1) \cdot \mathbf{v}$ so that (VS1) gives the required membership of $-\mathbf{v}$ in V.[22] Furthermore, from $\{\mathbf{v}, -\mathbf{v}\}$ both belonging to a vector space V, via (VS2) we know in addition that $\mathbf{0} \in V$. Table 3.1 gives some examples of vector spaces.

Notice that while the sets described in Table 3.1(a) and (b) are infinite, those given in Table 3.1(c) and (d) are *finite*. For case (d) V is

$$\{< 0,0 >, < 0,1 >, < 0,2 >, < 0,3 >,$$
$$< 2,0 >, < 2,1 >, < 2,2 >, < 2,3 >\}$$

Arithmetic operations are modulo 4 so that

$$(-1) \mod 4 = 3 \in \mathbb{Z}_4 \,; \ (-2) \mod 4 = 2 \in \mathbb{Z}_4 \,; \ (-3) \mod 4 = 1 \in \mathbb{Z}_4.$$

---

[21]Structures $(\mathbb{T}, +, \cdot)$ that satisfy (G1–G9) are, formally, called *fields*. Those $(\mathbb{T}, +, \cdot)$ meeting the conditions (G1–G5) and (G8) are referred to as *rings*: the form $(\mathbb{Z}, +, \cdot)$ describes a ring.

[22]Notice we assume $(\mathbb{T}, +, \cdot)$ is such that the (negative of) the multiplicative identity, 1, (i.e. -1) whose presence in $\mathbb{T}$ is ensured by (G4) and (G7) obeys $(-1) \cdot \alpha = -\alpha$ for all $\alpha \in \mathbb{T}$.

Table 3.1: Vector Space Examples

–	$\mathbb{T}$	+	$\cdot$	$V \subseteq \mathbb{T}^k$
a.	$\mathbb{R}$	+	$\cdot$	$\mathbb{R}^k$
b.	$\mathbb{Q}$	+	$\cdot$	$\mathbb{Q}^k$
c.	$\mathbb{Z}_{256}$	$+ \mod 256$	$(\cdot) \mod 256$	$\mathbb{Z}_{256}^3$
d.	$\mathbb{Z}_4$	$+ \mod 4$	$(\cdot) \mod 4$	$\{<p,q>: p = 2m,\ m \in \mathbb{Z}_4\}$

We may check (by direct computation) that this is, indeed, a vector space satisfying both conditions (VS1) and (VS2): the key requirement for $\mathbf{u}$ to be in V
is that u_1 is even. Since a scalar multiple (from $\mathbb{Z}_4$) of an even value is again
an even number and adding two even numbers gives an even number, hence
(VS1) and (VS2) hold.

It is worth noting that the vectors defined in Table 3.1(d) may be organized
into $(\mathbf{u}, -\mathbf{u})$ pairs as shown below.

$$
\begin{array}{cc}
\mathbf{u} & -\mathbf{u} \\
<0,0> & <0,0> \\
<0,1> & <0,3> \\
<0,2> & <0,2> \\
<0,3> & <0,1> \\
<2,0> & <2,0> \\
<2,1> & <2,3> \\
<2,2> & <2,2> \\
<2,3> & <2,1>
\end{array}
$$

Observe that (in addition to the rather vapid case of the zero vector being
its own negative) it is perfectly in order for other vectors to have the property of
being their own negative: i.e. there is nothing unusual about the cases $< 0, 2 >$
and $< 2, 2 >$.

We also, at this stage, note the significance of case (c) in computational
settings: the vector space $\mathbb{Z}_{256}^3$ describes those 3-vectors that may arise in the
RGB colour coding scheme that we mentioned briefly at the start of this Chapter.

We now turn to two important ideas that we will meet several times when
we present Matrix Algebra in greater depth in Chapter 7: the *dimension* of a
vector space and the idea of a *basis* set of vectors.

The thinking underlying these related concepts may, in an informal sense,
be given as "describing all of the vectors in a particular vector space, via a

minimal subset of these". The *number* of vectors in such a minimal set defines the *dimension* introduced earlier with the notation dim V at the start of this section. Any minimal set is called a *basis* (plural *bases*) of V.[23]

Of course in the case that V is *finite* it is not hard to see that V *does* have a basis: suppose we choose B, our initial basis, to be V itself. Either B is already minimal so that dim $V_{\bullet} = |V|$ or (since not minimal) we just select an appropriate (strict) subset of V. For the two finite vector spaces just introduced we have the bases given within Table 3.2.

Table 3.2: Bases of Finite Vector Spaces

	Basis (B)	Dimension
Table 3.1(c)	$\{< 0, 0, 255 >, < 0, 255, 0 >, < 255, 0, 0 >\}$	3
Table 3.1(d)	$\{< 0, 1 >, < 2, 0 >\}$	2

It may seem less clear, however, that these notions of basis and dimension can be justified when it comes to vector spaces containing infinitely many vectors, e.g. those such as Table 3.1 (a) (involving $\mathbb{R}^k$) and Table 3.1 (b) (similarly, using $\mathbb{Q}^k$)[24]. In order to gain some appreciation of the structures involved we look rather closer at what is intended by this informal notion of "describing all of the vectors $\cdots$ via a (*minimal*) subset of these". Here the central idea is that of *linear combinations* of a set of vectors.

Description 3. *Let* $U = \{\mathbf{u}_1, \mathbf{u}_2, \ldots, \mathbf{u}_t\}$ *be a set of vectors in* $\mathbb{T}^k$: U *is not required to be a vector space, but is simply an arbitrary set of k-vectors. A linear combination formed from* U *is given by a collection* $[\alpha_1, \alpha_2, \ldots, \alpha_t] \in \mathbb{T}^t$ *and is the vector*

$$\sum_{i=1}^{t} \alpha_i \mathbf{u}_i$$

Now suppose that V is a vector space and that U (in Description 3) is a subset of vectors in U. Then we know, courtesy of the properties (VS1) and (VS2) enjoyed by vector spaces, that *any* linear combination of the vectors in U also belongs to V. Thus, our notion of "minimal subset (of V) capable of describing all of the vectors in V" can be captured through the following:

---

[23]Notice the use of the indefinite article: there may (and, indeed, for vector spaces containing *infinitely many* vectors, **will**) be more than one choice of basis.

[24]We point out that it is *not necessarily* the case that a putative (finite) basis $B_k^{\mathbb{R}}$ for $\mathbb{R}^k$ would provide such a basis for $\mathbb{Q}^k$ or vice-versa: that $B_k^{\mathbb{Q}}$ a basis for $\mathbb{Q}^k$ is, *ipso facto*, also a basis for $\mathbb{R}^k$.

A subset, B, of a vector space V, is called a **basis** of V if B satisfies,

B1. Given any $\mathbf{v} \in V$, there is a linear combination of the vectors in B which equals $\mathbf{v}$. The technical name for this behaviour is we say that "B *spans* V".

B2. If B' is a strict subset of B then there is some vector $\mathbf{v} \in V$ that **cannot** be expressed as a linear combination of the vectors in B'.

Hence property (B1) ensures that all vectors in the vector space can be defined as linear combinations of B while (B2) guarantees that all of the vectors in B are needed to guarantee this degree of coverage. For a vector space V with a basis B the dimension of V is the *number* of vectors in B, i.e. $\dim V = |B|$.

And that would seem to be all that is required except for the fact there is one minor technical issue. This is a rather subtle aspect of the concept of *minimal* **set** of objects with a specific property.

We have defined dimension (minimal set) in terms of number of vectors. As is well-known, it is possible to choose two subsets, R and S say, of some set P for which: both R and S have some property (with respect to P); $|R| < |S|$, however, R is not a subset of S; no strict subset of either R or S have the property referred to with respect to P. If we were to consider the property of being a basis then it may seem that this gives two conflicting choices for dimension: namely as $|R|$ or $|S|$. Notice that S satisfies (B2) as we have described it. In fact it is not too difficult to argue that this apparent conflict cannot arise.

We first introduce the important notion of *linear independence*.

A set, B, of vectors from $\mathbb{T}^n$ is called *linearly independent* if it not possible to form any $\mathbf{v} \in B$ through a linear combination of those vectors in $B \setminus \{\mathbf{v}\}$.

Now it is clear from this definition that the vectors that form a basis, B, must be linearly independent since were it not so we could remove some vector ($\mathbf{u}$ say) from B and the set $B \setminus \{\mathbf{u}\}$ would still be a spanning set of vectors. For letting $< \alpha_1, \alpha_2, \ldots, \alpha_k >$ be the scalar multiples with which

$$\mathbf{u} = \sum_{\mathbf{v}_i \in B \setminus \{\mathbf{u}\}} \alpha_i \mathbf{v}_i$$

We could then take any linear combination $< \beta_1, \beta_2, \ldots, \beta_k, \gamma >$ of B and replace

$$\gamma \mathbf{u} + \sum_{\mathbf{v}_i \in B \setminus \{\mathbf{u}\}} \beta_i \mathbf{v}_i$$

by the identical computation

$$\gamma \sum_{\mathbf{v}_i \in B \setminus \{\mathbf{u}\}} \alpha_i \mathbf{v}_i + \sum_{\mathbf{v}_i \in B \setminus \{\mathbf{u}\}} \beta_i \mathbf{v}_i$$

which is a linear combination of $B \setminus \{\mathbf{u}\}$: specifically the combination

$$\sum_{\mathbf{v}_i \in B \setminus \{\mathbf{u}\}} (\gamma \alpha_i + \beta_i) \mathbf{v}_i$$

Thus, if B is not linearly independent then B cannot satisfy (B2) and, therefore, is not a basis.

Now dealing with the different size 'bases' issues is straightforward. For were it to be the case that B and D are different bases of some vector space V and $|B| < |D|$, e.g.

$$\begin{aligned} B &= \langle \mathbf{x}_1, \mathbf{x}_2, \ldots, \mathbf{x}_t \rangle \\ D &= \langle \mathbf{y}_1, \mathbf{y}_2, \ldots, \mathbf{y}_r \rangle \end{aligned} \quad (r < t)$$

D is (assumed to be) a basis and so every $\mathbf{x}_i \in B$ can be described by some linear combination of D:

$$\mathbf{x}_i = \sum_{k=1}^{r} \alpha_k \mathbf{y}_k$$

B is also (assumed to be) a basis, so, similarly, every $\mathbf{y}_k \in D$ can be described by some linear combination of B

$$\mathbf{y}_k = \sum_{m=1}^{t} \beta_m \mathbf{x}_m$$

But now, combining these two expressions we see that

$$\mathbf{x}_i = \sum_{k=1}^{r} \alpha_k \left(\sum_{m=1}^{t} \beta_m \mathbf{x}_m \right)$$

After some rearrangement,

$$\left(1 - \sum_{k=1}^{r} \alpha_k \right) \mathbf{x}_i = \sum_{j \neq i} \gamma_j \mathbf{x}_j$$

(Here $\gamma_j \in \mathbb{T}$ and is the scalar multiple of $\mathbf{x}_j$ that would result after simplifying.)

In other words, B is **not** a basis since its members are not linearly independent.

We have presented bases for two finite vector spaces (the cases (c) and (d) in Table 3.1). What, however, if our vector space V contains infinitely many vectors, e.g. the examples (a) and (b) in Table 3.1. Despite the fact that there are infinitely many distinct vectors to be spanned we can, for these cases, identify a finite basis. In fact, we have already seen this basis when we discussed notational matters in Section 3.3: the *standard basis vectors*, $\mathbf{e}_k$. Recall that, $\mathbf{e}_k$ is the n-vector from $\mathbb{Z}^n$ for which

$$\mathbf{e}_k \;=\; <\; \underbrace{0,\, 0,\, \ldots,\, 0}_{k-1 \text{ times}},\, 1,\, \underbrace{0,\, 0,\, \ldots,\, 0}_{n-k \text{ times}}\; >$$

Property 3. *For every $n \in \mathbb{N}$ the set*

$$\{\mathbf{e}_1,\, \mathbf{e}_2, \ldots, \mathbf{e}_k, \ldots, \mathbf{e}_n\}$$

defines a basis for $\mathbb{R}^n$ and $\mathbb{Q}^n$.

In principle, if we are processing graphical objects on a display we can do so using only the n standard basis vectors: any position can be constructed in terms of adding scalar multiples of these basis vectors. The fact that all n distinct standard basis vectors are required to span $\mathbb{R}^n$ tells us that $\dim \mathbb{R}^n = n$ providing one justification for the terminology n-dimensional. It should be noted, however, that there are vector space examples that cannot be defined through a **finite** basis.[25]

In summary, we have just seen the following concepts:

C1. **Vector space**: a set of vectors closed under operations of scalar multiplication and addition.

C2. **Dimension**: for a vector space, V, $\dim V$ is the **size** of the smallest subset of V which *spans* V.

C3. **Linear combination** (l.c.): for a set of vectors, D, a linear combination of vectors in D is the outcome of adding scalar multiples, δ_i, of individual vectors $\mathbf{d}_i$ in D. That is to say, a vector $\sum_{\mathbf{d}_i \in D} \delta_i \mathbf{d}_i$.

C4. **Linear independence** (l.i.) of a set of vectors: a set of vectors, U, being *linearly independent* if no vector $\mathbf{u} \in U$ can be formed as a linear combination of the vectors $U \setminus \{\mathbf{u}\}$. A set of a vectors without this property being *linearly dependent* (l.d.).

---

[25] See Endnote 6

C5. **Basis** of a vector space V: a subset, B of V containing $\dim V$ linearly independent vectors and which, as a consequence, allows any vector $\mathbf{u} \in V$ to be formed by a linear combination of B.

We note one aspect of (C5) which we have not discussed in depth. Namely for any vector space, V, for which $\dim V$ is finite, when we select **any** l.i. subset, B of V with $|B| = \dim V$, this subset is guaranteed to be a basis of V. As a corollary of this behaviour notice that if we choose any set, W, containing $\dim V + 1$ (or more) vectors from a vector space V then W cannot be l.i. and so we can find some $\mathbf{w} \in W$ which can be written as a linear combination of those vectors in $W \setminus \{\mathbf{w}\}$. One further consequence arising from (C5), is that the **only** linear combination of a basis B that results in $\mathbf{0}$ is that in which **all** of the scalar multiples involved (i.e. the α_i) are 0.

As one final observation, although (from the examples we have given) it may seem that $\dim V$ is just a very roundabout way of saying "the number of components defining $\mathbf{v} \in V$" this is not the case. There are many naturally arising examples of vector spaces $V \subset \mathbb{R}^n$ for which $\dim V < n$. To take a (rather trivial) example, consider $V \subset \mathbb{R}^3$ given by

$$V = \{ <\alpha, \alpha, \alpha> \ : \ \alpha \in \mathbb{R}\}$$

The reader may easily verify that V contains infinitely many members and also $\dim V = 1$.

3.5   A first look at Matrix Algebra

We now turn to a topic, also concerned with this general idea of using ordered structures, that will be discussed in much greater depth within Chapter 7: the concept of *matrix*. Our principal motivation within this part of the book is the intimate connection between matrix and matrix-vector processes and those concerned with realizing graphical effects in contexts such as Computer-aided design (or CAD) and basic (in the standard rather than programming language sense) computer games. To these ends much of the relevant matrix background is concerned with small forms: that is to say, 2×2 and 3×3 matrices. In Section 3.7 we shall see how particular animation effects such as moving a shape from one position to another, shrinking and expanding a shape, as well as rotation through a given (counterclockwise) angle about the origin can be achieved by describing these operations in terms of multiplying matrices by vectors: the vector will be defined by coordinates in 2 or 3 dimensional space (as would be the convention when interpreted by graphical displays); the changes to these vectors being defined by appropriate matrix forms.

In an extremely informal sense we can think of a (2 or 3 dimensional) matrix as an ordered collection of (2 or 3 dimensional) vectors: just as, at the start of this Chapter we presented such vectors as an ordered collection of (Real) numbers.

We begin by presenting the general definition of what will subsequently be referred to as an $n \times m$ *matrix*. As with our vector environment, although the underlying numerical structure we will be working with is $\mathbb{R}$ or $\mathbb{Q}$, we give this in terms of arbitrary numerical types $(\mathbb{T}, +, \cdot)$ assumed to observe the stipulations of (G1)–(G9) from earlier.

Description 4. *Let n and $m \in \mathbb{N}$. An $n \times m$-matrix over $\mathbb{T}$, $\mathbf{A}$, consists of n rows denoted $\mathbf{a}_1$, $\mathbf{a}_2$, ..., $\mathbf{a}_n$. Each row is an m-vector over $\mathbb{T}$, i.e. $\mathbf{a}_k \in \mathbb{T}^m$.*

*The quantity $n \times m$ is referred to as the **order** of the matrix. By convention, such a matrix may be denoted using $[a_{ij}]$ so describing the j'th component from the i'th row.*

*The entries a_{ii} $(1 \leq i \leq n)$ are called the **diagonal** entries of the $n \times n$ matrix $\mathbf{A}$. Should it be the case that $a_{ii} \neq 0$ for each i and $a_{ij} = 0$ whenever $i \neq j$, the corresponding matrix, $\mathbf{A}$ is called a **diagonal matrix**. The m-vector*

$$< a_{k1}, \ a_{k2}, \ldots, a_{km} >$$

*is called the k-th **row** of $\mathbf{A}$ while the n-vector*

$$< a_{1k}, \ a_{2k}, \ldots, a_{nk} >$$

*is called the k-th **column** of $\mathbf{A}$. An $n \times n$ matrix, $[a_{ij}]$ in which $a_{ij} = a_{ji}$ for every choice $1 \leq i, \ j \leq n$ is known as a **symmetric matrix**.*[26]

Although almost all of our examples will have $n = m$ (*square* matrices)[27] there is, by no means a requirement that this be so. For small values of n an explicit representation of the matrix is often used. So in the case of 2×2 matrices we have

$$\mathbf{A} \ = \ \begin{pmatrix} a_{11} & a_{12} \\ a_{21} & a_{22} \end{pmatrix}$$

---

[26]Symmetric matrices are of great importance in CS as a natural representation for *undirected n-vertex graphs*. The class of symmetric matrices has many useful computational properties some of which will be discussed in Section 7.4 of Chapter 7.

[27]A notable exception will be presented in Section 7.4.4 of Chapter 7.

While, in the 3×3 case

$$
\mathbf{A} \;=\; \left(\begin{array}{ccc} a_{11} & a_{12} & a_{13} \\ a_{21} & a_{22} & a_{23} \\ a_{31} & a_{32} & a_{33} \end{array} \right)
$$

We will use this convention in presenting the applications described in Section 3.7.

When comparing two $n \times m$ matrices, $\mathbf{A} = [a_{ij}]$ and $\mathbf{B} = [b_{ij}]$ (similarly to vector comparison) we write $\mathbf{A} \leq \mathbf{B}$ whenever $a_{ij} \leq b_{ij}$ (for every $1 \leq i \leq n$ and $1 \leq j \leq m$); $\mathbf{A} < \mathbf{B}$ should $\mathbf{A} \leq \mathbf{B}$ and there is at least one case in which $a_{ij} < b_{ij}$; $\mathbf{A} = \mathbf{B}$ if $a_{ij} = b_{ij}$ (again, for every $1 \leq i \leq n$ and $1 \leq j \leq m$); and $\mathbf{A} \neq \mathbf{B}$ whenever there is some case in which $a_{ij} \neq b_{ij}$. Here we find another behavioural link with n-vectors. As we saw, the set of n-vectors in $\mathbb{T}^n$ cannot be completely ordered; so also the set of $n \times m$ matrices with elements from $\mathbb{T}$: given two $n \times m$ matrices, $\mathbf{A}$ and $\mathbf{B}$ it is *not guaranteed to hold* that $\mathbf{A} < \mathbf{B}$ **or** $\mathbf{B} < \mathbf{A}$ **or** $\mathbf{A} = \mathbf{B}$.

Just as we did with polynomials (in Section 2.5) and vectors, we begin by describing the operations of **matrix addition** and **scalar multiplication**.

Matrix Addition

Given two $n \times m$ matrices, $\mathbf{A} = [a_{ij}]$ and $\mathbf{B} = [b_{ij}]$ the result of adding $\mathbf{A}$ and $\mathbf{B}$ is the $n \times m$ matrix $\mathbf{C}$ given through

$$
c_{ij} \;=\; a_{ij} + b_{ij}
$$

So that, exactly as vector addition, matrix addition is given as the outcome of adding respective components. In terms of our informal description of a matrix as n rows of m-vectors, the operation of addition may be seen as the result of n separate m-vector additions. As with the case of vector addition only being well-defined when the number of components in the two vectors is equal, so too matrix addition is well-defined only for matrices containing the same number of *rows* **and** the same number of *columns*.

Matrix Scalar Multiplication

Here again the form of $\alpha \mathbf{A}$ for an $n \times m$ matrix, $\mathbf{A} = [a_{ij}]$ and scalar $\alpha \in \mathbb{T}$ is obtained in a similar style to that used in defining scalar multiplication for n-vectors $\mathbf{u} \in \mathbb{T}^n$. The $n \times m$ matrix $\mathbf{C} = [c_{ij}]$ corresponding to $\alpha \mathbf{A}$ having

components
$$c_{ij} \;=\; \alpha a_{ij}$$

Similarly to our interpretation of matrix addition as the outcome of n separate m-vector additions so too matrix scalar multiplication can be treated as n separate scalar multiplications (by the same $\alpha \in \mathbb{T}$) of m-vectors.

Matrix Transpose

A useful operation which occurs in many of the contexts we shall meet subsequently is very loosely described as swopping the rows and columns of a matrix. In more precise terms, given an $n \times m$ matrix, $\mathbf{A} = [a_{ij}]$, its *transpose matrix*, denoted $\mathbf{A}^\top$, is the $m \times n$ matrix $\mathbf{A}^\top = [a_{ij}^\top]$ for which $a_{ij}^\top = a_{ji}$. Hence, the first column of $\mathbf{A}$ forms the first row of $\mathbf{A}^\top$, the second column of $\mathbf{A}$ describes the second row of $\mathbf{A}^\top$ and so on.

For example, if $\mathbf{A}$ is the 4×6 matrix

$$\mathbf{A} \;=\; \begin{pmatrix} 1 & 1 & 1 & 1 & 1 & 1 \\ 2 & 2 & 2 & 2 & 2 & 2 \\ 3 & 3 & 3 & 3 & 3 & 3 \\ 4 & 4 & 4 & 4 & 4 & 4 \end{pmatrix}$$

Then its transpose, $\mathbf{A}^\top$ is the 6×4 matrix

$$\mathbf{A}^\top \;=\; \begin{pmatrix} 1 & 2 & 3 & 4 \\ 1 & 2 & 3 & 4 \\ 1 & 2 & 3 & 4 \\ 1 & 2 & 3 & 4 \\ 1 & 2 & 3 & 4 \\ 1 & 2 & 3 & 4 \end{pmatrix}$$

If $\mathbf{A}$ is a symmetric matrix then it should be clear that $\mathbf{A} = \mathbf{A}^\top$.

Matrix Product

Unlike its vector counterpart the concept of the matrix $\mathbf{C}$ obtained as the product of two matrices $\mathbf{A}$ and $\mathbf{B}$ is less subject to the viscissitudes of interpretation that afflict the definition of vector product. That said there are some aspects which must be considered in its definition which, while not approaching the dot product or cross product level of complication in defining vector product, are of some significance.

Firstly a matrix, $\mathbf{C}$, corresponding to the product of an $n \times m$ matrix $\mathbf{A}$ by an $r \times s$ matrix $\mathbf{B}$ is *only* well-defined when the number of **columns** in $\mathbf{A}$ (m) is equal to the number of **rows** in $\mathbf{B}$ (r). The outcome, $\mathbf{C}$, will then be an $n \times s$ matrix. While it is, of course, the case that if $\mathbf{A}$ and $\mathbf{B}$ are both *square* matrices (with the same number of rows) then this condition will always be satisfied, unlike standard **scalar** multiplication i.e. the operation $\cdot$ in $(\mathbb{T}, +, \cdot)$ whereas the product of two scalars in $\mathbb{T}$ is always properly defined, the product of two *matrices* may not be.

In order to assist with understanding the general case, we first look at the outcome of multiplying two 2×2 matrices.

2×2 **matrix product**

For 2×2 matrices,

$$\mathbf{A} = \begin{pmatrix} a_{11} & a_{12} \\ a_{21} & a_{22} \end{pmatrix} \; ; \; \mathbf{B} = \begin{pmatrix} b_{11} & b_{12} \\ b_{21} & b_{22} \end{pmatrix}$$

The product, $\mathbf{C} = \mathbf{AB}$, is

$$\mathbf{C} = \begin{pmatrix} a_{11} \cdot b_{11} + a_{12} \cdot b_{21} & a_{11} \cdot b_{12} + a_{12} \cdot b_{22} \\ a_{21} \cdot b_{11} + a_{22} \cdot b_{21} & a_{21} \cdot b_{12} + a_{22} \cdot b_{22} \end{pmatrix}$$

We identify one immediate important property of matrix product by examining the result of $\mathbf{D} = \mathbf{BA}$. This is,

$$\mathbf{D} = \begin{pmatrix} b_{11} \cdot a_{11} + b_{12} \cdot a_{21} & b_{11} \cdot a_{12} + b_{12} \cdot a_{22} \\ b_{21} \cdot a_{11} + b_{22} \cdot a_{21} & b_{21} \cdot a_{12} + b_{22} \cdot a_{22} \end{pmatrix}$$

In general we find that,

$$\begin{aligned} a_{11} \cdot b_{11} + a_{12} \cdot b_{21} &\neq b_{11} \cdot a_{11} + b_{12} \cdot a_{21} \quad \textbf{AND} \\ a_{11} \cdot b_{12} + a_{12} \cdot b_{22} &\neq b_{11} \cdot a_{12} + b_{12} \cdot a_{22} \quad \textbf{AND} \\ a_{21} \cdot b_{11} + a_{22} \cdot b_{21} &\neq b_{21} \cdot a_{11} + b_{22} \cdot a_{21} \quad \textbf{AND} \\ a_{21} \cdot b_{12} + a_{22} \cdot b_{22} &\neq b_{21} \cdot a_{12} + b_{22} \cdot a_{22} \end{aligned}$$

For example, with

$$\mathbf{A} = \begin{pmatrix} 1 & 2 \\ 3 & 4 \end{pmatrix} \; ; \; \mathbf{B} = \begin{pmatrix} 5 & 6 \\ 7 & 8 \end{pmatrix}$$

We get

$$\mathbf{AB} = \begin{pmatrix} 19 & 22 \\ 43 & 50 \end{pmatrix} \; ; \; \mathbf{BA} = \begin{pmatrix} 23 & 34 \\ 31 & 46 \end{pmatrix}$$

Matrix product is, what is called, a *non-commutative* operation: typically, $\mathbf{AB} \neq \mathbf{BA}$.[28] This is a rather more extreme case than the one previous instance of a non-commutative operation seen, namely the cross product of two 3-vectors, $\mathbf{x}$ and $\mathbf{y}$. Referring to Figure 3.7 we saw that the 3-vector $\mathbf{x} \times \mathbf{y}$ differs from the 3-vector $\mathbf{y} \times \mathbf{x}$ *only* in its direction, i.e. $\mathbf{x} \times \mathbf{y} = -\mathbf{y} \times \mathbf{x}$: the *size* of both is identical.

Looking in more detail at what happens with 2×2 matrix product we notice one feature that is central to the development needed to define general matrix products. Consider the specific element c_{ij} $(1 \leq i, j \leq 2)$ of $\mathbf{C}$ when the product of $\mathbf{A} = [a_{ij}]$ with $\mathbf{B} = [b_{ij}]$ is constructed.

$$c_{ij} = a_{i1} \cdot b_{1j} + a_{i2} \cdot b_{2j}$$

The result is found through "multiplying successive elements in **row** i (of $\mathbf{A}$) with the corresponding elements from **column** j (of $\mathbf{B}$) and adding the results". That is, in determining c_{ij} we multiply the first component of row i in $\mathbf{A}$ by the first component of column j in $\mathbf{B}$; then add the outcome of multiplying the second component of row i by the second component of column j, $\cdots$, in general adding to the total already accrued, the result of multiplying the kth component of row i by the kth component of column j.

We can summarize this process as follows. Let $\mathbf{A} = [a_{ij}]$ be a $p \times q$ matrix; let $\mathbf{B} = [b_{ij}]$ be a $q \times r$ matrix. The matrix, $\mathbf{C} = [c_{ij}]$ obtained as the matrix product $\mathbf{AB}$ is a $p \times r$ matrix in which

$$c_{ij} = \sum_{k=1}^{q} a_{ik} \cdot b_{kj}$$

Now in spite of the superficially involved notational intricacy that this structure may appear to possess, we have in fact already met the processes involved when we described the dot (scalar) product operation on two n-vectors. We have seen that the operations of matrix addition and scalar multiplication can be treated as performing these separately on the individual rows of the corresponding matrices. What about the case of matrix **product**?

Suppose we have a $p \times q$ matrix $\mathbf{A} = [a_{ij}]$ and a $q \times r$ matrix $\mathbf{B} = [b_{ij}]$. The k'th **row** of $\mathbf{A}$ can be seen as the q-vector denoted $\mathbf{a}_k$ at the start of this

---

[28] An exception is the class of symmetric matrices. If $\mathbf{A}$ and $\mathbf{B}$ are symmetric matrices (with the same order) then $\mathbf{AB} = \mathbf{BA}$.

section. Similarly we have a q-vector given by the kth row of the **transpose** of B: this we can denote as $b_k^\top$. What about the kth row of $C = AB$? There are p such rows

$$\mathbf{c}_i \;=\; < c_{i1}, c_{i2}, \;\ldots, \; c_{ir} >$$

with

$$c_{ij} \;=\; \sum_{k=1}^{q} a_{ik} \cdot b_{kj} \;=\; \mathbf{a}_i \cdot \mathbf{b}_j^\top$$

In other words, the value of c_{ij} is simply the dot product of the q-vectors $\mathbf{a}_i$ and $\mathbf{b}_j^\top$.

Determinants

Although we will meet a much more detailed treatment in Chapter 7 it is useful to introduce the idea of matrix *determinants* for 2×2 matrices at this point. We first present one particular 2×2 matrix: the identity matrix I_2. This matrix has its diagonal entries equal to 1 and other entries equal to 0. That is,

$$\mathbf{I}_2 \;=\; \begin{pmatrix} 1 & 0 \\ 0 & 1 \end{pmatrix}$$

The term "identity matrix" is justified by the following, easily verified, property. Given any 2×2 matrix, A it holds that

$$\mathbf{A}\mathbf{I}_2 \;=\; \mathbf{I}_2\mathbf{A} \;=\; \mathbf{A}$$

Such behaviour allows us to raise the question of *inverse* matrices. Suppose that A is a 2×2 matrix. The *inverse* of A, denoted A^{-1}, is that matrix for which

$$\mathbf{A}\mathbf{A}^{-1} \;=\; \mathbf{A}^{-1}\mathbf{A} \;=\; \mathbf{I}_2$$

There is one complication: such a matrix may *not exist*. Hence there are 2×2 matrices (and, as we shall see in Chapter 7, $n \times n$ matrices) lacking an inverse of this form. In the 2×2 case checking whether a given matrix has a defined inverse is easily accomplished by evaluating the quantity called the **determinant**, denoted det A or, as we shall use on occasion, $|A|$. In particular, for any 2×2 matrix, A

$$A^{-1} \text{ exists } \textbf{if and only if } \det A \neq 0$$

Having seen this, two further questions arise: how is the "determinant of a 2×2 matrix" formally defined? and, knowing that A^{-1} *does* exist, how is it computed?

Taking the first of these,

$$\left| \begin{pmatrix} a_{11} & a_{12} \\ a_{21} & a_{22} \end{pmatrix} \right| = a_{11}a_{22} - a_{12}a_{21}$$

And the second question? Should the 2×2 matrix $\mathbf{A} = [a_{ij}]$ be such that $a_{11}a_{22} - a_{12}a_{21} \neq 0$, then $\mathbf{A}^{-1}$ is just

$$\begin{pmatrix} a_{11} & a_{12} \\ a_{21} & a_{22} \end{pmatrix}^{-1} = \frac{1}{a_{11}a_{22} - a_{12}a_{21}} \begin{pmatrix} a_{22} & -a_{12} \\ -a_{21} & a_{11} \end{pmatrix}$$

The Cross Product revisited

We have now met sufficient material to make sense of the *vector* form of the cross product. Recalling that the cross product of $\mathbf{u}$ and $\mathbf{v} \in \mathbb{R}^3$ is another 3-vector, letting

$$\mathbf{u} = <u_1, u_2, u_3>$$
$$\mathbf{v} = <v_1, v_2, v_3>$$

The 3-vector, $\mathbf{w} = <w_1, w_2, w_3>$ given by $\mathbf{u} \times \mathbf{v}$ is the linear combination of $\{\mathbf{e}_1, \mathbf{e}_2, \mathbf{e}_3\}$ (the standard basis vectors for $\mathbb{R}^3$) formed as

$$\mathbf{w} = \left| \begin{pmatrix} u_2 & u_3 \\ v_2 & v_3 \end{pmatrix} \right| \mathbf{e}_1 - \left| \begin{pmatrix} u_1 & u_3 \\ v_1 & v_3 \end{pmatrix} \right| \mathbf{e}_2 + \left| \begin{pmatrix} u_1 & u_2 \\ v_1 & v_2 \end{pmatrix} \right| \mathbf{e}_3$$

We now turn to a very specific collection of matrix products and their rôle: these are the cases in which the product of an $n \times n$ matrix $\mathbf{A}$ with (the transpose of) an n-vector, $\mathbf{x}$ occurs.[29]

3.6 Linear (and non-linear) Transformations

The notion of *Transformation* of a vector space, V, is intimately linked with that of forming a vector by means of multiplying some matrix, $\mathbf{A}$, by a vector belonging to V. One computational process that we often need concerns taking members of some vector space, V, and mapping these to elements in another vector space U. There are many reasons why we may wish to go through such

---

[29] As has been hinted in the earlier discussions, we may treat an n-vector as $1 \times n$ matrix. In such settings in order for the product of a matrix with a vector to be well-defined we have to use **column** vectors: the column vector corresponding to the n-vector ($1 \times n$ matrix) $\mathbf{x}$ being the $n \times 1$ matrix $\mathbf{x}^{\top}$, so that with the $n \times n$ matrix, $\mathbf{A}$, the product $\mathbf{A}\mathbf{x}^{T}$ is (also) a column vector: one with n components.

processes: some computational tasks may be more easily carried out working directly with V, however, the actual realization and implementation of these tasks requires using U. Here is one of the common settings for such problems. We have seen that $\mathbb{R}^3$ (and, indeed, $\mathbb{Q}^3$) defines a vector space with dimension 3. It has also been argued that $\mathbb{R}^3$, via the Cartesian 3-dimensional (xyz)-axes, can be presented in a style amenable to shape manipulation and visualization. If we wish to demonstrate these capabilities on a *graphical display*, however, there is a problem: such displays are flat, 2-dimensional environments so we have to find a mechanism by which 3-dimensional references can be depicted in 2-dimensions. One solution is to find a way of mapping from the vector space $\mathbb{R}^3$ to the vector space $\mathbb{R}^2$ which allows 3-dimensional manipulations to be processed *entirely* in $\mathbb{R}^3$ with the outcome then translated to $\mathbb{R}^2$ this translation being the only additional computation needed. That is to say, suppose we wish to illustrate a cube rotating around one of its corners on a (2-dimensional) graphical display, we would carry out the following.

a. Determine the 3-vectors defining the 8 corners and 12 edges of the cube.

b. Fix the order in which the 12 edges (each edge having a starting coordinate at some corner and an end coordinate in another) of the cube will be drawn.[30]

c. Find the points in $\mathbb{R}^2$ these should be mapped to when displaying.

d. Draw the cube on the 2-dimensional display using these data.

e. Recalculate the 3-vectors to apply in step (a) after rotation through some number of degrees.

f. Repeat (c–e) until finished.

We discuss some of these effects in Section 3.7, but before doing so we need to look at the various types of transformation, their properties, and their relationship with matrix-vector products.

---

[30]It is *impossible* to arrange this ordering of the 12 edges so that all three of the following hold,

a. each edge is drawn exactly once;

b. the starting point of the k'th edge is the end point of the $(k-1)$'st edge; **and**

c. the 12th edge ends at the start point of the first.

In fact, there is not even a method by which both (a) and (b) combined can be accomplished. This need not affect a translation from 3 to 2 dimensions. See Endnote 7 for one possible arrangement.

Linear Transformations

Suppose that $\mathbf{u}$, $\mathbf{v}$ are vectors for the sake of argument in $\mathbb{R}^n$ although our principal interest will be the case $\mathbb{R}^3$. Also let $\alpha \in \mathbb{R}$ be an arbitrary scalar. Finally let us assume that $G \subseteq \mathbb{R}^n$ and $H \subseteq \mathbb{R}^n$ are two (not necessarily distinct) vector spaces with $\mathbf{u}$ and $\mathbf{v}$ both belonging to G.

A **transformation**, T, from the vector space, G to the vector space H (formally, we write this as $T : G \to H$) specifies for each vector $\mathbf{w} \in G$ a corresponding *unique* vector denoted $T(\mathbf{w}) \in H$.

This, of course, is a very general notion, and should G contain infinitely many vectors there will be infinitely many different transformations that could be defined.[31]

Nearly all such transformations will, however, be of little interest and behave in a style which is computationally unhelfpul. This, therefore, raises the question "what properties would we find useful for T, a transformation between two vector spaces, to have?".

There are two immediate properties that turn out to be of considerable use in actually *implementing* (i.e. making effective computational use of) a transformation. For two vectors $\mathbf{u}$ and $\mathbf{v} \in G$, by virtue of the fact that G is a vector space, we know that $\mathbf{u} + \mathbf{v} \in G$. Similarly, for $\alpha \in \mathbb{R}$, again by virtue of G being a vector space, we know that $\alpha\mathbf{u} \in G$. For T to be "useful" we would like to be able to relate $T(\mathbf{u}), T(\mathbf{v}) \in H$ to the vectors

$$
\begin{aligned}
T(\mathbf{u}) + T(\mathbf{v}) &\in H \\
T(\mathbf{u} + \mathbf{v}) &\in H \\
T(\alpha\mathbf{u}) &\in H \\
\alpha T(\mathbf{u}) &\in H
\end{aligned}
$$

The property of T being a *linear* transformation provides this utility.

A mapping from a vector space G to a vector space H, $T : G \to H$, is a *linear transformation* if for each $\mathbf{u}$, $\mathbf{v}$ in G and each $\alpha \in \mathbb{R}$ we have

LT1. $T(\mathbf{u} + \mathbf{v}) = T(\mathbf{u}) + T(\mathbf{v})$.

LT2. $T(\alpha\mathbf{u}) = \alpha T(\mathbf{u})$.

So (LT1) indicates that it is unimportant, with respect to the vector in H that results, whether we first add $\mathbf{u}$ and $\mathbf{v}$ and apply T to the resulting vector in

---

[31]We note one important point: distinct vectors $\mathbf{x}$ and $\mathbf{y} \in G$ may be mapped by T onto the **same** vector in H. A transformation merely has to define **exactly** one $T(\mathbf{x}) \in H$ for each $x \in G$. It follows that the "infinitely many transformations" environment requires only G to be infinite but does not require H to be so. See the example in Endnote 8.

G or apply T separately to $\mathbf{u}$ and $\mathbf{v}$ and then add the resulting vectors in H. Similarly, (LT2) shows that there is no difference between applying T to a scalar multiple of $\mathbf{u} \in G$ and forming the equivalent scalar multiple of T applied directly to $\mathbf{u}$, i.e. the vector $T(\mathbf{u}) \in H$.

Now consider a vector space G which is formed by a subset of n-vectors from $\mathbb{R}^n$. Let us suppose that $\dim G = p$ and

$$U = \{ \mathbf{u}_1, \mathbf{u}_2, \ldots, \mathbf{u}_p \}$$

describes a basis of G. Now consider *any* linear transformation, T, from G to another vector space H.

From the fact that U is a basis for G and that T satisfies (LT1) and (LT2) we know that we can take any $\mathbf{v} \in G$ and find scalars $[\alpha_1, \ldots, \alpha_p]$ from $\mathbb{R}$ for which

$$\mathbf{v} = \sum_{i=1}^{p} \alpha_i \mathbf{u}_i$$

so that

$$T(\mathbf{v}) = \sum_{i=1}^{p} \alpha_i T(\mathbf{u}_i)$$

In other words the collection of vectors

$$\{ T(\mathbf{u}_1), T(\mathbf{u}_2), \ldots, T(\mathbf{u}_p) \}$$

spans the subset of vectors within H that can be mapped onto by T.

Before developing one very significant enrichment of these ideas: that of the *matrix*, $\mathbf{M}_T$ defining a linear transformation, T, we first present an important class of linear transformations called the **coordinates** with respect to a basis of a linear space.

Choose

$$U = \{ \mathbf{u}_1, \mathbf{u}_2, \ldots, \mathbf{u}_p \}$$

as a basis of G, and also set

$$V = \{ \mathbf{v}_1, \mathbf{v}_2, \ldots, \mathbf{v}_q \}$$

as a basis of H.

Now, since U is a basis any $\mathbf{u} \in G$ can be described in a unique manner by a p-vector, $\mathcal{C}_U(\mathbf{u})$, with

$$\mathcal{C}_U(\mathbf{u}) = <\alpha_1, \alpha_2, \ldots, \alpha_p> \in \mathbb{R}^p$$

and

$$\mathbf{u} \;=\; \sum_{i=1}^{p} \alpha_i \mathbf{u}_i$$

We refer to $\mathcal{C}_U(\mathbf{u})$ as the *coordinate* mapped to by $\mathbf{u}$.

In exactly the same way using the basis V for H, any $\mathbf{v} \in H$ is described by a unique q-vector, $\mathcal{C}_V(\mathbf{v})$, with

$$\mathcal{C}_V(\mathbf{v}) \;=\; < \beta_1, \beta_2, \ldots, \beta_q > \in \mathbb{R}^q$$

and

$$\mathbf{v} \;=\; \sum_{j=1}^{q} \beta_i \mathbf{v}_j$$

Both $\mathcal{C}_U \; : \; U \to \mathbb{R}^p$ and $\mathcal{C}_V \; : \; V \to \mathbb{R}^q$ are **linear transformations**. This yields the picture below

$$
\begin{array}{ccc}
G & \xrightarrow{T} & H \\
\mathcal{C}_U \downarrow & & \downarrow \mathcal{C}_V \\
\mathbb{R}^p & & \mathbb{R}^q
\end{array}
$$

It should be noted that when working with the vector space $\mathbb{R}^n$ and the standard basis $E_n = \{\mathbf{e}_1, \ldots, \mathbf{e}_n\}$, the coordinates to which $\mathbf{x} \in \mathbb{R}^n$ is mapped are simply the vector $\mathbf{x}$ itself, i.e. $\mathcal{C}_{E_n}(\mathbf{x}) = \mathbf{x}$.

In summary given $\mathbf{u}$ belonging to a vector space U having $\dim U = p$ we may represent $\mathbf{u}$ with respect to *any* basis of U by the *unique* (with respect to the chosen basis) p-vector in $\mathbb{R}^p$ corresponding to its coordinates.

From the perspective of the applications discussed in Section 3.7 one crucial property of linear transformations is that of representation via a matrix. Computationally this allows us to implement the transformation producing $T(\mathbf{x})$ as a matrix-vector product using a matrix $\mathbf{M}$ for which $\mathbf{M}\mathbf{x}^\top = (T(\mathbf{x}))^\top$.

If there is some linear transformation which we wish to implement in such a style, this raises the question: how do we construct the matrix $\mathbf{M}$ concerned?

To see how to do this given the vector spaces G with basis $U \subseteq \mathbb{R}^p$, H with basis $V \subseteq \mathbb{R}^q$, and $T \; : \; G \to H$ a linear transformation, consider the $q \times p$ matrix whose k'th **column** ($1 \le k \le p$) is

$$\mathbf{m}_k \;=\; \mathcal{C}_V(T(\mathbf{u}_k))^\top$$

In other words, "the $q \times 1$ column vector formed by the coordinates (with respect to V) of T applied to the k'th basis vector ($\mathbf{u}_k$) in U".

Writing, the q-vector $\mathcal{C}_V(T(\mathbf{u}_k))$ using

$$\mathcal{C}_V(T(\mathbf{u}_k)) \;=\; \mathbf{m}_k \;=\; < \alpha_1^k, \alpha_2^k, \ldots, \alpha_q^k > \; \in \mathbb{R}^q$$

Depicting this in full as a matrix $\mathbf{M}$,

$$\mathbf{M} \;=\; \begin{pmatrix} \alpha_1^1 & \alpha_1^2 & \cdots & \alpha_1^k & \cdots & \alpha_1^p \\ \alpha_2^1 & \alpha_2^2 & \cdots & \alpha_2^k & \cdots & \alpha_2^p \\ \cdots & \cdots & \cdots & \cdots & \cdots & \cdots \\ \alpha_i^1 & \alpha_i^2 & \cdots & \alpha_i^k & \cdots & \alpha_i^p \\ \cdots & \cdots & \cdots & \cdots & \cdots & \cdots \\ \alpha_q^1 & \alpha_q^2 & \cdots & \alpha_q^k & \cdots & \alpha_q^p \end{pmatrix}$$

What is the outcome of multiplying $\mathbf{M}$ by $\mathbf{x}^\top$ ($\mathbf{M}$ having order $q \times p$ and $\mathbf{x}^\top$ order $p \times 1$) with $\mathbf{x} \in G$? The outcome will, of course, be some $q \times 1$ column vector, $\mathbf{y}^\top$, but what can we actually state about the vector $\mathbf{y} \in \mathbb{R}^q$?

A bit of algebraic passage work

$$
\begin{aligned}
\mathbf{M}\mathbf{x}^T \;&=\; \sum_{i=1}^{p} x_i \mathbf{m}_i \\
&=\; \sum_{i=1}^{p} x_i (\mathcal{C}_V(T(\mathbf{u}_i)))^\top \\
&=\; \sum_{i=1}^{p} (\mathcal{C}_V(T(x_i\mathbf{u}_i)))^\top \\
&=\; \left(\mathcal{C}_V \left(\sum_{i=1}^{p} T(x_i\mathbf{u}_i) \right) \right)^\top \\
&=\; (\mathcal{C}_V(T(\mathbf{x})))^\top \\
&=\; \mathbf{y}^\top
\end{aligned}
$$

So that the outcome $\mathbf{M}\mathbf{x}^\top$ is the $q \times 1$ column vector $\mathbf{y}^\top$ with $\mathbf{y} \in \mathbb{R}^q$ the uniquely defined coordinates (with respect to the basis V of H) of $T(\mathbf{x}) \in H$. In total $\mathbf{M}$ completely describes the action of the linear transformation T so justifying its description as the *matrix of the linear transformation T*.

It is worth noting that the validation of $\mathbf{M}$ relies very heavily on the fact that T **is** a linear transformation allowing us to equate "a summation of T applied to a collection of vectors" with "T applied to the outcome of the sum of these vectors"; similarly at a number of stages we substitute "scalar multiple of T applied to a vector" using "T applied to a scalar multiple of the vector".

Finally although the notions of "coordinate mapping with respect to a given basis" might appear to complicate matters unnecessarily, this is not so much of an issue with respect to the actual examples we look at in Section 3.7. Here the underlying vector spaces will be $\mathbb{R}^n$ (with n typically 3 or 4) so allowing the standard basis E_n to underpin the notion of coordinates of a vector.

As a small example which may serve to demystify some of the algebraic esoterica, suppose we consider any linear transformation $T : \mathbb{R}^3 \to \mathbb{R}^3$, such as will be typical of the cases looked at in Section 3.7.

We know that

$$\{\mathbf{e}_1, \mathbf{e}_2, \mathbf{e}_3\} = \{< 1, 0, 0 >, \ < 0, 1, 0 >, \ < 0, 0, 1 >\}$$

is a basis for $\mathbb{R}^3$. To construct a 3×3 matrix, $\mathbf{M}$, corresponding to T we proceed as follows:

M1. Compute $T(< 1, 0, 0 >)$, $T(< 0, 1, 0 >)$ and $T(< 0, 0, 1 >)$. Denote the resulting 3-vectors by

$$\begin{array}{rcccl}
\mathbf{d}_1 & = & T(< 1, 0, 0 >) & = & < d_{11}, \ d_{12}, \ d_{13} > \in \mathbb{R}^3 \\
\mathbf{d}_2 & = & T(< 0, 1, 0 >) & = & < d_{21}, \ d_{22}, \ d_{23} > \in \mathbb{R}^3 \\
\mathbf{d}_3 & = & T(< 0, 0, 1 >) & = & < d_{31}, \ d_{32}, \ d_{33} > \in \mathbb{R}^3
\end{array}$$

M2. As we noted earlier the coordinates, $\mathcal{C}_{\mathbb{R}^3}$ of $\mathbf{d}_i$ with respect to the standard basis are simply the 3-vector $\mathbf{d}_i$ itself. Forming the matrix described with columns corresponding to these coordinates, we get

$$\mathbf{M} = (\ \mathbf{d}_1^\top \ ; \ \mathbf{d}_2^\top \ ; \ \mathbf{d}_3^\top \ ) = \begin{pmatrix} d_{11} & d_{21} & d_{31} \\ d_{12} & d_{22} & d_{32} \\ d_{13} & d_{32} & d_{33} \end{pmatrix}$$

To check this is correct, let's look at the effect of multiplying $\mathbf{x}^\top$ for some $\mathbf{x} \in \mathbb{R}^3$. Writing $\mathbf{x} = < x_1, x_2, x_3 >$:

$$\begin{pmatrix} d_{11} & d_{21} & d_{31} \\ d_{12} & d_{22} & d_{32} \\ d_{13} & d_{23} & d_{33} \end{pmatrix} \begin{pmatrix} x_1 \\ x_2 \\ x_3 \end{pmatrix} = \begin{pmatrix} < d_{11}, \ d_{21}, \ d_{31} > \cdot \mathbf{x} \\ < d_{12}, \ d_{22}, \ d_{32} > \cdot \mathbf{x} \\ < d_{13}, \ d_{23}, \ d_{33} > \cdot \mathbf{x} \end{pmatrix}$$

$$= \begin{pmatrix} x_1 \cdot d_{11} + x_2 \cdot d_{21} + x_3 \cdot d_{31} \\ x_1 \cdot d_{12} + x_2 \cdot d_{22} + x_3 \cdot d_{32} \\ x_1 \cdot d_{13} + x_2 \cdot d_{23} + x_3 \cdot d_{33} \end{pmatrix}$$

$$= \ x_1 T(\mathbf{e}_1)^\top + x_2 T(\mathbf{e}_2)^\top + x_3 T(\mathbf{e}_3)^\top$$

$$= \ T(< x_1, x_2, x_3 >)^\top$$

So that the outcome is, as required, $T(\mathbf{x})$.

Affine Transformations

Much of the technical baggage applied to implement graphical effects would be redundant were it the case that everything one might conceivably wish to animate or depict could be expressed as a process of manipulating objects via linear transformations. As one imagines many readers going onto to study advanced computer graphics will discover, unfortunately (?) this is **not** the case. Furthermore the "not a linear transformation" behaviour is more than just some recondite property exhibited by a handful of artificially constructed examples whose presence in actual applications is at best unlikely. There is, at least one, very basic 2-D effect that cannot be described in terms of linear transformation from $\mathbb{R}^2$ onto $\mathbb{R}^2$. Consider the process in Figure 3.11.

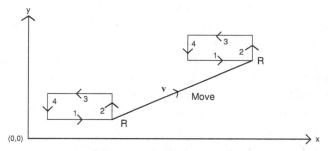

Figure 3.11: Moving a shape in 2 dimensions

The rectangle, labelled R, is drawn with 4 edges in the order indicated by the numbered labels and we wish to change where it is displayed from its starting position to the one resulting by "following the direction" of the vector $\mathbf{v} \in \mathbb{R}^2$. The obvious solution is, of course, to apply the relevant transformation $M : \mathbb{R}^2 \to \mathbb{R}^2$ for which

$$M(\mathbf{x}) = \mathbf{x} + \mathbf{v}$$

Obvious this may be, linear it is not: choose, e.g. $\mathbf{x} =< 2, 9 >$ and $\alpha = 3$ then

$$3M(\mathbf{x}) =< 6, 27 > +3\mathbf{v} \neq < 6, 27 > +\mathbf{v} = M(3\mathbf{x})$$

(except in the vacuous case $\mathbf{v} =< 0, 0 >$).

We may condense the two requirements (LT1) and (LT2) for $T : G \to H$ to be a linear transformation between vector spaces G and H into the single condition that for every $\alpha, \beta \in \mathbb{R}$ and $\mathbf{u}, \mathbf{v} \in G$ it holds,

$$T(\alpha\mathbf{u} + \beta\mathbf{v}) = \alpha T(\mathbf{u}) + \beta T(\mathbf{v})$$

The class of **affine** transformations, are those which satisfy, for every $\alpha, \beta \in \mathbb{R}$ having $\alpha + \beta = 1$ and every $\mathbf{u}, \mathbf{v} \in G$

$$T(\alpha\mathbf{u} + \beta\mathbf{v}) = \alpha T(\mathbf{u}) + \beta T(\mathbf{v})$$

The operation of *vector translation*, as $M(\mathbf{x}) = \mathbf{x} + \mathbf{v}$ is called, is an *affine* but not a linear transformation. Notice that every linear transformation is an affine transformation (the former perforce satisfying the $\alpha + \beta = 1$ precondition), however (as we have just seen) there are affine transformations that are **not** linear transformations.

That as elementary an operation as moving a shape from one position to another in 2-dimensions cannot be achieved by using a 2×2 matrix might appear to weaken by some margin the case for using matrix-vector products to achieve a graphical effect. There is, however, a technique we can apply to get around this problem: instead of insisting on describing 2-dimensional effects via 2×2 matrices we use 3×3**-matrices** and what are referred to as "*homogeneous coordinates*". A similar approach allows us to use 4×4-matrices to mimic the effect of 3-dimensional *non-linear* transformations of which the analogous translation effect for points in $\mathbb{R}^3$ is one such transformation. In basic terms the *homogeneous coordinate* corresponding to $(p, q) \in \mathbb{R}^2$ is the coordinate $(p, q, 1) \in \mathbb{R}^3$. Similarly, the homogeneous coordinate corresponding to $(p, q, r) \in \mathbb{R}^3$ is the 4-dimensional coordinate $(p, q, r, 1) \in \mathbb{R}^4$.

Returning to our notion of affine transformations which includes instances which are not linear transformations.

Let us look at the outcome of translating a point $(p, q) \in \mathbb{R}^2$ using the vector $< s, t > \in \mathbb{R}^2$. The transformation, M, should be such that

$$M(< p, q >) = < p + s, q + t >$$

Suppose instead of (p, q) and (s, t) we use the equivalent *homogeneous* coordinates, i.e. $(p, q, 1)$ and $< s, t, 1 >$. The result should be the homogeneous coordinate corresponding to $(p + s, q + t)$: in other words $(p + s, q + t, 1)$. The new transformation, let us call it $M_{\mathbf{v}}^h$, now maps from $\mathbb{R}^3$ to $\mathbb{R}^3$ and must satisfy

$$M_{\mathbf{v}}^h(< x, y, 1 >) = < x + v_1, y + v_2, 1 >$$

Is it possible to achieve the effect described by $M_{\mathbf{v}}^h$ using a 3×3-matrix with which to form a product of $< x, y, 1 >^\top$? The following, as the reader may easily verify, achieves precisely this:

$$\mathbf{M_v w}^\top = < w_1 + v_1, w_2 + v_2, 1 >^\top$$

for every $< v_1, v_2, 1 > \in \mathbb{R}^3$ and $< w_1, w_2, 1 > \in \mathbb{R}^3$. Here

$$\mathbf{M_v} = \begin{pmatrix} 1 & 0 & v_1 \\ 0 & 1 & v_2 \\ 0 & 0 & 1 \end{pmatrix}$$

In the case of 3-dimensional translation, that is moving a point $< p, q, r >$ to a new point $< p, q, r > + \mathbf{v}$ we may realize this effect using a 4×4 matrix whose final column is $< v_1, v_2, v_3, 1 >^\top$ applied to the homogeneous coordinate $(p, q, r, 1)$.

A Brief Note on Projection and Perspective

There is one further class of transformations of great importance in constructing "realistic" 3-dimensional depictions which, as it turns out, are neither linear nor affine. These may be, informally, described as transformations arising through attempts to reproduce *perspective*. In such effects we wish to emulate the real-world phenomenon of "an object appears to be smaller the more distant it is from the viewer" in terms of how 3-dimensional objects actually appear on a screen. The study of projection covers a huge range of techniques of relevance to technical drawing, computer graphics, CAD, etc. Since our aim, in this chapter, is to present a flavour of the uses of vectors and matrices as these might arise in computational areas (i.e. this textbook is not intended as a substitute for advanced graphics texts) we refer those wishing to look in greater depth at this field (in particular perspective and projection in 3-D) to standard texts on Computer Graphics, that of Foley, van Dam *et al.* [90] being a particularly excellent example.

3.7 Application to Computer Graphics and Animation

Table 3.3 presents three common 2-dimensional graphical manipulations: translating an object to a new position on the display; scaling (both expanding and shrinking) the size of the object; and, "flipping" (i.e. reflecting) an object in both horizontal and vertical planes.

Also, often applied are rotation about the origin by a given angle and "shearing" by which the bounding rectangle containing the graphical object is skewed (horizontally, vertically, or both) with the internal angles of the rectangle changing from $90°$ to θ. This process is illustrated Figure 3.12.

In (A) a "Horizontal shear through a counterclockwise angle of θ" is used.

In (B) a "Horizontal shear through a clockwise angle of θ" is used.

Table 3.3: A Clowder of 2-D Graphics Effects

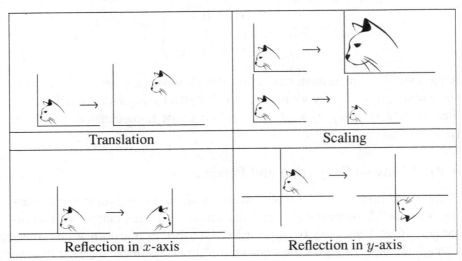

Translation	Scaling
Reflection in x-axis	Reflection in y-axis

(C) and (D) illustrate *Vertical* shears.

Finally (E) gives one example of combining both horizontal and vertical shearing.

All of the effects shown over Table 3.3 and Figure 3.12 can be realized by computing the product of a 3-vector $< x, y, 1 >$ with a 3×3-matrix. We give these matrices below.

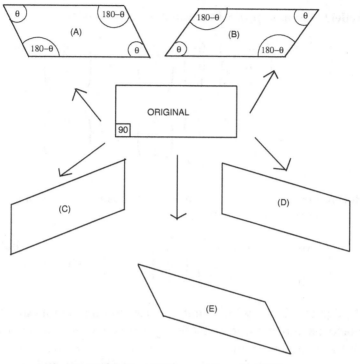

Figure 3.12: Five Different Shearing Effects

Translate a point $< p, q >$ to the point $< p + r, q + s >$ (p, q, r and $s \in \mathbb{R}$)

$$\begin{pmatrix} 1 & 0 & r \\ 0 & 1 & s \\ 0 & 0 & 1 \end{pmatrix} \begin{pmatrix} p \\ q \\ 1 \end{pmatrix} = \begin{pmatrix} p + r \\ q + s \\ 1 \end{pmatrix}$$

Scale (shrink or expand) the vector $< p, q >$ (in standard position) by $\alpha \in \mathbb{R}$.

$$\begin{pmatrix} \alpha & 0 & 0 \\ 0 & \alpha & 0 \\ 0 & 0 & 1 \end{pmatrix} \begin{pmatrix} p \\ q \\ 1 \end{pmatrix} = \begin{pmatrix} \alpha p \\ \alpha q \\ 1 \end{pmatrix}$$

Reflect a point $< p, q >$ in the x-axis (resp. y-axis).

$$\begin{pmatrix} -1 & 0 & 0 \\ 0 & 1 & 0 \\ 0 & 0 & 1 \end{pmatrix} \begin{pmatrix} p \\ q \\ 1 \end{pmatrix} = \begin{pmatrix} -p \\ q \\ 1 \end{pmatrix}$$

$$\begin{pmatrix} 1 & 0 & 0 \\ 0 & -1 & 0 \\ 0 & 0 & 1 \end{pmatrix} \begin{pmatrix} p \\ q \\ 1 \end{pmatrix} = \begin{pmatrix} p \\ -q \\ 1 \end{pmatrix}$$

Rotate the vector $< p, q >$ (in standard position) by an angle $\theta°$ *counterclockwise* around $< 0, 0 >$.

$$\begin{pmatrix} \cos\theta & -\sin\theta & 0 \\ \sin\theta & \cos\theta & 0 \\ 0 & 0 & 1 \end{pmatrix} \begin{pmatrix} p \\ q \\ 1 \end{pmatrix} = \begin{pmatrix} p\cos\theta - q\sin\theta \\ p\sin\theta + q\cos\theta \\ 1 \end{pmatrix}$$

Notice that if we wish to think of rotation through an angle $\varphi°$ in a **clockwise** direction, then φ (clockwise) is $360 - \varphi$ counterclockwise. Using the trigonometric identities $\cos(360 - \varphi) = \cos\varphi$ and $\sin(360 - \varphi) = -\sin\varphi$ allows us to make the appropriate substitution.

Shear (both X-shear and Y-shear)

Although Figure 3.12 presents the operation of shearing as involving an angular translation, in terms of describing the required matrix form it may be rather more useful to look at the construction in Figure 3.13

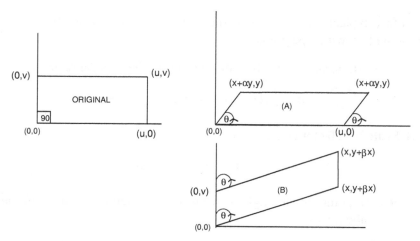

Figure 3.13: Another view of X (A) and Y (B) Shears

In the case of an X-shear the effect results in the y-coordinate of a point being unchanged while the (relevant) x-coordinates, (u, v) say, become some value $u + \alpha v$ with $\alpha \in \mathbb{R}$ defining the actual shear used. Similarly for Y-shears, now the x-coordinates are unchanged with (again relevant) y-coordinates, (u, v) moving to some position $v + \beta u$. The matrices realizing these effects are

X-shear

$$\begin{pmatrix} 1 & \alpha & 0 \\ 0 & 1 & 0 \\ 0 & 0 & 1 \end{pmatrix} \begin{pmatrix} u \\ v \\ 1 \end{pmatrix} = \begin{pmatrix} u + \alpha v \\ v \\ 1 \end{pmatrix}$$

Y-shear

$$\begin{pmatrix} 1 & 0 & 0 \\ \beta & 1 & 0 \\ 0 & 0 & 1 \end{pmatrix} \begin{pmatrix} u \\ v \\ 1 \end{pmatrix} = \begin{pmatrix} u \\ v + \beta u \\ 1 \end{pmatrix}$$

Notice that in these transformations the final coordinate (x, y) to which an input coordinate, (u, v), will be mapped is

$$(x, y) = (u + \alpha v, v) \quad X\text{-shear by factor } \alpha$$
$$(x, y) = (u, v + \beta u) \quad Y\text{-shear by factor } \beta$$

In fact, typical 2-D effects would be implemented by a suitable combination of the following operations:

M **Move** (translate) points by a distance (p, q). That is the mapping

$$M_{<p,q>}(< x, y >) =< x + p, y + q > .$$

S **Scale** by a factor $\alpha \in \mathbb{R}$.

$$S_\alpha(< x, y >) =< \alpha x, \alpha y > .$$

R **Rotate** points by an angle θ (measured counterclockwise from the x-axis) about $(0, 0)$.

$$R_\theta(< x, y >) =< x \cos \theta - y \sin \theta, x \sin \theta + y \cos \theta > .$$

By "suitable combination" we mean the following: given

$$\underline{\mathbf{P}} \;=\; \{\mathbf{P}_1, \mathbf{P}_2, \ldots, \mathbf{P}_k\}$$

a set of 3×3 matrices which can be used to "realize an effect" equivalent to $\mathbf{Q}\mathbf{x}^\top$ for $\mathbf{x} =< x, y, 1 >\in \mathbb{R}^3$ it is *not necessarily* the case that,

$$\mathbf{Q} \;=\; \prod_{i=1}^{k} \mathbf{P}_i$$

The **order** in which successive $\mathbf{P}_i$ are applied is important: matrix multiplication is, as we have seen, not in general commutative.

The principle complicating operation in this respect is that of *translate*. It is not hard to construct examples demonstrating choices of $< p, q >\in \mathbb{R}^2$, $\alpha \in \mathbb{R}$ and angles θ under which

$$\mathbf{M}_{<p,q>}\mathbf{S}_\alpha \;\neq\; \mathbf{S}_\alpha\mathbf{M}_{<p,q>}$$
$$\mathbf{M}_{<p,q>}\mathbf{R}_\theta \;\neq\; \mathbf{R}_\theta\mathbf{M}_{<p,q>}$$

"Translate followed by scaling" may have a different outcome from "scaling followed by translation".

Similarly, "Translate followed by rotation" may not produce the same result as "rotation followed by translation".

In contrast, however, irrespective of choices for $< \alpha, \beta >\in \mathbb{R}^2$, angles $< \theta, \psi >$ and movements $< p, q >$, $< r, s >$ it is unimportant in which order the effects: Rotate-then-scale, Rotate-then-Rotate, Scale-then-Scale, and Translate-then-translate are applied. In other words,

$$
\begin{aligned}
\mathbf{R}_\theta \mathbf{S}_\alpha &= \mathbf{S}_\alpha \mathbf{R}_\theta \\
\mathbf{R}_\theta \mathbf{R}_\psi &= \mathbf{R}_\psi \mathbf{R}_\theta &= \mathbf{R}_{\theta+\psi} \\
\mathbf{S}_\alpha \mathbf{S}_\beta &= \mathbf{S}_\beta \mathbf{S}_\alpha &= \mathbf{S}_{\alpha\cdot\beta} \\
\mathbf{M}_{<p,q>} \mathbf{M}_{<r,s>} &= \mathbf{M}_{<r,s>} \mathbf{M}_{<p,q>} &= \mathbf{M}_{<p+r,q+s>}
\end{aligned}
$$

For more complicated effects achieved as the outcome of a "Rotate-Scale-Translate" sequence, one often used device is to perform (although not *directly displaying* all of the stages) these with respect to the origin. Thus, suppose it has been decided to implement how the point (u, v) will be modified by applying to $< u, v, 1 >^\top$ the 3×3 matrix product $\mathbf{P}_k \mathbf{P}_{k-1} \mathbf{P}_{k-2} \cdots \mathbf{P}_2 \mathbf{P}_1$: that is the outcome representing $T(< u, v, 1 >)$ will be,

$$
(\mathbf{P}_k \mathbf{P}_{k-1} \mathbf{P}_{k-2} \cdots \mathbf{P}_2 \mathbf{P}_1) < u, v, 1 >^\top
$$

We may assume that, in this sequence, adjacent "rotate-then-scale" matrices have been collapsed into a single 3×3 matrix, i.e.

$$
\{\mathbf{R}_\theta \mathbf{S}_\alpha, \ \mathbf{S}_\alpha \mathbf{R}_\theta\}
$$

have been replaced by the equivalent 3×3 matrix resulting from computing the product directly. Notice that this allows us to assume that $\underline{\mathbf{P}}$ has the structure

$$
\mathbf{M}_{<x_k,y_k>} \, \mathbf{L}_{k-1} \, \mathbf{M}_{<x_{k-1},y_{k-1}>} \, \mathbf{L}_{k-2} \, \mathbf{M}_{<x_{k-3},y_{k-3}>} \mathbf{L}_{k-4} \cdots \mathbf{L}_2 \mathbf{M}_{<x_1,y_1>}
$$

Here $\mathbf{L}_j$ is the result of collapsing adjacent scaling and rotation matrices into single 3×3 matrices, so that the effect is implemented by "translate-then-(scale/rotate)-then-translate-$\cdots$-then-(scale/rotate)-then-translate".

Notice that we can always ensure the first matrix applied (and the last) is a translation simply by using $\mathbf{M}_{<0,0>}$ which translates $< x, y, 1 >$ to $< x + 0, y + 0, 1 >$, i.e. has no effect.

The main complication that arises is that the rotation matrices are defined with respect to rotation *about the origin*. To see why this might create a difficulty consider the situation in Figure 3.14.

If we wish to rotate the rectangle labelled C through $90°$ counterclockwise about the point (u, v) the new position displayed should be that corresponding to the rectangle labelled C'. The matrix $\mathbf{R}_{90°}$ while operating in a correct fashion for the rectangle labelled D (so that it produces D') will not have the required effect if applied directly to the corners of C. In order to overcome

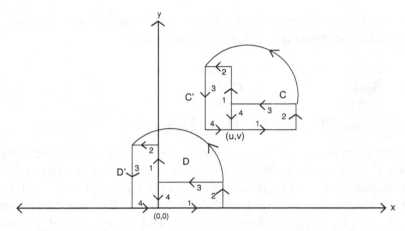

Figure 3.14: Rotation about $< 0, 0 >$ and arbritrary point

the problem we first apply the rotation as if C **were located at** D (to give D') and **then** translate D' to the position C''. We can do this by applying $\mathbf{R}_{90°}$ to each of the four corners, translating these points, and then drawing the edges of the rectangle in the same order as illustrated by the numbered labels in Figure 3.14. This imposes a slight overhead in implementation, however, the final translation need only be carried out when the rectangle is displayed, e.g. if in addition to rotation we then wanted to expand by a factor α, we can do this on D' prior to translating back. In total we would first apply the translation $\mathbf{M}_{<-u,-v>}$ to each corner of C (so taking the "origin corner" (u, v) to the "actual" origin); then carry out the specified rotations and scaling on the new corner points (noting that these can be collapsed into a *single* 3×3 matrix vector product) and *then* apply $\mathbf{M}_{<u,v>}$ to each of the four corners of the resulting rectangle. These corners and the order specified for individual edges uniquely determine what will be displayed.

For completeness, we summarize the 4×4 matrices applied to accomplish translation and scaling. Let us denote the mapping by,

$$M^3_{<p,q,r>}(< x, y, z >) \quad = \quad < x + p, y + q, z + r >$$
$$S^3_{\alpha}(< x, y, z >) \quad = \quad < \alpha x, \alpha y, \alpha z >$$

The 4×4 matrices have a very similar structure to those used for $2D$

effects,

$$\mathbf{M}_{<p,q,r>} = \begin{pmatrix} 1 & 0 & 0 & p \\ 0 & 1 & 0 & q \\ 0 & 0 & 1 & r \\ 0 & 0 & 0 & 1 \end{pmatrix}$$

So that the product of $\mathbf{M}_{<p,q,r>}$ with $< x, y, z, 1 >^\top$ is $< x + p, y + q, z + r, 1 >^\top$.

$$\mathbf{S}_\alpha = \begin{pmatrix} \alpha & 0 & 0 & 0 \\ 0 & \alpha & 0 & 0 \\ 0 & 0 & \alpha & 0 \\ 0 & 0 & 0 & 1 \end{pmatrix}$$

Yielding the product of $\mathbf{S}_\alpha$ with $< x, y, z, 1 >^\top$ as $< \alpha x, \alpha y, \alpha z, 1 >^\top$.

Rotation is a little more involved: when discussing $\mathbf{R}_\theta$, the 3×3 matrix used for rotation in the (x, y)-plane, we were able to fix $(0, 0)$ as the point to which the rotation of (u, v) was considered, as depicted in Figure 3.15.

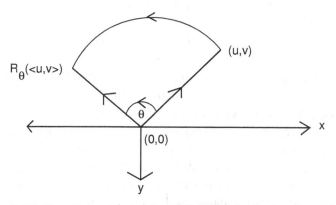

Figure 3.15: Rotation of (u, v) by $\theta°$ counterclockwise about $(0, 0)$.

We can deal with rotation about arbitrary points as discussed earlier following Figure 3.14.

In three dimensions we have the concept of "*rotation about a **line**"*. For example in Figure 3.16

If, analogously to the $2D$ we wish to have a standard reference line (the rôle played by $(0, 0)$ in the $2D$ case) then we must be able to express the outcome for rotation about an **arbitrary** line in terms of rotation about the reference. This is a rather more complicated process than that of "inverting a translation" used in $2D$. We will, therefore, be content to fix our reference line as the z-axis

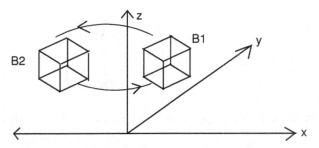

Figure 3.16: Rotation of cube about about a line

(that is the line described by the (set of) vectors $\{< 0, 0, z > \; : \; z \in \mathbb{R}\}$), however avoid any more extensive treatment.

Rotation of $< u, v, w >$ through $\theta°$ around the z-axis.

$$\mathbf{R}_\theta = \begin{pmatrix} \cos\theta & -\sin\theta & 0 & 0 \\ \sin\theta & \cos\theta & 0 & 0 \\ 0 & 0 & 1 & 0 \\ 0 & 0 & 0 & 1 \end{pmatrix}$$

The reader may find it useful to compare with the 3×3 matrix for rotation in $2D$ to develop corresponding 4×4 matrices for rotation around x and y axes.

We conclude this overview of how matrix-vector products are applied in Computer Graphics, by considering one example of such approaches that can be used to manipulate *colour*. As we mentioned earlier the colour of a picture cell (or *pixel*) can be viewed as a 3-vector with components drawn from $\mathbb{Z}_{256}$ and the operations $+$ and $\cdot$ being standard arithmetic module 256. A common photographic and colour manipulation is that of creating the **negative** of an image.

In terms of transformation $T_\neg(< r, g, b >)$ replaces the 3-vector $< r, g, b >$ by $< 255, 255, 255 > - < r, g, b >$, that is to say with $< 255 - r, 255 - g, 255 - b >$. Now, although the corresponding vector transformation $T_\neg$ is not a linear transformation, it is affine and so by operating on 4-vectors $< r, g, b, 1 >$ it can be implemented using a 4×4 matrix.

$$\mathbf{C} = \begin{pmatrix} -1 & 0 & 0 & 255 \\ 0 & -1 & 0 & 255 \\ 0 & 0 & -1 & 255 \\ 0 & 0 & 0 & 1 \end{pmatrix}$$

with which it is easily verified that $\mathbf{C} < r, g, b, 1 >^\top \; = \; T_\neg(< r, g, b >)^\top$ recalling that arithmetic is *modular* in this instance.

3.8 Summary

A number of ideas have been introduced in this chapter several of which will be built on in subsequent chapters. In particular we have presented the concept of n-**vector** defined within $(\mathbb{T}, +, \cdot)$ and considered how operations of vector addition and scalar for $\alpha \in \mathbb{T}$ are described. These led to in a similar style to the treatment of polynomials from $\mathbb{T}[X]$ to possible formulations of vector product. The important notion of **vector space** together with attributes of such was then considered, leading to a preliminary lead in to uses and properties of matrices. We concluded by describing the concept of transformations between vector spaces and demonstrated that the concept of transformation plays an important part in capturing basic graphical display effects. Although we have developed this aspect in great depth, the relationship between matrix-vector products and graphics is also central to the specialist discipline of **Computational Geometry**, whose concerns, among others, relate heavily to matters such as "hidden surface detection".

Matrices will be met again, in rather greater detail, in Chapter 7.

3.9 Projects

1. Develop a "retro 1970s" Computer Game (e.g. tennis) in which movements are controlled from a keyboard (for example by using the $\{\leftarrow, \rightarrow, \uparrow, \downarrow\}$ keys) to control a "racquet". This will intercept a puck whose movement is controlled by the program. In such contexts the graphics and animation effects are realized in $2D$ via the methods discussed in Section 3.7.

3.10 Endnotes

1. It is not surprising, given its nature and the fact that almost all of the
   key breakthroughs in the subject had been made prior to 1970, that the
   core material of Automata and Formal Language Theory as presented on
   introductory undergraduate courses has not changed significantly in half
   a century: one could, in principle, use standards such as Minsky [168]
   (from 1967) as a supporting text, some may harbour a lingering nostal-
   gia for the depth and detail of Hopcroft and Ullman [122] (from 1979),
   while yet others prefer the more student-friendly approach of Hopcroft,
   Motwani and Ullman [121] (of 2001). In this field there are a huge variety of differing texts and styles of presentation, however whether written
   in the late 1960s or mid 2010s, very similar ground is covered and the
   essential core remains identical.[32]

   Rather more of a surprise, in my personal experience having studied in
   the late 1970s and subsequently taught such material to undergraduates
   (1984 and between 2011–17), is to find a similar, admittedly less pronounced, pattern in practical arenas of Computer Science. A standard
   Operating Systems textbook from the mid 1970s, e.g. Lister [158] or
   Barron [21] is not hugely distinctive in its central focus from a latter day
   standard such as Silberschatz, Galvin and Gagne [214].[33] Similarly, the
   mechanics of high-level programming language compilers, (even without making allowances for new developments such as object-orientation
   etc.) could be presented using classic 1970s texts such as Gries [108] or
   Aho & Ullman [3] almost as effectively as the most recent presentations
   e.g. Halsey [113]. Even within as rapidly changing a field as AI one may
   identify a reasonable degree of common interest between *ur*-texts such
   as Bundy [38] and modern standards such as Russell and Norvig [201]:
   the contemporary emergence of machine learning and uncertain reasoning being significant absences (for reasons that are self-evident) in the
   former.

---

[32]One trusts the reader notes the author's restraint in not referring to [68].

[33]In O/S development, the important shift has been from the monolithic shared access mainframe environments dominating computational provision until the late 1990s to the stand-alone
personal single-user configurations of the present. Nonetheless this, often, just raises a rephrasing of *scale* rather than fundamental method. For example memory management and virtual
memory that had (when first mooted) concerned relative measures of Megabytes vs. Kilobytes
(back-up disk and main memory) now deal with quantities of Terabytes (hard disk) vs. Giga-
bytes (cache memory): *plus ça change plus c'est la même chose.*

Comparing the treatments of database design and implementation as given in a popular mid-1970s text such as Kroenke [147] to those being used barely a decade later, e.g. Ullman [237] let alone such textbooks as may be seen as standard today, e.g. Connolly & Begg [48] reveals enormous differences not only in emphasis but in what is essential, core, material. Seeing the DL/1 language ([147, Chapter 5]) or the CODA-SYL DBTG model ([147, Chapter 6]) in the light of the now all conquering Relational Model confirms only too clearly that (to paraphrase L. P. Hartley) the past is, indeed, a foreign country, they did things differently there.

2. *"we cannot say that* 'x < y' *or* 'y < x' *or* 'x = y' *must be the case.":* Here, of course, we are referring to the specific form of $x \leq y$ that is presented in the text. This "component-wise comparison" is not the only possible definition that might be used for $x \leq y$. One widely used method, that has many applications in computational settings, is known as *lexicographic* ordering. Not only does this provide a complete ordering of $\mathbb{T}^n$ (assuming that, as is the case for $\mathbb{T} \in \{\mathbb{N}, \mathbb{W}, \mathbb{Z}, \mathbb{Q}, \mathbb{R}\}$, $\mathbb{T}$ itself may be completely ordered) it also allows a coherent method of comparing vectors $x \in \mathbb{T}^m$ with $y \in \mathbb{T}^n$ even when $m \neq n$. Given $x \in \mathbb{T}^m$ and $y \in \mathbb{T}^n$ we write $x <_{\text{lex}} y$ should one of the following be true.

   a. If $x_1 < y_1$ then $x <_{\text{lex}} y$.

   b. If there is an index, k, with $1 \leq k < m$, and $x_i = y_i$ for each component with index $1 \leq i < k$ **but** $x_k < y_k$ then $x <_{\text{lex}} y$.

   c. If $x_i = y_i$ for every $1 \leq i \leq m$ and $m < n$ then $x <_{\text{lex}} y$.

This may be recognised as the standard dictionary ordering of words in a language.

3. The Euclidean (or L_2) measure for defining vector size is just one of many approaches. While undoubtedly the most widely used in computational settings, particularly in those elements of vector algebra contributing to computational geometry and computer graphics it is worth mentioning a generalization of this: the L_p-metric where $p \in \mathbb{R}$ with $p \neq 0$. Given a vector $x \in \mathbb{R}^n$ its size in the L_p measure (denoted $\|x\|_p$) is

$$\|x\|_p = \left(\sum_{k=1}^{n} |x_k|^p \right)^{\frac{1}{p}}$$

The case $p = 1$ corresponds to the *Manhattan distance* referring to New York street layout. Here in moving from the origin $(0, 0)$ to a point (x, y) one may either move "x places along then y places up" or "y places up then x places along": giving, in both cases, a total distance of $|x| + |y|$. Generalizing to n-vectors the L_1 measure describes movement from $(0, 0, \dots, 0)$ to $(x_1, x_2, \dots, x_n)$ via a sequence of n straight-lines each move in the sequence ensuring that a component whose value is 0 at the current position is changed to the corresponding x_i value.

The L_p concept can be defined with respect to $p = 0$ or even $p = \infty$. Most cases other than $p = 1$ and $p = 2$ have, however, very little computational interest.

4. The technical form for cross product could, in principle, be defined for n-vectors with arbitrary $n \in \mathbb{N}$. There are, however, issues not only with geometric analogies but also algebraic complications. Aside from 3-vectors, only 7-vectors (via treatment as *octonions*) are well-behaved. The 3-vector cross product finds an important development in *quaternions* (see Chapter 5) a formalism of huge importance in powerful graphics processing methods. To the best of my knowledge, no computational advantage is found with octonions.

5. "*…are referred to as 'left handed'.*": One finds a similar wording (e.g. "A three-dimensional coordinate system in which the axes satisfy the right-hand rule is called a right-handed coordinate system, while one that does not is called a left-handed coordinate system."[34]) in many references.

It is symptomatic of the lateralist bias in language that "left handed systems" are characterized not by virtue of some positive quality but simply by the attribute of "not being right handed". The continuing prevalence of such linguistic prejudice, when one considers the significant strides taken to eradicate all manner of once common usages falling foul of various -isms (racism, sexism, ageism, etc.) from everyday speech, is at the very least surprising and, at worst, only too indicative of a rancid hypocrisy polluting the mindset of those claiming to promote a "politically correct" agendum. Perhaps, this comment seems like an overstatement? Possibly a *sinister*, incor*rect*, *gauche*, mala*droit* over-reaction that lacks *rect*itude and is couched without *dexter*ity? This may be so, but $10\% +$ of the population could well think otherwise.

---

[34]from `http://mathworld.wolfram.com/Right-HandRule.html`.

Throughout the so-called "developed world" there are still many (naturally left handed) people who will recall the barbaric practices adopted in junior schools in vain attempts to force gripping a pen right handed in order to learn handwriting. Even today, the academic who, ignoring student clamour for the *panem et circenses* of powerpoint and video, continues to present impromptu written notes, will, in the event of their being left handed, have to contend with a mass of whining and bleating.[35] One notes, out of interest, that at least one aspect of the symbolism underpinning this prejudice in Renaissance depictions of the Crucifixion has no supporting basis: namely the "Penitent and unrepentant thieves" (Dismas and Gestas in the apocryphal Gospel of Nicodemus). Only St. Luke's Gospel reports their speech (23:39–43), however, no suggestion of left or right is offered.

6. If we consider the coefficients of polynomials having degree $< n$ in $\mathbb{R}[X]$ (for a bounded n) then this allows us to view the "set of polynomials with Real coefficients and degree less than n" as a vector space in the sense that $(\mathbb{R}, +, \cdot)$ satisfies the necessary properties as too does scalar multiplication and addition of polynomials. In this setting, the polynomials $\{1, x, x^2, \ldots, x^{n-1}\}$ are a basis for the corresponding space. If, however, we move to the set of **all** polynomials in $\mathbb{R}[X]$ (i.e. without fixing a degree bound) then although still a vector space, the structure is not a *finite dimensional* vector space. Of course using $\{1, x, x^2, \ldots, x^{n-1}\}$ simply corresponds to the standard basis for $\mathbb{R}^n$ just by considering the respective coefficients. Similarly the "vector space of all polynomials" is (subject to the necessary and one hopes self-evident modifications required to the definition of vector addition)[36] analogous to the vector space $\cup_{n=1}^{\infty} \mathbb{R}^n$.

---

[35]To anyone who doubts the existence of these attitudes, the disgusting pseudo-religious ranting that may be found on

http://www.landoverbaptist.net/showthread.php?t=49703

may prove enlightening. On a lighter note identifying what W. C. Fields, Fidel Castro, Albert Einstein, Bart Simpson and (of course!) Kermit the Frog have in common seems like an entertaining trivia question. Strangely the organization outing this collection fails to mention *The Simpsons* most famous left hander: Ned Flanders the proprietor of the short-lived Leftorium. Aficionados of the series on perusing this list will have little difficulty seeing the reason for the "oversight".

[36]In order to ensure that the outcome of adding $\mathbf{u} \in \mathbb{R}^n$ to $\mathbf{v} \in \mathbb{R}^m$ ($m < n$) is a vector $\mathbf{w} \in \mathbb{R}^n$: here a variant of the method to add polynomials of differing degree can be adopted.

7. Consider the cube with sides of length 1 as shown in Figure 3.17. We use the multiple arrows on some edges to indicate that these are drawn in separate phases, hence single arrows are drawn first in ascending order of the number label; then double, triple and, finally, quadruple arrows.

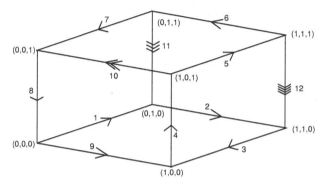

Figure 3.17: Traversing the edges of a unit cube.

8. On the notion of "infinitely many transformations": At the risk of presenting an example which will confirm many in-built prejudices about mathematical thinking in general and linear algebra in particular, consider the vector space, H, formed from $(\mathbb{Z}_2, +, \cdot)$ where arithmetic is modulo 2, i.e. binary with $H = \{< 0 >, < 1 >\}$.[37] Now choose G to be the vector space $\mathbb{R}^2$. There are, obviously, infinitely many vectors in G and, with respect to our very general description of transformation, for each $\mathbf{x} \in G$ we can have either $T(\mathbf{x}) = < 0 > \in H$ or $T(\mathbf{x}) = < 1 > \in H$. Whatever is chosen as $T(\mathbf{x})$ has no implications for what could be chosen for $T(\mathbf{y})$ (when $\mathbf{y} \neq \mathbf{x}$). Hence, over the whole vector space formed by G we have infinitely many different transformations onto the (finite) vector space H.

---

[37]Note the distinction between the 1-**vectors** $\{< 0 >, < 1 >\}$ comprising H and the **scalars**, $\{0, 1\}$ defining $\mathbb{Z}_2$.

Chapter 4

The world in motion
A Basic Introduction to Calculus

All changed, changed utterly: A terrible beauty is born.

Easter 1916
W. B. YEATS (1865-1939)

4.1   The origins of Differential Calculus

The concept and perceptions of Calculus, in both the form with which we are principally concerned in this chapter – Differential Calculus – and that of Integral Calculus, are sometimes perceived as representing a higher plateau of technical difficulty. It is possible that this creates some level of apprehension, and it would be fair to state that in comparison with many of the ideas we have so far encountered the underlying themes do encompass a number of more advanced notions.

This being so, it is worth devoting some space to the following questions, prior to embarking on discussing the formal apparatus involved in their resolution. In particular,

QC1. What **does** the study of Calculus concern?

QC2. Why are special techniques **needed** to address the issues arising in (QC1)?

QC3. What are the areas of **Computer Science** for which the methodology of Calculus is essential?

Calculus is concerned with the study of *change*. How do we determine the *speed* of a vehicle after it has been *accelerating* (increasing its speed at a given rate) for a certain amount of time? How do we *predict* the *next occurrence* of some astronomical phenomenon? How do we calculate when (or, indeed, if) the *spread of a contagious disease* will affect such a *proportion of the population* as to necessitate e.g. quarantine or other intervention? What factors can be used in deciding to *discontinue investment* in a particular enterprise on the grounds that its *return* has *reached a peak* and further investment would, at best, be fruitless, at worst, result in loss? As every child is aware, the **distance** a ball can be thrown *accurately* varies with a number of parameters from factors such as the force with which the object is propelled, to, perhaps, less obvious influences such as the *angle* at which it is projected. That such come into play is (at least subliminally) understood by those engaged in sports events (javelin, shot putt, rugby, football,[1] cricket, basketball, etc.) through to the military practice, dating back to ancient times, of lobbing objects at targets, e.g. via slings, catapults, bow and arrow, cannon and so on.[2]

In fact, Calculus is rather more than concerned with simply modelling change but, in particular, with seemingly more abstruse concepts such as the *rate* at which change affects objects and, especially, capturing changes by increasingly smaller and smaller amounts. Thus, the origins of the field now known as *Integral Calculus* lie in the measurement of line lengths, areas and volumes. Of course, these are easy enough if the line is a straight edge between two points, but what if the line is that formed by a "parabola" which is, in fact, the whole distance that would be traversed by an object propelled at a given speed and angle. Easy enough, also, if the area is a rectangle or the volume a cuboid, but what if we are faced with, say, the area spanned by a curve between two points where it intersects the x-axis?[3] What if our volume is that marked out by rotating a flat surface?[4] The classical technique developed by the Greek scholars Eudoxus of Cnidus (*fl.* 4th century BC) and Archimedes (*ca.* 225BC) is known as the "Method of Exhaustion" and provides the raw material for what would (the best part of 2000 years later) form the basis of integral calculus as recognized today.

---

[1]Meaning, of course, proper football, i.e. that which is referred to as "soccer" elsewhere.

[2]If one looks at the advertized programmes of study at many forces colleges one often finds quite extensive mathematical material either as prerequisite or taught, e.g. West Point, (https://www.usma.edu/math/).

[3]For example, if we have a curve mapped out through (x, y) coordinates related by $y = 9 - x^2$, this will intersect the x-axis (i.e. have $y = 0$) for the two values $x = -3$ and $x = 3$.

[4]For instance, in crafting a vase on a potter's wheel the volume of the object produced can be viewed in this fashion.

It is useful, briefly to look at the thoughts underlying the "Method of Exhaustion". In essence the idea is very simple: suppose we want to find the area covered within a particular marked out space. We start out by "fitting" the largest square (or equilateral triangle or rectangle or other shape whose area we know how to compute) we can into the space. It is unlikely (unless the "measurement problem" is effectively trivial) that we will cover the entirety of the region of interest. So we take *smaller* squares (or triangles or rectangles) and we get a *better* estimate of the region area. Progressing from S_1^2 (the original square of side, S_1) to some number, r say, of squares of area S_2^2: rS_2^2 (r squares with side length $S_2 < S_1$) covers more of the region we are trying to measure, so that less of this is unaccounted for than with the single square of area S_1^2. But why stop this process at S_2? There will still be sections of the region of interest not covered and so, noting the improvement from S_1 to S_2 i.e. with squares of *shorter* side length, we go on to squares of side length $S_3 < S_2$ and then $S_4 < S_3$ and then $\cdots$.

And then?

The achievement of Eudoxus, Archimedes and their $17th$ century (AD) successors is in making precise and hence, **computationally effective** what should happen at the stage "*and then* $\cdots$". Making *computational* sense of, what in effect is the issue "how sensibly to interpret the addition of more and more (but smaller and smaller) quantities", lies at the heart of Integral Calculus. We shall look at these ideas in greater depth within Section 4.9.

It is also worth mentioning one point where we have already seen this problem of "adding smaller and smaller quantities infinitely often": in Section 2.2 and Algorithm 2.2. Here we illustrated how to form the decimal expansion of any $q \in \mathbb{Q}$ for which $0 < q < 1$. A potential issue that arose is the possibility of such expansions being *infinite* depending on the value of q, e.g. cases such as $1/3$, $1/7$, etc. What is actually meant by saying that the infinite sequence $.r_1 r_2 \cdots r_k r_{k+1} \cdots$ "represents" the Rational q in such cases? Formally that

$$q = \sum_{k=0}^{\infty} \frac{r_k}{10^k}$$

This is a sum containing infinitely many terms with successive terms becoming smaller and smaller $(r_k/10^k) > (r_{k+1}/10^{k+1})$.

Integration originates in a problem that is computationally well grounded: measurement of lengths, areas, and volumes where there is no clear-cut approach to doing so e.g. akin to the notion of vector size, or multiplying 2 (and 3 in the case of volumes) Natural numbers.

What, however, about Differential Calculus? Where do we find these ideas of gleaning information about behaviour of a larger environment through consideration of accumulated increasingly smaller (but proliferating) changes, arising **in reality**? In order to gain some preliminary insight, consider the following scenarios.

DC1. A vehicle climbs to the summit of a hill whose height (after travelling M metres *horizontally*) is $3M^2$. If the vehicle starts at the foot of the hill which is at sea-level (i.e. height 0 metres) and (after descending from the peak) returns to sea-level having travelled an equivalent of 300 metres horizontally, how high is the hill at its peak?

DC2. An arrow travels a total distance (from its starting position) of 400 metres. If the archer has positioned the bow to launch the arrow at an angle of $60°$ (measured relative to the horizontal), what is the highest height the arrow reaches?

Our first observation is that both (DC1) and (DC2) are what are called *Optimization* settings. In both cases we are trying to discover the *maximum* value (subject to some side constraints) governing particular behaviours: the *maximum height* of, respectively a hill and an arrow.

We shall see that Differential Calculus provides a powerful suite of tools by which these and other such problems can be handled. Central to the approach is being able to describe "the line touching a curve at a given point".[5] With respect to the two questions raised above and, more generally, for problems of this type the line in question has a particular form: it is **parallel** to the x-axis *and* makes contact with (i.e. touches) the curve characterizing the behaviour being investigated. The battery of approaches provided within Differential Calculus offer elegant mechanisms for studying such touching lines. As with the "Method of Exhaustion" underlying the formal structure of Integral Calculus, in analyzing the character of "lines touching a curve", a key rôle is played by studying behaviour as a whole via behaviour presented in terms of increasingly small changes.

Our very informal discussion of the preceding paragraphs will, one hopes, give some kind of sense of the range and scope of matters with which Calculus is typically concerned. In brief, the study of phenomena that are modelled in terms of some sense of change and the "rate" at which such changes arise. Solution techniques thence leading to algorithmic approaches to optimization problems, area and volume measurement, etc.

---

[5] See Endnote 1.

Why, however, do we need a "new collection of techniques" to deliver these ends? Reviewing what we have looked at so far in this book, we have seen divers approaches by which the nature of "Number" is described, leading, subsequently to the concept and manipulation of what were called *polynomials*: Chapter 2. Having noted the lack of structure within these objects, we continued by presenting a collection of forms (vectors and matrices) by which some sense of order is provided: Chapter 3. These forms, however, overlook one element of importance: they are *static* and *fixed*. While some initial treatment of how structures change was offered at the conclusion of Chapter 3 through the use of "matrix-vector product", it is unclear to what degree this offers a solution method for questions such as (DC1) and (DC2).

We wrote of vectors as objects having "direction and size" but not, in terms of basic attributes, *position*. Let us look at the question posed in (DC2) in a little more detail. Consider Figure 4.1.

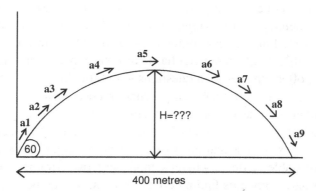

Figure 4.1: A "difficult" measurement problem

In principle in determining what the value of H is, we wish to inspect how the vectors, **ai** representing the "arrow length and direction" change as it progresses from the point at which it is unleashed, through its zenith and thence returns to ground. The successive changes, however, as is clear from Figure 4.1 do not capture the **same** vector. For example, **a1** the starting vector has a different *direction* (although identical size) from **a5** (where the greatest height is attained) and both differ from **a9**. The diagram separates the individual vectors from the trajectory drawn. Suppose, however, we had depicted the scenario with the arrows "overlapping" the path taken? Of course this will not be an "exact fit": the path is curved and the arrow vector a straight edge. In fact the path we wish to study is that of "the points on the curve touched by the arrow as it moves". We have no apparatus yet to address such questions. The techniques of Differential Calculus will provide precisely these.

Turning to the question raised in (QC3): the areas of **Computer Science** for which the methodology of Calculus is essential, we have already discussed one of these, namely *Optimization Problems*. Although this is not the only such area it is certainly one of the most important. In this class of problems we have an environment, typically described by a *function*, f, reporting values in $\mathbb{R}$ given input(s) to its *arguments*, of which there may be more than one: formally the environment is $f : \mathbb{R}^n \to \mathbb{R}$, the function arguments being $< x_1, x_2, \ldots, x_n >$. The aim is to find those values in $\mathbb{R}$, $< \alpha_1, \alpha_2, \ldots, \alpha_n >$ that should be assigned to the arguments so as to *maximize* (or, in the case of minimization problems, *minimize*) the value $f(\alpha_1, \alpha_2, \ldots, \alpha_n)$. Often it is the case that there are additional constraints placed on the allowable choices for $< \alpha_1, \ldots, \alpha_n >$: that specific values must lie within a given range; that some combination of the values must equal a given setting, e.g. for a 3 variable instance that the product $\alpha_1 \cdot \alpha_2 \cdot \alpha_3 = \beta \in \mathbb{R}$. The two examples presented both concern identifying a maximum value for the settings defined. Provided the function describing the environment has a suitable form (one typical case being where only a single parameter has to be determined), via differential calculus we can, often, answer such questions with little difficulty. These include settings such as: trade-offs between production costs, investment in machinery, and retail costs so as to maximize profit margins; estimating when a drug administered intravenously will reach its maximum level of concentration dependent on factors such as natural wastage, patient weight, initial dose. Even within multivariable settings, whereby more than one parameter is to be set, significant progress towards finding effective solutions can be made using the arsenal of techniques provided by Differential Calculus. As one final aspect which we will need in applying these methods, we will, again, encounter but in a much more general form than previously the idea of "roots of a function". In Section 2.4, we met this idea with respect to functions whose form was that of a "polynomial of degree k". Using methods grounded in Differential Calculus provides one approach to identifying roots of polynomials having degree exceeding 4.[6]

These are, of course, very far from an exhaustive list of areas where Calculus is an essential method within Computer Science. As we noted in Chapter 1, extensive use of Calculus in the form of "Differential Equations" and their solution is standard in Physics and Electrical Engineering. We do not, however, require methods of this degree of sophistication relative to the topics we will

---

[6]Recall, as discussed in Section 2.5, degree 4 (quartic) polynomials represent the highest degree whose roots can be explored through "closed form" expressions.

look at in this Chapter. To begin our overview, we must return to these notions of *"function"* and *"line"*.

4.2 Functions, Lines and Derivatives

We have referred to the concept of "function" a number of times already: both explicitly, above, when presenting the form taken by Optimization Problems, but also implicitly, for example with respect to the concept of "polynomial form" in Section 2.4 and, perhaps less obviously, via the idea of "vector space transformations" in Section 3.6. Given this and the fact that we assume the reader has, at least, an intuitive understanding of the concept of "function" our main intention at this point is to fix exactly what we shall understand by this term in the remainder of the chapter.

The intuitive concept of a "function f" is as an object that "takes values from some set of allowed values" $\mathcal{D}$ say and "reports values within some set of output possibilities" $\mathcal{R}$ say. In other words, a *function*, f, *maps* inputs from a *domain*, $\mathcal{D}$, to outputs within a *range* $\mathcal{R}$. In terse form: $f : \mathcal{D} \to \mathcal{R}$.

In our initial development we will be exclusively concerned with *functions over the Real numbers*, that is $f : \mathbb{R} \to \mathbb{R}$. Regarding notational conventions, for arbitrary functions we use lower-case letters such as f, g, h, etc.; x for the function input or *argument* as we shall subsequently refer to it and where it is useful to do so, y for the function result. Hence writing, $y = f(x)$, $y = x^3$, $y = \cos x$ etc. This allows us to present the behaviour even of quite intricate functions via a $2D$-plot within (xy)-Cartesian coordinate schemes: for each value of x that is of interest, we mark the point $(x, f(x))$ on our coordinate axes. At this stage the principal defining property of a function that should be remembered is: a function maps any x to **at most** one $f(x)$. If the value $f(x)$ is defined[7] then it is **uniquely** defined.

Table 4.1 presents a few examples.

Looking at some selected examples of these, we get the diagrams of Table 4.2.

Notice that these have very different behaviours: the first two trigonometric functions (sin and cos) oscillate between -1 and 1; the third case ($\tan x$), however, while also being periodic[8] can take any value in $\mathbb{R}$. The function x^{-1}

---

[7]As we will see, again, simply because $f : \mathbb{R} \to \mathbb{R}$ does not necessarily entail $f(x)$ having a "sensible" outcome for every $x \in \mathbb{R}$.

[8]We say that f is a *periodic* function if there is a (positive) $\alpha \in \mathbb{R}$ for which $f(x) = f(x + \alpha)$ with every x. The three standard trigonometric functions are all periodic using the value $\alpha = 360°$.

Table 4.1: Some Examples of Functions

	Definition	Description
a.	$y = x$	Identity
b.	$y = 5x + 1$	Simple linear function
c.	$y = x^2$	Simple polynomial (squaring)
d.	$y = x^4 - 3x^2 + 1$	Polynomial of degree 4
e.	$y = x^{-1}$	Reciprocal
f.	$y = x^{\sqrt{3}} + 2$	More complicated powering function (I).
g.	$y = x^\pi + x^{0.5}$	More complicated powering function. (II)
h.	$y = \sin x$	Trigonometric function (sin)
i.	$y = \cos x$	Trigonometric function (cos)
j.	$y = \tan x$	Trigonometric function (tan)
k.	$y = \exp x$	Exponential function (also e^x)
l.	$y = \log x$	("Natural") logarithm.

"jumps" from $x < 0$ to $x > 0$ but its behaviour at $x = 0$ is unclear. The exponential function ($\exp x$) increases very quickly while $\log x$ increases at quite a sedate rate. Finally the two polynomial examples (x^2 and $x^4 - 3x^2 + 1$) have markedly different behaviour, both distinctive from the "linear function" $5x + 1$.

Of these examples, Table 4.2 (b) has a fairly clear simple form. The outcome y prescribed by the line $y = 5x + 1$ increases as x increases, and, more than this, the *rate* at which $y = f(x)$ gets larger follow a very precisely defined pattern. Taking the sequence of x values: $< 1, 2, 3, 4, 5 >$ the corresponding y values are $< 6, 11, 16, 21, 26 >$ and as we look at the **ratio** of $f(x)$ to x this gets closer and closer to 5. The class of functions defined by cases such as (a) and (b) are known as *linear functions* and the relationship between the input argument (x) and the function value (y) is determined by two parameters: the multiple of x setting the rate of increase (or decrease) as the dominating determining factor for the value of y; and the *constant* additive offset. In total a linear function is any function that is captured by the relationship,

$$y = m \cdot x + c \quad m, c \in \mathbb{R}$$

The value m is called the **gradient** of the line, and, informally, describes its slope by how much y increases relative to increases in x. The notion of gradient will, of course, be familiar to motorists and pedestrians: the amount of

Table 4.2: Selected Plots of Functions in Table 4.1

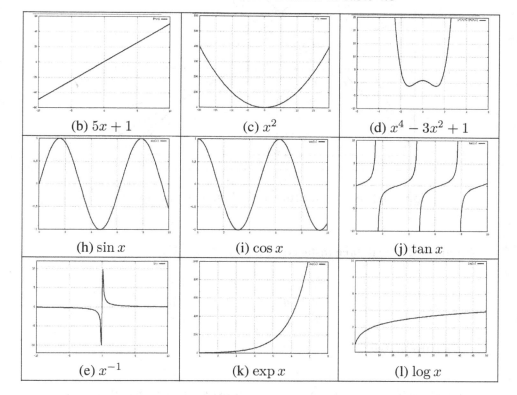

(b) $5x + 1$	(c) x^2	(d) $x^4 - 3x^2 + 1$
(h) $\sin x$	(i) $\cos x$	(j) $\tan x$
(e) x^{-1}	(k) $\exp x$	(l) $\log x$

effort expended in climbing a "hill with a one-in-six (1 : 6) gradient" is rather more than that expended when the gradient is "one-in-twenty" (1 : 20)".

Now this concept of "*linear function*" has an extremely important rôle with respect to the development of differential calculus and the application to optimization. Look again at Figure 4.1, but now let's think of the arrow trajectory being marked out by lines which touch the curve of interest as show in Figure 4.2.

As the arrow ascends along the trajectory the lines touching the path change from $L1$ to $L2$ then $L3$; as it descends these lines become $L5$ then $L6$ then $L7$. At its maximum height the line touching this point is $L4$. Now if we look at the line functions then these first three cases are of the form

$$
\begin{aligned}
L1 \quad y &= m_1 x + C_1 \\
L2 \quad y &= m_2 x + C_2 \\
L3 \quad y &= m_3 x + C_3
\end{aligned}
$$

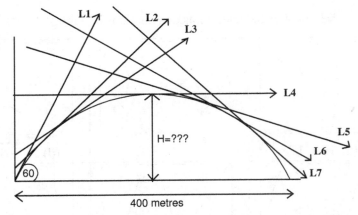

Figure 4.2: Arrow direction from Figure 4.1 as "touching lines"

Similarly the final three instances are,

$$
\begin{array}{llll}
L5 & y & = & m_5 x + C_5 \\
L6 & y & = & m_6 x + C_6 \\
L7 & y & = & m_7 x + C_7
\end{array}
$$

and, in the middle,

$$y = m_4 x + C_4$$

Now the values of m_i when $1 \leq i \leq 3$ **must** be greater than 0: as x increases in value so too does y.

Similarly the values of m_i when $5 \leq i \leq 7$ **must** be *less* than 0: as x increases in value y **decreases**. In other words,

$$
\begin{array}{llll}
\text{if } p > q & \text{then} & m_i \cdot p > m_i \cdot q & 1 \leq i \leq 3 \\
\text{if } p > q & \text{then} & m_i \cdot p < m_i \cdot q & 5 \leq i \leq 7
\end{array}
$$

And for the middle case, $L4$, *irrespective of how x changes* the corresponding value of y is unaffected: $m_4 = 0$ and, thus, $y = C_4$ in this case. What, however, is C_4? The line in question ($L4$) touches the path traced out by the arrow at its highest point and, therefore, since it **touches** this curve the value of $m_4 x + C_4$ must be **exactly the same as** the corresponding y value on the trajectory itself. In other words $C_4 = H$ the height we are trying to determine.

In total we have blocked out a strategy with which to attack question (DC2). Namely, assuming that we know $y = r(x)$ the function describing the path taken by the arrow,

S1. Determine the **function**, $\tau(x)$ for which the gradient of the line touching $r(x)$ when $x = p$ is $\tau(p)$, that is the corresponding line function is

$$y = \tau(p) \cdot x + (r(p) - \tau(p) \cdot p).$$

S2. Find which value(s) of x result in the gradient being 0, i.e. for which the touching line is parallel to the x-axis. These values are those for which $\tau(x) = 0$.

S3. Now letting z be one such value, i.e. $\tau(z) = 0$, find the maximum height by computing $r(z)$.

Strategy this may indeed be, but there are rather too many gaps at the moment for us seriously to regard it as an effective one. For example, (S1) sets the challenge of determining a specific function with a very particular behaviour in respect of the function with which we started. Although (S2) is a problem we have met earlier in the particular case when $\tau(x)$ would be a polynomial function we only discussed some very restricted instances of its solution. We have also hinted at a complication that will arise and be resolved in Section 4.4, namely: if there are multiple distinct z for which $\tau(z) = 0$, how do we identify the value we are actually interested in discovering? Finally, (S3) concerns *evaluating* a given function (the $r(z)$ of the problem that we are attempting to maximize) using a specific value: this, in contrast to (S1) and, to some degree (S2), one would hope, ought not to set too onerous a challenge.

The methodology underpinning answering (S1) was fundamental to the development of differential calculus. It is to this that we now turn.

To begin, however, we first recall that one sub-problem to be solved is that of finding the unique line function $y = m \cdot x + c$ joining two points (x_1, y_1) and (x_2, y_2). Let us assume that $x_2 > x_1$. In essence the gradient, m, simply describes "how much the value y **should** change relative to how much the value x **has** changed".

If we are looking at the line on which both (x_1, y_1) and (x_2, y_2) lie, we know that the "change from x_1 to x_2" produces a corresponding "change in y_1 to y_2. Thus, given that "y_1 **should** become y_2 when x_1 **has** become x_2" we know that

$$m = \frac{y_2 - y_1}{x_2 - x_1}$$

All we need to determine now is the offset value c. Our line function is $y = m \cdot x + c$, so that when $x = 0$ the corresponding value of y will be c. Since, however, we are dealing with a *straight* line the gradient m which we have just calculated will be exactly the same when we move from $(0, c)$ to (x_1, y_1) to (x_2, y_2). Hence, c must be such that

$$\frac{y_1 - c}{x_1 - 0} = \frac{y_2 - y_1}{x_2 - x_1} = m$$

In other words (after going through the necessary algebraic hackwork)

$$c = y_1 - m \cdot x_1$$

The argument is depicted in Figure 4.3

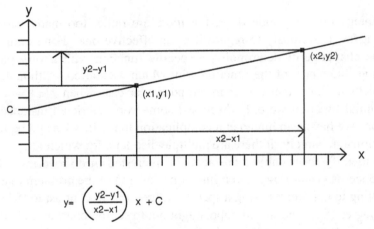

$$y = \left(\frac{y2-y1}{x2-x1}\right) x + C$$

Figure 4.3: The line between two points

Notice that if we already know m *and* a point (p, q) on the line of interest, then the line function is easily shown to be

$$y = m \cdot x + (q - m \cdot p)$$

In summary,

Given	Corresponding Line Function
(x_1, y_1) (x_2, y_2) $x_1 \neq x_2$	$y = \left(\dfrac{y_2 - y_1}{x_2 - x_1}\right) \cdot x + \left(y_1 - \left(\dfrac{y_2 - y_1}{x_2 - x_1}\right) \cdot x_1\right)$
m (p, q)	$y = m \cdot x + (q - m \cdot p)$

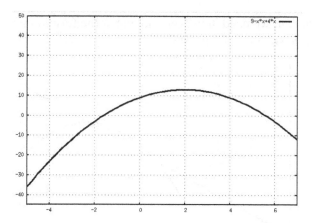

Figure 4.4: Example Maximization Problem

Let us now focus our discussion looking at the function $f(x) = 9 - x^2 + 4x$ for a running example. Its plot (between $x = -5$ and $x = 7$) is given in Figure 4.4

We have argued that, in order to find the value at which this function $(9 - x^2 + 4x)$ attains its maximum we should start by constructing the function $\tau(x)$ which for each value of x reports the gradient of the "line touching the point $(x, 9 - x^2 + 4x)$". Let's choose some arbitrary value, $x = 1$ say, and try to find the gradient of the line touching the point $(1, 12)$. One approach we could take is to select a value "close to 1", $x = 2$ say, and look at the line between the points $(1, 12)$ and $(2, 13)$. This gives the outcome depicted in Figure 4.5.

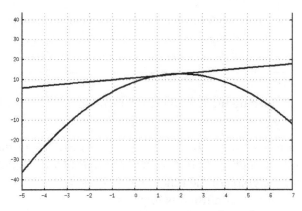

Figure 4.5: Approximating the line touching $(1, 12)$ on $9 - x^2 + 4x$

This looks on the scale used to be a "reasonable" approximation to the line and hence gradient we need, however, looking at the form rather more closely, gives the picture shown in Figure 4.6.

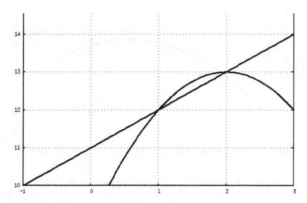

Figure 4.6: More detailed view of line from Figure 4.5

Maybe we should use an x value closer to 1 than 2, such as 1.5 say? Now the line between $(1, 12)$ and $(1.5, 12.75)$ is as shown in Figure 4.7.

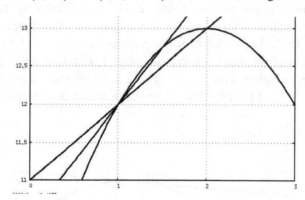

Figure 4.7: Replacing the line to $(1, 12)$ using the line from $(1.5, 11.5)$.

Once again this seems to be a "closer approximation" to the line whose function we are attempting to derive, namely that of the "line touching the point $(1, 12)$ for the graph of the function $9 - x^2 + 4x$".

Table 4.3 appears to confirm this impression

Table 4.3: Line Functions getting "closer" to the line touching $(1, 12)$

x	$y = m \cdot x + c$	m	$x - 1$
2	$x + 11$	1	1
1.5	$1.5 \cdot x + 10.5$	1.5	0.5
1.25	$1.75 \cdot x + 10.25$	1.75	0.25
1.05	$1.95 \cdot x + 9.05$	1.95	0.05
$\cdots$	$\cdots$	$\cdots$	$\cdots$
$1 + \delta$	$\left(\frac{2\delta - \delta^2}{\delta}\right) \cdot x + \left(12 - \frac{2\delta - \delta^2}{\delta}\right)$	$\frac{2\delta - \delta^2}{\delta}$	δ

Look at the final line of Table 4.3. This is telling us that: with the choice $1 + \delta$, the **gradient** of the line between

$$(1, 12) \text{ and } (1 + \delta, 9 - (1 + \delta)^2 + 4(1 + \delta))$$

is

$$\frac{(9 - (1 + \delta)^2 + 4(1 + \delta)) - (9 - 1^2 + 4 \cdot 1)}{1 + \delta - 1}$$

In an "ideal setting" the gradient of the line we **actually** want is that which touches the point $(1, 12)$ on the curve $9 - x^2 + 4x$ and we could find this simply by choosing $\delta = 0$ in the expression above. We **cannot**, however, proceed so directly: in fixing $\delta = 0$ and unravelling the expression this unravelment[9] will require the denominator $1 + \delta - 1$ to be evaluated and this will be 0: it is somewhat frowned upon by formalists to concoct derivations whose "validity" presumes divisions by zero.

We can, however, work around this minor inconvenience: although we cannot let δ **equal** 0, provided that it is non-zero we are free to manipulate δ in any "permitted" deductive style. Meaning?

---

[9]See Endnote 2.

A bit more algebraic passage work

$$\overbrace{\text{As we let } \delta \text{ become very very small (but } \textbf{never reach } 0)}$$

$$\text{written } \lim_{\delta \to 0}$$

$$\lim_{\delta \to 0} \frac{(9 - (1+\delta)^2 + 4(1+\delta)) - (9 - 1^2 + 4 \cdot 1)}{(1+\delta) - 1} =$$

$$\lim_{\delta \to 0} \frac{(9 - (1 + 2\delta + \delta^2) + 4 + 4\delta) - 12}{\delta} =$$

$$\lim_{\delta \to 0} \frac{12 - 2\delta - \delta^2 + 4\delta - 12}{\delta} =$$

$$\lim_{\delta \to 0} \frac{2\delta - \delta^2}{\delta} =$$

$$\lim_{\delta \to 0} \frac{\delta(2 - \delta)}{\delta} =$$

$$\lim_{\delta \to 0} (2 - \delta) = 2$$

And we have not only removed δ from the denominator but, in fact, removed **all** dependence whatsoever on δ. The crucial point in this derivation is the step:

$$\lim_{\delta \to 0} \frac{\delta(2 - \delta)}{\delta} = \lim_{\delta \to 0} (2 - \delta)$$

We are may legitimately "cancel out" δ because it **never equals** 0.
We have just demonstrated that,
"The gradient of the line touching the point $(1, 12)$ on the graph of the function

$$9 - x^2 + 4x$$

is 2".

And we have derived the gradient of the line touching the curve $9 - x^2 + 4x$ for a **specific** x, namely $x = 1$ and the point $(1, 12)$. We want, however, to do more than this: to construct the **function**, $\tau(x)$, reporting the gradient of the line touching $9 - x^2 + 4x$ **for every possible choice of**, x, i.e. not merely $x = 1$.

We have, however, more than sufficient background now to do precisely this. Look at how we discovered $\tau(1) = 2$: we started with a point "close to"

1 (2 in this instance) and calculated the gradient of the line joining $(1, 12)$ to $(2, 13)$. Noting that this looked like a decent but far from perfect estimate, we continued by looking at points closer and closer to our x of interest: 1.5 then 1.25 then 1.05, in each case getting more accurate estimates. So we decided to examine how **arbitrary** points close to 1 behaved, forming these as $1 + \delta$ and deriving the gradient of the line connecting $(1 + \delta, 9 - (1 + \delta)^2 + 4(1 + \delta))$ as δ was allowed to become arbitrarily small without ever attaining the value 0.

This gave us our solution for $x = 1$. Why not attempt the same approach for **any** value of x? That is to say: in order to compute the gradient of the line touching $(x, 9 - x^2 + 4x)$ look at the behaviour of the line joining

$$(x, 9 - x^2 + 4x) \text{ to } (x + \delta, 9 - (x + \delta)^2 + 4(x + \delta))$$

as δ is allowed to become arbitrarily small.

Recalling that the gradient of the relevant line is

$$\frac{(9 - (x + \delta)^2 + 4(x + \delta)) - (9 - x^2 + 4 \cdot x)}{(x + \delta) - x}$$

We have:

yet more algebraic passage work

$$
\begin{aligned}
\lim_{\delta \to 0} \frac{(9 - (x + \delta)^2 + 4(x + \delta)) - (9 - x^2 + 4 \cdot x)}{(x + \delta) - x} &= \\
\lim_{\delta \to 0} \frac{(9 - (x^2 + 2\delta \cdot x + \delta^2) + 4x + 4\delta) - 9 + x^2 - 4x}{\delta} &= \\
\lim_{\delta \to 0} \frac{-2\delta \cdot x - \delta^2 + 4\delta}{\delta} &= \\
\lim_{\delta \to 0} \frac{\delta(-2 \cdot x - \delta + 4)}{\delta} &= \\
\lim_{\delta \to 0} (-2x + 4 - \delta) &= 4 - 2x
\end{aligned}
$$

We have just discovered that
"the gradient of the line touching the point

$$(x, 9 - x^2 + 4x)$$

on the graph of the function

$$f(x) = 9 - x^2 + 4x$$

is given by the function $\tau(x) = 4 - 2x$".

We do not write "$\tau(x)$", since we want to relate the behaviour of the gradient function to any function, $f(x)$. The notation[10] that we use is: $f'(x)$ and when it is helpful to do so via the convention of writing $y = f(x)$ also,

$$\frac{dy}{dx}$$

The **function,** $f'(x)$ is known as the

(first) **derivative** of $f(x)$ with respect to x.

Our discussion above has demonstrated the construction of a function $(4 - 2x)$ that reports the gradient of lines touching $(x, f(x))$ for arbitrary $x \in \mathbb{R}$ and the function $f(x) = 9 - x^2 + 4x$: the arguments applied to show the gradient at $(1, 12)$ is 2 generalize, without too much additional effort, to arguments applicable to $(x, f(x))$. We have gone from *one* point with *one* function to **all** points for *one* function.

What we are leading up to is the derivation of such in a style that at least in principle will allow us to determine the gradient of the line touching $(x, f(x))$ for *all* $x \in \mathbb{R}$ **and** *all* $f : \mathbb{R} \to \mathbb{R}$.

It is at this juncture that we encounter one of the more problematic issues in differential calculus: we cannot, in fact, achieve such a goal for **every** function $f : \mathbb{R} \to \mathbb{R}$. We cannot even achieve it for that limited[11] collection of instances for which we can compute an outcome, $f(x)$, by an *algorithmic* process.

In order to extend the techniques described over the previous pages to other functions, the minimum requirement is that such functions are "*well-behaved*". What constitutes a function $f : \mathbb{R} \to \mathbb{R}$ as being a well-behaved function is a matter of considerable importance in the formal study of these methods within Pure Mathematics. It is, beyond pointing out some examples of ill-behaved functions, not a matter of such critical importance with respect to computational techniques, any more than the arcane subtleties involved in interpreting lim are crucial to computational understanding.[12]

A function may be well-behaved for every $x \in \mathbb{R}$ (as our example case $f(x) = 9 - x^2 + 4x$ is); it may be well-behaved for values of x satisfying a specific criterion but ill-behaved for those values of x failing in this respect.

---

[10]See Endnote 3.

[11]See Endnote 4.

[12]Sufficient thereto is regarding $\lim_{x \to \alpha}$ ($\alpha \in \mathbb{R} \cup \{\infty\}$) as "$x$ gets closer and closer to α but **never equals** it".

Such cases may involve merely a finite number of instances, e.g. $f(x) = x^{-1}$ is ill-behaved only for the case $x = 0$ or it may be ill-behaved infinitely often, e.g. the trigonometric function $\tan x$ which has undefined behaviour whenever $x = (2k - 1) \cdot 90°$ for every $k \in \mathbb{N}$.

These caveats in mind, let us look at enriching those techniques presented in order to discover the gradient of the line touching $(x, f(x))$ when $f(x) = 9 - x^2 + 4x$ for every x, to all "well-behaved" $f : \mathbb{R} \to \mathbb{R}$ and arguments, x, at which $f(x)$ is well-behaved.

The key move when we reviewed the gradients of lines touching $f(x) = 9 - x^2 + 4x$ at points $(x, f(x))$ was to consider the changes to the gradient of the line joining

$$(x, 9 - x^2 + 4x) \text{ to } (x + \delta, 9 - (x + \delta)^2 + 4(x + \delta))$$

In other words, the gradient of the line joining $(x, f(x))$ to $(x + \delta, f(x + \delta))$. Now it is utterly of no consequence whatsoever that with $f(x) = 9 - x^2 + 4x$ we are presented with a functional and computationally effective description of $f(x)$: we know how to express the gradient of the line joining to specified points and our ignorance of the relevant $f(x)$ is unimportant.

This gradient is,

$$\frac{f(x + \delta) - f(x)}{x + \delta - x} = \frac{f(x + \delta) - f(x)}{\delta}$$

This we wish to consider as δ gets arbitrarily close to but without reaching 0. That is, the gradient function which we have denoted $f'(x)$ is simply,

$$f'(x) = \lim_{\delta \to 0} \frac{f(x + \delta) - f(x)}{\delta}$$

So we have seen that with the well-behaved $f(x) = 9 - x^2 + 4x$ we obtain $f'(x) = 4 - 2x$. Choosing the example from Table 4.1(b): $f(x) = 5x + 1$, we get

$$\lim_{\delta \to 0} \frac{5(x + \delta) + 1 - (5x + 1)}{\delta} = \lim_{\delta \to 0} \frac{5\delta}{\delta}$$
$$= 5$$

Example Table 4.1(d) with $f(x) = x^4 - 3x^2 + 1$ is a little bit more work but within the scope of what has been seen so far in this book. The, rather tedious, manipulation of $f(x + \delta)$ producing

$$x^4 + 4x^3\delta + 6x^2\delta^2 + 4x\delta^3 + \delta^4 - -3(x^2 + 2x\delta + \delta^2) + 1$$

Leading (eventually) after simplifying and cancellation to the outcome

$$f'(x) \; = \; 3x^3 - 6x$$

But what of those cases in Table 4.1(e–l)? We have already seen that Table 4.1(e,j) are not well-behaved: the former when $x = 0$ the latter with $x = (2k - 1)90°$. Does this mean that we are unable to find the corresponding derivatives? Similarly Table 4.1(l) with $f(x) = \log x$ presents a function that is ill-defined whenever $x \leq 0$. Is it possible to find the derivative of this? Or of the two "powering functions" (Table 4.1(f,g))? Or even the trignonometric functions $\sin x$ and $\cos x$?

Fortunately we do not need to concern ourselves with (what were once known as) "first principles" methods to derive the appropriate $f'(x)$ forms.[13]

In the following section we shall see that demands of "first principles" techniques are more than obviated by applying a few standard rules. These suffice to cater for the vast majority of cases that arise in practical circumstances.

4.3 Standard differentiation rules

There are very few cases that one will meet in practical contexts that are not covered by some combination of the rules in Table 4.4.

It is stressed that understanding of these rules and their underlying principles is more important than being able to commit them eidetically to memory.[14] The reader will notice that some of these rules are easily derived from "first principles methods" whereas other are rather more opaque. For example, taking the rule for constant functions, these being such that $f(x) = c$ so reporting the same value ($c \in \mathbb{R}$) irrespective of the input argument x. Using the methods presented at the end of Section 4.2 we see that

$$\lim_{\delta \to 0} \frac{f(x + \delta) - f(x)}{\delta} \; = \; \lim_{\delta \to 0} \frac{c - c}{\delta} = 0$$

---

[13]The English (and Scottish) secondary educational systems having joined the civilized world in using the metric system and S.I. units from the mid-1960s found themselves unable to pose traditional calculation questions such as: "how many pecks can be contained in a tank having the form of an open trapezoidal prism with length 5 feet, height 2 yards, base width 71 inches, and top width half a chain? If the tank is filled with grain from two funnels one dispensing at the rate of 1½ bushels every 7 minutes, the other at 2¾ quarts every 2 minutes, how long will it take to be filled?" as part of public examination papers. The (pupil) benefits accruing from this change were more than offset by subsequent demands to "find the first derivative of the function $x^2(x^5 + 2)$ *from first principles.*

[14]See Endnote 5.

Table 4.4: 8 Simple Rules for Finding a First Derivative

Function form $h(x)$	Rule name	First Derivative $h'(x)$
c	*Constant*	0
$f(x) + g(x)$	*Sum*	$f'(x) + g'(x)$
$f(x) \cdot g(x)$	*Product*	$f'(x) \cdot g(x) + f(x) \cdot g'(x)$
$\frac{f(x)}{g(x)}$	*Quotient*	$\frac{f'(x)g(x) - f(x)g'(x)}{g(x)g(x)}$
$f(g(x))$	*Composition*	$f'(g(x)) \cdot g'(x)$
x^α	*Polynomial*	$\alpha \cdot x^{\alpha-1}$ (for all $\alpha \in \mathbb{R}$)
$\sin x$ (resp. $\cos x$)	*Trig.*	$\cos x$ (resp. $-\sin x$)
$\exp x$ (resp. $\log x$)	*Exponent (Log.)*	$\exp x$ (resp. x^{-1})

On the other hand treatment of $f(x) = x^\alpha$ (even in the special case of $\alpha \in \mathbb{N}$) requires a combinatorial result known as the *Binomial Theorem*, the most general form of which is usually attributed to Newton.[15] In this case "first principles" techniques use a rather roundabout analysis of $(1 + (x - 1))^\alpha$ to deal with x^α: we have already given a hint of the approach when we, briefly, reviewed the case $f(x) = x^4 - 3x^2 + 1$ in Section 4.2.

In this Section rather than indulging in haruspication concerning the whys and wherefores affecting first principles applications, it may be rather more useful to consider some examples of applying Table 4.4.

The function $\tan x$

This is not given with the other trigonometric functions in Table 4.4 but in the case $f(x) = \tan x$ we can combine the *Quotient Rule* and both *Trigonometric Rules*. Recall that,

$$\tan x = \frac{\sin x}{\cos x}$$

So (using the Leibnizian notation dy/dx) we get via the Quotient Rule

$$\frac{d \tan x}{dx} = \frac{\left(\frac{d \sin x}{dx}\right) \cos x - \sin x \left(\frac{d \cos x}{dx}\right)}{\cos x \cos x}$$

Now applying the Trigonometric Rules yields,

$$\frac{d \tan x}{dx} = \frac{\cos x \cos x - (-\sin x \sin x)}{\cos x \cos x}$$

---

[15] As remarked in Section 1.2 we neither assume nor require this level of background preparedness.

In other words

$$\frac{d\tan x}{dx} = \frac{\cos^2 x + \sin^2 x}{\cos^2 x} = \frac{1}{\cos^2 x}$$

via the standard trigonometric identity $\cos^2 x + \sin^2 x = 1$.

Composing Functions: $\exp(-\alpha x^2)$

Functions of the form $\exp(-\alpha f(x))$ with $\alpha \in \mathbb{R}$ are one of the contributing elements that have been seen to arise in experimental studies of medication effectiveness. In discussing Optimization contexts, one of the examples that was mentioned concerned the time taken for a given dosage (administered intravenously) to reach its maximum concentration. We shall see similar behaviour when presenting a particular instance of this problem from medical research, specifically Seng *et al.* [209].

For the function $h(x) = \exp(-\alpha x^2)$, we can view this as $h(x) = f(g(x))$ allowing the *Composition Rule* (also known as the *Chain Rule*) to be used by taking $f(x) = \exp(x)\ g(x) = -\alpha x^2$. Now, from $h'(x) = f'(g(x)) \cdot g'(x)$ we have,

$$
\begin{aligned}
f'(x) &= \exp(x) & \text{Exponential Rule}\\
g'(x) &= -2\alpha x & \text{Polynomial, Product and Constant Rules}\\
h'(x) &= -2\alpha x \exp(-\alpha x^2)
\end{aligned}
$$

Notice that we are being a little pedantic in deriving $g'(x)$ via three distinct rules:

$$g'(x) = \frac{d(-\alpha)}{dx} \cdot x^2 + (-\alpha) \cdot \frac{d(x^2)}{dx}$$

The constant rule (applied to $-\alpha$) eliminates the first term, so that applying the polynomial rule to x^2 gives $-2\alpha x$ as the contribution for $g'(x)$.

In total, although the algebraic contortions that can arise in some cases may look a little daunting, in general, where we face the task of identifying an optimizing setting or demonstrating that no such setting is possible when dealing with functions having only a *single* argument the rules in Table 4.4 offer powerful enough approaches coupled, on occasion with some standard relations between functions, e.g. as we used in looking at the derivative of $\tan x$ for almost all practically arising computational cases. As we shall see in Section 4.10, this is very far from being so in the case of *Integral Calculus* where some considerable ingenuity is often needed.[16]

---

[16]Or, for more indolent individuals such as myself, recourse to [186].

4.4   Turning Points and the Second Derivative Test

In the previous Section we described a strategy (S1–S3) by which a particular maximization problem could be tackled. In order to discover the optimal value ("optimal" being "maximal" in the specific case presented) of a function, $f(x)$, we proceed by: first constructing the function describing the "*gradient of the line touching the point* $(x, f(x))$". This we argued was the function, denoted $f'(x)$, corresponding to the "**first** derivative of $f(x)$". The possible solution values, those z for which $f(x)$ attains its optima, were, in stage (S2) of our strategy, claimed to be those for which $f'(z) = 0$.

Some informal justification that these **are**, indeed, the values we should examine further in optimizing $f(x)$ was given with respect to Figure 4.2: the function $f'(x)$ describes the gradient of lines touching the graph of $f(x)$ at the point $(x, f(x))$; so should z be such that $f'(z) = 0$ then the line in question has gradient 0. What does "a line having gradient equal to 0" mean? That the line is **parallel** to the x axis. In addition, however, what can we say about points such as $z - \alpha$ and $z + \alpha$ for positive $\alpha \in \mathbb{R}$? Assuming as in the example from Figure 4.2 our function is "well-behaved", we can certainly state that for some "small enough" α neither $f'(z - \alpha) = 0$ nor $f'(z + \alpha) = 0$ and, even further, choosing any positive $\beta < \alpha$ we have, similarly, $f'(z - \beta) \neq 0$ and $f'(z + \beta) \neq 0$. are true.[17]

Taking this behaviour – "if $f'(z) = 0$ then there is some positive $\alpha \in \mathbb{R}$ for which neither $f'(z - \alpha) = 0$ nor $f'(z + \alpha) = 0$ hold; and similarly for positive $\beta \in \mathbb{R}$ with $\beta < \alpha$" – as a given, how does this allow us to investigate further the behaviour of $f(z)$ and, most importantly, relate this behaviour to notions of maximum and minimum value?

If the gradient of the line touching $(z - \alpha, f(z - \alpha))$ is not zero it is either **greater than** 0 or **less than** 0;

If the gradient of the line touching $(z + \alpha, f(z + \alpha))$ is not zero it is either **greater than** 0 or **less than** 0;

And as we already know the gradient of the line touching $(z, f(z))$ **is** zero.

This leaves us with four possible behaviours to consider for z and the surrounding region using our presumed α:

B1. $f'(z - \alpha) > 0$; $f'(z) = 0$; $f'(z + \alpha) < 0$;

B2. $f'(z - \alpha) < 0$; $f'(z) = 0$; $f'(z + \alpha) > 0$;

B3. $f'(z - \alpha) > 0$; $f'(z) = 0$; $f'(z + \alpha) > 0$;

---

[17] See Endnote 6 for a more detailed discussion of this assertion.

B4. $f'(z - \alpha) < 0$; $f'(z) = 0$; $f'(z + \alpha) < 0$;

Cases (B3) and (B4) both of which are perfectly possible with naturally arising, "well-behaved" functions, e.g. $f(x) = (x-1)^3$ are a little troublesome and we will ignore such instances.

The significant examples are (B1) and (B2): (B1) corresponds to what happens in our arrow flight example related to (DC2) as illustrated in Figure 4.2. We have seen that a *positive* gradient as would be indicated by $f'(z - \alpha) > 0$ is a function whose value **increases** as x increases. Similarly, a *negative* gradient the case $f'(z + \alpha) < 0$ describes a function whose value **decreases** as x increases.

So, in Case (B1) we have: the line function touching $(z - \alpha, f(z - \alpha))$ is increasing but that touching $(z + \alpha, f(z + \alpha))$ is a decreasing function: and hence $f(z)$ must define a local[18] **maximum**.

By similar reasoning in Case (B2) we have: the line function touching $(z - \alpha, f(z - \alpha))$ is a decreasing function but that touching $(z + \alpha, f(z + \alpha))$ is an increasing function: and hence $f(z)$ must define a local **minimum**.

An illustration is given in Figure 4.8

The key question now is: how do or even more fundamental *can* we distinguish case (B1) from (B2)?

In order to answer this question we need to look at an entity whose existence is hinted at in the usage "**first** derivative of $f(x)$": the **second** derivative of $f(x)$. The derivative of $f(x)$ is a *function*: $f' : \mathbb{R} \to \mathbb{R}$. This function could, in theory, itself have a derivative. In the event that this property holds the resulting function, denoted $f''(x)$ is called the **second** derivative of f. In principle this process "$f^{(k)}$ is a function – the k'th derivative of f – whose derivative is $f^{(k+1)}$ called the '$k + 1$st derivative' of f" could continue indefinitely. For example consulting Table 4.4 we see that the function $f(x) = x^{-1}$ may be differentiated infinitely often with its kth derivative being a different function from that described by its $(k - 1)$st derivative. On the other hand taking $f(x) = x^3$ we get

$$f'(x) = 3x^2 \ ; \ f''(x) = 6x \ ; \ f'''(x) = 6 \ ; \ f''''(x) = 0$$

after which no change occurs.

---

[18]The notion of "local" simply indicates that we are focused on a range of x values, e.g. consider the function in Table 4.2(d): the "bump" in the function plot somewhere between $x = -2$ and $x = 2$ is a local maximum but, as is clear from the plot does not describe the maximum attainable value.

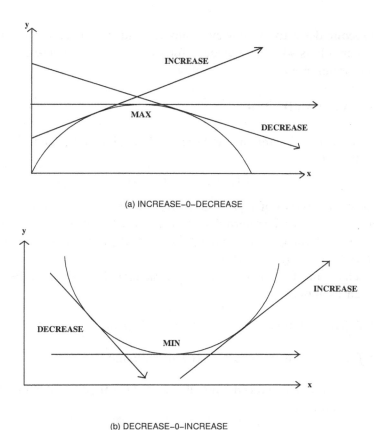

(a) INCREASE–0–DECREASE

(b) DECREASE–0–INCREASE

Figure 4.8: Increase–max–decrease & Decrease–min–increase touching lines.

As can be seen the accumulation of primes (i.e. $'$) becomes unwieldly and although the form $f^{(k)}$ offers a solution there is some danger of this being misinterpreted, $f^{(k)}$ often being used to express

$$f^{(k)}(x) \;\; = \;\; \underbrace{f(f(f(\ldots(x))))}_{k \text{ times}}$$

For so-called *higher derivatives* we shall often prefer the form popularized by Leibniz, i.e.

$$\frac{d^k x}{dy^k}$$

Typically it is rarely needed in computing contexts to consider third and higher order derivatives.

The **second** derivative is, however, another matter: inspecting the behaviour of $f''(x)$ can tell us whether a value α for which $f'(\alpha) = 0$ describes a local maximum or minimum.

The Second Derivative Test

For a function, $f(x)$ having first and second derivatives $f'(x)$ and $f''(x)$, suppose that the **set**

$$\{\alpha_1,\ \alpha_2, \ldots, \alpha_r, \ldots\}$$

describes all of the *roots* of $f'(x)$, i.e. those values for which $f'(\alpha) = 0$. These roots will subsequently be referred to as the *turning points* of $f(x)$. Notice that there be infinitely many such turning points, e.g. if $f(x) = \sin x$; this set may also be **empty**, e.g. $f(x) = \exp x$.

The behaviour of $f(x)$ at $x = \alpha_k$ is characterized by which of the following three cases applies.

SD1. If $f''(\alpha_k) < 0$ then $f(\alpha_k)$ is a (local) *maximum*.

SD2. If $f''(\alpha_k) > 0$ then $f(\alpha_k)$ is a (local) *minimum*.

SD3. If $f''(\alpha_k) = 0$ then it is not possible to deduce anything about the (local) behaviour of $f(\alpha_k)$.

Some Examples of Using the Second Derivative Test

The running example used to present the concept of "first derivative of $f(x)$" was the function depicted in Figure 4.4: $f(x) = 9 - x^2 + 4x$.

It is clear (from the diagram) that $f(x)$ has exactly one turning point and that this is a maximum.[19]

Often it is the case that we will not have a diagrammatic depiction to provide such information. In any event we can confirm that $f(x)$ does behave as our intuition suggests.

We have already seen that,

$$f'(x) \;=\; 4 \,-\, 2x$$

The identity $f'(x) = 0$ yields exactly one turning point: $4 - 2x = 0$ when $x = 2$. Now looking at $f''(x)$ we see $f''(x) = -2$. Applying the Second

---

[19]In fact, in this example, a **global**, more general than merely local, maximum.

Derivative Test, we get $f''(x) < 0$ (for every x) and so $f(2) = 13$ is the maximum value the function $9 - x^2 + 4x$ reaches.

As a rather less trivial example, we have the case of Table 4.2(d),

$$f(x) = x^4 - 3x^2 + 1$$

Again, from the diagram, we can see by inspection that this has 3 turning points. To identify these first construct $f'(x)$.

$$f'(x) = 4x^3 - 6x = x(4x^2 - 6)$$

It is not difficult to see that this yields the turning points as $\{-\sqrt{1.5}, 0, \sqrt{1.5}\}$. Which of these are maxima or minima? Looking at $f''(x)$ gives

$$f''(x) = 12x^2 - 6$$

With which: $f''(-\sqrt{1.5}) = 12 > 0$; $f''(0) = -6 < 0$; and $f''(\sqrt{1.5}) = 12 > 0$. The turning points $\{-\sqrt{1.5}, \sqrt{1.5}\}$ are minima, $f(-\sqrt{1.5}) = f(\sqrt{1.5}) = 1.25$; that corresponding to $x = 0$ is a local maximum with $f(0) = 1$.[20]

These outcomes are straightforward to verify when, as with the cases Figure 4.4 and Table 4.2(d), we have a diagrammatic view of the function's behaviour. Suppose, however, we are not so fortunate? Consider,

$$f(x) = 3x^{0.5} - 2x^{1.5}$$

We first notice that this is only well-behaved (as a function $f : \mathbb{R} \to \mathbb{R}$) whenever $x \geq 0$.[21] Secondly, in order to satisfy the requirement that the result of a function *if* it is defined then it is *uniquely* defined, we need to interpret $x^{0.5}$ as being the **positive** value, α, for which $\alpha^2 = x$.

Taking these into account, we find $f'(x)$ (defined whenever $x \geq 0$) to be

$$f'(x) = \frac{3}{2x^{0.5}} - 3x^{0.5}$$

In this case, $f'(x) = 0$ when

$$3x^{0.5} = \frac{3}{2x^{0.5}}$$

---

[20]In this case we have a distinction between "local" and "global": 0 falling between $-\sqrt{1.5}$ and $\sqrt{1.5}$ (both of which are *global* minima), $f(x)$ increases with x from one minimal value $(-\sqrt{1.5})$ up to the (local) maximum (0) and as x continues to increase, $f(x)$ gets smaller until reaching the other global minimum ($\sqrt{1.5}$). Thereafter $x > \sqrt{1.5}$, $f(x)$ increases as x does.

[21]There are methods, using techniques from Chapter 5 that would allow this to be considered for any $x \in \mathbb{R}$, however we do not consider these in this book.

In other words when

$$3x = \frac{3}{2}$$

i.e. $x = 0.5$.

So we know that $f(x)$ has a single turning point ($x = 0.5$). Is it a minimum, maximum or are we unable to determine this?

Looking at $f''(x)$ we get,

$$f''(x) = \frac{-3}{4x^{1.5}} - \frac{3}{2x^{0.5}}$$

and $f''(0.5) \sim -4.24$. Since $f''(0.5) < 0$, the function $3x^{0.5} - 2x^{1.5}$ has its (global in this instance) maximum when $x = 0.5$ giving $f(0.5) = \sqrt{2}$.

4.5   Differential Calculus and Optimization

In this subsection we look at 4 different optimization questions and see how the methods introduced in the previous sections aid in deriving solutions.

Software Development Planning

A standard issue in product development concerns balancing investment in personnel responsible for design and delivery against the functionality offered. Thus in areas such as specialist software packages (e.g. antivirus and malware detection software, scientific and mathematical computation) up to the level of new Operating System platforms decisions are taken concerning what features need to be included. While including many non-standard elements may make the final product more marketable the drawback is that this will require longer development time and hence increase the product cost. On the other hand, too few features may result in a product that is difficult to promote.

In a very simplified setting some resolution of these issues could be attempted by determining the size of team who will develop things. Here is one (rather artificial) example.

The **MegaHard Software Company** wants to determine the cost at which to launch its new *Casement XI* Operating System: this cost will be set in order to maximize MegaHard's profit while taking into account the development costs. In such scenarios the more developers involved in the design and implementation of *Casement XI* the greater its costs will be albeit with improved functionality for the system. On the other hand, while a small development team will result in reduced costs there is an increased risk of the system eventually needing significant and expensive repairs and patches. It is decided to assign t individuals to work on the system, who after an initial training and orientation course costing \$131 per person will be deployed in teams to give an overall **project build value** $B(t)$. This value will determine the cost of purchasing a legal copy of *Casement XI* once it is ready for release, so that it will retail at $\$B(t)$.

$$B(t) = \frac{131t}{10} + \frac{t(3451 - 634t)}{2350}$$

How many people, t, should MegaHard employ in order to *maximize* this value and so determine its supply price for *Casement XI*?

The League of Legends PC Game

Although, superficially, more complicated the problem below is very similar to our previous example.

In this game players have a Health score (H) and available armour score (A). Depending on these players have an *effective health* (E) given through

$$E = \frac{H(100 + A)}{100}$$

Players may purchase additional Health and Armour units at a given cost of 2.5 tokens for Health and 18 tokens for armour. How should an initial allocation of T tokens be used to maximize E?

Medication Effectiveness

Drugs such as caffeine are absorbed into the bloodstream over a period of time given a single dose during which some of the drug will be be eliminated. Using α for the absorption rate; β for elimination rate, the concentration for an initial dosage D after time t is known to be given by the function,

$$c(t) \;=\; \frac{D}{1 - \beta/\alpha} \left(\frac{1}{\exp(\alpha t)} - \frac{1}{\exp(\beta t)} \right)$$

How long does it take for the concentration to be maximal?

This is the example given in Seng *et al.* [209] mentioned earlier.

Employment Practice

As a final example we have another instance where the underlying functions involved are not simple polynomial forms.

A large corporation engages a consultant to assess the **utility** of its employees in terms of the number of years an individual has been working for the corporation. The consultant reports that this ought to be calculated by the formula

$$U(x) \;=\; \alpha(\log x)^2 \;-\; \beta(\log x)^3$$

Here x is the number of **years** an individual has been employed.

α is a constant meant to capture "contribution and impact" that will vary according to whether an employee is a senior manager, Junior manager or Worker.

β is a constant related to the overall salary (i.e. cost to the corporation) of the employee.

The consultant recommends setting these constants to give the following specific **utility formulae**

Employee Category	Utility Formula Used
senior manager	$U(x) = 80(\log x)^2 - 12(\log x)^3$
Junior manager	$U(x) = 25(\log x)^2 - 6(\log x)^3$
Worker	$U(x) = 12(\log x)^2 - 4(\log x)^3$

After accepting these recommendations the corporation decides that in order to improve its productivity, employment contracts will **only** be issued for the number of years taken to **maximize** the employee's utility, after which the contract will lapse. Under this scheme, for how many years will an employment contract run when

a. The employee is a Worker?

b. The employee is a Junior manager?

c. The person is a (senior) manager?

Software Development Problem

The function we are attempting to maximize is,

$$B(t) = \frac{131t}{10} + \frac{t(3451 - 634t)}{2350}$$

Notice that this is exactly the same as,

$$B(t) = \frac{131t}{10} + \frac{3451t}{2350} - \frac{634t^2}{2350}$$

Our first step is to construct $B'(t)$. Since $B(t)$ is a polynomial of degree 2 in t, we see that

$$B'(t) = \left(\frac{131}{10} + \frac{3451}{2350}\right) - \frac{1268t}{2350}$$

We now need to find the turning points, i.e. those values of t under which $B'(t) = 0$. These are the values for which

$$\frac{1268t}{2350} = \left(\frac{131}{10} + \frac{3451}{2350}\right)$$

In other words when t satisfies,

$$t = \frac{2350}{1268}\left(\frac{131}{10} + \frac{3451}{2350}\right) = \frac{2350}{1268}\left(\frac{30785 + 3451}{2350}\right) = \frac{34236}{1268} = 27$$

Notice, applying the second derivative test, that $t = 27$ **is** a maximizing value: $B''(t) = (-1268/2350) < 0$. The value $t = 27$ justifies a retail cost of just under \$197 for *Casement XI*.

The League of Legends PC Game

On first inspection it may seem unclear how to maximize the function

$$E = \frac{H(100 + A)}{100}$$

given some number of tokens, T, to spend over health (H) and armour (A) units. The critical point to note is that we can express the number of armour units that can be purchased in terms of the number of tokens *remaining* after some quantity of health units have been purchased. We are given that health units cost 2.5 tokens, so if we start with T tokens and purchase x units of health then we have **exactly** $T - 2.5x$ tokens available to spend on armour. This amount allows the purchase of

$$\frac{T - 2.5x}{18}$$

units of armour. So we can recast our optimization problem in terms of "given T tokens how many units of health (x) should be purchased in order to maximize $E(x)$?" Here $E(x)$ is defined through

$$E(x) = \frac{x(100 + (T - 2.5x)/18)}{100}$$

Carrying out some rearrangement we obtain

$$E(x) = \left(1 + \frac{T}{1800}\right)x - \frac{2.5x^2}{1800}$$

Notice that this is subject to the constraint that if x units of health are to be purchased then we must have sufficient available initial tokens to allow this, i.e. $2.5x \leq T$.

We can regard T the initial allocation of tokens as a constant and focus on finding the maximizing x for the expression.

As before we start by finding $E'(x)$ noting that our expression for $E(x)$ is again a polynomial of degree 2 in x.

$$E'(x) = \left(1 + \frac{T}{1800}\right) - \frac{5x}{1800} = \frac{1800 + T - 5x}{1800}$$

The turning points are when $E'(x) = 0$ arising when $1800 + T - 5x = 0$, that is when

$$x = \frac{1800 + T}{5} = 360 + \frac{T}{5}$$

Again this choice maximizes $E(x)$ since, checking $E''(x)$ we find

$$E''(x) \;=\; \frac{-5}{1800} \;<\; 0$$

Thus given T tokens to start, in order to maximize effective health we should purchase $360 + (T/5)$ health units spending the remaining

$$T - \left(900 + \frac{T}{2}\right) \;=\; \frac{T}{2} - 900$$

on armour units.

Medication Effectiveness

In this and our final example we move away from optimizing simple polynomial functions. In the example instance given we are looking to find a setting for t (in terms of given constant values α, β, and D) that will maximize the function

$$c(t) \;=\; \frac{D}{1 - \beta/\alpha} \left(\frac{1}{\exp(\alpha t)} - \frac{1}{\exp(\beta t)}\right)$$

We follow exactly the same strategy used in the previous two examples. First construct the derivative $c'(t)$. As we saw with our example of applying the *Composition Rule*, the terms $\exp(-\alpha t)$ and $\exp(-\beta t)$ can be dealt with by viewing these as functions of the form $f(g(x))$ in which $f(x) = \exp x$ and $g(x) = -\gamma x$ where γ will be either α or β. In this way we find

$$c'(t) \;=\; \frac{D}{1 - \beta/\alpha} \left(\frac{-\alpha}{\exp(\alpha t)} + \frac{\beta}{\exp(\beta t)}\right)$$

So that,

$$c'(t) \;=\; \frac{D}{1 - \beta/\alpha} \left(\frac{-\alpha \exp(\beta t) + \beta \exp(\alpha t)}{\exp(\alpha t) \exp(\beta t)}\right)$$

Now there is one very useful property of the function $\exp(x)$ that we can use: for every $x \in \mathbb{R}$, $\exp x > 0$. This means that, in determining when $c'(t) = 0$, we do not have to be concerned with the denominator term $\exp(\alpha t) \exp(\beta t)$: it will always exceed 0. Furthermore, the multiplicative term $D/(1 - \beta/\alpha)$ is independent of t, i.e. constant. In total when considering when $c'(t) = 0$ we need only look at the term

$$-\alpha \exp(\beta t) + \beta \exp(\alpha t)$$

and identify values of t for which this is 0. That is such that

$$\beta \exp(\alpha t) = \alpha \exp(\beta t)$$

In other words,

$$\frac{\exp(\beta t)}{\exp(\alpha t)} = \frac{\beta}{\alpha}$$

$$\exp((\beta - \alpha)t) = \frac{\beta}{\alpha}$$

In order to simplify the term $\exp((\ldots)t)$ we can just take (Natural) logarithms of both sides[22] to obtain that t must satisfy

$$t = \frac{\log \beta - \log \alpha}{\beta - \alpha}$$

in order that $c'(t) = 0$. We leave it as an exercise for the reader to verify that $c''(t) < 0$ when t has this value.

This expression for t may be found (with different notational conventions used) in Seng *et al.* [209, p. 108, col. 2].

Employment Practice

In this example we again have a function involving variable (t), Real constants (α, β) but using the log function. We note that when we refer to log unless explicitly stated otherwise we intend what are referred to as *Natural* logarithms (base e) rather than "*Common*" logs (base 10) often occurring in school use or base 2 which frequently arises in Computer Science contexts in the analysis of algorithm behaviour.

In the example presented the basic function is

$$U(x) = \alpha(\log x)^2 - \beta(\log x)^3$$

for which, depending on the specific choices of α and β, we are looking for maximum values of x.

We proceed as before, first forming $U'(x)$. The function $(\log x)^k$ we can handle via the *Composition Rule* writing it as $f(g(x))$ with $g(x) = \log x$ and $f(x) = x^k$. This gives

$$U'(x) = \frac{2\alpha \log x}{x} - \frac{3\beta(\log x)^2}{x}$$

---

[22]That is log to the base e = $\exp(1)$.

Noting that $\log x$ is ill-behaved when $x \leq 0$, in order to resolve $U'(x) = 0$ we need to find x satisfying

$$2\alpha \log x \; - \; 3\beta(\log x)^2 \;\; = \;\; 0$$

In other words having

$$(2\alpha \; - \; 3\beta \log x) \cdot \log x \;\; = \;\; 0$$

One immediate case is $x = 1$, since $\log 1 = 0$. We will look at this particular case subsequently, but there is also the possibility

$$2\alpha \; - \; 3\beta \log x \;\; = \;\; 0$$

That is,

$$\log x \;\; = \;\; \frac{2\alpha}{3\beta}$$

Recalling that log is Natural we obtain our second turning point as

$$x \;\; = \;\; \exp\left(\frac{2\alpha}{3\beta}\right)$$

When $x = 1$, we find $U(x) = 0$ irrespective of α and β. For the choice

$$x \;\; = \;\; \exp\left(\frac{2\alpha}{3\beta}\right)$$

we find

$$U(x) \;\; = \;\; \alpha \left(\frac{2\alpha}{3\beta}\right)^2 \; - \; \beta \left(\frac{2\alpha}{3\beta}\right)^3$$

which is

$$\frac{4\alpha^3}{9\beta^2} \; - \; \frac{8\alpha^3}{27\beta^2} \;\; = \;\; \frac{4\alpha^3}{27\beta^2}$$

Noting that α, β are positive (in the particular cases presented) with

$$x \;\; = \;\; \exp\left(\frac{2\alpha}{3\beta}\right)$$

$U(x) > 0$ and larger than $U(1) = 0$. We may thus answer the three cases arising by focussing on the former case.[23]

Looking at the three different settings for α and β gives the breakdown below.

---

[23] We could also, of course, analyze the behaviour of $U''(x)$, however it is not **always** needed to use the second derivative in order to discern the behaviour of a function at particular points.

a. **Workers**: $\alpha = 12$; $\beta = 4$.

   Maximizing value $x = \exp(24/12) \sim 7.4$.

Workers contracts will be nullified after 7 years.

b. **Junior managers**: $\alpha = 25$; $\beta = 6$.

   Maximizing value $x = \exp(50/18) \sim 16.1$.

Junior managers cease to be useful after 16 years.

c. **senior managers**: $\alpha = 80$; $\beta = 12$.

   Maximizing value $x = \exp(160/36) \sim 85.2$.

Once appointed, the formula alleges that senior managers continue to serve some purpose for 85 years.

4.6 . Digging out roots using Derivatives

In Section 2.4 the concept of "polynomial expression" was presented together with the notion of the *roots* of a polynomial. Given $p_n(x)$ a polynomial of degree n in x it was argued that $p_n(x)$ has n roots. This was subject to two caveats: n roots does not imply n **distinct** roots; and, there are polynomials with "roots", α, that are "not Real". This second point we will elaborate upon in more detail in Chapter 5. The first point tells us that, considering the graph plotted for a polynomial function, $p_n(x)$, we can deduce that this curve has *at most* $n - 1$ turning points.

Why is this? The first derivative, p'_n of p_n is a degree $n - 1$ polynomial and the roots of this polynomial, being the values α for which $p'_n(\alpha) = 0$, as we have seen define the turning points of $p_n(x)$. Of course, the qualification "*at most*" is necessary for the two reasons just presented: some roots may have multiplicity greater than 1 (hence defining only one turning point despite the multiple occurrence); some roots do not define "turning points" consistent with our functions being over $\mathbb{R}$.

Although there are methods such as those outlined in Section 2.5 that allow us to treat some limited collection of cases there are three major weaknesses to these:

W1. These are computationally very intensive for all but low degree polynomials. For example the "Rational Root Test" requires procedures to factorize $q \in \mathbb{N}$ a problem for which no "easily implementable" fast algorithms exist.[24]

W2. The polynomial manipulation methods presented in Section 2.5 concerned polynomials in $\mathbb{Q}[X]$: we may wish to find roots of polynomials in $\mathbb{R}[X]$.

W3. Looking at the final two "Optimization Examples" presented at the end of the previous section we may, in fact, want to do rather more than merely find "roots of polynomials in $\mathbb{R}[X]$": we may wish to find "roots of arbitrary $f : \mathbb{R} \to \mathbb{R}$" or (at least) of those $f(x)$ for which we can construct its first derivative $f'(x)$.

The study of root finding methods has a very long history and several algorithms, some specialized to polynomials in $\mathbb{R}[X]$, e.g. the widely used Jenkins–Traub Algorithm [128, 129] or Laguerre's Method, discussed in Hansen and Patrick [116] others applicable to arbitrary (i.e. non-polynomial) functions.[25] This second group includes classical techniques such as Newton's Method also referred to as Newton-Raphson, the Bisection Method, Secant Method and Halley's Method. Further sub-divisions of the approaches include those which are most effective on single argument functions i.e. deal with finding $\alpha \in \mathbb{R}$ for which $f(\alpha) = 0$ and those suitable for functions of more than one argument i.e. can be used to identify $\mathbf{a} = < \alpha_1, \ldots, \alpha_n >$ for which $f : \mathbb{R}^n \to \mathbb{R}$ will satisfy $f(\mathbf{a}) = 0$.

The specialized mathematical discipline of *Numerical Analysis* (see. e.g. Stoer and Bulirsch [224]) deals, among other issues, with root finding techniques.[26]

We will briefly present an overview of two methods – one of each type – to give a flavour of how first and second derivatives of a function, $f(x)$, can be exploited in finding the roots of f. Despite its widespread adoption in practical systems the complexities underlying the Jenkins-Traub method of [128, 129] render its presentation beyond the scope of this text. Similarly, given that our aim is to show how derivatives may be exploited in solving computational problems outside the immediate context of Optimization we will limit our attention to single argument functions.

---

[24] See Endnote 7.

[25] Although most such algorithms require the function itself to satisfy certain preconditions.

[26] The study of Numerical Analysis played a very significant part in the growth of Computer Science as a recognized scientific field. Further elaboration is given in Endnote 8.

Classifying root finding methods

In addition to the categories "Single argument" and "Multivariable", "polynomial methods" and "general functions" there are a number of features arising in classifying different approaches. Some methods are what are called *direct*: these produce solutions taking a number of steps (run-time) that can be predetermined. The closed-form expressions that were described for quadratics and cubics in Section 2.5 are examples of direct methods. There are, however, only a small and limited selection of such techniques. The two methods we shall look at are examples of *iterative methods*. The approach used in such methods is the following: we have our starting function, $f(x)$ for which we wish to identify $\alpha \in \mathbb{R}$ yielding $f(\alpha) = 0$; we have (here we will be rather informal and opaque) a defined procedure, G which produces another *function* given f.[27] The final element which often has a critical effect on the time taken to produce a solution is a starting value, $\beta_0 \in \mathbb{R}$ which defines a guess at a potential root. In iterative methods the next value, β_1, is produced as the outcome of applying the function, $G(f)$, constructed from f to β_0 so that its outcome (β_1) provides the value with which to continue. In general β_k (the guess used at the kth *iteration*) is the result of evaluating $G(f)(\beta_{k-1})$. In a very informal sense different iterative methods are distinguished by the exact way in which the transforming functional, G, is specified.

Now there are some quite obvious questions arising with such iterative methods: how do we choose the "initial guess"? how does this choice affect the behaviour of the process? how do we know when to stop the process of iterating new values? etc.

These questions relate to the other quality distinguishing iterative methods: their *convergence rate*. Again we will avoid a formal technical exposition merely noting that "convergence" describes "how quickly" i.e. the number of iterations a method approaches a solution, i.e. putative root. Standard ways of capturing convergence are with respect to the number of bits that become known as the method proceeds. For instance, suppose β_0 is our first guess at a root of f but $|f(\beta_0)| = \delta > 0$. With a good iterative method we hope that $|f(\beta_1)| = \delta_1 > 0$ **and** $\delta_1 < \delta_0$: informally, "β_1 is closer to being a root of f".

The two methods we shall look at are *Halley's Method* and *Laguerre's Method*. The latter is particularly effective as a means of finding Real roots of polynomials whereas the former can be applied to general (subject to some technical conditions) functions. We mention, that as demonstrated in the study

---

[27]In effect such G map from functions to functions; G has domain and range the set f : $\mathbb{R} \to \mathbb{R}$.

of Hansen and Patrick [116], these and many other approaches such as Newton's may be considered as specific cases resulting by setting a parameter, α, to instantiate a more general approach, e.g. Newton's method results by letting this parameter become arbitrarily large (i.e. more formally by considering behaviour as $\alpha \to \infty$); Laguerres's with $\alpha = 1/(n-1)$ (degree n polynomials); and Halley's via $\alpha = -1$.[28] Although adaptations are possible to multivariable instances we concentrate on single variable functions.

Halley's Method for Finding Roots

Halley's Method deals with finding solutions for x with which $f(x) = 0$ when $f : \mathbb{R} \to \mathbb{R}$ satisfies certain conditions. It was discovered by the English astronomer and mathematician Edmond Halley (1656–1741/2)[29] who also analyzed the periodicity of the comet named in his honour [112].

In order to be applicable Halley's method to find roots of $f(x)$ requires not only that $f'(x)$ exists but also that $f''(x)$ is "well-behaved", existence being an essential prerequisite for being well-behaved.

Suppose that x_0 is the first guess we use for a root of $f(x)$. Of course if we are exceptionally fortunate then $f(x_0)$ will be 0 and we need only look at the function $f(x)/(x - x_0)$ to seek further roots of $f(x)$. Typically, however, we will not be so fortunate. Halley's Method, described in Algorithm 4.1, describes one approach to refining the initial estimate.

Halley's Method is an effective approach to identifying roots of functions which are not polynomial in form. For example consider

$$f(x) = \sin x + 2x \cos x$$

Using the Table of Rules given in Table 4.4 we find

$$f'(x) = 3 \cos x - 2x \sin x$$

and

$$f''(x) = -5 \sin x - 2x \cos x$$

Applying Halley's Method with an initial $x_0 = 3.5$, gives

---

[28] All three of these are given in Hansen and Patrick [116, p. 260].

[29] The calendar year ambiguity arises from two sources: one the change in the start of the Legal year (now 1st January but until 1752 (England); and 1600 (Scotland) was fixed as 25th March); the second being British tardiness in adopting the Gregorian (as opposed to the Julian) calendar. Despite having been accepted in continental Europe by the end of the 16th Century, it was not recognized for British dating conventions until 1752 as decreed in the U.K. "*Calendar (New Style) Act*" of 1750. The date of Halley's death is 1741 ("Old style" calendar) but 1742 ("New style" calendar).

Algorithm 4.1. Halley's Method for finding roots of $f(x)$

1: $k := 0$;

2: $x_0 :=$ Initial guess;

3: **repeat**

4:
$$x_{k+1} \ := \ x_k \ - \ \frac{2f(x_k)f'(x_k)}{2(f'(x_k))^2 - f(x_k)f''(x_k)}$$

5:    $k := k + 1$;

6: **until** $|f(x_k)| < \varepsilon$ or $k > MAX$

7: $\{\varepsilon$ is a "tolerance level", e.g. $\varepsilon \sim 10^{-12}$ indicating that the approximation x_k is good enough.$\}$

8: $\{MAX$ is a cut-off point to ensure the algorithm does not iterate "indefinitely" without finding a root.$\}$

Table 4.5: Halley's Method applied to $f(x) = \sin x + 2x \cos x$ with $x_0 = 3.5$

k	x_k	$f(x_k)$
0	3.5	-6.90598
1	3.415189628925223	-6.846521
2	3.16221915777742	-6.343718
3	2.526174835597002	-3.548107
4	1.9118785011014694	-0.336681
5	1.836752811192699	-6.741792×10^{-4}
6	1.8365972031536533	$-6.6177064 \times 10^{-12}$
7	1.8365972031521258	$-5.551115 \times 10^{-16}$

Laguerre's Method for Polynomial Roots

Although one could use Halley's or any general root approximation approach with polynomials, because of specific algebraic properties it is often the case that special-purpose techniques perform in a superior manner. One example of such a method is Laguerre's Method, which has been observed in experimental studies to hone in (i.e. *"converge"*) to *at least one* root, α, of a degree n polynomial, $p_n(x)$ very rapidly irrespective how distant the initial guess, x_0, may be from α. Hence even if $|\alpha - x_0|$ is large, Laguerre's method can be successfully adopted.[30]

---

[30]A more detailed discussion of this point may be found in Hansen and Patrick [116, pp. 260–261].

Algorithm 4.2. Laguerre's Method for finding roots of polynomials $p(x)$

1: $k := 0$;
2: $x_0 :=$ Initial guess;
3: **repeat**
4:
$$\beta := \frac{p'(x_k)}{p(x_k)}$$
$\{p'(x)$ has degree $n-1.\}$
5:
$$\gamma := \beta^2 - \frac{p''(x_k)}{p(x_k)}$$
6:
$$\alpha := \frac{n}{\max\{\beta + \sqrt{(n-1)(n\gamma - \beta^2)},\ \beta - \sqrt{(n-1)(n\gamma - \beta^2)}\}}$$
7: $\quad x_{k+1} := x_k - \alpha$;
8: $\quad k := k+1$;
9: **until** $|p(x_k)| < \varepsilon$ or $k > MAX$

Example Comparison of the Two Methods – Polynomial Roots

Considering the degree 5 polynomial

$$p_5(x) = x^5 + x^4 - 9x^3 - 9x^2 + 14x + 14$$

Its first and second derivatives are

$$\begin{aligned} p'(x) &= 5x^4 + 4x^3 - 27x^2 - 18x + 14 \\ p''(x) &= 20x^3 + 12x^2 - 54x - 18 \end{aligned}$$

All of the roots of this polynomial turns out to be in $\mathbb{R}$: it can be shown to be the result of expanding[31]

$$(x+1) \cdot (x^2 - 2) \cdot (x^2 - 7).$$

One standard approach to choosing a good starting guess is to look for two values – x^- and x^+ – for which $f(x^-) < 0$ and $f(x^+) > 0$: assuming that $x^- < x^+$ (and, in more general instances, that $f(x)$ is well-behaved) we know

---

[31]Recall the example is for illustrative purposes. Normally such a factorization will not be known in advance.

that at some stage between x^- and x^+ the function f must be 0.[32] We can then start by choosing x_0 as the value "half-way between x^- and x^+".

Looking at the factorization just given we see that $p(2) = 3\cdot2\cdot(-3) = -18$ and $p(0) = 1\cdot(-2)\cdot(-7) = 14$. So we expect there to be root, α, of $p(x)$ with $0 < \alpha < 2$. Choosing the intermediate initial guess, x_0 to be 1, Halley's Method produces

Table 4.6: Halley's Method applied to $p_5(x)$ with $x_0 = 1$

k	x_k	$p_5(x_k)$
0	1.0	12.0
1	1.3646408839779005	1.673581
2	1.4141493080791265	0.002194
3	1.4142135623729548	4.786394×10^{-12}
4	1.414213562373095	3.552714×10^{15}

With Laguerre's Method we obtain the outcome presented in Table 4.7.

Table 4.7: Laguerre's Method applied to $p_5(x)$ with $x_0 = 1$

k	x_k	$p_5(x_k)$
0	1.0	12.0
1	0.45303693571090875	17.719702
2	−0.30290085570204517	9.189633
3	−0.8371455139932192	1.332773
4	−0.993568039394002	0.03917
5	−0.9999993388269698	3.967044×10^{-6}
6	−1.0000000000000002	$-1.998401 \times 10^{-15}$

Notice that the same starting guess ($x_0 = 1$) produces two **different** roots:

$$\alpha \sim \sqrt{2} \text{ (Halley's) and } \alpha \sim -1 \text{ (Laguerre's).}$$

In both cases our initial guess is "close" to a root: 1 vs. ~ 1.414 with Halley's method; 1 vs. -1 with Laguerre.

A second point of interest is the behaviour of Laguerre's method after processing the initial guess $x_0 = 1$. The next estimate generated is $x_1 \sim 0.453036936$. While $p_5(1.0) = 12.0$, the second estimate has $p_5(0.453036936) \sim$

---

[32]See Endnote 9.

17.72: "further away" from being a root. After this hiccough, however, successive x_i are such that $|p(x_{i+1})| < |p(x_i)|$. What we find (and Laguerre's approach is not unique in displaying such phenomena) is that iterative algorithms may not be *monotonic*: it is possible that estimates appear to be "further away" from a solution before some order of convergence results. The extent to which this behaviour arises in respect of Algorithm 4.2 is a combination of the polynomial being processed and the initial choice x_0: Algorithm 4.2 will, however, **always** find a root.

Sometimes, however, we do not have much to guide the choice of the initial x_0. If we choose $x_0 = 1000.0$, say, this value is not "close to" any root of $p_5(x)$.

Now Halley's Method performs as presented in Table 4.8.

Table 4.8: Halley's Method applied to $p_5(x)$ with $x_0 = 1000.0$

k	x_k	$p_5(x_k)$
0	1000.0	1.000991×10^{15}
1	666.601462849891	1.3181764×10^{14}
2	444.3365035301291	1.735867×10^{13}
3	296.16096301603864	2.285906×10^{12}
4	197.37891983051617	3.01022×10^{11}
5	131.5267044869558	3.963996×10^{10}
6	87.62895763848634	5.219838×10^9
7	58.36941045522328	6.873148×10^8
8	38.871522217483445	9.048928×10^7
9	25.885759288374075	1.190987×10^7
10	17.24808752258769	1566428.836518
11	11.519484304415112	205677.727309
12	7.746513194073952	26895.002158
13	5.30329938349298	3478.727176
14	3.788891862070474	435.237732
15	2.961658792629953	47.520306
16	2.669202043728096	2.34364
17	2.6457703666441525	0.001838
18	2.645751311064601	9.947598×10^{-13}
19	2.6457513110645907	0.0

In comparison, Laguerre's Method produces the outcome given within Table 4.9

Table 4.9: Laguerre's Method applied to $p_5(x)$ with $x_0 = 1000.0$

k	x_k	$p_5(x_k)$
0	1000.0	1.000991×10^{15}
1	3.6690354864682604	345.808578
2	2.6796696661634227	3.443341
3	2.6457559579768617	4.482328×10^{-4}
4	2.6457513110645907	0.0

In both cases the methods arrive at the same root $\alpha \sim \sqrt{7}$.

As we noted earlier, in principle we could use either method to find (approximations to) all roots by constructing the quotient polynomial $p_5(x)/(x - \alpha)$.

It is important to be aware of a subtle technical issue with Algorithm 4.2 and many other methods. This issue arises in many root finding approaches and, in the case of Algorithm 4.2 concerns l. 6, specifically the computation

$$\sqrt{(n-1)(n\gamma - \beta^2)}$$

A number of iterative approaches require computation of square roots and one of the advantages of Halley's Method is in avoiding this requirement. What, however, if it is the case that $n\gamma - \beta^2$ is **negative**? This is a matter that we deal with in the next chapter, noting for now that far from being an obstacle to its use, coping with such behaviour provides a further advantage.

Summary of Root Finding Techniques

Finding roots of functions is, as we have seen in Section 4.4, an important stage in solving optimization questions: when the function describing the environment in which an optimization issue is modelled can be differentiated (or at least its first derivative is well-defined within a specific relevant interval) the roots of the first derivative, those α for which $f'(\alpha) = 0$, determine local minima and maxima. As we saw in Section 2.5, finding roots of even highly structured functions such as polynomial forms is non-trivial except in some very limited cases. The selected methods discussed above are only two examples from the many that have been proposed. A common feature of these and other general techniques, however, is that in addition to providing an approach to the application of calculus in optimization, differential calculus actually underpins the effectiveness of the methods in themselves. Both Laguerre's and

Halley's Method are derived through studying function behaviour in terms of first and second derivatives. Newton's approach, which we did not discuss in depth, also relies heavily on iterating towards solutions by means of evaluating $f'(x)$ at successive approximations.

4.7 Dealing with several variables

Over the preceding sections we have concentrated on the importance of Differential Calculus in Computer Science as a powerful mechanism with which to address optimization issues. Yet, in some respects, the nature of the problems we have been looking at is, while one would not go the extreme of describing as artificial nonetheless fails to embrace one very important aspect of typical "real world" scenarios: the problems and related functions required only a **single** parameter value to be identified. In typical applications, however, we often need to identify settings for several parameters **simultaneously**.

In other words rather than looking for a value $\alpha \in \mathbb{R}$ that maximizes $f(\alpha)$ we may face the challenge of our underlying function having domain $\mathbb{R}^k$ (for some $k \in \mathbb{N}$ greater than 1) and need to find values $\mathbf{a} = <\alpha_1, \alpha_2, \ldots, \alpha_k>$ for which $f(\mathbf{a})$ is an optimal setting for $f(x_1, x_2, \ldots, x_k)$.

In presenting an overview of how differential calculus affords one approach to multivariable optimization problems we will focus on 2 variable functions. The extension to n-variable cases is, in the main, a straightforward development of these.

Let us begin by returning to the geometric view of functions with which we opened our initial presentation in Section 4.2. A function of a **single** variable, $f(x)$, associates a value, $y = f(x)$, with each $x \in \mathbb{R}$: viewing the pairs (x, y) within the 2-dimensional xy Cartesian coordinate axes, allows us to picture the function behaviour within a selected range, $\alpha \leq x \leq \beta$ say, through the curve traced out by the pairs $(x, f(x))$ as x assumes every value between α and β. Working from this visualization led to the concept of interpreting what was to be understood by "the line touching the point $(x, f(x))$ on the curve $f(x)$". We saw that this line or more precisely its **gradient** provided information about how $f(x)$ behaved and, in particular, the Real-valued function that reported "the gradient of the line touching $(x, f(x))$ given x" could be used as means of determining when $f(x)$ attained (locally) minimal and maximal values. This function – "the gradient of the line touching $(x, f(x))$ given x" – we termed the *first derivative of* $f(x)$ denoted by $f'(x)$ or dy/dx. We additionally saw that the values of x of interest, i.e. local optima, are captured by those $\alpha \in \mathbb{R}$ for which $f'(\alpha) = 0$.

In 2 variable settings, functions $f \;:\; \mathbb{R}^2 \rightarrow \mathbb{R}$, we can no longer exploit the geometric analogy of "behaviour" **in the plane**. We can, however, look for an interpretation of what such a function describes as a 3 **dimensional entity**.

Figure 4.9 displays part of the **surface** (with x and y between -2 and 2) mapped out by the function

$$z = f(x, y) = -(3x^2 + 2y^2 + xy)$$

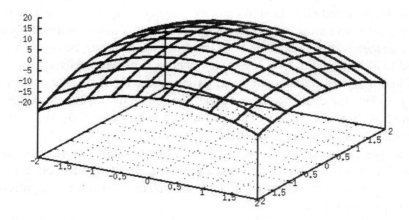

Figure 4.9: The function $z = -(3x^2 + 2y^2 + xy)$ between $-2 \le x, y \le 2$

There are a few observations we can make about the manner in which this surface changes:

OS1. For a **fixed** value of x (α say) a "line within this surface" describes the behaviour of the **single** variable function of y:

$$z = f(\alpha, y) = -(3\alpha^2 + 2y^2 + \alpha y).$$

OS2. From (OS1) using techniques we have already met we can construct a function that describes the **gradient** of "the line touching the curve $f(\alpha, y)$": that is to say the *first derivative* of $f(\alpha, y)$.

It follows that *for any fixed α there is **some** β_α that optimizes $f(\alpha, \beta_\alpha)$.*

OS3. Similarly with a fixed value of y (β say) some line within this surface describes the behaviour of the single variable function of x:

$$z = f(x, \beta) = -(3x^2 + 2\beta^2 + \beta x).$$

From (OS3) using techniques we have already met we can construct a function that describes the **gradient** of "the line touching the curve $f(x, \beta)$": that is to say the *first derivative* of $f(x, \beta)$.

It follows that *for any fixed β there is **some** α_β that optimizes $f(\alpha_\beta, \beta)$*.

OS4. By inspection of Figure 4.9, we see there is **some** choice (α, β) for (x, y) which **maximizes**

$$z = f(\alpha, \beta) = -(3\alpha^2 + 2\beta^2 + \alpha\beta).$$

Suppose we try and "combine" the effects deduced from (OS1) and (OS3)? We have a function $(f'(\alpha, y))$ describing the behaviour i.e. gradient of a line obtained by setting the x argument to a constant and another function $(f'(x, \beta))$ also describing a gradient function: that relating to setting the y argument to a constant. We would like to use these in such a way as to solve the question posed by (OS4), namely: what are the values (α, β) that maximize $f(x, y)$?

The concept of **partial derivative** allows us to make more precise exactly what is meant by "combine" in the paragraph above. Informally, "the *partial derivative* of $y = f(x_1, x_2, \ldots, x_n)$ with respect to x_i" is derived by treating each of the variables $< x_1, \ldots, x_{i-1}, x_{i+1}, \ldots, x_n >$ as **if it were a constant** (α_i say) and then forming the first derivative of the **single variable** function $f(\alpha_1, \ldots, \alpha_{i-1}, x_i, \alpha_{i+1}, \ldots, \alpha_n)$.[33]

In total, our two variable function $z = f(x, y)$ has two partial (first) derivatives: one with respect to the variable x and the other with respect to the variable y. In order to distinguish the two the former is denoted $\partial z / \partial x$ (also $\partial f / \partial x$ and f_x) and the latter $\partial z / \partial y$ (alternative notations being $\partial f / \partial y$ and f_y). Now we do not require any further rules in order to form such partial derivatives with respect to a single variable. Those we have presented already suffice.

---

[33]The **explicit** naming of constants, α_i, is not used in practice, we use it here solely to provide some insight into the formal definition.

What are the partial derivatives of $f(x, y)$ with respect to x and y for the specific function presented? Simply

$$\frac{\partial f}{\partial x} = -6x - y$$

$$\frac{\partial f}{\partial y} = -4y - x$$

Notice that, with any $\beta \in \mathbb{R}$, the first of these is **exactly** the same as

$$f'(x, \beta) = -6x - \beta$$

Similarly, with any $\alpha \in \mathbb{R}$, the second is **exactly** the same as

$$f'(\alpha, y) = -4y - \alpha$$

This, very informally, justifies our description of constructing the partial derivative of $f(x_1, x_2, \ldots, x_n)$ with respect to x_i as a process involving treating all variables other than x_i as constants.

Now, we know already how to find optimal values for x and y of the functions $f(x, \beta)$ and $f(\alpha, y)$: form $f'(x, \beta)$ and $f'(\alpha, y)$; find their roots and test the sign of the second derivative at these roots. Overall we see that $f'(x, \beta) = 0$ when $x = -\beta/6$ and $f'(\alpha, y) = 0$ when $y = -\alpha/4$. Furthermore $f''(x, \beta) = -6$ and $f''(\alpha, y) = -4$ so that these are "maxima". We have, however, one important question to deal with:

How (if at all) do we find **simultaneous** valuations for x and y that will optimize $f(x, y)$?

We know that for any fixed value (α) of x the choice $y = -\alpha/4$ will maximize.

We, also, know that for any fixed value (β) of y the choice $x = -\beta/6$ will maximize.

Finding a setting (α, β) which **is** a critical point of $f(x, y)$ and hence a potential maixmum or minimum involves identifying roots α of $\partial f / \partial x$ **and** roots β of $\partial f / \partial y$.

In other words we are faced with the problem of solving a *system of simultaneous equations* involving two variables:

$$\frac{\partial f}{\partial x}(x, y) = 0$$

$$\frac{\partial f}{\partial y}(x, y) = 0$$

In studying the nature of those critical points that may be found, just as in the single variable case we applied the "Second Derivative Test" (Section 4.4), in the multivariable case we need to look at "second order partial derivatives". What is meant by this?

The function $\partial z/\partial x = -6x - y$ is a function of **two** arguments and has, therefore, via our discussion so far two partial derivatives: one with respect to x the other with respect to y.

$$\frac{\partial^2 z}{\partial x^2} = \frac{\partial(-6x - y)}{\partial x} = -6$$

$$\frac{\partial^2 z}{\partial y \partial x} = \frac{\partial(-6x - y)}{\partial y} = -1$$

Similarly, $\partial z/\partial y = -4y - x$, being also a function of two arguments, has two partial derivatives

$$\frac{\partial^2 z}{\partial x \partial y} = \frac{\partial(-4y - x)}{\partial x} = -1$$

$$\frac{\partial^2 z}{\partial y^2} = \frac{\partial(-4y - x)}{\partial y} = -4$$

These four functions, which may also be denoted $\{f_{xx}, f_{yx}, f_{xy}, f_{yy}\}$, describe all[34] of the information needed to analyze optima. Notice that this is not only for the specific example $f(x, y) = -(3x^2 + 2y^2 + xy)$ considered but also, in principle **any** function $f : \mathbb{R}^2 \to \mathbb{R}$ subject, of course, to the usual "good behaviour" assumptions.

In order further to consider the nature of critical points we need to examine the behaviour of

$$D(x, y) = \frac{\partial^2 f}{\partial x^2} \frac{\partial^2 f}{\partial y^2} - \left(\frac{\partial^2 f}{\partial x \partial y}\right)^2$$

Or, using our alternative notation,

$$D(x, y) = f_{xx} f_{yy} - f_{xy}^2$$

Before considering how $D(x, y)$ is used we deal with one apparent lacuna in its definition: only three ($\{f_{xx}, f_{xy}, f_{yy}\}$) from the four possible second order

---

[34]In some cases further analysis of a function's behaviour may be needed, however, given that we are concerned only to give a basic introduction we will gloss over this detail.

partial derivatives feature, what has happened with f_{yx}?

Recall that f_{xy} is the

"partial derivative of f_y with respect to x, f_y being the partial derivative of f with respect to y".

and f_{yx} is the

"partial derivative of f_x with respect to y, f_x being the partial derivative of f with respect to x"

In writing $D(x,y) = f_{xx}f_{yy} - f_{xy}^2$ we are not "ignoring" the contribution of f_{yx}: we simply exploit the fact that f_{yx} and f_{xy} are the **same** function. Whether we first form the partial derivative of f with respect to x and then form the partial derivative of the result with respect to y (f_{yx}) or form the partial derivative of f with respect to y and then form the partial derivative of the result with respect to x (f_{xy}) makes no difference: the same function results. In consequence we have three **equivalent** formulations for $D(x,y)$.

$$D(x,y) = \begin{cases} f_{xx}f_{yy} - f_{xy}^2 \\ f_{xx}f_{yy} - f_{yx}^2 \\ f_{xx}f_{yy} - f_{xy}f_{yx} \end{cases}$$

To summarize, in tackling an optimization problem concerning a function of two arguments, $f(x,y)$, we can proceed in the following style.

T1. Construct the partial derivatives $\partial f/\partial x$ and $\partial f/\partial y$ with respect to x and y of $f(x,y)$.

T2. Determine the critical points of $f(x,y)$ by identifying those roots α of $\partial f/\partial x$ and β of $\partial f/\partial y$ with which

$$\frac{\partial f}{\partial x}(\alpha, \beta) = 0$$
$$\frac{\partial f}{\partial y}(\alpha, \beta) = 0$$

T3. Construct the function $D(x,y) = f_{xx}f_{yy} - f_{xy}^2$ of second order partial derivatives of $f(x,y)$ and consider the values of $D(\alpha, \beta)$ and $f_{xx}(\alpha, \beta)$ in order to classify the critical points identified in (T2).

It remains only to elaborate on what is involved in realizing (T3). Recall that, in the single variable function case, whether $f(\alpha)$ was a (local) maximum or (local) minimum relied on evaluating $f''(\alpha)$: when $f''(\alpha) < 0$ then $f(\alpha)$ was a maximum; when $f''(\alpha) > 0$, $f(\alpha)$ was a minimum; when $f''(\alpha) = 0$ we were unable to conclude anything about the behaviour of $f(\alpha)$.

A similar but marginally more involved collection of conditions governs the treatment of $f(\alpha, \beta)$ when (α, β) is a critical point.
If $D(\alpha, \beta) \leq 0$ we are unable to claim that $f(\alpha, \beta)$ is either a maximal or minimal outcome.

If $D(\alpha, \beta) > 0$ **and** $f_{xx}(\alpha, \beta) > 0$ then $f(\alpha, \beta)$ is a minimum.

If $D(\alpha, \beta) > 0$ **and** $f_{xx}(\alpha, \beta) < 0$ then $f(\alpha, \beta)$ is a maximum.

It should be noted that there is no asymmetry in this treatment, i.e. although we have expressed the conditions relative to $f_{xx}(\alpha, \beta)$ we might equally have chosen to do so via exactly the same conditions using $f_{yy}(\alpha, \beta)$. For suppose it were the case that $f_{xx}(\alpha, \beta) \geq 0$ but $f_{yy}(\alpha, \beta) \leq 0$ (or *vice-versa*)? Then in such instances we would be unable to investigate the nature of the critical point (α, β) any further since:

$$D(\alpha, \beta) = f_{xx}f_{yy} - f_{xy}^2 \leq -f_{xy}^2 \leq 0.$$

Returning to our example $f(x, y) = -(3x^2 + 2y^2 + xy)$, let us work through the mechanisms described in (T1)–(T3) using (if applicable, i.e. $D(x, y) > 0$) the analytical tool provided by the more complicated "second derivative test" just presented.

$$f(x, y) = -(3x^2 + 2y^2 + xy)$$

Step T1: Constructing the two partial derivatives of $f(x, y)$.
As we saw earlier,

$$\frac{\partial f}{\partial x} = -6x - y$$
$$\frac{\partial f}{\partial y} = -4y - x$$

Step T2: Finding critical points. We have to identify solutions (α, β) for (x, y) that satisfy the system of two equations

$$
\begin{aligned}
-6x - y &= 0 \quad (f_x(x, y) = 0) \\
-x - 4y &= 0 \quad (f_y(x, y) = 0)
\end{aligned}
$$

It is not too difficult to see that the only solution for this system is $x = y = 0$.

Step T3: Construction of $D(x, y)$ and its behaviour at critical points.

We have seen that

$$f_{xx} = \frac{\partial^2 f}{\partial x^2} = -6$$

$$f_{xy} = f_{yx} = \frac{\partial^2 f}{\partial x \partial y} = -1$$

$$f_{yy} = \frac{\partial^2 f}{\partial y^2} = -4$$

Hence,

$$
\begin{aligned}
D(x, y) &= f_{xx} f_{yy} - (f_{xy})^2 \\
&= (-6)(-4) - (-1)^2 \\
&= 23
\end{aligned}
$$

So $D(x, y)$ is a positive constant value telling us that $D(0, 0) > 0$ and that the critical point $(0, 0)$ can be further examined as to whether it is a maximal or minimal value. Here we evaluate f_{xx} at the point $(0, 0)$.

$$f_{xx}(0, 0) = -6$$

The function f_{xx} is a negative constant value and, therefore, $(0, 0)$ is a maximizing point for the function $f(x, y) = -(3x^2 + 2y^2 + xy)$.

3 or more variables

Most of the concepts introduced in the preceding subsection carry over to the case of 3 or more variables.

Thus, if $f : \mathbb{R}^m \to \mathbb{R}$ with arguments $\mathbf{x} =< x_1, \ldots, x_m >$ we have m (first order) partial derivatives

$$\left\{ \frac{\partial f}{\partial x_1}, \frac{\partial f}{\partial x_2}, \ldots, \frac{\partial f}{\partial x_m} \right\}$$

Identifying critical points of $f(\mathbf{x})$ hinges on finding solutions for the system of m equations

$$\left\{ \frac{\partial f}{\partial x_i} \right\} (\mathbf{x}) = 0$$

Analysis of critical points in higher dimensions involves an analogue of the "second derivative" style methods already discussed. Notice that our formulation of $D(x, y)$ (the 2-variable case) can also be presented in terms of a structure that was introduced in Section 3.5: the *determinant* of a 2×2-matrix.

Suppose we write the four second order partial derivatives of $f(x, y)$ in the form

$$H_2 = \begin{pmatrix} f_{xx} & f_{xy} \\ f_{yx} & f_{yy} \end{pmatrix}$$

Then

$$\det \mathbf{H}_2 \; = \; f_{xx}f_{yy} \, - \, f_{xy}f_{yx} \; = \; D(x, y)$$

As we shall describe in Chapter 7, the idea of "matrix determinant" extends to arbitrary $m \times m$ matrices. Forming the symmetric[35] matrix $\mathbf{H}_m$ as $[\, f_{x_i x_j} \,]$, i.e.

$$\mathbf{H}_m \; = \; \begin{pmatrix} f_{x_1 x_1} & f_{x_1 x_2} & \cdots & f_{x_1 x_{m-1}} & f_{x_1 x_m} \\ f_{x_2 x_1} & f_{x_2 x_2} & \cdots & f_{x_2 x_{m-1}} & f_{x_2 x_m} \\ \vdots & \vdots & \ddots & \vdots & \vdots \\ f_{x_{m-1} x_1} & f_{x_{m-1} x_2} & \cdots & f_{x_{m-1} x_{m-1}} & f_{x_{m-1} x_m} \\ f_{x_m x_1} & f_{x_m x_2} & \cdots & f_{x_m x_{m-1}} & f_{x_m x_m} \end{pmatrix}$$

of all second order partial derivatives of $f(\mathbf{x})$ and analyzing the behaviour of $\det \mathbf{H}_m$ is one important approach to m-variable optimization problems. The matrix $\mathbf{H}_m$ is called the *Hessian* (sometimes this terminology is used to refer to its determinant only). The Hessian is of considerable importance not only in optimization contexts but also in sophisticated image processing and computer vision methods.

2 variable optimization example – Management Avarice

Context:

Having cravenly accepted the widely vilified metrics imposed as part of a government "Teaching Quality Assessment" exercise, a university senior management cabal finds that, despite its supine acquiescence, the outcome of an initial trial of the scheme is "a bit of a disappointment" i.e. the university concerned has been given a humiliatingly low score.

Desperate to avoid relegation to the University ranking equivalent of Football's Isthmian League Division 2 (South) and anxious to achieve bragging

---

[35]This follows from our observation that $f_{x_i x_j} = f_{x_j x_i}$.

rights over Stotfold Higher Academy of Fertiliser Technology an institute which had been awarded the highest score by the exercise in recognition of SHAFT's innovative collaboration with (the other) MIT (Minnesota Institute of Taxidermy), the management decide that success in a forthcoming exercise will only be attained by a thorough overhaul of the means by which resources are allocated to areas of activity.

After much debate the managerial outfit decide that the total annual university budget, B, should be divided under two general headings.

M. The **Managerial Covetousness Fund** under which senior management can continue to indulge in the sybaritic incontinence of squandering public money on a lifestyle involving first-class travel to "educational strategy conferences" such being usually hosted in Miami, Las Vegas, Acapulco, etc., penthouse suites in 5-star hotel accommodation, and "entertaining" others of their ilk with vats of vintage wines and orgiastic gourmandizing in expensive restaurants.

W. After taking care of M, some proportion of the remaining budget will be spent on fripperies such as Building maintenance, cleaning, Student Welfare, and academics in that order of priority.

The management come to the conclusion that an optimal allocation in the sense of maximizing the university prospects of doing well in the next teaching quality assessment, will be that which **maximizes**

$$\mathrm{TEF}(m, w) = \frac{mw}{w^4 + m^3 + \alpha}$$

where $\alpha \in \mathbb{N}$ is a **constant**, m is the quantity allocated under M and w the quantity used for W.

Question: What are the values, m_α and w_α (as functions of the constant α) that will maximize $\mathrm{TEF}(m, w)$?

Analysis:

First notice that the choice of (m, w) that maximizes $\mathrm{TEF}(m, w)$ is exactly the same as that which **minimizes**

$$\mathrm{FET}(m, w) = \frac{1}{\mathrm{TEF}(m, w)} = \frac{w^3}{m} + \frac{m^2}{w} + \frac{\alpha}{mw}$$

Given the structure of FET(m, w) we focus on minimizing this function.

Step 1: Finding the first-order partial derivatives of FET(m, w)

$$
\begin{aligned}
\frac{\partial \text{FET}}{\partial m} &= \frac{-w^3}{m^2} + \frac{2m}{w} - \frac{\alpha}{m^2 w} \\
&= \frac{2m^3 - w^4 - \alpha}{m^2 w}
\end{aligned}
$$

$$
\begin{aligned}
\frac{\partial \text{FET}}{\partial w} &= \frac{3w^2}{m} - \frac{m^2}{w^2} - \frac{\alpha}{mw^2} \\
&= \frac{3w^4 - m^3 - \alpha}{mw^2}
\end{aligned}
$$

Step 2: Finding the critical points of FET(m, w)

We may ignore the denominators ($m^2 w$ and mw^2) and concentrate on finding (m_α, w_α) with which

$$
\begin{aligned}
2m_\alpha^3 - w_\alpha^4 - \alpha &= 0 \\
3w_\alpha^4 - m_\alpha^3 - \alpha &= 0
\end{aligned}
$$

These will require

$$
\begin{aligned}
w_\alpha^4 &= 2m_\alpha^3 - \alpha \\
3w_\alpha^4 &= m_\alpha^3 + \alpha
\end{aligned}
$$

Giving

$$
m_\alpha = (0.8\alpha)^{1/3} \ ; \ w_\alpha = (0.6\alpha)^{1/4}
$$

Step 3: Analysing the critical points

We need to look at the second-order partial derivatives,

$$
\left\{ \frac{\partial^2 \text{FET}}{\partial m^2}, \frac{\partial^2 \text{FET}}{\partial w^2}, \frac{\partial^2 \text{FET}}{\partial m \partial w} \right\}
$$

and show (for the point (m_α, w_α) just identified) that

$$
\left(\left(\frac{\partial^2 \text{FET}}{\partial m^2} \right) \left(\frac{\partial^2 \text{FET}}{\partial w^2} \right) - \left(\frac{\partial^2 \text{FET}}{\partial m \partial w} \right)^2 \right) (m_\alpha, w_\alpha) > 0
$$

and

$$\left(\frac{\partial^2 \text{FET}}{\partial m^2}\right)(m_\alpha, w_\alpha) > 0$$

$$\frac{\partial^2 \text{FET}}{\partial m^2} = \frac{2w^3}{m^3} + \frac{2}{w} + \frac{2\alpha}{m^3 w}$$
$$= \frac{2(w^4 + m^3 + \alpha)}{m^3 w}$$

$$\frac{\partial^2 \text{FET}}{\partial w^2} = \frac{6w}{m} + \frac{2m^2}{w^3} + \frac{2\alpha}{mw^3}$$
$$= \frac{2(3w^4 + m^3 + \alpha)}{mw^3}$$

$$\frac{\partial^2 \text{FET}}{\partial m \partial w} = \frac{-3w^2}{m^2} - \frac{2m}{w^2} + \frac{\alpha}{m^2 w^2}$$
$$= \frac{-3w^4 - 2m^3 + \alpha}{m^2 w^2}$$

From which

$$\frac{\partial^2 \text{FET}}{\partial w^2} \cdot \frac{\partial^2 \text{FET}}{\partial m^2} = \frac{4(3w^4 + m^3 + \alpha)(w^4 + m^3 + \alpha)}{m^4 w^4}$$

$$\left(\frac{\partial^2 \text{FET}}{\partial m \partial w}\right)^2 = \frac{(-3w^4 - 2m^3 + \alpha)^2}{m^4 w^4}$$

Substituting $(0.6\alpha)^{1/4}$ for w and $(0.8\alpha)^{1/3}$ for m gives

$$\left(\frac{\partial^2 \text{FET}}{\partial w^2} \cdot \frac{\partial^2 \text{FET}}{\partial m^2}\right)(m, w) = \frac{4(1.8\alpha + 0.8\alpha + \alpha)(0.6\alpha + 0.8\alpha + \alpha)}{(0.8\alpha)^{4/3}(0.6\alpha)}$$

$$= \frac{34.56\alpha^2}{(0.8\alpha)^{1/3} \cdot 0.48\alpha^2}$$

$$= \left(\frac{34.56}{0.48 \cdot 0.8^{1/3}}\right)\alpha^{-1/3}$$

$$\geq 77\alpha^{-1/3}$$

Similarly,

$$\left(\frac{\partial^2 \text{FET}}{\partial m \partial w}\right)^2 (m, w) \;=\; \frac{(-1.8\alpha - 1.2\alpha + \alpha)^2}{(0.8\alpha)^{4/3}(0.6\alpha)}$$

$$=\; \frac{4}{(0.8)^{4/3} \cdot 0.6 \cdot \alpha^{1/3}}$$

$$\leq\; 9\alpha^{-1/3}$$

Hence (since $77 > 9$) we see that

$$\left(\left(\frac{\partial^2 \text{FET}}{\partial m^2}\right)\left(\frac{\partial^2 \text{FET}}{\partial w^2}\right) \;-\; \left(\frac{\partial^2 \text{FET}}{\partial m \partial w}\right)^2\right)(m_\alpha, w_\alpha) \;>\; 0$$

Finally we note that $((0.8\alpha)^{1/3}, (0.6\alpha)^{1/4})$ is a minimal point since $\partial^2 \text{FET}/\partial m^2$ is always positive.

4.8   Summary of Differential Calculus in CS

The brief commentary on treatments of multivariable functions just presented, completes our presentation of one extremely important methodology for CS: differential calculus. We have seen how the approach taken to the analysis of single variable functions offers a powerful suite of methods by which optimal (minimal or maximal) settings can be determined. Although this process requires identifying the roots of specific functions (i.e. solving the equation $f'(x) = 0$), here again ideas from differential calculus provide a series of methods that allow approximations to such roots to be obtained reasonably efficiently. The basis for optimization studies established for single variable functions provides much of the supporting machinery when more than one variable is involved: critical points as roots of specific derivatives, analysis of the nature of critical points via second derivatives, etc.

In the remaining sections of this chapter we turn to the other main element of calculus and one, as we have remarked in our introduction, that has its origins in classical questions of measurement and volume estimation: Integral Calculus.

4.9   Overview of Integral Calculus

The driving motivation supporting the development of those methods that sub-sequently emerged as Integral Calculus was, as has been noted, measurement. In Chapter 2 we asserted that the fundamental *computational* question is, "How do I measure this object?". The arsenal of techniques offered by Integral Calculus are particularly powerful in those cases where "this object" is a 2-dimensional surface and the concept of "measure" is to calculate its area. We can, in addition, turn the methods provided by Integral Calculus to the mea-surement of *length* (that is where we are dealing with other than straight lines) and *volume*.

On first inspection, while one would hope the computational importance of Integral Calculus is evident through the examples just given, it may seem odd that we deal with this topic as part of a chapter whose focus so far has been dominated by *Differential* Calculus and its computational use. The idea of derivative yields insight into how a function acts, this insight often being of such depth as to validate statements about the nature of optimal instantiations of its arguments. In terms of their respective spheres of application in compu-tation, however, Differential and Integral Calculus may seem rather disparate conceits, sharing only the commonality of "Calculus" in their titles.[36] In fact, as we shall see, the view of "function behaviour" afforded through the method-ology of Differential Calculus is intimately linked to the treatment of functions in the context of integration and measurement.

In order to get a sense of this relationship between Differential and Integral approaches let us consider the following problem.

Given the curve depicted in Figure 4.10 what is the area of the region highlighted?

The curve within which the shaded area of Figure 4.10 lies is that of the function $f(x) = x^2$. In total we are being asked to calculate the area marked out by four "sides", namely:

S1. The line between the coordinates $(6, 0)$ and $(14, 0)$.

S2. The line from $(6, 0)$ to $(6, 36)$.

S3. The line from $(14, 0)$ to $(14, 196)$.

S4. The **curved** segment between $(6, 36)$ and $(14, 196)$.

---

[36]The use of "calculus" as a technical term is, of course, not limited to Mathematics. One other important scientific field in which the technicality "calculus" arises being Medicine.

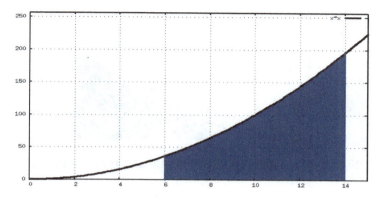

Figure 4.10: Area Computation Problem

Now if the specification of (S4) were to be "the **line** from $(6, 36)$ to $(14, 196)$" then the area measurement exercise would present no difficulty: the area would be easily calculated as $8 \cdot 36 + 0.5 \cdot 8 \cdot (196 - 36)$ i.e. 928.

The specified fourth side is, however, **not** a (straight) line between these two points: it is the portion of the x^2 **curve** between them. It is not hard to see that 928 **over estimates** the area required.

In Section 4.1 we mentioned the "Method of Exhaustion" discovered and refined by the Greek scholars Eudoxus of Cnidus and Archimedes between the 3rd and 4th centuries BC. The connection between Integral Calculus (as a mensuration device) and Differential Calculus (as an analytic tool for modelling the behaviour of functions) is given by examining the Method of Exhaustion applied to problems such as the one under consideration.

We know how to determine the area of a rectangle with sides having lengths W and H: it is simply $W \cdot H$.

Inspecting Figure 4.10, it is clear that the entire area of interest is contained within a rectangle with $H = 196$ and $W = 8$; furthermore it contains a rectangle, also with $W = 8$ but $H = 36$, as shown in Figure 4.11.

Of course we can do better: the entire region is contained within **two** rectangles having $W = 4$ and heights 100 and 196; and it contains two rectangles with $W = 4$ and heights 36 and 100 as shown in Figure 4.12

The Method of Exhaustion would have this process continued "indefinitely": for our immediate graphical purposes neither realistic nor necessary. Intead let us look at what these processes are achieving in greater depth.

We have two approaches to estimating the area: one produces too big an answer, the other too small an outcome.

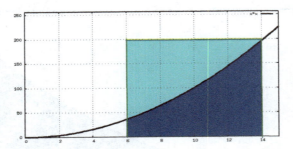

Figure 4.11: Upper and Lower Estimates for Area Problem

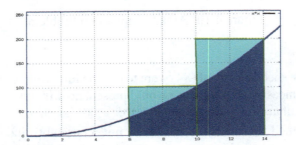

Figure 4.12: Improved Upper and Lower Estimates for Area Problem

The error in both approaches, that is to say the amount by which the first overshoots and the second undercounts, is reduced by reducing W: the base of the rectangle in both methods.

Within the line (S1) we can fit $(14 - 6)/w$ rectangles having base w. If we did so what would the corresponding upper $U(w)$ and lower $L(w)$ estimates become?

Using $A(x^2, a, b)$ to denote the area spanned by the curve $f(x) = x^2$ between $x = a$ and $x = b$ we have seen that

$$L(w) \leq A(x^2, 6, 14) \leq U(w)$$

Looking at the "sum the area of rectangles with base w" consequences we see

$$L(w) = \sum_{k=1}^{8/w} w \cdot (6 + (k-1)w)^2 \quad ; \quad U(w) = \sum_{k=1}^{8/w} w \cdot (6 + kw)^2$$

In general (with a minor notational abuse),

$$L(w, a, b) = \sum_{k=1}^{(b-a)/w} w \cdot (a + (k-1)w)^2 \quad ; \quad U(w, a, b) = \sum_{k=1}^{(b-a)/w} w \cdot (a + kw)^2$$

Of course, "ideally" we wish to consider the "extreme" case $w = 0$. In our first principles approaches to constructing the gradient function of $f(x)$ in Section 4.2 we used

$$\lim_{\delta \to 0} \frac{f(x + \delta) - f(x)}{\delta}$$

So expressing the idea of letting δ become arbitraily close to but **never reaching** 0. Let's introduce the idea of letting $w \to 0$ in our expression for $U(w, a, b)$ to get

$$A(x^2, a, b) = \lim_{w \to 0} U(w, a, b) = \lim_{w \to 0} \sum_{k=1}^{(b-a)/w} w \cdot (a + kw)^2$$

This form does not seem to be particularly helpful: unlike the "first principles" derivations from Section 4.2 there does not appear to be a clear route to eliminating the "division by w" which is hampering further expansion.

It is at this point we can establish a powerful link between the processes of differentation and integration. What do we **know** about the function $f(x) = x^2$?

For one thing that

$$x^2 = \frac{d(x^3/3)}{dx}$$

The notation dy/dx is a shorthand for a very sophisticated idea: when we write $x^2 = d(x^3/3)/dx$ what we are stating is that

$$x^2 = \lim_{\delta \to 0} \frac{(x + \delta)^3/3 - (x^3)/3}{\delta} = \lim_{\delta \to 0} \frac{(x + \delta)^3 - x^3}{3\delta}$$

In the expression just presented we have $\lim_{\delta \to 0}$; in our "area expression" we have $\lim_{w \to 0}$.

Why not use the **same** symbol, h say in both and also write N for $(b-a)/h$. The result is

$$A(x^2, a, b) = \lim_{h \to 0} U(h, a, b) = \lim_{h \to 0} \sum_{k=1}^{N} h \cdot \left(\frac{(a + kh + h)^3 - (a + kh)^3}{3h} \right)$$

We can now indulge in

Even more algebraic passage work

$$U(h, a, b) \quad = \quad \lim_{h \to 0} \sum_{k=1}^{N} h(a + kh)^2 \tag{4.1}$$

$$= \quad \lim_{h \to 0} \sum_{k=1}^{N} h\left(\frac{(a + kh + h)^3 - (a + kh)^3}{3h}\right) \tag{4.2}$$

$$= \quad \lim_{h \to 0} \sum_{k=1}^{N} \frac{(a + kh + h)^3 - (a + kh)^3}{3} \tag{4.3}$$

$$= \quad \lim_{h \to 0} \sum_{k=1}^{N} \frac{(a + (k + 1)h)^3 - (a + kh)^3}{3} \tag{4.4}$$

$$(\dagger) \quad = \quad \lim_{h \to 0} \frac{(a + (N + 1)h)^3 - (a + h)^3}{3} \tag{4.5}$$

$$= \quad \lim_{h \to 0} \frac{(a + (b - a)h/h + h)^3 - (a + h)^3}{3} \tag{4.6}$$

$$= \quad \lim_{h \to 0} \frac{(a + b - a + h)^3 - (a + h)^3}{3} \quad = \quad \frac{b^3 - a^3}{3} \tag{4.7}$$

The line (4.5) of this "derivation" highlighted with (†) marks the stage where an apparent infinite sum is reduced to just **two single terms**: one of these arising from the first term in the sum $(-(a + h)^3/3)$ the other from the final $(k = N)$ contribution $((a + (N + 1)h)^3/3)$. How does this simplification arise? It happens because the **positive** contribution when $1 \le k < N$, i.e. $(a + (k + 1)h)^3/3$ is exactly the same as the **negative** contribution when $2 \le k \le N$, i.e. $(a + kh)^3/3$.

Taking stock of what we have just seen, the area we are trying to compute, $A(x^2, 6, 14)$ in the specific instance and $A(x^2, a, b)$ for general regions of the curve $f(x) = x^2$ is completely defined by

$$A(x^2, a, b) \quad = \quad \frac{b^3}{3} - \frac{a^3}{3}$$

Now in this case a crucial stage was in substituting (for x^2) in the area calculation the function $(x^3/3)$ whose first derivative was x^2. It was this function, $x^3/3$ that remained after working through all of the consequences of summing over the area contributions of rectangles having increasingly smaller base lengths, i.e. the term $h \cdot (a + kh)^2$.

In applying the substitution, however, we exploited the fact that $x^3/3$ and x^2 has a specific relationship: previously in the context of differential calculus we would have said "x^2 is the first derivative of $x^3/3$". Reflecting the use in area measurement or what we will now refer to as *Integral* Calculus, we can now, also, express this relationship as

$x^3/3$ is the **anti-derivative** of x^2.

We have established a baseline for developing these ideas. Our illustration concerned the specific function $f(x) = x^2$. We may, however, have to contend with some arbitrary function $f : \mathbb{R} \to \mathbb{R}$ and, for instance, issues such as determining the area spanned by the curve of $f(x)$ between two values a and b with $a < b$.

In such cases we can look for a function $F : \mathbb{R} \to \mathbb{R}$ with the property that

$$\frac{dF}{dx} = f(x)$$

Such a function F is called an **anti-derivative** of $f(x)$.

A particular notational convention is used to capture the relationship between $f(x)$, informally the source of an area measurement problem and $F(x)$ the solution anti-derivative function. We write

$$F(x) = \int f(x)dx$$

The symbol $\int$ being called the "integration operator".

The form presented is called an **indefinite** integral. In the case that we analyzed of computing a specific area between two x values, we have the notation that indicates a **definite** integral, i.e.

$$F(b) - F(a) = \int_a^b f(x)dx$$

Before discussing this distinction in more detail we first clarify the general relation between $F(x)$ (the anti-derivative of f) with regard to the specific example ($x^3/3$ the anti-derivative of x^2) and the justifying analysis for the area problem presented in Figure 4.10 being $(14^3 - 6^3)/3 = 842\frac{2}{3}$.

If we look at the process described starting in Equation 4.1 although it refers to $(x^2, x^3/3)$ as the (function, anti-derivative) pair throughout its development we never replace or expand terms of the form $(a + rh)^3$. The cancellation or other simplifications of these, e.g. at (4.5), do not depend in any way on the fact that the underlying $F(x)$ is $x^3/3$. This behaviour tells us that, provided $dF/dx = f(x)$ in carrying out the "sum of rectangle areas" computation (between 4.2 and 4.4) we can replace the term $f(a + rh)$ by

$$\lim_{h \to 0} \frac{F(a + rh + h) - F(a + rh)}{h}$$

without affecting the conclusion. In other words the final stage reached (in 4.7) will be $F(b) - F(a)$.

Going back to the concept of "definite" versus "indefinite" integrals, the latter idea arises because if it **is** the case that we can describe $F(x)$ with which $dF/dx = f(x)$ then we can describe infinitely many such $F(x)$. The reason being that for any $\alpha \in \mathbb{R}$

$$\frac{dF}{dx} = \frac{d(F + \alpha)}{dx} = f(x)$$

The "indefinite" integral formulation allows us to focus on the **function** $F(x)$ independent of additive constant factors. Reflecting such usage we will when presenting for example $\int f'(x)dx$, write

$$\int f'(x)dx = f(x)$$

rather than

$$\int f'(x)dx = f(x) + C$$

Of course, for the application to area measurement, we are dealing with a calculation between two defined points: $x = a$ and $x = b$ and so these must be specified within the notation presented.

4.10   Standard integration rules

As in the case of forming first derivatives we do not have to be concerned with "first principles" methods, so too we have a number of general rules that can be adopted in integrating various functions. These are given in Table 4.10 below

There are three omissions from this collection when we compare to the earlier collection: we have no analogue of the product, quotient or chain rule. There are techniques which allow, in some cases, these to be mimicked, e.g. from the fact that

$$\frac{d(f \cdot g)}{dx} = \frac{df}{dx} \cdot g + f \cdot \frac{dg}{dx}$$

as described in the Product Rule of Table 4.4, we can deduce

$$\int (f'(x)g(x) + f(x)g'(x))dx = f(x)g(x)$$

Table 4.10: 8 Not so Simple Rules for Finding an Anti-derivative

Function form $h(x)$	Rule name	Anti-derivative $\int h(x)dx$
$\alpha \cdot f(x)$	Scalar Product	$\alpha \cdot \int f(x)dx$
$f(x) + g(x)$	Sum	$\int f(x)dx + \int g(x)dx$
x^n	Polynomial	$\frac{x^{n+1}}{n+1}$ $(n \neq -1)$
x^{-1}	Reciprocal	$\log x$
$\sin x$	Trigonometric I	$-\cos x$
$\cos x$	Trigonometric II	$\sin x$
$\exp x$	Exponential	$\exp x$
$\log x$	(Natural) Logarithm	$x \log x - x$

and so, using the Integration Sum Rule from the previous slide:

$$\int f'(x)g(x)dx = f(x)g(x) - \int f(x)g'(x)dx$$

This can be useful in those cases where a function $h(x)$ can be "easily" described as a product of the form $f'(x)g(x)$.

The creativity that is very often needed to find anti-derivatives contrasts sharply with what is, despite the occasional expressive intricacy, in the case of differentiation a fairly mechanical process. Rather than dwell on the more tedious aspects of techniques such "Integration by Parts" and "Substitution" we will be content to note, again, the existence of numerous standard texts supplying required outcomes, e.g. Petit-Bois [186].

We also note one significant problem aspect which (although examples exist) we have not encountered in the case of Differential Calculus: there are a number of commonly arising functions for which it is not possible to formulate (in a simple closed-form) their anti-derivative. For example $f(x) = \sqrt{\sin x}$, functions describing applications in statistics and probability theory such as those relating to various probability distributions.

Typically, while it often arises that we cannot process relevant expressions by *algebraic* legerdemain and must resort to numerical approximations, the methodology prescribed by integral calculus offers a powerful tool for analyzing computational settings expressed as "an (infinite) sum of infinitesimally small quantities". Among such instances we find,

1. Typical or "average" value. Although we shall look at statistical notions of average in much greater detail within Chapter 6, it is worth briefly considering how our notion of definite integral allows this to be calculated. At first inspection, questions such as "what is the average value of $x^3 + \log x$ between two given points" may look rather strange. In fact, if we consider settings where an object is moving at a given rate prescribed by a function (e.g. a car accelerating by some fixed amount) then questions such as "what is the vehicle's average speed" are well-motivated. Here the solution is prescribed in a very straightforward manner. The average value of the function $f(x)$ between $x = \alpha$ and $x = \beta$, $A(\alpha, \beta)$, is just

$$A(\alpha, \beta) \;=\; \frac{1}{\beta - \alpha} \int_\alpha^\beta f(x)dx$$

2. Determining the **length of a curve segment**. When $f(x)$ is some Real-valued function and we wish to determine the length of its path between two values α and β e.g. in the trajectory followed by a projectile (Problem DC2 earlier), the total distance travelled along the path would be twice the distance travelled from ground level to zenith. In this case we can analyze the result by considering the curve as broken down into smaller and smaller line segments just as we studied area through use of rectangular tiles. We know how to describe the length of a **line** between $(x, f(x))$ and $(x + h, f(x + h))$ since this is

$$\sqrt{h^2 + (f(x + h) - f(x))^2}$$

so the path length, $L(\alpha, \beta)$ is

$$\lim_{h \to 0} \sum_{k=0}^{\frac{\beta - \alpha}{h}} \sqrt{h^2 + (f(\alpha + (k + 1)h) - f(x + kh))^2}$$

While the expression above looks somewhat involved, after some manipulation it can be shown to be equivalent to

$$L(\alpha, \beta) \;=\; \int_\alpha^\beta \sqrt{1 + f'(x)^2}dx$$

For example, consider the quarter-circle of radius 1 centered at $(0, 0)$. Any x lying between 0 and 1 maps to the point $f(x)$ on this curve with

$$f(x) \;=\; \sqrt{1 - x^2}$$

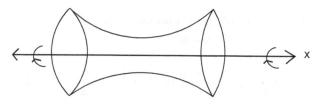

Figure 4.13: 3-dimensional volume by rotating $f(x)$

The length, $L(0, 1)$, of this quarter arc is given by

$$L(0,1) \;=\; \int_0^1 \sqrt{\left(1 + \left(\frac{d(\sqrt{1-x^2})}{dx}\right)^2\right)}\, dx \;=\; \int_0^1 \frac{dx}{\sqrt{1-x^2}}$$

From [186, p. 45, l. 2],

$$\int \frac{dx}{\sqrt{1-x^2}} \;=\; \sin^{-1} x$$

That is, the inverse sine function. As a result

$$\int_0^1 \frac{dx}{\sqrt{1-x^2}} \;=\; \sin^{-1} 1 \;-\; \sin^{-1} 0 \;=\; \frac{\pi}{2}$$

Confirming our expectation that the circumference of the circle is $\pi \cdot d = 2\pi$.

3. Volume calculation. We can view certain 3-dimensional objects as obtained by rotating the curve traced out by $f(x)$ around the x-axis, e.g. as shown in Figure 4.13.

   Just as we used rectangles to cover the area spanned by the curve of $f(x)$ and examined how this changed as the rectangle base approached 0, a similar technique (this time using cylinders to bound the volume spanned) allows us to derive that the volume, $V(\alpha, \beta)$ covered by rotating the curve of $f(x)$ between $x = \alpha$ and $x = \beta$ is

   $$V(\alpha, \beta) \;=\; \pi \int_\alpha^\beta f(x)^2 dx$$

   For example, a half-sphere with radius 1 is the shape obtained rotating the quarter circle drawn between $x = 0$ and $x = 1$. As we have seen earlier $f(x)$ describing points on this curve is $f(x) = \sqrt{1-x^2}$ so that our expression above becomes

$$V(0,1) = \pi \int_0^1 (\sqrt{1-x^2})^2 dx = \pi \left[x - \frac{x^3}{3} \right]_0^1 = \pi \left(1 - \frac{1}{3} \right) = \frac{2\pi}{3}$$

4.11 Summary

From the range of examples presented both differential and integral calculus have a range of important applications in Computer Science. The techniques provided for the treatment of functions in differential calculus provide a valuable approach to tackling optimization questions a central study of significance in CS. While there are some technical complications that arise in integral calculus, here again we have an powerful basis with which to handle what we have described as the fundamental computational concern: that of measurement.

4.12 Projects

1. Extend the suite of polynomial operations from Section 2.8(2) to include reporting the polynomials corresponding to the first and second derivatives.

2. Implement algorithms for,

   a. Halley's root-finding method. (Algorithm 4.1)

   b. Laguerre's method for finding roots of polynomials. (Algorithm 4.2) Here you should make use the methods implemented for differentiating polynomials.

   What conclusions can be drawn regarding the performance of these algorithms. Does your implementation of Algorithm 4.2 sometimes "go wrong". What do you think the reasons for such failure are?

4.13 Endnotes

1. *"the line **touching** a curve at a given point"*: There will, I have little doubt, be readers who are more used to the terminology "the tangent to a function at a specified point". I see little point in continuing to proliferate Latinisms where there is no pressing need to do so. Newton and his contemporaries published and wrote in Latin as the language of educated discourse at the time. The vast majority of work disseminated in the present day is likely to be available in English. Outside Latin-American ballroom dancing and the subject matter of painting by artists such as Titian, Bronzino, and Corregio,[37] there is no good reason for replacing "touch" and "touching" with *"tango"* or *"tangere"* or *"tangent"*.

2. *"unravelment"*: Yes, this is a legitimate British (and U.S.) English word and yes it is one of those pretentious usages (of a nature similar to "divers" which some readers may have noted and is **not** a misprint for "diverse") that one occasionally indulges.

3. *"notation that we use ..."* There are at least 3 conventions that are in use to denote "the first derivative of $f(x)$ with respect to x". In addition to $f'(x)$ and dy/dx the style $\dot{x}$ may be found (principally in Physics and Mechanics textbooks, e.g. Smith and Smith [216, p. 14]). The form $\dot{x}$ is from Newton ([175, p. 5], [176, pp. 313–18]). This for reasons that will become clear is notoriously cumbersome and awkward to use, a fact recognized by the English mathematician and Computational pioneer Charles Babbage, who was vocal in his criticism of English universities (especially Cambridge where Newton had worked) continuing to favour "dot-age" over the dy/dx style of Leibniz (a co-discoverer of Calculus).[38] The form $f'(x)$ is usually credited to the French mathematician, Joseph Lagrange [150, pp. 25–26].

4. *"that limited collection of instances ..."*: As the reader has no doubt gathered (certainly having considered the "infinitely many transformations" example from Endnote 8 of Chapter 3), there are infinitely many

---

[37] Using the Vulgate text of *John 20:17*.

[38] Regarding the phenomenon of *plus ça change plus c'est la même chose*, mentioned with respect to O/S development in Endnote 1 of Chapter 3, another example is furnished by Babbage's encounter with the asinine stupidity of politicians. He reports (in [17]) "On two occasions I have been asked [by members of Parliament], 'Pray, Mr. Babbage, if you put into the machine wrong figures, will the right answers come out?' I am not able rightly to apprehend the kind of confusion of ideas that could provoke such a question.".

different functions that accept some $x \in \mathbb{R}$ as input argument and return some $y \in \mathbb{R}$ as result. One (infinite) sub-class of these are those functions $f : \mathbb{N} \to \{0, 1\}$: so-called *predicates*. One of the most significant achievements in the study of Computation is that not only are there infinitely many functions of this type for which no **algorithmic process** exists but there are, in fact, very precisely specified functions with this behaviour. This is one of the breakthroughs demonstrated by the noted English mathematician, Computer Scientist and contributor to Artificial Intelligence, Alan Turing, cf. Turing [236]. Of course if one cannot even describe a function *computationally* there is little sense (outside some exercise in *gedankenerfahrung*) attempting to capture "the gradient of a line touching a point on (the curve of) that function".

5. It is important and useful, in the longer term to have at least an intuitive sense of **how** results are derived but pointless, unless hopes are entertained that such can form the basis of a Music-hall novelty act to worry about being able parrot-style to repeat these rules and examples of their use effortlessly. It is counterproductive in the extreme to acquire and, indeed, even to invest any effort in so acquiring, an ability to do the latter without any sense of the former. With respect to putative openings in the entertainment industry it may help to remember that decades of TV "talent" shows have regaled their audiences with singers (representative of every style and genre and running the gamut of ages from pre-school to pensioner), comedians, conjurers, contortionists, ventriloquists, illusionists, impressionists (of people, animals, birds, and arbitrary sounds), jugglers, bird acts (canaries, budgerigars, parakeets, pigeons and doves), rodent performers (white mice, hamsters, guinea-pigs and gerbils), dance acts, dog acts, dancing dog acts, "singing" dancing dog acts etc. Not one, however, has seen fit to offer for public approbation the spectacle of a performer applying product, quotient and chain rules to hyperbolic functions (with or without safety net). Given that it took almost half a century of UK TV broadcasts for the sight of an individual doing "live arithmetic" to be found "interesting", the openings for calculus savants are unpromising even where such virtuosi are canine.

6. "*Assuming our function is 'well-behaved', we can certainly state that for some 'small enough' $\alpha > 0$ neither $f'(z - \beta) = 0$ nor $f(z + \beta) = 0$ (whenever $0 < \beta \leq \alpha$) are true.*": Formally justifying this claim, which is valid in a very general and loose sense (for "well-behaved" functions) provides the source of much of the precise and technically sophisticated

analysis that is involved in a thorough and rigorous treatment of Differential Calculus. Of course one could just adopt a (somewhat underhand) formulation along the lines of "the function $f(x)$ is said to be *well-behaved* (at z) if should it be the case that $f'(z) = 0$ then there is some $\alpha > 0$ for which $f'(z - \beta) \neq 0$ **and** $f'(z + \beta) \neq 0$ whenever $0 < \beta \leq \alpha$".

One of the most important contributions to intellectual progress that has been achieved through (modern) Pure Mathematics is not only in exposing why "definitions" of this form are woefully inept and unusable but also in (at least attempting to) substitute language that is precise. The reader who wishes to look in greater depth at how this notion of "well-behaved" is approached via quite deep concepts of "differentiability" and "continuity" (as well as the concomitant formal treatment of "limits" that arises) is directed to the pages of any one of the many excellent Mathematics texts available, amongst which there are not many (that I am aware of) that do better than the classic Spivak [219].

This level of detail is unimportant regarding those applications of Calculus in Computer Science with which we are concerned. This is **not**, however, to relegate such precision to the status as having no importance at all. As I observed in the Preface, the rationale for looking at specific subjects varies with the direct concerns of the audience. In respect of the need for exactness and precision in terminology it is worth quoting the great English mathematician and philosopher Bertrand Russell:

> "Let us enumerate a few of the errors that infected mathematics in the time of Hegel. $\cdots$ There was no definition of continuity, and no known method of dealing with the paradoxes of infinite number. The accepted proofs of fundamental propositions in the differential and integral calculus were all fallacious. $\cdots$ The resulting puzzles were all cleared up $\cdots$ not by heroic philosophic doctrines such as that of Kant or that of Hegel but by patient attention to detail." (Russell [200, p. 369])

In other words, a clear and unambiguous context is **necessary** in order to ensure that the outcome of subsequent applications is well grounded and justifiable. A thorough and intimate understanding of such subtleties is, however, not needed in order to apply those technologies in themselves: one can *use* a smart phone to test applications code; one does not require a deep understanding of mobile phone frequencies, chip design and haptic screen technology in order to do so.

7. *"no 'easily implementable' fast algorithms"*: The problem given $m \in \mathbb{N}$ of returning two Natural numbers p, $q \geq 2$ such that $m = p \cdot q$ or, failing such, reporting that m is a Prime number, is known as *"Integer Factorization"*. There is a long history of algorithmic studies of this problem. Adopting the standard approach used in the formal Computer Science discipline known as Computational Complexity Theory, efficient algorithms are considered to be those that a) always report correct answers for any instance; b) do so in "time polynomial in $\log_2 m$", i.e. in at most $(\log_2 m)^k$ steps for some constant k. The significance of $\log_2 m$ is that this is the number of **bits** needed to encode m in binary. Despite considerable efforts, to date no such algorithms have been discovered. Brent [31] gives a good overview of work and progress on integer factorization up to the turn of the century. The non-existence of "fast algorithms" or, at least, "non-awareness of such" is an aspect of computational study that has been recognized and formally investigated for over half a century. The qualification used, however, is *"easily implementable'*: there **are** fast (i.e. "polynomial time") algorithms solving Integer Factorization, but these are for *Quantum Computers*. The concept of Quantum Computation was introduced by the physicist David Deutsch in [62]. It would be fair to say that this model deriving its basis from work in Theoretical Physics and its power from the phenomenon of *"superposition"* in Quantum Theory, whereby two "states" exist simultaneously in the same locale, was of primarily theoretical interest. Then in 1999, Peter Shor in [213] described a fast algorithm for Integer Factorization within this model. To date, however, while there has been significant investment towards constructing quantum computation devices, there is, as yet, no known efficient simulation of these by "standard" computers so whether Shor's algorithm can be realized outside the quantum domain is unclear.

8. Numerical Analysis for many years was a required study as part of a Computer Science degree programme. In the U.K. a number of University CS Departments grew out of Numerical Analysis (and Operational Research or, as it is now usually dubbed, Optimization Theory) groups working within existing Mathematics Departments. Among such are The University of Cambridge through the pioneering work of the distinguished figure of Maurice Wilkes and The University of Liverpool.

Wilkes acknowledges the rôle played by computational aids in an almost throwaway aside to his 1947 paper [253]: "The numerical results given in this paper were obtained on the differential analyzer in the Mathematical Laboratory, Cambridge" [253, p. 98]. More extensive presentations of the supporting computer technology were offered in papers presented between 1948 and 1949 [256, 257].

9. "$f(x^-) < 0$ and $f(x^+) > 0$: assuming that $x^- < x^+ \cdots$ we know that at some stage between x^- and x^+ the function f must be 0": The more general form of the assertion made here states if α, β are values in $\mathbb{R}$ with $\alpha < \beta$, and $f(x)$ is "well-behaved" for each γ with $\alpha \leq \gamma \leq \beta$ then for **every** δ with $f(\alpha) \leq \delta \leq f(\beta)$ there is **some** ε between α and β with which $f(\varepsilon) = \delta$. Formally this defines the *Intermediate Value Theorem*. While it appears to be "intuitively obvious" establishing the validity of the Intermediate Value Theorem is not possible without assuming some other "intuitively obvious" claim, e.g. Rolle's Theorem which is described in most standard Calculus textbooks, e.g. Spivak [219] or through divers so-called "Completeness Constructions of $\mathbb{R}$", see e.g. Myhill [173], Dedekind [56, 57]. This is one aspect that presents significant philosophical challenges in careful treatments of what $\alpha \in \mathbb{R}$ says about the nature of α, cf. Richman [194].

Chapter 5

An unorthodox view of number *Complex Numbers*

Gott weiß, wie das geschah?

Die Meistersinger von Nürnberg Act 3, Sc. 1
RICHARD WAGNER (1813–1883)

5.1   Introductory Comments

The dark and sombre string phrases pervading the prelude to the final act of Wagner's *Die Meistersinger von Nürnberg*, haunting and brooding, set a melancholic atmosphere that lingers through much of the opening scene (broken only by the short comic interlude involving the apprentice of the principal character Hans Sachs). This atmosphere begins to lighten towards the conclusion of the great baritone aria known as the *Wahnlied* in which Sachs reflects morosely on the events of the previous night: a minor misunderstanding had led to increasingly acrimonious and strident verbal exchanges before erupting in a public brawl during the course of which the town clerk was physically assaulted. Unable to fathom the process by which a trivial incident could turn so quickly into violent altercation, Sachs can only offer, as much in puzzled bemusement as despair, the question with which this chapter opens: *"Gott weiß, wie das geschah?"* ("God knows how that came about!").

One looks at the ramifications and sometimes rather obstructive consequences of Complex Number Theory, particularly in the light of what has been seen already, and while this is perhaps a little uncharitable, one feels, on occasion, some considerable empathy with Sachs' question.

Consider again the range of number types that we presented in Chapter 2 and Section 2.2 therein. We begin with the aptly named *"Natural* numbers": these serving a well-founded purpose in allowing us to **count**. We add the deep and subtle idea of "representing an absence of quantity": the number 0 and thus obtain what were called the *Whole* numbers. We recognize that there are occasions where it is helpful to "count backwards" so leading to our concept of *integer*. Finally by dint of looking at the respective amounts resulting by comparing two numbers we obtain the *Rational* numbers. Throughout these developments we always remain within a finite environment whose elements we can *physically relate* to *measurable* objects.

And then we encounter a difficulty: rationality is not enough and there seem to be quantities to which we can give a physical interpretation but not one which allows expression as a ratio of two Natural numbers. In the present day we do not (one hopes) feel particularly uncomfortable with the thought of "quantities inexpressible as a ratio of two numbers". To the mathematicians of classical Greek times, however, such irrationals created huge philosophical issues some inkling of which may be gleaned in the terminology used to name such quantities: $\alpha\lambda o\gamma o\varsigma$, ("inexpressible" literally "having no word for"). The existence of irrationals also raises the niggling issues of "continuous vs. discrete", paradoxes of limits, and the infinite.[1]

The outcome of these inconveniences is the Real numbers. These, however, still maintain some tangible link with the "physical world" and offer many even though not all of the beneficial aspects provided by the Rationals: we can **order** them, making precise exactly what is meant by one Real number α being less than another Real number β. And while we face a computational representation issue (discussed in Endnote 5 of Chapter 2) on balance the *modelling* benefits accruing through use of the continuum may be felt to outweigh this. Indeed by separating out the *algebraic numbers* we could recover, in principle, the possibility of finite representation schemes. Even the cases of transcendental (i.e. non-algebraic Real numbers) can, in a select number of instances, be described in a finite manner: from π as the "circumference of a circle with unit diameter", to more ornate forms "e as the base of Natural logarithms."[2] In total, in spite of some of the suspicion with which "irrational" quantities were viewed by mathematicians of the Pythagorean school, we can work around

---

[1]For more discussion of the reactions to this and other innovations see Endnote 1.

[2]If we wish to become enmired once more in "limits" a more helpful definition of e may be as $\lim_{n\to\infty}(1 + n^{-1})^n$.

or ignore the more esoteric aspects of troublesome behaviour. We also gain one important new idea: the suite of operations we can perform on numerical quantities is enriched from the basic $\{+, -, \cdot, /\}$ to include powering involving arbitrary values i.e. x^y.

Except, of course, this supposed enrichment raises a new difficulty: just as we faced a problem in identifying p, $q \in \mathbb{N}$ with the property that $(p/q)^2 = 2$ now we face coming to terms with interpreting $(-1)^{1/2}$. The former problem we recast as that of finding the root of a given polynomial leading to our x as the solution to $x^2 - 2 = 0$ and, eventually, to the treatment of general polynomial forms and their roots. If we attempt a similar approach to the latter problem we face seeking a solution x that satisfies $x^2 + 1 = 0$. The operation of squaring **always** produces a **non-negative** outcome, so outside of a philosophical conceit the notion of a "Real" number x whose square is negative leads nowhere. So we must resign ourselves to the situation that there are polynomials $(x^2 + 1)$ that have no roots. In fact what we must be resigned to is the situation of there being polynomials ($x^2 + 1$ for instance) that have *no roots belonging to* $\mathbb{R}$. Degree n polynomials we have stated have (*pace* multiplicity) n roots. And thus the central question we have to address (assuming it is addressed at all) is: what **are** the two roots of $x^2 + 1$?

This qualification "assuming it is addressed at all" is not intended as a casual aside. Developing a rigorous interpretation of what it means for a value x to be such that $x^2 + 1 = 0$ involves facing several very non-trivial challenges. Slightly to preempt some aspects of these (although we will not expand detailed technicalities referring the reader, whose curiosity is piqued, to works such as the lucid presentation in Priestley [191]) one consequence entailed is a new approach to Calculus especially in its Integral form. Answering the question "what are the two roots of $x^2 + 1$?" also poses some philosophical issues concerning the aims and rationale of mathematics as an intellectual pursuit. Although our concern is with *computational exploitation* rather than *mathematical subtleties* the philosophical doubts carry across: often it is tempting in the pursuit of mathematical advances to retreat to the comparative comfort and security of elementary methods.[3] That this does not always happen suggests there are significant formal gains to be had. As we hope to demonstrate through applications in algorithmics and AI such gains carry through to CS.

---

[3]The adjective "elementary" is used here in neither a disparaging nor derogatory sense but with its precise technical meaning as "requiring only the use of the Real Numbers": "elementary" is not a synonym for "easy" and just as one can find "easy" arguments which are not elementary, so too there are "elementary" techniques which are technically demanding, e.g. Cavaretta [43].

The basic device used in resolving the question

"what are the two roots of $x^2 + 1$?"

is staggeringly simple;[4] its consequences, on the other hand, are anything but: *Gott weiß, wie das geschah?*

5.2   Historical origins: "awkward polynomials"

As we have emphasized above, but ignored in Chapter 2, although we claim that "polynomials of degree k have k roots" there are instances which seem to challenge this assertion. For example,

$$x^2 + 1$$
$$x^2 - 2x + 2$$
$$x^3 - 8$$
$$x^3 - 27$$
$$\ldots$$

The first two cases have no roots in $\mathbb{R}$ whatsoever; the last two only one root in $\mathbb{R}$ (2 and 3 respectively). So, to rephrase the question with which the opening section of this chapter concluded, what has happened to the "other two roots"?

The (an?) answer to this question was, as is usually attributed, offered by Gerolamo Cardano in a work to which we have already referred: the *Artis magnae, sive de regulis algebraicis* [42]. Cardano's proposal is not to look for solutions in $\mathbb{R}$ (there are none), but rather to consider what are the properties we wish solutions to have. With respect to our first "awkward polynomial" we already know one such property: that its root should be such that, when squared, the result is -1.

The description "its root should be such that, when squared, the result is -1" is rather long-winded. Instead of this, let's propose using a symbol, $\imath$ say, to represent this idea. Meaning that $\imath$ denotes an entity obeying

$$\imath^2 \;=\; (-\imath)^2 \;=\; -1$$

And with this convention we have the two roots of $x^2 + 1$: they are simply $\{\imath, -\imath\}$. **And** we have our two roots of $x^2 - 2x + 2$: $1 + \imath$ and $1 - \imath$.

---

[4]To such an extent that, on more than one occasion, I have noticed it viewed by students with suspicion as a "cheat".

Indeed, as well as the Real root we now recover the missing two roots of $x^3 - 8$:

$$\{-1 + \sqrt{3}\imath, -1 - \sqrt{3}\imath\}$$

and those of $x^3 - 27$:

$$\{-1.5 + 0.5\sqrt{27}\imath, \; -1.5 - 0.5\sqrt{27}\imath\}.$$

Overall by "inventing a notation" ($\imath$) for the object with the properties we want, we have immediately solved our "all degree k polynomials have k roots" quandary.

This "invention of a notation to solve a problem" was treated with some suspicion by Cardano's contemporaries and successors. So one finds figures such as the eminent French mathematician and philosopher René Descartes (of Cartesian coordinate system renown) writing in 1637 [60]:

> "For any equation one can imagine as many roots [as its degree would suggest], but in many cases no quantity exists which corresponds to what one imagines."

Descartes' disdain and scepticism regarding this object $\imath$ survives in terminology still in use today[5]: $\imath$ and the structures that depend on its use are "Imaginary" numbers.

Descartes' concerns may seem unreasonable to latter-day audiences. Nonetheless, the mechanism by which we (courtesy of Cardano) now deal with the roots of $x^2 + 1$, does, I think, raise some legitimate doubts.[6]

We may summarize a core philosophical objection as:

> "In order to deal with $\sqrt{-1}$ we resort to 'inventing' a name ($\imath$) for this object. We do not address the problem itself. This entity, $\imath$, is a subterfuge not a solution, it has no 'meaning'. Such sleight-of-hand raises, in particular, one key question: if, faced with a problem insoluble by 'legitimate' methods, we simply 'invent a convenient solution' then doesn't this call into question mathematics as an intellectual pursuit? Every time we are faced with a difficulty we can just follow the precedent set by $\imath$ and devise a convenient notational device to overcome the problem."

---

[5] Although not, one has the impression, as prevalent as half a century ago.

[6] As mentioned in the opening section, using $\imath$ as the "solution" to $\sqrt{-1}$ has, in my experience, been viewed with a degree of suspicion by students.

The views expressed above do, I think, merit some attention. When as distinguished a figure as Descartes continues to express doubts about using $\imath$ almost a century after Cardano's promulgation of the concept[7]; when Descartes' opinion continues to be reflected in contemporary (albeit increasingly anachronistic) terminology, then there is, perhaps, a need to comment on the sources.

To paraphrase the "philosophical commentary" above this raises two objections to the shorthand $\imath = \sqrt{-1}$.

O1. To write $\imath = \sqrt{-1}$ doesn't "mean anything".

O2. To invent a symbol is not "solving a problem": $\imath$ is an artefact and its use sets a precedent incompatible with the ethos of mathematical thinking.

There is no entirely satisfactory answer to (O1) that I am aware of. How "meaning" becomes associated with notation is a matter more properly devolved to the domain of "Philosophy of Mathematics". In any event, if meaning is sought then, in so much as $\imath$ must "mean" something, one could rebut (O1) simply by **defining** $\imath$ to be "the object whose value when squared is -1". To the best of my knowledge no use of $\imath$ be it in Science or Engineering or even Mathematics, treats $\imath$ in any greater depth or differently from what such a definition indicates.

Regarding (O2), to make use of $\imath$ does not "**establish** a precedent": using a "symbol" to describe the properties of an object follows a very long tradition of expressing uncapturable entities by notational conventions. The School of Pythagoras had difficulties becoming reconciled to the reality of entities inexpressible as a ratio between two Natural numbers. In the present day (indeed even in Cardano's age) $\sqrt{2}$ and its irrationality (*pace* some logical paradoxes) is accepted without question. To which a counterobjection that may arise is that $\sqrt{2}$ has a physical and finite interpretation: the length of the diagonal of a square with unit sides or as a solution to the identity $x^2 - 2 = 0$. Against this claim, however, we may mention the abstraction π: true this also has a physical interpretation (the circumference of a circle with unit diameter), but other than via divers recherché and arcane infinite series (e.g. $\pi = 4\sum_{k=1}^{\infty} \frac{(-1)^{k-1}}{2k-1}$) neither finite numerical nor even root of a polynomial in $\mathbb{Q}[X]$ interpretation.

In fact we use π exactly as it has been used for over two and half thousand years: as a placeholder to describe a collection of properties originating in the ratio between a circle's circumference and its diameter, so that when, for

---

[7]See Endnote 2.

example we write

$$\pi = 4 \sum_{k=1}^{\infty} \frac{(-1)^{k-1}}{2k - 1} \quad \text{or} \quad \pi = \sqrt{6 \cdot \sum_{k=1}^{\infty} \frac{1}{k^2}}$$

all we are doing is stating that "the expression on the left-hand side (the circumference of a circle with diameter 1) **is equivalent** to the expression on the right be it 4 times an alternating sum of the reciprocals of odd numbers or the square root of 6 times the sum of reciprocals of squares".

So we **already** use π (and e the "base of Natural logarithms", and φ for the Golden Ratio and γ the "Harmonic Number" etc etc.) as such placeholder signs and this is precisely how $\imath$ will be used. In other words $\imath$ is just a novel shorthand (i.e. a symbol describing a collection of properties) and there are no exotic agenda attaching to such usage. Here it is, again, worth quoting the famous English philosopher and mathematician Bertrand Russell:

> "One result $\cdots$ is to dethrone mathematics from the lofty place that is had occupied since Pythagoras and Plato $\cdots$ thus mathematical knowledge ceases to be mysterious. It is all of the same nature as the 'great truth' that there are three feet in a yard."

Russell [199, pp. 785–786]

We, however, neither read nor write this textbook as Mathematicians but as Computer Scientists. What has been said in this section is to stress the fact that $\imath$ is no more than a simple notational device whose manipulation turns out to offer considerable **computational** benefits: in advanced graphics, in image analysis, in the study of algorithm behaviour and in AI. Before we can examine these advantages in depth we first turn to a more detailed treatment of the subject with which this Chapter is concerned: the properties and manipulation of what we will henceforward refer to as **Complex numbers.**[8]

---

[8]Whether the description "Complex" is superior to the presently unfashionable "Imaginary" is, I think, somewhat debatable. I quite like the suggestion of one first year student given during a lecture discussion. He proposed "unreal number": an idea which expresses the property accurately without any hint that the nature of these objects is somewhat dubious or exotic. The adjective "Complex" with its connotations of difficulty and intricacy, gives the impression of rather esoteric concerns. One hopes to show, particularly when dealing with algorithmic gains, that such impressions are unwarranted.

5.3 Basic properties and operations

Just as we did in the case of polynomial operations (Section 2.5), vectors (Section 3.3) and matrices (Section 3.5) we start by looking at the basic arithmetic operations involving Complex numbers.

First, however, we present a more rigorous definition and some notational conventions to be used.

Hence we use z to describe an arbitrary Complex number. Although later in Section 5.4 we will see a number of other representations for z, to begin with we use the following.

A Complex number, z, is a **pair** (α, β) of values from $\mathbb{R}$. The number z expresses

$$z = \alpha + \imath\beta$$

In this

  i. $\imath$ has the property that $(-\imath)^2 = (\imath)^2 = -1$.

 ii. $\alpha \in \mathbb{R}$ is called the **Real** part of z and is denoted by $\Re(z)$.

iii. $\beta \in \mathbb{R}$ is called the **Imaginary** part of z and denoted by $\Im(z)$.

Hence we may write either

$$z = \alpha + \imath\beta$$

or

$$z = \Re(z) + \imath\Im(z)$$

The notation $\mathbb{C}$ is used to describe the set of all Complex numbers, i.e. equivalently pairs $(\alpha, \beta) \in \mathbb{R}^2$.

Associated with every Complex value, z, is another Complex number, denoted, $\overline{z}$ known as the **complex conjugate** of z.

$$\text{When } z = \alpha + \imath\beta \text{ then } \overline{z} = \alpha - \imath\beta$$

The conjugate operation replaces (α, β) by the pair $(\alpha, -\beta)$.

Earlier, when discussing $\alpha \in \mathbb{R}$ for which $\alpha < 0$ we introduced the idea of "*modulus*" also called "absolute value". Thinking of $\alpha \in \mathbb{R}$ as a 1-vector, $< \alpha >$ we see that

$$|\alpha| = \|< \alpha >\| = \sqrt{(\alpha^2)}$$

where the "$\sqrt{...}$" reports the positive square root of α^2, i.e. $+\alpha$.

The analogous operation, in the case of $z \in \mathbb{C}$, is also denoted using $|z|$ and, when $z = \alpha + \imath\beta$,

$$|z| = \sqrt{\alpha^2 + \beta^2}$$

Notice that $|z| = |\bar{z}|$ and that, if we view the values $\alpha = \Re(z)$, $\beta = \Im(z)$ as describing a vector $< \alpha, \beta > \in \mathbb{R}^2$, then

$$|z| = \|< \alpha, \beta >\| = \sqrt{\alpha^2 + \beta^2}$$

Complex Addition and Scalar Multiplication

Before proceeding to the marginally more involved ideas of multiplication and division of two Complex numbers, we present the comparatively straightforward ideas of *addition* and *scalar multiplication*.

Given $u \in \mathbb{C}$ and $v \in \mathbb{C}$, the outcome $z = u + v$ of adding the two is the Complex number,

$$z = (\Re(u) + \Re(v)) + \imath(\Im(u) + \Im(v))$$

So that $\Re(z)$ is obtained by adding the corresponding Real parts of u and v while $\Im(z)$, in the same way, is found by adding the Imaginary parts. Looking at the contributions from u and v in terms of vectors in $\mathbb{R}^2$, i.e. with $u = \alpha + \imath\beta$, $v = \gamma + \imath\delta$, we get

$$z = < \alpha, \beta > + < \gamma, \delta >$$

In other words Complex addition can be treated as no different from vector addition. We find a similar behaviour with respect to scalar multiplication. Suppose that $\varepsilon \in \mathbb{R}$ and $u \in \mathbb{C}$. The result of muliplying u by ε is the Complex number, z for which

$$z = \varepsilon\Re(u) + \imath\varepsilon\Im(u)$$

So (conjugate aside), by viewing the components of $z \in \mathbb{C}$ as a vector in $\mathbb{R}^2$, that is the vector $< \Re(z), \Im(z) >$ these operations have the same definition as those as addition, scalar multiplication, and size that we met earlier in Section 3.3.

Complex Multiplication

The operation of multiplying two Complex numbers, however, has a rather closer resemblance to the process of multiplying polynomials as deriving from

Section 2.5. In this case, however, we now, for the first time, exploit the notational convention $i^2 = -1$

Given $u = \alpha + i\beta$ and $v = \gamma + i\delta$ their product $z = u \cdot v$ is,

$$
\begin{aligned}
z &= (\alpha + i\beta) \cdot (\gamma + i\delta) \\
&= \alpha \cdot \gamma + i(\delta \cdot \alpha + \beta \cdot \gamma) + (i \cdot i) \cdot \beta \cdot \delta \\
&= (\alpha \cdot \gamma - \beta \cdot \delta) + i(\alpha \cdot \delta + \beta \cdot \gamma)
\end{aligned}
$$

This we can see as the same process for determining the three coefficients $< c_0, c_1, c_2 >$ when computing the polynomial

$$(a \cdot x + b)(c \cdot x + d)$$

so that $c_0 = b \cdot d$ ($\beta \cdot \delta$ above); $c_1 = a \cdot d + b \cdot c$ ($\alpha \cdot \delta + \beta \cdot \gamma$) and $c_2 = a \cdot c$ ($\alpha \cdot \gamma$).

The changes to the actual combinations from $\{\alpha, \beta, \gamma, \delta\}$ are accounted for by noting that the term $\beta \cdot \delta$ is multiplied by $i \cdot i = i^2 = -1$, so with $z = u \cdot v$ we obtain,

$$
\begin{aligned}
\Re(z) &= \Re(u) \cdot \Re(v) - \Im(u) \cdot \Im(v) &= \alpha \cdot \gamma - \beta \cdot \delta \\
\Im(z) &= \Re(u) \cdot \Im(v) + \Im(u) \cdot \Re(v) &= \alpha \cdot \delta + \beta \cdot \gamma
\end{aligned}
$$

Complex Division

When we come to the process of division, the Complex number z obtained through division of $u \in \mathbb{C}$ by $v \in \mathbb{C}$, here we begin to meet some rather more involved ideas.

First notice that, exactly as in the case of defining x/y (for $x, y \in \mathbb{R}$) where the qualification $y \neq 0$ is imposed, we need to rule out certain choices of $v \in \mathbb{C}$ in order that u/v is well-defined. For the process of Complex division these exceptions are that u/v is defined *only* for those v having $|v| \neq 0$. Notice this is an identical condition to $\Re(v) \neq 0$ or $\Im(v) \neq 0$: $|v| = 0 \Rightarrow \sqrt{\Re(v)^2 + \Im(v)^2} = 0$ which (given that $\alpha^2 \geq 0$ for $\alpha \in \mathbb{R}$) can only be the case when both $\Re(v) = 0$ and $\Im(v) = 0$.

Continuing with the analogy of division by an element of $\mathbb{R}$, an alternative view of x/y is that it is just $x \cdot y^{-1}$ with y^{-1} (the *reciprocal* of y) defined through $1/y$.

Given that we know how to **multiply** two Complex numbers, adopting a similar view reduces the problem of defining the computational meaning of Complex division, u/v, to that of finding an interpretation of v^{-1} (i.e. $1/v$) as an element of $\mathbb{C}$.

When $z = \alpha + \imath\beta$ with $|z| \neq 0$ the object z^{-1} is given through

$$\frac{1}{z} = \frac{\Re(z)}{|z|^2} - \imath\left(\frac{\Im(z)}{|z|^2}\right)$$

This, in fact, reduces to a much simpler form,

$$z^{-1} = \frac{\alpha}{\alpha^2 + \beta^2} - \frac{\imath\beta}{\alpha^2 + \beta^2} = \frac{\alpha - \imath\beta}{\alpha^2 + \beta^2} = \frac{\overline{z}}{|z|^2}$$

That this has the desired properties, e.g. for $z = \alpha + \imath\beta$ we have $z \cdot z^{-1} = 1$ is easily demonstrated,

$$z \cdot z^{-1} = \frac{z \cdot \overline{z}}{|z|^2} = \frac{(\alpha + \imath\beta)(\alpha - \imath\beta)}{\alpha^2 + \beta^2} = \frac{\alpha^2 - (\imath^2)\beta^2}{\alpha^2 + \beta^2} = \frac{\alpha^2 + \beta^2}{\alpha^2 + \beta^2} = 1$$

Notice the relationship between z, $\overline{z}$ and $|z|$ that features here,

$$z \cdot \overline{z} = (\alpha + \imath\beta)(\alpha - \imath\beta) = \alpha^2 - (\imath^2)\beta^2 = \alpha^2 + \beta^2 = |z|^2$$

In other words, for every $z \in \mathbb{C}$

$$z \cdot \overline{z} = |z|^2$$

To summarize given $u = \alpha + \imath\beta$ and $v = \gamma + \imath\delta \in \mathbb{C}$ and $\varepsilon \in \mathbb{R}$ we have seen,

C1. $\overline{u} = \alpha - \imath\beta$.

C2. $|u| = \sqrt{\alpha^2 + \beta^2}$.

C3. $u + v = (\alpha + \gamma) + \imath(\beta + \delta)$.

C4. $\varepsilon \cdot u = \varepsilon\alpha + \imath\varepsilon\beta$.

C5. $u \cdot v = (\alpha\gamma - \beta\delta) + \imath(\alpha\delta + \beta\gamma)$.

C6. $u/v = (u \cdot \overline{v})/|v|^2$ (when $|v| \neq 0$).

We observe two further properties of $\mathbb{C}$ before continuing to explore differing representations. Firstly, all of the relationships described behave in exactly the same manner when $\Im(z) = 0$, that is when $z \in \mathbb{R}$. Secondly, just as with the case of vectors from $\mathbb{R}^k$ (as was argued in Section 3.3) we find it is **not** possible completely to order $\mathbb{C}$. In other words, given u, $v \in \mathbb{C}$ we have no defined concept of $u < v$.

5.4 A multiplicity of forms

One of the most troublesome and helpful features provided by the formalism offered by Complex numbers is its versatility in respect of the many equivalent representations. In the discussion of operations on Complex numbers just presented we have already made use of one such equivalence: the Complex number $\alpha + \imath\beta$ can be treated as the 2-vector $< \alpha, \beta >\in \mathbb{R}^2$. This convention, however, is only one of many possibilities. In this section we shall look at some other alternatives.

Matrix Form

Given $z = \alpha + \imath\beta \in \mathbb{C}$ the operations just described can be presented in terms of using 2×2 matrices. Writing

$$
\mathbf{M}_z = \begin{pmatrix} \alpha & -\beta \\ \beta & \alpha \end{pmatrix}
$$

It is easily seen that $\mathbf{M}_{\bar{z}} = \mathbf{M}_z^\top$, i.e. the matrix of the conjugate of z ($\mathbf{M}_{\bar{z}}$) is the transpose of the matrix of z. Similarly we have,

$$
\begin{aligned}
\mathbf{M}_u + \mathbf{M}_v &= \mathbf{M}_{u+v} \\
\varepsilon \cdot \mathbf{M}_z &= \mathbf{M}_{\varepsilon \cdot z} \\
\mathbf{M}_u \cdot \mathbf{M}_v &= \mathbf{M}_{u \cdot v} \\
|z|^2 &= \det \mathbf{M}_z
\end{aligned}
$$

Argand diagrams

The depiction of $z \in \mathbb{C}$ by an *Argand diagram* was popularized in the 1813 paper of the Swiss autodidact Jean-Robert Argand (1768–1822), cf. Argand [13].[9] It exploits the connection between viewing z as a pair of values, (α, β) from $\mathbb{R}$ and the explicit representation and treatment of such pairs as 2-**vectors**, $< \alpha, \beta >$ in the **Complex plane**.

The concept of "Complex Plane" provides a valuable approach underpinning many aspects of the geometric properties of $\mathbb{C}$. Here the idea is very similar to the 2-dimensional coordinate scheme that we have seen already, however, instead of labelling the horizontal and vertical axes by x and y we make explicit the link to $\mathbb{C}$ by using $\Re$ (to replace x) and $\Im$ (for y).

---

[9]Originally, however, the work of the Danish mathematician Caspar Wessel (1745–1818) and presented in Wessel [255].

Using Argand diagrams establishes a direct link between the results of *adding* two Complex numbers, u and v, and adding two 2-vectors: the Complex number $< \Re(u) + \Re(v), \Im(u) + \Im(v) >$ is just the (2-vector) resulting from vector addition (as described in Section 3.3) when we consider the 2-vector, $< \Re(v), \Im(v) >$ to follow the end-point of the 2-vector $< \Re(u), \Im(u) >$, i.e. while the latter may appear in what we dubbed "standard position" the former $< \Re(v), \Im(v) >$, recalling that "position" is not a vector attribute, would be drawn from where $< \Re(u), \Im(u) >$ ended. We may, in a similar way, interpret scalar multiplication of $< \Re(z), \Im(z) >$ with this in standard position within an Argand diagram in exactly the same way as scalar multiplication of a 2-vector in $\mathbb{R}^2$.

Just as the length of the 2-vector $\| < \alpha, \beta > \|$ was defined to be the outcome $\sqrt{\alpha^2 + \beta^2}$ so too the modulus $|\alpha + \imath\beta|$ of $z = \alpha + \imath\beta$ in $\mathbb{C}$ is simply $\sqrt{\alpha^2 + \beta^2}$. Overall Argand diagrams provide exact geometric interpretations of addition, scaling and modulus.

In addition, however, Argand diagrams also provide us with a geometric interpretation of *conjugate*, the operation that substitutes for $z = \alpha + \imath\beta$ the Complex number $\overline{z} = \alpha - \imath\beta$. Noting that the "vertical axis" is labelled $\Im$, the conjugate operation replaces the geometric depiction of z, by its **reflection** in the $\Re$-axis.

Argand diagrams, however, do not provide the most convenient approach to interpreting operations such as $u \cdot v$ or u/v. Looking at a trigonometric form arising from Argand diagrams whereby we consider the angle, θ, formed by the vector $< \Re(z), \Im(z) >$ with respect to the $\Re$-axis, does however, offer such a mechanism. This is the scheme referred to as *polar coordinate representation* which we now go on to describe.

Polar Coordinates

The method of **polar coordinates** again uses two elements to describe a vector. Although we did not do so when discussing vectors in the 2-dimensional Cartesian system, the representation can be applied equally effectively in that context. Among standard usages of the latter setting are to define positions on the 2-d screens used in radar and air-traffic control.

In polar coordinates the elements do not correspond to distances along the axes but rather to a distance and an **angle**.

Consider Figure 5.1

The Complex number, z, is defined by two values (both in $\mathbb{R}$): $z = (r, \theta)$. Here r is the size, $|z|$ of z, and θ the angle measured counterclockwise between

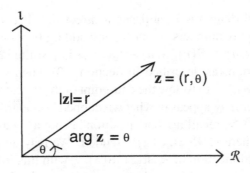

Figure 5.1: Polar Coordinates

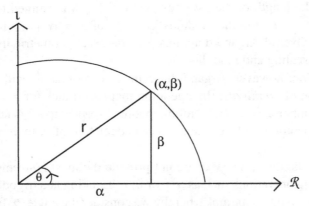

Figure 5.2: Polar vs Argand Form

the $\mathfrak{R}$ axis and the vector **z**. This angle is called the **phase** of z and is denoted by $\arg z$.

The standard convention for angular measurement in Complex numbers is to express angles in **radians** rather than, as we have so far adopted, *degrees*. In radian measures, the angle spanned in a full sweep of a line, L from the centre to the circumference moving counterclockwise from its starting position back is 2π radians: equivalently $360°$. Converting from radians to degrees involves a simple constant factor multiplication, i.e. based on $360° = 2\pi$ radians,

$$\theta° = \frac{\theta \cdot \pi}{180} \text{ rad } ; \ \theta \text{ rad } = \left(\frac{180\theta}{\pi}\right)°$$

Looking at polar coordinate form with respect to Argand diagrams we get the view in Figure 5.2.

From which we get,

$$\cos \theta = \alpha/r$$
$$\sin \theta = \beta/r$$

So that the polar coordinate (r, θ) in the Complex plane corresponds to the Complex number

$$r \cos \theta + \imath r \sin \theta$$

That is to say the vector $< r \cos \theta, r \sin \theta >$ in Argand diagram notation.

Thus, for the three forms we have introduced, i.e.

$$z = \alpha + \imath \beta$$
$$\text{Argand} \quad < \alpha, \beta >$$
$$\text{Polar} \quad (r, \theta)$$

it is straightforward to change between the three.

Standard to Argand: Given $z = \alpha + \imath \beta \in \mathbb{C}$ its Argand form is $< \alpha, \beta >$.

Argand to Polar: Given the vector $< \alpha, \beta >$ in the Complex plane, its polar coordinate form (r, θ) has

$$r = |z| = \sqrt{\alpha^2 + \beta^2}$$

$$\arg z = \theta = \cos^{-1} \frac{\alpha}{|z|} = \sin^{-1} \frac{\beta}{|z|}$$

Exponent (Euler) form

The exponent or **Euler form** for $z \in \mathbb{C}$ was a discovery of the noted Swiss mathematician Leonhard Euler[10] (1707–1783) appearing in 1748 [82, Chapter 8]. This establishes a powerful link between three apparently very disparate ideas: trignonometric functions, exponential (and, by implication, logarithm) and Complex numbers.

Central to this representation is Euler's discovery that for every $x \in \mathbb{R}$,

$$e^{\imath x} = \cos x + \imath \sin x$$

Now suppose, instead of $x \in \mathbb{R}$, we consider what this formula tells us about a value θ in radians,[11]

$$e^{\imath \theta} = \cos \theta + \imath \sin \theta$$

---

[10]See Endnote 3.
[11]See Endnote 4, regarding $\theta = \pi$.

For $z = \alpha + \imath\beta \in \mathbb{C}$, the Euler form for z, indicates that

$$
\begin{aligned}
z &= |z|e^{\imath \arg z} \\
&= \sqrt{\alpha^2 + \beta^2}\, e^{\imath \cos^{-1}\left(\frac{\alpha}{\sqrt{\alpha^2+\beta^2}}\right)} \\
&= \sqrt{\alpha^2 + \beta^2}\, e^{\imath \sin^{-1}\left(\frac{\beta}{\sqrt{\alpha^2+\beta^2}}\right)} \\
&= |z|(\cos \arg z + \imath \sin \arg z)
\end{aligned}
$$

The distinguished physicist, Richard Feynman, has described the relationship

$$e^{\imath\theta} = \cos\theta + \imath\sin\theta$$

as "the most remarkable formula in mathematics" (Feynman [85]).

We shall see some of the powerful uses of Euler's form over the next few sections, however, for now we observe that all five ($\alpha + \imath\beta$, 2×2 matrices, Argand diagrams, Polar coordinates, and Euler form) are interchangeable.

We have earlier commented that while the effects on $z \in \mathbb{C}$ of some operations (addition and scalar multiplication) are easily described by Argand diagrams others, particularly Complex multiplication, as less clear.

Looking at Complex multiplication of u, $v \in \mathbb{C}$ using Euler form not only is particularly straightforward but also reveals some useful insight into polar coordinates.

Suppose we write $\arg u = \varphi_u$, $\arg v = \varphi_v$, $u = |u|e^{\imath\varphi_u}$, and $v = |v|e^{\imath\varphi_v}$. We have easily,

$$u \cdot v = |u| \cdot |v|e^{\imath(\varphi_u+\varphi_v)} = |u \cdot v|e^{\imath(\varphi_u+\varphi_v)}$$

In this formula justifying that the size ($|\ldots|$) accruing from the product of u and v is simply the product of their respective ($|u|$, $|v|$) sizes is straightforward.

What may seem rather less obvious is the implied relationship

$$\arg u \cdot v = \arg u + \arg v$$

This, however, is what follows directly from Euler's formula.

Summary of different schemes

In what we have just described there are a variety of different mechanisms we can use to expand upon $z \in \mathbb{C}$. We have looked at five of these, namely

C1. $z \in \mathbb{C}$ is viewed as 2×2 matrix of Real numbers,

$$\mathbf{M}_z = \begin{pmatrix} \Re(z) & -\Im(z) \\ \Im(z) & \Re(z) \end{pmatrix}$$

C2. $z \in \mathbb{C}$ is a **pair**, (α, β) of Real numbers, with manipulation of z following the reading $z = \alpha + \imath\beta$ where $\imath^2 = (-\imath)^2 = -1$.

C3. $z \in \mathbb{C}$ is a **vector**, $< \alpha, \beta >$ depicted on an *Argand diagram*. The latter being a 2-dimensional coordinate system wherein axes are labelled $\Re$ (replacing x) and $\Im$ (replacing y). The size of z is the length of the vector used.

C4. $z \in \mathbb{C}$ is, again, a pair $z = (r, \theta)$, interpreted as a position drawn using **polar coordinates**. As with (C3), the component r is the size of the corresponding vector. The second element, θ (also denoted by $\arg z$) is the angle (in radians) measuring counterclockwise from the horizontal ($\Re$) axis to the vector z.

C5. $z \in \mathbb{C}$ is described by the Euler form, $z = |z|e^{\imath \arg z}$, leading to $z = |z|(\cos \arg z + \imath \sin \arg z)$.

We have presented an outline justifying how any one of these may be translated into any of the others, a property indicating the versatility and range of methods available for manipulating $z \in \mathbb{C}$. As we shall see, however, many computational applications build on the powerful consequences of Euler's representation, one of which we mention in passing stems from the fact that given any $\alpha \in \mathbb{R}$,[12]

$$(\cos \theta + \imath \sin \theta)^\alpha = \cos \alpha\theta + \imath \sin \alpha\theta$$

---

[12]The original formulation (applicable only to $n \in \mathbb{N}$) is attributed to the French mathematician Abraham de Moivre (1667–1754) and dates from 1707. Euler is credited with the extension from $n \in \mathbb{N}$ to $\alpha \in \mathbb{R}$. The statement of the relationship using only $\mathbb{N}$ is, often, called De Moivre's Formula.

5.5   Complex Numbers and powers

We have seen that a number of standard operations (scalar multiplication, addition, size) adapt to $\mathbb{C}$ with little difficulty. We have (so far) just a single new operation (Complex conjugate) but this not only poses no great computational challenge but also has a natural geometric interpretation as the reflection of a vector. Complex Product and Division are more involved but, in the former case, far less so than the difficulties raised in defining "cross product of vectors". These operations are also the first cases in which the interpretation $i^2 = -1$ is used.

So the reader may feel justified asking wherein lie the obstacles referred to earlier. One such complication, and the focus of the next sections is the operation of raising a given value, x say, to a power y. That is not only in computing x^y but also in presenting a coherent interpretation of what x^y means.

The properties of α^β when both are in $\mathbb{R}$ are easily summarized.

RP1. If the **base** (α) is non-negative then $\alpha^\beta \in \mathbb{R}$ for any $\beta \in \mathbb{R}$.

RP2. If $\beta \in \mathbb{Z}$ then $\alpha^\beta \in \mathbb{R}$ for every $\alpha \in \mathbb{R}$.

RP3. For every $\alpha \in \mathbb{R}$ it holds that $\alpha^0 = 1$.

RP4. If $\alpha^\beta \in \mathbb{R}$ and $\alpha^\gamma \in \mathbb{R}$ then $\alpha^\beta \cdot \alpha^\gamma = \alpha^{\beta+\gamma}$.

RP5. If $\delta = \alpha^\beta \in \mathbb{R}$ and $\delta^\gamma \in \mathbb{R}$ then $\delta^\gamma = (\alpha^\beta)^\gamma = \alpha^{\beta \cdot \gamma}$.

When we move to the realm where at least one of $\alpha \in \mathbb{C}$ or $\beta \in \mathbb{C}$ or $\gamma \in \mathbb{C}$ is the case it **cannot** (in general) be assumed all of these hold.

Here is a very simple example of such: consider the number $(e^{2\pi i})^i$.
Using the "multiply powers" approach, that is, $(\alpha^\beta)^\gamma = \alpha^{\beta \cdot \gamma}$.

$$(e^{2\pi i})^i \;=\; e^{2\pi i \cdot i} \;=\; e^{2\pi \cdot i^2} \;=\; e^{-2\pi}$$

Taking the Euler form of $e^{2\pi i}$ we get

$$
\begin{aligned}
(e^{2\pi i})^i &= (\cos 2\pi + i \sin 2\pi)^i \\
&= (\cos 2\pi)^i \\
&= 1^i \\
&= 1 \\
&\neq e^{-2\pi}
\end{aligned}
$$

The example just presented shows that considerable care is required when dealing with u^v where one (or both) of u and v belong to $\mathbb{C}$. The particular case $u \in \mathbb{C} \setminus \mathbb{R}$ and $v \in \mathbb{C} \setminus \mathbb{R}$, i.e. $\Im(u) \neq 0$, $\Im(v) \neq 0$ has a number of subtleties which we will avoid elaborating upon.[13]

We distinguish two specific cases which are of importance regarding powers involving Complex numbers.

First case: u^v when $u \in \mathbb{R}$, $u > 0$, $\Im(v) \neq 0$.

We may exploit the property that when u satisfies the conditions stipulated

$$u = e^{\log u} \quad .$$

(where $\log$ is, of course, using the base e of Natural logarithms.)

In such cases, the "multiply exponents" substitution $(\alpha^\beta)^\gamma = \alpha^{\beta \cdot \gamma}$ can be used irrespective of the fact that $\Im(v) \neq 0$ to give

$$u^v = (e^{\log u})^v = e^{v \cdot \log u}$$

Writing $v = \alpha + \imath\beta$, now shows that $z = u^v$ satisfies

$$\Re(z) = e^{\alpha \log u} \cos(\beta \log u) \; ; \Im(z) = e^{\alpha \log u} \sin(\beta \log u)$$

With

$$|z| = e^{\alpha \log u} \; ; \quad \arg z = \beta \log u$$

Second case: u^v when $\Im(u) \neq 0$, $v \in \mathbb{Q}$.

We may assume that $v > 0$ for otherwise we may simply compute $u^{-1} \in \mathbb{C}$ and analyze $(u^{-1})^{-v}$.

We know that $v = p/q$ for p and $q \in \mathbb{N}$. Now we can, by rewriting the expression $u^{p/q}$ focus attention on the single case $p = 1$.

$$u^v = u^{\frac{p}{q}} = (u^p)^{\frac{1}{q}}$$

Notice that writing $u = |u|e^{\imath \arg u}$ we obtain, via Euler's and De Moivre's Formulae,

$$
\begin{aligned}
u^p &= (|u|e^{\imath \arg u})^p \\
&= |u|^p (\cos \arg u + \imath \sin \arg u)^p \\
&= |u|^p (\cos p \arg u + \imath \sin p \arg u)
\end{aligned}
$$

In total the computation of u^v when $\Im(u) \neq 0$, $v \in \mathbb{Q}$ reduces to computing the "q'th root of u".

---

[13]Our primary reason for reviewing the formalism of Complex numbers concerns their application to **computational** settings. For almost all of these instances $u \in \mathbb{R}$ or $v \in \mathbb{R}$ suffice.

Once again some complications arise.

The concept of what is understood by "the k'th root of z" when $z \in \mathbb{C}$ is coloured by a number of subtleties, not arising in our earlier consideration of "the k'th root of α" when $\alpha \in \mathbb{R}$ and $\alpha \geq 0$. One of these subtleties is that, for $z \in \mathbb{C}$, $k \in \mathbb{N}$ there are **infinitely many** "sensible" forms that $z^{1/k}$, the "k'th root of z", may take: there are as we have defined $\mathbb{R}$ "only" 2 square roots of 4 ($\{-2, 2\}$). The "infinity of k'th roots" for $z \in \mathbb{C}$ requires us to focus and filter out a selection.

It is not difficult to see where this infinitude of solutions, w for which $w^k = v$ arises. Suppose $\arg w = \theta$, then from Euler's Form

$$
\begin{aligned}
w &= |w|e^{i\theta} \\
&= |w|(\cos\theta + i\sin\theta)
\end{aligned}
$$

But, as we have already observed in Section 4.2 (fn. 8), sin and cos are **periodic** functions. For every choice of $m \in \mathbb{Z}$,

$$
\cos\theta = \cos(\theta + 2m\pi) \quad ; \quad \sin\theta = \sin(\theta + 2m\pi)
$$

So that if w is a "q'th root of v" then any u having $|u| = |w|$ and $\arg u = \arg w + 2m\pi$ for some $m \in \mathbb{Z}$ is also a "q'th root of v".

The solution to this rather irksome behaviour is to focus on a particular **range** of values for $\arg z$. We know that $\cos\theta = \cos(\theta + 2m\pi)$, and similarly for sin. When we manipulate $z \in \mathbb{C}$ (say in the context of finding $\sqrt{z}$) we force $\arg z$ to be such that $0 \leq \arg z < 2\pi$. In other words, suppose $\arg z = 2m\pi + \theta$ with θ some value less that 2π. Recalling the geometric interpretation of $\arg z$ as the angle in radians measuring counterclockwise from the $\Re$-axis to the vector $< \Re(z), \Im(z) >$, $\arg z = 2m\pi + \theta$ is just expressing the angle concerned in terms of rotating through a **full circle** from the $\Re$ axis to itself and doing so m times. Having achieved an angle of $2m\pi$, $\arg z$ simply rotates a further θ radians counterclockwise. Of course in terms of the vector actually described we do not need to birl around m times: we could just proceed (from the $\Re$-axis) to reach z by rotating an angle of θ. We thus define, what is called the **principal value** of $\arg z$ to be θ such that $0 \leq \theta < 2\pi$ and $\arg z = \theta + 2m\pi$ for some $m \in \mathbb{Z}$.[14]

In our subsequent development, unless explicitly stated to the contrary, we assume that z is specified with its principal value for $\arg z$.

We now look briefly at interpreting $\sqrt{z}$ when $z \in \mathbb{C}$:

---

[14]Notice, in terms of our geometrical view, $m < 0$ corresponds to rotation in a clockwise rather than counterclockwise direction.

If $\Im(z) = 0$ **and** $\Re(z) < 0$: $z = \alpha$

Since $z = (-1)|\alpha|$, the two options for $\sqrt{z}$ are $\{\imath\sqrt{|\alpha|}, -\imath\sqrt{|\alpha|}\}$.

If $\Im(z) \neq 0$

We expect there to be two solutions $\{u_1, u_2\}$ for $\sqrt{z}$ in the sense that $0 \leq \arg u_i < 2\pi$.

To see how these must behave, consider any $u \in \mathbb{C}$ with $u^2 = z$. Letting $\arg z = \varphi$, $\arg u = \theta$

$$u^2 = \left(|u|e^{\imath\theta}\right)^2 = |u|e^{\imath 2\theta} = |z|e^{\imath\varphi}$$

From which we see that $|u| = \sqrt{|z|}$.[15] What about $\arg u$? One obvious choice is $\varphi/2$ giving one root of z as $\sqrt{|z|}e^{\imath\varphi/2}$. There is, however, one additional choice

$$\sqrt{|z|}\, e^{\imath(\varphi/2+\pi)}$$

Since we know $0 \leq \varphi < 2\pi$ it follows that $0 \leq \varphi/2 < \pi$ and hence the argument, θ, of this root satisfies $\pi \leq \theta < 2\pi$.

5.6 Primitive roots of Unity

In Chapter 2 we met the concept of roots of a *polynomial*: those α for which $p_k(\alpha) = 0$. In Section 4.6 (particularly when considering Halley's Method) we saw that this idea of "root" is a general attribute of functions $f : \mathbb{R} \to \mathbb{R}$: again, those α for which $f(\alpha) = 0$. Throughout the opening sections of the present chapter we have emphasized the source of Complex numbers as being an attempt to define what is meant by the "roots" of polynomials such as x^2+1. These we have seen to be the values $z \in \mathbb{C}$ with which $p_k(z) = 0$, entirely in keeping with our earlier concept bearing in mind that $\mathbb{R} \subset \mathbb{C}$: the set $\mathbb{R}$ being just those members, z of $\mathbb{C}$ having $\Im(z) = 0$.

When we discuss **primitive** roots of Complex numbers the sense in which the word "root" is used is rather closer in spirit to usages such as "square root" or "cubic root" etc. True we moved to the use with which "root" has been invoked most often by interpreting the "square root of α as "that value of x for which $x^2 - \alpha = 0$", i.e. as a root of a quadratic, and it may seem unnecessarily

---

[15]We do not need to consider the negative square root: $|\ldots|$ is always non-negative.

obfuscating to return to our earlier "square root", "cube root", "k'th root" form rather than continue with the "root of a function" form we have been using.

In presenting ideas of "primitive roots" by far the most powerful application of these is that of primitive roots of unity. These are exploited in a rich variety of methods arising from what is called the Discrete Fourier Transform. We conclude our overview of the technical background to Complex numbers by presenting the ideas underpinning "primitive roots of unity".

Consider any $k \in \mathbb{N}$. In the "real" world the Natural number 1 has a single distinct k'th root (if k is odd) and 2 distinct k'th roots (if k is even). For example if $k = 4$

$$(1)^{\frac{1}{4}} \in \{-1, 1\} \quad \text{since } (-1)^4 = 1 \text{ and } 1^4 = 1$$

and there are no other solutions in $\mathbb{R}$.

Similarly when $k = 7$,

$$(1)^{\frac{1}{7}} \in \{1\} \text{ since } (1)^7 = 1$$

and, again, there are no other solutions in $\mathbb{R}$.

The degree 4 polynomial $x^4 - 1$ has, however, **four distinct** roots: $\{-1, 1, -\imath, \imath\}$.

The degree 7 polynomial $x^7 - 1$ also has a further six distinct roots all of these in $\mathbb{C}$.

The idea of what we call a **primitive n'th root of unity** is to describe, in a succinct and, what will be a computationally powerful style, all of the n roots of $x^n - 1$.

We know, already that $1^n = 1$. Suppose we look at 1 as a Complex number expressed in Euler form

$$1 = e^{0 \cdot \imath}$$

Notice we use the principal value form for $\arg 1$, i.e. $\arg 1 = 0$.

So that

$$e^{0 \cdot \frac{2\pi \imath}{n}}$$

is an n'th root of 1 and we have found one root through $e^{2k\pi \imath / n}$ with $k = 0$. What if we chose $k = 1$, or $k = 2$, and so on?

$$
\begin{aligned}
k &= 0 && \text{gives the root } \alpha_0 && e^{0 \cdot \frac{2\pi i}{n}} \\
k &= 1 && \text{gives the root } \alpha_1 && e^{1 \cdot \frac{2 \cdot \pi i}{n}} \\
k &= 2 && \text{gives the root } \alpha_2 && e^{2 \cdot \frac{2 \cdot \pi i}{n}} \\
& \quad \cdots \\
k &= i && \text{gives the root } \alpha_i && e^{i \cdot \frac{2 \cdot \pi i}{n}} \\
k &= n-1 && \text{gives the root } \alpha_{n-1} && e^{(n-1) \cdot \frac{2 \cdot \pi i}{n}}
\end{aligned}
$$

What can we deduce about the n values $< \alpha_0, \alpha_1, \ldots, \alpha_k, \ldots, \alpha_{n-1} >$ where $0 \le k \le n - 1$?

Firstly that $(\alpha_k)^n = 1$:

$$
\begin{aligned}
\alpha_k^n &= \left(\cos \left(k \cdot \frac{2\pi}{n} \right) + i \sin \left(k \cdot \frac{2\pi}{n} \right) \right)^n \\
&= \cos(2k\pi) + i \sin(2k\pi) \\
&= \cos 0 + i \sin 0 \\
&= 1
\end{aligned}
$$

So that the collection $\{\alpha_k \ : \ 0 \le k < n\}$ gives n roots of the polynomial $x^n - 1$: and these are **distinct** roots in the sense that if $i \ne j$ then (at least) one of $\Re(\alpha_i) \ne \Re(\alpha_j)$ or $\Im(\alpha_i) \ne \Im(\alpha_j)$ holds.

To see this notice that $\arg \alpha_k = 2k\pi/n$ hence the structures described use the principal value. It is clear that $|\alpha_k| = 1$ hence,

$$
\alpha_k = \cos \left(\frac{2k\pi}{n} \right) + i \sin \left(\frac{2k\pi}{n} \right)
$$

Whence,

$$
\Re(\alpha_k) = \cos \left(\frac{2k\pi}{n} \right) \ ; \ \Im(\alpha_k) = \sin \left(\frac{2k\pi}{n} \right)
$$

and both $\Re(\alpha_i) \ne \Re(\alpha_j)$ **and** $\Im(\alpha_i) \ne \Im(\alpha_j)$ whenever $i \ne j$

So not only does $\{\alpha_k : 0 \le k \le n - 1\}$ describe n roots of $x^n - 1$ it describes n **different** roots.

While the form $e^{2k\pi/n}$ may look rather cumbersome, often for suitable n this has a basic simplification. For example consider $x^4 - 1$. We know this has 4 roots and these are

$$
\{e^{\frac{0\pi \cdot i}{4}}, e^{\frac{2\pi \cdot i}{4}}, e^{\frac{4\pi \cdot i}{4}}, e^{\frac{6\pi \cdot i}{4}}\}
$$

which are easily verified from Euler's formula to be simply $\{1, i, -1, -i\}$.

5.7 Summary of Complex Power Operations

As we have noted, manipulation of expressions involving powers of Complex numbers requires considerable care to be exercised. This is not only in accounting for multiple solutions (the determination of the root $\sqrt{|z|}\, e^{\imath(\varphi/2+\pi)}$ of $z \in \mathbb{C}$ relies on observing that $\arg z$ behaves in a similar manner to $\arg z + 2\pi$) but also in the fact that many of the standard identities that hold for α^β when both α and β are in $\mathbb{R}$ can no longer be relied upon when Complex numbers are involved. We have already illustrated the pitfalls in interpreting $(e^{2\pi\imath})^\imath$, and a number of supposed paradoxes, e.g. Steiner, Clausen & Abel [222] with Complex powers are, in fact, through invalid assumptions concerning the behaviour of e^x.

These complications reach a new level of intricacy when we attempt (as we have not done and will not do in this text) to give a rigorous basis for the concept of "logarithm of $z \in \mathbb{C}$".

5.8 A selection of computational uses

Having presented a basic overview of Complex numbers – their properties, operations on, and differing representation approaches – we now look at some important computational applications. In some cases, given the fact that rather more advanced theory is required, we will be content to outline at a rather informal and high-level where the use of Complex analysis is developed: the principal example in this instance concerns quite sophisticated results used in what is called "average-case" analysis of algorithms and structures. In other instances, in particular application of the Discrete Fourier Transform we present rather more detailed discussion, noting that the background required for a basic appreciation has already been discussed.

First, however, we deal with the issue raised with respect to one polynomial root finding approach earlier.

Laguerre's Method Redux

In Section 4.6 we looked at some methods for finding roots, i.e. given $f : \mathbb{R} \to \mathbb{R}$ identifying those α for which $f(\alpha) = 0$. One of the methods we described – Laguerre's Method presented in Algorithm 4.2 – was effective when $f(x)$ belonged to the class of functions $\mathbb{R}[X]$ of bounded degree polynomials having coefficients drawn from $\mathbb{R}$.

We noted, however, one possible problem with Laguerre's method also arising in other approaches, Halley's in Algorithm 4.1 being an important exception: some stages of the computation required the computation of square roots. Specifically having computed values β and γ associated with $p_n(x)$, its first two derivatives and a current estimate of a root the computation of

$$\sqrt{(n-1)(n\gamma - \beta^2)}$$

was demanded. It was suggested that were $(n\gamma - \beta^2)$ to be negative there might be problems. This, however, is only the case if $p_n(x)$ is being evaluated with $x \in \mathbb{R}$. Of course, as we have seen there are polynomials for which this assumption would lead to Laguerre's method failing to find any roots at all. In fact, we can apply Laguerre's method to find **Complex** as well as Real roots.

To proceed in this way we have to make some (very minor) changes in implementing Algorithm 4.2. The most important of these is, of course, the fact that when $\{p(x), p'(x), p''(x)\}$ are evaluated (in ll. 4 and 5 of Algorithm 4.2) we must now allow the polynomial argument to be a member of $\mathbb{C}$ rather than just $\mathbb{R}$. Computationally this is no significant issue. If, for example, the form (x, y) (both in $\mathbb{R}$) is used to describe $z = x + \imath y$ then the computation of $p(z)$ will correspond to that of a function, $f_p : \mathbb{R}^2 \to \mathbb{R}^2$, i.e. taking pairs of values from $\mathbb{R}$ as arguments and reporting a pair of values (again from $\mathbb{R}$) as result. Now the value β (computed in l. 4 of Algorithm 4.2) through

$$\beta := \frac{p'(x_k)}{p(x_k)}$$

will be a value in $\mathbb{C}$ obtained by **dividing** $p'(x_k) \in \mathbb{C}$ by $p(x_k) \in \mathbb{C}$. In principle we could replace the explicit use of division by rewriting this computation as

$$\frac{p'(x_k) \cdot \overline{p(x_k)}}{|p(x_k)|^2}$$

so that the division is by an element in $\mathbb{R}$. We have similar adjustments in l. 5 when processing

$$\gamma := \beta^2 - \frac{p''(x_k)}{p(x_k)}$$

The final stage of the algorithm requiring some modification of l. 7, i.e. the calculation of α as

$$\frac{n}{\max\{\beta + \sqrt{(n-1)(n\gamma - \beta^2)},\ \beta - \sqrt{(n-1)(n\gamma - \beta^2)}\}}$$

Recalling that $(n-1)(n\gamma-\beta^2)$ is being treated as an element of $\mathbb{C}$ the outcome

$$\sqrt{(n-1)(n\gamma-\beta^2)}$$

must be treated as an element of $\mathbb{C}$.

Suppose we write

$$z = \beta + \sqrt{(n-1)(n\gamma-\beta^2)}$$
$$w = \beta - \sqrt{(n-1)(n\gamma-\beta^2)}$$

Then we see that $w = \bar{z}$. Since $|z| = |w|$ the maximization is achieved through $\sqrt{|z|}e^{i\arg z/2}$.

One further point of interest exploitable in Laguerre's approach, but also in general, is that having found $z \in \mathbb{C}$ to be a root of $p(x)$ this, immediately, provides another root: the conjugate, $\bar{z}$. Thus for any polynomial $p(x) \in \mathbb{C}[X]$ we have $p(z) = 0$ if and only if $p(\bar{z}) = 0$. In simplifying $p(x)$ in order to find all roots, once we have found $z \in \mathbb{C}$ as a root, we can factor out $(x-z)(x-\bar{z})$ a quantity which we have seen is $x^2 - 2\Re(z)x + |z|^2 \in \mathbb{R}[X]$.

Quaternions

Strictly speaking the formalism of *quaternions* is not so much an application of Complex numbers but rather an enrichment made possible from the precedent of the supporting theory in Complex numbers. Here we introduce the main components involved and discuss some important applications of the idea in computer graphics.

The formal structure of quaternions was discovered in 1843 by the Irish mathematician and astronomer William Hamilton (1805–1865) appearing in 1848 [114].[16]

In addition to the notion of quaternions, the importance of Hamilton's contribution to computational issues is recognized in the terminology "*Hamiltonian path*" and "*Hamiltonian cycle*".[17]

One of the most powerful applications of quaternions to computer graphics is in displaying the movement of 3-dimensional objects through 3-dimensional spaces. Of course, in principle, exactly the same processes can be implemented

---

[16]Although a very similar structure was presented by the French mathematician Benjamin Olinde Rodrigues in his 1840 paper published in [196]. The German scientist, Carl Friedrich Gauss (1777–1855) had also discovered related methods by 1819: Gauss' work, however, did not appear in print until 1900 [99].

[17]The latter underpins the formulation of the well-known Optimization task now known as the *Travelling Salesperson Problem*.

with reference to the standard Cartesian coordinate system and appropriate matrix-vector computations, much as we described in Section 3.7, but there is a difficulty: in order to ensure accurate and realistic displays of such objects care has to be taken to apply a consistent orientation for the "frame of reference" with which computations are performed. Very often this necessitates applying computationally involved operations by which an effect is achieved through repeated "translate-realize-translate" processes, i.e. translate a system of coordinates to a more convenient operational context, realize the effect intended in the new system, translate back to the coordinate system from which the displayed object is determined. This process is feasible for animating 2-dimensional effects but for 3-dimensional displays it quickly becomes cumbersome for all but the most basic effects e.g. scaling. The mechanisms provided by **Quaternion Algebra** offer one solution.

In this subsection we give an overview of how quaternions are defined and summarize the advantages of the approach in the context of 3-D graphics. We will not give an extensive account of the latter methods for which detail we direct the interested reader to the papers of Shoemake [212], Jüttler [131], and Pletinckx [188].

Basic Form and Operations

Just as $z \in \mathbb{C}$ can be thought of as a point (x, y) through the form $z = x + \imath y$ ($\imath$ describing an object for which $\imath^2 = -1$), a quaternion q is described by a point in $\mathbb{R}^4$: (w, x, y, z). The relationship between q and (w, x, y, z) being

$$q = w + \imath x + \jmath y + k z$$

The components $\{\imath, \jmath, k\}$ are considered as satisfying the identities,

$$\imath^2 = \jmath^2 = k^2 = -1$$
$$\jmath k = -k\jmath = \imath$$
$$k\imath = -\imath k = \jmath$$
$$\imath \jmath = -\jmath\imath = k$$

The notation $\mathbb{H}$ is often used to describe the set of all quaternions or, equivalently, subject to the manipulation rules just given the relevant subset of $\mathbb{R}^4$.

A useful view of $q \in \mathbb{H}$ is as a pair $[\alpha, \mathbf{v}]$ in which $\mathbf{v}$ is a vector in $\mathbb{R}^3$ and $\alpha \in \mathbb{R}$ a scalar value. All of the operations we have seen so far with respect to vectors and $\mathbb{C}$, i.e. scalar multiplication, addition and subtraction, adapt to the 4-vectors given by quaternions.

The notions of **conjugate** $\overline{q}$ and size $\|q\|$ are given for $q = w + \imath x + \jmath y + kz$ by

$$\overline{q} = w - \imath x - \jmath y - kz$$

$$\|q\| = \sqrt{w^2 + x^2 + y^2 + z^2}$$

An important subclass of quaternions being the **unit** quaternions: those for which $\|q\| = 1$. Hamilton in [114] was looking to develop the analogy from "Complex numbers (x, y) as points in 2-space" to similar treatments of points (x, y, z) in 3-space. The approach of quaternions as exemplified by the relationships just given offers a mechanism by which not only is addition, scalar multiplication and subtraction easily defined but also operations corresponding to the **product** of quaternions $(q_1 \cdot q_2)$ and the idea of q^{-1}. A significant difference between the interpretation of $q_1 \cdot q_2$ (when q_1 and q_2 are in $\mathbb{H}$) compared to the case where both are in $\mathbb{C}$ (i.e. that at least two of $\{x, y, z\}$ equal 0) is that whereas $u \cdot v = v \cdot u$ when u and v are in $\mathbb{C}$, the product of quaternions q_1 and q_2 may be such that

$$q_1 \cdot q_2 \neq q_2 \cdot q_1$$

Using the "scalar-vector" pair presentation of quaternions, the product of $q_1 = [\alpha, \mathbf{v}]$ and $q_2 = [\beta, \mathbf{w}]$ is

$$q_1 \cdot q_2 = [\alpha\beta - \mathbf{v} \cdot \mathbf{w}, \ \alpha\mathbf{w} + \beta\mathbf{v} + \mathbf{v} \times \mathbf{w}]$$

Notice this exploits both the dot (scalar) product and cross product of $\mathbf{v}_1$ and $\mathbf{v}_2$. The cross product component $\mathbf{v}_1 \times \mathbf{v}_2$ is where potentially the issue $q_1 \cdot q_2 \neq q_2 \cdot q_1$ can arise: as we saw in Chapter 3 the vector cross product (for $\mathbf{v}$ and $\mathbf{w} \in \mathbb{R}^3$) is such that $\mathbf{v} \times \mathbf{w} = -\mathbf{w} \times \mathbf{v}$.

Again, in a very similar style to the form of z^{-1} for $z \in \mathbb{C}$, the notion of "reciprocal of a quaternion", q^{-1} for $q = [\alpha, \mathbf{v}]$ (with the usual exception that $\|q\| \neq 0$) is given through

$$q^{-1} = \frac{\overline{q}}{\|q\|^2}$$

In summary, with $q_1 = [\alpha, \mathbf{v}]$ and $q_2 = [\beta, \mathbf{w}]$ both in $\mathbb{H}$

Operation	Definition
$\varepsilon \cdot q$	$[\varepsilon \cdot \alpha, \varepsilon \cdot \mathbf{v}]$
$\overline{q}$	$[\alpha, -\mathbf{v}]$
$\|q\|$	$\sqrt{\alpha^2 + \|\mathbf{v}\|^2}$
$q_1 + q_2$	$[\alpha + \beta, \mathbf{v} + \mathbf{w}]$
$q_1 \cdot q_2$	$[\alpha\beta - \mathbf{v} \cdot \mathbf{w}, \ \alpha\mathbf{w} + \beta\mathbf{v} + \mathbf{v} \times \mathbf{w}]$
q^{-1}	$\dfrac{\overline{q}}{\|q\|}$

Now all of this is, from an algebraic viewpoint, very pretty and elegant, however such aesthetic niceties tell us nothing about the process of **applying** quaternions in the context of graphics.

We will not give a full account of the gains offered through manipulating quaternions (directing the interested reader to the references given earlier), however, we will give a taste of one particular use.

As has been suggested, displaying and calculating operations involving **rotations** in 3-dimensions is rather a trying process using classical so-called Euler angles[18]: rotations of an object involving two or more separate stages have to be applied in a precisely specified order the matrices defining the relevant transformations being ham-strung by the non-commutativity of matrix product; rigid objects do not change shape as they move so any realistic animation of, say, a solid cube tumbling through space must take account of this fact. In addition classical "rotation matrix" techniques are prone to suffer from the phenomenon of *"Gimbal lock"* whereby noting that 3 different angles can be specified should one of these become 90° it becomes impossible due to the behaviour of the trigonometric functions governing the changes to alter the others.

Prior to the application of quaternion approaches, the typical method used to animate movement of, say, a solid cube would be: identify one reference or "fixed" point e.g. a corner of the cube; translate to a given coordinate of interest; apply the famous discovery of Euler that *any* rotation can be expressed as a **single** rotation about this fixed point, a "line of points" called the rotation axis.

Now if we think of $\mathbf{v} = <\alpha, \beta, \gamma>$ defining the vector in the xyz-Cartesian system describing this rotation axis and we wish to see what a point

---

[18]Informally, these define the orientation of objects by three angles relative to a fixed coordinate system.

(x, y, z) should be translated to when rotating by $\theta°$ around this axis, then classical methods tell us that it is the outcome of multiplying $(x, y, z)^\top$ by the matrix

$$\begin{pmatrix} \alpha^2(1 - \cos\theta) + \cos\theta & \alpha\beta(1 - \cos\theta) - \gamma\sin\theta & \alpha\gamma(1 - \cos\theta) + \beta\sin\theta \\ \alpha\beta(1 - \cos\theta) + \gamma\sin\theta & \beta^2(1 - \cos\theta) + \cos\theta & \beta\gamma(1 - \cos\theta) - \alpha\sin\theta \\ \alpha\gamma(1 - \cos\theta) - \beta\sin\theta & \beta\gamma(1 - \cos\theta) + \alpha\sin\theta & \gamma^2(1 - \cos\theta) + \cos\theta \end{pmatrix}$$

What if we use quaternions instead? Consider the quaternion q_θ specified as

$$q_\theta = [\cos(\theta/2), \sin(\theta/2)\mathbf{v}]$$

Notice that
$$\|q_\theta\| = \sqrt{\cos^2(\theta/2) + \|\mathbf{v}\|^2 \sin^2(\theta/2)}$$

Recalling that $\mathbf{v}$ is describing an **axis** of rotation (i.e. infinite line of points) we can always choose $\mathbf{v}$ to have $\|\mathbf{v}\| = 1$. Doing so we see that the quaternion q_θ is a **unit** quaternion.

And the effect we wish to realize, i.e. the result of applying the rotation to (x, y, z)? Using the mapping

$$R_q : \{[0, \mathbf{w}] \in \mathbb{H}\} \rightarrow \{[0, \mathbf{w}] \in \mathbb{H}\}$$

the computation of "rotate $\mathbf{w}$ (i.e. $[0, \mathbf{w}]$) through $\theta°$ around the axis specified by $\mathbf{v}$ (i.e. $q_\theta = [\cos(\theta/2), \sin(\theta/2)\mathbf{v}])$" is expressed through the quaternion calculation

$$R_q([0, \mathbf{w}]) = q_\theta \cdot [0, \mathbf{w}] \cdot q_\theta^{-1} = q_\theta \cdot [0, \mathbf{w}] \cdot \overline{q_\theta}$$

Furthermore in addition to avoiding the potential issues (Gimbal lock etc.) of rotation matrices, the quaternion approach is a *linear transformation*, cf. Section 3.6 and for q_1, q_2 of the form $[0, \mathbf{v}] \in \mathbb{H}$

$$R_q(\alpha \cdot q_1 + q_2) = \alpha_1 R_q(q_1) + R_q(q_2)$$

Depicting movement and animation within 3-dimensions on a graphics display is just one application of quaternions as a basic component for modern computer graphics support. One also finds sophisticated uses in the task of "rendering": the action of displaying an object with a "smooth" rather than obviously approximated by regular polygons surface. For this, and similar developments we refer the interested reader to Pletinckx [188, Section 7] and the books by Kuipers [149] or Vince [242].

Properties of typical structures

Counting is, as we have stressed in several places already within this text, a ubiquitous and core process within computation. The first developments of electronic (or at least automated) assistance with counting activities one can trace back at least as far as Hollerith's tabulating device [120] and its use in reducing the manual overhead involved in processing census data. So we find "counting" as an activity arising in applications such as accounting, census taking, pay-roll processing and handled by spreadsheets and databases. The matter of counting also arises in computational settings such as programming numerical approximation methods and the analysis of data from large-scale scientific enterprises. There is, however, also a rather less direct use of "counting" in CS: in the specialist discipline of Algorithmics. At its most basic level we would be concerned with questions such as "How many **steps** does this program take to deliver its answer?". For example, "how long" a specific sorting algorithm takes to process **any** collection of n numbers into increasing order. Having answered such questions for a single approach one may then turn to the question of whether whatever bound had been demonstrated could be improved upon. Such questions, and the techniques used in both designing and analyzing algorithms are, of course, core material within the delivery of first-year "Algorithm and Data Structures" courses and have been so going back to the earliest study of CS as a degree-level subject. A wealth of textbooks being available as support.[19]

There is, however, usually a common treatment of what is understood by "how many steps does this program take to deliver its answer?": such considerations tend to be with respect to what are called **worst-case** scenarios, i.e. very informally "what is the *maximum* amount of time that I will have to wait?". As we shall examine in rather more depth in the next chapter there is, however, another view that could be taken of "How many **steps** does this program take to deliver its answer?": not worst-case but **on average**. In such contexts our interest is in assessing the "typical" performance of a method not its pessimal[20] behaviour. Arguably, consideration of typical as opposed to worst possible run-time gives a more realistic sense of how a given approach

---

[19]e.g. Long standing texts such as Aho, Hopcroft and Ullman [2] an edition which still many prefer to its successor from 1983 [4]. Comprehensive classics such as the 3 volume (to date) work of Knuth [144, 145, 146] and modern treatments such as Cormen, Leiserson *et al.* [51].

[20]*vide.* the observation opening Endnote 2, Chapter 4. The first use of the adjective "pessimal" is not (as has been claimed) from 1960s Stanford: it appears as early as 1640, cf. Cobbett and Hansard[46, p. 692]. Usage in print can be traced at least as far back as a paper of Sassa and Tokio [204, p. 336] from 1921.

would work in practice. Often a worst-case view may rule out or be used as an argument against their adoption, algorithms which are "feasible" in practice, worst-case instances being unlikely to surface in real scenarios.

There is one significant advantage of "worst-case" analysis by comparison with "average-case" study: the former is (usually) relatively straightforward; the latter, however, can be technically extremely challenging and non-trivial. We shall look at some of the issues that arise from a statistical perspective in studying average-case run-time of algorithms in the next Chapter. For the present we, very briefly, look at one approach that can be used and which has its supporting rationale from deep results in Complex Analysis.

A truism: algorithms operate on **input data**. It is reasonable, therefore, to consider the typical performance of an algorithm in terms of typical characteristics of its input. For example the nature of sorting algorithms via the nature of collections of n numbers; that of an algorithm for traversing binary trees via the nature of binary trees. In this way attention is shifted from "algorithms" to particular combinatorial objects and their structure. The problem of sorting is, in essence, that of rearranging a *permutation* of $p_1 p_2 \cdots p_n$ into the order $1, 2, \ldots, n$ and so, in principle, the typical performance of a sorting algorithm could be gauged by answering the question "how many of the objects in a typical permutation are in the wrong position?" or, more formally: "given $p_1 p_2 \cdots p_n$ what is $|\{ k : p_k \neq k \}|$?".[21] Similarly, for the example of tree traversal a relevant measure might be "the maximum number of nodes from the tree root to a leaf node": the tree *height*.

It follows that one approach we could use to estimate average case properties is: determine the number of objects of a particular **size** (n) that might arise as inputs, e.g. for our sorting example this would be $n! = \prod_{k=1}^{n} k$; denote this quantity by $N(n)$; determine the number of objects of size n for which some measure is k e.g. the number of permutations of size n with k elements "out-of-place"; the number of n node binary trees with height k; denote this quantity by A_{nk}. Having assessed these the average value of our quantity of interest which will give some insight into the average algorithm run time is

$$\frac{1}{N(n)} \sum_k k A_{nk}$$

So that our "average run-time" problem becomes simply a matter of counting objects with a given character.

---

[21]This, of course, is not the only way in which "dis-orderedness" can be defined. Other styles include counting the number of pairs (i, j) for which $i < j$ and $p_i > p_j$.

A very well established approach to this counting of objects task is the approach (still widely taught on many "Discrete Methods for CS" modules) of **Generating Functions**. A very comprehensive treatment of the ideas underlying the theory of generating functions may be found in the text of Flajolet and Sedgewick [87]. In simple terms, a generating function for some infinite sequence of numbers e.g. the total number of n-node binary trees for each $n \in \mathbb{N}$, describes this sequence by

$$G(z) = \sum_{n=1}^{\infty} a_n z^n$$

The form $G(z)$ captures the fact that the "the coefficient of z^n" is the value of the n'th sequence member a_n.

On first inspection this representation doesn't seem particularly helpful. The power of generating functions arises by the validity of standard manipulations applied to them. For example, $G(z)$ is a *function* of z. So, in theory we could differentiate it with respect to z getting

$$\frac{dG}{dz} = \sum_{n=1}^{\infty} n a_n z^{n-1}$$

Now suppose we could express the number of objects of size n in terms of some function of the number of objects of a smaller size? For example, consider a binary tree with n nodes. It has a root (1 node), a Left hand tree (l nodes) and a right hand tree (r nodes). It must be the case, however, that $n = 1 + l + r$. So we see, letting t_n be the number of n-node binary trees, that $t_1 = 1$, $t_2 = 0$ and for $n \geq 3$,

$$t_n = \sum_{k=1}^{n-1} t_k \cdot t_{n-1-k}$$

and its generating function, $B(z)$ satisfies

$$B(z) = \sum_{n=1}^{\infty} t_n z^n = 1 + \sum_{n=3}^{\infty} \sum_{j=1}^{n-1} t_j t_{n-1-j} z^n$$

Leading to

$$B(z) = 1 + \sum_{n=3}^{\infty} \sum_{j=1}^{n-1} t_j z^j t_{n-1-j} z^{n-1-j} = 1 + z \left(\sum_{j=1}^{\infty} t_j z^j \right) \left(\sum_{k=1}^{\infty} t_k z^k \right)$$

[A little sleight-of-hand is involved here: a "left-hand tree" with j nodes can be paired via the root node with any "right-hand tree" having k nodes, for any value of $k \geq 1$.]

In other words, $B(z) = 1 + zB^2(z)$. Now from $B(z) = 1 + zB^2(z)$ the following rearrangement can be justified

$$B(z) = \frac{1 - \sqrt{1 - 4z}}{2z}$$

So that the coefficient of z^n in the function on the right hand side is exactly the number of n-node binary trees, i.e. t_n. After some further trickery we obtain

$$t_n = \frac{(2n)!}{n!(n+1)!}$$

The use of z as the formal variable in $G(z)$ is not a coincidence. The legitimacy of the operations applied to the infinite series represented by a generating function is established through analysis of Complex numbers.

This reaches a new level of sophistication, however, when used in conjunction with deep results from Complex Analysis and methods such as Singularity analysis. A full discussion of these is, unfortunately, beyond the scope of this text. An excellent treatment of the general approach can be found in survey article by Vitter and Flajolet [243].

The Discrete Fourier Transform and its use

The **Fourier Transform** is a method that is used extensively in applications involving signal processing. In this section we are interested in one variant called the *Discrete Fourier Transform* (DFT).[22]

The formal structure of the DFT involves the use of Primitive Roots of Unity.[23]

---

[22]This is also called the *Finite* Fourier Transform (FFT) in some texts. We avoid this form partly because of the confusion that has been noted with the algorithmic approach called the *fast* Fourier Transform (also, sometimes, abbreviated to FFT) or FFFT, i.e. Fast Finite Fourier Transform.

[23]The style "primitive root" is reserved for operations in $\mathbb{C}$. Rather confusingly, there is a very similar notion known as a "*principal* root of unity" which arises in the context of modular arithmetic: when considering the structure $(\mathbb{Z}_k, +, \cdot)$ of modulo k arithmetic over $\{0, 1, 2, \ldots, k-1\}$ a "**principal** n'th root of unity" is a value $\alpha \in \mathbb{Z}_k$ for which $\alpha^n = 1$ and for every $r < n$, $\sum_{j=0}^{n-1} \alpha^{rj} = 0$. When considering some applications of the DFT the actual form being used involves *principal* (rather than *primitive*) roots of unity, however, this is not something which we need worry about in discussing the DFT here.

After presenting the formal definition of the DFT we look at two very different applications. The first of these is in image compression, where the tranformation of the image via DFT methods, results in reduced storage overheads while it is hoped not impairing too significantly the quality of the reconstituted image.

The second application is to the development of fast integer arithmetic algorithms. As was described, very briefly, in Section 2.5, there is a close link between the process of "determining the coefficients resulting from multiplying two polynomials" and "computing the representation in some number base b of the product of two integers represented in base b". We shall illustrate how the properties of the DFT can be exploited in computer arithmetic.

Finally we look at the actual algorithmic problem of **computing** the DFT. Here we describe the famous Cooley-Tukey algorithm developed for this purpose and described in [50].

The Discrete Fourier Transform - definition & properties

The Discrete Fourier Transform defines a mapping from an n-vector of Complex numbers
$$\mathbf{x} \;=\; < x_0, x_1, \ldots, x_{n-1} > \in \mathbb{C}^n$$
The reason for indexing the individual components $0, 1, \ldots, n-1$ rather than $1, 2, \ldots, n$ is merely to simplify the notation in the actual specification.

This mapping is denoted $\mathcal{F}(\mathbf{x})$ and with
$$\mathcal{F}(\mathbf{x}) =< y_0, y_1, \ldots, y_{n-1} >$$
the specific $y_t \in \mathbb{C}$ are given by
$$y_t \;=\; \sum_{k=0}^{n-1} x_k \cdot e^{\frac{-2\pi i t k}{n}}$$

Notice that, although this is a one dimensional structure in that it describes a mapping from $\mathbb{C}^n$ to $\mathbb{C}^n$, it is not difficult to extend to two dimensional forms i.e. $n \times n$ **matrices** with entries from $\mathbb{C}$.

Thus if we have

$$\mathbf{M} \;=\; \begin{pmatrix} x_{00} & x_{01} & \cdots & x_{0,n-2} & x_{0,n-1} \\ x_{10} & x_{11} & \cdots & x_{1,n-2} & x_{1,n-1} \\ \vdots & \vdots & \ddots & \vdots & \vdots \\ x_{n-2,0} & x_{n-2,1} & \cdots & x_{n-2,n-2} & x_{n-2,n-1} \\ x_{n-1,0} & x_{n-1,1} & \cdots & x_{n-1,n-2} & x_{n-1,n-1} \end{pmatrix}$$

then the 2-dimensional DFT, $\mathcal{F}_2$ replaces $x_{p,q}$ by

$$\mathcal{F}_2(x_{p,q}) = \sum_{k=0}^{n-1} \sum_{r=0}^{n-1} x_{p,q} \cdot e^{-i2\pi\left(\frac{kp}{n} + \frac{rq}{n}\right)}$$

so giving a direct correspondence with the form of $\mathcal{F}(x_k)$

This matrix form is particularly of interest in image compression applications since encoding of images (via say .jpg) can be viewed as a matrix of pixel values in which these values describe the characteristics e.g. colour using RGB or other conventions such as the YC_bC_r method of brightness/blue/red.

Before going on to present some general properties of $\mathcal{F}(\mathbf{x})$ it is worth looking at

$$y_t = \sum_{k=0}^{n-1} x_k \cdot e^{\frac{-2\pi i t k}{n}}$$

and the relationship with primitive roots of unity. Consider the component,

$$e^{\frac{-2\pi i t k}{n}}$$

Recalling that the object we denoted $\alpha_k = e^{2\pi i k/n}$ in Section 5.6 satisfied $(\alpha_k)^n = 1$ what can we say about the objects which we will denote, ω_k, for which

$$\omega_k = e^{\frac{-2\pi i k}{n}}$$

It is not hard to see that $\omega_k = (\alpha_k)^{-1}$ and since $|\alpha_k| = 1$ we see that

$$\omega_k = \overline{\alpha_k}$$

Furthermore,

$$\begin{aligned}
(\omega_k)^n &= \left(\frac{1}{\alpha_k}\right)^n \\
&= \frac{1}{(\alpha_k)^n} \\
&= 1
\end{aligned}$$

Since α_k is a primitive n'th root of unity. So we see that the set

$$\{\omega_k : 0 \leq k < n\}$$

presents an alternative set of n primitive n'th roots of unity.

Notice that both $\{\alpha_k : 0 \leq k < n\}$ and $\{\omega_k : 0 \leq k < n\}$ with $\omega_k = \overline{\alpha_k}$ defining two sets of solutions to $z^n - 1 = 0$ does not contradict our "degree

n polynomials have n roots" property. These sets are not different but **exactly the same**. To see this, noting that $|\alpha_i| = |\omega_j| = 1$ for every α_i and ω_j, we just need to show that for each ω_k there is exactly one α_r for which $\arg \omega_k = \arg \alpha_j$. Notice that in specifying ω_j we do not use our convention of adopting the principal argument so that in the description $\arg \omega_k \leq 0$. To demonstrate the mapping it suffices to note that $\alpha_0 = \omega_0$ and if we take ω_k ($1 \leq k < n$) then

$$\arg \omega_k = \frac{-2\pi k}{n}$$

Howevever,

$$\frac{-2\pi k}{n} + 2\pi = \frac{2\pi(n-k)}{n} = \arg \alpha_{n-k}$$

so that ω_k (when $1 \leq k < n - 1$) is the same element of $\mathbb{C}$ as α_{n-k}.

Having dealt with this apparent difficulty, let us return to the properties of $\mathcal{F}$ and the output y_t. Since $t \in \mathbb{W}$ we can legitimately write

$$\left(e^{\frac{-2\pi \imath k}{n}}\right)^t = (\omega_k)^t$$

So our expression for y_t is just

$$y_t = \sum_{k=0}^{n-1} x_k (\omega_k)^t$$

One consequence is that the entire DFT process can be presented as a matrix-vector product. Note that the matrix rows and columns are indexed starting from 0, i.e. in referring to the (i, j) entry we have $0 \leq i < n$ and $0 \leq j < n$.

$$\begin{pmatrix} y_0 \\ y_1 \\ y_t \\ \cdots \\ y_{n-1} \end{pmatrix} = \begin{pmatrix} (\omega_0)^0 & (\omega_1)^0 & \cdots & (\omega_{n-2})^0 & (\omega_{n-1})^0 \\ (\omega_0)^1 & (\omega_1)^1 & \cdots & (\omega_{n-2})^1 & (\omega_{n-1})^1 \\ \vdots & \vdots & \ddots & \vdots & \vdots \\ (\omega_0)^{n-2} & (\omega_1)^{n-2} & \cdots & (\omega_{n-2})^{n-2} & (\omega_{n-1})^{n-2} \\ (\omega_0)^{n-1} & (\omega_1)^{n-1} & \cdots & (\omega_{n-2})^{n-1} & (\omega_{n-1})^{n-1} \end{pmatrix} \begin{pmatrix} x_0 \\ x_1 \\ x_t \\ \cdots \\ x_{n-1} \end{pmatrix}$$

The matrix form of $\mathcal{F}_2$ can be treated similarly by taking successive rows at a time.

In fact recalling that ω_r is simply $e^{r \cdot (\imath 2\pi/n)}$ we can just use $\omega = e^{\imath 2\pi/n}$ and write

$$\begin{pmatrix} y_0 \\ y_1 \\ y_t \\ \cdots \\ y_{n-1} \end{pmatrix} = \begin{pmatrix} \omega^0 & \omega^0 & \cdots & \omega^0 & \omega^0 \\ \omega^0 & \omega^1 & \cdots & \omega^{n-2} & \omega^{n-1} \\ \vdots & \vdots & \ddots & \vdots & \vdots \\ \omega^0 & \omega^{n-2} & \cdots & \omega^{(n-2)(n-2)} & \omega^{(n-2)(n-1)} \\ \omega^0 & \omega^{n-1} & \cdots & \omega^{(n-1)(n-2)} & \omega^{(n-1)(n-1)} \end{pmatrix} \begin{pmatrix} x_0 \\ x_1 \\ x_t \\ \cdots \\ x_{n-1} \end{pmatrix}$$

So that the (i, j) entry of the matrix is ω^{ij}

Important Computational Properties of the DFT

The DFT has a number of properties which prove to be very powerful in algorithms exploiting it. We summarize a few of these below. In the sequel, $\mathbf{x}$ and $\mathbf{y}$ are n-vectors drawn from $\mathbb{C}^n$ and $\varepsilon \in \mathbb{R}$ an arbitrary scalar value.

Linearity

$$\mathcal{F}(\varepsilon \mathbf{x} + \mathbf{y}) \;=\; \varepsilon \mathcal{F}(\mathbf{x}) + \mathcal{F}(\mathbf{y})$$

In other words, $\mathcal{F} : \mathbb{C}^n \to \mathbb{C}^n$ is a linear transformation.

Inverse Transform

Suppose we have been given $\mathbf{y}$ and know that there is *some* $\mathbf{x} \in \mathbb{C}^n$ for which $\mathbf{y} = \mathcal{F}(\mathbf{x})$. How do we recover $\mathbf{x}$ if we have only been provided with $\mathbf{y}$? The **inverse transform**, $\mathcal{F}^{-1}$ reports the value $x_t \in \mathbb{C}$ as[24]

$$x_t \;=\; \frac{1}{n} \sum_{k=0}^{n-1} y_k e^{\frac{2\pi \imath k t}{n}}$$

It is worth expanding this in a similar style to that in which we considered the form $\mathcal{F}$. First notice that the Complex value $e^{2\pi \imath k t / n}$ is, as before, a primitive root of unity. In fact it is the value, $(\alpha_k)^t$ with α_k that value presented in Section 5.6. From our introduction to $\mathcal{F}$ we have seen that $\alpha_{n-k} = \omega_k$, i.e. $\alpha_k = \omega_{n-k}$ and, of course, $\alpha_0 = \omega_0$. Thus, in order to use a consistent style of reference to the primitive roots of unity involved, instead of writing

$$x_t \;=\; \frac{1}{n} \sum_{k=0}^{n-1} y_k \alpha_k^t$$

we may re-write the expression for x_t as

$$x_t \;=\; \frac{1}{n} \sum_{k=0}^{n-1} y_k (\omega_{n-k})^t \;=\; \frac{1}{n} \sum_{k=0}^{n-1} y_k \omega^{(n-k)t}$$

---

[24]Recall the indexing convention used has $0 \leq t < n$.

where, in the first summation we have $\omega_n = \omega_0$.

Returning to the matrix-vector product view of $\mathcal{F}(\mathbf{x})$ we find $\mathcal{F}^{-1}(\mathbf{y})$ is described by the matrix-vector product

$$
\frac{1}{n}
\begin{pmatrix}
\omega^0 & \omega^0 & \cdots & \omega^0 & \omega^0 \\
\omega^n & \omega^{(n-1)} & \cdots & \omega^2 & \omega^1 \\
\vdots & \vdots & \ddots & \vdots & \vdots \\
\omega^{n(n-2)} & \omega^{(n-1)(n-2)} & \cdots & \omega^{2(n-2)} & \omega^{n-2} \\
\omega^{n(n-1)} & \omega^{(n-1)(n-1)} & \cdots & \omega^{2(n-1)} & \omega^{n-1}
\end{pmatrix}
\begin{pmatrix}
y_0 \\
y_1 \\
y_t \\
\cdots \\
y_{n-1}
\end{pmatrix}
$$

Denoting by $\mathbf{M}_{\mathcal{F}}$ the matrix describing the DFT itself, i.e. for which $\mathbf{y} = \mathcal{F}(\mathbf{x})$ is computed by the matrix-vector product $\mathbf{M}_{\mathcal{F}} \cdot \mathbf{x}^{\top}$ and using $\mathbf{M}_{\mathcal{F}^{-1}}$ for the matrix giving the inverse transform, we see that

$$
\mathbf{x} \;=\; \mathbf{M}_{\mathcal{F}^{-1}} \mathbf{M}_{\mathcal{F}} \cdot \mathbf{x} \;=\; \mathbf{M}_{\mathcal{F}} \mathbf{M}_{\mathcal{F}^{-1}} \mathbf{x}
$$

The fact that the inverse mapping exists and is readily computable offers significant advantages: we can carry out operations using the transformed structure of vectors and then reconstruct the representative object in the system of interest, e.g. in image compression techniques, the compression details are performed after applying $\mathcal{F}$ to rows of a matrix describing the image and the image itself (for display) is rebuilt by using the inverse transform, As we shall see in the final application we present of the DFT these ideas lead to especially notable results when combined with the **Convolution** of two n-vectors.

The Convolution Property

We have already, although not named as such, met this apparently "new" idea of "the convolution of two vectors": in Section 2.5 when describing the process of finding the coefficients of the polynomial formed by multiplying $p_n(x)$ and $q_m(x)$.

In order to simplify our description let $\mathbf{x} \in \mathbb{C}^{2n}$ and $\mathbf{y} \in \mathbb{C}^{2n}$ but with the condition imposed that the vectors in $\mathbb{C}^{2n}$ we focus upon have the form

$$\mathbf{u} = <\underbrace{0, 0, \ldots, 0,}_{n \text{ times}} u_{n-1}, u_{n-2}, \ldots, u_1, u_0 >$$

so that these describe "degenerate" polynomials of degree $2n - 1$, $p_{2n-1}(x)$ within $\mathbb{C}[X]$, i.e.

$$p_{2n-1}(x) = \sum_{k=0}^{2n-1} u_k x^k$$

Given $\mathbf{u}$ describing the coefficients of $p_{2n-1}(x)$ and $\mathbf{v}$ describing the coefficients of $q_{2n-1}(x)$, as we have seen already, their product $p_{2n-1}(x)q_{2n-1}(x)$ is a polynomial of degree $2(2n - 1)$ with coefficients,

$$\mathbf{w} = <w_{2(2n-1)}, w_{2(2n-1)-1}, w_{2(2n-1)-2}, \ldots, w_2, w_1, w_0 >$$

We have seen that these coefficients are related to those from $\mathbf{u}$ and $\mathbf{v}$ by

$$w_k = \sum_{i=0}^{k} u_i \cdot v_{k-i}$$

The operation of determining these values is called the **convolution** of $\mathbf{u}$ and $\mathbf{v}$.

Notice that the coefficients w_k when $k \geq 2n$ are all 0: in each of the contributing $u_i v_{k-i}$ terms, we will have either $u_i = 0$ ($i \geq 2n$) or $v_i = 0$ ($i < 2n$, since $k - i \geq 2n$). In this case we regard $\mathbf{w}$ as the $2n$-vector whose components are

$$\mathbf{w} = <w_{2n-1}, w_{2n-2}, \ldots, w_2, w_1, w_0 >$$

We use the notation

$$\mathbf{w} = \mathbf{u} \otimes \mathbf{v}$$

to describe the fact that $\mathbf{w}$ is obtained as the convolution of $\mathbf{u}$ and $\mathbf{v}$, so that (recalling our convention for $\mathbf{u}$ and $\mathbf{v}$), the convolution operator as we have defined it, describes a vector in $\mathbb{C}^{2n}$ i.e. $\mathbf{w}$ given two vectors $\mathbf{u}$ and $\mathbf{v}$ in $\mathbb{C}^{2n}$.

One final operation: given $\mathbf{u}$ and $\mathbf{v}$ in $\mathbb{C}^n$, $\mathbf{u} \diamond \mathbf{v}$ is the vector, $\mathbf{w} \in \mathbb{C}^n$ with i'th component w_i defined by $u_i \cdot v_i$, i.e. by component-wise multiplication

The Discrete Fourier Transform allows this convolution to be described in a particularly elegant manner.

$$\mathbf{w} \;=\; \mathbf{u} \otimes \mathbf{v} \;=\; \mathcal{F}^{-1}(\mathcal{F}(\mathbf{u}) \diamond \mathcal{F}(\mathbf{v}))$$

So we can obtain the convolution of $\mathbf{u}$ and $\mathbf{v}$ by:

1. First compute the DFT of $\mathbf{u}$ and $\mathbf{v}$, i.e. $\mathcal{F}(\mathbf{u})$, $\mathcal{F}(\mathbf{v})$.

2. Then compute the component-wise multiplication ($\diamond$) of these vectors.

3. Compute the inverse DFT of the result.

Having seen some of the important characteristics of the Discrete Fourier Transform, let us now turn to its use in some Computing applications.

DFT and Image Compression

When sending or storing digital photographs the amount of space these occupy is a major consideration. Very large images, although potentially having better quality, will take longer to transmit (e.g. via a smart phone messaging application) and the amount of data forwarded may result in some noticeable expense. Even storing such images may, at some point, lead to difficult decisions when the storage medium is near full capacity, concerning whether to delete a photograph or move to an alternative back-up store. Against such problems techniques by which the space used to describe essential information within an image are of great importance. In realizing such methods a number of factors come into the play: the amount of space occupied by the compressed image, the efficiency with which compression and decompression can be carried out, and, not least, the quality of the reconstituted compressed image itself. With respect to the last of these, several compression methods are what is referred as "lossy": information (which cannot be recovered) is discarded in order to save space with the hope that the quality of the result is not significantly impaired. In Section 7.4 we shall see one approach to Image Compression deriving from the so-called "Spectral analysis" of image information. In this section we look at how the Discrete Fourier Transform offers an alternative method of image compression.[25]

---

[25]The DFT is only one of several transform type methods. Another widely-used in practice is the *Discrete Cosine Transform* (DCT). This differs from DFT principally in the nature of the actual transformation applied to the integer values describing pixels in an image.

The rationale for Fourier Transform compression approaches comes from the continuous variant's application in signal processing. Here the transform is interpreted as translating from a "a collection of values over some time period" e.g. the amplitude/height of a wave signal, into "a collection of frequencies": the former is sometimes referred to as the *spatial domain* and the latter as the *frequency domain*. Noting the limits of human optical powers, it is often the case that "high frequencies" do not give much information about an image whereas the bulk of information about an image's content is covered by a band of relatively low frequencies. Hence in DFT compression methods the idea is, having translated from the "spatial domain" to the "frequency domain", to discard "high frequency" data and reform the image via the inverse Fourier transform with the data that remains. In total this method involves the following stages.

C1. Given the image S with height h and width w partition this image into separate **blocks** of size $k \times k$ for some value $k \in \mathbb{N}$. The choice $k = 8$ is often used.

C2. For each $k \times k$ block, S_r compute the DFT of the entries in S_r.

C3. This is the "compression step" also called the "**quantization**" step. Using a fixed $k \times k$ quantization matrix, $\mathbf{Q}$ having entries drawn from $\mathbb{N}$, replace each component, s_{ij} of S_r by the rounded value of s_{ij}/q_{ij}.

C4. Recover the new image by computing the inverse DFT of each of the quantized blocks, S_r.

Notice that the DFT translation defined in step (C2) can be performed on each row of the block S_r at at a time rather than applying the matrix DFT given earlier.

This method presumes that a particular image encoding scheme is used in order for the quantization matrix to achieve good results. Specifically that the YC_bC_r format is used. In this (similar to the RGB convention described at the start of Chapter 3) the value of an image pixel is presented as three separate 8 bit values: Y defining the pixel brightness; C_b the amount of blue used; and C_r the amount of red. Hence S comprises three *channels* of data each channel being a value in $\mathbb{Z}_{256}$: typically entries are translated to values in the range -128 to 127 by subtracting 128.

Although, in principle, arbitrary values of block size could be used, the choice of 8×8 has been very widely analyzed. In this case the quantization matrix below has been found through empirical study to perform effectively. We refer to Cabeen and Gent [40] for further background.

$$\begin{pmatrix}
16 & 11 & 10 & 16 & 24 & 40 & 51 & 61 \\
12 & 12 & 14 & 19 & 26 & 58 & 60 & 55 \\
14 & 13 & 16 & 24 & 40 & 57 & 69 & 56 \\
14 & 17 & 22 & 29 & 51 & 87 & 80 & 62 \\
18 & 22 & 37 & 56 & 68 & 109 & 103 & 77 \\
24 & 35 & 55 & 64 & 81 & 104 & 113 & 92 \\
49 & 64 & 78 & 87 & 103 & 121 & 120 & 101 \\
72 & 92 & 95 & 98 & 112 & 100 & 103 & 99
\end{pmatrix}$$

Further discussion of image compression and noise reduction in images by transform methods may be found in Buades, Coll and Morel [36]. The use of the Discrete Cosine Transform is also discussed in Strang [226].

DFT and Large number Arithmetic.

We know from primary (junior) school[26] how to **multiply** two given values p and $q \in \mathbb{W}$.

Assuming the convention of decimal representation we may write

$$\begin{aligned}
p &= p_{r-1} \quad p_{r-2} \quad \cdots \quad p_1 \quad p_0 \\
q &= q_{r-1} \quad q_{r-2} \quad \cdots \quad q_1 \quad q_0
\end{aligned}$$

so that $p \in \mathbb{W}$ and $q \in \mathbb{W}$ are described through

$$p = \sum_{k=0}^{r-1} 10^k p_k \quad ; \quad q = \sum_{k=0}^{r-1} 10^k q_k$$

with the product $p \cdot q$ obtained by calculating successively for each m between 0 and $r-1$ the representations,

$$l_m = c_{r-1}(q_m \cdot p_{r-1} + c_{r-2})(q_m \cdot p_{r-2} + c_{r-3}) \cdots (q_m \cdot p_1 + c_0)(q_m \cdot p_1) \cdot \underbrace{00 \ldots 0}_{m \text{ times}}$$

where c_j denotes the "carry-forward" that might have resulted from the previous computation, e.g. where $p_0 = 8$ and $q_m = 6$ then $c_0 = 4$ arising from the calculation $q_m \cdot p_0 = 48$. The actual representation of the result is then obtained through the calculation

$$l_0 + l_1 + \cdots + l_{m-2} + l_{m-1}$$

---

[26]*pace* the comments of fn. 30 from Chapter 2.

For example if $p = 62$ and $q = 81$ then

$$
\begin{aligned}
l_0 &= 062 \\
l_1 &= 4960
\end{aligned}
$$

In which:

$q_0 \cdot p_0 = 1 \cdot 2 = 2$; $c_0 = 0$; $q_0 \cdot p_1 + c_0 = 1 \cdot 6 + 0 = 6$; $c_1 = 0$.

For l_1

$q_1 \cdot p_0 = 8 \cdot 2 = 16$ giving $c_0 = 1$; $q_1 \cdot p_1 + c_0 = 8 \cdot 6 + 1 = 49$ so that $c_1 = 4$ and $l_1 = 4960$.

Adding l_1 and l_2 yields the answer 5022, i.e. $62 \cdot 81$.

Even without the opacity created through our minimalist abstract description above this seems rather a tedious and laborious exercise. It is also a rather time-consuming one. Inspecting the number of basic arithmetic operations involved, the process of constructing the representation of $p \cdot q$, p and q being two n-digit numbers, is dominated by the $n \cdot n = n^2$ individual multiplications of single digits by single digits in forming each l_k i.e. overall each p_i in p is multiplied at some stage by each q_j in q.

It may appear that this method taking around n^2 steps to compute the product of two n-digit numbers is really a "don't-care". The function n^2, certainly in formal analysis of algorithm performance, exhibits what is called "polynomial growth" and the qualifying exponent (2) is fairly small. In any event, given that for the purposes of program implementation the multiplication of the contents of two memory locations will be done as part of the basic machine hardware allowing values of potentially $2^{32} - 1$ (roughly 4.3 (U.S.) billion) to be processed.[27] In typical small-scale applications 4.3×10^9 looks more than sufficient. The problem, however, is not "typical small-scale applications": it is very atypical and very large-scale studies. It is often the case that in processing data arising even in modest size scientific experiments, e.g. as might be conducted in Chemistry, Particle Physics, Genetics, etc. one is faced with computations involving manipulation of values requiring several thousands of bits. Another arena were extremely large numerical quantities are commonplace is that of Cryptography: both encryption and (legitimate) decryption require processes in which the larger the numerical quantities supporting these are the more secure, in principle, the system is.

---

[27]This estimate is based on 64-bit architectures so that the product of two 32-bit values will always be accommodatable in 64 bits.

There are three features that arise in such settings. It is rarely feasible to implement special purpose hardware methods: if a scientific study is conducted only once the cost of developing a special-purpose processor dedicated to say 5000 bit arithmetic is somewhat extravagant. Secondly, even if such costs are "reasonable" this does not eliminate considerations of design efficiency. There are widely studied methods of translating "efficient algorithmic solutions" to "efficient hardware realizations". We refer the reader to [67] for a more detailed discussion of these. Overall such translations motivate searching for better i.e. faster techniques.

Finally, although n^2 in terms of software operations is moderate if $n \sim 64$, it is far from being so when $n \sim 4096$: the former leads to a few thousand operations; the latter to over sixteen million. If it is possible to replace the n^2 technique with, for instance one attaining $n^{1.5}$ then the number drops from sixteen million to around a quarter of a million (in the 64 bit case the reduction is to around five hundred). If we are able to go further and achieve $n^{1.25}$ then the consequent demands are of the order of tens of thousands ($\sim 33,000$) as opposed to tens of millions.

If we look at the description of "classical school multiplication" just presented we see that even though only single digit operations are involved its main bottleneck is the total number of multiplications used. Of course we might try and do something a little more clever. Perhaps we could see where the classical Computer Science paradigm "divide-and-conquer" leads in offering a recursive approach. Following this route we might write assuming we have an even number of digits, i.e. $r = 2n$

$$X \;=\; (x_{2n-1}\cdots x_{(n+1)}x_n) \cdot 10^n \;+\; (x_{n-1}x_{n-2}\cdots x_1 x_0) \;=\; A \cdot 10^n + B$$

and similarly for Y

$$Y \;=\; (y_{2n-1}\cdots y_{(n+1)}y_n) \cdot 10^n \;+\; (y_{n-1}y_{n-2}\cdots y_1 y_0) \;=\; C \cdot 10^n + D$$

So that the result of multiplying two $2n$-digit numbers X and Y is described in terms of multiplications involving four n-digit numbers: A, B, C, and D. That is via,

$$X{\cdot}Y = (A{\cdot}10^n + B){\cdot}(C{\cdot}10^n + D) = (A{\cdot}C){\cdot}10^{2n} + (A{\cdot}D + B{\cdot}C){\cdot}10^n + (B{\cdot}D)$$

So, as no doubt the reader will recall from treatments of analyzing divide-and-conquer methods,[28] we see that the product of two $2n$-digit numbers is

---

[28] Another topic that is, often found on Discrete Methods courses in CS.

expressed in terms of four products of two n-digit numbers (AC, AD, BC and BD): and this whole process still requires about n^2 operations.

We can do better. One of the landmark and surprising achievements going back to the early "formal" study of algorithms dates from 1962: the algorithm discovered by Anatoly Karatsuba and presented in [137].

Karatsuba's discovery was that we do not need to use four "high-level" multiplications to compute $\{AC, AD, BC, BD\}$: we can do this with three and a few extra single digit additions, but not so many as will influence the overall cost adversely.

How do we do this? The method is illustrated in Figure 5.3.

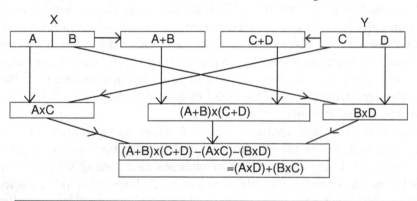

Figure 5.3: The Karatsuba Multiplication Algorithm

Looking at the structure of Karatsuba's algorithm we no longer need four high-level multiplications, that is involving n-digit numbers: we can obtain these using only three. Namely

$$A \cdot C$$
$$B \cdot D$$
$$(A + B) \cdot (C + D) - A \cdot C - B \cdot D \;=\; A \cdot D + B \cdot C$$

The "middle pair" ($\{AD, BC\}$) are obtained simultaneously by subtracting the "outer pairs" ($\{AC, BD\}$) (which do require computing) from the seemingly redundant computation of $(A + B) \cdot (C + D)$. At the cost of four extra high-level additions ($\{A + B, C + D, -AC, -BD\}$) we save one multiplication: but this equates to saving one recursive call so that overall Karatsuba's algorithm multiplies two n-digit numbers taking about $n^{\log_2 3} \sim n^{1.59}$ steps.

Why stop at splitting the input $2n$-digits forms into four n-digit values? If we split each $3n$-digit number into **three** parts say $\{A, B, E\}$ and $\{C, D, F\}$ in principle **nine** high-level multiplication of two n-digit values would be needed from relevant expansion of

$$(A \cdot 10^{2n} + B \cdot 10^n + E) \cdot (C \cdot 10^{2n} + D \cdot 10^n + F)$$

but if these nine could by similar legerdemain be achieved by some mixture of **five** high-level multiplications (and some extra additions and subtractions) then the resulting method would achieve $n^{\log_3 5} \sim n^{1.46}$ steps and do even better. Or if we could reduce the sixteen "obvious" high-level multiplications when splitting into four down to **seven** then our algorithm would do still better: $n^{\log_4 7} \sim n^{1.404}$.

One could play this game endlessly trying to find clever ways to perform the k^2 high-level multiplications arising by splitting a $k \cdot n$-digit number into k separate n-digit parts using T contortions of these parts with T such that $\log_k T < \log_{k-1} S$. Here S is the "best" result that had been attained for division into $k - 1$ sections.

There are three drawbacks to this endless play scenario: as we increase the number of sections involved the search for the cleverest combination of these, the combination that leads to fewest high-level multiplications, becomes increasingly onerous; the extra manipulations needed in the way of additions and subtractions while not affecting α in the n^α run-time begin to affect the overall run-time in the sense that these give $K n^\alpha$ **but** K becomes notably large but constant relative to n. Finally the actual gains made become increasingly minuscule: it is one thing to gain an improvement of 1.59 over 2 and with only a tolerably small overhead, it is quite another to gain an improvement of, say, 1.200000001 over 1.200000002 and with significantly more effort required in the reconstruction of results.

These are **not** needed and the recognition that such efforts are unnecessary brings us back to the topic and focus of this subsection: the discrete Fourier Transform.

The intricate and "needle-in-a-haystack" contortions involved in finding how to perform an "obvious" k^2 high-level multiplications using a number, T say, that is sufficiently small to give an asymptotic performance gain, come about because typically $k \in \mathbb{N}$, i.e k is a **constant** value independent of the number of positions used to represent the values being multiplied.

The way through this morass of hunting for increasingly ornate ways of "doing k^2 by T" was discovered by Arnold Schönhage and Volker Strassen and appeared in 1971 [207]: almost a decade after Karatsuba's pioneering insight. The Schönhage-Strassen algorithm for multiplying n-digit numbers still proceeds by taking each input and splitting it into subsections but now the **number** of such parts is no longer a constant, it depends on n. In addition reassembling the result makes extensive use of the discrete Fourer Transform and the associated Convolution property.

To see how this approach works, let us start with two n-bit values, X and Y as before, writing

$$\begin{aligned} X &= x_{n-1}x_{n-2}\cdots x_1 x_0 \\ Y &= y_{n-1}y_{n-2}\cdots y_1 y_0 \end{aligned}$$

Suppose that in a similar style to what we have seen already $n = rm$ and we divide each of these into m "r bit chunks", which we denote A_i (for X) and B_j (for Y)

$$\begin{aligned} X &= A_{m-1}\cdot A_{m-2}\cdots A_1 \cdot A_0 \\ Y &= B_{m-1}\cdot B_{m-2}\cdots B_1 \cdot B_0 \end{aligned}$$

Each chunk describes some value in $\mathbb{W}$ which can be written in binary using r bits. Furthermore we can recover the number represented by X through the computation,

$$X = \sum_{k=0}^{m-1}(A_k)\cdot 2^k \; ; \; Y = \sum_{k=0}^{m-1}(B_k)\cdot 2^k$$

Notice that the values $a_k \in \mathbb{W}$ and $b_k \in \mathbb{W}$ corresponding to A_k and B_k can be thought of as **coefficients** in a **polynomial** having degree $m-1$. That is

$$p_{m-1}(x) = \sum_{k=0}^{m-1}a_k x^k \; ; \; q_{m-1}(x) = \sum_{k=0}^{m-1}b_k x^k$$

so that $X = p_{m-1}(2)$ and $Y = q_{m-1}(2)$ and, most importantly,

$$X \cdot Y = p_{m-1}(2)\cdot q_{m-1}(2) = (p_{m-1}\cdot q_{m-1})(2)$$

If we compute the product of the two **polynomials**, p_{m-1} and q_{m-1}, and evaluate the resulting polynomial when $x = 2$ then we have found the result of multiplying X and Y.

We know how to multiply two polynomials. In fact, if we make some minor changes to these polynomials to consider both as "degenerate" polynomials having degree $2(m-1)$, i.e. consider the set of coefficients of $p(x)$ to be

$$\mathbf{a} = \underbrace{< 0, 0, \ldots, 0}_{m-1 \text{ times}}, a_{m-1}, a_{m-2}, \ldots, a_1, a_0 >$$

and those of q to be,

$$\mathbf{b} = < \underbrace{0, 0, \ldots, 0}_{m-1 \text{ times}}, b_{m-1}, b_{m-2}, \ldots, b_1, b_0 >$$

then the coefficients that we require are,

$$\mathbf{c} = < c_{2(m-1)}, c_{2(m-1)-1}, \ldots, c_2, c_1, c_0 >$$

and

$$\mathbf{c} = \mathbf{a} \otimes \mathbf{b} = \mathcal{F}^{-1}(\mathcal{F}(\mathbf{a}) \diamond \mathcal{F}(\mathbf{b}))$$

In summary, having chosen r

SS1. Split the n-bits describing X and Y into m parts, each containing r bits. Call these A_k (for X) and B_k (for Y) where $0 \leq k \leq m-1$.

SS2. Form the $2(m-1)$ coefficient vectors, in which a_i (resp. b_i) are the values (in $\mathbb{W}$) whose binary representation is A_i (resp. B_i).

$$\mathbf{a} = < \underbrace{0, 0, \ldots, 0}_{m-1 \text{ times}}, a_{m-1}, a_{m-2}, \ldots, a_1, a_0 >$$

and those of q to be,

$$\mathbf{b} = < \underbrace{0, 0, \ldots, 0}_{m-1 \text{ times}}, b_{m-1}, b_{m-2}, \ldots, b_1, b_0 >$$

SS3. Compute the convolution, $\mathbf{a} \otimes \mathbf{b}$ by taking the discrete Fourier transform of each, **recursively** performing pairwise multiplication of components (that occur in applying the operation $\diamond$) in $\mathcal{F}(\mathbf{a})$ with $\mathcal{F}(\mathbf{b})$.

SS4. Obtain the outcome $(X \cdot Y)$ by applying the inverse discrete Fourier transform, $\mathcal{F}^{-1}$ to $\mathcal{F}(\mathbf{a}) \diamond \mathcal{F}(\mathbf{b})$.

There are a couple of minor details, one of which is: what are the "best" values of r and m to use? The analysis offered in [207] shows that choosing r and m to be roughly equal yields the best outcome. In other words given n-bit integers fixing $r \sim m \sim \sqrt{n}$ and combined with an efficient realization of both DFT and its inverse, results in the number of operations required to compute the product of two n-bit numbers being of the order of $n \log_2 n \log_2 \log_2 n$. If we examine what the effect is with $n = 4096$, the case which needed ca. sixteen million steps with n^2 techniques, the result is a computation taking of the order of $200,000$ operations.

There is, of course, another qualification in the description above: our condition "combined with an efficient realization of both DFT and its inverse". We discuss this in the next subsection, however, to conclude this overview it is worth returning to one point we hinted at earlier in the matter of terminology. The DFT and its inverse use the behaviour of what we have called "Primitive roots of Unity": the α and the ω of the notational description. There is, therefore, one obvious issue: integer multiplication is a process of taking a pair $(X, Y$ in the presentation) of Whole numbers and computing a Whole number as result. These primitive roots of unity are, however, elements in $\mathbb{C}$. Now although we could in theory compute transform and inverse via a suitable handling of pairs of Real numbers, i.e. with $\omega = \gamma + \iota\delta$ for suitable (γ, δ) it would seem likely that such techniques would inevitably lead to creeping numerical errors in the outcome. This is not so much an issue in applications such as the image compression methods of the previous subsection, but is extremely undesirable as a side-effect of **integer** multiplication. There is, however, a means of avoiding such complications: by working with *principal roots* of unity and modular arithmetic.

Recall from fn. 22 earlier a **principal n'th root of unity** in $(\mathbb{Z}_m, +, \cdot)$, is a value which we will continue to denote by ω for which $\omega^n = 1$ and for every $r < n$, $\sum_{j=0}^{n-1} \omega^{rj} = 0$. It is important to remember that arithmetic operations in this setting are performed modulo m. A well-known result from the analysis of algebraic structures shows the following which is of considerable use in "bit-level" implementations of DFT.

If $n = 2^m$ ($m \in \mathbb{N}$) and $(\omega)^{n/2} = t - 1$ with respect to arithmetic in $(\mathbb{Z}_t, +, \cdot)$ then ω is a principal n'th root of unity.

For example, using $n = 8$, $\omega^4 = -1$ (i.e. $t - 1$ in $\mathbb{Z}_t$) for $\omega = 2$ and $t = 17$: $2^4 = 16$, $2^8 = 256 = 1$ modulo 17: $256 = 15 \cdot 17 + 1$. Carrying out computation of DFT and its inverse working with principal roots of unity e.g. recasting the expressions given for ω and performing arithmetic in $(\mathbb{Z}_m, +, \cdot)$ preserves all of the relationships and properties in particular the Convolution property. In implementations of Schönhage-Strassen's method the approach using modular arithmetic and suitable principal n'th roots is used.

All we need now is an efficient method of computing the DFT.

The Cooley-Tukey Fast DFT Algorithm

The Cooley-Tukey algorithm for fast computation of the DFT appeared in [50]. This is a recursive method, allowing $\mathcal{F}(\mathbf{x})$ for $\mathbf{x} \in \mathbb{C}^n$ to be evaluated in of the order of $n \log_2 n$ operations: an operation being a "Complex multiplication followed by a Complex addition" ([50, p. 297]). This performance efficiency is mirrored when the basis for defining the DFT is $(\mathbb{Z}_m, +, \cdot)$ and a principal root of unity, ω as discussed in the previous section with respect to implementations of the Schönhage-Strassen algorithm.

The key idea is exploit symmetries arising from the property that $\omega^n = 1$ whether working in $(\mathbb{Z}_m, +, \cdot)$ or $\mathbb{C}$ so allowing explicit matrix multiplication that is through $\mathcal{F}(\mathbf{x}) = \mathbf{M}_{\mathcal{F}}\mathbf{x}^\top$ to be avoided. We shall refer to ω as a primitive rather than principal root, noting however, that all of the development used when viewing $\omega \in \mathbb{C}$ applies equally when viewing $\omega \in \mathbb{Z}_m$.

In order to track the thinking underpinning the algorithm, consider $\mathbf{M}_{\mathcal{F}}$ when $n = 8$.

$$
\mathbf{M}_{\mathcal{F}} = \begin{pmatrix}
\omega^0 & \omega^0 & \omega^0 & \omega^0 & \omega^0 & \omega^0 & \omega^0 & \omega^0 \\
\omega^0 & \omega^1 & \omega^2 & \omega^3 & \omega^4 & \omega^5 & \omega^6 & \omega^7 \\
\omega^0 & \omega^2 & \omega^4 & \omega^6 & \omega^8 & \omega^{10} & \omega^{12} & \omega^{14} \\
\omega^0 & \omega^3 & \omega^6 & \omega^9 & \omega^{12} & \omega^{15} & \omega^{18} & \omega^{21} \\
\omega^0 & \omega^4 & \omega^8 & \omega^{12} & \omega^{16} & \omega^{20} & \omega^{24} & \omega^{28} \\
\omega^0 & \omega^5 & \omega^{10} & \omega^{15} & \omega^{20} & \omega^{25} & \omega^{30} & \omega^{35} \\
\omega^0 & \omega^6 & \omega^{12} & \omega^{18} & \omega^{24} & \omega^{30} & \omega^{36} & \omega^{42} \\
\omega^0 & \omega^7 & \omega^{14} & \omega^{21} & \omega^{28} & \omega^{35} & \omega^{42} & \omega^{49}
\end{pmatrix}
$$

Recall that the value in the i'th row and j'th column is ω^{ij} and that we index rows and columns $0 \leq i < n, 0 \leq j < n$.

Now there are a couple of "obvious" points we can note about this matrix. Firstly since ω is a primitive (eighth) root of unity ω^t is exactly the same as $\omega^{t \mod 8}$, e.g. $\omega^{17} = \omega \cdot (\omega^8)^2 = \omega; \omega^{24} = (\omega^8)^3 = \omega^0$.

Suppose we go through the matrix just given and apply all of these simplifications. The result is,

$$
\begin{pmatrix}
\omega^0 & \omega^0 & \omega^0 & \omega^0 & \omega^0 & \omega^0 & \omega^0 & \omega^0 \\
\omega^0 & \omega^1 & \omega^2 & \omega^3 & \omega^4 & \omega^5 & \omega^6 & \omega^7 \\
\omega^0 & \omega^2 & \omega^4 & \omega^6 & \omega^0 & \omega^2 & \omega^4 & \omega^6 \\
\omega^0 & \omega^3 & \omega^6 & \omega^1 & \omega^4 & \omega^7 & \omega^2 & \omega^5 \\
\omega^0 & \omega^4 & \omega^0 & \omega^4 & \omega^0 & \omega^4 & \omega^0 & \omega^4 \\
\omega^0 & \omega^5 & \omega^2 & \omega^7 & \omega^4 & \omega^1 & \omega^6 & \omega^3 \\
\omega^0 & \omega^6 & \omega^4 & \omega^2 & \omega^0 & \omega^6 & \omega^4 & \omega^2 \\
\omega^0 & \omega^7 & \omega^6 & \omega^5 & \omega^4 & \omega^3 & \omega^2 & \omega^1
\end{pmatrix}
$$

Now, instead of ω^{2k} ($0 \leq k < n/2$) let us write α^k and, instead of ω^{2k+1} write $\omega\alpha^k$, where $\alpha = \omega^2$. This, apparently trivial alteration produces

$$
\begin{pmatrix}
0 & \alpha^0 & \alpha^0 & \alpha^0 & \alpha^0 & \alpha^0 & \alpha^0 & \alpha^0 & \alpha^0 \\
1 & \alpha^0 & \omega\alpha^0 & \alpha^1 & \omega\alpha^1 & \alpha^2 & \omega\alpha^2 & \alpha^3 & \omega\alpha^3 \\
2 & \alpha^0 & \alpha^1 & \alpha^2 & \alpha^3 & \alpha^0 & \alpha^1 & \alpha^2 & \alpha^3 \\
3 & \alpha^0 & \omega\alpha^1 & \alpha^3 & \omega\alpha^0 & \alpha^2 & \omega\alpha^3 & \alpha^1 & \omega\alpha^2 \\
4 & \alpha^0 & \alpha^2 & \alpha^0 & \alpha^2 & \alpha^0 & \alpha^2 & \alpha^0 & \alpha^2 \\
5 & \alpha^0 & \omega\alpha^2 & \alpha^1 & \omega\alpha^3 & \alpha^2 & \omega\alpha^0 & \alpha^3 & \omega\alpha^1 \\
6 & \alpha^0 & \alpha^3 & \alpha^2 & \alpha^0 & \alpha^0 & \alpha^3 & \alpha^2 & \alpha^1 \\
7 & \alpha^0 & \omega\alpha^3 & \alpha^3 & \omega\alpha^2 & \alpha^2 & \omega\alpha^1 & \alpha^1 & \omega\alpha^0 \\
\hline
 & 0 & 1 & 2 & 3 & 4 & 5 & 6 & 7
\end{pmatrix}
$$

Now this matrix could be viewed as four 4×4 matrices:

Matrix Notation	Rows	Columns
$\mathbf{M}_{first,even}$	$\{0,1,2,3\}$	$\{0,2,4,6\}$
$\mathbf{M}_{first,odd}$	$\{0,1,2,3\}$	$\{1,3,5,7\}$
$\mathbf{M}_{second,even}$	$\{4,5,6,7\}$	$\{0,2,4,6\}$
$\mathbf{M}_{second,odd}$	$\{4,5,6,7\}$	$\{1,3,5,7\}$

And, now we see the reasoning behind these rewrites. What is the matrix $\mathbf{M}_{first,even}$?

$$
\mathbf{M}_{first,even} =
\begin{pmatrix}
0 & \alpha^0 & \alpha^0 & \alpha^0 & \alpha^0 \\
1 & \alpha^0 & \alpha^1 & \alpha^2 & \alpha^3 \\
2 & \alpha^0 & \alpha^2 & \alpha^0 & \alpha^2 \\
3 & \alpha^0 & \alpha^3 & \alpha^2 & \alpha^1 \\
\hline
 & 0 & 2 & 4 & 6
\end{pmatrix}
$$

and the matrices, $\mathbf{M}_{first,odd}$, $\mathbf{M}_{second,even}$ and $\mathbf{M}_{second,odd}$?

$$
\mathbf{M}_{first,odd} =
\begin{pmatrix}
0 & \alpha^0 & \alpha^0 & \alpha^0 & \alpha^0 \\
1 & \omega\alpha^0 & \omega\alpha^1 & \omega\alpha^2 & \omega\alpha^3 \\
2 & \alpha^1 & \alpha^3 & \alpha^1 & \alpha^3 \\
3 & \omega\alpha^1 & \omega\alpha^0 & \omega\alpha^3 & \omega\alpha^2 \\
\hline
 & 1 & 3 & 5 & 7
\end{pmatrix}
$$

$$
\mathbf{M}_{second,even} =
\begin{pmatrix}
4 & \alpha^0 & \alpha^0 & \alpha^0 & \alpha^0 \\
5 & \alpha^0 & \alpha^1 & \alpha^2 & \alpha^3 \\
6 & \alpha^0 & \alpha^2 & \alpha^0 & \alpha^2 \\
7 & \alpha^0 & \alpha^3 & \alpha^2 & \alpha^1 \\
\hline
 & 0 & 2 & 4 & 6
\end{pmatrix}
$$

$$
\mathbf{M}_{second,odd} = \begin{pmatrix}
4 & \alpha^2 & \alpha^2 & \alpha^2 & \alpha^2 \\
5 & \omega\alpha^2 & \omega\alpha^3 & \omega\alpha^0 & \omega\alpha^1 \\
6 & \alpha^3 & \alpha^0 & \alpha^0 & \alpha^1 \\
7 & \omega\alpha^3 & \omega\alpha^2 & \omega\alpha^1 & \omega\alpha^0 \\
\hline
 & 1 & 3 & 5 & 7
\end{pmatrix}
$$

The first observation is that $\mathbf{M}_{first,even}$ and $\mathbf{M}_{second,even}$ are identical. We can, however, go further: ω we recall, was a primitive eightth root of unity, and hence ω^2 is a primitive **fourth** root of unity. We have, however, in the matrix we will now denote $\mathbf{M}_{e,\alpha,4}$ written $\alpha = \omega^2$ and made the required substitutions. That matrix $\mathbf{M}_{\mathcal{F}}^{\beta}$ corresponding to the four element DFT using a primitive fourth root of unity, β, is

$$
\mathbf{M}_{\mathcal{F}}^{\beta} = \begin{pmatrix}
\beta^0 & \beta^0 & \beta^0 & \beta^0 \\
\beta^0 & \beta^1 & \beta^2 & \beta^3 \\
\beta^0 & \beta^2 & \beta^4 & \beta^6 \\
\beta^0 & \beta^3 & \beta^6 & \beta^9
\end{pmatrix} = \begin{pmatrix}
\beta^0 & \beta^0 & \beta^0 & \beta^0 \\
\beta^0 & \beta^1 & \beta^2 & \beta^3 \\
\beta^0 & \beta^2 & \beta^0 & \beta^2 \\
\beta^0 & \beta^3 & \beta^2 & \beta^1
\end{pmatrix}
$$

after making the simplifications arising from $\beta^4 = 1$. This matrix is exactly the same that would result were we to use α as our primitive fourth root of unity: $\alpha = \omega^2$, **is** a primitive fourth root of unity, from which it follows that

$$
\begin{aligned}
\mathbf{M}_{e,\alpha,4} < x_0, x_2, x_4, x_6 >^{\top} &= \mathcal{F}_4(< x_0, x_2, x_4, x_6 >) \\
\mathbf{M}_{e,\alpha,4} < x_1, x_3, x_5, x_7 >^{\top} &= \mathcal{F}_4(< x_1, x_3, x_5, x_7 >)
\end{aligned}
$$

What, however about $\mathbf{M}_{first,odd}$ and $\mathbf{M}_{second,odd}$? We can see that $\mathbf{M}_{first,odd}$ and $\mathbf{M}_{second,odd}$ differ.

$$
\mathbf{M}_{first,odd} = \begin{pmatrix}
0 & \alpha^0 & \alpha^0 & \alpha^0 & \alpha^0 \\
1 & \omega\alpha^0 & \omega\alpha^1 & \omega\alpha^2 & \omega\alpha^3 \\
2 & \alpha^1 & \alpha^2 & \alpha^1 & \alpha^3 \\
3 & \omega\alpha^1 & \omega\alpha^0 & \omega\alpha^3 & \omega\alpha^2 \\
\hline
 & 1 & 3 & 5 & 7
\end{pmatrix}
$$

$$
\mathbf{M}_{second,odd} = \begin{pmatrix}
4 & \alpha^2 & \alpha^2 & \alpha^2 & \alpha^2 \\
5 & \omega\alpha^2 & \omega\alpha^3 & \omega\alpha^0 & \omega\alpha^1 \\
6 & \alpha^3 & \alpha^0 & \alpha^0 & \alpha^1 \\
7 & \omega\alpha^3 & \omega\alpha^2 & \omega\alpha^1 & \omega\alpha^0 \\
\hline
 & 1 & 3 & 5 & 7
\end{pmatrix}
$$

We know, however, that

$$
\alpha^2 = \omega^4 = e^{4\frac{2\pi i}{8}} = e^{\pi i} = -1
$$

So exploiting this relationship in $\mathbf{M}_{second,odd}$ gives

$$\mathbf{M}_{second,odd} = (-1)\cdot \begin{pmatrix} \alpha^0 & \alpha^0 & \alpha^0 & \alpha^0 \\ \omega\alpha^0 & \omega\alpha^1 & \omega\alpha^0 & \omega\alpha^3 \\ \alpha^1 & \alpha^0 & \alpha^0 & \alpha^1 \\ \omega\alpha^1 & \omega\alpha^0 & \omega\alpha^1 & \omega\alpha^0 \end{pmatrix}$$

and hence $\mathbf{M}_{first,odd} = -\mathbf{M}_{second,odd}$. In summary, if we re-ordered the columns of our eight component DFT matrix we would have

$$\mathbf{R} = \left(\begin{array}{c|cc} \mathbf{0\text{--}3} & \mathbf{M}_{e,4,\alpha} & \mathbf{M}_{odd} \\ \mathbf{4\text{--}7} & \mathbf{M}_{e,4,\alpha} & -\mathbf{M}_{odd} \\ \hline & [0,2,4,6] & [1,3,5,7] \end{array} \right)$$

Now using $\mathbf{M}_{\mathcal{F},2^n,\omega}$ to denote the DFT matrix for the 2^n component transform with respect to a primitive root of unity, ω, that is with which $\omega^{2^n} = 1$, we have just seen that

$$\mathbf{M}_{\mathcal{F},8,\omega}\mathbf{x}^\top = \begin{pmatrix} \mathbf{M}_{\mathcal{F},4,\omega^2} & \mathbf{M}_{\mathcal{F},4,\omega^2}^{\omega-adjust} \\ \mathbf{M}_{\mathcal{F},4,\omega^2} & -\mathbf{M}_{\mathcal{F},4,\omega^2}^{\omega-adjust} \end{pmatrix} \begin{pmatrix} x_0 \\ x_2 \\ x_4 \\ x_6 \\ x_1 \\ x_3 \\ x_5 \\ x_7 \end{pmatrix}$$

where $\mathbf{M}_{\mathcal{F},4,\omega^2}^{\omega-adjust}$ is the matrix $\mathbf{M}_{\mathcal{F},4,\omega^2}$ in which the entries in odd numbered rows are multiplied by ω. In general, we have

$$\mathbf{M}_{\mathcal{F},2^n,\omega}\mathbf{x}^\top = \begin{pmatrix} \mathbf{M}_{\mathcal{F},2^{n-1},\omega^2} & \mathbf{M}_{\mathcal{F},2^{n-1},\omega^2}^{\omega-adjust} \\ \mathbf{M}_{\mathcal{F},2^{n-1},\omega^2} & -\mathbf{M}_{\mathcal{F},2^{n-1},\omega^2}^{\omega-adjust} \end{pmatrix} \begin{pmatrix} x_0 \\ \vdots \\ x_{2i} \\ \vdots \\ x_{2^n-2} \\ x_1 \\ \vdots \\ x_{2i-1} \\ \vdots \\ x_{2^n-1} \end{pmatrix}$$

Algorithm 5.1. The fast DFT Method: DFT($\mathbf{x}, n, \omega$)

1: **Input:** $\mathbf{x} = < x_0, x_1, \ldots, x_{n-1} >$; ω;
2: **requires:** $n = 2^m$ ($m \in \mathbb{W}$); ω a primitive n'th root of unity.
3: **Output:** $\mathcal{F}_n^\omega(\mathbf{x})$
4: **if** $n = 1$ **then**
5:    **return** x_0;
6: **end if**
7: $\mathbf{a} := \; < x_0, x_2, \ldots, x_{2i}, \ldots, x_{n-2} >$; {$\mathbf{a}$ holds even indices of $\mathbf{x}$}
8: $\mathbf{b} := \; < x_1, x_3, \ldots, x_{2i+1}, \ldots, x_{n-1}$; {$\mathbf{b}$ holds the odd indices of $\mathbf{x}$}
9: $\mathbf{a} := \; \text{DFT}(\mathbf{a}, n/2, \omega^2)$;
10: $\mathbf{b} := \; \text{DFT}(\mathbf{b}, n/2, \omega^2)$;
11: $\alpha := 1; k := 0$;
12: **while** $k < n/2$ **do**
13:    $y_k := a_k + \alpha \cdot b_k$;
14:    $y_{n/2+k} := a_k - \alpha \cdot b_k$;
15:    $\alpha := \alpha \cdot \omega$;
16:    $k := k + 1$;
17: **end while**
18: **return** $\mathbf{y}$

We quickly review the computation of $\mathcal{F}^{-1}$. Noting our earlier connection between the form of the inverse matrix $\mathbf{M}_{\mathcal{F}^{-1}}$ and the transform matrix itself, the computation of $\mathcal{F}^{-1}$ turns out to be relatively straightforward. Recalling that Algorithm 5.1 specifies n, $\mathbf{x}$ and ω as parameters the inverse is obtained via Algorithm 5.2.

Algorithm 5.2. Fast inverse DFT method: IDFT($\mathbf{y}, n, \omega$)

1: **Input:** $\mathbf{y} = < y_0, y_1, \ldots, y_{n-1} >$; ω;
2: **requires:** $n = 2^m$ ($m \in \mathbb{W}$); ω a primitive n'th root of unity.
3: **Output:** $\mathcal{F}_n^{-1}(\mathbf{y})$
4: $\mathbf{x} = \text{DFT}(\mathbf{y}, n, \omega^{n-1})$;
5: $k := 0$;
6: **while** $k < n$ **do**
7:    $x_k := (\omega^n/n) \cdot x_k$;
8:    $k := k + 1$;
9: **end while**
10: **return** $\mathbf{x}$

As one final use of DFT in CS, the potential for exploiting its properties in the area of algorithmic composition has been explored by Amiot [10, 11]. This specialist field of AI is where we find another use of Complex number properties: these are considered in the next subsection.

Music through chaos

It is tempting to dismiss the use of AI in particular and, indeed, computational technology in general within creative enterprises, as a somewhat lazy and undemanding aesthetic approach. If mindless jingles or ephemeral doggerel can be produced by recourse to judiciously chosen initial settings and the click of a mouse or press of the return key, then wherein lies any artistic challenge? But, of course, the serious user of such methods looks to produce neither jingle nor doggerel.[29]

There is a long history of creative artists using "non-obviously artistic" means to guide creative processes. As far back as the 18th Century, Mozart defined an aleatory compositional approach (The Musical Dice Game) whereby coherent precomposed snippets of music could be stitched together to create a satisfying whole despite its individual components being selected at random. In the 20th Century extramusical devices are seen in a variety of works. Ottorino Respighi in the *I pini del Gianicolo* movement of *Pini di Roma* (1924) imbeds a gramophone record of birdsong to colour the atmosphere of the piece itself. The Brazilian composer, Heitor Villa-Lobos builds his short piano study *New York Skyline* (W407 from 1939) around the architectural profile of the eponymous city and by graphing this physical outline onto a musical score determines pitch values. The U.S. composer John Cage in the 5 movement *Imaginary Landscapes* created between 1939 and 1952 engages artefacts ranging from turntables (Nos. 1 and 3), through to magnetic tape recordings (No. 5) and radio sets (No. 4, "scored" for 24 performers using 12 radios). The use of electronic tape is a frequent device in works of Edgar Varese (*Déserts* written between 1950 and 1954, *Poème électronique* from 1957–8). Shortwave radio receivers feature again in Stockhausen's *Spiral* and *Kurzwellen* both from 1968. The use of mechanical and/or aleatory elements (dice, radio sets etc.) has been an established process dating back over 200 years. Even outside the arena of musical creativity one finds randomized elements arising. The major works of the abstract expressionist painter Jackson Pollock between 1947 and

---

[29]Although, from some subjective viewpoints, this *might* be the outcome, my point is that such is not the *intention*.

1950 are, in essence "randomly created".[30] The *Anthropometry* of the French artist Yves Klein involved naked models daubed and drenched in paint[31] being dragged and dragging themselves around blank canvases with, again, unpredictable results. Finally randomly guided creative efforts are a central technique in Surrealist writing, e.g. the *decoupé* method in which a text is cut up and randomly put together again in order to build the final work.

Against this rich and varied background it is, therefore, unsurprising that several composers have sought to explore the possibilities that computational techniques bring to creative works: Ligeti, Boulez, Xenakis, Berio and many others. It is here that a very specialized application of Complex Number Theory arises: as a constructive technique for *fractal* sets.

Fractals, Computer Art and $\mathbb{C}$

The concept of *fractal dimension* originates from the work of Mandelbrot [161]. We focus on the principal qualities of interest.

The idea of "*dimension*" is familiar within everyday objects: points have "dimension 0", lines "dimension 1", (plane) surfaces "dimension 2", volumes "dimension 3". Outside specialized areas of Physics it is not usually the case that dimensionality above 3 arises in practice. In the cases just described there is one common feature; the normal concept of dimension is as a *Whole number*, however, fractal dimensions arise when this Whole number convention is insufficient. For objects which are interpreted as having *fractional* dimensions. With conventional notions of dimension there is a relation between dimension and *scaling*. So, suppose for example, we have a line which is 1 metre in length. If we have a 1 metre measuring stick we need apply this exactly once to determine the line's length. If our measuring stick is only half a metre long then it must be applied twice. In general, every time the *length* of the measuring rule is reduced to a half of what it was previously it must be applied twice as often.[32] Typically if we examine how the number of applications (N) changes as the available length is scaled by some factor, ε say, for a line this is $N = 1/\varepsilon = \varepsilon^{-1}$. We find a similar pattern going from lines to, e.g. squares and cubes. A square of side length 4 metres can be regarded as formed by

---

[30]Although it would, perhaps, be more accurate to describe these as produced independently of conscious control and direction.

[31]An important aspect of Klein's "Painting Ritual" being the use of his patent shade IKB (International Klein Blue).

[32]There is nothing significant or special about our use of 2 and reduction by $1/2$: a similar pattern would be observed by continually reducing the length of measuring stick to $1/k$ for Natural numbers $k > 1$.

16 squares of side length 1 metre. These in turn comprise 16 squares of side length 0.25 metres so that the initial 4×4 square contains $256 = 16^2$ squares of side length 0.25. Just as with the line example we have a relationship between N the total number of squares contained within the initial object and ε the scaling factor: for a square $N = 1/\varepsilon^2 = \varepsilon^{-2}$. Again, were we measuring "the number of cubes in a given cube" (N) using progressively smaller cubes i.e. scaling down by a factor ε on successive measurements we would find $N = \varepsilon^{-3}$. In general, for an object in D dimensions the "number of applications" (N) required to "measure" the object using a device of size K then εK, $\varepsilon^2 K$ etc increases according to $N \propto \varepsilon^{-D}$: that is, N is proportional to some power of the "scaling measure" ε.

The idea of "measurement by counting the number of objects of given form within a larger object" raises one of the key properties linking "fractal dimension" and aesthetic perceptions: that of so-called *"self-similarity"*, We can think of a square as comprising "smaller" squares and itself forming a part of a "larger" square. Similarly we could view an equilateral triangle in terms of it containing smaller and smaller equilateral triangles. Informally self-similarity within a structure, S expresses the idea that S is built from "smaller" *identical* or "near-identical" copies of S) and the same construction process can be extended to build "larger" objects of which S is a component. Thus "squares" can be expressed as built from smaller squares, equilateral triangles, in the same way, analyzed as formed from equilateral triangles and being capable of embedding in larger such objects.

This property is found in many natural structures and has been extensively studied. Examples are found in geological formations, e.g. Batty [22]; biology and medicine, see e.g. Havlin *et al.* [117] and the recent collection of Nonnenmacher, Losa and Weiber [177]; and within other physical sciences, see e.g. Stanley and Ostrowsky [220].

The investigation of fractal elements within creative arts dates back to at least the 1940s. An early advocate of their use in music composition was Joseph Schillinger whose system was presented in the 1946 volume [205]. Further exploration of the properties of Complex number sequences extending Schillinger's work was undertaken by Elaine Walker [249] who contributed to technology for reproducing "Chaos Melody" i.e. compositions resulting through Complex sequence generation and Sukumaran & Thiyagarajan [230].

Another important use has been in attempting to find a rationale as to why particular musical creations are more "appealing" than others. In the latter context the rôle of fractal dimension has proved to be of some interest.

Investigating this question, Voss & Clarke [247] examine the character-

istics of "spectral density" a measurement that can be interpreted in terms
of fractal dimension of the sounds in various musical genres. In extremely
loose terms, their findings can be summarized as classifying "sound streams"
as falling into one of three categories: so-called "$1/f^0$" noise, equating to
the phenomenen of "white" noise; $1/f^2$ noise or "Brownian" noise; and finally, $1/f^1$ noise. The experimental studies of Voss and Clarke led them to
the conclusion that the first two categories ($1/f^0$ and $1/f^2$) are found unap-
pealing. In contrast, patterns exhibiting $1/f$ behaviour were regarded as aes-
thetically satisfying by their audience. The fractal dimension as measured in
"randomly generated" $1/f$-noise has been used to underpin algorithmic composition methods. The article by Martin Gardner [96] offers a lucid summary
of Voss and Clarke's work together with an overview of a "random $1/f$-noise
generator".

In such creative work a key approach is to build structures reflecting fractal sets, and among the most commonly used are the **Mandelbrot Set** and the
Julia-Fatou sets of Julia [130] and Fatou [83] dating from the early 20th century. Where do operations on $\mathbb{C}$ come into these methods? Manipulation of
$\mathbb{C}$ turns out to be central to the generation of sequences by iterating a function over $\mathbb{C}$ that can be mapped directly onto such fractal set structures. We
can take such sequences and associate these directly with musical pitch values.
Let us first look at how Complex number sequences are used to mimic fractal
sets.

From $\mathbb{C}$ to Fractal Sets

Underlying both Mandelbrot and Julia-Fatou sets are the behaviour of Com-
plex valued functions, $f : \mathbb{C} \to \mathbb{C}$ and, in particular the value obtained over a
large number of iterations.

A standard way of looking at these sets is to consider a region in the Complex Plane and how different points within this region are affected by successively evaluating f. Overall one has for (x, y) in the region of interest a
repeated computation in which $z_0 = (x, y)$, $z_{n+1} = f(z_n)$. The functions and
points that are of interest are those for which no matter how many iterations
$f(f(f(\ldots)))$ are carried out the size i.e. $|z|$)of the output $z \in \mathbb{C}$ is always
bounded.

The **Mandelbrot set**, $\mathcal{M}$, is the subset of $\mathbb{C}$ for which

$$\mathcal{M} = \{ c : \text{For all } n \ |z_{n+1}| \leq 2 \text{ with } z_0 = 0 \text{ and } z_{n+1} = z_n^2 + c \}$$

A standard way (approximately) to compute $\mathcal{M}$ is, having fixed the rectangular
region within the Complex plane, the usual choice being that section in which

$-2.5 \leq \Re(z) \leq 1.0$ and $-1.0 \leq \Im(z) \leq 1.0$, to go through the sequence of iterations as described in Algorithm 5.3. These assign a value, $v(p)$ in $\{0, 1\}$ (equivalently a colour, $\chi(p)$, $\{\textbf{white}, \textbf{black}\}$) to each point p according to whether $p \in \mathcal{M}$ ($\chi(p) = \textbf{black}$, $v(p) = 1$) or $p \notin \mathcal{M}$ ($\chi(p) = \textbf{white}$, $v(p) = 0$).[33]

Algorithm 5.3. Approximation of Mandelbrot Set, $\mathcal{M}$, in Complex Plane

---

1: Set x_{start} and x_{end} {$\Re$ boundary of rectangular region};
2: Set y_{start} and y_{end} {$\Im$ boundary of rectangular region};
3: $M := 10000$; {M is maximum number of iterations for each point tested.}
4: $xmax :=$ Number of points on $\Re$-axis considered;
5: $ymax :=$ Number of points on $\Im$-axis consisdered;
6: {A total of $xmax \cdot ymax$ values are fixed. Individual points (x, y) will be scaled to lie within the rectangular region of the Complex Plane used.}
7: $x_{inc} := (x_{end} - x_{start})/xmax$; {Increment between successive x values}
8: $y_{inc} := (y_{end} - y_{start})/ymax$; {Increment between successive x values}
9: $x := x_{start}$;
10: **repeat**
11:   **repeat**
12:     $y := y_{start}$;
13:     $k := 0$;
14:     $z := (0.0, 0.0)$; $c := (x, y)$
15:     **repeat**
16:       $z := z^2 + c$;
17:       $k := k + 1$;
18:     **until** $k > M$ or $|z| > 2$
19:     **if** $|z| \leq 2$ and $k > M$ **then**
20:       $\chi(<x, y>) = \textbf{black}$
21:     **else**
22:       $\chi(<x, y>) = \textbf{white}$
23:     **end if**
24:     $y := y + y_{inc}$;
25:   **until** $y > ymax$
26:   $x := x + x_{inc}$;
27: **until** $x > xmax$

---

[33]More sophisticated colour mappings, generally used for graphical displays of $\mathcal{M}$ have been used. For our immediate purposes a straightforward Boolean perspective suffices.

Figure 5.4: The Mandelbrot Set, $\mathcal{M}$

The output produced, using a granularity of 5000×5000 is illustrated in Figure 5.4

In Sukumaran & Thiyagarajan [230] mapping of $\mathcal{M}$ to musical pitches is discussed. Rather more scope for creativity is, however, presented in Walker's used of Julia-Fatou sets [249, Figures 23, 24, pp. 23–24].

The main difference is in the nature of the Complex function being iterated. Within the Mandelbrot set construction, points, c, in the Complex plane are classified, after iterating sufficiently often, the function $z_{n+1} = (z_n)^2 + c$, starting **always** from an initial value $z_0 = 0$.

Overall, as observed by Walker [249, p. 22], the Mandelbrot set determines the status of each $c \in \mathbb{C}$ with respect to iterations of $z_{n+1} = z_n^2 + c$ and a **fixed** starting value of $z_0 = 0$. The Julia set construction is defined for arbitrary[34] functions $f : \mathbb{C} \to \mathbb{C}$. Although those $f(z) = z^2 + c$ have particularly interesting behaviour, the classification is not with respect to c and a **single** starting value of z as in the Mandelbrot structure: each $c \in \mathbb{C}$ yields a different Julia set. In realizing this behaviour in terms of a musical score, Walker adopts the convention whereby the function $z_{n+1} = r \cdot e^{z_n}$ is applied. In these instances initial z_0 are specified by $\alpha = \Re(z)$ and $\beta = \Im(z)$. Similarly $\Re(r)$ and $\Im(r)$

---

[34]Strictly speaking some technical conditions must be satisfied, however, if $p(x) \in \mathbb{C}[X]$, and $q(x) \in \mathbb{C}[X]$ with $q(x) \neq 0$ then $f(z) = p(z)/q(z)$ is always suitable.

are under control of the composer. In total the next "notes" are specified from

$$z_{n+1} = (\alpha + \imath\beta)e^{z_n}$$

with four starting parameters (α, β) and $z_0 = \gamma + \imath\delta$. The output melody consists of two simultaneous sections corresponding to $\Re(z)$ and $\Im(z)$. Each corresponding Real value being mapped to a (MIDI) note value between 0 and 127 ([249, p. 25]).

As a compositional method, these provide basic generation of melodic elements i.e. note pitch values. Walker's ideas are used as the support for a performance instrument in which having built the basic Chaos Melody line, improvization of rhythm, dynamics, and tempo can be added.

Voss' $1/f$-music Algorithm

We conclude this overview by giving a description of Voss' "random $1/f$-music" generator as described originally in Gardener[96]. Although not directly exploiting properties of $\mathbb{C}$ the algorithm is of interest for its relationship to fractal dimension which we have seen can be analyzed using $\mathbb{C}$ and for allowing a more "traditional" mapping to music scores.

The technique is a sophisticated combination of "random dice throwing" and binary representation. Using k dice (standard dice having face values between 1 and 6 and $k \geq 2$) any total between k (all dice land showing 1) and $6k$ (all dice land showing 6) might result on throwing these. The $5k + 1$ possibilities determine the collection of available pitch values. One method, suggested in Gardener's article, is to set the initial value (throwing exactly k) to be the middle key on a piano and going rightwards number succeeding keys in order. Alternative labellings are, of course, equally usable.

Having fixed the number of dice as k, the initial score is produced over 2^k rounds.

List the numbers 0 to $2^k - 1$ in binary e.g. using k columns. For example with four dice, 21 individual notes would be available by throwing between 4 and 24. The numbers 0 through 15 being given as

$Number$	$D1$	$D2$	$D3$	$D4$
0	0	0	0	0
1	0	0	0	1
2	0	0	1	0
3	0	0	1	1
4	0	1	0	0
5	0	1	0	1
6	0	1	1	0
7	0	1	1	1
8	1	0	0	0
9	1	0	0	1
10	1	0	1	0
11	1	0	1	1
12	1	1	0	0
13	1	1	0	1
14	1	1	1	0
15	1	1	1	1

Next (starting at line $000\ldots0$) generate a random number in $\mathbb{N}$ between k and $6k$ by simulating throwing k dice: a straightforward algorithmic simulation. This value determines the first note, i.e. if $2k$ is the outcome then this will be the note labelled $2k$ earlier.

For each of remaining rounds. If one has just completed round r and about to simulate round $r+1$, identify the positions which change between the binary representation of r and that of $r+1$.

Throw **only** the dice corresponding to these positions (leaving the others unchanged) and calculate the new total. For example if at round 6 using four dice one had thrown $D1 = 4$, $D2 = 3$, $D3 = 6$ and $D4 = 1$ for a total of 14, then for round 7 only $D4$ would be cast ($(6)_2 = 0110$ and $(7)_2 = 0111$ only $D4$ changes). If the new throw led to $D4 = 6$ the note corresponding to this round would be $4 + 3 + 6 + 6 = 19$.

Continue this process until having completed round $2^k - 1$ whereupon the composition can continue from 0. Noting that $2^k - 1$ and 0 have no positions with a common value, this corresponds to rethrowing all k dice for the next round.

It is worth noting that although superficially only concerned with pitch values, the same approach can be brought to bear with respect to note duration and other score aspects.

Figure 5.5: Untitled piece produced by Voss' $1/f$-method

In Figure 5.5 a very basic example melodic line generated by this algorithm is presented (using a 4 dice setting)

Although having in this case a quite simple structure, using $1/f$ methods we could in theory combine this with standard approaches to vary the structure.[35]

5.9   Summary

It may be that, at first sight, the forms and properties offered by Complex numbers are concerned with a problem ("what are the roots of $x^2 + 1$?") that is unimportant and fail to find a solution to it: the "i is an invention" proposal discussed in the opening pages of this Chapter. Our primary aim has been, not to wrestle with philosophical *mathematical* worries which are irrelevant to the exploitation of Complex number in *Computer Science* but rather to advance a case, based on a number of quite diverse examples of their use, that $\mathbb{C}$ and its properties have proved to be of signal importance in computational settings.

Thus we have seen that when considering the most general case of single variable polynomials, i.e. the set $\mathbb{C}[X]$ which includes $\mathbb{Q}[X]$, the problem of finding roots of polynomials can be handled just as effectively using the methods described in Chapter 4. In particular the fundamental issue that gave rise to the theory of Complex Numbers, namely the existence of polynomials with roots outside $\mathbb{R}$ can be resolved by very minor adjustments to algorithms such as Laguerre's method.

The questions raised by providing a **geometric** interpretation of $\mathbb{C}$ had a powerful influence on the formulation of the concept of quaternions. These objects offer a powerful suite of methods by which quite sophisticated 3D graphics effects can be realized without the computational worries that arise through trying to enrich the techniques presented in Chapter 3.

---

[35]An extremely rudimentary example as well as some further comments on this approach are given in Endnote 5.

Although considerations of space prevented a detailed technical exposition, we have also seen that $\mathbb{C}$ or, more accurately, the validation of the techniques adopted that Complex analysis provides, gives one mechanism for addressing difficult questions with regard to how intricate combinatorial forms typically behave. In the next Chapter we shall consider a less analytic approach to such questions.

One of the most significant ideas arising in Complex analysis is that of the **Fourier Transform**. As we noted, this can be presented in both continuous and discrete versions. The former is of huge importance in the world of signal analysis a key activity e.g. in acoustics, optical transmission, radio wave properties within the discipline of Electrical Engineering.[36]

We have seen that using the discrete form of the Fourier transform offers significant benefits not only to a traditional signal processing problem, namely, that of reducing the amount of data needed to store and transmit a digital image without noticeable reduction in quality, but also in applications to efficient large-scale Computer Arithmetic. By developing the approach initiated in the discoveries of Karatsuba from [137], combining these with the efficient DFT computation method from Cooley and Tukey [50], we are able, as demonstrated by Schönhage and Strassen in [207] to achieve a total number of bit operations to multiply two n-bit values that is of the order of $n \log_2 n \log_2 \log_2 n$. This represents a considerable saving, once n is of modest size, over the standard school methods that require n^2 steps. Of course it may be objected that the DFT realization used by Schönhage and Strassen does not require any awareness of $\mathbb{C}$ and its properties: the arithmetic operations exploit the algebraic structure and behaviour of $(\mathbb{Z}_m, +, \cdot)$ at least as much as anything gained from $\mathbb{C}$. In response to such claims, however, we may note the following. The fact that computation is performed in $(\mathbb{Z}_m, +, \cdot)$ is largely irrelevant to the origins of the **discrete** Fourier transform. The DFT is, as we noted, a discrete form of the *continuous* Fourier transform. Much of the analysis of how the DFT operates can be motivated and couched in terms of related behaviour in the continuous form. Certainly in terms of presenting a description of the workings of the algorithm in [50] it could be argued that such descriptions are less opaque taking $\mathbb{C}$ and primitive n'th roots as a foundation than $\mathbb{Z}_m$ and *principal* n'th roots.

---

[36]The Russian writer, Vassily Aksyonov, in his epic novel chronicling the thirty years of Stalin's regime and its effect on one family, has one character boasting of progress achieved by 1925: *"Revolutionary ardor is already a thing of the past . . . It is not Marxism that will triumph, but electrical engineering . . ."*. [6, p. 8]. Whether the triumph of electrical engineering is to be preferred to the triumph of Marxism, one must leave readers to decide for themselves.

Finally we reviewed how the behaviour of specific Complex valued functions can be exploited in the realm of Computer Creativity: specifically through linking $f(z)$ that always remain bounded given certain initial conditions to the notion of fractal dimension and sets and, thence, to the ideas exploited in work of many composers of using Complex numbers within these as a means of mapping to music. Given the link to fractal dimension we also presented the "$1/f$-music algorithm" discovered by Voss and described in Gardner [96] giving a very simple example of output it might generate.

From the examples we have just sketched, we can see that $\mathbb{C}$ is rather more than some nebulous affectation of interest only to Pure Mathematicians. This set, its behaviour, and both methods inspired by (quaternions, $1/f$-music algorithms) and directly reliant upon $\mathbb{C}$ (roots of polynomials in $\mathbb{R}[X]$, properties of generating functions, the continuous and discrete Fourier Transforms) describe mechanisms by which basic Computational tasks can be addressed: without some appreciation of $\mathbb{C}$, it may be argued that, for example, no understanding of DFT is easily acquired. While it is true that there are aspects, e.g. the behaviour of w^z when both w and z are Complex which may appear to create unwanted complications, the benefits, I would claim, outweigh the difficulties. Quoting, again, from that same aria which gives the opening line of this Chapter:

> "*denn lässt er uns nicht ruhn,*
> [⋯]
> *so sei's um solche Werk',*
> *die selten vor gemeinen Dingen,*
> *und nie ohn ein'gen Wahn gelingen.*"[37]

(R. Wagner, *Die Meistersinger von Nürnberg*, Act III).

---

[37](very freely) "if we must bear such things then let them influence those works which are seldom realized easily, and never without some delusion"

5.10 Projects

1. Extend your previous realization of Laguerre's method to handle Complex roots.

2. Implement the Cooley-Tukey algorithm for DFT computation. Using your implementation

   a. Examine its effectiveness as a means of "noise reduction" in digital images.

   b. Implement the Schönhage-Strassen fast integer multiplication algorithm.

3. Using a more involved colour mapping scheme, generate graphical outputs for Julia sets when iterating different functions $f : \mathbb{C} \to \mathbb{C}$. For example, having determined that $|f(z)| > 2$ after k iterations from a starting value, z_0 fix the pixel colour for z_0 based on the value of k.

4. Implement Voss' $1/f$-music algorithm as described above. If you are able to construct sound files (e.g. `.mp3`) from the output do you agree this supports Voss' conjecture that "$1/f$-noise" is intrinsically appealing?

5.11   Endnotes

1. The philosopher Zeno of Elea (ca. 490–430 B.C.) formulated a set of 4 logical paradoxes effectively apparently demonstrating the impossibility of movement that call into question the validity of a fundamental assumption of ancient Greek mathematics: "all quantities can be described in terms of *discrete indivisible* elements". The fact that numbers such as "the length of the side of a square having area equal to 2" cannot be so described: that $2^{1/2}$ is irrational challenges this perception.

   Kline [143, p. 32] retells the traditional account of the fate of Hippasus of Metapontum to whom the demonstration that $\sqrt{2}$ cannot be expressed as the ratio of two Natural numbers has been attributed: announcing his discovery while at sea, this news was ill-received by his fellow Pythagoreans whose response was to throw Hippasus overboard by reason of him

   > "... *having produced an element in the universe which denied the ... doctrine that all phenomena in the universe can be reduced to Whole numbers and their ratios.*".

   This version of Hippasus' end together with the supporting reasons and the albeit fanciful alleged fate of Paolo Valmes and its rationalization (described in Endnote 9 of Chapter 2) perhaps seem rather discouraging precedents to those with ambitions to undertake original mathematical research. John Steinbeck gives a wryly humorous account of reactions to technological, scientific and social innovations since prehistoric times in [221] (reprinted in the collection Aldiss [7]). The fate of the apocryphal discoverer of the process of making earthenware pottery ("Harry") being reported as exciting the reaction:

   > "*They had to hang Harry head down over a bonfire. Nobody can put a knife in the status quo and get away with it.* ".

   In the story Steinbeck suggests violent, hostile, and negative reactions are the inevitable consequences of innovation irrespective of how beneficial such innovation may be. Referring to the possibility of such reactions leading to humans becoming extinct Steinbeck, however, concludes on an upbeat note

"If we do, we're stupider than the cave people and I don't think we are. I think we're just exactly as stupid and that's pretty bright in the long run."

Nonetheless Steinbeck's sardonic aside *"Nobody can put a knife in the status quo and get away with it"* is borne out by numerous real examples. The evidence for Hippasus' fate may be thin; the evidence for that of Valmes non-existent, however, as is well documented the scientist, mathematician and cosmologist Giordano Bruno (1548–1600) was burnt at the stake in Rome following a seven year trial and imprisonment for among other "offences" promoting the idea of a "plurality of worlds". The contributions of the French scientist, Antoine Lavoisier (1743–1794) to chemistry and biology failed to move the Revolutionary Tribunal which ordered his execution on charges of embezzlement.[38]

The *"Nobody can put a knife in the status quo and get away with it"* phenomenom has blighted scientific progress throughout the twentieth century. The perversion of scientific orthodoxy in the Third Reich and the fate of those who objected has been widely documented, see e.g. Remmert [193] (Mathematics), Beyerchen [28] (Physics), and Chasseguet-Smirgel [44] (Psychoanalysis). Under Stalin, Tofimir Lysenko, e.g. [160, 159] championed Lysenkoism, a now discredited view of agronomics virulently hostile to the theory of genetics.[39] This, as a consequence of Stalin's support for Lysenkoism, led to the persecution of noted figures such as Georgii Karpechenko (died in prison 1941), Gregory Levitsky (executed in 1941), Nikolai Vavilov (arrested 1940, died 1943 from dystrophy in condemned cell), and many others: a detailed review of this period and its negative effects on Biological research under Stalin is presented in Sofyer [217],

---

[38]The often quoted rejection of Lavoisier's case by the presiding judge Jean-Baptiste Coffinhal in the words *"La République n'a pas besoin de savants ni de chimistes"* (loosely, "The Republic needs neither sages nor chemists"), almost certainly, never happened, cf. the commentary of the Socialist writer and anarchist apologist James Guillaume (1844-1916) reproduced in the Marxist historical review *Les Cahiers du mouvement ouvrier continuent* [110], and the discussion in Duveen [75, p. 62, col. 2] which acknowledges Guillaume's research into the supporting evidence for this quote.

[39]e.g. "I do not accept Mendelism . . . I do not consider formal Mendelian-Morganist genetics a science . . . We object to . . . rubbish and lies in science, we discard the static, formal tenets of Mendelism-Morganism" (Lysenko writing in 1952 quoted in Sofyer [217, p. 725, col. 1]

2. *"doubts about using i almost a century after Cardano's promulgation of the concept"*: Many generally accepted but counter-intuitive ideas from modern theory are less than one hundred year old: Gödel's demonstration that there are true theorems that cannot be proved to be so (1931, Gödel [103]); Turing's argument that there are well-defined computational problems for which no algorithmic process exist has already been mentioned in this text and dates from 1936, Turing [236]. Even outside the arena of mathematics, in the physical sciences, Heisenberg [118] in 1927 had, through the Uncertainty Principle, shown the impossibility of complete **and** accurate empirical studies. Although figures such as Wittgenstein continued to have difficulties accepting the consequences of Gödel's discovery[40], it causes little disquiet today.

3. Mispronunciation of surnames is a habit that, personally, one finds singularly irritating: Euler is "Oil-er" (as in the former NFL team) or "Oi-lur" (as in Millwall FC supporter's chant): it is **not** "Ewe-ler" or "You-ler" (as in female sheep or second person pronoun). One has long given up hope of Stevenson's Dr. Jekyll being pronounced accurately: *Jee-*kil, as confirmed by Stevenson himself and correctly used in Rouben Mamoulian's 1931 film version rather than Jeck-ill, a mis-usage that seems to originate in the (vastly inferior for reasons in addition to linguistic incompetence) Victor Fleming adaptation from 1941.

4. The Complex number $e^{i\pi}$. The apotheosis of late seventies geek-chic was, undoubtedly, the spectacle, commonly seen in UK Student Union facilities of usually male Engineering undergraduate students sporting t-shirts encrusted with the slogan *"I am number $-e^{i\pi}$"* in the apparent belief that such coruscating wit and Olympian awareness regarding the subtleties of Complex analysis would attract the enraptured awe and perennial respect of their contemporaries: it didn't.

5. Recalling our basic $1/f$-music example in Figure 5.5, using further $1/f$ and standard techniques this could be developed as Figure 5.6.

   There are a few points of interest concerning this approach. For example:

   a) Characteristics of different numbers of dice: while more dice offer a greater range of pitches (e.g. four as in our example, can work

---

[40]See e.g. Wittgenstein [258, I, Appendix 3, para. 8–9, V. paras. 24, 46, 47], the 2000 article by Floyd and Putnam [88], and the 1991 commentary from Dunne [68, pp 126–129].

Figure 5.6: Variant of Figure 5.5

from a basis of 21 distinct tones used over sixteen rounds whereas three provide 16 over eight). The random nature of the output, however, may lead to scores with uncomfortably larger intervals.

b) Note duration and time signatures: here again there is no clear idea how to vary and manipulate these measures.

As a very basic indication, Figure 5.7 gives the unadjusted form of a short "three dice" example.

Figure 5.7: Voss $1/f$ algorithm using 3 dice

Chapter 6

Computing as experiment
Statistics and Data Analysis

Probability is the bane of the age.

Casanova's Chinese Restaurant (vol. 5 of *A Dance to the Music of Time*)
ANTHONY POWELL (1905–2000)

6.1 Probability theory v. statistics: differences

If the choice of quotation opening this Chapter seems to offer a rather jaun-
diced view of its subject matter then I should point out that this was not (entirely) my intention in choosing it. It is used largely to emphasize and, one
hopes dispel a popular misconception about two disciplines: Probability Theory with which we are concerned only in so much as some key ideas are essential and not otherwise; and Statistics with which we are very much concerned
in this particular Chapter. The conflation and misidentification of these two
arenas as essentially the same subject some preferring the former name as
seeming more exotic and challenging when compared to what are perceived
to be the mundane and prosaic connotations of the latter, while not quite as
heinous as that of identifying "arithmetic" with Mathematics[1] is, I consider
damaging to the conduct of both. It is harmful to the pursuit of Statistics by
bringing into its ken activities which have no practical locus with respect to

---

[1]A particular order of infantilism which I have commented upon earlier in the Preface to
this volume.

their use. It is unhelpful to Probability Theory in consequence of such identification having the effect of reducing important technical nuances e.g. the Borel-Cantelli properties of infinite sequences of Bernoulli trials, Martingales, spectral treatment of ergodic processes, etc.[2] to the myopic level of those who see only studies that can be directly applied as having any value.

So there is on the one side the formal Mathematical study of Probability Theory and, on the other, a collection of ideas, techniques and processes that are essential to the proper and correct analysis of *any* empirical study: be it in the realm of psephology, or data pertaining to evidence for climate change or consumer purchasing trends or the outcome of particle accelerator experiments. That is to say, on the other side, we have Statistics.

Probability Theory is not Statistics and Statistics is not Probability Theory. The aim of this introductory section is to elaborate in more detail on precisely where these differences lie.

In order to describe the concerns of *Probability Theory*, a good concise summary of these is given in the introduction to the classic text of Feller [84]:

"Probability is a mathematical discipline with aims akin to those, for example, of geometry or analytical mechanics." Feller [84, p. 1].

The text continues to breakdown this study into three separate but interacting components: the formal logical and axiomatic theory; the intuition underpinning the formal ideas; and the relationship to applications. With regard to the last of these, Feller notes ([84, p. 1–2])

"In applications, the abstract mathematical models serve as tools and different models can describe the same empirical situation. *The manner in which mathematical theories are applied does not depend on preconceived ideas; it is a purposeful technique depending on, and changing with, experience.*" (emphasis in the original)

In other words, Probability Theory provides some rigorous basis for the handling of a number of intuitive ideas ("chance", "likely outcome", "typical result", "independent events" etc.). This basis offers a sound underpinning and means of justifying claims that may be made when applying techniques: so, for example, the turf-accountant's setting of the initial starting prices offered is based on statistical methodologies using existing data ("form", nature of the racecourse, distance of the race itself). Less predictable settings e.g. the likely amount to be won when placing a stake at roulette, or playing a fruit-machine are not subject to analysis by the viscissitudes of prior form and must rely upon studying how likely particular events may be to occur: a roulette game in which a correct number paid out exactly the same amount as its correct parity

---

[2]The reader should feel unconcerned by my deliberate failure to elaborate these.

i.e. odd or even would be unlikely to attract much interest from clients since there would be no incentive to gamble on the "less likely" outcome.

So in the discipline of Probability Theory, core questions of importance are, among others

a. How to associate *quantitative* measures with each of a set of possible occurences? Are there properties that such measures **must** observe in order that particular analytic techniques are valid?

b. What are the qualities of "sets of possible outcomes" it is reasonable to assume?

c. How do or, more fundamentally, **can** we describe all of the possible outcomes in such a way that these can be treated in a coherent, meaningful, and consistent fashion?

It is not, of course, suggested that these are the only such issues that arise in a formal mathematical treatment of Probability Theory. They are, however, of interest in distinguishing a few matters of significance.

What, on the other hand, does the discipline of Statistics concern? As a rather banal observation one might consider Statistics to concern "the use of the techniques and theory of Probability to model and reason about settings in everyday life". Here in making an assertion about the "likely occurence of some incident" one is **not** making a mathematically certain statement. Consider, for example, the following context.

A casino operates a roulette table on which a standard roulette wheel with 37 slots numbered 0 to 36 is used.

Q1. What are the chances of a specific number r ($0 \leq r \leq 36$) occurring on a given play?

Q2. If two players each stake £1 one on "even" and the other on "odd" and the House wins all stakes whenever 0 lands, how much is the House "likely to win/lose" after n consecutive plays?

Q3. A player bets on even occurring on each of 50 games. At the end of this the player has "only" £20 from an amount of £50 staked. Is the player justified in regarding the game as "unfair"? Would the player be justified in such an assumption if left with only £30 or £10? Would the House have good reason to suspect malpractice if a player had an amount of £70 or £90 after the game had concluded?

Now (Q1) and (Q2) are issues within the domain of Probability Theory: the conclusions apply to an abstract, environment independent, analysis of what one would expect to happen in an ideal context: e.g. that the wheel is perfectly balanced, and rotates at the same speed behaving independently of forces such as friction and air resistance.

Question 3, however, is an issue properly addressed by Statistical methods: the situation considered is that of a specific game in a single environment. In order to answer the questions posed, one must have a *model* of what one expects to happen: here the basis for such a model is via Probability Theory **and** a basis for assessing whether an *actual* outcome (being left with only £30 from £50) is so unlikely as to justify suspicions.

In Q3, we have a key question arising from empirical studies: we have obtained a collection of *numerical data*; based on these data we posit a particular model of behaviour; after gathering further data we compare these with our model. What bases do we have for confirming that our model based on the "old data" is incompatible with these "new data"? Questions of this form arise in, among other contexts,

a. Analysis of climate data. Historical weather records e.g. dating back several centuries, ("old data") indicate a particular pattern of seasonal temperatures and weather. Information collected over recent decades ("new data") suggest long-term changes in this pattern are underway. How do we assess evidence based on the disparity between these two for the change being the result of human rather than natural activity?

b. On the morning[3] of a General Election, newspaper polls predict the division of MPs between the major parties based on a survey of voters ("old data"). Subsequently based on so-called exit polls, ("new data") television news programmes postulate a completely different result. What, if any, conclusions can be drawn?

c. Product quality control. Based on sampling manufacturing output, a seller of electrical batteries, claims that a typical $1.5V$ battery will have a continuous use lifetime of 2 weeks ("old data"). Consumers complain that, in their experience, the typical lifetime is under 10 days ("new data"). Is the manufacturer exaggerating or have consumers just been unfortunate?

---

[3]One peculiarity of U.K. electoral law, as opposed to a tradition in many continental European states, is that there is no "cut-off" time for publishing such polls.

Well-known examples of the failure to apply accurate interpretative methods to statistical data include the inaccurate prediction of both the 1936 (Landon defeats Roosevelt) and 1948 (Dewey defeats Truman) U.S. Presidential elections. The former based on a two million respondent postal survey conducted by the U.S. *Literary Digest*.[4]

Outdoing even politics in its studied mendacity (no easy accomplishment) advertizing is one of the most common sources of statistical abuse. Among the more notorious examples one finds Colgate's "80% of dentists recommend ..." campaign being censured by the U.K.'s Advertizing Standards Authority (ASA) (2007); in September 2012, the U.S. Food and Drug Administration (FDA); warned *Lancôme* (a division of *L'Oreal*) concerning a claim that its products "see significant deep wrinkle reduction in UV damaged skin" and this had been "clinically proven". The bleach and detergent brand Domestos has faced criticism leading to product recall in 2013 by South African regulators over its "Kills 99.9% of all germs" slogan although the same nonsense has featured in U.K. promotions with only superficial alterations (e.g. from "all germs" to "all *known* germs") and without objection for the best part of forty years.

Statistical claims allegedly "backed up" by supporting evidence provide one major source of deliberate and wilful misuse.[5] So it is not uncommon to see misuse of statistics and logic propounded often by politicians whose grasp of basic numeracy is, usually, rather limited.[6] For example, in arguments such as:

C1. It is the intention of Government to reduce by a significant degree the number of motor vehicle accidents that result in fatalities.

C2. Analysis of police and hospital casualty records, shows that in 10% of serious automobile accidents, the driver of at least one of the vehicles involved was under 14 years old.

C3. It therefore follows, that the other 90% of such incidents must have involved driver(s) over the age of 14.

---

[4]The subsequent domination of "Gallup polls" in political surveys, is in no small part down to Gallup's accurate prediction of the actual outcome from a basis of only $50,000$ samples.

[5]A fact known by the 19th century, from which the famous statement "There are lies, damned lies, and statistics" dates. This has been variously attributed to, among others the Duke of Wellington and Benjamin Disraeli.

[6]*cf.* Babbage's experience as recalled in Chapter 4, fn. 38.

C4. Hence, in order effectively to deliver this policy, legislation will be introduced making it a criminal offence for anyone above the age of 14 to be in control of a motor vehicle.

We shall look at some of the more common misuses and statistical fallacies in Section 6.9.

In a legitimate application, however, the principal questions may be summarized relative to the following: "what evidence does the result of this experiment provide for or against the model that the experiment was designed to test?". The classical "scientific method" provides one framework for addressing such questions. It is this which we now, briefly review.

6.2   Classical scientific experimental method

It has been a long-established methodology in the "traditional" sciences (by which we shall intend Chemistry, Physics, and Biology) that in seeking to formulate, test, and defend a given model of reality such is accomplished through a rigorous and precisely defined approach. This approach, consisting of a series of separate stages, is known as *Scientific Method*.

Hence, taking examples from each of these disciplines, typical, historical, well-known instances are:

From **Physics**: in order to examine the behaviour of light, in particular what enabled light waves to travel through space, in keeping with the accepted *model* that waves required a medium to move through, physicists had *hypothesized* a structure called the *"ether"* towards the end of the 19th century. If the existence of the ether were a reality, then light travelling through it would result in various peripheral effects occuring. The U.S. physicist Albert Michelson, initially in [163] and then in conjunction with Edward Morley [164] devised *experiments* by which these effects could be detected. On analyzing the outcome, it was eventually realized that a *revision* to the putative model was needed.

From **Chemistry**: studying hypotheses of the Soviet chemist Alexander Oparin and the English scientist, J. B. S. Haldane, the U.S. scientists Stanley Miller and Harold Urey devised an experiment to simulate what were believed to be conditions necessary for chemical compounds essential to organic life-forms to develop. Their model recreated in miniature, atmospheric and water states from approximately a billion years previously. The outcome, reported in the papers [166, 167] recreates a number of the basic building blocks (amino acids) needed, and provides a basis for more detailed empirical studies, e.g. Oró and Kamat [179].

From **Biology**: an experiment was designed by the medical researchers Oswald Avery, Colin MacLeod, and Maclyn McCarty to test a theory that changes in the biochemical structure of bacteria were effected by DNA rather than as had been thought by the action of proteins. The findings of the Avery-MacLeod-McCarty study being reported in [15].

From **Behavioural Psychology**: two very famous (notorious?) studies on human behaviour were conducted by the psychologists Stanley Milgram [165] examining stimuli to perform distasteful actions and, in order to gauge reactions of individuals under "peer-group divisions", Philip Zimbardo: the widely commented upon Stanford Prison Experiment [261].

Now the range of activities being outlined above are in very different and distinctive areas. Nevertheless we can identify common high-level aspects emphasized in our review of the Michelson-Morley experiments, in all of them.

In each case we have an *hypothesis* being investigated: that light waves moving through space will disturb the "ether"; that electrical reactions with simple compounds will over time lead to the basic building blocks for life-forms being generated; that bacteria in the particular study mentioned, a strain of *pneumococcus* will be altered by DNA; that ordinary, intelligent, humans will, under sufficient provocation act in a manner that they would consider unthinkable under usual conditions (the Milgram and Zimbardo experiments).

In order further to study these hypotheses an *experimental structure* is devised.

After conducting the experiment (which may take some considerable time, e.g. Miller's experiment originally carried out in 1953, was found to be yielding novel outcomes even as recently as 2007) its *results* are analyzed with the conclusions being held either to *validate* the hypothesis e.g. the Avery-MacLeod-McCarty experiment, debatably the Milgram and Zimbardo studies, or necessitate a *revision* of the hypothesis e.g. the Michelson-Morley experiment, with consequential further *experimental* study in order to examine the new claims.

In total we have, in the classical scientific disciplines, a process of advancing the state of knowledge that involves the following stages:

S1. **Observation**: consider details of the phenomenon being studied, e.g. how should a wave in motion behave?

S2. **Hypothesis**: construct a *model* consistent with data observed that explains and would allow future behaviour to be predicted. e.g. since light waves moving through the ether would have side-effects, the hypothesis formed accounts for such changes in the ether.

S3. **Experiment**: design an experiment by which the validity of the hypothesis can be examined. e.g. if the ether is perturbed then it must be perturbed by a measurable amount. Construct an experiment which allows some estimation of this perturbation to be made.

S4. **Analysis**: having conducted the experiment review the data obtained. Do these confirm the hypothesis? do they indicate that the hypothesis cannot be valid? The data from the Michelson-Morley experiment was not able to confirm that the ether and light waves behaved in the manner predicted.

S5. **Revise**: if the empirical data suggest that the model is unlikely to be accurate, what specific aspects of this appear to be incorrect? If some support for the hypothesis is given from experimental results, is it possible to refine the experiment and hypothesis to get a "better" view?

[**Note**: one other aspect of importance, which we will not discuss, is *reproducibility*: would the same experiment with the same configuration produce the same results?]

One crucial methodology colouring the interpretation of (S4) and any modifications with respect to (S2) arising as a result is Statistics. Our hypothesis in S2 may be based on numerical data e.g. climate records, concentration of specific chemical substances in a compound, measured velocities noted via (S1). Our experiment may generate or otherwise accrue further numerical data. One major statistical concept is that of "degree of confidence": informally this allows the derivation of quantitative estimates describing to what extent those data produced in conducting the experiment are consistent with those predicted by the hypothesis. If wildly divergent it is likely that the hypothesis must be revised. The interaction between model, hypothesis, experiment and theory, is succinctly commented upon in Grossman's novel from which I quoted in Chapter 1:

"The laboratory experiments had been intended to confirm the predictions of the theory. They had failed to do this. The contradiction between the experimental results and the theory naturally led him to doubt the accuracy of the experiments. A theory that had been elaborated on the basis of decades of work by many researchers, a theory that had then explained many things in subsequent experimental results, seemed quite unshakeable. Repetition of the experiments had $\cdots$ still failed to correspond with what the theory predicted. Even the most generous allowance for inaccuracy $\cdots$ could in no way account for such large discrepancies."

V. Grossman [109, Part 2, Chap. 6] (trans. R. Chandler)

The methodology defined over stages (S1)–(S5) and minor variants of this has proved extremely effective as a process for scientific study and advance for over five centuries. The main conceit of the present Chapter is that, just as Physics, Chemistry, Biology, Pyschology, etc., Computer Science has a valid treatment as an *experimental* discipline, in which the "model-experiment-revise" cycle implicit within (S1)–(S5) can be applied. There may, however, appear to be one apparent flaw in this claim. Before moving onto the technical discussion of Statistics we must first deal with this aspect.

6.3 It's not about "machines": artefact & algorithm

Physicists are concerned, among other interests, with the nature of "matter" (solid, liquid, gas): "states of matter" are *natural* as opposed to artificial or manufactured phenomena.

Chemists may consider properties of compounds e.g. molecular structure: again, such are *natural* "real-world" phenomena.

The interests of Biologists are, self-evidently, linked to the study of one collection of natural phenomena.

What of Computer Science? What does the study of Computer Science involve? Clearly and, perhaps, somewhat tautologously just as "Physics is concerned with aspects of the Physical world" and "Chemistry with the aspects of the constituency of chemical compounds" and "Biology with living i.e. biological organisms" so too

Computer Science concerns the study of Computers.

And with this statement a problem arises if we seek, as this Chapter does, to argue a case for Computer Science as an experimental discipline. Computers are **machines**: artificial, designed and built through human efforts. What

Computers, emphatically are **not** are a "natural phenomenon". This, of course, has nothing to do with the technology of computational devices and exactly the same statement holds true whether we are concerned with abacus, soroban, slide rules, Pascalines, Schickard's Calculating Clock, or Leibniz' Stepped Reckoner or any of the various aids and devices that have emerged to assist with calculation over the course of three millenia. So to speak of the study of "machines and mechanical objects" as an "experimental discipline" appears rather bizarre, to make no more sense than the investigation of "gardening tools" would make as an "experimental study" within the genuinely scientific study of Botany.

The arguments put forward in the preceding paragraph are, of course, justified. They are, however, predicated upon a fundamental misconception: Computer Science does **not** concern the "study of Comput**ers**".

Computer Science concerns the study of Comput**ation**.

Now one could debate the extent which "computation" or more accurately "computational process" defines a "natural phenomenon", however, in setting out the case for experimental methods playing a rôle in the study and advancement of Computer Science, such debate is unnecessary.

Consider, rather, the following **real** computational issues.

E1. Assess the **average-case** run-time of an *algorithm*.

E2. In AI, an important sub-field is that of *Machine Learning*. Within this one often has to determine "how well" a *learning algorithm* recognizes and correctly classifies examples: such cases may range from simple patterns to complex face recognition cases.

E3. Review how changes in system parameters change the behaviour of a *scheduling algorithm*, e.g. changes to page size settings, number of pages loaded by default for a given process.

E4. Gauge the robustness of a *concurrent algorithm* given **random** processor breakdown.

E5. Model the reliability of a *network routing algorithm* in the presence of **random** link ie "machine–to–machine" connection failures.

E6. Predict the robustness of a given software package with respect to the presence of program errors.

E7. Assess the performance of a malware/virus detection and removal suite.

Notice that every single one of these is concerned with assessing the character of a specific *computational* process when operating within some environment. The issues arising in (E1) we discussed, briefly, in the previous chapter. Assessment of system performance under given parameters has been a long established area of CS dating back to the late 1960s, e.g. in studying questions such as "given a main or as it is now RAM memory of size T how many pages i.e. division of T into P blocks of size K should this be split? too large a choice of K leads to available resources being under used; too small a choice results in performance degradation as a result of bookkeeping overheads. The issue discussed in (E6) may seem rather strange, however, has an extensive empirical methodology underpinning it, see e.g. Veevers [239], Veevers & Marshall [240].

So we see that, although not having as extensive a history as the use of empirical study within the traditional sciences, nonetheless there is an abundance of scenarios where experiment is not merely an appropriate process to adopt, but in fact may well be the *only* feasible technique: in principle one could formally analyze how well a machine-learning algorithm performs, but in practice a more convincing demonstration of its merits may be by exhibiting its success with respect to some benchmark suite of examples. We have, in fact, already mentioned one example of empirical assessment earlier in this text: as one method of gauging the performance of root finding techniques with respect to how rapidly these converge to a solution, e.g. our very basic comparison of the behaviours of Halley's and Laguerre's methods presented over Tables 4.6–4.9.

It is worth noting here an additional advantage of empirical demonstration over formal analytic proof: the latter even when correct may seem opaque, hard to understand and therefore unconvincing. The former especially when supported via some graphical illustration is perceived to have greater clarity and thence advances a stronger case for a claim. This facet is, of course, very well recognized in advertizing contexts: it is unlikely that anyone would feel convinced by a rigorous analytic proof that "8 out of 10 cats preferred . . ." even where such a thing to be possible, yet some hand-waving, nice graphics (e.g. bar chart describing alleged levels of feline satisfaction with divers products) will, on occasion, prove to be effective.

To summarize, in the computational settings enumerated under the examples (E1) through (E7) and, in general, we have the following basic elements easily mapped to stages of the methodology presented within (S1) through (S5) earlier.

A. Some sense of the *properties* of how **input data** is selected.

B. A consideration of **what** is being measured and **why**.

C. Some model against which genuine distinctive behaviour can **reasonably** be distinguished from mere coincidence: this provides the principal tool the use of which allows us either to seek a new hypothesis ("our results *post* experiment are so far away from what our hypothesis *predicted* would happen that our hypothesis must be wrong"') or continue to hold faith with the model we proposed ("we have been unable to obtain a set a results that are inconsistent with our model. Therefore, *pro tem*, we can continue to use this model as a true reflection of reality for the purposes of prognostication").

The reader may wonder at the rather verbose and seemingly over-cautious reading of what point (C) involves. As we look at some basic notions common to both Probability Theory and Statistics it is hoped that the need for such care will become apparent.

Now having focussed on motivational context over the past few pages let us turn to the actual quantitative and formal ideas at the heart of Statistics.

6.4   Basic statistical concepts

In this section we introduce some concrete formalisms which are subsequently exploited in the use of experimental studies with CS.

Population and distribution

When we conduct an experimental study there are two underlying entities we have to consider.

A1. The set of objects from which input data for the experiment are drawn. For example, if we are looking at the typical run-time of an algorithm this set would be the range of all possible inputs to the algorithm. When studying how robust a concurrent algorithm is with respect to individual processors failing (example (E4) above) this set might be either all of the distinct ways in which a collection of processors could be linked in effect, all possible **graph** structures. Alternatively, with respect to (E4) we may wish to focus on a specific set of processor interconnection schemes e.g. mapping to binary tree forms. Again, for settings such as that presented in (E2), this set might be the different collections or even just a *single* set of items we are interested in the algorithm classifying.

A2. The likelihood, that is the **probability**, that a given item from this set is chosen. For example, in the "typical run-time of an algorithm" case this probability would express the chances that a specific input to the algorithm occurs. In the processor network setting some combination of a given graph form being used *and* the chances of some specified collection of processors in the architecture fail. In the machine-learning example, the probability that a given "training example" is chosen.

The set of objects referred to within (A1) is called a **population**. Now this can be exactly the same as its standard natural language equivalent e.g. "the set of all individuals living in a specific location" or a more abstract entity e.g. "the set of all Natural numbers less than 20", "the six possible outcomes of throwing a single die", "the two possible results of tossing a coin".

It is also the case (although, typically in the examples we look at this will not be the case) that populations may contain infinitely many members, e.g. "the set of **all** Natural numbers", "the set of all binary trees", "the set of all directed graphs".

Such infinite populations are of interest if we are trying to extrapolate claims about behaviour in general, however, often we can do so by considering finite subsets of the population qualified by some parameter. So rather than "the population of all binary trees" we would consider "the population of all binary trees with exactly or at most n nodes".

Now suppose for the sake of initial presentation we have some population, Ω, containing exactly n, for some $n \in \mathbb{N}$ members

$$\Omega = \{t_1, t_2, \ldots, t_n\}$$

The concept arising in (A2) concerns how we determine what the chances of choosing $t_k \in \Omega$ are. For example, if we are considering the population $T = \{1, 2, 3, 4, 5, 6\}$ of outcomes from throwing a single die, then if the die is fair we would expect that each outcome is equally likely, i.e.

$$Prob[t_k] = \frac{1}{6} \text{ for each } t_k \in \Omega$$

In other words for each **outcome**, $t_k \in \Omega$, *the probability* of the die landing t_k is exactly $1/6$. Having introduced the concept in the sequel we shall write $\mathbf{P}[x]$ rather than $Prob[x]$. Now we are, of course, not restricted to "fair situations": simply because a die, D, has six different faces or a coin, C, two different sides does not necessarily mean that $\mathbf{P}[\text{C lands heads}]$ is exactly the same as $\mathbf{P}[\text{C lands tails}]$. We may wish to consider **biased** outcomes, those in which

$$\Omega = \{x_1, x_2, \ldots, x_n\}$$

is the population of interest, but

$$\mathbf{P}[x_k \in \Omega] \neq \frac{1}{n}$$

The notion of *probability distribution* over a population offers a means of capturing such bias.

A **probability distribution**, D over a population Ω associates a **probability**, $\mathbf{P}_D[x]$ with each member of x. In other words, D maps each $x \in \Omega$ to a value, $\mathbf{P}_D[x] \in \mathbb{R}$. As is probably quite evident, not every such mapping constitutes a probability distribution. There are two basic criteria D must satisfy in order to be regarded as such.

D1. For each $x \in \Omega, 0 \leq \mathbf{P}_D[x] \leq 1$. Every $x \in \Omega$ is assigned a **probability** of being chosen by D.

D2.
$$\sum_{x \in \Omega} \mathbf{P}_D[x] = 1$$

It is **certain** that **some** member of Ω will be selected under the distribution D.

That special distribution in which for $\Omega = \{x_1, x_2, \ldots, x_n\}$, $\mathbf{P}_D[x] = 1/n$ with every $x \in \Omega$ is called the **uniform** or, also, an **unbiased** distribution.

It may seem strange to consider anything other than uniform distributions but there are many well motivated settings in which we will wish to do precisely that.

Here are a few such examples.

Example 1:

A consumer survey is collating data involving individuals in a particular locale. Here the population is $X = \{x_1, \ldots, x_{2000}\}$. This population covers everyone living in the location, however, the group on whose behalf the survey is conducted is largely interested in the views of those living in the more affluent areas who comprise 5% of the population: $\{x_1, x_2, \ldots, x_{40}\}$ say. The chances of targetting is therefore set using the biased distribution

$$\mathbf{P}_D[x_i] = \begin{cases} 1/50 & \text{if} \quad 1 \leq i \leq 40 \text{ i.e. } x \text{ is affluent} \\ 1/9800 & \text{if} \quad 41 \leq i \leq 2000 \text{ i.e } x \text{ is not affluent} \end{cases}$$

Notice that, as may be easily verified the sum over all individual probabilities is 1, i.e. condition (D2) is met.

Example 2

An algorithm is claimed to solve the problem of deciding if an input graph has a *Hamiltonian cycle* quickly on average.[7] This claim is verified by assessessing its performance against graphs chosen at random. The probability distribution used to choose test graphs is unbiased. The algorithm, however, does not perform well when applied to "typical" graphs that arise in applications. The reason for the apparent discrepancy is that using a uniform distribution favours graphs which are *dense*: the number of links is large relative to the number of nodes, and the algorithm itself is particularly effective when given dense graphs as input. In practice, however, graphs arising in applications tend to be *"sparse"*: the number of links is small relative to the number of nodes. In such cases the method does not perform as strongly. Thus in assessing how good the typical behaviour of a graph based method is there is a strong case especially if the algorithm is being promoted for use in real settings for reviewing its behaviour not with respect to unbiased distributions but with respect to those which favour "sparse graphs".

Example 3

The prospective users of a data indexing tool which uses a binary tree structure to store and order records, allege that this tool is too slow having conducted an experimental evaluation of its behaviour on random binary trees. The study, however, has been carried out using a uniform distribution e.g. via the algorithm of Atkinson and Sack [14]. Typical binary trees tend to have paths from their root to a leaf node which are quite long. Similarly to the previous graph example, binary trees as they arise in "real applications" e.g. database indexing are shallow the depth of an n-node tree being around $\log_2 n$ rather than the $\sim \sqrt{n}$ in the uniform case. When assessed against a biased distribution

---

[7]See Endnote 1.

favouring "shallow binary trees" e.g. the so-called "binary search tree model", cf. [195], [63] the method performs much better.

As regards the situation described in this example, a study of the difference between "uniform" and "biased" outcomes relative to binary tree forms representing digital systems may be found in Dunne and Leng [73].

Random variables

Within the previous subsection we have introduced the key ideas of *population* – the set of cases from which the data used in empirical studies are drawn – and that of a defined *distribution* over the population. The latter notion recognizes as exemplified in the three examples presented at the conclusion that there are occasions for which "fair's got nothing to do with it".[8] Sometimes the most misleading results are those obtained by analyzing outcomes from the uniform distribution.

The probability distribution defined for use with a population informs us how we should *sample* that population's members. Of course, ideally, we would like to perform an experimental study to which **every** member of the population analyzed contributes. Unfortunately, and a central motivating reason for statistical methods, this is rarely a feasible option: polling organizations attempting to gauge the outcome of an election cannot, in general, ask every single member of an electorate what their intentions are.[9]

Typically the reasons why such exhaustive analysis is unrealistic is simply the sheer size of the underlying population. The notion of probability distribution is one method of limiting attention to "a few cases" without, however, distorting the outcomes deduced.

So notions of population and distribution help us in selecting specific elements to test, however, these ideas do not tell us how to **evaluate** an item that has been chosen. In order to address this issue we need the concept of **random variable**.

The idea underlying this is very simple: given a population, Ω, implicitly every element $x \in \Omega$, has some value concerning which we wish to estimate how the population as a whole behaves. In other words, we have some function, f (we limit attention to numerical instances) that reports a value for each $x \in \Omega$, that is $f : \Omega \to \mathbb{R}$.

---

[8]As observed by the character William Munny in Eastwood's film *Unforgiven*.

[9]In fact, recalling the wrongful prediction of the 1936 Landon v. Roosevelt U.S. Presidential election by the magazine *Literary Digest* based on a sample of two million compared with the correct call made by Gallup from a sample of fifty thousand, it is far from being the case that "the more members of a population contribute the more accurate the results will be".

Now in conducting a study of Ω we are, in effect, not dealing with the individual members of Ω *per se*, but with the collection

$$\{f(x_1),\ f(x_2),\ \ldots,\ f(x_n)\}$$

and so we could think of our probability distribution, D, as choosing a member $f(x_i)$ following the strictures laid out by D. In other words, choose $x \in \Omega$ with $\mathbf{P}_D[x]$ and having done so evaluate the chosen x according to f. With such a view, f is a random value (variable) according to how our distribution D tells us to choose x. It is important to note especially in considering measures such as average value that the value of the random variable r_f is a characteristic of the probability distribution, D. That is, if Ω is sampled according to two different distributions, D_1 and D_2 the value of $r_f(x)$ does not change for any specific $x \in \Omega$. What will change, as we shall see in the next subsection are the statistical measures derived for the population with respect to the distribution used.

In more formal language we have:

A **random variable** is a function, $X\ :\ \Omega \to \mathbb{R}$ associating a Real value with each member of the population Ω. Instead of considering distributions with respect to a population Ω, we can view these as **functions** of random variables on Ω.

It is important here to be clear that a **random variable** (for which we will denote an arbitrary case by X) is mapping from elements of a population Ω to Real values, so that when we write for some $x \in \mathbb{R}$ "$\mathbf{P}[X \leq x]$" this is a shorthand for "the probability that we have chosen some $\omega \in \Omega$ for which the random variable X returns a value $X(\omega)$ that is at most x".

The **distribution function** of a random variable, X, is defined to be the function $F : \mathbb{R} \to [0, 1]$ such that

$$F(x) = \mathbf{P}[X(\omega) \leq x]$$

in other words F captures the probability that we will choose from Ω an element, ω, for which $X(\omega) \leq x$. Subsequently we will not write $X(\omega)$ for $\omega \in \Omega$ when describing the action of a random variable within a given population, leaving this relationship to be implicitly present.

Distribution functions turn out to be useful in studying a number of general types of random variable that we will elaborate in Section 6.6, especially in those instances where we can identify some function, $f : \mathbb{R} \to \mathbb{R}^{\geq 0}$ i.e. the set of non-negative Real numbers with which

$$F(x) = \int_{-\infty}^{x} f(t)dt$$

A random variable, X is called **discrete** if with each distinct outcome, $X(\omega)$ of $\omega \in \Omega$ we can associate a **unique** $n \in \mathbb{N}$. It is important to note that this is **not** equivalent to stating that X maps from Ω to $\mathbb{N}$ although any random variable $X : \Omega \to \mathbb{N}$ or even $X : \Omega \to \mathbb{Q}$ is a discrete random variable. Formally, if V is the possibly infinite set of possible outcomes to which X maps Ω, then for X to be discrete, then V must be **countable**.

Some examples

Suppose the population is $\Omega = \{1, 2, 3, 4, 5, 6\}$ is the set of outcomes that may result when throwing a single die.

Random variables that could be of interest are,

D1. The number corresponding to the result thrown so that $X(x) = x$ for each $x \in \Omega$.

D2. Whether the result is a high number or a low number so that $X = \{0, 1\}$ and

$$X(x) = \begin{cases} 0 & \text{if} \quad x \in \{1, 2, 3\} \\ 1 & \text{if} \quad x \in \{4, 5, 6\} \end{cases}$$

D3. Whether the result is odd or even, so that again $X = \{0, 1\}$ and

$$X(x) = \begin{cases} 0 & \text{if} \quad x \in \{1, 3, 5\} \\ 1 & \text{if} \quad x \in \{2, 4, 6\} \end{cases}$$

D4. The square of the number thrown if it is both high and even; its square root if both low and odd, and the number itself if neither holds.

Here, $X = \{1, 2, \sqrt{3}, 16, 5, 36\}$ arising from

$$X(x) = \begin{cases} \sqrt{x} & \text{if} \quad x \in \{1, 3\} \\ x^2 & \text{if} \quad x \in \{4, 6\} \\ x & \text{if} \quad x \in \{2, 5\} \end{cases}$$

Notice that these are all **discrete** random variables.

Expectation, mode & median

We now wish to combine these elements – population, distribution and random variable – in order to focus on questions such as:

Q1. Given a population, Ω with n members, a random variable, X over Ω what value should we **expect** X, i.e. $X(\omega)$ to have when some distribution D is used?

Q2. Suppose we wish to **forecast** what will happen when we choose members from Ω according to D, e.g. by claims such as "the typical value of X when we conduct an **experiment** involving Ω will be 'close to' the value calculated in (Q1)". What methods are there to assess the correctness of such forecasts?

The matter raised under (Q2) can, in essence, be summarized very informally as: "if I conduct some experiment that yields a collection of numerical data, how can I assess these data relative to what I expected the result to be?".

Expected Value of a random variable

Given

$$\Omega = \{t_1, t_2, \ldots, t_n\}$$

and a random variable $X \; : \; \Omega \to \mathbb{R}$ the **expected value** of $X \in \Omega$ when selected via a distribution D is denoted by $\mathbf{E}[X]$ and defined to be

$$\mathbf{E}[X] = \sum_{t \in \Omega} \mathbf{P}_D[t] \cdot X(t)$$

For example, suppose, to avoid encumbering notation unduly, we write

$$X = \{x_1, x_2, \ldots, x_n\} = \{X(t_1), \ldots, X(t_n)\}$$

so that we may use

$$\mathbf{E}[X] = \sum_{i=1}^{n} \mathbf{P}_D[x_i] \cdot x_i$$

For our examples from earlier, we have in the special case of the uniform distribution,

$$\mathbf{E}[X] = \frac{1}{n} \sum_{i=1}^{n} x_i$$

For instance, returning to throws of single die in which the random variable is the number thrown.

If the die is fair then $\mathbf{P}[x = k] = 1/6$, and we expect to throw

$$\mathbf{E}[\{1, 2, 3, 4, 5, 6\}] \;=\; \frac{1 + 2 + 3 + 4 + 5 + 6}{6} \;=\; \frac{21}{6} \;=\; 3.5$$

We return to this example again, not because of its intrinsic importance but rather to illustrate an important point about this notion of "expectation" also called "average" or "mean" value. A die has six possible outcomes with each outcome a value in $\mathbb{N}$. Against this it may look somewhat peculiar to claim "the expected outcome when we throw a fair die is 3.5".

We have to be careful when interpreting what $\mathbf{E}[X] = x$ means. It is not necessarily the case that $x \in X$. In fact, when dealing with finite subsets T of $\mathbb{R}$, typically we find that $\mathbf{E}[T] \notin T$. What this notion of expected outcome attempts to describe is what we **expect** to happen over a large number of tests.

For example, suppose we threw the single die N times and added the total achieved. This total would always be at least N (we throw 1 on every single occasion) and would never exceed $6N$ (throwing 6 every time). If we look at the possible outcomes after N throws, we see it is that subset of $\mathbb{N}$ described by

$$X_N \;=\; \{\, k \,:\, N \,\le k \le\, 6N \,\}$$

For example when $N = 2$ or $N = 3$, we have

$$
\begin{aligned}
X_1 &= \{1, 2, 3, 4, 5, 6\} \\
X_2 &= \{2, 3, 4, 5, 6, 7, 8, 9, 10, 11, 12\} \\
X_3 &= \{3, 4, 5, 6, 7, 8, 9, 10, 11, 12, 13, 14, 15, 16, 17, 18\}
\end{aligned}
$$

Returning to the definition of $\mathbf{E}[X]$ we have seen that $\mathbf{E}[X_1] = 3.5$ and by looking at the 36 ways in which throwing a die twice in succession can land it not difficult to show that $\mathbf{E}[X_2] = 7$, and similarly, $\mathbf{E}[X_3] = 10.5$.

In general if we look at the expected outcome after throwing the die N times we find this to be $3.5N$. Overall the assertion $\mathbf{E}[X] = 3.5$ is not a claim about what will **definitely** happen after a **single** throw but rather a claim about how the die will behave if fair over a large number of throws. In Probability Theory such intuitive beliefs are formalized within a device called *The Law of Large Numbers*.

Property 4. *(The Law of Large Numbers) Let X be a discrete random variable over Ω and $\mathbf{E}[X]$ its expected value. Let Ω_N be the population Ω^N of possible outcomes resulting by choosing from Ω on N separate occasions. Given $\omega = \omega_1\omega_2\cdots\omega_N \in \Omega_N$, the discrete random variable $X_N : \Omega_N \to \mathbb{R}$ is*

$$X_N(\omega_1\omega_2\cdots\omega_N) = \sum_{i=1}^{N} X(\omega_i)$$

$$\frac{\mathbf{E}[X_N]}{N} \underset{N\to\infty}{\to} \mathbf{E}[X]$$

In other words "the more times we sample from Ω ($N \to \infty$) averaging the total outcome ($\mathbf{E}[X_N]/N$) the closer and closer we approach to the expected outcome of a single trial ($\mathbf{E}[X]$)".

To conclude this subsection we briefly mention two measures that are often used in addition to that of expectation: the **mode** and **median**.

If we take a given population, Ω, and look at applying some random variable, X, to its members then the **mode** of $< X(\omega_1), X(\omega_2), \ldots, X(\omega_n) >$ is simply that value, $X(\omega)$ that occurs most often. For example if Ω is a set of students and $X : \Omega \to \mathbb{W}$ the marks obtained by these in an exam[10] then the mode would be the mark that most students received, e.g. from $< 1, 1, 2, 4, 7, 8, 12 >$ the mode is 1 and expected mark 5.

The **median** of $< X(\omega_1), X(\omega_2), \ldots, X(\omega_n) >$ is found by arranging the $X(\omega_i)$ into ascending order and selecting the result which occurs in the middle. Formally if

$$< y_1, y_2, \ldots, y_n >$$

is the result of ordering

$$< X(\omega_1), X(\omega_2), \ldots, X(\omega_n) >$$

then the median value is $y_{n/2}$ if n is even or $y_{(n+1)/2}$ if n is odd. In our example we have the median is 4.

It is worth noting that the median is, often, a better indicator of "typical value" than expectation. In clinical studies, e.g. Mueller *et al.* [172], Salovin *et al.*[203, Table, p. 3] median figures are often given in addition to averages. Another example of such is the common political practice of quoting "typical

---

[10]Of course, in an ideal setting the range for X would be $\mathbb{N}$.

earnings" using expectation as a base. Suppose within a population one has

100, 000 people earning	£7, 000 *per annum*
10, 000 people earning	£70, 000 *per annum*
1, 000 people being paid	£700, 000 *per annum*
100 people being paid	£7, 000, 000 *per annum*

The expected annual salary is

$$\frac{100,000 \cdot 7000 + 10,000 \cdot 70,000 + 1000 \cdot 700,000 + 100 \cdot 7,000,000}{100,000 + 10,000 + 1,000 + 100}$$

Which gives a result of $\sim$ £25, 503.

The median and in fact also mode salary is that earned by the amount occurring at position 55, 550, i.e. £7000.

The concept of expectation formalizes the intuitive idea of what the typical value of a random variable is after sampling from a given population. In principle, the notion of expectation might seem sufficient to use as a measure of gauging empirical data: our experiment hypothesizes that the outcome of an experiment will be κ posited as the expected value of the population; conducting the experiment produces some value λ; if λ is very different from κ we conclude that our hypothesis that the expected value would be κ is unsubstantiated. Notice that we can improve our confidence in whatever judgement we reach via Property 4 by calculating λ as the outcome of running the experiment N times producing $\{\lambda_i : 1 \leq i \leq N\}$ with $\lambda = (\sum \lambda_i)/N$.

Independence & Conditional Probability

One of the most common sources of erroneous statistical analysis is to treat two outcomes, X and Y say, in a style suggesting that $\mathbf{P}[X]$ can be treated entirely separately from $\mathbf{P}[Y]$. While such may, indeed, be the case, it is not hard to find examples where such treatments are flawed, being based on an invalid assumption that X and Y are **independent** outcomes.

To see what this notion of "independence" concerns consider the following two groups of examples in which X and Y are two outcomes relative to the context described.

I1. A fair die is thrown fifty times: X is the event that it lands showing 1 on the first throw; Y is the event that it lands showing 6 on the fiftieth throw.

I2. A fair coin is thrown twice: X is the event that it lands HH or TT; Y is the event that it lands HT or TH.

I3. An individual finds it exciting to log details of cars using a busy road: X is the event that the first car seen is Green; Y is the event that the second car spotted is Orange.

I4. With respect to one academic session: X is the event "Over 90% of University of Liverpool C.S. students graduated with a classified Honours degree"; Y is the event "Under 5% of Harvard Law students graduated *summa cum laude*".

D1. Dealing from a standard 52 card deck: X is the event "Player A receives the first card which is a Red King"; Y is the event "Player B receives after the remainder of the pack is reshuffled the second card which is a Red King".

D2. Railway station schedules: X is the event "There is a signal failure at Crewe"; Y is the event "The train from Liverpool Lime St. to London Euston is delayed".

D3. Respecting the itinerary of a coach tour company: X is the event "Today is Tuesday"; Y is the event "The coach is in Brussels".

The situations described in (I1)–(I4) are examples of **independent events**: the probability of Y occurring is unaffected by whether X has or has not occurred: in (I1) $\mathbf{P}[X] = \mathbf{P}[Y] = 1/6$; in (I2) $\mathbf{P}[X] = \mathbf{P}[Y] = 1/2$: to see this it is sufficient to observe that there are four possible outcomes $\{HH, HT, TH, TT\}$ any one of which has probability $1/4$ of being the result. In (I3) whether an Orange car is spotted is simply a function of the number of Orange cars being driven around at the time not of the number of Green cars about. Finally, in (I4) one would hope it is self-evident that whatever it is that does governs the academic ability of Harvard Law students it is not the academic ability of contemporaneous Liverpool CS students.

In (D1)–(D3) we have a rather different setting: in each case the probability of the event Y is **dependent** on whether or not the event X has occurred. In (D1), there are only two Red Kings in a standard deck so X occurs with probability $1/26$. Whether Y happens, however, will be either with probability

$1/51$ (X **has** happened) or with probability $2/51$ (X did not happen). Notice that if we change X to "Player A receives the first card which is a **Black** King" while keeping Y as before, then X and Y are **still** dependent: $\mathbf{P}[X] = 1/26$ but $\mathbf{P}[Y]$ is $1/51$ (X did not happen as A received a Red King); or $\mathbf{P}[Y]$ is $2/51$: either X happened so leaving the chances of Y unchanged, or X did not happen but A received no Kings of any colour.

In (D2) X has a bearing on Y in that Liverpool–London trains pass through Crewe, even allowing for the fact that there may be delays for reasons other than signal failure. If Y is changed to "The train from Liverpool Lime St. to Wallasey is delayed" then X and Y can be considered as independent: Liverpool–Wallasey services not being routed through Crewe.

A discussion of (D3) may be found in work of Mel Stuart from 1969.[11]

The distinction between independent and dependent outcomes is of some importance when considering the likelihood of **both** X and Y occurring.

Independent events

If X and Y are independent then

$$\mathbf{P}[X \text{ and } Y] \;=\; \mathbf{P}[X] \cdot \mathbf{P}[Y]$$

Dependent Events

If X and Y are dependent then $\mathbf{P}[Y|X]$ denotes "the probability that Y happens given that the event X **has** happened" and is called the **conditional probability** of Y given X.

$$\mathbf{P}[X \text{ and } Y] \;=\; \mathbf{P}[X]\mathbf{P}[Y|X]$$

In order to extract $\mathbf{P}[Y|X]$ this, of course, requires $\mathbf{P}[X] \neq 0$.

Notice that using the convention X^C as a shorthand for the event "X does not occur", we can see that

$$\mathbf{P}[Y] \;=\; \mathbf{P}[Y|X] + \mathbf{P}[Y|X^C] \;=\; \frac{\mathbf{P}[X \text{ and } Y]}{\mathbf{P}[X]} + \frac{\mathbf{P}[X^C \text{ and } Y]}{\mathbf{P}[X^C]}$$

---

[11]*vide.* https://www.imdb.com/title/tt0064471/.

Variance & standard deviation

There is one obvious problem with the informal approach described at the end of Section 6.3: what is meant by "is very different from"? In order to answer this question we must look rather closer at the notion of "probability of choosing from a sample population" and introduce the key idea of **variance**.

Probability distributions as "area under a curve"

So far we have been regarding the idea of random variables as leading to a finite set of outcomes: we have a finite population, choose according to some distribution a member of this population and evaluate a function of interest for this choice. While this view is adequate for small-scale studies in which all information about the population and its properties is available or, at worst, can be calculated, in larger scale studies we may need to refine our approach. For example,

P1. Distributions capturing the number of successes in a large number of **independent** trials, e.g. the number of times a coin lands tails in N throws where N may be several 100s or even several 1000s.

P2. Distributions describing the spread of marks obtained in an exam taken by potentially several hundreds of thousands of students, e.g. the U.S. SAT tests; English GCSE and A-levels; Scots Highers and CSYS.

A number of ideas are used to describe (P1) one of the most important of these being the **Binomial Distribution**.

To see how this operates, consider tossing a fair coin N times. Since it **is** a fair coin we would expect two things to hold:

• The likelihood the coin lands heads on exactly k occasions from the N is exactly the same as the likelihood the coin lands tails on exactly k occasions.

• The number of times the coin lands heads will be about the same as the number of times the coin lands tails.

Now if we denote by

$b(N, k)$ = The probability of a fair coin landing H exactly k times in N

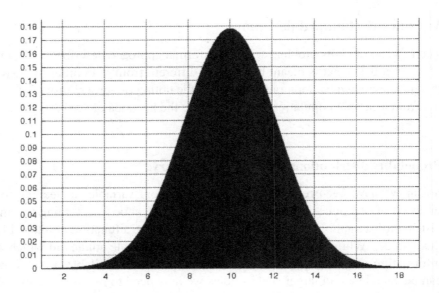

Figure 6.1: Outcomes for Fair Coin (20 throws)

Then,

$$b(N, k) \; = \; \left(\begin{array}{c} N \\ k \end{array} \right) \frac{1}{2^N}$$

What do the values $b(N, k)$ look like when we chart all of these for k between 0 and N? Should $N = 20$ we get Figure 6.1.

When $N = 100$ we get Figure 6.2.

We note that the functions actually plotted in these Figures are defined over the whole **Real** number interval of values between 0 and N otherwise the diagram would consist of a sequence of discrete steps. In fact what is depicted in Figures 6.1 and 6.2 is a *continuous* equivalent of Binomial Coefficients.

In both diagrams the horizontal axis gives the number of Heads thrown and the Vertical axis reports the probability that these events arise. In both cases the peak probability is for exactly half of the throws to have the same result: when $k = 10$ (Figure 6.1) this probability is ~ 0.18; when $k = 50$ (Figure 6.2) it is ~ 0.08. Noting our earlier expression for $b(N, k)$ it is not too difficult[12]

---

[12]This is via the approximation known as Stirling's formula from [223]:

$$n! \sim \sqrt{2\pi n} \cdot (n/e)^n$$

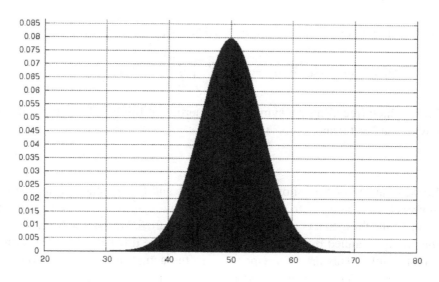

Figure 6.2: Outcomes for Fair Coin (100 throws)

to show that

$$b(N, N/2) \sim \sqrt{\frac{2}{\pi N}}$$

A second aspect of great importance in analyzing the behaviour of experiments whose underlying distribution is similar is the **shape** of the curve itself. In both instances and in general we have a symmetrical "bell–shape" centred about the middle point, $k = 10$ or $k = 50$ **and** the further away a given outcome is from this mid-point the more unlikely it is to occur.

Suppose we look at the event "more than k Heads occur" equivalently, "tails results at most $N - k - 1$ times". Looking at $b(n, k)$ we see that the likelihood of these are

$$b(N, > k) = \frac{1}{2^N} \sum_{i=k+1}^{N} \binom{N}{i}$$

This is rather cumbersome to manipulate, however one useful trick is to apply instead of the discrete form of $b(N, k)$ a continuous function equivalent. Denoting this continuous version by $F(n, t)$ which coincides with $b(n, k)$ whenever $t \in \mathbb{W}$, and $t \leq n$, it can be shown that,

$$F(n, > t) = \mathbf{P}[> t \text{ successes in } n] = (n-t) \binom{n}{t} \int_0^{0.5} x^{n-t-1}(1-x)^t dx$$

As an aside, notice when $t = n$ we see that $F(n, n > n)$ is

$$\mathbf{P}[> n \text{ successes in } n] = 0 \begin{pmatrix} n \\ n \end{pmatrix} \int_0^{0.5} x^{-1}(1-x)^n dx = 0$$

From which (recalling the symmetry properties) it follows that the chances of having "at least 0 successes" is

$$1 - F(n, > n) = 1$$

Looking at the picture shown in Figures 6.1 and 6.2 we can begin to see an approach to dealing with this question of how to measure "is very different from". One thing that is very apparent from Figure 6.2 is that the "area beneath the curve" spanned by throwing Heads 65 or more times out of 100 is almost unnoticeable. This area corresponding to the actual probability of so doing, i.e $F(100, > 64)$ is such that were we actually to throw 65 Heads on 100 throws it would seem more likely that the coin being used was **not** fair rather than that we had just been fortunate. Here, the parameters of importance are 100 (the number of trials); 50 (the expected number of Heads) and 65 (the actual number): 65 is sufficiently different from 50 in the context of 100 tests as to raise suspicions of an unfair coin being used. What we'd like to do is capture a general notion of these ideas: the concepts of **variance** and **standard deviation** allow us to do so.

Variance describes how spread out different outcomes are relative to their probability of occurrence. It thus offers a more refined view of how a random variable acts. Given a population, random variable X and probability distribution

$$X = \{x_1, x_2, \ldots, x_n\} \; ; \; D : X \to \mathbb{R}$$

we have seen that the expected outcome of X under D is

$$\mathbf{E}[X] = \sum_{k=1}^n x_i \mathbf{P}_D[X_i]$$

The **variance** of X under D is

$$Var(X) = \sum_{i=1}^n x_i^2 \mathbf{P}_D[x_i] - \mathbf{E}[X]^2 = \mathbf{E}[X^2] - \mathbf{E}[X]^2$$

In other words we consider the random variables comprising the collection $X^2 = \{x^2 : x \in X\}$; compute its expected value ($\mathbf{E}[X^2]$) and subtract from this the square of the expected value of X ($\mathbf{E}[X]^2$).

Returning to our single die case, with $X = \{1, 2, 3, 4, 5, 6\}$. We have seen that under the uniform distribution, $\mathbf{E}[X] = 3.5$. To compute $Var(X)$ in the uniform case we have $X^2 = \{1, 4, 9, 16, 25, 36\}$ so that $\mathbf{E}[X^2] \sim 15.17$ and $\mathbf{E}[X]^2 = 12.25$ giving $Var(X) = 15.17 - 12.25 \sim 2.92$. If we consider a distribution D with which

$$\mathbf{P}_D[x] = \begin{cases} 0 & \text{if} \quad x \in \{2, 3, 4, 5\} \\ 0.5 & \text{if} \quad x \in \{1, 6\} \end{cases}$$

Then, again $\mathbf{E}[X] = 3.5$. The variance under D, however, is now

$$\mathbf{E}[X^2] - 12.25 = (0.5 + 0 + 0 + 0 + 0 + 18) - 12.25 = 6.25$$

Despite the two distributions having identical expectations, the more polarized case where only 1 (lowest) and 6 (highest) outcomes are possible has larger variance.

Rather than applying variance directly as a measure of "distance from expected outcome" a structure known as **standard deviation** is used. In its purest form the Standard Deviation in X with $|X| = N$ with respect to D (which we denote by σ) is simply $\sigma = \sqrt{Var(X)}$. This suffices for many statistical studies even in those cases where it is not strictly accurate.

We measure how unexpected the outcome of an experiment is with respect to *the number of standard deviations by which the outcome differs from what was expected.*

An "idealized setting" for this is the q-test.

Let us assume that we have,

Q1. A population, Ω, random variable X and distribution, D, for which it is hypothesized that $\mathbf{E}[X] = \mu$.

Q2. The **known** standard deviation of X with respect to D: σ.

Q3. An experimental outcome obtained by choosing a sample, Y, from X using D and computing

$$\tau = \sum_{y \in Y} y \mathbf{P}_D[y]$$

For example in our coin throwing example using 100 throws in order to test the hypothesis that the coin used is fair, we would have

$\Omega = \{< H, T >^{100}\}$	:	the possible sequences of H and T
$X = \{0, 1, 2, \ldots, 100\}$	:	X counts the number of H
$\mathbf{P}[X(\omega) = k] = 2^{-100} \begin{pmatrix} 100 \\ k \end{pmatrix}$	:	The coin is hypothesized to be fair
$\sigma = 5$	:	Can be computed directly or, using $\sigma = \sqrt{N \cdot \mathbf{P}[H] \cdot \mathbf{P}[T]}$.
$\mu = 50$	:	we expect to see H 50 times.
τ	:	The **actual** number of times H occurs in 100 throws.

Having obtained all of these data, the q-test computes the value

$$q = \frac{|\mu - \tau|}{\sigma}$$

So that q measures the "number of standard deviations (σ) by which the result (τ) differs from the expected outcome (μ)".

We can relate specific numbers of standard deviations to levels of likelihood for the events described occurring. For example suppose we wish to look again at the initial hypothesis in the event of the experimental outcome having "only a 5% possibility" of being consistent with the hypothesis. As we did with our "throwing a single coin" examples (Figures 6.1 and 6.2) we can have a function, $f : \mathbb{R} \to [0, 1]$ describing the distribution so that $f(x) \equiv \mathbf{P}_D[x]$. Assuming this function is symmetric about its expected value, i.e. $f(\mathbf{E}[X] - \alpha) = f(\mathbf{E}[X] + \alpha)$, then we have,

$$\int_{-\infty}^{\infty} f(x) dx = 1$$

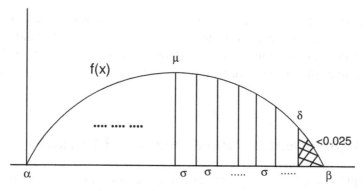

Figure 6.3: Counting number of standard deviations

[**Note:** the $(-\infty, \infty)$ range is just to ensure all possible Real values are accounted for, in general we will have some lower limit (α) and upper limit (β), e.g. for Figure 6.2, $\alpha = 0$, $\beta = 100$, and thence

$$\int_{\alpha}^{\beta} f(x)dx = 1$$

]

All that is then required in order to decide the number of standard deviations defining "only a 5% possibility" is (writing μ instead of $\mathbf{E}[X]$) to find that value δ with which

$$\int_{\mu-\delta}^{\mu+\delta} f(x)dx \geq 0.95$$

This is illustrated very informally in Figure 6.3.

The "number of standard deviations" is: δ/σ.

Suppose we have an outcome τ and $\tau - \mu \geq \sigma \cdot (\delta/\sigma)$. Then

$$\int_{\tau}^{\beta} f(x)dx \leq \int_{\mu+\sigma\cdot(\delta/\sigma)}^{\beta} f(x)dx$$

$$= \int_{\mu+\delta}^{\beta} f(x)dx$$

$$\leq \frac{0.05}{2} = 0.025$$

It should be noted that as suggested by the $|\mu - \tau|$ description in the q-test form we use the assumed symmetry of f to cater for both possible extremes: an outcome much larger than anticipated and one much smaller.

In Section 6.8 we consider standard **confidence levels** that have been used and how these are interpreted in terms of actual numbers of standard deviations. In the next section we look at how the notion of Standard deviation requires some adjustment in order to provide a useful measure in experimental analysis.

6.5 Adjustment to "Pure" Standard Deviation

In principle, the q-test offers a rough guideline in practice it is rarely the case other than toy games of chance settings that it can be used directly: the assumption that the standard deviation is known or can be computed easily being unreasonable.

In Statistics the fact that it is not always feasible to obtain an exact measure of the true standard deviation leads to the question of methods to estimate it. Thus we have two distinct notions

SD1. The standard deviation of the entire population being studied: this is our value σ from the previous section and to which **every** member of the population contributes.

SD2. The **estimated** Standard Deviation found by **sampling** the population.

In this section we wish to consider (SD2) and the corrections that can be applied in order to render the computational results nearer to the true Standard deviation, i.e. as captured within (SD1).

In order to distinguish the two we use σ to denote the standard deviation as a computation involving every member of the population. We now, however, use s_N for the estimate obtained by sampling N members of X.

The main conceit underpinning how (SD2) is obtained is that if we choose N members of the population then under certain conditions these can be used as the basis for estimating σ.

In total given the population, X, suppose we sample N elements from X, i.e. choose, $Y = <\ y_i\ :\ y_i \in X >$ with $1 \le i \le N$.

The **estimated** Standard Deviation of X is found by first computing $\mathbf{E}[Y]$

$$\mathbf{E}[Y] = \frac{1}{n} \sum_{i=1}^{N} y_i$$

and then taking the square root of the **estimated variance** so that

$$s_N = \frac{1}{\sqrt{N}} \sqrt{\sum_{i=1}^{N} (y_i - \mathbf{E}[Y])^2}$$

We note that some texts use an alternative form with $1/\sqrt{N-1}$ being the factor qualifying $\sqrt{\sum_y (y - \mathbf{E}[Y])^2}$, a process referred to as *Bessel's Correction*. This has some importance as a method of trying to correct for the disparity between the true standard deviation i.e. σ and the fact that only a finite sample is being used to estimate σ in the computation of s_N. We will, however, forgo detailed discussion of the subtleties and potential problems in adopting such corrections, merely noting that the form

$$s_N^{\mathrm{B}} = \sqrt{\frac{1}{N-1} \sum_{i=1}^{N} (y_i^2 - \mathbf{E}[Y]^2)}$$

as we will use to denote the estimate of standard deviation with Bessel's correction can be formally justified through analytic considerations showing that

$$s_N = \sqrt{\frac{1}{N} \sum_{i=1}^{N} (y_i^2 - \mathbf{E}[Y]^2)}$$

often *underestimates* the true value of σ.

Table 6.1 summarizes these parameters.

Table 6.1: Statistical Measures

Name	Notation	Definition
Expected/Mean/Average value	$\mathbf{E}[X]$	$\sum_{x \in X} x \cdot \mathbf{P}[x]$
Variance	$Var(X)$	$\mathbf{E}[X^2] - \mathbf{E}[X]^2$
Standard Deviation	σ	$\sqrt{Var(X)}$
Sample SD	s_N	$\sqrt{\frac{1}{N} \sum_{i=1}^{N} (y_i - \mathbf{E}[Y])^2}$
(Bessel) corrected SD	s_N^B	$\sqrt{\frac{1}{N-1} \sum_{i=1}^{N} (y_i - \mathbf{E}[Y])^2}$

Example: Exam Marks

As a very basic illustration of the difference Bessel's correction can produce, consider the following toy example.

In a population, X, of 1000 students we have

3 students	with mark :	0
50 students	with mark :	1
50 students	with mark :	2
100 students	with mark :	3
100 students	with mark :	4
200 students	with mark :	5
200 students	with mark :	6
150 students	with mark :	7
100 students	with mark :	8
40 students	with mark :	9
7 students	with mark :	10

Performing a "brute force" computation of $\mathbf{E}[X]$ we see that

$$\mathbf{E}[X] \;=\; 5.33 \;\;; \;\; \mathbf{E}[X^2] \;=\; 32.64$$

So that

$$Var(X) \;\sim\; 4.23 \;\;; \;\; \sigma \;=\; 2.06$$

Now, suppose we chose 10 from the $1,000$ at random. Assuming each student is equally likely to be selected it is not hard to see that

$$\mathbf{P}[y] \;=\; \begin{cases} 3/1000 & \text{if} \quad y's \text{ mark is } 0 \\ 1/20 & \text{if} \quad y's \text{ mark is } 1 \\ 1/20 & \text{if} \quad y's \text{ mark is } 2 \\ 1/10 & \text{if} \quad y's \text{ mark is } 3 \\ 1/10 & \text{if} \quad y's \text{ mark is } 4 \\ 1/5 & \text{if} \quad y's \text{ mark is } 5 \\ 1/5 & \text{if} \quad y's \text{ mark is } 6 \\ 3/20 & \text{if} \quad y's \text{ mark is } 7 \\ 1/10 & \text{if} \quad y's \text{ mark is } 8 \\ 1/25 & \text{if} \quad y's \text{ mark is } 9 \\ 7/1000 & \text{if} \quad y's \text{ mark is } 10 \end{cases}$$

Let us assume the ten chosen cases are

$$Y =< 1, 3, 0, 4, 5, 1, 5, 2, 6, 3 >$$

This sample has $\mathbf{E}[Y] = 3$ and using, s_{10} we get

$$s_{10} \;=\; \sqrt{\frac{1}{10}\sum_{i=1}^{10}(y_i - 3)^2} \;\sim\; 1.89$$

With, however, s_N^{B} we obtain

$$s_N^{\mathrm{B}} \;=\; \sqrt{\frac{1}{9}\sum_{i=1}^{10}(y_i - 3)^2} \;=\; 2$$

So that with this particular sample using the correction by $N-1$ i.e. 9 we obtain an estimate of σ which is closer to that computed without the correction, i.e $\sigma = 2.06$ and estimates of 1.89 and 2.

Using either s_N or the Bessel correction s_N^{B} instead of σ, allows a more finely tuned investigation of how a sample, Y, of size N compares to an hypothesized mean value, μ, by computing a t-value.

T1. Find

$$\tau = \frac{1}{N} \sum_{i=1}^{N} y_i$$

T2. Compute

$$(s_N^B)^2 = \frac{1}{N-1} \sum_{i=1}^{N} (y_i - \tau)^2$$

T3. The t-**value** is

$$t = \sqrt{N} \left(\frac{\tau - \mu}{s_N^B} \right)$$

We consider how this is used when we review the concepts of significance and confidence in Section 6.8.

6.6   The Normal and some discrete distributions

We now wish to consider a small number of distributions which arise very frequently in statistical studies. So much so that a common assumption in particular environments some of which we mentioned earlier in this chapter is that events within these follow the pattern indicated by appropriately parameterized instances of one of these. In such settings one aim of statistical studies is accurately to estimate the **exact** values of such parameters.

We begin with one of the most important and oft-occuring such cases.

The Normal Distribution $\mathcal{N}(\mu, \sigma^2)$

In general, $\mathcal{N}(\mu, \sigma^2)$ is characterized by two parameters:

μ : the Real value defining the **mean** of the distribution (that we earlier dubbed expectation).

σ^2 : the Real value defining the **variance** of the distribution.

If we are looking at the likelihood of some value $x \in \mathbb{R}$ then $\mathcal{N}(\mu, \sigma^2)$ defines this to be

$$f(x) = \frac{1}{\sigma\sqrt{2\pi}} e^{\frac{-(x-\mu)^2}{2\sigma^2}}$$

Of course what we are typically interested in studying is the likelihood of an experiment having an outcome falling between some range of values, e.g. as in our coin throwing example from earlier.

In these cases we want to look at reviewing $\alpha \leq x \leq \beta$,

$$\frac{1}{\sigma\sqrt{2\pi}} \int_{\alpha}^{\beta} e^{\frac{-(x-\mu)^2}{2\sigma^2}} \, dx$$

Of course, typically outside formal studies in probability we are not looking **explicitly to evaluate** expressions such as these. Having postulated an experimental context which is believed to be described by some $\mathcal{N}(\mu, \sigma^2)$ our primary interest will be in trying to estimate both μ and σ^2 using some test sample, Y, and thence drawing conclusions about general behaviour.

Normal distributions are often found or assumed to describe

1. the range of marks obtained by students in an exam.

2. the heights of adult females in a country.

3. currency exchange rates over a given period of time: the not universallly accepted Black–Scholes model [29].

In the remainder of this sub-section we consider three important **discrete** probability distributions which arise very frequently in applications.

The Binomial Distribution

Although we earlier considered some features of the Binomial distribution when discussing modelling distributions via definite integrals, for completeness we consider its aspects here, focussing on its importance as a discrete distribution.

The Binomial Distribution captures the behaviour of sequences of events in which each separate event reports one of two outcomes. Conventionally these outcomes are seen as **Success** (the result is 1) or **Failure** (the result is 0). Generally the Binomial distribution models the number of sucessess one might have within some number of trials. We have, already, seen one such example in the case of throwing a coin on N occasions: sometimes the coin will land **H**eads (success) at others it will land **T**ails (failure).

In this distribution one has,

B1. An (experimental) event or outcome, e, in which $\mathbf{P}[e = 1] = p$ and $\mathbf{P}[e = 0] = 1 - p$ where p is a fixed probability. In the "fair coin throw" example $p = 0.5$.

B2. The outcomes of successive trials are **independent**, so that even if there has been a run of N successes, the probability $\mathbf{P}[e_{N+1}]$ of the $(N+1)$'st trial as being successful is still p.

With these notions, any Binomial distribution is characterized by two parameters: n the total number of trials conducted, and p $(0 \leq p \leq 1)$ the probability that the outcome is success, i.e. $\mathbf{P}[e = 1] = p$.

The Geometric Distribution

Suppose we have some state of affairs we wish to bring about and whose eventuality will lead to ceasing attempts to achieve a further occurrence. For example, we might participate in a raffle in which

a. There are 1000 tickets available

b. We choose one ticket at random.

c. If our chosen ticket does not win then we replace it (i.e. return to the stock of 1000 tickets) and start all over again from (b).

d. If our chosen ticket does win then we cease playing.

In such contexts a natural question that arises is the number of attempts (i.e. the number of times step (b) is repeated) we might expect to be made before succeeding, i.e. step (d) is activated.

Settings such as this result in what is called the **Geometric Distribution**. The characteristics of events described by Geometric distribtions are that we have a probability, p, with which

$$\begin{aligned}
\mathbf{P}[\text{success on the \textbf{first} trial}] &= p \\
\mathbf{P}[\text{success on the \textbf{second} trial}] &= (1-p)p \\
\mathbf{P}[\text{success on the \textbf{third} trial}] &= (1-p)^2 p \\
&\cdots \\
\mathbf{P}[\text{success on the \textbf{n}'th trial}] &= (1-p)^{n-1} p
\end{aligned}$$

Notice that, as with the Binomial Distribution, events are independent in the sense the number of earlier failures does not reduce (or increase) the probability that the outcome of the next trial will change.

The Poisson Distribution

The **Poisson Distribution** arises in more dynamic contexts than those met above. In this case we are attempting to model the occurrence of events over some time interval. For example,

P1. The number of times a web site is accessed over a period of weeks.

P2. The number of "page faults" generated within some time frame.

P3. The number of births between $00:00$ and $05:00$ in a maternity hospital.

P4. The number of phone calls received at a Customer Services centre.

P5. The number of fatalities caused by horse kicks in a cavalry unit.[13]

The Poisson distribution arises through considering the behaviour of a particular class of discrete random variables. A **Poisson random variable**, X, is characterized by a single parameter $\lambda > 0$ and concerns activities whose outcome is $\{0, 1, \ldots, k, \ldots\}$. Specifically a discrete random variable is defined by a Poisson distribution with parameter $\lambda > 0$ if

$$\text{For } k \in \mathbb{W} \quad \mathbf{P}[X = k] \quad = \quad \frac{\lambda^k e^{-\lambda}}{k!}$$

Very often events that display the following behaviours can be modelled using Poisson distributions.

a. There is no upper limit on the number of times an event may occur within a given time.

b. Occurrences are independent, i.e. the fact that there has been one incident in an hour does not change the probability of a second incident within the hour happening.

c. The rate of incidents is constant, i.e. if 5 happen in one minute then 300 happen in one hour.

d. There is a minimum time interval δ with the property that for all times, t, either no event occurs in the interval $[t, t + \delta]$ or **exactly one** event occurs in this interval.

---

[13]This is one of the classic 19th century applications undertaken by the Russian economist Ladislaus Bortkiewicz (1868–1931) who promoted important uses of the Poisson distribution in [244].

Looking at the examples in (P1)–(P5), although it is not **guaranteed** that (a)–(d) will hold, the aim of modelling these cases via Poisson random variables is that, in principle (a)–(d) can be considered as defining typical behaviour. So we have, in (P1): (a) holds (number of hits on a web page is only limited by technological rather than statistical issues); (b) holds, at least at a primitive modelling level, since one user may access a page without any regard for what another is doing; (c) is perhaps arguable but can be used as a "working hypothesis"; finally (d) is the case as a side-effect of technology. What the interval δ actually is ($1\mu s$ or $1\ nano$) is irrelevant. Similarly with (P2) while other factors could distort the number of page faults viewing these as obeying a Poisson process at least gives a first approximation to how a system behaves.

Summary of Discrete Probability Distributions

In Table 6.2 we state, without proof, how the measures $\mathbf{P}[X]$, $\mathbf{E}[X]$, etc. behave with respect to the three discrete distributions just outlined.
    Within this Table,

A. describes the **Binomial** distribution.

B. the **Geometric** distribution.

C. the **Poisson** distribution.

Table 6.2: Characteristics of Discrete Probability Distributions

		$\mathbf{P}[X=k]$	$\mathbf{E}[X]$	$Var(X)$
A.	(n,p)	At least k successes in n trials $\mathbf{P}[(n,k)] = \sum_{i=k}^{n}\binom{n}{i}p^i(1-p)^{n-i}$	np	$np(1-p)$
B.	$p \neq 0$	success at test k after $k-1$ fails $\mathbf{P}[k]=(1-p)^{k-1}p$	p^{-1}	$(1-p)/p^2$
C.	$\lambda > 0$	k observations $\mathbf{P}[k]=\lambda^k e^{-\lambda}/k!$	λ	λ

6.7 Moments and their application

One is reluctant to do anything so obvious, at this juncture, as to quote from *Hamlet*.[14] Suppose we wish to demonstrate that some object "almost certainly" exists or does not exist? Problems of this type arise repeatedly in Computer Science. For example, in graph-colouring where one wishes to assign colours to graph nodes in such a way that no two adjacent nodes[15] are given identical colours, we may want to know when it is likely that four or more colours will be needed. Similarly in the realm of Boolean logic we may be interested in conditions under which logical formulae under inspection are **unsatisfiable**.[16] Questions such as these were investigated by probabilistic methods with, among other rationales, the aim of validating empirical observations concerning algorithms for, what are believed to be, computationally challenging classification problems.[17]

Among such empirical work and algorithmic study one has Larrabee [151], Freeman [91] Petford and Welsh [185] and many others.

A powerful technique by which analytically to investigate such concerns is through examining the "moments of the supporting distribution". Considering the most general form of such, the *k'th moment* (respectively k'th **central moment**) of the random variable X is denoted by m_k (resp. μ_k) ($k \in \mathbb{N}$) and given by

$$
\begin{aligned}
m_k &= \mathbf{E}[X^k] \\
\mu_k &= \mathbf{E}[(X - \mathbf{E}[X])^k]
\end{aligned}
$$

Why should these help with questions of the type raised at the opening of this Section? One insight giving an answer is a relationship between the expected value of a random variable being at least some quantity and the moments of the distribution: the relationship named, in honour of the Soviet mathematician Andrey Markov, the **Markov Inequality**.[18]

Markov's Inequality simply observes that for any $t > 0$,

$$
\mathbf{P}[X \geq t] \leq \frac{\mathbf{E}[X]}{t}
$$

---

[14]*"And enterprises of great pitch and moment// With this regard their currents turn awry,// And lose the name of action."*

[15]That is to say with an edge connecting them.

[16]Meaning that regardless of how we choose truth values for the variables the formula will never evaluate to **true**.

[17]For a more formal description we refer the reader, again, to Endnote 1.

[18]Although this relationship was actually discovered by Markov's teacher, Pafnuty Chebyshev.

which may be generalized to

$$\mathbf{P}[X \geq t] \ \leq \ \frac{m_k}{t^k}$$

Now suppose we have a particular means of constructing random graphs by which we can vary the likely number of edges that will be in the resulting constructions. Suppose, further, we wish to know how dense (that is the ratio of number of edges to number of nodes) the graphs ought to be in order for there to be a "high chance" that we **cannot** properly colour these with, say three, colours. All we need to do is the following,

C1. Find a **lower** estimate on the expected number of different ways we can three colour a typical graph produced by our random generator.

C2. Choose the "edge density" parameter in such a way that this expected number is zero.

For we then have

$$\begin{aligned}\mathbf{P}[G \text{ has } \textbf{at least} \text{ one colouring}] \ &\leq \\ \mathbf{E}[\text{The number of colourings of } G] \ &\rightarrow 0\end{aligned}$$

since we have parameterized our algorithm in order for this to be the case.

Of course in applying this approach there are some problems that must be dealt with, not least amongst which is addressing the counting problem in (C1). To give a flavour of how this can be tackled in practice we look at the simple example of determining how dense a random graph needs to be in order for it not to be possible properly to colour it with at most three colours.

First we describe our random graph model which is essentially a Binomial distribution. If we have n nodes then there are exactly $n(n-1)/2$ possible edges (noting that we exclude links from nodes to themselves). Suppose, independently of all other choices, having fixed a probability $p(n)$ we include an edge between node i and node j with probability $p(n)$ and exclude it with probability $1 - p(n)$. The chance of any graph with exactly t edges from the $N = n(n-1)/2$ possible being the result is precisely

$$\left(\begin{array}{c} N \\ t \end{array} \right) p(n)^t (1 - p(n))^{N-t}$$

and (since we are dealing with a Binomial distribution) we see from Table 6.2 that the expected number of edges is $N \cdot p(n)$. We need, however, to obtain an

upper estimate of the number of ways such a randomly chosen graph could be coloured with exactly three colours.

It we had no edges at all in our graph then there would be 3^n legal colourings since any node could be given any of the three colours. Every time, however, we choose there to be an edge between i and j this means that we must use **different** colours so that, with a single edge graph there are $2 \times 3^{n-1}$ legal colourings: $n - 1$ of the nodes can be coloured arbitrarily but (depending on the colour chosen for node i) there will only be two choices for node j. If we add a second edge the number of allowable colourings will be **at most** $2^2 \cdot 3^{n-2}$: $n - 2$ nodes are unrestricted but (again depending on where the two edges are located) the other two nodes will be limited. To see this, the possible configurations for the two edges are that neither has a common node (e.g. $\{1, 2\}$, $\{3, 4\}$) giving 3^{n-2} (all but $\{1, 3\}$ say) and 4 ways for $\{1, 3\}$) or both edges have a common node (e.g. $\{1, 2\}$, $\{1, 3\}$). In this case, we have complete freedom in colouring all but 2 and 3 (contributing 3^{n-2}) and exactly 2 choices for each of 2 and 3.

Now if we continue looking at the effect of adding a random edge to a graph with at most $\chi(m)$ legal colourings (m being the number of edges added so far) then we see that every new edge reduces the number of legal colourings by $1/3$, i.e.

$$\chi(m) \leq \begin{cases} 3^n & \text{if} \quad m = 0 \\ (2/3)\chi(m-1) & \text{if} \quad m > 0 \end{cases}$$

So that $\chi(m) \leq (2/3)^m 3^n$. It is, one hopes, obvious that the **expected** number of legal colourings in our random m edge graph is, therefore, bounded above by $\chi(m)$. This tells us, courtesy of Markov's inequality that

$\mathbf{P}[G$ chosen at random with $m = N \times p(n)$ edges is 3-colourable] $\leq$
$\mathbf{E}[$Number of legal 3 colourings of $G] \qquad \leq \chi(m)$

And hence,

$\mathbf{P}[G$ chosen at random with $m = N \times p(n)$ edges is 3-colourable] $\leq \dfrac{2^m 3^n}{3^m}$

With m chosen so that 3^m grows faster (technically is "asymptotically larger") than $2^m 3^n$ this expected number and the associated probability will go to 0.

A suitable choice of m turns out to be $\sim 5.419n$, so that a randomly constructed graph with an expected number of edges exceeding $5.419n$ will have a probability of being 3-colourable close to 0.[19]

---

[19]The value $c \sim 5.419$ is found as the solution to $3(2/3)^{c/2} = 1$.

It should be noted that this is a very crude and basic analysis and that rather more careful counting analyses are needed in order to improve the bound. Even a very limited improvement to 5.20566 requires some involved algebraic and combinatorial contortions, c.f. Dunne and Zito [74].

The *First Moment Method*, as this technique is called allows us to study behaviour of random variables via $\mathbf{P}[X > 0] \leq \mathbf{E}[X]$. In other words bounding from above the probability of existence. If we wish to obtain a **lower** bound on this quantity, the *Second Moment method* provides one avenue, since we may show, when X is a random variable having **finite** variance, that

$$\mathbf{P}[X > 0] \geq \frac{\mathbf{E}[X]^2}{\mathbf{E}[X^2]}$$

Higher moments are rather rarer although one important contribution is that of Berger [26] who considers fourth moments.

6.8   Confidence and hypothesis testing

So far we have considered various methods by which we can produce an estimate of what the true standard deviation σ within some population happens to be, in order to compare an average value calculated for a sample from the population with a value (μ) that is *hypothesized* to be the population mean.

It has been indicated that the notion of "number of standard deviations from the mean" provides one approach to assessing whether the hypothesis "the mean of this population is μ" is tenable.

In this section our aim is more fully to develop these ideas. In particular we wish precisely to formulate concepts such as "statistical significance" and "confidence level". We discuss how these are derived and the various pitfalls that can arise in their use.

We first introduce some terminology.

- The **Null hypothesis** (N.H.) is the claim that is being studied, e.g. the mean of this population **is** μ.

- A **confidence interval** for the mean specifies two items of information:

    C1. A **confidence level** describing the minimum probability for which the sample study is held to be consistent with the Null hypothesis.

    C2. A **range** by which the analysis of the sampled data should produce a result consistent with (C1)

- The **significance level** describes the level of probability for the sample data result being so unlikely relative to the Null hypothesis that the Null hypothesis is rejected,

- An experimental conclusion results in a **Type I error** if the Null hypothesis is, indeed, true but it is rejected.

- An experimental conclusion results in a **Type II error** if the Null hypothesis is invalid, however, the experimental study fails to produce sufficient evidence to allow its rejection.

For example, returning to the test for fairness of a coin thrown one hundred times that we discussed earlier in Section 6.4.

- The Null hypothesis is that the coin is fair, i.e. "it will land H fifty times out of the one hundred".

- We looked at confidence intervals in which the confidence level was set at 0.95 with the range being $50 \pm 5d$, recall that $\sigma = 5$ i.e. N.H. will be regarded as consistent with throwing the coin one hundred times if the number of times it lands H is at least $50 - 5d$ and at most $50 + 5d$. Note that the specific value of d that is to say the actual number of standard deviations involved is one of the questions we deal with in this section.

- The significance level was 0.05 also, often expressed as 5%: "the chance of our experiment producing a result outside the range of interest **and** the coin used being fair is less than 0.05: sufficiently low as to justify rejecting N.H, i.e the coin **is** unfair."

- A Type I error would be: the coin is fair but lands H so often in our one hundred trials that it is concluded not to be so.

- A Type II error would be: the coin is biased but the number of times H is seen is insufficiently different from fifty the number we expect to see that there is insufficient support for claiming bias."

We will discuss, later in this section, potential reasons for Type I and II errors, however, at this point our interest will focus on the matter of fixing confidence intervals. Reviewing the background we will work within we have

a. An underlying population, Ω, being investigated.

b. A **single** sample Y chosen from Ω or equivalently a collection of observations Y.

c. A distribution model into which Ω is assumed to fit. For example that Ω has a Normal distribution $\mathcal{N}(\mu, \sigma^2)$ or that the events observed in forming Y presume Ω is consistent with a Poisson process having a parameter λ.

d. The Null hypothesis is with respect to the unknown mean, μ working with Normally distributed data or λ with assumed Poisson processes.

e. The goal is to assess the extent to which Y is consistent with N.H.

f. In addressing (e) we want to fix an **interval** centred around $\mathbf{E}[Y]$, i.e. choose some value, α and consider the behaviour of Ω in the interval $[\mathbf{E}[Y] - \alpha, \mathbf{E}[Y] + \alpha]$.

g. Set a minimum level of confidence, C with $0 \leq C \leq 1$. This will be such that, in order to reject N.H, not only does μ lie outside the interval $[\mathbf{E}[Y] - \alpha, \mathbf{E}[Y] + \alpha]$ but would fall in a region consistent with the N.H. having at most $(1 - C)/2$ likelihood.

Looking at this template, the key question that arises is how to determine the appropriate confidence interval.

In empirical studies three so-called confidence levels are widely used: $C = 0.95$ (95% confidence); $C = 0.99$ (99% confidence); and $C = 0.999$ (99.9% confidence).

Keeping with these, the problem is to identify $\alpha(n, C)$ (n being the sample size of Y) for which: if μ (the hypothesized mean) does **not** fall within the region $[\mathbf{E}[Y] - \alpha(n, C), \mathbf{E}[Y] + \alpha(n, C)]$ then that μ **is** the true mean holds with probability at most $1 - C$.

Suppose we are dealing with data drawn from a presumed Normal Distribution $\mathcal{N}(\mu, \sigma^2)$. It is unlikely that either μ or σ are actually known so we must rely on estimates.

At the conclusion of Section 6.5 we introduced the t-value

$$ t = \sqrt{N} \left(\frac{\tau - \mu}{s_N^B} \right) $$

where μ is the hypothesized mean of the Normally distribution population, Ω, N is the number of samples in Y drawn from Ω with $\tau = \mathbf{E}[Y]$ and

$$ s_N^B = \sqrt{\frac{1}{N-1} \sum_{i=1}^{N} (y_i - \mathbf{E}[Y])^2} $$

the Bessel corrected estimate of the Standard deviation.

Depending on what level of C has been set, the status of N.H. can be gauged by determining the upper and lower levels for the mean as

$$\tau \pm t_{N-1} \frac{s_N^B}{\sqrt{N}}$$

The quantity t_{N-1} is derived from the so-called Student's t-distribution originating from [229].[20]

The actual value to use depends on,

T1 The number of **degrees of freedom** (D.F.). This being another term for the quantity $N - 1$.

T2. The confidence level required. This is our value C from earlier.

Now although it is possible explicitly to describe how to calculate $t(\text{D.F.}, C)$ a standard approach is to consider precomputed tables.[21]

One final point of importance is the distinction between 1-tailed and 2-tailed tests. In the former, a confidence level C is capturing one of the two cases $\tau-$ or $\tau+$ whereas the latter describes both. In consequence there is a distinction between "95% confidence 1-tail" the N.H is rejected if the conjectured mean falls into the, say, uppermost 5% region and "95% confidence 2-tail" the N.H is rejected if the conjectured mean falls into **either** the upper 2.5% region or the lower 2.5% region.

For example, suppose we were dealing with a population believed to follow the Normal Distribution $\mathcal{N}(0, 0.4)$ as shown in Figure 6.4

The 95% confidence region with 2-tails is depicted in Figure 6.5.

---

[20]"Student" is not used in the adjectival sense of "suitable for undergraduates" but was the pseudonym under which its discoverer, the English statistician William Sealy Gosset published. Gosset originally developed this in connection with quality control in the production of Guinness. Publication under a pseudonym was needed given the negative view of his employers to dissemination of ideas.

[21]Features to compute $t(\text{D.F.}, 0.95)$, etc. are now standard addenda to scientific and statistical calculators.

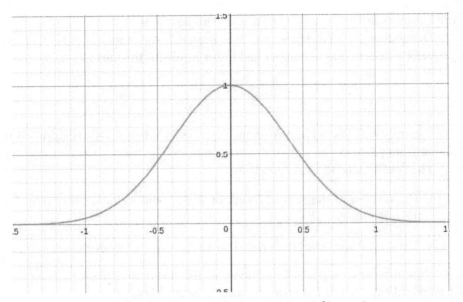

Figure 6.4: The Normal Distribution $\mathcal{N}(0, 0.4)$

To summarize, to evaluate a presumed Normally distributed population $\mathcal{N}(\mu, \sigma^2)$ where neither μ nor σ is known. To carry out a 95% confidence evaluation w.r.t. 2-tails.

1. Fix the sample **size**, N.

2. Select Y of size N cases.

3. Compute $\tau = \mathbf{E}[Y]$ and s_N^B.

4. Determine t_{N-1} the relevant t-value for 95% confidence.

5. The population mean μ is such that

$$\tau - t_{N-1}\frac{s_N^B}{\sqrt{N}} \leq \mu \leq \tau + t_{N-1}\frac{s_N^B}{\sqrt{N}}$$

with 95% confidence.

The discussion above considers environments where the population is assumed to follow a Normal distribution, $\mathcal{N}(\mu, \sigma^2)$. We have noticed that this is symmetric about the value $x = \mu$. For the other class of distributions that arise

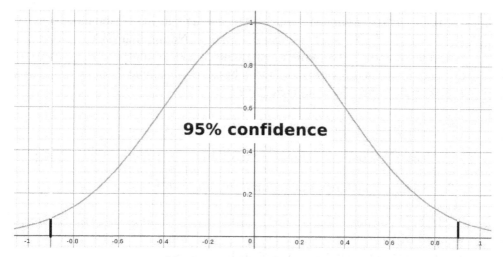

Figure 6.5: The 95% confidence region (2-tailed) for $\mathcal{N}(0, 0.4)$

often in empirical studies – the Poisson distribution – this symmetry is usually not present.

In Figure 6.6 we give the extended to $\mathbb{R}$ plot of probabilities in the Poisson distribution for the case $\lambda = 3$.

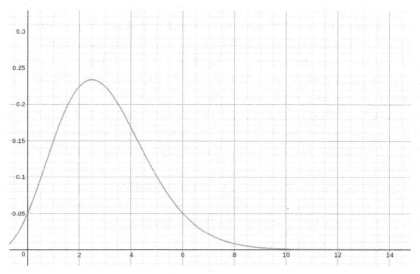

Figure 6.6: The Poisson process with $\lambda = 3$

If we wish to examine statistics relative to a putative Poisson model having $\mathbf{P}[k] = (\lambda^k e^{-k})/k!$ we can do so as follows. Noting that $\mathbf{E}[X] = \lambda$ for X a random variable with a Poisson distribution and, similarly $\sigma = \sqrt{\lambda}$, we can estimate upper and lower limits for λ based on a sample Y of observations. For example, with 95% confidence intervals,

P1. Compute $\tau = \mathbf{E}[Y]$ and $s = \sqrt{\tau/N}$.

P2. The 95% confidence lower limit for λ is: $\tau - 1.96s$.

P3. The 95% confidence upper limit for λ is: $\tau + 1.96s$.

It should be noted that the constant 1.96 can in a similar way to that which we used with t-tests be improved in a variety of ways, see e.g. Patil and Kulkarni [181] for a comparative study of such methods.

Comparing two samples – Welch's Test

While the confidence intervals obtained through applying the t-test are, quite robust as a mechanism for testing hypotheses regarding the behaviour of **single** samples drawn from a **single** population there is a presumption which sometimes renders it less reliable when we wish to compare the behaviour of two **different** samples, e.g. if we want to compare the typical performance of two different software methods and hypotheses that their average run-time is comparable. This comes from there being an underlying assumption that the two samples have similar variance. Where it is the case that the variances are different, testing a Null hypothesis stating $|\mu_1 - \mu_2| = 0$ where μ_1 and μ_2 are the hypothesized population means, requires some subtle modifications. The statistical test discovered by Bernard Welch ([254]) offers, an admittedly more complicated, development of the t-test that can reliably deal with questions about the comparative means of two or, indeed, more samples. In common with the t-test it is assumed that the underlying populations are both normaly distributed.

If we have populations Ω_1 and Ω_2, concerning which we have chosen samples $Y_1 \subset \Omega_1$ and $Y_2 \subset \Omega_2$: it is not required or assumed that Y_1 and Y_2 are equal sizes, Welch's test involves the following preliminary computations to be carried out.

$$t_w = \frac{\tau_1 - \tau_2}{\sqrt{\frac{s_1^2}{N_1} + \frac{s_2^2}{N_2}}}$$

$$df_w \sim \frac{(s_1^2/N_1 + s_2^2/N_2)^2}{\frac{(s_1^2/N_1)^2}{N_1-1} + \frac{(s_2^2/N_2)^2}{N_2-1}}$$

In these expressions s_1^2 and s_2^2 are the Bessel corrected sample variances ($s_{N_i}^2$) for the sample sets Y_1 and Y_2 and τ_1 (respectively τ_2) the sample means. The value df_w approximates the number of degrees of freedom for the test.

In total, suppose we look at Ω_1 and Ω_2 of which we can only assume that both are normally distributed, the former with respect to $\mathcal{N}(\mu_1, \sigma_1^2)$ and the latter with respect to $\mathcal{N}(\mu_2, \sigma^2)$.

We set as N.H. the assertion $\mu_1 = \mu_2$ and take samples Y_1 from Ω_1 and Y_2 from Ω_2. If we are working with a 95% confidence interval, we calculate

W1.

$$\tau_1 = \frac{1}{N_1} \sum_{y \in Y_1} y \; ; \; \tau_2 = \frac{1}{N_2} \sum_{y \in Y_2} y$$

W2.

$$s_1^2 = \frac{1}{N_1 - 1} \sum_{y \in Y_1} (y - \tau_1)^2 \; ; \; s_2^2 = \frac{1}{N_2 - 1} \sum_{y \in Y_2} (y - \tau_2)^2$$

W3.

$$df_w = \frac{(s_1^2/N_1 + s_2^2/N_2)^2}{\frac{(s_1^2/N_1)^2}{N_1-1} + \frac{(s_2^2/N_2)^2}{N_2-1}}$$

W4. The $(1 - \alpha)$ confidence interval for $\mu_1 = \mu_2$ e.g. $\alpha = 0.05$ is

$$(\tau_1 - \tau_2) \pm t(\alpha, df_w)\sqrt{\frac{s_1^2}{N_1} + \frac{s_2^2}{N_2}}$$

Here $t(\alpha, df_w)$ is the 1 or 2-tail test value as required t-distribution confidence factor. Often, recognizing that $df_w \notin \mathbb{N}$ the calculated value is rounded down to the nearest integer.

We conclude this section by briefly discussing potential sources of Type I ("N.H. wrongly rejected") and Type II ("N.H. wrongly accepted") errors. One of the main reasons for the popularity of 95% as a confidence interval is that, while not foolproof, it has a tendency to minimize occurrences of such errors.

Using 99% or even 99.9% reduces the likelihood of Type I errors since the threshold set is so high that if N.H. is valid it is rather less likely to be thrown out by an unfortunate sampling anomaly. It is the case, however, that this degree of robustness increases the chance of Type II errors: an hypothesis that is correctly rejected because the tested average μ lies in the $95.1 - 95.2\%$ region will be wrongly accepted with 99% confidence levels.

On the other hand, Type I errors may be more likely with lower acceptance thresholds. Welch's test is recognized as less prone to Type I errors, see e.g. Wang [252].

One technique that can be used to reduce although not eliminate completely Type I errors when using 95% intervals is that of conducting several independent sampling experiments, so that if e.g. five samples of size 25 all indicate N.H. should be rejected there is some likelihood although not certainty that this is a correct conclusion.

We note that Type I and Type II errors are inevitable consequences of statistical processes: while these may arise through fallacious application of techniques these are not, in themselves, fallacies. Misapplications and questionable reasoning via statistics is the topic reviewed in the next section.

6.9   Statistical fallacies and misuse

We now consider some of the more common fallacious beliefs and abuses of statistics and probabilistic reasoning. A very readable and informal presentation of these topics may be found in Darrell Huff's classic text originally from 1954 [124].

Bigger is not the same as better: large vs. small

We have noted in several places that it is, usually, impractical to query *every* member of a population Ω. It might seem that, in the absence of exhaustive data, the best approach is to try and sample as many members as possible. Such an approach, however, does not necessarily provide more reliable results.

We have already mentioned one instance where a "large sample" led to an inaccurate prediction, despite a "small sample" making a correct forecast: the 1936, U.S. Presidential election, in which one survey of two million individuals led to it being claimed that the Republican Alfred Landon would defeat the incumbent president F. D. Roosevelt with 57% of the popular vote whereas the latter retained office achieving 62% of the vote. With respect to the same election Gallup, on the basis of $50,000$ samples correctly predicted that Roosevelt would win. In this specific case it is clear that "more data" does not always result in better predictions.

It is not too difficult with hindsight to see reasons for this discrepancy. The two million element sample was not only biased, but arguably, biased in a manner that favoured the candidate predicted to win. Why was this? It was conducted by a periodical the now defunct *Literary Digest* who conducted its survey by soliciting by post the opinions of **ten** million people drawing the names not randomly but through merging lists of phone directories, club memberships, magazine subscribers. One immediate issue with this base is that it leant towards people likely to support the Republican platform over the social agenda promoted by Roosevelt, i.e. financially secure with disposable income at a level to afford private club subscriptions and magazines.[22]   In contrast, despite being barely 1% of the target size, Gallup's study, by avoiding inherent bias was not subject to these problems.

Another problem, also to some degree affecting the tendency reported, with the *Literary Digest* poll, was the fact that although over ten million opinions were solicited, just over two million replies in the form of a "dummy ballot paper" to be posted to the magazine's offices were received: a number of those targetted may have dismissed the survey paper as junk mail; others may have been reluctant to invest the time and postage costs involved in completing the survey.

In selecting a sample from a population what is important is not to maximize its size but to minimize any inherent sources of bias in its members. This fact is now recognized by psephologists who have refined methodologies to focus on voter intentions in marginal constituencies in the U.K. Such constituencies describe areas which often change between elections. Other foci for studying voter intentions are ideas such as target seats: the constituencies which parties consider they need to be successful in order to continue or take over government; and in the U.S. the concept of "swing states" or "bellwether states". The U.S. polling organizations recognizing that many states consistently vote in the same way over a number of elections. Bellwether states are those which have a history of returning in favour of the eventual successful presidential candidate.[23]

---

[22]It should be remembered that in 1936 the effects of the 1929 Wall St. crash were still evident so that expenditure on club dues and reading matter particularly given levels of unemployment would be something of a luxury.

[23]For example, Missouri has voted in favour of the winning candidate in every U.S. election except 1956 since 1904.

Summary: Larger sample sizes do not necessarily lead to more accurate empirical analyses compared to smaller samples. In sampling from a population a key element is to try and filter out bias.

Post hoc ergo propter hoc and Causality fallacies

Suppose we have two studies of, say, an Operating system's activity. The first (Study A) suggests that

"85% of student users are compiling programs written in the language BAD-SOFT[24] between the hours of $13 : 00$ and $15 : 00$."

The second (Study B) suggests

"After $15 : 00$ the system exhibits 95% fewer total page faults than between $13 : 00$ and $15 : 00$."

It is concluded that

"Use of BADSOFT results in a significant deterioration in overall system performance."

This, of course, is a standard logical reasoning fallacy: simply because an event, Y, is observed following an event X does not, necessarily mean that "X causes Y". Although in the scenario it *could* be the case that the events in A are linked to the events in B there may be other reasons. For example there may be other activity between $13 : 00$ and $15 : 00$ which, once ceased, leads to better system performance e.g. possibly daily back-ups are scheduled at this time since it is considered unimportant if student activity is disrupted.

Summary: Simply because an event Y frequently occurs in close proximity to another event X is not sufficient to justify the assertion "X caused Y". The occurrence of Y may have arisen on account of other factors, so that at the very least, before "X caused Y" can be considered defensible other causes of Y may require exploration.

---

[24]There is, of course, no such programming language: one is reluctant to traduce any currently or, indeed, historically widely-used high-level languages.

Outlier effects

In some ways this is similar to the "average versus median" effect we noted earlier in Section 6.4. Consider the following three statements

S1. The rôle and responsibilities of a University Vice-Chancellor[25] are similar to those of the Chief Executive Officer (CEO) of a large company.

S2. The average CEO receives six times as much in annual salary as is paid to the average VC.

S3. Therefore, in view of (S1) and (S2), University VCs are fully justified and, indeed, exhibiting considerable restraint in asking for annual salary increases of 400%.

While one could debate the extent to which (S1) is valid, the potential flaw in the statistical argument being used to promote vice-cancellarian cupidity, is the assessment by which (S2) is reached. Suppose one has a group[26] of 10 VCs

3 of whom are paid	£200,000
1 who receives	£250,000
4 of whom are paid	£350,000
2 of whom are paid	£475,000

Comparing with a selection of 10 CEOs sampled at random, one finds

4 of whom are paid	£500,000
2 of whom receive	£650,000
3 of whom are paid	£450,000
1 who is paid	£15,000,000

The average VC salary is £320,000. The average CEO salary from the sample is, on the other hand, £1,965,000 or about ~ 6.14 times as much. To this extent there may appear to be some justification for the assertion advanced under (S3). Suppose, however, we replace the CEO being paid £15,000,000 with one whose annual renumeration is £700,000. The average CEO pay is now £535,000 only ~ 1.67 times higher.

The computation of "average CEO pay" is distorted by a single outlier: the contributing figure of £15,000,000.

---

[25]"Vice" in this context means "in place of" and not, despite several examples to the contrary "possessed of questionable moral standards".

[26]I am unsure of what the collective noun for such a group is, although there would seem judging from UK performance to be strong arguments for "a craven of VCs".

One danger in making statistical claims regarding average quantities on the basis of comparisons between groups is that "averages" can be affected by such outliers. While using median rather than average can go some way to avoiding the issue, e.g. in the example median VC pay is £350,000 whereas median CEO pay in both cases is £500,000, it is not hard to construct misleading example with apparently disparate medians and averages arising from a single outlier in one sample.

Notice if we consider the values of s_N^B for these samples we get

$$s_{10}^B \sim £105,278 \quad \text{VCs}$$
$$s_{10}^B \sim £4,580,639 \quad \text{CEOs}$$

From which it is clear that CEO levels of renumeration are considerably more dispersed: presenting the argument in terms of **all** of average pay, median pay **and** standard deviation or variance would give a far less convincing case: $(320,000; 350,000; 105,278)$ against $(1,965,000; 500,000; 4,580,639)$: median values are similar and CEO pay while being higher on average is considerably more widely dispersed.

Summary: Averages may be distorted by a small number of extremely low or extremely high value samples, these being called *outliers*. In attempting to reason from two sets of data drawn from distinct populations parameters in addition to the average of both samples need to considered.

Reading too much into results: overgeneralizing

If a statistical claim is supported having looked at a sample Y of a population Ω, irrespective of the strength of support for the claim within Y it would be fallacious to assume the same holds for the population Ω as a whole. For example, suppose a University CS department consults undergraduates studying on its degree programmes regarding which from {C#, JAVA, PYTHON, ADA, PASCAL} should be used as the basis for Algorithms and software applications modules. Even in the event that 99% of respondent students indicated a preference for, say, C# this cannot be used to assert that **all** students prefer C# to other options: the survey has been limited to undergraduate CS specialists, however students from different programmes could have very different opinions as to what should be taught on introductory programming modules; similarly Masters' CS students could have opinions distinct from UG students.

Summary: Deductions from empirical studies, if based on a sample, Y, from a *sub-population*, Ω' within a larger population, Ω do not give a basis for generalization to Ω. In fact, these may not even provide a good foundation for generalizing to Ω',

Proving the Null Hypothesis

The typical context we have considered for experimental study involves presumed Normally distributed populations, Ω, e.g. falling into some distribution $\mathcal{N}(\mu, \sigma^2)$, and a sample, Y, of N members of Ω. If we have already hypothesized a mean value, μ' say, then the N.H. asserts "The mean of the underlying Normal distribution is μ'". Should, however, this turn out to be consistent with the analysis of Y, then it does **not** constitute a **proof** that N.H. holds: merely that the sample Y provides insufficient ground to reject N.H.. Similarly, if Y were such that the hypothesized mean μ' did not lie within the region $\mathbf{E}[Y] \pm st(Y)$ where $st(Y)$ is the statistic, e.g. t-value calculated using T, again such does not constitute a **proof** that N.H. is false: only that the sample chosen provides some support for querying its validity, however other samples may behave in a different manner.

Summary: Experimental investigation of an hypothesis does not categorically prove or disprove that hypothesis. Analysis of empirical findings can only provide some degree of evidential backing for its rejection or demonstrate that insufficient grounds have been found to claim it does not hold.

6.10   Selected example cases

We discussed some motivating reasons and difficulties with assessing average-case performance when looking at when looking at ways in which $\mathbb{C}$ has been adopted in CS in Section 5.8.

If we can model the distribution of input instances and have some knowledge of an algorithm's **asymptotic** behaviour, then one could use empirical analysis, of the form we have been discussing, to glean some information about the **constant** typically qualifying the asymptotic performance.

Constant Factors in Quicksort Implementations

As a very basic example consider the sorting method known as Quicksort, discovered by Hoare [119]. It is known that the **average** number of comparisons used by the algorithm to sort n items is $O(n \log n)$. One common objection to the notation $O(\ldots)$ is that this can hide information about the usability of methods since should the constant factor qualifying $f(n)$ in $O(f(n))$ be unreasonably large then the fact that the application can be solved in "$O(f(n))$" may be of little more than theoretical interest as opposed to affording a realistic solution. A well-known example of this is the $O(\log n)$ parallel time sorting approach from Ajtai, Komlós, and Szemerédi [5].

In demonstrating that the constant factor qualifying $n \log_e n$ for Quicksort is moderate we could proceed via an analytic demonstration. Some sense of the intricacy of argument required here may be found in the paper of Fill and Janson [86] which considers similar problems.

Alternatively we can try and form some empirical conclusions.[27]

The very superficial study below demonstrates this approach for one implementation of Quicksort.

In this we consider random permutations of n items.[28] Thus we have as the underlying population Ω_n,

$$\Omega_n = \{\underline{\pi} = < \pi_1 \pi_2 \cdots \pi_n > \; : \; \underline{\pi} \text{ is an ordering of } < 1, 2, 3, \cdots, n >\}$$

For each n we consider a sample of 50 elements $Y_n \subset \Omega_n$ and determine the average number of comparisons taken to order the permutation normalizing this value by the known asymptotic value $n \log_e n$. So the implicit random variable $X : \Omega_n \to \mathbb{R}$ is

$$X(\underline{\pi} \in \Omega_n) = \frac{\text{Number of comparison steps used by Quicksort on } \underline{\pi}}{n \cdot \log_e n}$$

Using a 95% 1-tail confidence interval, we have 49 degrees of freedom and $t_{49} \sim 1.68$. Table 6.3 summarizes the results from the experiment where n ranges between 10 and 200 in steps of 10.

This suggests a constant factor, qualifying $n \log_e n$ between 1.34 averaging the lower limits, which we recall are derived independently of n and with 50 samples in every case and 1.4 in a similar style by averaging the upper limits.

---

[27]Notice that one important aspect of this approach is that, although not providing a rigorous formal proof of behaviour it may suggest directions that formal analyses could consider, e.g. if experimental study of an $O(t(n))$ average run-time algorithm suggests a constant factor $K = 1000$, there may be little point in trying to prove behaviour of $K = 1/2$.

[28]Some detail is being glossed over in viewing the demands made of a sorting algorithm relative to a random permutation as "normally distributed".

Table 6.3: Experimental Outcomes for Quicksort Comparisons

n	$Mean\ (\tau)$	s_{50}^{B}	Lower Limit	Upper Limit
10	1.03	0.12	1.0	1.06
20	1.15	0.13	1.11	1.18
30	1.25	0.18	1.21	1.30
40	1.26	0.12	1.23	1.30
50	1.33	0.15	1.30	1.37
60	1.34	0.12	1.31	1.37
70	1.38	0.18	1.35	1.41
80	1.39	0.16	1.35	1.43
90	1.39	0.16	1.36	1.42
100	1.41	0.11	1.39	1.44
110	1.45	0.14	1.41	1.48
120	1.41	0.12	1.38	1.44
130	1.43	0.12	1.40	1.46
140	1.43	0.12	1.40	1.46
150	1.49	0.12	1.46	1.51
160	1.44	0.12	1.41	1.47
170	1.44	0.1	1.42	1.46
180	1.49	0.12	1.46	1.52
190	1.47	0.1	1.44	1.50
200	1.44	0.1	1.42	1.47

It is worth, however, recalling that there are several factors that may skew this particular study (again, we emphasize that the aim in presenting this particular example is to give a brief illustration of how experimental means may be used in analyzing algorithm behaviour and not to make rigorously verifiable assertions about the outcome). Among these one finds:

S1. A specific "naive" implementation of Quicksort is used.[29] More sophisticated realizations would be likely to show different outcomes.

S2. The sample population, Ω_n is restricted to permutations of $< 1, 2, 3, \ldots, n >$ so that the items being ordered are always **distinct**. It has been observed by several researchers that Quicksort's comparison counts are affected by factors such as

[29]For readers familiar with the basic mechanics of Quicksort one aspect of this naivety is that the "pivot" location is always chosen as the first element.

a. The proportion of items which are identical.

b. How "disordered" the list of items is initially: a standard "folk-lore theorem" being that the worst-case instance is for collections which are already sorted in reverse order.

Exam strategy and the Geometric Distribution

A University department decides that, in order to relieve the pressures occasioned through significant student numbers, exams will be based around Multiple Choice Question (MCQ) papers. The following procedures are adopted.

1. Papers will contain N questions, each with k options, exactly one of which will be the correct answer.

2. The correct answers are always ("roughly") evenly distributed, so that for any MCQ paper with N questions and k options per question, for each choice c in $\{1, 2, \ldots k\} \sim N/k$ questions will have c as its correct answer.

3. To achieve a passing score on a paper at least some number, t, from the N questions must be answered correctly.

4. In order to comply with the bizarre diktats arising from the, increasingly eccentric, pronouncements of the institution's Academic "Quality" Office, there will be no upper limit on the number of attempts that an exam may be resat, although it is understood that "different" question papers will be used in further sittings.

The parameters N, k and t are decided by the setter of a given paper subject, of course, to the constraint $0 \leq t \leq N$.

Suppose a (not especially diligent) student decides to adopt the following "study strategy". Since the student is only interested in eventually attaining a passing mark, he[30] decides to avoid actually revising, relying instead on the generous provision for resit opportunities and luck. Having been informed of the parameters (N, k, t) the student decides that when the exam takes place he will:

---

[30] Although one tries to avoid gender-specific pronouns as far as possible, from my personal experience while I have encountered many male students who might adopt the strategy about to be described, I cannot say I have met any female student so indolent.

a. Smuggle a fair k-sided die into the Exam Hall.

b. Determine what answer to select based on rolling this die.

c. Each successive question will result in a further roll of the die.

Question: If a student adopts this strategy, how may times would he expect to take the exam before reaching a passing standard?

Analysis: First notice that attempts at successive papers may be seen as independent. This is because given the assumption that correct answers are evenly distributed over possible options as specified in (2) with the strategy chosen, the probability $\mathbf{P}[1]$ of passing on the first attempt depends only on the parameters (N, k, t). Noting that the probability of guessing a **single** answer correctly follows a Binomial distribution, as can be seen by noting it to be $1/k$ while that of an incorrect answer is $(k-1)/k$. In total,

$$\mathbf{P}[1] \;=\; \sum_{i=t}^{N} \binom{N}{i} \frac{1}{k^i}\left(1-\frac{1}{k}\right)^{N-i}$$

which is

$$\mathbf{P}[1] \;=\; 1 \,-\, \sum_{i=0}^{t-1} \binom{N}{i} \frac{1}{k^i}\left(1-\frac{1}{k}\right)^{N-i}$$

Referring to Table 6.2, we see that the expected number of attempts to reach a passing level is $1/\mathbf{P}[1]$, i.e.

$$\left(1 \,-\, \sum_{i=0}^{t-1} \binom{N}{i} \frac{1}{k^i}\left(1-\frac{1}{k}\right)^{N-i}\right)^{-1}$$

For example with parameters (N, k, t) set to $(20, 8, 4)$ we get

$$\mathbf{P}[1] \;=\; 1 \,-\, \left(\frac{7}{8}\right)^{20}\left(1+\frac{20}{7}+\frac{190}{49}+\frac{1140}{343}\right)$$

the terms within $(\cdots)$ being,

$$\left\{\binom{20}{0}\frac{1}{7^0},\binom{20}{1}\frac{1}{7^1},\binom{20}{2}\frac{1}{7^2},\binom{20}{3}\frac{1}{7^3}\right\}$$

corresponding to to the number of ways in which no questions are answered correctly, exactly one, or exactly two or exactly three questions have the correct option chosen.

Unravelling the calculations gives,

$$\mathbf{P}[1] \ \sim \ 1 \ - \ 0.07 \cdot (1 + 2.86 + 3.88 + 3.32) \ \sim \ 0.23$$

so that a student adopting this strategy would expect to take between four and five attempts before succeeding (the actual value being ~ 4.35).

Notice that, as one would expect, setting a higher threshold, e.g. by increasing k and/or t, would result in a reduced chance of passing at first attempt (the quantity described by $\mathbf{P}[1]$) and thus a higher number of expected attempts. Similarly, lowering the bar, e.g. by fewer options and/or reduced passing standard, would correspondingly lower the expected number of attempts.

Web-page "Hits"

Looking to interest advertizers in buying space on their web site, a company indicates the number of hits received per day in the first six months of its launch. This provides 168 data points, which are presented in a pitch to advertizers as Table 6.4.

Although some interest is expressed many potential advertizers are concerned that, after the initial interest has worn off the rate of hits will decline. In response the web site developers claim that "significant" increase is apparent from data collected in the last fortnight, presenting the further figures in Table 6.5.

Question: Are the developers justified in claiming a "significant" increase?

Analysis

Assume that the incidence of web page accesses is described by a Poisson random variable with parameter, λ. We wish to determine the following values.

1. An estimate for λ based on the first 168 items of data.

2. A confidence interval say for the 95% region giving lower and upper estimates for the expected number of hits in a 168 day period.

3. Since we have an additional fortnight of data ($168 = 14 \times 12$) the result of comparing the average number of hits in the fortnight just observed against the bounds derived in (2) **divided by** 12.

Table 6.4: Daily Web page Access Per Week over Six Months

Wk	Sun	Mon	Tues	Wed	Thurs	Fri	Sat
1	730	749	726	732	763	751	749
2	786	755	747	737	734	749	720
3	744	723	765	770	726	798	768
4	798	731	714	724	756	745	749
5	703	733	754	711	744	759	760
6	756	763	694	701	718	779	746
7	762	738	740	774	711	765	785
8	712	777	775	763	719	773	755
9	764	751	740	741	733	751	731
10	732	742	706	753	705	734	744
11	765	709	730	715	754	715	730
12	735	737	784	743	717	781	792
13	776	721	749	793	755	784	743
14	784	739	682	713	714	746	718
15	697	718	810	792	721	744	790
16	755	745	736	754	757	761	781
17	708	740	665	751	739	743	769
18	737	679	721	732	729	690	745
19	754	727	802	714	722	731	722
20	732	754	746	772	746	722	729
21	749	755	758	740	767	734	702
22	713	760	752	749	691	685	746
23	745	774	779	741	737	780	733
24	702	793	716	738	800	736	778

For (1), we find $\lambda = 124895$: this is the **total** number of hits observed in the 168 day interval. This gives an **estimated** standard deviation of $s = \sqrt{124895} \sim 353.4$. Notice that given the total number of observations it is usually considered unneccesary to make any adjustment, i.e. s_N is a good enough estimate of the true standard deviation in a Poisson random variable when $N > 20$. We now find the 95% confidence interval to be

$$124895 \pm 1.96\sqrt{124895} = 124895 \pm 692.67$$

This, however, is for a total observation period of 168 days, so we need to divide by 12 to form a view of what is expected to happen over a period of a

Table 6.5: Recent Web page Access in past Fortnight

Wk	Sun	Mon	Tues	Wed	Thurs	Fri	Sat
1	830	779	926	932	763	791	789
2	986	955	887	1057	834	780	920

fortnight.

$$\frac{124895 \pm 692.67}{12} = 10407.91 \pm 57.72 \sim (10350.19, 10465.63)$$

So that in the fortnight following the initial data set we would expect to see between $10,350$ and $10,466$ further hits.

The actual number seen is $12,229$ so that there is, indeed, some justification for developers' assertions.

If, however, the figures for the past fortnight were as given in Table 6.6, then the total number (10375) would be insufficiently high or low to justify claims about aberrant patterns of behaviour.

Table 6.6: Revised Page Access I

Wk	Sun	Mon	Tues	Wed	Thurs	Fri	Sat
1	708	663	811	802	647	672	654
2	865	830	732	911	718	623	739

Similarly, a pattern of hits of the nature of Table 6.7, although only marginally outside the lower confidence limit (10317) would provide some cause for potential advertizers to think the site's popularity had peaked.

Table 6.7: Revised Page Access II

Wk	Sun	Mon	Tues	Wed	Thurs	Fri	Sat
1	704	653	801	805	644	671	662
2	860	831	722	905	712	613	734

Poisson with Small Data sets

In the previous example the basis for studying the claims of "significant" increase in occurrence was a relatively large quantity of data: having observed over $120,000$ incidents. If, in treating K known occurrences as a Poisson process we have $K > 20$, a typical assumption used is that the process is accurately captured with the Poisson parameter λ set to K. What, however, if we only have a small amount of data? In this case, we can still try to establish confidence intervals for how we expect the process to behave but must now make corrections to allow for the fact that K may not be the exact Poisson parameter.

Here is a rather frivolous example of such analysis.

The UK, having yet to come to terms with latter-day civilized standards, maintains a system of "Honours awards" doled out on two regular occasions annually whereby allegedly noteworthy contributions are accorded some state sponsored award.

In attempts to court public favour an increasing number of these are given each year to popular figures: comedians, soap opera actors, pop stars, singers, sports players,[31] in addition to the usual sops to political hacks, time-serving civil servants, and commercial interests. A further, seemingly increasing, trend is the award of higher level honours to individuals in university administration with the excuse being that the award is for "services to higher education".[32]

Question: A cursory Google search (December 2018) shows that between 2012 and 2017 a total of nine serving or just retired university vice-chancellors were given a knighthood or its equivalent. In 2018 there have already been five such awards. Is this increase significant?

Analysis: Suppose we conjecture that awards of a particular level (CBE or DBE) within a given field (university administration) follow a Poisson process. In this case we have nine observations in a lustrum (five year period). Hypoth-

---

[31] Irrespective of whether anything has actually been contributed. The Australian cricketer, Shane Warne, remarking on the confetti like sprinkling of awards to a victorious England team reproached one such recipient (Paul Collingwood) with the observation "You got an MBE, right? For scoring seven at The Oval? It's an embarrassment."

[32] One can only presume that "service" is being used with the sense common to the discipline of animal husbandry given the number of British universities that have been well and truly "serviced" by vice-chancellors.

esizing that $\lambda = 9$, the 95% confidence interval[33] gives using the correction needed from the low level of sample size.

$$4.12 \leq \lambda \leq 17.08$$

This, however, is over a five year period so in order to give the interval for a single year we divide by five to get $(0.82, 3.42)$ suggesting with generous rounding to integer values that the number of incidents expected to be seen is between 1 and 4. The actual number (5) could be viewed as significant.[34]

Exam standards Comparison

A tabloid newspaper runs a series of stories under a headline blaring that "Students opt for soft subjects to get high grades". The basis of the claim being that large numbers of secondary school students have chosen to take, allegedly easy, A-level subjects such as *Media Studies* in preference to, again allegedly, hard traditional academic disciplines such as *Physics*. The reason offered for such a choice is that it is "easier" to obtain high grades in the former than in the latter.

Question: Are there reasonable grounds based on numbers of students and achieved grades for this allegation?

Analysis

In order to examine these claims take as a Null Hypothesis: "the average raw mark achieved on a Media Studies A-level paper is equal to the average raw mark obtained on a Physics A-level paper."

The underlying populations i.e. those engaged in Media Studies, and those concerned with Physics are likely to comprise different sets of students.[35] Notice that although, as is standard in such settings, the random variables corresponding to

$$X_1 = \{ X_1(\omega) : \omega \text{ is a Media Studies student and } X_1 \text{ their mark. } \}$$
$$X_2 = \{ X_2(\omega) : \omega \text{ is a Physics student and } X_2 \text{ their mark. } \}$$

---

[33]Using methods from Patil and Kulkarni [181].

[34]A possible reason for this leap, recalling the rôle of politicians in the nomination process, may be found within the discussion of collective nouns from fn. 21 earlier.

[35]There may, of course, be some overlap, however it seems unlikely that either set is properly contained within the other.

may be assumed to be normally distributed via $\mathcal{N}(\mu_1, \sigma_1^2)$ and $\mathcal{N}(\mu_2, \sigma_2^2)$ we have no reason to assume similar let alone identical variances. Furthermore the basis of the tabloid noise is that $\mu_1 \gg \mu_2$.

Taking Y_1 from Ω_1 we might collect raw marks of 25 students,

$$Y_1 = \begin{array}{l} \{31, 25, 79, 72, 55, 68, 49, 85, 25, 13, 100, 95, 24, 94, \\ 100, 87, 30, 97, 71, 71, 63, 34, 99, 53, 55\} \end{array}$$

For Y_2 from Ω_2 we might have raw marks sampled from 15 students,

$$Y_2 = \{5, 88, 29, 93, 61, 56, 82, 82, 65, 29, 94, 28, 49, 50, 8\}$$

Applying Welch's test using a 95% confidence interval we get with Y_1

$$\tau_1 = 63.0 \ ; \ s_1^2 \sim 792.17$$

And for Y_2

$$\tau_2 = 54.6 \ ; \ s_2^2 \sim 892.68$$

These values lead to

$$df_w = \frac{(s_1^2/N_1 + s_2^2/N_2)^2}{\frac{(s_1^2/N_1)^2}{N_1-1} + \frac{(s_2^2/N_2)^2}{N_2-1}}$$

which is

$$df_w \sim 28.21$$

Rounding this down allows $t(95\%, 28) \sim 1.7$ to be used in determining the confidence interval for our N.H that $\mu_1 - \mu_2 = 0$,

$$(\tau_1 - \tau_2) \ \pm \ t(95\%, 28) \cdot 9.55$$

The value 9.55 being the result of

$$\sqrt{\frac{s_1^2}{25} + \frac{s_2^2}{15}} = \sqrt{\frac{792.17}{25} + \frac{892.68}{15}} \sim \sqrt{91.2}$$

With which we have a range of $(-7.84, 24.64)$ for the difference between average Media studies mark and average Physics mark based on the data collected. Since $\mu_1 - \mu_2 = 0$ (i.e. no difference in performance) falls within this range we have insufficient cause to reject the N.H.. It should be noted, however, that the sample sizes are small and both have relatively high standard deviation.

6.11   Statistics & CS – Summary

The potential for experimental methods arises in many areas of CS. These may be direct contexts such as assessing the typical performance of an algorithm to rather less obvious settings such as the popularity of a given web site. Here statistical techniques are of fundamental importance in providing supporting evidence for specific claims involving data analysis. Thus one has a battery of methods treating properties of distributions and random variables and an extensive theory of confidence assessment and hypothesis testing.

In the next section of this Chapter, our aim is to look at another important aspect of data analysis: techniques to support claims that a series of discrete observations fit into a given pattern of behaviour.

6.12 Finding a fit: Interpolation and Extrapolation

In the final section of this Chapter we deal with an issue that not only arises in interpreting empirical data but also frequently features in CS disciplines such as average-case analysis of algorithms, machine learning and data science.

Underlying aims of interpolation

The context of these problems can be summarized in the following way. We have a collection of **data points** describing the outputs (y values) obtained over a series of experiments (x values). Since (x, y) may be viewed as 2-dimensional Cartesian coordinates we wish to do at least one of

E. **Extrapolation**: find a function $y = f(x)$ that gives a good fit to the observed data points **and** a good prediction of the y values that would be output for those values of x outside the study range.

I. **Interpolation**: find the best function $y = f(x)$ that smoothly connects the (x, y) pairs for the observed data points. Notice that we are less concerned in this case with what happens outside the region $x_{\min}$ and $x_{\max}$, i.e. the smallest and largest values of x considered.

For example,

a. Using input sizes of $n = 10$ up to $n = 200$ in steps of 10 two algorithms, T_1 and T_2, for producing random binary trees with n leaf nodes are run fifty times with the outputs being analyzed in terms of the tree **depths**, i.e the maximum number of links seen when traversing a path from the root node to a leaf. These data are presented as

Y1. The **mean** depth for each method: $< \tau_1^n, \tau_2^n >$.

Y2. The **maximum** depth seen for each method: $< \max_1^n, \max_2^n >$.

Y3. The **minimum** depth seen for each method: $< \min_1^n, \min_2^n >$.

Assuming that T_1 is such that every n leaf binary tree is equally likely i.e. implements the uniform distribution and T_2 realizes the *binary search tree* (BST) distribution, what function(s) best describe

$$\Delta_1(n) = \tau_1^n \text{ and } \Delta_2(n) = \tau_2^n?$$

b. A **scatter plot** displays points on a 2-dimensional coordinate system, these being for instance "Distance (Km) walked in a day" (Horizontal axis) against "Weight in Kg" (Vertical axis); or "Number of hours spent studying on a module" (Horizontal axis) against "Score achieved in a test" (Vertical axis). What defines the best straight line for such data?

Overview

The general form of the question being addressed is that we have an assumed to be ordered set of **data values** in $\mathbb{R}$,

$$X_n \ = \ < x_1, \ x_2, \ \cdots, \ x_n > \quad \text{(here } x_i \ < \ x_{i+1})$$

For each of these we have found a corresponding **observation value** in $\mathbb{R}$,

$$Y_n \ = \ < y_1, \ y_2, \ \cdots, \ y_n >$$

We are looking for the "best", function $F \ : \ \mathbb{R} \ \rightarrow \ \mathbb{R}$ for which $F(x_i) \sim y_i$ for every one of the $(data, obvn)$ pairs. Now there will, of course, be infinitely many F with this property, so one of the key challenges of this field is in defining what is meant by "best".

Consider the example set of $(data, obvn)$ pairs in Table 6.8.

Table 6.8: Example Data–Observation Pairs

–	1	2	3	4	5	6	7	8
Data (x)	1.5	2.4	3.6	4.2	4.8	5.7	6.3	7.9
Obs. (y)	1.2	1.5	1.9	2.0	2.2	2.4	2.5	2.8

We could start by plotting these points, to get Figure 6.7

In principle any of the four alternatives in Table 6.9 might be suitable.

In order to choose which is the best model of the data given we must start by deciding what are desirable properties of F.

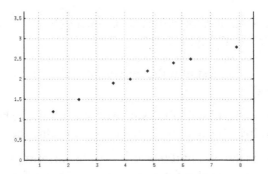

Figure 6.7: Plot of data in Table 6.8

Table 6.9: Four possible fits for Table 6.8

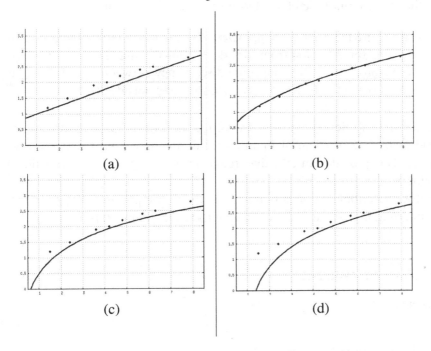

(a)

(b)

(c)

(d)

D1. The source data could have been produced by observing phenomena
which are subject to noise, e.g. a robot sensor recording levels of ambi-
ent sound over a period of twenty-fours hours. In such environments the
$(data, obvn)$ pairs require some statistical assessment of inherent error
in the **source**.

D2. There are a number of different parameters that could be adopted in defining "best fit", e.g.

 P1. $F(x)$ is the best fit if the **maximum** value of $|y_i - F(x_i)|$ is **minimized**.

 P2. $F(x)$ is the best fit if the sum over the difference between the modelled (by F) value for x_i and observed value for x_i is minimized.

 P3. $F(x)$ is the best fit if the sum over the **absolute values** of the modelled (by F) value for x_i and observed value for x_i is minimized.

D3. Is the function F intended to predict outcomes for x outside the data range? This would be the case if claims are made that $F(x)$ describes the average run-time of an algorithm using X_n as experimental data.

D4. Is it required that $F(x_i) = y_i$ **exactly** i.e. the function must be such that no scope for deviation from the $(data, obvn)$ sample is acceptable? Or are we prepared to tolerate some discrepancy between $F(x_i)$ and y_i if $F(x)$ turns out to be a good predictor of cases outside X_n?

In the next section we present one of the most extensively used methods for addressing the problem of finding best fit solutions: the **Least Squares Method**. This provides an effective treatment for a wide range of functional behaviours.

Before describing its operation in more detail, we present some terminology capturing, in particular, the notions introduced within (P1)-(P3).

Regression and Residuals

The expression,

$$y \;=\; F(x)$$

is called the **regression equation** of the observation y on data x. The function, $F : \mathbb{R} \to \mathbb{R}$, **approximates** or is an **approximation for** (X_n, Y_n) with the values $F(x_i)$ being denoted $\hat{y}_i$. Notice that at this stage we do not insist for every or indeed *any* value that $\hat{y}_i = y_i$.

The possible difference between $\hat{y}_i$ (the value for x_i reported by the approximation F) and y_i (the value for x_i reported in the data set being modelled), motivates the important concept of **residual**. With the pair $< X_n, Y_n >$

we associate a third collection R_n its exact specification varying with the approximation F. The **residual**, r_i for $< x_i, y_i >$ approximated by F is

$$r_i \; = \; y_i - F(x_i) \quad \equiv \quad r_i \; = \; y_i - \hat{y}_i$$

In terms of the ideas of best fit given by (P1)–(P3) the concept of residual defines these as

P1. Find $F : \mathbb{R} \to \mathbb{R}$ such that $\max |r_i|$ is minimized.

P2. Find $F : \mathbb{R} \to \mathbb{R}$ such that $\sum r_i$ is minimized.

P3. Find $F : \mathbb{R} \to \mathbb{R}$ such that $\sum |r_i|$ is minimized.

In the Least Squares Method, F is constructed to minimize $\sum r_i^2$.

Least Squares approaches

When looking for an approximation, F, very often the most suitable choice will depend on fixing some auxiliary parameters in order to get the best outcome. So we may find, among others, the following examples

R1. $F(x)$ is a **linear function** of x.

R2. $F(x)$ is a **polynomial function** of degree $k > 1$ in x.

R3. $F(x)$ is a **Real power** (x^p).

R4. $F(x)$ is an **exponential** function.

R5. $F(x)$ is a **logarithmic** function.

R6. $F(x)$ is a **linear rational function**, i.e $F(x) = O(1/x)$.

A common property and one of considerable importance in applying the Least Squares Method is each case can be characterized in a general form by some vector of **constant** values, $\mathbf{u} \in \mathbb{R}^t$ $(t \in \mathbb{N})$.
Revisiting (R1)–(R6) we find

R1. $F(x)$ is a **linear function**: $\mathbf{u} \in \mathbb{R}^2$ so that[36]

$$F(x, \mathbf{u}) = u_1 x + u_2.$$

R2. $F(x)$ is a **polynomial function** of degree $k > 1$: $\mathbf{u} \in \mathbb{R}^{k+1}$ with

$$F(x, \mathbf{u}) \;=\; \sum_{i=1}^{k+1} u_{i-1} x^{i-1}.$$

R3. $F(x)$ is a **Real power** (x^p): $\mathbf{u} \in \mathbb{R}^2$ and

$$F(x, \mathbf{u}) \;=\; u_1 x^{u_2}.$$

R4. $F(x)$ is an **exponential** function: $\mathbf{u} \in \mathbb{R}^2$ and

$$F(x, \mathbf{u}) \;=\; u_1 e^{u_2 x}.$$

R5. $F(x)$ is a **logarithmic** function: $\mathbf{u} \in \mathbb{R}^2$ and

$$F(x, \mathbf{u}) \;=\; u_1 \log_e x + u_2.$$

R6. $F(x)$ is a **linear rational function**: $\mathbf{u} \in \mathbb{R}^2$ and

$$F(x, \mathbf{u}) \;=\; \frac{1}{u_1 x + u_2}.$$

So we see that the best fit problem reduces, having fixed on the category to be used for $F(x, \mathbf{u})$, to identifying an appropriate $\mathbf{u} \in \mathbb{R}^k$. It should be noticed that one can, in principle, attempt to fit an arbitrary approximation $F(x, \mathbf{u})$ to the data (X_n, Y_n) and, in some instances, more involved F may be the most suitable. Having noted this, however, we shall in the next section concentrate on the simplest such case, i.e fitting a linear function to the data set. This, very

---

[36]Recalling from Section 4.2 that any linear function of x is described by a relationship of the form $y = m \cdot x + c$.

often in practice, offers a good enough solution. As we shall also see, although superficially outside the regime of linear regression it is sometimes possible to recast identifying F, e.g. for F a logarithmic function, in terms of finding a related linear function $G(x, \mathbf{u})$. We look at assessing the quality of fit in the final section of this Chapter where the idea of **correlation coefficient** and calculation of these, is described.

For the remainder of this section we focus on the general methodology used in Least Squares Methods, i.e. without making assumptions about the exact nature of the approximation $F(x, \mathbf{u})$.

Derivation of Least Squares Approximation

We recall that the thinking underpinning Least Squares Methods is to find an approximation function which, henceforward we will denote in the form $F(x, \mathbf{u})$, by which

$$\sum_{i=1}^{n} r_i^2$$

is minimized. What does this indicate relative to $F(x, \mathbf{u})$ and (X_n, Y_n)? Simply that,

$$\sum_{i=1}^{n} (y_i - F(x_i, \mathbf{u}))^2$$

is minimized.

Now in these subexpressions $(y_i - F(x_i, \mathbf{u}))^2$ we are looking to choose **constant** values $\mathbf{u} \in \mathbb{R}^k$. We already know the values for each x_i and y_i, since they are simply our $(data, obvn)$ pairs. What we are trying to find is that setting of $\mathbf{u}$ resulting in

$$\sum_{i=1}^{n} (y_i - F(x_i, \mathbf{u}))^2$$

attaining its minimum value relative to the known values for (X_n, Y_n). In other words we just need to consider minimization of a function of $\mathbf{u}$. In total the problem reduces to,

Find $\mathbf{u} \in \mathbb{R}^k$ such that $\Psi(\mathbf{u})$ is minimal with $\Psi : \mathbb{R}^k \to \mathbb{R}$ and

$$\Psi(\mathbf{u}) = \sum_{i=1}^{n} (y_i - F(x_i, \mathbf{u}))^2$$

And this problem, finding an instantiation of parameters under which a function attains its minimum value, we have seen before: in Section 4.5 with $\mathbf{u} \in \mathbb{R}^1$ and, more immediately relevant to the present context, in Section 4.7.

Overall, having chosen our approximation model, $F(x, \mathbf{u})$ we have the following procedure to go through.

LS1. Construct the function of $\mathbf{u}$ only described through

$$\Psi(\mathbf{u}) = \sum_{i=1}^{n} (y_i - F(x_i, \mathbf{u}))^2$$

LS2. Find the k **partial derivatives** of $\Psi(\mathbf{u})$, that is

$$\left[\frac{\partial \Psi}{\partial u_1}, \frac{\partial \Psi}{\partial u_2}, \dots, \frac{\partial \Psi}{\partial u_k} \right]$$

LS3. The solution for $\mathbf{u} \in \mathbb{R}^k$ is that choice for which

$$\left\{ \frac{\partial \Psi}{\partial u_1}, \frac{\partial \Psi}{\partial u_2}, \dots, \frac{\partial \Psi}{\partial u_k} \right\} (u_1, u_2, \dots, u_k) = \mathbf{0}$$

In other words, as found by solving the system of k equations,

$$\left\{ \sum_{i=1}^{n} \left[(y_i - F(x_i, \mathbf{u})) \frac{\partial F(x_i, \mathbf{u})}{\partial u_k} \right] \right\}_{1 \leq k \leq n} = 0$$

[Notice that although the function considered has the form $\sum \varphi(\mathbf{u})^2$, with partial derivatives $2 \sum \partial \varphi / \partial u_i$ since we are primarily interested in instantiations of u_i under which all of these are zero the constant multiple (2) is irrelevant.]

Now, although in principle, such systems can be processed for arbitrary $k \in \mathbb{N}$, computationally these can be quite demanding. This fact provides one motivation, when adopting Least Squares Methods, for trying to find approximation models $F(x, \mathbf{u})$ for which $\mathbf{u} \in \mathbb{R}^2$. With the exception of degree $k \geq 2$ polynomials all of the instances from (R1)–(R6) can be so defined.

Fitting a line: Linear Regression

Returning to the optimizing choice for $\mathbf{u} =< u_1, u_2 >$ derived at the conclusion of the previous section, we can completely describe $\mathbf{u}$ given the $(data, obvn)$ pairs and the characterization of linear functions through $F(x, u_1, u_2) = u_1 x + u_2$: in other words given (X_n, Y_n) we can construct a closed form solution for $< u_1, u_2 >$ expressing the outcome solely in terms of the known constant pairs from (X_n, Y_n).

It may be found helpful to work through this process.

Looking back to the specification of $\Psi(u_1, u_2)$ we see that

$$
\begin{aligned}
\Psi(u_1, u_2) &= \sum_{i=1}^{n} (y_i - F(x_i, u_1, u_2))^2 \\
&= \sum_{i=1}^{n} (y_i - u_1 x_i - u_2)^2 \\
\frac{\partial \Psi}{\partial u_1} &= -2 \sum_{i=1}^{n} (y_i - u_1 x_i - u_2) \cdot x_i \\
\frac{\partial \Psi}{\partial u_2} &= -2 \sum_{i=1}^{n} (y_i - u_1 x_i - u_2)
\end{aligned}
$$

Here we use the composition rule: $[f(g(x))]' = f'(g(x)) \cdot g'(x)$, with $f(x) = x^2$ and $g(x) = (y_i - u_1 x_i - u_2)$, cf. Table 4.4 in Section 4.3.

Recalling the procedure for optimizing functions of more than one variable described in Section 4.7, we first obtain expressions for u_1 and u_2 that simultaneously make each of the partial derivatives take the value 0.

$$
\begin{aligned}
\sum_{i=1}^{n} (y_i - u_1 x_i - u_2) \cdot x_i &= 0 \\
\sum_{i=1}^{n} (y_i - u_1 x_i - u_2) &= 0
\end{aligned}
$$

Rearranging these two expressions it is not hard to see that the task is equivalent to finding u_1 and u_2 that satisfy

$$u_1 \sum_{i=1}^{n} x_i^2 + u_2 \sum_{i=1}^{n} x_i - \sum_{i=1}^{n} x_i y_i = 0$$

$$u_1 \sum_{i=1}^{n} x_i + n u_2 - \sum_{i=1}^{n} y_i = 0$$

The terms involving x_i and y_i are independent of u_1 and u_2 forming, as they do, part of the input data, i.e. these are the $(data, obvn)$ pairs.

In order to simplify the notation being used, we write W_x, W_y, W_{xy} and W_{xx} with

$$W_x = \sum_{i=1}^{n} x_i \quad ; \quad W_y = \sum_{i=1}^{n} y_i$$

$$W_{xy} = \sum_{i=1}^{n} x_i y_i \quad ; \quad W_{xx} = \sum_{i=1}^{n} x_i^2$$

So that we are left with solving,

$$u_1 W_{xx} + u_2 W_x - W_{xy} = 0$$
$$u_1 W_x + n u_2 - W_y = 0$$

Which leads to

$$u_1 = \frac{n W_{xy} - W_x W_y}{n W_{xx} - (W_x)^2}$$

$$u_2 = \frac{W_{xx} W_y - W_{xy} W_x}{n W_{xx} - (W_x)^2}$$

Putting everything together, we have just seen that:

For a set of data (X_n) and observations (Y_n) the line function

$$y = mx + c$$

defined by the Least Squares approximation which **minimizes** the sum of the squares of the *residuals*, has gradient m with

$$m = \frac{n\sum_{i=1}^n x_i y_i - (\sum_{i=1}^n x_i)(\sum_{i=1}^n y_i)}{n\sum_{i=1}^n x_i^2 - (\sum_{i=1}^n x_i)^2}$$

and offset, c, with

$$c = \frac{(\sum_{i=1}^n x_i^2)(\sum_{i=1}^n y_i) - (\sum_{i=1}^n x_i y_i)(\sum_{i=1}^n x_i)}{n\sum_{i=1}^n x_i^2 - (\sum_{i=1}^n x_i)^2}$$

Summarizing the mechanisms for applying the Least Squares method to identify a best fit line function, we have:

F1. Data $X_n \subset \mathbb{R}^n$ and observations $Y_n \subset \mathbb{R}^n$: y_i is the outcome seen with respect to the stimulus x_i.

F2. To find the best fit line function $y = mx + c$ via the Least Squares technique:

F2.1. Compute

$$W_x = \sum_{i=1}^n x_i \quad \text{and} \quad W_y = \sum_{i=1}^n y_i$$

F2.2. Compute

$$W_{xy} = \sum_{i=1}^n x_i y_i \quad ; \quad W_{xx} = \sum_{i=1}^n x_i^2$$

F2.3. The gradient of the best fit line is

$$m = \frac{nW_{xy} - W_x W_y}{nW_{xx} - (W_x)^2}$$

F2.4. The offset of the best fit line is

$$c = \frac{W_{xx}W_y - W_{xy}W_x}{nW_{xx} - (W_x)^2}$$

Before considering Least Squares approach with respect to some of the other function models in (R1)–(R6), we first illustrate its application to finding a line function for the $(data, obvn)$ collection for our earlier example.

In this instance we had $n = 8$ and $(data, obvn)$ pairs from Table 6.8. Applying the template above,

a.

$$W_x = 36.4 \; ; \; W_y = 16.5 \; ; \; W_{xy} = 82.75 \; ; \; W_{xx} = 196.24$$

b.

$$m = \frac{8 \cdot 82.75 - 36.4 \cdot 16.5}{8 \cdot 196.24 - 36.4^2} = \frac{61.4}{244.96} \sim 0.2507$$

c.

$$c = \frac{196.24 \cdot 16.5 - 82.75 \cdot 36.4}{8 \cdot 196.24 - 36.4^2} = \frac{225.86}{244.96} \sim 0.922$$

d. The best fit line function for these data is, therefore

$$y = 0.2507 \cdot x + 0.922$$

This is depicted in Figure 6.8.

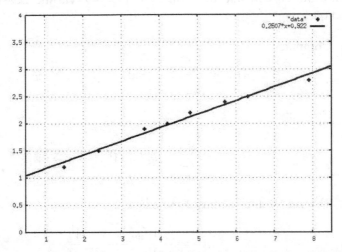

Figure 6.8: The line function found by Least Squares for Table 6.8

There is one small detail which we have not discussed. In the presentation of using partial derivatives in order to address two variable optimization problems from Section 4.7 a variant of the second derivative test for discerning the existence and nature of critical points was introduced. For completeness we examine this in the context of linear regression by Least Squares.

Using the variables u_1 and u_2 we recall this analysis considered

$$D(u_1, u_2) = \frac{\partial^2 \Psi}{\partial u_1^2} \cdot \frac{\partial^2 \Psi}{\partial u_2^2} - \left(\frac{\partial^2 \Psi}{\partial u_1 \partial u_2} \right)^2$$

We have seen that

$$\frac{\partial \Psi}{\partial u_1} = -2 \sum_{i=1}^{n} (y_i - u_1 x_i - u_2) \cdot x_i$$

$$\frac{\partial \Psi}{\partial u_2} = -2 \sum_{i=1}^{n} (y_i - u_1 x_i - u_2)$$

Hence,

$$\frac{\partial^2 \Psi}{\partial u_1^2} = 2W_{xx}$$

$$\frac{\partial^2 \Psi}{\partial u_2^2} = 2n$$

$$\frac{\partial^2 \Psi}{\partial u_1 \partial u_2} = 2W_x$$

Notice that these are independent of whatever values u_1 and u_2 may have been found. So that,

$$D(u_1, u_2) = 4nW_{xx} - 4W_x^2$$

This is required to be positive, i.e.

$$n \sum_{i=1}^{n} x_i^2 > \left(\sum_{i=1}^{n} x_i \right)^2$$

In which event $< u_1, u_2 >$ provides a best-fit should

$$\frac{\partial^2 \Psi}{\partial u_1^2} = 2W_{xx}$$

be positive.

This latter condition will always hold: W_{xx} is a sum of squares. To demonstrate that

$$n \sum_{i=1}^{n} x_i^2 \; > \; \left(\sum_{i=1}^{n} x_i \right)^2$$

while easy enough on a case-by-case basis that is to say using explicit instantiations of X_n it turns out to be surprisingly non-trivial to demonstrate in general. For this reason we omit the argument that $D(u_1, u_2) > 0$ for every $X_n \in \mathbb{R}^n$.[37]

Selected Non-linear models

While many of the cases seen in practice provide $(data, obvn)$ sets to which some linear function can be used as an approximation model, this is very far from being universally so. One may especially in analysing average case characteristics be faced with data collections for which the plotted data e.g. as we did in Figure 6.7 are more suitably explored using other of the models from (R1)–(R6).

We can, of course, proceed in exactly the same manner as we did with linear regression to identify the minimizing setting for $< u_1, u_2 >$: form the appropriate system of k partial derivatives of $F(x, \mathbf{u})$ and identify the setting of $\mathbf{u}$ that makes all of these take the value 0.

An alternative approach, however, is to try and reformulate the model for which a solution is sought as a linear function model. We now consider a few examples of such an approach, noting that in all of these we are dealing with **two** auxiliary parameters as before, i.e. $\mathbf{u}$ for which we are trying to find an optimizing setting is in $\mathbb{R}^2$.

Case 1: Powers of positive Real numbers: $F(x, \mathbf{u}) \; = \; u_1 x^{u_2}$

This is also known as **Geometric regression**. We assume that only positive x values feature in our data set. Suppose we consider

$$\log_e F(x, \mathbf{u}) \; = \; \log_e(u_1 x^{u_2}) \; = \; u_2 \cdot \log_e x \; + \; \log_e u_1$$

The function "$u_2 \cdot \log_e x \; + \; \log_e u_1$" is a linear function of $\log_e x$ and may be viewed as a linear approximating model for $\log_e F(x, \mathbf{u})$, We can, therefore adopt the following approach to finding the Least Squares geometric regression model for $F(x, \mathbf{u}) \; = \; u_1 x^{u_2}$.

---

[37]Or, rather more accurately, for all cases other than sets comprising a **single** value.

S1. Replace (X_n, Y_n) by

$$
\begin{aligned}
P_n &= \{\, p_i \; : \; p_i = \log_e x_i \,\} \\
Q_n &= \{\, q_i \; : \; q_i = \log_e y_i \,\}
\end{aligned}
$$

S2. Find $\mathbf{v} \in \mathbb{R}^2$ which is a linear Least Squares best fit for,

$$
q = v_1 p + v_2
$$

That is, using $\hat{q}_i$ for $v_1 p_i + v_2$ the choice $\mathbf{v}$ minimizes the sum of squares of the residuals

$$
\sum_{i=1}^{n} (q_i - \hat{q}_i)^2
$$

S3. Having found $< v_1, v_2 >$ we can use

$$
\begin{aligned}
u_1 &= e^{v_2} \\
u_2 &= v_1
\end{aligned}
$$

We can validate these replacements by noting that

$$
\begin{array}{llll}
F(x, \mathbf{u}) &= u_1 x^{u_2} & \text{Initial model} \\
\log_e F(x, \mathbf{u}) &= u_2 \cdot \log_e x + \log_e u_1 & \text{Linear model} \\
G(p, \mathbf{v}) &= v_1 p + v_2 & \text{with } p = \log_e x \\
F(x, \mathbf{u}) &= e^{v_1 \log_e x + v_2} \\
F(x, \mathbf{u}) &= e^{v_2} x^{v_1} & \text{i.e. } u_1 = e^{v_2}, u_2 = v_1.
\end{array}
$$

Example: Suppose instead of the linear Least Squares fit for our example,

–	1	2	3	4	5	6	7	8
X	1.5	2.4	3.6	4.2	4.8	5.7	6.3	7.9
Y	1.2	1.5	1.9	2.0	2.2	2.4	2.5	2.8

which we saw to be

$$y = 0.2507 \cdot x + 0.922$$

we see if we can find a better fit to these data via the model

$$F(x, u_1, u_2) = u_1 x^{u_2}.$$

Following the steps defined via (S1)–(S3), we start by replacing the (X, Y) table with Table 6.10

Table 6.10: Substitution by $\log_e$ in Table 6.8

–	1	2	3	4	5	6	7	8
P	0.405	0.875	1.281	1.435	1.569	1.74	1.841	2.067
Q	0.182	0.405	0.642	0.693	0.788	0.874	0.916	1.03

For the quantities, which we continue to denote $\{W_x, W_y, W_{xx}, W_{xy}\}$ we now obtain

$$W_x = 11.213 \; ; \; W_y = 5.53 \; ; \; W_{xy} = 8.81744 \; ; \; W_{xx} = 17.780967$$

Leading to

$$v_1 = \frac{8.53163}{16.516367} \sim 0.516556 \; ; \; v_2 = \frac{-0.54120721}{16.516367} \sim -0.032767927$$

So that, the final model, $F(x, u_1, u_2)$ is

$$u_1 = 0.967763125 \; ; \; u_2 = 0.516556$$

and

$$F(x) = 0.967763125 x^{0.516556}$$

The resulting mapping against the data from Table 6.8 is shown compared to Figure 6.8 in Table 6.11.

It is worth commenting on the fact that the fit to observed data using the function found by geometric regression seems closer than that found by linear regression. There is a very simple reason for this: when composing the

Table 6.11: Comparison of Linear and Geometric Regression for Table 6.8

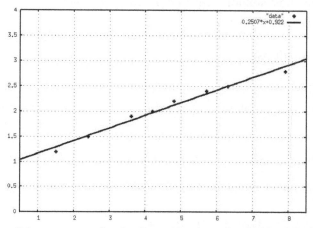

Linear regression by Least Squares for Table 6.8

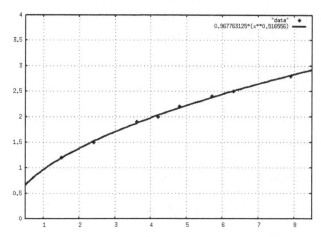

Geometric regression by Least Squares for Table 6.8

example in Table 6.8 the actual y_i function used was $\sqrt{x_i}$ with the outcome rounded to two places. This is, in fact, the curve plotted in Table 6.9(b) where no rounding of $\sqrt{x}$ is applied.

We present this example to illustrate the difficulties that arise in defending hypotheses such as "$F(x)$ is **the** best fit for the outcome described by (X_n, Y_n)". It may, assuming the technical apparatus has been applied correctly, very well be the case that "$F(x)$ is **a** best fit" with respect to some approximation model, however, the approximation model used e.g. linear versus geometric may not be the most suitable. Given more extensive data alternative interpretations may suggest themselves.

Case 2: Exponential Functions

The form of the approximation model used in this case is $F(x, \mathbf{u}) = u_1 e^{u_2 x}$. We can, however, express the problem of optimizing the choice of $\mathbf{u}$ in terms of linear regression.

$$\log_e F(x, \mathbf{u}) = \log_e u_1 + u_2 x$$

So rather than finding optimal settings of $F(x, \mathbf{u})$ we can use the **linear** function,

$$G(x, v_1, v_2) = u_2 x + \log_e u_1 = v_1 x + v_2$$

We can then consider $\log_e y_i$ from our observation and minimize the sum of squares of residuals from $\hat{y}_i = v_1 x_i + v_2$ by linear Least Squares. We then use the substitution $u_1 = e^{v_2}$ and $u_2 = v_1$ to give

$$\log_e F(x, \mathbf{u}) = v_2 + v_1 x$$

Hence

$$F(x, u_1, u_2) = e^{\log_e F(x, \mathbf{u})} = e^{v_2} e^{v_1 x} = u_1 e^{u_2 x}$$

Case 3: Logarithmic Functions

The form of the approximation model used now is

$$F(x, \mathbf{u}) = u_1 \log_e x + u_2.$$

To describe this in terms of linear Least Squares, it suffices to replace each x_i in the data set by $\log_e x_i$ leaving the observation set, Y_n unchanged. The model we are now trying to fit is simply

$$G(\log_e x, u_1, u_2) = u_1 \log_e x + u_2$$

So we can treat this as a standard linear regression problem, using the values $\mathbf{u}$ to give the solution

$$F(x, \mathbf{u}) = u_1 \log_e x + u_2$$

Case 4: Linear Rational Functions

Here the approximation model takes the form

$$F(x, \mathbf{u}) = \frac{1}{u_1 x + u_2}$$

In this we can use a similar device to that described in Case 3. Defining

$$G(x, u_1, u_2) = \frac{1}{F(x, u_1, u_2)} = u_1 x + u_2$$

instead of the observation set Y_n we replace each y_i by $1/y_i$ assuming, of course, that no y_i has the value zero then then $\mathbf{u} \in \mathbb{R}^2$ giving the best Least Squares fit minimizing

$$\sum_{i=1}^{n} \left(\frac{1}{y_i} - (u_1 x_i + u_2) \right)^2$$

is also the optimal fit for

$$\sum_{i=1}^{n} \left(y_i - \frac{1}{u_1 x_i + u_2} \right)^2$$

Fitting a curve: Polynomial Interpolation

The case of fitting data to arbitrary polynomials in $\mathbb{R}[X]$ has quite an extensive history, see, e.g. Gautschi [100] for a good overview of this. To begin we consider one approach, and then discuss why linear or, at worst, quadratic and general geometric regression methods may sometimes be preferable.

Given (X_n, Y_n) as previously, where it is assumed

$$x_{\min} = x_1 < x_2 < \cdots < x_i < x_{i+1} < \cdots < x_n = x_{\max}$$

the problem of **Polynomial Interpolation** is to find $p(x) \in \mathbb{R}[X]$ for which

PI1. $\deg p(x)$ is minimal.

PI2. $p(x_i) = y_i$ for every x_i in X_n.

The condition stipulated in (PI2) means that, unlike the Least Squares methods we have been considering, **no deviation** from the observation, y_i, for **any** data point x_i is allowed.

The classical method is known as **Lagrange Interpolation**.

Given n **distinct** $(data, obvn)$ pairs (X_n, Y_n) there is a **unique** polynomial $p(x) \in \mathbb{R}[X]$ having degree at most $n - 1$ and for which $y_i = p(x_i)$ with all (x_i, y_i) pairs.

Not only does an appropriate polynomial **exist** but we can also describe a computational process to construct it. Such is presented in Algorithm 6.1.

Algorithm 6.1. Polynomial Interpolation from (X_n, Y_n)

1: **for** Each k, $1 \le k \le n$ **do**

2:    Compute:

$$l_k(x) \quad := \quad \prod_{1 \le i \ne k \le n} \frac{x - x_i}{x_k - x_i}$$

3:    $\{l_k(x)$ are called the **Lagrange Polynomials**$\}$

4: **end for**

5: **return** the polynomial $p(x)$ given by

6:

$$p(x) \quad := \quad \sum_{i=1}^{n} y_i l_i(x)$$

Before discussing its advantages and other features, we look at a small example.

Suppose we have three points,

$$(X_3, Y_3) = \{ (1,8), (2,5), (3,10) \}$$

The method of Algorithm 6.1, first constructs the three Lagrange polynomials

$$l_1(x) = \frac{x-2}{1-2} \cdot \frac{x-3}{1-3} = \frac{x^2 - 5x + 6}{2}$$

$$l_2(x) = \frac{x-1}{2-1} \cdot \frac{x-3}{2-3} = \frac{x^2 - 4x + 3}{-1}$$

$$l_3(x) = \frac{x-1}{3-1} \cdot \frac{x-2}{3-2} = \frac{x^2 - 3x + 2}{2}$$

The polynomial returned is then

$$\frac{8 \cdot (x^2 - 5x + 6)}{2} - \frac{5 \cdot (x^2 - 4x + 3)}{1} + \frac{10 \cdot (x^2 - 3x + 2)}{2}$$

That is,

$$4 \cdot (x^2 - 5x + 6) - 5 \cdot (x^2 - 4x + 3) + 5 \cdot (x^2 - 3x + 2)$$

which simplifies to

$$p(x) = 4x^2 - 15x + 19$$

From which $p(1) = 8$, $p(2) = 5$, and $p(3) = 10$ are easily confirmed.

While minimizing the number of basic operations involved in actual realizations of Lagrange Interpolation requires careful implementation, overall the efficiency of this method is not a major drawback.

There are, however, other subtle difficulties which can make interpolation of a polynomial of appropriate degree exactly to fit (X_n, Y_n) via Lagrange interpolation problematic. Suppose that $p_{n-1}(x) \in \mathbb{R}[X]$ is the Lagrange interpolant polynomial constructed for (X_n, Y_n). That is to say, $p_{n-1}(x_i) = y_i$ for every x in X_n. It could be the case that the $(data, obvn)$ pairs from which (X_n, Y_n) were derived would, if more data were analyzed, describe behaviour which is not a polynomial but actually some function $f(x)$. In such instances $p_{n-1}(x)$, while exact for the observations that led to its construction, is just an approximation to $f(x)$, the true functional behaviour. While, in principle, more data points will admit a closer approximation to $f(x)$ this will be achieved at the cost of the corresponding polynomial having higher degree.

Overall if $f(x)$ is the true function that would capture, exactly, **all** $(data, obvn)$ sets and $p_n(x)$ the degree n polynomial that has been discovered, then we are interested in the behaviour of $|f(x) - p_n(x)|$ either in the worst-case or through some notion of "on average". A quite deep and extensive analysis of interpolation by polynomials and the error arising has evolved. We refer the interested reader to any standard text on Numerical Analysis for further details, e.g. that of Stoer and Bulirsch [224, pp. 37–144] or Isaacson and Keller [126]. In these studies the nature of $f(x)$ may be that of a trigonometric function, e.g. $f(x) = \cos x + \sin^2 x$ or a rational function of x such as $1/(5x^2 + 1)$. We note that finding polynomial functions $p(x) \in \mathbb{R}[X]$ is only one interpolation direction. Of huge importance in signal processing and Electrical Engineering contexts is the problem of *trigonometric interpolation*. Here the aim is to find vectors $\mathbf{u} \in \mathbb{R}^{n+1}$ and $\mathbf{v} \in \mathbb{R}^n$ for which given (X_n, Y_n)

$$\varphi(x) = u_0 + \sum_{k=1}^{n} u_k \cos(kx) + v_k \sin(kx)$$

will satisfy $\varphi(x_i) = y_i$ for each $1 \le i \le n$.[38] These and similar problems are, however, outside the scope of the present book.

Another reason why it may not be practical to use Lagrange interpolation to find a polynomial capturing n data points is the behaviour of degree n polynomials: we have seen that such will have $n - 1$ critical points, leading to the function potentially flipping between increasing and decreasing outputs and within comparatively short intervals. Such outcomes may be alleviated to an extent by dividing the data set into small sections of two or three pairs each. For example, instead of fitting a degree $n - 1$ polynomial to (X_n, Y_n) the data are split into

$$(\{< x_1, y_1 >, < x_2, y_2 >\}, \{< x_2, y_2 >, < x_3, y_3 >\}, \cdots,$$
$$\{< x_i, y_i >, < x_{i+1}, y_{i+1} >\}, \{< x_{i+1}, y_{i+1} >, < x_{i+2}, y_{i+2} >\}, \cdots,$$
$$\{< x_{n-1}, y_{n-1} >, < x_n, y_n >\})$$

and in this instance lines are mapped to the pairs in each section, and in the case of three items a quadratic function is used.

The resulting approximation model may, however, be rather "disjointed" and not offer a reasonable basis for extrapolation unlike the linear regression by least squares methods. It may also be noted that when considering, say the average case of an algorithm's runtime we are less concerned with lower order

---

[38] The vectors, $\mathbf{u}$ and $\mathbf{v}$ may also be chosen from $\mathbb{C}^n$. This variant is very closely related to the properties underpinning the Fourier Transform discussed in Section 5.8.

coefficients and much more so with **asymptotic** performance. That is, if this is of the order of n^3 while the coefficient of n^3 in the polynomial interpolated is of interest, this is less so for other coefficients.

In the light of these concerns we will conclude our review of data fitting methods by considering the Least Squares method with respect to **quadratic** functions.

Quadratic Regression

As a brief recap when using Least Squares methods for Quadratic regression we have,

Q1. The n $(data, obvn)$ pairs specified by (X_n, Y_n).

Q2. We are looking for the choice of **three** values, $< u_0, u_1, u_2 >$ defining the quadratic

$$p(x) = u_2 x^2 + u_1 x + u_0$$

for which

$$\Psi(u_0.u_1, u_2) = \sum_{i=1}^{n} (y_i - u_2 x_i^2 - u_1 x_i - u_0)^2$$

   is **minimized**

In this setting we will have a set of three first order partial derivatives to examine with respect to identifying critical points. Specifically the solutions of

$$\left\{ \frac{\partial \Psi}{\partial u_0}, \frac{\partial \Psi}{\partial u_1}, \frac{\partial \Psi}{\partial u_2} \right\} = 0$$

In other words such that,

$$\frac{\partial \Psi}{\partial u_0} = -2 \sum_{i=1}^{n} (y_i - u_2 x_i^2 - u_1 x_i - u_0)$$

$$\frac{\partial \Psi}{\partial u_1} = -2 \sum_{i=1}^{n} x_i (y_i - u_2 x_i^2 - u_1 x_i - u_0)$$

$$\frac{\partial \Psi}{\partial u_2} = -2 \sum_{i=1}^{n} x_i^2 (y_i - u_2 x_i^2 - u_1 x_i - u_0)$$

simultaneously equal zero.

Recalling our notational conventions,

$$W_x = \sum_{i=1}^{n} x_i \; ; \; W_y = \sum_{i=1}^{n} y_i$$

$$W_{xy} = \sum_{i=1}^{n} x_i y_i \; ; \; W_{xx} = \sum_{i=1}^{n} x_i^2$$

we add to these

$$W_{xxy} = \sum_{i=1}^{n} x_i^2 y_i \; ; \; W_{xxx} = \sum_{i=1}^{n} x_i^3 \; ; \; W_{4x} = \sum_{i=1}^{n} x_i^4$$

so that the three values we require are the solutions of

$$
\begin{aligned}
W_y &= u_2 W_{xx} + u_1 W_x + n u_0 \\
W_{xy} &= u_2 W_{xxx} + u_1 W_{xx} + u_0 W_x \\
W_{xxy} &= u_2 W_{4x} + u_1 W_{xxx} + u_0 W_{xx}
\end{aligned}
$$

These can be considered as the matrix problem of finding the column vector $< u_0, u_1, u_2 >^{\top}$ with

$$
\begin{pmatrix}
n & W_x & W_{xx} \\
W_x & W_{xx} & W_{xxx} \\
W_{xx} & W_{xxx} & W_{4x}
\end{pmatrix}
\begin{pmatrix}
u_0 \\
u_1 \\
u_2
\end{pmatrix}
=
\begin{pmatrix}
W_y \\
W_{xy} \\
W_{xxy}
\end{pmatrix}
$$

We have seen the Least Squares solution for linear regression in terms of finding $< u_1, u_2 >^{\top}$ viewed as

$$
\begin{pmatrix}
W_{xx} & W_x \\
W_x & n
\end{pmatrix}
\begin{pmatrix}
u_1 \\
u_2
\end{pmatrix}
=
\begin{pmatrix}
W_{xy} \\
W_y
\end{pmatrix}
$$

and derived the solution via

$$
\begin{pmatrix}
u_1 \\
u_2
\end{pmatrix}
=
\frac{1}{n W_{xx} - (W_x)^2}
\begin{pmatrix}
W_{xx} & -W_x \\
-W_x & n
\end{pmatrix}
\begin{pmatrix}
W_{xy} \\
W_y
\end{pmatrix}
$$

We can identify a solution for $< u_0, u_1, u_2 >^{\top}$ in the quadratic case by finding the inverse of the 3×3 matrix formed. In the next chapter we look at this computational process.

How good a fit is it?

The concept of "scatter plot" concerns the display of two collections of data formed as pairs of (x, y) points. Such diagrams are frequently used to investigate links between seemingly unconnected items. For example, x may be an individual's height and y that individual's weight. The scatter plot in this case would typically contain points corresponding to people of different height and similar weight and vice versa. Alternatively, x may represent weekly expenditure at a local supermarket, and y the total spent on dairy products. Again in such settings different amounts of total spending may map to the same quantities of product and, in the same way, the amount dedicated to particular types of produce may be identical for cases where the overall spending differs.

An immediate consequence, distinguishing data analysis from scatter plots and the concepts of regression and curve fitting reviewed in the previous section, is that the depiction on a two-dimensional coordinate scheme of individual data points may be rather more amorphous than cases such as that in Figure 6.7. In that example, not only do we have distinct data values (X_n is a **set**) but also in the main distinct observation outcomes: while not invariably so it is frequently the case that Y_n is also a set. As indicated with our examples, neither assumption can be made with respect to information reported through a scatter plot.

In such circumstances a common approach, in attempting to justify a causal link between x and y values is to derive a line function that fits the available data in a reasonable fashion.[39] Such an approach raises two questions.

Q1. Given a set of N points $S = \{< x_i, y_i >\ :\ 1 \le i \le N\}$ what is the best linear function covering S?

Q2. Having identified $f(x) = mx + c$ as the best function, how do we assess the extent to which $f(x)$ captures the data in S?

The methods by which (Q1) is addressed are similar to those developed in our discussion of linear regression. The second question, however, requires a new concept: that of **correlation coefficient**. Informally, correlation coefficients give a **quantitative** measure of how well the line function chosen matches the source data: if this has a relatively low absolute value than we can argue that there is little connection between the observed x_i and y_i values (the data is said to be **poorly correlated**). On the other hand, if the absolute value of such

---

[39]We limit attention to linear functions, however, in principle non-linear cases could also be adopted.

a correlation coefficient is close to the maximum attainable[40] then there is a good case for arguing that the x and y values are connected as measured by the best line function.

In total, bearing in mind that we focus on 2 part structures $\{(x_i, y_i) : 1 \leq i \leq N\}$, we can distinguish five possibilities.

CSP The data have a **strong positive** correlation.

CSN The data have a **strong negative** correlation.

CWP The data have a **weak positive** correlation.

CWN The data have a **weak negative** correlation.

CZ The data are **uncorrelated**.

Figure 6.9 shows these five possibilities for different scatter plots.

In Figure 6.9(a) the data are **strongly positively** correlated: the points are close to the best fit linear function which is an increasing function of x.
In Figure 6.9(b) the data are **strongly negatively** correlated: the points are close to the best fit linear function but this is now a decreasing function of x.
In Figure 6.9(c) the data are **weakly positively** correlated: the points are spread around the best fit linear function an increasing function of x.
In Figure 6.9(d) the data are **weakly negatively** correlated: the points are also spread around the best fit linear function a decreasing function of x.
In Figure 6.9(e) the data are **uncorrelated**: the best fit line has zero gradient (is parallel to the x axis).

In terms of support for extrapolating behaviour outside the range of x_i values, (CSP) and (CSN) provide the strongest evidence. In the former case the output y increases in value with x, in the latter it decreases. For (CSP) and (CSN) the quantitative measure of **correlation coefficient** should be close to 1 (CSP) or -1 (CSN).

Such support is less evident in (CWP) and (CWN). The data are less clearly mapped around the best fit line. In such cases one might expect a correlation coefficient to be above 0.5 (CWP) or under -0.5 (CWN).

The final example provides no support at all for linking x and y values. Here we would expect the correlation coefficient to be close to 0.

---

[40]Typically for the cases we look at such correlation coefficients will have a theoretical minimum of 0 (poor correlation) and maximum of 1 (strong correlation).

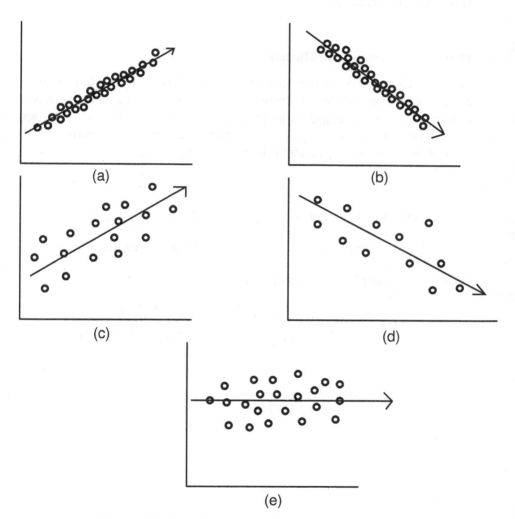

Figure 6.9: Correlation Behaviour in Scatter Plots

In order to estimate in which of these five categories sample data may fall, an oft used technique is to calculate its **Pearson Correlation Coefficient** an overview of the background is presented in Pearson [182] and the related **Determination Coefficient**.

Pearson's Correlation Coefficient

Pearson's Correlation Coefficient conventionally denoted by R brings statistical considerations not directly treated within the Least Squares methods discussed earlier. Its principal assumption is that $\{(x_i, y_i) : 1 \le i \le N\}$ are linearly related, and thus may be viewed through a best fit line function.[41]

Formally, letting X_N be **all** of the contributing x_i, i.e.

$$X_N \quad = \quad < x_1, \, x_2, \ldots, \, x_{N-1}, \, x_N > \quad \text{there is some } (x_i, y) \in S$$

Note the use of $< \ldots >$ rather than $\{\ldots\}$. Similarly

$$Y_N \quad = \quad < y_1, \, y_2, \ldots, \, y_{N-1}, \, y_N > \quad \text{there is some } (x, y_i) \in S$$

R_{XY} or more simply, R is computed as

$$R_{XY} \;=\; \frac{\sum_{i=1}^{N} (x_i - \mathbf{E}[X_N])(y_i - \mathbf{E}[Y_N])}{\left(\sqrt{\sum_{i=1}^{N} (x_i - \mathbf{E}[X_N])^2 \sum_{i=1}^{N}(y_i - \mathbf{E}[Y_N])^2}\right)}$$

---

[41]Notice that although in the analysis of linear regression we have, implicitly, assumed that X_n and Y_n are **sets**, the regression approach continues to be valid provided that $NW_{xx} - (W_x)^2 \neq 0$. Here N represents the total number of distinct **points** and the summation contributing to W_{xx} and W_x uses **all** contributing x_i, e.g. if the underlying scatter plot set, S, contains say $(4,6)$ and $(4,3)$ then W_{xx} will have **two** contributions from $16 = 4^2$ as, similarly, W_x will have two contributions of 4. It can be shown that $NW_{xx} - (W_x)^2 = 0$ only for the trivial instance of every x_i being the same.

[**Caveat**: There is some rather unfortunate confusion created by a small number of non-Statistics experts misquoting the denominator in this formula as

$$\sqrt{\sum_{i=1}^{N}(x_i - \mathbf{E}[X_N])^2(y_i - \mathbf{E}[Y_N])^2},$$

which, as one is confident the reader who has reached this far will realize, is **not** equivalent to

$$\sqrt{\sum_{i=1}^{N}(x_i - \mathbf{E}[X_N])^2 \sum_{i=1}^{N}(y_i - \mathbf{E}[Y_N])^2}$$

Despite this slip, at least one such source does describe the computational process accurately.]

Now this formula for R_{XY} may look rather intricate and computationally involved, however, if we look back to Table 6.1, it turns out we may express R_{XY} in a rather less ornate form.

Firstly, let us use

$$\mathbf{E}[X_N] = \frac{1}{N}\sum_{i=1}^{n} x_i \quad \text{and} \quad \mathbf{E}[Y_N] = \frac{1}{N}\sum_{i=1}^{n} y_i$$

We can then referring to Table 6.1 see that

$$\sum_{i=1}^{N}(x_i - \mathbf{E}[X_N])^2 = N \cdot \left(\frac{1}{N}\sum_{i=1}^{N}(x_i - \mathbf{E}[X_N])^2\right) = N \cdot [s_N(X_N)]^2$$

Similarly

$$\sum_{i=1}^{N}(y_i - \mathbf{E}[Y_N])^2 = N \cdot \left(\frac{1}{N}\sum_{i=1}^{N}(y_i - \mathbf{E}[Y_N])^2\right) = N \cdot [s_N(Y_N)]^2$$

where we recall that s_N is the *Sample Standard Deviation* which is computed for each of the collections X_N and Y_N.

Overall we may simplify the formula for R_{XY} by writing

$$R_{XY} = \frac{\sum_{i=1}^{N}(x_i - \mathbf{E}[X_N])(y_i - \mathbf{E}[Y_N])}{N s_N(X_N) s_N(Y_N)}$$

Notice that we use a substitution leading to Sample Standard Deviation, however, in principle, we could also rearrange matters to give the Bessel corrected form. While such is adopted by a number of authors we will eschew any further complication here.

In fact by using a rather relaxed notation[42] with

$$\mathbf{E}[XY] \;=\; \frac{1}{N}\sum_{i=1}^{N} x_i y_i$$

That is, similarly to the convention $\mathbf{E}[X^2]$ describing the expected value of the square of **individual** contributions, so too $\mathbf{E}[XY]$ is the expected value of the component-wise product of, again individual, components from X_N and Y_N.

Using this notation, it is not too hard to see that $\sum(x_i - \mathbf{E}[X])(y_i - \mathbf{E}[Y])$ is

$$
\begin{aligned}
&= \; \sum(x_i y_i - \mathbf{E}[X]\sum y_i - \mathbf{E}[Y]\sum x_i + \sum \mathbf{E}[X]\mathbf{E}[Y]) \\
&= \; N\mathbf{E}[XY] - 2N\mathbf{E}[X]\mathbf{E}[Y] + N\mathbf{E}[X]\mathbf{E}[Y] \\
&= \; N(\mathbf{E}[XY] - \mathbf{E}[X]\mathbf{E}[Y])
\end{aligned}
$$

So that,

$$R_{XY} \;=\; \frac{\mathbf{E}[XY] - \mathbf{E}[X]\mathbf{E}[Y]}{s_N(X)s_N(Y)}$$

In a very similar fashion to the relationship between variance and Standard Deviation, in which the former is **always** non-negative, a concept called the **Determination Coefficient** is sometimes given as an alternative if the direction of correlation as positive or negative is clear. This is simply the value R_{XY}^2.

Spearman's Rank Correlation

The focus of Pearson's Correlation Coefficient presumes that we are primarily interested in the relationship between X_N and Y_N as **numerical** data. What, however, if we have "values" for these collections which are not numerical? For example, our pairing is

$$\{(\text{orange}, \text{mini}), (\text{red}, \text{astra}), (\text{black}, \text{chevy}), (\text{pink}, \text{cadillac})\}$$

We have a sense of **preference** or **rank** for both components, e.g.

$$\text{orange} \prec \text{red} \prec \text{black} \prec \text{pink}$$
$$\text{astra} \prec \text{chevy} \prec \text{cadillac} \prec \text{mini}$$

---

[42] XY here is, in fact just the dot product of the vectors X, Y in $\mathbb{R}^N$, cf. Section 3.3.

Where the chief interest lies is the extent to which our ranking of the first (X) component agrees with the ranking of the second (Y) component. The *Spearman Rank Correlation Coefficient* presented in Spearman [218] offers one approach to comparing how much distinct rankings are in agreement.

We have two versions: one in which no two items in either collection have the same rank referred to as having **no tied** ranks and, the other, in which some items in one or more of X_N and Y_N are considered equal: having **tied** ranks.

In the former case, assume that the X_N data are ranked as $rank(x_i) = i$. First compute the value

$$D_{XY} = \sum_{i=1}^{N} d_i^2$$

where

$$d_i = i - rank(y_i)$$

In other words the difference between the ranking of x_i with respect to X_N and the ranking of y_i with respect to Y_N. In our four pair example we might have,

$$
\begin{aligned}
rank(\text{mini}) &= 4 \\
rank(\text{astra}) &= 1 \\
rank(\text{chevy}) &= 2 \\
rank(\text{cadillac}) &= 3
\end{aligned}
$$

Leading to,

$$D_{XY} = (-3)^2 + (1)^2 + (1)^2 + (1)^2 = 12$$

The **Spearman Rank Correlation Coefficient** with no tied ranks, ρ_{XY} for (X_N, Y_N) is

$$\rho_{XY} = 1 - \frac{6D_{XY}}{N(N^2 - 1)}$$

Noting that D_{XY} is (obviously!) at least 0 and (less obviously) is largest when

$$rank(i) = \begin{cases} N - i + 1 & \text{if} \quad i \leq \lfloor N/2 \rfloor \\ i - 1 - N & \text{if} \quad i > \lfloor N/2 \rfloor \end{cases}$$

Informally this is the ranking in which the highest ranked x is associated with the lowest rank y, the second highest x with the second lowest y, and so on continuing to the lowest ranked x being linked to the highest rank y.

Some rather tedious algebraic manipulation shows that

$$-1 \leq \rho_{XY} \leq 1$$

An outcome $\rho_{XY} = 1$ indicates complete agreement in the rankings of X_N and their partner Y_N: highest x associated with highest y, etc. An outcome $\rho_{XY} = -1$ as suggested by the informal description indicates total disagreement concerning the relative ranking of X_N and the Y_N cases associated with these.[43]

For the small four pair example we find

$$\rho_{XY} = 1 - \frac{6 \cdot 12}{4 \cdot (4^2 - 1)} = 1 - \frac{72}{60} = -0.2$$

where we to exchange $rank(astra)$ with $rank(cadillac)$, i.e. use $rank(astra) = 3$, $rank(cadillac) = 1$ then D_{XY} would become

$$D_{XY} = (-3)^2 + (-1)^2 + 1^2 + 3^2 = 20$$

leading to

$$\rho_{XY} = 1 - \frac{6 \cdot 20}{4 \cdot (4^2 - 1)} = 1 - \frac{120}{60} = -1$$

Thus resulting in a maximal disagreement about relative rankings.

Spearman Rank Correlation with tied ranks

A number of approaches have been used to deal with the case of two or more data items having the same rank. To illustrate, suppose we have the data rankings of Table 6.12 in which we have both X_N **and** Y_N with tied ranks.

Table 6.12: Example of Tied Ranking Data

i	1	2	3	4	5	6	7	8
$rank(x_i)$	1	2	3	3	5	6	6	8
$rank(y_i)$	2	4	8	2	6	4	7	1

One method to resolve the unseparated items is to replace the value given to t items each having rank k e.g. in Table 6.12, x_5 and x_6 are two data with rank 2 and y_1 and y_2 also have rank 2, with other values.

Now if we have N items but less than N values then some items must be ranked equally and therefore some Natural rank values must be absent. In this

---

[43]Alternatively we can interpret $\rho_{XY} = -1$ as complete agreement that the ordering of X_N is the **reverse** of the ranking of Y_N.

case we just replace the values by the **average** of the **tied positions**, e.g. if the second, third and fourth items all have rank 2 then the next ordered rank value would be 5: so we replace 2 by $(2+3+4)/3$, i.e. 3.

In our example this would lead to Table 6.13.

Table 6.13: Resolving X_N and Y_N Tied Ranking

Order i	1	2	3	4	5	6	7	8
Order $rank(x_i)$	1	2	3	3	5	6	6	8
New $rank(x_i)$	1	2	3.5	3.5	5	6.5	6.5	8
Order $rank(y_i)$	1	2	2	4	4	6	7	8
New (sorted) $rank(y_i)$	1	2.5	2.5	4.5	4.5	6	7	8
i	1	2	3	4	5	6	7	8
Data X_N	1	2	3.5	3.5	5	6.5	6.5	8
New Y_N	2.5	4.5	8	2.5	6	4.5	7	1

Although one could calculate the Rank Correlation coefficient using the data after resolving ties, that is by applying ρ_{XY} to these, a more trustworthy alternative is to apply a variant of Pearson's Correlation described earlier. Thus using $r(x_i)$ and $r(y_i)$ to denote the ranking values, this computes Rank Correlation as,

$$\rho_{XY} = \frac{\sum_{i=1}^{N}(r(x_i) - \mathbf{E}[r(x_i)])(r(y_i) - \mathbf{E}[r(y_i)])}{\sqrt{\sum_{i=1}^{N}(r(x_i) - \mathbf{E}[r(x_i)])^2 \sum_{i=1}^{N}(r(y_i) - \mathbf{E}[r(y_i)])^2}}$$

Comparing the two approaches with the example.

Spearman's method gives:

$$D_{xy} = (-1.5)^2+(-2.5)^2+(-4.5)^2+(1)^2+(1)^2+(2)^2+(-0.5)^2+(7)^2 = 84$$

Leading to

$$\rho_{XY} = 1 - \frac{6 \cdot 84}{8 \cdot 63} = 1 - \frac{504}{504} = 0$$

Using the modified Pearson coefficient method.

$$\mathbf{E}[r(x_i)] = 4.5 \; ; \; \mathbf{E}[r(y_i)] = 4.5$$

$$\sum_{i=1}^{8}(r(x_i) - 4.5)^2 = 41 \; ; \; \sum_{i=1}^{8}(r(y_i) - 4.5)^2 = 41$$

Table 6.14: Average Depth

m	BST	m	BST	m	BST	m	BST
50	11.701	100	14.278	150	15.618	200	16.741
250	17.666	300	18.553	350	18.808	400	19.59
450	19.926	500	20.395	550	20.623	600	20.946
650	21.481	700	21.588	750	21.911	800	22.106
850	22.4	900	22.62	950	22.791	1000	22.973
1050	23.276	1100	23.371	1150	23.565	1200	23.833
1250	23.778	1300	23.985	1350	24.306	1400	24.483

$$\sum_{i=1}^{8}(r(x_i) - 4.5)(r(y_i) - 4.5) \quad = \quad -3$$

So that, with this $\rho_{XY} \sim \ -0.073170732$. Although relatively low, the data have *some* level of rank correlation.

To conclude we note that there are a number of approaches that have been studied to compare ranking correlation both in data $\{(x_i, y_i)\ 1 \leq i \leq N\}$ where both X_N and Y_N are sets and when ties are present. One such widely adopted method is that of Kendall [140].

6.13   Example Regression & Correlation Cases

We conclude this chapter by presenting two worked through examples of the techniques we have just discussed.

Binary Tree Depths

In order to estimate typical depths of binary trees under the **binary search tree** distribution, a random collection of these were analyzed. The results are presented in Table 6.14

Details: m is the number of *leaf* nodes so that $n = 2m - 1$ gives the total number of nodes in a binary tree with m leaves. For each number of leaf nodes, 500 cases were randomly generated. The binary search-tree method is a standard approach and has been analyzed by Robson [195] and Devroye [63].

Figure 6.10 shows the data points.

The analysis presented in Robson [195] indicates that under the BST distribution tree depth increases logarithmically with the number of nodes. Con-

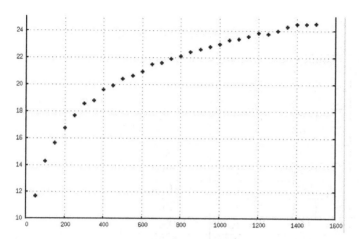

Figure 6.10: Average Depth – BST

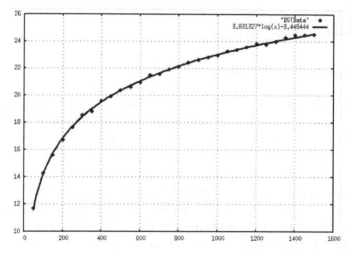

Figure 6.11: Best Fit estimate for BST Data in Table 6.14.

sidering $D(n, u_1, u_2) = u_1 \log n + u_2$ against the outcome presented in Table 6.14, we find a Least Squares estimate of

$$D_{\text{BST}}(n) \sim 3.83132 \log_e n - 3.445444$$

This is depicted in Figure 6.11

Table 6.15: Letter Frequencies in Text

Letter	Occurrences	Letter	Occurrences
A	1184	B	230
C	397	D	548
E	1877	F	338
G	248	H	900
I	999	J	23
K	87	L	564
M	381	N	1014
O	1124	P	256
Q	16	R	935
S	900	T	1425
U	452	V	181
W	352	X	26
Y	274	Z	2

Zipf's Law in Text Analysis

Zipf's Law was proposed in [262, 263] and is an empirically based observation about the relative frequency of occurrence of lexical data, e.g. letters, words, word and sentence lengths, in a collection. Thus, suppose one orders all words $< w_1, w_2, \ldots, w_k, \ldots >$ in a text by their usage frequency, i.e. w_1 is the most commonly used word, w_2 the second most, etc. Given any word w in the text let r_w be its rank and $f(r_w)$ its frequency of occurrence. Zipf's Law asserts $f(r_w) \propto r_w^{-\alpha}$ for $\alpha \sim 1$. In other words, the "second most frequent word" occurs roughly half as often as the most frequent word; the "k'th most common word" occurs proportionate to $1/k^\alpha$ within a text. Zipf's Law is empirically supported by a number of studies. A good overview of Zipf's Law in text and linguistic analysis may be found in Piantadosi [187].

In [72] some empirical analysis of Zipf's Law as it occurs in a specific class of texts is examined.[44] The **letter** ranking, for one sample, gives the outcome in Table 6.15.[45]

This leads to the letter ranking and corresponding frequency mapping of Table 6.16.

---

[44]The collection consists of examples of persuasive oratory.

[45]The text in question being that of Thomas Paine's pamphlet *The Crisis* from December 1776.

Table 6.16: Letter Ranking from Table 6.15

Rank	Letter	Occurrences	Rank	Letter	Occurrences
1	E	1877	2	T	1425
3	A	1184	4	O	1124
5	N	1014	6	I	999
7	R	935	8	S	900
9	H	900	10	L	564
11	D	548	12	U	452
13	C	397	14	M	381
15	W	352	16	F	338
17	Y	274	18	P	256
19	G	248	20	B	230
21	V	181	22	K	87
23	X	26	24	J	23
25	Q	16	26	Z	2

The same text is examined in [72] with respect to word incidences: there are a total of $3,439$ words of which $1,054$ are distinct. Assigning rank 1 to the most frequent word, 2 to the second most common, etc., the pattern for the first few ranks and the number of occurrences is found to be as Table 6.17.

Looking at a scatter plot of rank order (x-axis) to frequency (y-axis) gives the picture in Figure 6.12 (letters) and Figure 6.13 (words)

Examining the best-fit line function for the letter data gives

$$y = -60.88308x + 1388.57538$$

Figure 6.14 matches this linear function against the data from Figure 6.12.

The Pearson correlation coefficient is $R = -0.9465$ indicating these data fall into the category of having a strong negative correlation. The basis of Zipf's Law, however, does not assert a **linear** relationship between rank and frequency but rather that rank (x) occurs with frequency proportional to $x^{-\alpha}$ for some α.

In specialist literature examining texts e.g. Eftekhari [76] an approach adopted to studying such α is to look at the scatter plot given by viewing

$$-\log k \ (x\text{-axis}) \text{ vs. } \log\left\{\frac{occ(k)}{Total}\%\right\}$$

That is on a $\log-\log$ scale of "Rank k" against "number of occurrences of items of rank k as a **percentage** of all tokens in the input".

Table 6.17: Word Ranking

Rank	#	Rank	#	Rank	#	Rank	#
1	204	2	118	3	106	4	102
5	90	6	59	7	55	8	46
9	45	10	42	11	37	12	35
13	34	14	32	15	31	16	29
17	29	18	27	19	25	20	24
21	23	22	23	23	22	24	22
25	22	26	21	27	21	28	19
29	18	30	17	31	17	32	16
33	16	34	16	35	16	36	16
37	15	38	14	39	13	40	12
41	12	42	12	43	12	44	12
45	12	46	12	47	11	48	11
49	11	50	11	51	11	52	11
53	10	54	10	55	10	56	10
57	10	58	10	59	9	60	9
...	...	...	...	362	1	363	1
...	...	...	...	...	...	1054	1

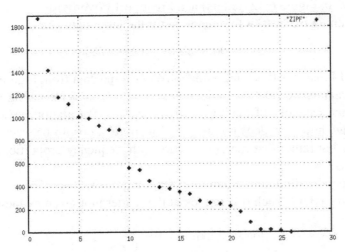

Figure 6.12: Letter Rank v. Frequency

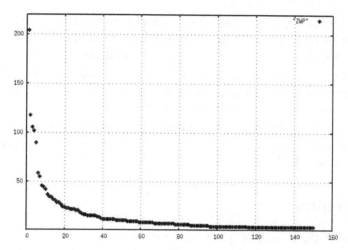

Figure 6.13: Word Rank v. Frequency

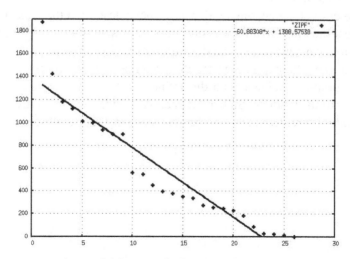

Figure 6.14: Best-fit line for Figure 6.12

The gradient of the best-fit line which will be negative provides a good approximation to the value $-\alpha$.

We refer the interested reader to the papers mentioned for a more detailed discussion of how R^2 and regression methods are applied to estimate α for the cases described. Specifically and as can be demonstrated directly using Geometric regression we find $\alpha \sim -1.4193$ (letter) and $\alpha \sim -0.8296$ (word). A significant advantage of converting to a "$\log - \log$-scale" is that it allows the notions of correlation coefficients e.g. Pearson's to be reviewed since the assumption of there being a linear relationship is justified: x in our original use will be viewed as $\log x$ on a $\log - \log$-axis; similarly $x^{-\alpha}$ will be examined as $-\alpha \log x$ on the "$\log y$" axis.

6.14 Summary

The focus of the preceding pages has been with regard to questions arising in data analysis concerning both identifying functions that map input data to observed outcomes and in providing support that such functions are, indeed, reasonable models. The former area, covering the fields of interpolation and regression analysis, has an extensive supporting literature from which we have only discussed a very small number of techniques: principally the important Least Squares Method.

In the case of supporting evidence we have described the concept of "correlation coefficients" and their use in providing quantitative measures of how accurate a linear function is as a descriptor of observed data sets.

Within the Chapter as a whole the principal aim has to been to defend a view of Computer Science as a discipline in which experimental techniques are central to its conduct. Statistical analysis and the related activities of data fitting methods are, from this perspective, core methodologies.

6.15 Projects

1. Using the algorithm of Atkinson and Sack [14] investigate the behaviour of binary trees chosen according to the uniform distribution.

2. A number of models of random graph structures have been proposed ranging from that of Erdös and Rényi see e.g.[78]. to models focused on specific applications fields such as Newman *et al.* [174]. Compare the properties of randomly generated graphs using a selected number of such approaches.

6.16 Endnotes

1. "an input graph has a *Hamiltonian cycle* quickly on average.": The Hamiltonian Cycle problem asks of an input graph with nodes V and edges E, denoted by $G(V, E)$, whether it is possible to trace a circular sequence of edges i.e *path* or *cycle* which visits each node exactly once. The decision problem described is a well-known example of an **NP**–complete problem, a class of computational problems of considerable importance and studied within the CS discipline of Computational Complexity Theory. The study of these problems originates in work of Steven Cook [49] and independently of Cook's discoveries, Leonid Levin [154]. A comprehensive discussion of properties and problems known to belong to this collection may be found in Garey and Johnson [98]. The set of these contains an extensive range of widely varying computationally important problems, however, there are two significant features of interest regarding it: no "fast" worst-case algorithms have been discovered for **any** of its members; *if* such a method was discovered for just a **single** NP–complete problem then it would yield constructive fast methods for **all** members. Fast "average-case" methods are of great importance in trying to overcome the difficulties of "no fast general methods". In the particular case of Hamiltonian cycle detection a key breakthough was made through the discoveries of Dana Angluin and Les Valiant [12].

Chapter 7

Matrices revisited
Introduction to Spectral Methods

And one and all they had a longing to get away from this painfulness, this ceremony which had reminded them of things they could not bear to think about – to get away quickly and go about their business and forget.

The Man of Property (from *The Forsyte Saga*)
JOHN GALSWORTHY (1867–1933)

A choice of opening words which, one can but hope, does not reflect the feelings of too many readers. In Computer Science, much as the concept of number provides the fundamental object on which computational activity is based, so too that of *matrix* as a mechanism for organizing, presenting and processing numerical data is, to a great extent, almost as ubiquitous. So we have matrices as implicit forms used to describe images, graphs and networks, and statistical data. Of course often the presentational form is dubbed "table", however, whether dealing with a description of basic arithmetic process e.g. a multiplication table, Statistical tables such as t-test confidence values or conversion between different measurement systems e.g. Imperial to metric, Fahrenheit to Celsius, such devices may all be treated as *matrices*[1] in the formal sense introduced in Section 3.5 and which will be the primary focus of the current chapter.

Although some basic matrix mechanisms have been encountered earlier, a number of important new concepts will be presented. Not only will appropriate generalizations of notions such as determinant be reviewed but also the,

---

[1] See Endnote 1.

increasingly significant in computational settings, idea of spectral methods in Section 7.4. While the formal basis for this will be presented our main interest is with respect to three quite different uses of spectral analysis in addressing computational problems.

7.1 Operations on $n \times n$-matrices

We first recall the matrix processes introduced in Section 3.5. In this review $\varepsilon \in \mathbb{R}$ and $\mathbf{A} = [a_{ij}]$, $\mathbf{B} = [b_{ij}]$ are unless stated otherwise order $n \times n$ matrices with entries from $\mathbb{R}$.

Matrix Addition

$$\mathbf{A} + \mathbf{B} \;=\; [a_{ij} + b_{ij}] \;=\; \mathbf{B} + \mathbf{A}$$

Scalar Multiplication

$$\varepsilon \cdot \mathbf{A} \;=\; [\varepsilon \cdot a_{ij}] \;=\; \mathbf{A} \cdot \varepsilon$$

Transpose

For $\mathbf{A}$ an order $n \times m$ matrix, $\mathbf{A}^\top$ is the order $m \times n$ matrix with $[a_{ij}^\top] = [a_{ji}]$.

Matrix Product

For $\mathbf{A}$ an order $p \times q$ matrix and $\mathbf{B}$ an order $q \times r$ matrix, the matrix $\mathbf{C} = \mathbf{A} \cdot \mathbf{B}$ has order $p \times r$ with

$$c_{ij} \;=\; \sum_{k=1}^{q} a_{ik} b_{kj} \quad 1 \le i \le p, \; 1 \le j \le r$$

In general, a case which is, in any event, only defined for matrices $\mathbf{A}$ and $\mathbf{B}$ both having order $n \times n$ $\mathbf{AB} \neq \mathbf{BA}$.

7.2 Inverse Matrices and the Determinant

The concepts of matrix **inverse** and the **determinant** are central to the formation of eigenvalues as we shall see in Section 7.4. We introduced the structure of these in the case of 2×2 matrices in Section 3.5. We now turn to their definition with respect to $n \times n$ matrices. First we recall the matrix $\mathbf{I}_n$ the **identity**

matrix. This has order $n \times n$ and diagonal elements that is, (i, j) entries with $i = j$, all equal to 1 while every other value is set to 0.

For any $n \times n$ matrix, $\mathbf{A}$

$$\mathbf{A} \cdot \mathbf{I}_n \;=\; \mathbf{I}_n \cdot \mathbf{A} \;=\; \mathbf{A}$$

The concept of **inverse matrix** is only well-defined for square matrices i.e. of some order $n \times n$ and, given $\mathbf{A}$, posits a matrix, $\mathbf{A}^{-1}$ with which

$$\mathbf{A} \cdot \mathbf{A}^{-1} \;=\; \mathbf{A}^{-1} \cdot \mathbf{A} \;=\; \mathbf{I}_n$$

We have, subsequent to Section 3.5 met at least one setting where inverse matrices have powerful applications: in Section 4.7 and even more directly Section 6.12 with respect to Least Squares minimization, in identifying critical points for n variable functions via analysis of the function's n first-order partial derivatives.

There are, in fact, many applications, where the answer sought can be expressed as

a. an n-vector, $\mathbf{x} \in \mathbb{R}^n$ (the **solution**).

b. an $n \times n$ matrix, $\mathbf{A}$ (the **conditions**)

c. an n-vector $\mathbf{y} \in \mathbb{R}^n$ (the **objective**).

Where the solution $\mathbf{x}$ is not known, but is found in terms of $\mathbf{A}$ and $\mathbf{y}$ usually known constants to be that $\mathbf{x}$ for which

$$\mathbf{A}\mathbf{x}^\top \;=\; \mathbf{y}^\top$$

These define a system of *simultaneous equations* whose solution is obtained using $\mathbf{A}^{-1}$ via

$$\mathbf{x}^\top \;=\; \mathbf{A}^{-1} \cdot \mathbf{y}^\top$$

There may, however, be a problem: $\mathbf{A}^{-1}$ cannot be found since the necessary conditions for it to be defined are not satisfied. In the case of 2×2 matrices these necessary conditions are easily stated and, for any 2×2 matrix equally easily tested: if $\mathbf{A}$ is a 2×2 matrix then $\mathbf{A}^{-1}$ exists if and only if $\det \mathbf{A} \neq 0$, wherein $\det \mathbf{A} = a_{11}a_{22} - a_{12}a_{21}$. The quantity $\det \mathbf{A}$ being called the **determinant** of $\mathbf{A}$.

In the case of $n \times n$ matrices, it turns out we have an identical condition prescribing the existence of $\mathbf{A}^{-1}$. Namely

If $\mathbf{A}$ is any $n \times n$ matrix then there exists a matrix, $\mathbf{A}^{-1}$ for which

$$\mathbf{A} \cdot \mathbf{A}^{-1} = \mathbf{A}^{-1} \cdot \mathbf{A} = \mathbf{I}_n$$

if and only if $\det \mathbf{A} \neq 0$.

A property which raises two further questions.

DQ1. In the 2×2 case, $\det \mathbf{A} = a_{11}a_{22} - a_{12}a_{21}$, how do we compute $\det \mathbf{A}$ when $\mathbf{A}$ has order $n \times n$ with $n > 2$?

DQ2. The inverse matrix, $\mathbf{A}^{-1}$ was constructed for 2×2 matrices possessing such, as

$$\mathbf{A}^{-1} = \frac{1}{\det \mathbf{A}} \begin{pmatrix} a_{22} & -a_{12} \\ -a_{21} & a_{11} \end{pmatrix}$$

How is $\mathbf{A}^{-1}$ formed when $\mathbf{A}$ has order $n \times n$, $\det \mathbf{A} \neq 0$ and $n > 2$?

The questions above are more than just arbitrary generalizing from a notationally straightforward ($n = 2$) instance to what may well appear to be a rather convoluted solution (for $n > 2$). Not only is there a considerable gain in being able to formulate precisely what and how $\mathbf{A}^{-1}$ and $\det \mathbf{A}$ are captured for arbitrary n with respect to the simultaneous equation setting, but the algebraic formulation for $\det \mathbf{A}$ is central to the notion of eigenvalue as we shall see later in Section 7.4.

Computing $\det \mathbf{A}$.

In Computer Science the process of using an already solved base case such as $n = 2$ as the foundation for building solutions to larger cases such as $n = 3$, 4, etc. is very familiar.

In respect of $\det \mathbf{A}$ this is exactly the mechanism used: we know how $\det \mathbf{A}$ is captured for 2×2 matrices, and we will use the 2×2 solution to define $\det \mathbf{A}$ for order 3×3; and the 3×3 solution to build $\det \mathbf{A}$ for order 4×4 and so on.

At this point it is helpful to introduce one additional notational convention.

For an order $n \times n$ matrix, $\mathbf{A}$, given i and j with $1 \leq i,\ j \leq n$, the order $(n-1) \times (n-1)$ matrix, $\mathbf{A}_{ij}$ is formed by deleting the i'th row and j'th column of $\mathbf{A}$. For example if $\mathbf{D}$ is the 5×5 matrix

$$\mathbf{D} = \begin{pmatrix} 0 & 11 & 1 & 7 & 0 \\ 0 & 0 & 41 & 0 & 0 \\ 22 & 0 & 0 & 16 & 1 \\ 1 & 0 & 8 & 0 & 9 \\ 0 & 0 & 0 & 3 & 0 \end{pmatrix}$$

then $\mathbf{D}_{12}$ is the 4×4 matrix given by deleting the first row and second column of $\mathbf{D}$, i.e.

$$\mathbf{D}_{12} = \begin{pmatrix} 0 & 41 & 0 & 0 \\ 22 & 0 & 16 & 1 \\ 1 & 8 & 0 & 9 \\ 0 & 0 & 3 & 0 \end{pmatrix}$$

In terms of the formal description of matrix elements within $\mathbf{A}_{ij}$, if $\mathbf{B} = [b_{ij}]$ is the order $(n-1) \times (n-1)$ matrix corresponding to $\mathbf{A}_{pq}$ then

$$b_{ij} = \begin{cases} a_{ij} & \text{if} \quad i < p \text{ and } j < q \\ a_{i+1,j} & \text{if} \quad i \geq p \text{ and } j < q \\ a_{i,j+1} & \text{if} \quad i < p \text{ and } j \geq q \\ a_{i+1,j+1} & \text{if} \quad i \geq p \text{ and } j \geq q \end{cases}.$$

The determinant, $\det \mathbf{A}$ also denoted using $|\mathbf{A}|$ can be computed through

D1. If $n = 2$ ($\mathbf{A}$ is a 2×2-matrix),

$$\det \mathbf{A} = a_{11}a_{22} - a_{12}a_{21}$$

D2. If $n > 2$,

$$\det \mathbf{A} = \sum_{j=1}^{n} (-1)^{1+j} a_{1j} \det \mathbf{A}_{1j}$$

There are a number of devices that can be used, in particular instances, to simplify this somewhat cumbersome procedure. Many of these exploit one or more of the following properties of the determinant.

DP1. For any choice of k ($1 \leq k \leq n$)

$$\det \mathbf{A} = \sum_{j=1}^{n} (-1)^{k+j} a_{kj} \det \mathbf{A}_{kj}$$

Thus although the description in (D2) is given in terms of the first row, **any** row can be adopted.

DP2.
$$\det \mathbf{A} \;=\; \det \mathbf{A}^{\top}$$

Hence not only can any **row** be used but, in consequence of the transpose of $\mathbf{A}$ having the same determinant we can also use any **column** of $\mathbf{A}$. In this case the symbolic form for det $\mathbf{A}$ using the first column will be

$$\det \mathbf{A} \;=\; \sum_{i=1}^{n} (-1)^{1+i} a_{i1} \det \mathbf{A}_{i1}$$

We illustrate this process for a small (3×3) example. For larger examples a number of matrix manipulation packages are available: MATLAB provides determinant computation directly, as also does the PYTHON Linear Algebra subpackage of NUMPY (numpy.linalg). For JAVA implementation a wide range of Matrix manipulation procedures may be found within the Java Matrix suite (JAMA).[2]

Example 3×3 **determinant**

For the 3×3 matrix:
$$\mathbf{A} \;=\; \begin{pmatrix} 0 & 5 & 2 \\ 3 & 0 & 4 \\ 10 & 7 & 0 \end{pmatrix}$$

$$\mathbf{A}_{11} = \begin{pmatrix} 0 & 4 \\ 7 & 0 \end{pmatrix} ; \; \mathbf{A}_{12} = \begin{pmatrix} 3 & 4 \\ 10 & 0 \end{pmatrix} ; \; \mathbf{A}_{13} = \begin{pmatrix} 3 & 0 \\ 10 & 7 \end{pmatrix}$$

So that,
$$\det \mathbf{A}_{11} = -28 \; ; \;\; \det \mathbf{A}_{12} = -40 \; ; \;\; \det \mathbf{A}_{13} = 21$$

Combining the determinants found for $\{\mathbf{A}_{11}, \mathbf{A}_{12}, \mathbf{A}_{13}\}$ gives
$$\begin{aligned} \det \mathbf{A} &= (-1)^2 \cdot 0 \cdot (-28) + (-1)^3 \cdot 5 \cdot (-40) + (-1)^4 \cdot 2 \cdot (21) \\ &= 0 + 200 + 42 \\ &= 242 \end{aligned}$$

---

[2]This may be downloaded from http://math.nist.gov/javanumerics/jama/.

Matrix Inverse

We face a similar series of contortions in generalizing from the inverse of 2×2 matrices to those $n \times n$ when $n > 2$. In addition, however, we need the notion of the **adjoint**. The adjoint of $\mathbf{A}$ which we denote by $\mathrm{adj}\,\mathbf{A}$ is the $n \times n$ matrix $[\alpha_{ij}]$ in which

$$\alpha_{ij} \;=\; (-1)^{i+j}|\mathbf{A}_{ji}|$$

[Here it will be convenient to use the alternative $|\ldots|$ rather than $\det \mathbf{A}$.]

It is important to note the subscript ordering in the definition of α_{ij}: the element in the i'th row and j'th column of $\mathrm{adj}\,\mathbf{A}$ is defined using that matrix $\mathbf{A}_{ji}$ formed by deleting the j'th **row** and i'th **column** of $\mathbf{A}$.

Now, with this idea of adjoint matrix, it may be shown that whenever $|\mathbf{A}| \neq 0$ we have:

$$\mathbf{A}^{-1} \;=\; \left(\frac{1}{\det \mathbf{A}}\right) \mathrm{adj}\,\mathbf{A}$$

In other words, $[a_{ij}^{-1}]$ the (i,j) element within $\mathbf{A}^{-1}$ is

$$a_{ij}^{-1} \;=\; \frac{(-1)^{i+j}|\mathbf{A}_{ji}|}{|\mathbf{A}|}$$

As with computation of $\det \mathbf{A}$ there are some useful relationships linking $\mathbf{A}$, $\det \mathbf{A}$ and $\mathbf{A}^{\top}$. Before continuing with the small 3×3 example above, we summarize the more important of these.

$$
\begin{aligned}
\mathbf{A}\mathbf{A}^{\top} &= \mathbf{A}^{\top}\mathbf{A} \\
\mathbf{A}\mathbf{A}^{\top} &\ \text{is}\ \ \textbf{symmetric} \\
(\mathbf{A}\mathbf{B})^{\top} &= \mathbf{B}^{\top}\mathbf{A}^{\top} \\
\det \mathbf{A} &= \det \mathbf{A}^{\top} \\
\mathrm{adj}\,\mathbf{A} &= (\mathrm{adj}\,\mathbf{A}^{\top})^{\top} \\
(\mathbf{A}^{-1})^{\top} &= (\mathbf{A}^{\top})^{-1}
\end{aligned}
$$

Returning to our 3×3 example matrix,

$$\mathbf{A} \;=\; \begin{pmatrix} 0 & 5 & 2 \\ 3 & 0 & 4 \\ 10 & 7 & 0 \end{pmatrix}$$

We have already seen that $|\mathbf{A}| = 242$. For $\text{adj}\,\mathbf{A}$ we obtain,

$$
\begin{cases}
\alpha_{11} &=\ (-1)^2 \det \mathbf{A}_{11} = -28 \\
\alpha_{12} &=\ (-1)^3 \det \mathbf{A}_{21} = 14 \\
\alpha_{13} &=\ (-1)^4 \det \mathbf{A}_{31} = 20 \\
\alpha_{21} &=\ (-1)^3 \det \mathbf{A}_{12} = 40 \\
\alpha_{22} &=\ (-1)^4 \det \mathbf{A}_{22} = -20 \\
\alpha_{23} &=\ (-1)^5 \det \mathbf{A}_{32} = 6 \\
\alpha_{31} &=\ (-1)^4 \det \mathbf{A}_{13} = 21 \\
\alpha_{32} &=\ (-1)^5 \det \mathbf{A}_{23} = 50 \\
\alpha_{33} &=\ (-1)^2 \det \mathbf{A}_{33} = -15
\end{cases}
$$

Leading to

$$
\mathbf{A}^{-1} \;=\; \begin{pmatrix} 0 & 5 & 2 \\ 3 & 0 & 4 \\ 10 & 7 & 0 \end{pmatrix}^{-1} \;=\; \frac{1}{242} \begin{pmatrix} -28 & 14 & 20 \\ 40 & -20 & 6 \\ 21 & 50 & -15 \end{pmatrix}
$$

We leave the reader to verify that $\mathbf{A}\mathbf{A}^{-1} = \mathbf{A}^{-1}\mathbf{A} = \mathbf{I}_3$.

Triangular Matrices

The mechanisms just described can with larger "dense" matrices, that is those in which the number of non-zero elements is $\sim \tau n^2$ for some constant $\tau \in \mathbb{R}$, quickly become rather excessive. There is, however, a special class of Real-valued matrices for which $\det \mathbf{A}$ can be obtained with significantly less effort: the **triangular** matrices.

The $n \times n$ matrix $\mathbf{A}$ is said to be a **lower triangular** matrix if

$$
a_{ij} = 0 \text{ for } \textbf{every } (i, j) \text{ satisfying } 1 \le i < j \le n
$$

So that all but its diagonal elements, a_{ii} and those elements whose row index exceeds their column index will be 0.

$$
\begin{pmatrix}
a_{11} & 0 & \cdots & 0 & 0 \\
a_{21} & a_{22} & 0 & \cdots & 0 \\
\vdots & \cdots & a_{ii} & \cdots & 0 \\
\vdots & \cdots & \vdots & \ddots & \vdots \\
a_{n1} & a_{n2} & \cdots & a_{n,n-1} & a_{nn}
\end{pmatrix}
$$

A Lower Triangular Matrix

The $n \times n$ matrix $\mathbf{A}$ is said to be an **upper triangular** matrix if

$$a_{ij} = 0 \text{ for } \textbf{every } (i, j) \text{ satisfying } 1 \leq j < i \leq n$$

So that all but its diagonal elements, a_{ii} and those elements whose row index is less than their column index will be 0.

$$\begin{pmatrix} a_{11} & a_{12} & \cdots & a_{1,n-1} & a_{1n} \\ 0 & a_{22} & \cdots & \cdots & a_{2n} \\ 0 & \cdots & a_{ii} & \cdots & a_{in} \\ \vdots & \vdots & \vdots & \ddots & \vdots \\ 0 & 0 & \cdots & 0 & a_{nn} \end{pmatrix}$$

An Upper Triangular Matrix

An order $n \times n$ matrix $\mathbf{A}$ is a **triangular** matrix if $\mathbf{A}$ is one of upper triangular, or lower triangular or a diagonal matrix. Diagonal matrices are, it is easy to see, **both** upper and lower triangular.

The determinant of a triangular matrix has a particularly elegant form.

Property 5. *If $\mathbf{A}$ is an order $n \times n$ triangular matrix then,*

$$\det \mathbf{A} \;=\; \prod_{i=1}^{n} a_{ii}$$

Thus, from Property 5, in order to compute the determinant of a triangular matrix we simply need to multiply all of its diagonal elements.

The determinant as a sum of permutations

We include this development not because of its compuational utility but rather because it may be seen to provide a better insight into how $\det \mathbf{A}$ is manipulated in Section 7.4.

Let us look again at the **symbolic** outcome arising from our determinant computation **algorithm** within (D1)–(D2) above. Suppose we consider the following set of **mappings**

$$\pi \;:\; [1, 2, 3, \cdots, n-1, n] \to [1, 2, 3, \cdots, n]$$

so that $\pi(i)$ given some $i \in \mathbb{N}$ between 1 and n reports another value also in $\mathbb{N}$ and also between 1 and n.

The set

$$S_n \;=\; \{\, \pi \;:\; \pi : [1, 2, 3, \cdots, n] \to [1, 2, 3, \cdots, n]$$

is called the set of **permutations** of $\{1, 2, 3, \ldots, n\}$. Now if we take **any** $\pi \in S_n$ then $(i, \pi(i))$ selects a unique element within an order $n \times n$ matrix $\mathbf{A}$: namely that in the i'th row and $\pi(i)$'th column, i.e. $a_{i,\pi(i)}$.

Permutations can be **even**: meaning that

$$|\{ (i, j) \ : \ i < j \ \textbf{and} \ \pi(i) > \pi(j) \}| \ \text{is an } \textbf{even} \text{ number.}$$

Permutations can also be **odd**: meaning that

$$|\{ (i, j) \ : \ i < j \ \textbf{and} \ \pi(i) > \pi(j) \}| \ \text{is an } \textbf{odd} \text{ number.}$$

The **signum** of a permutation π denoted $\text{sgn}(\pi)$, is defined to be

$$\text{sgn}(\pi) \ = \ \begin{cases} 1 & \text{if} \quad \pi \text{ is an even permutation in } S_n \\ -1 & \text{if} \quad \pi \text{ is an odd permutation in } S_n \end{cases}$$

What does this idea offer with respect to the determinant of $\mathbf{A}$? Suppose we take any $\pi \in S_n$ and consider the product

$$\prod_{i=1}^{n} a_{i,\pi(i)}$$

In this case it can be shown that for any order $n \times n$ matrix $\mathbf{A}$

$$|\mathbf{A}| \ = \ \sum_{\pi \in S_n} \text{sgn}(\pi) \prod_{i=1}^{n} a_{i,\pi(i)}$$

We stress that this representation, while extremely helpful as a symbolic description, is unusable when n becomes moderately large as a **computational** approach.

7.3 Matrix Rank and the relationship to singularity

The concept of **rank** provides a, sometimes more direct, method by which one can determine if $\det \mathbf{A} = 0$. In Section 3.4 we introduced the structure referred to as a *vector space* denoting an arbitrary such space by V and saw that any vector space has an associated **dimension** being the minimum size of a set $U \subseteq V$ for which any vector $\mathbf{v} \in V$ can be constructed as a *linear combination* (Description 3 of Section 3.4) of the vectors in U. Such a set U being called a basis of V.

The matrices we are concerned with in this Chapter we consider as having n rows and columns: that is as a collection of n vectors from $\mathbb{R}^n$. Suppose we examine the rows of an arbitrary such matrix and discover that these n vectors are **not** linearly independent?[3] Since this is the case, we can identify a **strict** subset R of the rows of $\mathbf{A}$, $R = \{\mathbf{r}_1, \mathbf{r}_2, \ldots, \mathbf{r}_t\}$ say, **and** a row $\mathbf{a}_k \notin R$ of $\mathbf{A}$ for which

$$\sum_{i=1}^{t} \tau_i \mathbf{r}_i \; = \; \mathbf{a}_k \quad < \tau_1, \tau_2, \ldots, \tau_t > \in \mathbb{R}^t$$

Given $\mathbf{A}$ its **rank** is defined to be the minimum size of a subset R of the rows of $\mathbf{A}$ such some row of $\mathbf{A}$ that is not included is a linear combination of R. We use $\mathrm{rank}(\mathbf{A})$ to denote the rank of $\mathbf{A}$. Now it is, one hopes, obvious that $\mathrm{rank}(\mathbf{A})$ cannot exceed the number of rows in $\mathbf{A}$, i.e. for any $n \times n$ matrix, $\mathbf{A}$ $\mathrm{rank}(\mathbf{A}) \leq n$. If we have $R \subset \{\mathbf{a}_1, \ldots, \mathbf{a}_n\}$ and $\mathbf{a}_k \notin R$ for which $\mathbf{a}_k$ is a linear combination of R, then $\mathrm{rank}(\mathbf{A}) \leq |R| < n$. What does this tell us about $\det \mathbf{A}$? In answering this question we find one of the basic connections between Matrix Algebra as reviewed here and in Section 3.5 and Vector Algebra as it concerned much of Chapter 3.

Property 6. *For any $n \times n$ matrix, $\mathbf{A}$,*

$$\det \mathbf{A} \neq 0 \;\; \textit{if and only if} \;\; \mathrm{rank}(\mathbf{A}) = n$$

Thus, in principle, in order to establish that a given matrix is **singular** as matrices whose determinant is zero are called, those for which $\det \mathbf{A} \neq 0$ being termed **non-singular** it would suffice to find a strict subset of its rows from which one of the unselected rows can be reconstructed as a linear combination of the chosen.

In the light of Property 6 if we simply wish to decide whether $\det \mathbf{A} = 0$ or, looking ahead to Section 7.4, in identifying parameters which render a given matrix as one having determinant equal to zero, rather than wade through explicit computation of $\det \mathbf{A}$ via the steps presented in (D1) and (D2) earlier an alternative would be to identify a strict subset of rows, R say, for which some matrix row, a not among R, can be described as a linear combination of R.

One assistance in finding such a set of rows is offered through the idea of **elementary row operations**.

First notice that, via the specification of (DP1) we see the following holds.

---

[3]We focus on rows but much of what is developed here applies equally with respect to **columns**. Noting that our main interest is regarding conditions indicating that $\det \mathbf{A} = 0$, using the property $\det \mathbf{A} = \det \mathbf{A}^\top$ shows that any condition expressed solely in terms of matrix rows applies in an identical form to the condition applied solely to the matrix columns.

Property 7. *If* $\mathbf{A}$ *is an* $n \times n$ *matrix with some row* $\mathbf{a}$ *of* $\mathbf{A}$ *having* $\mathbf{a} = \mathbf{0}$ *i.e. the vector all of whose components are zero then* $\det \mathbf{A} = 0$.

And, of course, Property 7 also holds if we replace "row" by "column" and $\mathbf{0}$ by $\mathbf{0}^{\top}$.

We can develop Property 7 in a way which begins to make the links between "$\det \mathbf{A} = 0$", "$\mathrm{rank}(\mathbf{A}) < n$" and "some row of $\mathbf{A}$ is a linear combination of other rows of $\mathbf{A}$" rather clearer.

Property 8. *If* $\mathbf{A}$ *is an* $n \times n$ *matrix with distinct rows* $\mathbf{a}$ *and* $\mathbf{b}$ *such that* $\mathbf{a} = \varepsilon \mathbf{b}$ *for some* $\varepsilon \in \mathbb{R}$ *then* $\det \mathbf{A} = 0$.

Property 8 indicates that if $\mathbf{A}$ has two **identical** rows then $\det \mathbf{A} = 0$: choose $\varepsilon = 1$.

We now introduce the concept of **elementary row operations** on order $n \times n$ matrices[4] and the effect these have on $\det \mathbf{A}$.

Elementary row operations

The three elementary row operations for an order $n \times n$ matrix $\mathbf{A}$ are defined to be the following.

ER1. For distinct rows $\mathbf{a}_i$ and $\mathbf{a}_j$ of $\mathbf{A}$: swop $\mathbf{a}_i$ and $\mathbf{a}_j$. The resulting matrix we denote by $\mathbf{R}_{ij}(\mathbf{A})$. (SWOP)

ER2. For some $\varepsilon \in \mathbb{R}$, replace some row $\mathbf{a}_i$ of with $\varepsilon \mathbf{a}_i$. The new matrix is denoted $\mathbf{R}_i^{\varepsilon}(\mathbf{A})$. (SCALE)

ER3. For some $\varepsilon \in \mathbb{R}$ and row $\mathbf{a}_i$ replace a **different** row $\mathbf{a}_j$ with the row $\varepsilon \mathbf{a}_i + \mathbf{a}_j$. The new matrix is denoted $\mathbf{R}_{ij}^{\varepsilon}(\mathbf{A})$. (COMBINE)

It is, of course, not hard to see that $\mathbf{R}_{ij}(\mathbf{A}) = \mathbf{R}_{ji}(\mathbf{A})$.

Suppose that $\mathbf{S}_{ij}^{\varepsilon}(\mathbf{A})$ is the outcome of applying one of (ER1) through (ER3) to $\mathbf{A}$. What can we say about $\det \mathbf{S}_{ij}^{\varepsilon}(\mathbf{A})$? Property 9 answers this question.

---

[4]Such operations, as will be clear from the definition, are also well-defined for non-square matrices, however since our interest with such operations is in the context of non-trivial indicators of $\det \mathbf{A} = 0$ and for any non-square matrix, $\mathbf{B}$ while it is possible to define concepts of row $\mathrm{rank}(\mathbf{B})$ the notion of "$\det \mathbf{B}$" it leads to via Property 6 is somewhat vacuous.

Property 9.

DER1. $\det \mathbf{R}_{ij}(\mathbf{A}) = -\det \mathbf{A}$.

DER2. $\det \mathbf{R}_i^{\varepsilon}(\mathbf{A}) = \varepsilon \det \mathbf{A}$.

DER3. $\det \mathbf{R}_{ij}^{\varepsilon}(\mathbf{A}) = \det \mathbf{A}$.

So that the SWOP operation changes a positive determinant to a negative one and *vice-versa*; the SCALE operation multiplies the determinant by whatever scaling factor (ε) has been applied; and the COMBINE operation makes no difference to the determinant's value.[5]

Two $n \times n$ matrices, $\mathbf{A}$ and $\mathbf{B}$ are said to be **row-equivalent** if we can apply a finite sequence $S_1 S_2 \cdots S_t$ of elementary row operations to $\mathbf{A}$ with the resulting matrix being the matrix $\mathbf{B}$. Now, from the description given in Property 9 we have, immediately

Property 10. *If $\mathbf{A}$ and $\mathbf{B}$ are row-equivalent then there is some $\tau \in \mathbb{R}$ with $\tau \neq 0$ having $\det \mathbf{A} = \tau \det \mathbf{B}$.*

Properties 7, 8 and 10 now suggest the following (seemingly rather "hit-and-miss", however there are algorithms for directing the process efficiently) alternative determinant computation approach.

Given $\mathbf{A}$ apply elementary row and elementary column operations to reach a matrix $\mathbf{B}$ which satisfies at least one of the following conditions.

BC1. $\mathbf{B}$ has a zero row or a zero column. **OR**

BC2. $\mathbf{B}$ has two distinct rows, $\mathbf{b}_i$ and $\mathbf{b}_j$ with which for some ε, $\mathbf{b}_i = \varepsilon \mathbf{b}_j$. Equivalently $\mathbf{B}$ has two **columns** with this property. **OR**

BC3. $\mathbf{B}$ is a **triangular** matrix.

Should we be able to finish in state (BC1) or (BC2) then we know that $\det \mathbf{A} = 0$. Should we reach condition (BC3) then

$$\det \mathbf{A} = \tau \prod_{i=1}^{n} b_{ii}$$

---

[5]Notice the qualification that the rows be distinct within the specification of COMBINE is necessary. Otherwise, "combining" $\mathbf{a}_i$ with itself using a factor ε would replace $\mathbf{a}_i$ with $\varepsilon \mathbf{a}_i + \mathbf{a}_i = (1 + \varepsilon)\mathbf{a}_i$ so that $\mathbf{R}_{ii}^{\varepsilon}(\mathbf{A}) \equiv \mathbf{R}_i^{1+\varepsilon}(\mathbf{A})$: this, however, would contradict what we have stated the outcome of SCALE and that of COMBINE to be. Namely, multiply $\det \mathbf{A}$ by a factor of $1 + \varepsilon$ and $\det \mathbf{A}$ is unchanged.

where $\tau \in \mathbb{R}$ is the accumulated result of any scaling and swopping operations used in going from $\mathbf{A}$ to $\mathbf{B}$.

Recalling the form of the inverse matrix, the following property of triangular matrices shows that not only is the computation of $\det \mathbf{A}$ straightforward but also computation of $\mathbf{A}^{-1}$.

Property 11. *Suppose that* $\mathbf{A}$ *is an order* $n \times n$ ***upper*** *triangular matrix. Then all of the following properties hold for* $\mathbf{A}$.

UT1. $\mathbf{A}^{\top}$ *is a **lower** triangular matrix. Similarly, if* $\mathbf{A}$ *is a lower triangular matrix then* $\mathbf{A}^{\top}$ *is upper triangular.*

UT2. For any $1 \le i, j \le n$, *the matrix* $\mathbf{A}_{ij}$ *is also upper triangular.*

UT3. $\mathtt{adj}\,\mathbf{A}$ *is upper triangular.*

UT4. If $\det \mathbf{A} \ne 0$, *then* $\mathbf{A}^{-1}$ *is upper triangular.*

UT5. When $\mathbf{B}$ *is an order* $n \times n$ *upper triangular matrix then*

$$\mathbf{A} + \mathbf{B} \ and \ \mathbf{A} \cdot \mathbf{B}$$

are both upper triangular.

Notice that Property 11 allows the inverse to be computed via the description for $\mathbf{A}^{-1}$ given previously.

We conclude this overview by introducing the important relationship between matrices called **similarity**. In implementing some of the processes arising in the body of the next part of this chapter similarity offers a number of helpful devices.

Thus we say that the order $n \times n$ matrices, $\mathbf{A}$ and $\mathbf{B}$ are **similar** if there is a non-singular matrix, $\mathbf{T}$ for which

$$\mathbf{B} = \mathbf{T}^{-1} \cdot \mathbf{A} \cdot \mathbf{T}$$

Similarity provides a useful mechanism for arguing about collections of matrices much in the way that the concept of vector space provided with respect to collections of vectors.

7.4 Introduction to Spectral Analysis

A problem that arises in what may seem like a surprising number of applications concerns identifying n-vectors and values which have a specific relationship with respect to a given $n \times n$ Real-valued matrix. This relationship is described in Problem 2.

Problem 2. *Given* $\mathbf{A}$ *an order* $n \times n$ *matrix with Real elements, find*

*E1. All **scalar** values,* λ, *and*

E2. All n*-vectors,* $\mathbf{x}_\lambda$,

with which

$$\mathbf{A}\mathbf{x}_\lambda^\top = \lambda \cdot \mathbf{x}_\lambda^\top$$

It may be noted that although we concentrate on and specify explicitly in the Problem's description **matrices** with Real elements, we do not do so with regard to either λ or $\mathbf{x}_\lambda$. The fact that the domain of these items is not restricted within the problem definition is quite deliberate. It is **not** because repeatedly writing "with elements from $\mathbb{R}$" is felt to be at this stage of the text unnecessary or is becoming rather burdensome constantly to repeat. It is because, in the nature of the solutions we may find, these may take values from $\mathbb{C}$. And so, if the reader would be more comfortable with the most general statement[6] of Problem 2 then the entities sought within (E1) and (E2) are all **Complex** values $\lambda \in \mathbb{C}$ and all n-vectors, $\mathbf{x}_\lambda \in \mathbb{C}^n$ for which

$$\mathbf{A}\mathbf{x}_\lambda^\top = \lambda \cdot \mathbf{x}_\lambda^\top$$

Various terms have been used for the general study of the question raised in Problem 2. We will adopt that which is most widely used in Computer Science settings and is also frequently found in Chemistry, and that sphere of mathematical endeavours dedicated to studying the structure of graphs: we shall refer to this topic as **spectral analysis**. The reasons for this will be seen when we come to look at the nature of those $\lambda \in \mathbb{C}$ of interest. Spectral analysis is, rather tautologously, concerned with the "analysis of spectra" a word, which

---

[6]In fact, in order to be as general as possible here not only must solutions be allowed from $\mathbb{C}$ but also the domain in which we operate must, similarly, be extended to $\mathbb{C}$, i.e. to $n \times n$ matrices with elements from $\mathbb{C}$.

unlike instances such as "formula" is stll used, as standard for the plural of **spectrum**.[7]

That question raised by Problem 2 has an appealing mathematical elegance: it is simply stated *pace* the spectre of Complex numbers; it highlights a potentially again mathematically interesting connection between vectors and matrices. This, however, is not a mathematics text and our sole reason for looking at the matter raised in Problem 2 is on account of its **computational** importance. We will examine a small number of important computational uses of spectral methods in the final sections of this Chapter. For now, however, we note a few points of importance concerning such applications. I stress that a "small number" of computational applications are presented. To give a full and detailed description of **every** major and a few minor computational fields in which spectral techniques have proved beneficial would require a text at least of the length of the present one: machine learning, image analysis, computational argument, ranking problems particulary with reference to the world-wide web, computational game theory, data science, and growth patterns in social networks e.g. Facebook, twitter, etc. etc. Many of these fields are recent[8] developments. They have, however, had a huge impact on computational activity and, contrary to expectations, the formal support for many successful applications is not some arcane, technically intricate and deep mathematical result at least, would not be regarded as such in the present day: the basis is classical linear algebra dating back to more than a century ago. There is a strong argument that the predominance of Google as the search-engine of choice is due not so much to clever corporate machinations but far more to a standard item of high school[9] algebra. Before considering this, we begin by investigating Problem 2 in greater detail.

The concept of eigenvalue & eigenvector

Looking again at the task set in Problem 2, to find **scalars** and **vectors** having a particular relationship to a given **matrix**, it would be helpful if we could adopt a standard approach to solving identities. One way we could do this is, instead of writing $\mathbf{A}\mathbf{x}^\top = \lambda\mathbf{x}^\top$ we write

$$\mathbf{A}\mathbf{x}^\top - \lambda\mathbf{x}^\top = \mathbf{0}$$

[7]The plural of "formula" is, of course(!), "formula**e**" and not "formula*s*": it is regrettable, that the latter usage has begun to creep in heedless of grammatical accuracy. Not so, at present, with spectra, where I do not recall seeing the abomination "spectrums" in any published work.

[8]Reflecting one's age "recent" meaning "not around when I was an undergraduate".

[9]I use the US form "high school" rather than the British equivalent "secondary school" given the discoverers' nationality.

This is no great rearrangement: a simple device of rephrasing the identity we are trying to solve. We would, however, having made the change just given like to "factor out" the term $\mathbf{x}^\top$ on the left-hand side of this identity. The result would look something like

$$(\mathbf{A} - \lambda \cdot \textbf{??}) \cdot \mathbf{x}^\top = \mathbf{0}$$

What should be used for "**??**" in this reordering? Certainly, in order for the term to be combined with the $n \times n$ **matrix A** the result of the product involving a **scalar**, λ and the object "**??**" must be an $n \times n$ matrix. This leads to only one option for "**??**": it must be an $n \times n$ matrix and more particularly it must be the $n \times n$ **identity** matrix, $\mathbf{I}_n$. So, in total, Problem 2 becomes the task of finding scalars, λ, and associated vectors x for which

$$(\mathbf{A} - \lambda \cdot \mathbf{I}_n) \cdot \mathbf{x}^\top = \mathbf{0}.$$

And we have one immediate solution: **any** $\lambda \in \mathbb{C}$ will satisfy this identity, provided that $\mathbf{x} = \mathbf{0}$. Such solutions are of, at best, very little interest. The trivial solution $\mathbf{x} = \mathbf{0}$ comes about entirely independent of the matrix **A**. The cases we want to focus on are those λ for which

$$\mathbf{A} - \lambda \cdot \mathbf{I}_n = \mathbf{0}$$

[Here, of course, **0** on the right-hand side is the $n \times n$ zero **matrix**, rather than the n-**vector**, **0**.]

To investigate these, let us begin by making some further small changes. Consider the $n \times n$ matrix $\lambda \cdot \mathbf{I}_n$. This is a diagonal matrix: $\mathbf{I}_n$ is diagonal and all we have done is multiply by a scalar. Furthermore its diagonal entries all equal λ. So the matrix which we are trying to "make equal to **0** via judicious choice of λ is simply that obtained from **A** by subtracting λ from each diagonal element of **A**, i.e. a_{ii} is replaced by $a_{ii} - \lambda$ leaving everything else unchanged. The matrix, **A** has been given, so Problem 2 is recast as

"What are the values, λ, for which $\mathbf{A} - \lambda \cdot \mathbf{I}_n$ becomes the zero matrix?"

There is one collection of values that can be dismissed immediately: any λ which leads to a **non-singular** $\mathbf{A} - \lambda \cdot \mathbf{I}_n$.

Why is this the case? Suppose that λ results in a matrix, $\mathbf{B}_\lambda = \mathbf{A} - \lambda\mathbf{I}$, which is non-singular? This therefore means that $\mathbf{B}_\lambda$ has an inverse $\mathbf{B}_\lambda^{-1}$. Now it is a matter of no consequence what exact form $\mathbf{B}_\lambda^{-1}$ may take. All we need to look at are the ramifications of this inverse existing, relative to our original problem, i.e. Problem 2.

We have seen that those λ and $\mathbf{x}_\lambda$ for which $\mathbf{A}\mathbf{x}_\lambda^\top = \lambda \cdot \mathbf{x}_\lambda^\top$ are those satisfying,

$$(\mathbf{A} - \lambda\mathbf{I}) \cdot \mathbf{x}_\lambda^\top = \mathbf{0}^\top$$

That is to say, meeting the criterion $\mathbf{B}_\lambda\mathbf{x}_\lambda^\top = \mathbf{0}^\top$. Since $\mathbf{B}_\lambda$ is non-singular, it has an inverse and thence the allowable $\mathbf{x}_\lambda^\top$ are simply those obeying

$$\mathbf{B}_\lambda^{-1}\mathbf{B}_\lambda\mathbf{x}_\lambda^\top = \mathbf{B}_\lambda^{-1}\mathbf{0}^\top$$

In other words, since

$$\begin{aligned} \mathbf{B}_\lambda^{-1}\mathbf{B}_\lambda &= \mathbf{I} \quad &\text{and} \\ \mathbf{B}_\lambda^{-1}\mathbf{0}^\top &= \mathbf{0}^\top \quad &\text{and} \\ \mathbf{I} \cdot \mathbf{x}_\lambda^\top &= \mathbf{x}_\lambda^\top \end{aligned}$$

the only $\mathbf{x}_\lambda$ we have available is $\mathbf{x}_\lambda = \mathbf{0}$: precisely the collection of trivial solutions concerning which we have no interest.

Now, although it may not seem as such immediately, by dismissing those $\mathbf{B}_\lambda$ possessed of inverses, the question, Problem 2, of interest, becomes the simplification of Problem 3.

Problem 3. *Given an order $n \times n$ Real valued matrix, $\mathbf{A}$, find the values, λ, for which*

$$|\mathbf{A} - \lambda\mathbf{I}_n| = 0$$

We have now, courtesy of this recasting, a problem of identifying scalars of a particular type: those $\lambda \in \mathbb{C}$ related to a given matrix $\mathbf{A}$ that lead to $|\mathbf{A} - \lambda\mathbf{I}|$ being zero. We have described a computational process for evaluating $\det \mathbf{B}$ in the lead up to this section, however, there is an underlying assumption that the $n \times n$ matrices have fixed constant numerical values, and so computing $\det \mathbf{B}$ is an, admittedly onerous, easy algorithmic demand. In the context we are now dealing with however, that of Problem 3, we can now longer rely on the assumption that "everything is known that requires knowing" but must instead find an approach to capture the quantities we wish to identify. In order to do so, we must consider the determinant as a **symbolic** i.e. algebraic form.

The determinant as polynomial

Let us return to the world of 2×2 matrices and consider the solution of Problem 3 in this setting. We would be attempting to identify λ for which

$$\left| \begin{pmatrix} a_{11} & a_{12} \\ a_{21} & a_{22} \end{pmatrix} - \begin{pmatrix} \lambda & 0 \\ 0 & \lambda \end{pmatrix} \right| = 0$$

Carrying out the required expansions of $|\ldots|$, we would find these to be those satisfying

$$(a_{11} - \lambda)(a_{22} - \lambda) - a_{12}a_{21} = 0$$

In other words, for which

$$\lambda^2 - (a_{11} + a_{22})\lambda + (a_{11}a_{22} - a_{12}a_{21}) = 0$$

We are given those elements $< a_{11}, a_{12}, a_{21}, a_{22} >$ from $\mathbb{R}$ that define $\mathbf{A}$: these may be viewed as **constants**. So the expression we have just presented is of a nature we have seen before in this text, from six chapters and several hundred pages past, when discussing the application of differential calculus to optimization problems, when dealing with one motivation for the study of Complex Numbers: it is a **quadratic** expression, that is to say a **polynomial of degree two**, whose coefficients $< c_0, c_1, c_2 >$ are

$$< (a_{11}a_{22} - a_{12}a_{21}), -(a_{11} + a_{22}), 1 >$$

and whose **roots** are those values for λ which we seek.

Perhaps this coincidence of "roots of a degree 2 polynomial" and "solutions for λ of $|\mathbf{A} - \lambda \mathbf{I}_2| = 0$ is no more than that: a coincidence.

Earlier in this Chapter we saw that, using the idea of permutation, we could define the algebraic form for an $n \times n$ matrix, $\mathbf{A}$ when $n > 2$ through,

$$\det \mathbf{A} = \sum_{\pi \in S_n} \text{sgn}(\pi) \prod_{i=1}^{n} a_{i,\pi(i)}$$

here $\text{sgn}(\pi) \in \{-1, +1\}$ according to where π is an odd (resp. even) permutation. Suppose we denote by B_λ the matrix $\mathbf{A} - \lambda \mathbf{I}$. If we consider $\det \mathbf{B}_\lambda$ in terms of this permutation structure we see that

$$\det \mathbf{B}_\lambda = \sum_{\pi \in S_n} \text{sgn}(\pi) \prod_{i=1}^{n} b_{i,\pi(i)}$$

$$= \sum_{\pi \in S_n} \text{sgn}(\pi) \left(\prod_{i\,:\,\pi(i)=i} (a_{ii} - \lambda) \prod_{i\,:\,\pi(i)\neq i} a_{i,\pi(i)} \right)$$

If we simplified this expression, looking to identify coefficients of λ^k a number of properties would be apparent.

The polynomial that would result from $\mathbf{B}_\lambda = \mathbf{A} - \lambda\mathbf{I}$ is called the **characteristic polynomial** of $\mathbf{A}$ and denoted $\chi_{\mathbf{A}}(\lambda)$.

Property 12. *Suppose that $\chi_{\mathbf{A}}(\lambda)$ is the characteristic polynomial of the $n \times n$ Real valued matrix $\mathbf{A}$.*

CP1. $\chi_{\mathbf{A}}(\lambda)$ *is a degree n polynomial in λ.*

CP2. Letting
$$\{\lambda_1, \lambda_2, \cdots, \lambda_{n-1}, \lambda_n\}$$
be the collection[10] of values from $\mathbb{C}$ for which $\chi_{\mathbf{A}}(\lambda_i) = 0$, i.e. the n roots of $\chi_{\mathbf{A}}(\lambda)$.

Then $\lambda \in \mathbb{C}$ is a root of $\chi_{\mathbf{A}}$ if and only if λ is solution with respect to $\mathbf{A}$ for Problem 2. That is to say, λ is a root of $\chi_{\mathbf{A}}$ if and only if there is an n-vector, $\mathbf{x} \in \mathbb{C}^n$ with $\mathbf{x} \neq \mathbf{0}$ and $\mathbf{A}\mathbf{x}^\top = \lambda\mathbf{x}^\top$.

*The collection of roots of $\chi_{\mathbf{A}}(\lambda)$ are known as the **eigenvalues of the matrix** $\mathbf{A}$. If λ_i is an eigenvalue of $\mathbf{A}$, any non-zero n-vector $\mathbf{x} \in \mathbb{C}$ for which $\mathbf{A}\mathbf{x}^\top = \lambda\mathbf{x}^\top$ is an **eigenvector of the matrix** $\mathbf{A}$ with respect to the eigenvalue λ.*

It is worth commenting a little on the subtext of Property 12. In this result not only do we find the answer to our original Problem 2 we do so by linking concepts introduced in the opening Chapter of this volume: roots of polynomials. So just as it was argued using the idea of multiplicity that polynomials of degree n have exactly n roots, so too we see that a matrix of order $n \times n$ again exploiting the idea of multiplicity has exactly n eigenvalues. We see also, from this interpretation why it is that the domain from which eigenvalues of $\mathbf{A}$ and their associated eigenvectors cannot be limited to $\mathbb{R}$ (respectively to $\mathbb{R}^n$): some polynomials of degree n have roots in $\mathbb{C}$ and thence some order $n \times n$ matrices will have eigenvalues and associated eigenvectors drawn from $\mathbb{C}$ (respectively $\mathbb{C}^n$). In the computational applications we are reviewing (ranking of web pages and image compression) we do not need to be unduly concerned about eigenvalues in $\mathbb{C}$: either the associated matrices considered

---

[10]Notice we use "collection" and **not** "set": potentially some λ_i may be roots with multplicity, $\mu(\lambda_i) > 1$.

will be of a type which guarantee all eigenvalues and eigenvectors fall within $\mathbb{R}$ ($\mathbb{R}^n$) or we are interested only in the "largest" eigenvalue.[11]

In the following subsection we will elaborate in more detail on aspects of spectral properties and eigenvalues as we will meet these in applications.

Properties of eigenvalues

At the end of the previous subsection we referred to a notion of "largest eigenvalue". On first inspection defining such seems to present no difficulty. And, in the event that the spectrum of $\mathbf{A}$ consists solely of values from $\mathbb{R}$ it would seem even more apparent that there is no problem in stating what is meant by "the largest eigenvalue". As we noted, however, the spectrum of $\mathbf{A}$ corresponds to the n roots of a degree n polynomial: what we have called the characteristic polynomial of $\mathbf{A}$. And this polynomial may have roots within $\mathbb{C}$. Unlike $\mathbb{R}$ we cannot "order" $\mathbb{C}$ in the style we have been used to with other number forms. That is to say, given u, $w \in \mathbb{C}$ there is not a "sensible" meaning of $u < w$. For x, $y \in \mathbb{R}$ we know that under the usual numerical view of $<$ **exactly one of** "$x < y$, $x > y$ or $x = y$" is true. So before proceeding further with presenting properties of eigenvalues we introduce exactly how $\lambda_i \leq \lambda_j$, for two eigenvalues of $\mathbf{A}$, will be interpreted. Before doing so, we give some notational conventions.

For an order $n \times n$ matrix, $\mathbf{A}$ its collection of n eigenvalues, that is to say the **spectrum** of $\mathbf{A}$ is denoted $\sigma(\mathbf{A})$ and we write

$$\sigma(\mathbf{A}) = (\lambda_1, \lambda_2, \ldots, \lambda_n)$$

The conventional ordering of these is that,

$$i < j \implies |\lambda_i| \geq |\lambda_j|$$

Viewing $\sigma(\mathbf{A})$ as a point in $\mathbb{C}^n$ that is we do not, for the moment, distinguish Real from Complex, seeing the former as simply having $\Im(\lambda_i) = 0$ the reading of $|\lambda|$ is as the **modulus** so that

$$|\lambda| = \sqrt{\Re(\lambda)^2 + \Im(\lambda)^2}$$

---

[11]There are, however, a number of applications, often in the field of combinatorial graph theory, where the "second largest" or even "third largest" eigenvalues offer significant information about the structures from which they arise. These are beyond the scope of this text and we refer the interested reader to, for example, the comprehensive treatment of Brouwer and Haemers [34] particularly Chapter 4 of this text, or more specialized analyses such as Mojar [169], van den Heuvel [238], or Friedman [92].

It should be noted that if, say $\{-5, 2\} \subseteq \sigma(\mathbf{A})$ then this convention "order by decreasing value of the modulus" leads to $|-5| > |2|$ so that, in contrast to the usual ordering of $\mathbb{R}$, -5 is seen as a **larger** eigenvalue than 2. In a similar way $\lambda = a + \imath b$ with $a^2 + b^2 > 25$ would be treated as larger than -5.

There is one property of polynomial roots mentioned in Section 5.8 when discussing using Laguerre's root finding method which tells us that $\sigma(\mathbf{A})$ must contain an **even number** of λ for which $\Im(\lambda) \neq 0$, i.e.

$$|\{\, \lambda \in \sigma(\mathbf{A}) \; : \; \lambda \notin \mathbb{R} \,\}| \; = \; 2k \text{ for some } k \in \mathbb{W}$$

The reason for this being that if $\lambda \notin \mathbb{R}$ but $\lambda \in \sigma(\mathbf{A})$ (in other words $\chi_{\mathbf{A}}(\lambda) = 0$) then we also have $\overline{\lambda}$ its Complex conjugate which is also not in $\mathbb{R}$ and a root of the characteristic polynomial $\chi_{\mathbf{A}}$ so that $\overline{\lambda} \in \sigma(\mathbf{A})$.

In total the ordering of $\sigma(\mathbf{A})$ will be assumed to be

$$\underbrace{\lambda_1, \; \lambda_2, \cdots, \lambda_k}_{|\lambda_i| \geq |\lambda_{i+1}|} \cdots \qquad \underbrace{\lambda_k, \lambda_{k+1}}_{\text{if } \lambda_k = a + \imath b \notin \mathbb{R} \text{ then } \lambda_{k+1} = \overline{\lambda}_k = a - \imath b} \qquad \cdots \lambda_{n-1}, \; \lambda_n$$

Notice we do not "mix" values whose modulus is identical with the other conjugates, e.g. if

$$\{3 + 4\imath, 4 + 3\imath\} \subset \sigma(\mathbf{A})$$

then these would be described in the spectrum itself using

$$\cdots 4 + 3\imath, \; 4 - 3\imath, \; 3 + 4\imath, \; 3 - 4\imath \cdots \quad \textbf{or} \quad \cdots 3 + 4\imath, \; 3 - 4\imath, \; 4 + 3\imath, \; 4 - 3\imath \cdots$$
$$\text{but } \textbf{not}$$
$$\cdots 4 + 3\imath, \; 3 - 4\imath, \; 3 + 4\imath, \; 4 - 3\imath \cdots \quad \textbf{or} \quad \cdots 3 + 4\imath, \; 4 - 3\imath, \; 4 + 3\imath, \; 3 - 4\imath \cdots$$
$$\text{etc.}$$

We point out that the principal ordering convention of $\sigma(\mathbf{A})$ observes

$$|\lambda_1| \geq |\lambda_2| \geq \cdots \geq |\lambda_i| \geq |\lambda_{i+1}| \geq \cdot \geq |\lambda_n|$$

so that there is no universally accepted approach and typically no complications arising from different conventions as to matters such as: ordering of Complex conjugate pairs, ordering of Complex values having the same modulus but differing Real and Imaginary parts, e.g. $3 + 4\imath$ and $4 + 3\imath$; ordering of $\{\alpha, -\alpha\} \subset \mathbb{R}$.

The main consequence of such liberality is that some care needs to be observed when referring to objects such as "**the** *largest* eigenvalue of $\mathbf{A}$. We know that such is reported as λ_1, so that $|\lambda_1| \geq |\lambda_i|$ whenever $2 \leq i \leq n$.

If we wish to focus on their being a **unique** largest value we must do so in terms of $|\cdots|$. For example if $\lambda_1 = -5$ and $\lambda_2 = 5$ we do not have a unique largest eigenvalue in $\sigma(\mathbf{A})$ (notice this is independently of matters such as multiplicity: in this example even if both 5 and -5 have multiplicity 1 there is still not a unique largest value).

In order to separate such instances from "genuine" unique largest values, some further terminology is introduced.

Given $\sigma(\mathbf{A})$, λ_1 is the **dominant** eigenvalue if $|\lambda_1| > |\lambda_i|$ ($2 \leq i \leq n$). The **spectral radius** of $\mathbf{A}$, denoted, $\rho(\mathbf{A})$ is $|\lambda_1|$.

Notice the concept of "*spectral radius*" is well-defined irrespective of whether there is a **unique** largest eigenvalue. For our purposes, however, a dominant value must be unique. In both cases, of course, $\rho(\mathbf{A}) = |\lambda_1|$. For the computational settings in which spectral analysis plays an important rôle, we are, generally, interested in matrices with properties such as those enumerated below.

P1. $\sigma(\mathbf{A}) \in \mathbb{R}^n$. That is, the spectrum of $\mathbf{A}$ contains only values from $\mathbb{R}$.

P2. The largest value in $\sigma(\mathbf{A})$ is unique (and in $\mathbb{R}$). That is λ_1 has multiplicity 1 as a root of the characteristic polynomial, $\chi_{\mathbf{A}}$ of $\mathbf{A}$.

P3. There is an **eigenvector**, $\mathbf{x}_\lambda$ which satisfies at least one of

EV1. $\mathbf{x}_\lambda \in \mathbb{R}^n$. That is has only Real components.

EV2. $\mathbf{x}_\lambda \in \mathbb{R}^{n,\geq 0}$: has only **non-negative** components.

EV3. $\mathbf{x}_\lambda \in \mathbb{R}^{n,> 0}$: has only **positive** components.

In the next subsection we present the statement of a classical result under which condition (EV3) is satisfied for a particular class of matrices. We mention at this stage one other class which guarentees (EV1).

Property 13. *If $\mathbf{A}$ is an order $n \times n$ **symmetric** matrix with elements from $\mathbb{R}$ then*

S1. *The spectrum, $\sigma(\mathbf{A})$ of $\mathbf{A}$ consists only of $\mathbb{R}$ values.*

S2. *Let $\mathbf{x}_i$ be an eigenvector corresponding to the eigenvalue λ_i of a Real symmetric matrix, $\mathbf{A}$ i.e. $\mathbf{A} \cdot \mathbf{x}_i^\top = \lambda_i \mathbf{x}_i^\top$. There is a set,*

$$\mathbf{Or}(\mathbf{A}) = \{\mathbf{x}_1, \mathbf{x}_2, \ldots, \mathbf{x}_n\}$$

of n vectors for which

OA1. $\mathbf{x}_i \in \mathbb{R}^n$.

OA2. $\mathbf{x}_i$ *is an eigenvector of* $\mathbf{A}$ *with respect to the eigenvalue* λ_i.

OA3. *For every pair* $\mathbf{x}_i$ *and* $\mathbf{x}_j$ *of distinct n-vectors from* $\mathbf{Or}(\mathbf{A})$

$$\mathbf{x}_i \cdot \mathbf{x}_j = \sum_{k=1}^{n} \mathbf{x}_{i,k}\mathbf{x}_{j,k} = 0$$

That is the distinct pairs are **orthogonal**, *cf. Section 3.3 regarding properties of vector dot products.*

OA4. *Let* $\mathbf{Or}(\mathbf{A})$ *satisfy (OA1) through (OA3) and define the order* $n \times n$ *matrices,* $\mathbf{Q}$ *and* $\mathbf{L}$ *so that*

$$\mathbf{Q} = [\mathbf{x}_1^{\top}, \mathbf{x}_2^{\top}, \cdots, \mathbf{x}_k^{\top}, \cdots, \mathbf{x}_n^{\top}]$$

That is to say, the **columns** *of* $\mathbf{Q}$ *are formed from the transpose of successive eigenvectors as ordered by* $\sigma(\mathbf{A})$.

$$\mathbf{L} = [l_{ij}] = \begin{cases} \lambda_{ii} & if \quad i = j \\ 0 & if \quad i \neq j \end{cases}$$

so that $\mathbf{L}$ *is a diagonal matrix whose diagonal is formed by the ordering of* $\sigma(\mathbf{A})$.

$$\mathbf{A} = \mathbf{Q} \cdot \mathbf{L} \cdot \mathbf{Q}^{\top}$$

As has been our practice we do not provide a formal proof of this property. We note that the behaviour guaranteed by (S2) provides a useful method allowing these ideas to be extended to **non-square** matrices in a style which offers powerful applications in Data Science, Machine Learning and Image Compression. The approach adopted will be discussed in Section 7.6.

Before moving on to the main classical result providing sufficient existence conditions for (EV2) and (EV3) we mention some aspects of Spectral Analysis which we will not present directing interested readers to standard Linear Algebra texts. In particular, it may be noticed that the formulation of Problem 2 asked for n-vectors, $\mathbf{x}_\lambda$ relative to what we now call the eigenvalue λ with which

$$\mathbf{A}\mathbf{x}_\lambda^{\top} = \lambda\mathbf{x}_\lambda^{\top}$$

We could, however, also have phrased the desired $\mathbf{x}_\lambda$ to be such that

$$\mathbf{x}_\lambda \cdot \mathbf{A} = \lambda \cdot \mathbf{x}_\lambda$$

thereby obviating any mention of vector transposition. Formally, the notions of **left** with $\mathbf{x}$ a row vector and **right** the form $\mathbf{x}^\top$ eigenvectors are distinguished. There are very select cases where the distinction is significant, however, these do not arise in the applications we present. In summary when the phrase "an eigenvector, $\mathbf{x}$ of $\mathbf{A}$" occurs it is assumed that a **right** eigenvector is concerned.[12]. Similarly, despite its use in analysing **directed** graph forms, we will eschew elaboration of the so-called *Laplacian*, see e.g. Brouwer and Haemers [34, Secn. 3.9–10].

We conclude this subsection with a brief look at some algebraic properties that treat these concepts of "eigenvalue" and "eigenvector" from the perspective of *Vector spaces* as discussed in Section 3.4.

Property 14. *Given* $\mathbf{A}$ *a Real-valued* $n \times n$ *matrix with characteristic polynomial* $\chi_\mathbf{A}(\lambda)$ *the set* $\mathcal{E}_\mathbf{A}(\lambda)$ *are those* n-*vectors within* $\mathbb{C}^n$ *for which*

$$\mathcal{E}_\mathbf{A}(\lambda) \;=\; \{\, \mathbf{x} \in \mathbb{C}^n \,:\, \mathbf{A}\mathbf{x}^\top \,=\, \lambda\mathbf{x}^\top \,\} \;\cup\; \{\mathbf{0}\}$$

ES1. For each λ, $\mathcal{E}_\mathbf{A}(\lambda)$ *defines a **vector space**[13],*

*ES2. The **dimension** of* $\mathcal{E}_\mathbf{A}(\lambda)$ *is at most the the **multiplicity** of* λ *as a root of* $\chi_\mathbf{A}(\lambda)$.[14]

Although the applications we consider have no need to be concerned about the possibility of $\dim \mathcal{E}_\mathbf{A}(\lambda)$ **differing** from $\mu(\lambda)$ with respect to the characteristic polynomial of $\mathbf{A}$ the dimension of this vector space has important consequences in applications involving **ranking**: in such cases eigenvectors of λ for which $\dim \mathcal{E}_\mathbf{A}(\lambda) > 1$ could be interpreted as different orderings of the items being ranked.

---

[12]A further example of the attitudes criticised in Endnote 5 of Chapter 3

[13]Many specialist Linear algebra texts use the term "*eigenspace*" as alternative.

[14]The quantity $\dim \mathcal{E}_\mathbf{A}(\lambda)$ is usually referred to as the **geometric multiplicity** in contrast to **algebraic multiplicity** for the number of occurrences of λ as a root of $\chi_\mathbf{A}(\lambda)$.

The Perron-Frobenius Theorem

Our description above has given a brief overview of the ideas underpinning the concepts of eigenvalue and eigenvector. In applying these we would like to have a suite of instances with which statements such as those presented under (EV1) through (EV3) can be assured to hold of the matrices used. The **Perron-Frobenius Theorem**, the original form from Perron [184] and subsequently extended by Frobenius [93] offers precisely such assurances. We first consider the statement presented in [184].

Property 15. *Let* $\mathbf{A}$ *be an order* $n \times n$ *matrix, all of whose entries are **positive** Real numbers, i.e.* $a_{ij} > 0$. *Then*

P1. $\mathbf{A}$ *has a dominant, eigenvalue,* λ_{pf} *which is **positive**.*

P2. *There is an eigenvector,* $\mathbf{x}_{pf}$ *of* λ_{pf} *having **only positive** components, i.e.* $x_i > 0$ *for every* $1 \leq i \leq n$.

P3. *There are no eigenvectors for **any** other eigenvalue,* λ, *of* $\mathbf{A}$, *even with* $\lambda > 0$ *all of whose components are positive Reals with the exception of **scalar multiples** of* $\mathbf{x}_{pf}$. *In other words, if*

$$\mathbf{A}\mathbf{y}^{\top} = \lambda \mathbf{y}^{\top} \text{ and } y_i > 0 \text{ for every } i$$

then there is some $\alpha \in \mathbb{R}$, $\alpha \neq 0$ *for which*

$$\mathbf{y} = \alpha \cdot \mathbf{x}_{pf}$$

We recall our convention of interpreting "**dominant**" eigenvalues as requiring multiplicity 1, so that for a dominant eigenvalue the characteristic polynomial of $\mathbf{A}$ could be written as $(\lambda - \lambda_1) \cdot p_{n-1}(\lambda)$ wherein $p_{n-1}(\lambda)$ the degree $n - 1$ polynomial obtained by factoring out $(\lambda - \lambda_1)$ from $\chi_{\mathbf{A}}(\lambda)$ is such that $p_{n-1}(\lambda)(\lambda_1) \neq 0$, and the ordering convention by $|\cdots|$, not only is it the case that $|\lambda_1| > |\lambda_i|$ $(2 \leq i \leq n)$ but also by virtue of positivity, $\lambda_{pf} > |\lambda_i|$ when $2 \leq i \leq n$.

We refer to $\mathbf{x}_{pf}$ as the **dominant eigenvector**.

The reader puzzled by our use of a definite article to describe a single vector from an infinitude of such with identical properties (the vector $\alpha \cdot \mathbf{x}_{pf}$ when $\alpha > 0$ satisfying all of the stated criteria given for "the" dominant eigenvector $\mathbf{x}_{pf}$) should note that we take as a representative the **normalized vector**

$$\mathbf{x}_{pf} = \left(\sum_{i=1}^{n} x_i \right)^{-1} \mathbf{x}_{pf}$$

In this approach each component, x_i of $\mathbf{x}_{pf}$, is scaled by what we referred to in Endnote 3 of Chapter 3 as the "L_1 norm or Manhattan distance". With this choice of representative dominant eigenvector we have $\|\mathbf{x}_{pf}\|_1 = 1$.[15]

Property 15 guarantees the **existence** of both a positive dominant eigenvalue and associated positive eigenvector for matrices, $\mathbf{A}$, satisfying the precondition that $a_{ij} > 0$ for each element. Looking back to the notions of vector space and basis which we presented in Section 3.4 the property ensured through (P3) can be interpreted as "$\{\mathbf{x}_{pf}\}$ is a basis for the vector space of the subset $\mathbb{R}^n$ of vectors, $\mathbf{y}$ for which $\mathbf{A}\mathbf{y}^\top = \lambda_{pf}\mathbf{y}^\top$".

In trying to exploit Property 15 within computational settings we meet a difficulty: the requirement that $\mathbf{A}$ contain **only** positive elements. Consider one area where we might want to use a matrix representation and as a result take advantage of spectral results: graph theory. Even if we are considering graphs in which edges $\{p, q\}$ between nodes p and q are associated with *weights* ($w_{pq} \in \mathbb{R}$) whether we are looking at undirected graphs yielding symmetric matrices or directed graphs where the possibility $w_{pq} \neq w_{qp}$ arises, the prescription of universal positivity is not realistic in such cases: not only does it effectively require that there are connections between **every distinct** pair of nodes but even more so that there is a positive contribution modelled from each node to itself, i.e. $w_{ii} > 0$ since the modelling diagonal must also be positive. This last requirement, that $a_{ii} > 0$ severely limits the cases to which the pure Perron formulation in Property 15 can be applied. We can, however, overcome this inconvenience, courtesy of the enhancement of Perron's discovery found by Frobenius and presented in [93]. We first, however, require the concept of an order $n \times n$ matrix being **irreducible**.

Description 5. *Let $\mathbf{A}$ be order $n \times n$ matrix with **non-negative** elements from $\mathbb{R}$. The matrix, $\mathbf{A}$ is said to be **irreducible** if for each pair (i, j) (with $1 \leq i, j \leq n$) there is some $k \in \mathbb{N}$ for which the (i, j) element of $\mathbf{A}^k$ is positive. That is, denoting the elements of $\mathbf{A}^k$ as $[a_{ij}^k]$ we have $a_{ij}^k > 0$.*

We first note one important point about the wording of Description 5: "for each pair (i, j) (with $1 \leq i, j \leq n$) there is some $k \in \mathbb{N}$" does **not** mean the same as "there is some $k \in \mathbb{N}$ with which for each pair (i, j) (with $1 \leq i, j \leq n$)". In the latter case we need to find a value $k \in \mathbb{N}$ that has the desired behaviour for **every** a_{ij}^k simultaneously. Although this would imply the former interpretation, the condition we need to satisfy is rather less restrictive in that,

---

[15]On occasion it useful to use other metrics for normalization, one frequent choice being our standard approach to vector length: the L_2 or Euclidean distance.

in principle, we might have n^2 distinct choices of k over the different elements of $\mathbf{A}$.

We have, from the perspective of CS, one extremely important characterization of irreducible matrices.

Property 16. *Given an order $n \times n$ matrix, $\mathbf{A}$ whose elements are non-negative Reals, $\mathbf{A}$ is irreducible if and only if the **directed gr/ntsraph**, $D_{\mathbf{A}}(V, F)$ defined to have nodes $\{1, 2, \ldots, n\}$ and directed edges*

$$< i, j > \ \in \ F \ \ if \ and \ only \ if \ a_{ij} > 0$$

*is **strongly connected**.*

Now a directed graph is said to be *strongly connected* if we can take any pair of nodes, p and q say, and travel using **only** the directed links provided in F *from* node p *to* node q **and** we can also travel again using only those links in F *from* node q *to* node p. Many of the graphs and networks that arise in CS applications define strongly connected structures. We can, however, also observe that if we interpret an **undirected** graph as one in which for any pair of nodes, p and q, either there is no link at all between p and q i.e. the corresponding matrix entry is such that $a_{pq} = a_{qp} = 0$ **or** there is a link between p and q and a link between q and p i.e. $a_{pq} = a_{qp} > 0$ then this notion of "strong connectedness" within **directed** graphs now has a corresponding analogue with respect to **undirected** graphs. Just as we moved from matrices to graphs in Property 16 so too we can map from graphs (V, E) both directed and undirected to matrices.

$$a_{ij} = \begin{cases} 0 & \text{if} \quad < i, j > \notin E \\ 1 & \text{if} \quad < i, j > \in E \end{cases}$$

Now if our matrix is irreducible equivalently defines a strongly connected directed graph although we do not have **all** of those properties guaranteed within Perron's result for positive matrices sufficient of these continue as can be seen within Property 17.

Property 17. *If $\mathbf{A}$ is a non-negative and irreducible $n \times n$ matrix with elements drawn from $\mathbb{R}$ then*

F1. There is a unique positive $\lambda_{pf} \in \mathbb{R}$ such that λ_{pf} is an eigenvalue of $\mathbf{A}$.

*F2. There is an eigenvector, $\mathbf{x}_{pf}$ of λ_{pf} having **only positive** components*

F3. If $\mathbf{y}$ is a non-negative eigenvector of $\mathbf{A}$ then $\mathbf{A}\mathbf{y}^\top = \lambda_{pf}\mathbf{y}^\top$.

F4. If λ is any other eigenvalue of $\mathbf{A}$ then $|\lambda| \le \lambda_{pf}$.

One of the main differences between the two forms – Property 15 and 17 is in the relationship of $\lambda_1 = \lambda_{pf}$ to the other eigenvalues: in the Perron formulation we are guaranteed $\lambda_{pf} > |\lambda|$ for every $\lambda \in \sigma(\mathbf{A}) \setminus \{\lambda_{pf}\}$. In the Frobenius formulation we can only gaurantee $\lambda_{pf} \ge |\lambda|$ for every $\lambda \in \sigma(\mathbf{A}) \setminus \{\lambda_{pf}\}$. For example one possibility for irreducible but not positive $\mathbf{A}$ is that there are $\lambda \in \mathbb{C}$ with $\{\lambda, \overline{\lambda}\} \subset \sigma(\mathbf{A})$ and $\lambda_{pf} = |\lambda| = |\overline{\lambda}|$, one example is the 3×3 matrix

$$\mathbf{A} = \begin{pmatrix} 0 & 1 & 0 \\ 0 & 0 & 1 \\ 1 & 0 & 0 \end{pmatrix}$$

Looking at $\chi_{\mathbf{A}}(\lambda)$ we have

$$\chi_{\mathbf{A}}(\lambda) = \begin{vmatrix} -\lambda & 1 & 0 \\ 0 & -\lambda & 1 \\ 1 & 0 & -\lambda \end{vmatrix} = -\lambda^3 + 1$$

and eigenvalues $\{1, -0.5 + (\sqrt{3}/2)\imath, -0.5 - (\sqrt{3}/2)\imath\}$.

For those values in $\mathbb{C}$:

$$|-0.5 \pm (\sqrt{3}/2)\imath| = \sqrt{0.25 + 0.75} = 1$$

so that $\lambda_{pf} = |\lambda_2| = |\lambda_3|$.

These are minor technical irritations which one needs to be aware of but rarely affect those cases in which spectral methods are applied in CS.

To conclude this section we mention two important and useful results, the first of which, is of great importance in applying spectral analysis to ranking problems.

Property 18. *We say that a non-negative matrix, $\mathbf{A}$ is row (respectively column) stochastic if*

$$\text{For every } i \quad \sum_{j=1}^{n} a_{ij} = 1 \; ; \; (\text{respectively } \sum_{j=1}^{n} a_{ji} = 1)$$

If $\mathbf{A}$ is a row-stochastic matrix then 1 is an eigenvalue of $\mathbf{A}$ and $|\lambda| \le 1$ for all $\lambda \in \sigma(\mathbf{A})$.

We observe two things concerning Property 18: firstly this holds irrespective of whether $\mathbf{A}$ is irreducible; even if $\mathbf{A}$ is **not** irreducible $1 \in \sigma(\mathbf{A})$ with no other eigenvalue of $\mathbf{A}$ having greater size provided it is stochastic. Secondly, recalling that eigenvalues arise as roots of the characteristic polynomial, $\chi_{\mathbf{A}}$, from the fact that $\chi_{\mathbf{A}}(\lambda) \equiv \chi_{\mathbf{A}^\top}(\lambda)$ we see that $\mathbf{A}$ and $\mathbf{A}^\top$ have identical spectra: $\sigma(\mathbf{A}) \equiv \sigma(\mathbf{A}^\top)$, so as one consequence, Property 18 holds equally for **column stochastic** non-negative matrices.

The second result we mention provides extremely powerful approaches by which the range of values for $\lambda \in \sigma(\mathbf{A})$ may be bounded. This was discovered by the Soviet mathematician Semyon Gershgorin and is called the Gershgorin circle theorem. It first appeared in [101]. For its statement we must return once more to the Complex plane.

Property 19. *Consider any*[16] *order $n \times n$ matrix $\mathbf{A}$. For any row, $\mathbf{a}_i$ of $\mathbf{A}$ define the quantity*

$$R_i = \sum_{j \neq i} |a_{ij}|$$

that is, the sum of the moduli of elements in the i'th row with the exception of a_{ii}.

*The **Gershgorin circle with centre** a_{ii}, is the set of all **Complex** numbers*

$$\mathcal{G}(a_{ii}, R_i) = \{z \in \mathbb{C} : |a_{ii} - z| \leq R_i\}$$

So that the Gershgorin circle with centre a_{ii} can be thought of as all Complex numbers at a distance up to and including the circumference of a circle of radius R_i and centred at a_{ii}.

For any $\lambda \in \sigma(\mathbf{A})$ there is at least one i for which $\lambda \in \mathcal{G}(a_{ii}, R_i)$.

7.5 Computing Eigenvalues and Eigenvectors

The applications we describe require, at some stage, that an actual eigenvector corresponding to the dominant eigenvalue be computed. We describe one approach that has been widely used – the **Power Method** – although we point out that, in practice, there are some computational drawbacks resulting in alternatives being used. In respect of these the reader is directed to the technical survey of Golub and van der Vorst [105] for details.

The **Power Method** provides an effective if potentially time-consuming approach whereby two related computations can be handled. As with the techniques we looked at earlier for the problem of unearthing roots of polynomials

---

[16]We continue, in this statement to assume that $\mathbf{A}$ draws its elements from $\mathbb{R}$, however the full formal statement of Gershgorin's result is in terms of arbitrary Complex valued $n \times n$ matrices.

and, in the case of Halley's approach described in Section 4.6, arbitrary "well-behaved" functions the Power Method converges to solutions by repeatedly evaluating (iterating) a computation over an initial guess. For those matrices having a dominant eigenvalue, the power method is not only guaranteed to converge to an eigenvector for this value but may also be applied to find this value.

Overview of Problem

Given $\mathbf{A}$ an order $n \times n$ Real-valued matrix, which we *assume*[17] to have a dominant eigenvalue, we wish to compute

PM1. The dominant eigenvalue, λ of $\mathbf{A}$.

PM2. An eigenvector, $\mathbf{x}_\lambda$ for this eigenvalue.

Overview of the Power Method

Although we may not know what the precise form of $(\lambda, \mathbf{x}_\lambda)$ may be, given that the former should be an eigenvalue of $\mathbf{A}$ and the latter an eigenvector of that value, whatever this form may be the pair in question must satisfy

$$\mathbf{A}\mathbf{x}_\lambda^\top = \lambda \mathbf{x}_\lambda^\top$$

Now if some vector, $\mathbf{y}$ say, **is** an eigenvector of $\mathbf{A}$ with respect to λ then any Real scalar multiple e.g. $\alpha \mathbf{y}$ for some non-zero $\alpha \in \mathbb{R}$ is also such an eigenvector. That is to say, from

$$\mathbf{A}\mathbf{y}^\top = \lambda \mathbf{y}^\top \text{ and } \mathbf{A}(\alpha \mathbf{y}^\top) = \alpha \mathbf{A}\mathbf{y}^\top$$

$$\begin{aligned} \mathbf{A}(\alpha \mathbf{y}^\top) &= \alpha \cdot (\lambda \mathbf{y}^\top) \\ &= \lambda \cdot (\alpha \cdot \mathbf{y}^\top) \end{aligned}$$

it easily follows $\alpha \mathbf{y}$ is an eigenvector of $\mathbf{A}$ for λ.

So we know that any scalar multiple of an eigenvector of λ is, itself, also an eigenvector of λ.[18] The key observation underpinning the power method is that $\lambda \mathbf{x}_\lambda$ is a scalar multiple of the eigenvector $\mathbf{x}_\lambda$ and $\lambda^2 \mathbf{x}_\lambda$ also a scalar multiple, and in general $\lambda^k \mathbf{x}_\lambda$ is a scalar multiple, and thence eigenvector for λ, of the eigenvector $\mathbf{x}_\lambda$.

---

[17] The assumption is not necessary for the technique to construct **some** solution but is needed if we wish to ensure convergence of the method.

[18] A fact which, of course, is already apparent by virtue of Property 14(ES2).

Putting these together we get the basic method of Algorithm 7.1 for approximating a **dominant** eigenvector, i.e. an eigenvector of the dominant eigenvalue.

Algorithm 7.1. Building an approximation to a dominant eigenvector.

1: **Input A** $n \times n$ Real-valued matrix;
2: **Output:** (approximation) to a dominant eigenvector of **A**
3: $k := 0$; { Counter for number of iterations}
4: $x_0 := 1$; {Initial "guess"}
5: **repeat**
6:   $k := k + 1$;
7:   $x_k := \mathbf{A} \cdot x_{k-1}$;
8: **until** $k > MAX$ {Preset number of iterations to do}
9: **return** x_k;

For example consider the 3×3 matrix

$$\mathbf{A} = \begin{pmatrix} 4 & 3 & 1 \\ 1 & 6 & 2 \\ 1 & 4 & 2 \end{pmatrix}$$

Were we to analyse the characteristic polynomial of **A** we would be looking for roots of the cubic

$$\lambda^3 - 12\lambda^2 + 32\lambda - 14$$

These give $\sigma(\mathbf{A})$ as having only Real eigenvalues which are (rounding to 3 places)

$$\sigma(\mathbf{A}) = (8.381,\ 3.076,\ 0.543)$$

with representative eigenvectors

$$\begin{aligned} \mathbf{x}_{(8.381)} &= \ <1, 1.165, 0.887> \\ \mathbf{x}_{(3.076)} &= \ <1, -0.276, -0.096> \\ \mathbf{x}_{(0.543)} &= \ <1, -10.889, 29.21> \end{aligned}$$

Suppose we look at Algorithm 7.1 using $x_0 = <1, 1, 1>$.

k	$\mathbf{x}$	$x_1 \cdot (\mathbf{x}/x_1)$
0	$< 1, 1, 1 >$	$-$
1	$< 8, 9, 7 >$	$8 \cdot\ < 1, 1.125, 0.875 >$
2	$< 66, 76, 58 >$	$66 \cdot\ < 1, 1.152, 0.879 >$
3	$< 550, 638, 486 >$	$550 \cdot\ < 1, 1.16, 0.884 >$
4	$< 4600, 5350, 4074 >$	$4600 \cdot\ < 1, 1.163, 0.886 >$
5	$< 38524, 44848, 34148 >$	$38524 \cdot\ < 1, 1.164, 0.886 >$

We can identify one immediate issue. Not the rate of convergence, since after five iterations we are already close to a scalar multiple of a dominant eigenvector namely $< 1, 1.165, 0.887 >$ having found $< 1, 1.164, 0.886 >$. The minor issue is the rate at which the numerical quantities increase: after five iterations we are already handling integers of the order of tens of thousands, if we continued even for as small a number as a dozen iterations it is likely we would be faced with manipulating integers of the size of several tens of millions.

There is, however, a very straighforward way of overcoming this issue. We are simply looking for a **representative** dominant eigenvector so we could as suggested by the example iterate the process not with respect to $\mathbf{x}_k$ but with respect to a **scaled** variant of it. In order to reduce the accumulation of large values we may simply choose the scaling factor to be $\max\{|x_i|\}$, i.e. the largest modulus component of the current approximation. Implementing this step involves adding the line (after l. 7 of Algorithm 7.1)

$$\mathbf{x}_k \ := \ \frac{\mathbf{x}_k}{\max\{|x_i|\}}$$

Applying this modification we now get

k	$\mathbf{x}$	*Scaled* $\mathbf{x}$
0	$< 1, 1, 1 >$	$-$
1	$< 7, 9, 8 >$	$< 0.778, 1, 0.889, >$
2	$< 7.334, 8.445, 6.445 >$	$< 0.868, 1, 0.763 >$
3	$< 7.235, 8.394, 6.394 >$	$< 0.862, 1, 0.762 >$

Notice that if we modified the $\mathbf{x}$ found after $k = 3$, to scale x_1 to 1 we get

$$\frac{< 0.862, 1, 0.762 >}{0.862} \ = \ < 1, 1.16, 0.884 >$$

so we are already close to the "representative" dominant eigenvector.

The Rayleigh Quotient

Algorithm 7.1 and its refinement through scaling factors offer a reasonable approach to identifying a dominant **eigenvector**. In those applications wherein we are concerned not so much with the precise component **values**, x_i of such a vector **x** but rather more with the ordering of components within the vector[19] the power method with scaling already gives a usable technique.

So we have a method that can, under suitable constraints, be applied to construct an eigenvector. We have seen that eigenvalues are simply the roots of the characteristic polynomial of a matrix, a computational problem for which we have already seen two algorithmic approaches in Algorithm 4.1 (Halley's Method) and Algorithm 4.2 (Laguerre's method). There are some drawbacks to applying these or, indeed, the other techniques mentioned in Section 4.6 as a means of extracting the eigenvalues of **A**.

DR1. The actual root(s) found by these iterative methods are dependent on the method used and the initial "guess", cf. the behaviour of Halley's Method versus Laguerre's when both are presented with the same polynomial and use the same x_0 as starting point described in Table 4.6 and Table 4.7.

DR2. In order to apply Laguerre's method which can be adapted to identify roots in $\mathbb{C}$ it is necessary to **construct** the characteristic polynomial of **A**, i.e. the relevant coefficients of $\chi_{\mathbf{A}}$. This may be a very laborious process and yet is only a **precomputation** implemented ahead of the actual computation of interest, i.e. root/eigenvalue identification.

DR3. Although there are a number of applications one of which is discussed in the following section for which we wish to find **all** eigenvalues of **A**, it is often the case that we are only interested in the dominant or (failing the existence of a dominant value) a Real eigenvalue, λ, with maximal modulus. In principle, for an arbitrary **A**, Laguerre's method for example might have to be applied a number of times with $\chi_{\mathbf{A}}$ having the root most recently found factored out before we can be confident that the desired value has been found.

Ideally, we would like to have a means of computing eigenvalues or at worst the largest such directly from **A** obviating the need for intermediate methods involving, e.g. polynomial formulation, root finding techniques etc.

---

[19]i.e. the fact that x_1 has the largest value among $\{x_1, x_2, x_3, \ldots, x_n\}$ is of interest; the fact that $x_1 \sim 5.65123$ less so.

We can, however, do exactly that, and be confident the value identified is the dominant value should the spectrum of $\mathbf{A}$ more precisely the structure of $\mathbf{A}$ itself be such that we know that the dominant eigenvalue is well-defined. This is by exploiting the **Rayleigh quotient**. Given $\mathbf{A}$ and $\mathbf{x}$ an eigenvector of $\mathbf{A}$ with respect to some unknown eigenvalue λ the **Rayleigh quotient** is given by

$$\frac{\mathbf{A}\mathbf{x}^\top \cdot \mathbf{x}}{\mathbf{x} \cdot \mathbf{x}}$$

Now this expression is identical to the eigenvalue λ since

$$\mathbf{A}\mathbf{x} \cdot \mathbf{x}^\top = \lambda \mathbf{x} \cdot \mathbf{x}$$

So if we have already found a good approximation for a dominant eigenvector e.g. via one of the earlier methods the Rayleigh quotient provides a good approximation to the associated dominant eigenvalue. Thus, in our earlier example we found $< 1, 1.16, 0.884 >$ as an approximation. Calculating $\mathbf{A}\mathbf{x} \cdot \mathbf{x}$ gives 26.19715 whereas $\mathbf{x} \cdot \mathbf{x} = 3.127056$ giving an approximation to λ as 8.378 compared to the actual value identified from $\chi_{\mathbf{A}}(\lambda)$ as 8.381.

Finding other eigenvalues and eigenvectors

The examples above are focussed on finding an approximation to dominant eigenvectors and their associated eigenvalue. As we mentioned briefly (fn. 11 of this Chapter) there are applications were, although not neccesarily requiring **all** eigenvalues and representative eigenvectors, particular cases other than the dominant eigenvalue are of interest. In this subsection we give an overview of some widely studied computational methods that have been applied. We refer the reader who may be interested in such things as convergence and correctness proofs to more comprehensive texts on Numerical Methods, e.g. Isaacson and Keller [126, Ch. 4].

Inverse Power Method

There is one technically straightforward but computationally challenging approach we can use to find the **smallest** eigenvalue of $\mathbf{A}$. We saw in Section 7.2 that the following relationship holds between $\det \mathbf{A}$ and $\det \mathbf{A}^{-1}$ rather indirectly perforce our explicit statement that $\det \mathbf{A} = \det \mathbf{A}^T$.

Since it is the case that

$$\det \mathbf{A} = \det \mathbf{A}^T \quad \textbf{and} \ (\mathbf{A}^{-1})^\top \ = \ (\mathbf{A}^\top)^{-1}$$

or, in rather glib terms "the transpose of the inverse matrix is the same as the inverse of the transpose matrix" we see that

$$\det \mathbf{A}^{-1} \;=\; \det(\mathbf{A}^{-1})^{\top} \;=\; \det(\mathbf{A}^{\top})^{-1} \;=\; \det(\mathbf{A})^{-1} \;\equiv\; \frac{1}{\det \mathbf{A}}$$

It may, perhaps, be unclear how this mathematically pretty but computationally opaque relationship will help, however, suppose we know and have found e.g. by the power method from earlier the dominant eigenvalue, λ_1 and an associated eigenvector $\mathbf{x}$.

$$\mathbf{A}\mathbf{x} \;=\; \lambda_1 \mathbf{x}$$

If $\mathbf{A}$ is non-singular then it has an inverse matrix $\mathbf{A}^{-1}$ and

$$\mathbf{A}^{-1}\mathbf{A}\mathbf{x} \;=\; \mathbf{A}^{-1}\lambda_1 \mathbf{x}$$

Implying that

$$\mathbf{I}\mathbf{x} \;=\; \mathbf{A}^{-1}\lambda_1 \mathbf{x}$$

or, rearranging, that

$$\mathbf{A}^{-1}\mathbf{x} \;=\; \frac{1}{\lambda_1}\mathbf{x}$$

In other words, since λ_1 is the "largest" i.e. dominant eigenvalue of $\mathbf{A}$ we see that $1/\lambda_1$ is the **smallest** eigenvalue of $\mathbf{A}^{-1}$. Via this reasoning if we are able to find a dominant eigenvalue of the **inverse** matrix, $\mathbf{A}^{-1}$ then the reciprocal value must be the **smallest** eigenvalue of $\mathbf{A}$: applying the standard power method to $\mathbf{A}^{-1}$ allows us to find an approximation to this dominant eigenvalue.

This "compute an eigenvalue of a matrix, $\mathbf{B}$ related in some manner to our original matrix $\mathbf{A}$ in order to glean some information about other eigenvalues of $\mathbf{A}$" approach (in the instance just described, $\mathbf{B} = \mathbf{A}^{-1}$ and the eigenvalue, λ found to be the dominant eigenvalue of $\mathbf{B}$ is, in the form λ^{-1}, the smallest eigenvalue of $\mathbf{A}$), has rather more general application.

Start once more from the non-singular order $n \times n$ matrix, $\mathbf{A}$. Let the presumed unknown eigenvalues of $\mathbf{A}$ be

$$\sigma(\mathbf{A}) \;=\; (\lambda_1, \lambda_2, \dots, \lambda_n)$$

using that standard ordering whereby $|\lambda_i| \geq |\lambda_{i+1}|$. In addition let

$$\{\, \mathbf{x}_1, \mathbf{x}_2, \dots, \mathbf{x}_n \,\}$$

be corresponding eigenvectors, that is $\mathbf{A}\mathbf{x}_i^{\top} = \lambda_i \mathbf{x}_i^{\top}$. Now suppose we choose some $q \in \mathbb{C}$ for which the matrix $\mathbf{A} - q\mathbf{I}$ is **non-singular**. Notice provided q

is **not** an eigenvalue of $\mathbf{A}$ the matrix $\mathbf{B}_q = (\mathbf{A} - q\mathbf{I})^{-1}$ is well-defined, cf. our observations earlier in the chapter respecting eigenvalues, λ and the property $|\mathbf{A} - \lambda\mathbf{I}| \neq 0$.

The **Inverse Power Method** relies on Property 20.

Property 20. *Let* $q \in \mathbb{C}$ *be such that the matrix,* $\mathbf{B}_q = (\mathbf{A} - q\mathbf{I})^{-1}$ *is well-defined, i.e.* q *is **not** an eigenvalue of* $\mathbf{A}$.

$$\frac{1}{\lambda_i - q}$$

is the dominant eigenvalue of $\mathbf{B}_q$ *if and only if*

$$|\lambda_i - q| \text{ is **minimal** among } \lambda_i \in \sigma(\mathbf{A})$$

Thus Property 20 offers the following *modus operandum*.

To find an eigenvalue of $\mathbf{A}$ that is "closest to" some constant $q \in \mathbb{C}$.

IP1. If $q \in \sigma(\mathbf{A})$ then we have already found[20] the required eigenvalue.

IP2 Otherwise, that is $q \notin \sigma(\mathbf{A})$, form the matrix $\mathbf{A} - q\mathbf{I}$. This is non-singular and let $\mathbf{B}_q$ be its inverse matrix.

IP3. Find the dominant eigenvalue, μ of $\mathbf{B}_q$, e.g. by use of the standard power method.

IP4. From Property 20,

$$\lambda = \frac{1}{\mu} + q$$

is both an eigenvalue of $\mathbf{A}$ **and** the "closest such eigenvalue" to q.

Deflation

Although the power method allowing for inevitable numerical and rounding errors gives a route to constructing an eigenvector for the dominant eigenvalue and the concept of Rayleigh coefficient a means of identifying the dominant eigenvalue, the techniques underlying Inverse Power Methods raise computationally demanding issues: if $\mathbf{A}$ is "large", e.g. as is often the case in intensive

---

[20]If $q \in \sigma(\mathbf{A})$ then $|\mathbf{A} - q\mathbf{I}| = 0$ and we can verify this status for q either by direct construction of $\chi_{\mathbf{A}}$ allowing it to be shown that $\chi_{\mathbf{A}}(q) = 0$ or by showing the matrix $\mathbf{A} - q\mathbf{I}$ to be singular.

Physical experimental studies or in the computational discipline of Data Science, the underlying matrices may have order $10^5 \times 10^5$ or higher. In such cases, the requirement to compute $\mathbf{A}^{-1}$ may turn out to be unrealistically burdensome.

We can, often, avoid the need to look at characteristic polynomials and their roots or the overhead of constructing the inverse of large matrices through a general approach known as **deflation**. We have seen a, superficially, similar notion already when discussing the problem of **factorization** in Section 2.5. Given a polynomial of degree n ($p(x) \in \mathbb{Q}[X]$ for instance) we know that $p(x)$ has n roots. If we can identify **one** such root, α, then we reduce the problem, **deflate** as is sometimes used, to finding the remaining $n-1$ roots of $p(n)$ by "filtering out" the contribution from the fact that α is a root without affecting the remaining roots of $p(x)$. How was this achieved? We formed the polynomial of degree $n-1$ described by $q(x) = p(x)/(x-\alpha)$: the roots of $q(x)$ are all roots of $p(x)$ and, even if α has multiplicity exceeding one, the remaining such occurrences will continue to contribute to the roots of $q(x)$, e.g.

$$
\begin{aligned}
p(x) &= x^4 - 4x^3 + 6x^2 - 4x + 1 \\
&= (x-1)(x^3 - 3x^2 + 3x - 1) \\
&= (x-1)(x-1)(x^2 - 2x + 1)
\end{aligned}
$$

The root $x = 1$ has multiplicity four but the result of factoring out $(x-1)$ from the starting degree four polynomial, will be a cubic in which the root $x = 1$ has multiplicity three.

The thinking behind deflation as an eigenvalue discovery method is, having by some way or another, unearthed the dominant eigenvalue λ_1 and eigenvector $\mathbf{v}$, to obtain a new matrix, $\mathbf{B}$ via some (computationally inexpensive) operations on $\mathbf{A}$.

We first need to focus on a selected representative set of eigenvectors, and hence use the following assumptions.

AD1. $\sigma(\mathbf{A})$ has **no repeated eigenvalues**, i.e. $\mu(\lambda_i) = 1$ within the characteristic polynomial, $\chi_{\mathbf{A}}(\lambda)$.

AD2. We say that, $\mathbf{u}_i$ is a **representative eigenvector** for λ_i if $\mathbf{A}\mathbf{u}_i^\top = \lambda_i \mathbf{u}_i^\top$ and

$$
\|\mathbf{u}_i\|_2 = \sqrt{\sum_{k=1}^{n} u_{i,k}^2} = 1
$$

That is to say, $\mathbf{u}$ has been **normalized** with respect to the standard vector length metric, as described in Section 3.3.

Given these requirements we choose

$$\sigma(\mathbf{A}) = (\lambda_1, \lambda_2, \ldots, \lambda_n) \ |\lambda_1| > |\lambda_i| \ (2 \le i \le n)$$

and

$$\mathcal{R}(\mathbf{A}) = \{\mathbf{u}_1, \mathbf{u}_2, \ldots, \mathbf{u}_n\}$$

as the set of representative eigenvectors for $\mathbf{A}$. We need one, final aspect of such sets of representatives which we state without proof in Property 21.

Property 21. *For any set of representative eigenvectors,*

$$\{\mathbf{u}_1, \mathbf{u}_2, \ldots, \mathbf{u}_n\}$$

it holds that: $\mathbf{u}_i^\top \cdot \mathbf{u}_i = 1$ *and whenever* $i \ne j$ $\mathbf{u}_i^\top \cdot \mathbf{u}_j = \mathbf{u}_j^\top \cdot \mathbf{u}_i = 0$.

These desiderata to hand, we can now look at how $\mathbf{B}$ is defined from $< \mathbf{A}, \sigma(\mathbf{A}), \mathcal{R}(\mathbf{A}) >$. The matrix, $\mathbf{B}$ will have two properties of interest.

D1. If $\sigma(\mathbf{A}) = (\lambda_1, \lambda_2, \ldots, \lambda_n)$ then $\sigma(\mathbf{B}) = (\lambda_2, \lambda_3, \ldots, \lambda_n, 0)$.

D2. If $\mathbf{x}_i$ is an eigenvector of λ_i in $\mathbf{B}$ then $\mathbf{x}_i$ is an eigenvector of λ_i in $\mathbf{A}$.

Thus the largest eigenvalue (λ_1) in $\mathbf{A}$ contributes the smallest eigenvalue having been replaced by 0 in $\mathbf{B}$ and other eigenvalues remain unchanged.

To see how this is accomplished, assume e.g. by the power method that we have found ($\lambda_1, \mathbf{v}$) dominant eigenvalues and eigenvector for $\mathbf{A}$. Normalizing, $\mathbf{v}$ as the choice for $\mathbf{u}_1$ we now pick **any** n-vector, $\mathbf{y}$ that satisfies

$$\mathbf{y} \cdot \mathbf{u}_1^\top = 1$$

and form the matrix[21]

$$\mathbf{B} = \mathbf{A} - \lambda_1 \mathbf{u}_1^\top \mathbf{y}$$

Notice that $\mathbf{u}_1^\top \mathbf{y}$ is an order $n \times n$ matrix: the result of multiplying the $n \times 1$ column vector, $\mathbf{u}_1^\top$ by the $1 \times n$ row vector $\mathbf{y}$.

---

[21]Two points to note here are that, as an eigenvector of $\mathbf{A}$, $\mathbf{v} \ne 0$. Secondly it is **always** possible to define a suitable $\mathbf{y}$: different choices can lead to less numerically-skewed and faster converging methods. We will, however, not elaborate on this particular point.

What can we deduce about the matrix $\mathbf{B}$?

Properties of the "deflation matrix" B

We focus on a specific choice for $\mathbf{y}$ in order to satisfy the condition $\mathbf{y} \cdot \mathbf{u}_1^\top = 1$, specifically, exploiting one property of representative sets, the choice $\mathbf{y} = \mathbf{u}_1$.

B1. The value $0 \in \mathbb{R}$ is an eigenvalue of $\mathbf{B}$.[22]

B2. If $(\lambda_i, \mathbf{u}_i)$ is an eigenvalue/eigenvector pair with $\mathbf{A}$ $(i > 1)$ then $(\lambda_i, \mathbf{u}_i)$ is an eigenvalue/eigenvector pair with $\mathbf{B}$.

These relationships are easily verified when we recollect what it means for $(\lambda, \mathbf{x})$ to be an eigenvalue/eigenvector pair with $\mathbf{A}$ and the properties of the representative set, $\mathcal{R}$.

Let us look at (B1): $0 \in \mathbb{R}$ is an eigenvalue of $\mathbf{B}$ whose associated eigenvectors are those $\mathbf{x}$ for which $\mathbf{A}\mathbf{x} = \lambda_1 \mathbf{x}$, i.e. the eigenvectors of 0 in $\mathbf{B}$ were the eigenvectors of λ_1, the dominant eigenvalue from $\mathbf{A}$. Consider the effect of $\mathbf{B}\mathbf{u}^\top$ on a representative eigenvector $\mathbf{u} \in \mathcal{R}(\mathbf{A})$, Using $\mathbf{u}_i$ we get

$$
\begin{aligned}
\mathbf{B}\mathbf{u}_i^\top &= (\mathbf{A} - \lambda_1 \mathbf{u}_1^\top \mathbf{u}_1) \cdot \mathbf{u}_i^\top \\
&= \mathbf{A}\mathbf{u}_i^\top - \lambda_1 \mathbf{u}_1^\top \mathbf{u}_1 \mathbf{u}_i^\top \\
&= \lambda_i \mathbf{u}_i^\top - \lambda_1 \mathbf{u}_1^\top (\mathbf{u}_1 \mathbf{u}_i^\top)
\end{aligned}
$$

Now for $i = 1$ we get

$$
\mathbf{B}\mathbf{u}_1^\top = \lambda_1 \mathbf{u}_1^\top - \lambda_1 \mathbf{u}_1^\top (\mathbf{u}_1 \mathbf{u}_1^\top)
$$

But we have chosen $\mathbf{u}_1$ (that is the choice of $\mathbf{y}$ when we introduced $\mathbf{B}$) to be such that $(\mathbf{u}_1 \mathbf{u}_1^\top) = 1$ and so the we are left with

$$
\mathbf{B}\mathbf{u}_1^\top = \lambda_1 \mathbf{u}_1^\top - \lambda_1 \mathbf{u}_1^\top
$$

and thus, $\mathbf{B}\mathbf{u}_1^\top = 0$, i.e. $0 \in \sigma(\mathbf{B})$ and $\mathbf{u}_1$ is a representative eigenvector for this eigenvalue.

What of the other eigenvalues in $\sigma(\mathbf{A})$?

---

[22]We have no issue with eigen**values** which are zero: these are simply describing the non-trivial relationship $\mathbf{A}\mathbf{x}^\top = \mathbf{0}^\top$. Noting the ordering of eigenvalues by modulus, it should be clear that $|0| \leq |\lambda|$, i.e. if 0 is an eigenvalue then it is the **smallest** eigenvalue.

In these cases ($i \neq 1$) we obtain

$$\mathbf{B}\mathbf{u}_i^\top = \lambda_i \mathbf{u}_i^\top - \lambda_1 \mathbf{u}_1^\top (\mathbf{u}_1 \mathbf{u}_i^\top)$$

We now see the rationale for choosing $\mathcal{R}(\mathbf{A})$ as a representative set, since one of the principal properties of importance is,

$$\text{For all } i \neq j \ \mathbf{u}_i^\top \cdot \mathbf{u}_j = \mathbf{u}_j^\top \cdot \mathbf{u}_i = 0$$

reducing $\mathbf{B}\mathbf{u}_i^\top$ to be $\lambda_i \mathbf{u}_i^\top$, i.e. $\lambda_i \in \sigma(\mathbf{A})$ is an eigenvalue in $\sigma(\mathbf{B})$ and $\mathbf{u}_i$ an eigenvector of this with respect to $\mathbf{B}$.

In summary, for matrices and their spectra satisfying appropriate conditions (distinct eigenvalues being one such) we can recover all eigenvalues and a representative eigenvector for each by the following protocol.

D1. Given an assumed suitable $\mathbf{A}$ find $(\lambda_1, \mathbf{x}_1)$ the dominant eigenvalue and an eigenvector for it using, e.g. the Power Method.

D2. If not already in such a form, replace $\mathbf{x}_1$ by $\mathbf{u}_1$, its normalized by L_2 form, i.e

$$\mathbf{u}_1 = \frac{\mathbf{x}_1}{\|\mathbf{x}_1\|}$$

D3. Deflate $\mathbf{A}$ replacing it with

$$\mathbf{A} - \lambda_1 \mathbf{u}_1^\top \mathbf{u}_1$$

D4. Repeat from (D1) to identify λ_2, λ_3, etc and associated eigenvectors.

The choice of $\mathbf{y}$ as $\mathbf{u}_1$ is called Hotellings's Deflation, and is known to exhibit some undesirable effects as, for that matter do most Deflation techniques. An overview of different approaches may be found in Danisman *et al.* [53] who consider use in "*Principal Components Analysis*" an important methodology in the burgeoning discipline of Machine Learning.

Special Case: Symmetric Matrices

We conclude our overview of eigenvalue and eigenvector construction methods by commenting without detailed algorithmic discussion on one specific class of Real-valued matrices which are amenable to detailed spectral analysis, albeit with some non-trivial but far from excessive computational overheads: Real symmetric matrices.

We have already noted, in passing one or two advantageous aspects: if $\mathbf{A}$ is an order $n \times n$ symmetric matrix with values for $\mathbb{R}$, then $\sigma(\mathbf{A}) \in \mathbb{R}^n$, its spectrum comprises solely Real entries.

The property of symmetry is not some recherché never-arises-in-proper scenarios attribute: we have already seen its presence in the natural model of undirected graphs, and such continues to hold even if we allow Real edge weights. The matrix structure $\mathbf{PP}^\top$ is symmetric and is defined irrespective of whether the underpinning matrix, $\mathbf{P}$ is square: if $\mathbf{P}$ has order $r \times s$ then $\mathbf{PP}^\top$ has order $r \times r$. This aspect is usefully exploited within a matrix decomposition method that we shall see in more depth in the following section.

The significant algorithm in this respect is that of Jacobi [127], unfortunately there are a number of complications rendering a detailed presentation of Jacobi's method beyond the scope of this text. We will instead give an extremely superficial overview of its operation.

Jacobi's approach is motivated by a property which, if possessed of a matrix $\mathbf{A}$, renders the computation of its eigenvalues as straightforward as possible. We have alluded to this property earlier in our discussion of determinants and of calculating these: it is the property of a matrix being **triangular**. Now this is so whether we are dealing with upper triangular or lower triangular or even diagonal matrices, in all instances the matrix determinant is provided by finding the product of its diagonal, a_{ii} entries. If $\mathbf{A}$ is triangular then so also is the matrix $\mathbf{A} - \lambda\mathbf{I}$ whose symbolic form determinant describes $\chi_\mathbf{A}(\lambda)$ the characteristic polynomial of $\mathbf{A}$. And what is this polynomial? It is simply the result of expanding

$$\chi_\mathbf{A}(\lambda) \equiv \prod_{i=1}^{n}(a_{ii} - \lambda)$$

Eigenvalues are roots of polynomials and, in this case, no expansion is required: the eigenvalues of a triangular matrix are simply its diagonal entries[23] $\sigma(\mathbf{A}) = < a_{11}, a_{22}, \ldots, a_{nn} >$. And so questions such as "does this matrix have a dominant eigenvalue"? or "does this matrix have any repeated eigenvalues" or "eigenvalues of identical moduli" become essentially trivial: answering in the affirmative or negatively being a simple matter of inspecting the entries a_{ii}.

All of these properties give a very powerful motivation to proceed as follows: we have, courtesy of Property 9 and Property 10, a battery of techniques

---

[23]We are a little loose notationally here: the spectrum would involve **sorting** these entries into decreasing order.

by which we can manipulate matrices leaving their determinant affected only by a constant factor. We further know that concerted application of such methods will either result in a trivially singular matrix or a triangular one. The Jacobi eigenvalue algorithm is an approach to systematically taking a Real symmetric matrix and transforming it to a "nearly diagonal" matrix, in such a manner that its diagonal entries provide good approximations of the actual eigenvalues.

The nature of the manipulations applied (so-called "rotations") is technically quite sophisticated. The Jacobi algorithm is only one of many approaches to eigenvalue calculation through transforming the source matrix via various "decompositions". Space prohibits an extensive discussion of these, the more important of which are LDU in which A is given as the product of lower triangular (L) diagonal (D) and upper triangular (U) matrices; Cholesky (A is described as a product of two related matrices one of which is an upper triangular matrix with positive in the non-zero section Real entries). Detailed development sometimes but not invariably accompanied by algorithmic discussion may be found in most advanced Linear Algebra texts.

Summary

We have an extensive and varied range of techniques by which the dominant eigenvalues and accompanying eigenvectors may be approximated. In the computational applications we now move on to discuss such approximation usually suffices: we do not require exact values. Often in fact, as mentioned in places earlier in this chapter, we do not even need "values" at all: simply the awareness of how the components of an eigenvector with Real entries would be ordered.

As we move now to specific applications, this aspect is already apparent in the first such.

7.6 Applications of spectral methods in Computing

Our principal interest in eigenvalues and eigenvectors is not to be found in recondite algebraic subtleties. Our principal interest is the application of spectral
techniques as an effective and powerful *computational* device, and so it is to
this end that we conclude the chapter by looking at two classical mechanisms
in which the spectral theory of matrices has achieved great success. There are,
however, continuing new fields in which these ideas are found to have significant use. The final application we examine concerns one such arena.

The Google Page Rank Algorithm

The longer a technology is established the more blasé our attitudes towards it
become and we finds its presence less and less surprising. It is seen to be so
normal, as something so commonplace that the sense of astonishment that may
have greeted its advent disappears.

There was a time, as any of the generation born prior to 1975 will confirm,
that the World Wide Web did not exist. And yet that generation born after 1995
has never known a world lacking it. To have neither awareness nor experience
of an environment wherein the wealth of information now freely available via
mobile phone and tablet was inaccessible, is to those so placed, a terrible loss.
For such, the Web has always been there and its huge gains as well as its
attendant perils are taken for granted and it becomes impossible to reconcile
the fact that there was a point where one had to make do without its presence,
with one's own *personal* experience.

There is no starker indicator of this fact than the ease with which information on all manner of abstruse, eclectic subjects and questions can be obtained.
You want to know about some arcane topic in modern particle physics? Simply type (or speak!) a few judicious terms to the search engine of your choice
(π-meson, cyclotron, charm) and you will be deluged with as much and more
than you require. You are struggling to recall the name of a bit player from a
long defunct television soap opera? Simply supply the name of the programme
and you would be unfortunate if there is not some site dedicated to its entire
broadcast history.

And yet beneath such apparent ease of discovery lies a vast and sophisticated support structure pervading and snaking through the dense and unim-
peded anarchy that is the result of several billion personal web pages.

For in an environment where it would seem that all the world and their dog[24] have a personal web page, where many believe that vast numbers wait with baited breath for announcements of their every move and decision[25] this level of engagement raises one enormous and technically daunting challenge: in response to a query how do you report **only** those links having a bearing on the query posed? How, further, do you **order** the data discovered so that that which is **most relevant** is that which is reported **first**?

A web searcher that could even come *close* to dealing with such issues is already a significant breakthrough, but the web engine that time and time again actually delivers successfully will ultimately overhaul, leaving in its wake, all rival and all competing services: for much of the present century that search engine has been Google.

The triumphs from the dawn of the web, the Altavistas have been swept aside. Lycos limps on as a research project based at Carnegie-Mellon but has only a shadow of its former importance. The file transfer and search systems offered by Archie are retired followed, after a decent interval by Jughead. No longer do enquirers Ask Jeeves, in fact many do not even trouble to Ask.[26] Google has entered the English language as a neologism and even to one of conservative linguistic tastes, such as myself, the usages "I'll Google it" or "Have you tried Googling it?" no longer grate. True, Yahoo and Microsoft continue to push their own engines not without some degree of success but increasingly seem doomed to go the way of all search engines prior to Google. One cannot imagine Yahoo outside the pages of Swift, entering the language. Similarly even thinking of statements such as "I'll Bing it" or "Have you tried Binging" is to create an image that is risible.[27] In all seriousness, who would Bing when they could Google?

Google may not have been the **first**[28], but it is a truism in all manner of ac-

---

[24]One exempts cats from the implied rampant hysteria and narcissism.

[25]This level of self-introspection and delusion is, in my view, the only rational explanation for the success of phenomena such as twitter and Facebook.

[26]At the risk of stating the obvious all of these, Altavista, Lycos, Archie, Jughead, Ask Jeeves and its successor Ask were representative early mechanisms for trawling and gleaning data from the nascent Web.

[27]On teaching the material with which this section is concerned, one often checks as a lead-in which are the search engines of choice. A few diehards continue to Yahoo, however mention of Bing is usually the occasion of barely suppressed laughter.

[28]Many of the great breakthroughs such as natural language translation were realized by the now (sadly) defunct Altavista. Readers who have not encountered this particular engine, which in its prime looked set to dominate web services to the extent that Google does now, might be interested in the succinct timeline of Altavista's rise and demise that may found on, among others https://www.whoishostingthis.com/resources/history-search-engines/.

tivity, science, engineering, arts: being first is irrelevant, being **best**, is another matter entirely.

So it would seem reasonable to ask just why this is so. Corporate strategy? Possibly so, but one feels unlikely to explain the dominance. After all, for most of the 20th century, IBM was the primary market force, and one could argue this was in some part due not so much to its corporate activity but as much to product quality.[29]

Google achieves **two** outcomes, which we have hinted at as important above, **and** *ceteris paribus* does so efficiently:

G1. In response to basic search terms, e.g. "algorithmic complexity", a mass of links will be found **quickly**: the query in question reports thirteen million results in around one third of a second.

G2. These results are **ordered** so that the most **relevant** appear first. Again for the term just given, the first dozen are links to tutorial web pages or textbooks.

Many predecessors had gone some way to realizing the first of these, how-ever, few had had significant success with the second.[30]

And it is at this point where linear algebra and spectral analysis appears. For this "ordering" problem turns out to be no more than that of "ordering the components" within a **dominant eigenvector**.

Before going on to present the details, let us consider one further motivating context: finding relevant sources and attributions.

Consider the following two quotations.

Q1. "A university should be a place of light, of liberty, and of learning."

Q2. "I am much afraid that the Universities will prove to be the great gates of Hell."

---

[29]It was fashionable to sneer at some of IBM's activity, a tendency noticeable in the noisome critically overrated geek-fest that is 2001 *A space odyssey* wherein a plot device is claimed to originate as a play on the acronym IBM. Nevertheless some significant achievements are due to IBM not least among which were the contributions to realizing **effective** and usable high-level language compilers. Even today, the FORTRAN H compiler from the OS/370 development is recognized as a watershed.

[30]One of the main issues I recall from using Altavista in the late 1990s was that although the results reported had some relevance, often the ones of greatest interest would only be clear after trawling through sixty or seventy more "highly rated" by the search engine pages.

These, especially in the U.K the first, may sound vaguely familiar. And, in the of light of what has been written above there may be times when one is either curious about their provenance or in the context of scholarly work need to be able to pinpoint the exact date, place and occasion of their utterance. Until roughly the end of the twentieth century the only reliable way of so doing would be to trace the source in previously published work: to go to a specialist library. And, yet we have already highlighted two incidents where even this approach would not be entirely reliable: we may be fortunate enough to discover a **single** source, but this may be disputed by other works, and so we need to be aware if producing scholarly works of other sources, disputed claims (and the rationale for the dispute). We have seen the pitfalls of attributing "discoveries" to the non-existent Paolo Valmes[31] and something of the motivation for this piece of fiction. We have also mentioned, in passing, the oft-quoted but never said in reality, remarks of Jean Baptiste Coffinhal on the occasion of Lavoisier's trial.[32]

And so while there are still similar dangers (multiple disputed sources and versions), **if** we can glean as much data as possible we are better placed to comment on facts. This is the possibility that Google's search engine offers.[33]

The web as a large graph

We have argued that the principal challenges in retrieving information from the World wide web in response to a search query are twofold:

GC1. Identifying **relevant** links from a potential source comprising several millions of distinct items.

GC2. **Ordering** those items discovered in such a way that the **most useful** links appear **highest**.

We first need to have a reasonable model of the structure that is being trawled. This turns out to be relatively straightforward.

Description 6. *The **web graph**, is a directed graph structure (W, L) in which the nodes, W, correspond to individual web pages and $< w_i, w_j >$ is a directed edge in L if there is a (hyper)link from the page, w_i to the page w_j.*

---

[31]Endnote 9, Chapter 2.

[32]fn. 35, Chapter 5.

[33]I discuss the two quotations and their provenance in Endnotes 2 and 3 of this Chapter.

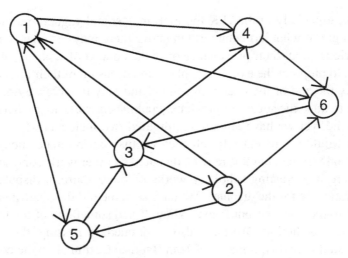

Figure 7.1: A world of six web pages

Now let us assume as is the case with all commercial web engines that
we have been able to collate as one, all or at least a significant proportion of
those web sites which seem relevant, e.g. if we are seeking information about
a particular technicality, e.g. Computational Argument, our raw data might
be as many pages as we can identify that contain the phrase "*Computational
Argument*" or, in addition those that contain the word "Argument" and its de-
clensions. While we would be unlikely to find ourselves in the position of
every page we have found linking directly to every other page found, it seems
a reasonable expectation that there would be some interconnection between
large groups: after all, these are all found to be "relevant" to the given technicality so it would not be surprising that, say, there would be mutual links
between an index page of active researchers and individual researchers and
organizations. We will return to the minor issue of pages that do not link to
others (as might happen with .jpg or .pdf files) a little later, however, as a
working example let us suppose that we have only discovered **six** pages, and
that their interconnection is as displayed in Figure 7.1.

The corresponding 6×6 matrix, which we will denote by $\mathbf{L}$. has entries which are either 0 or 1, and is

$$
\mathbf{L} = \begin{pmatrix}
0 & 0 & 0 & 1 & 1 & 1 \\
1 & 0 & 0 & 0 & 1 & 1 \\
1 & 1 & 0 & 1 & 1 & 0 \\
0 & 0 & 0 & 0 & 0 & 1 \\
0 & 0 & 1 & 0 & 0 & 0 \\
0 & 0 & 1 & 0 & 0 & 0
\end{pmatrix}
$$

A very superficial look at this network might appear to suggest that the most "important" i.e. relevant to the search being undertaken pages are 5 and 6: each of these is pointed to by three others and so, along the logic of "more followers on twitter means a more 'interesting' individual" one might wish to have these ranked highest. Hence, assigning a score to each page based on the number of links to it, **backlinks** as these are dubbed, gives us a first pass page score of

$$
\begin{bmatrix}
\text{Page} & \text{Score} \\
1 & 2 \\
2 & 1 \\
3 & 2 \\
4 & 2 \\
5 & 3 \\
6 & 3
\end{bmatrix}
$$

Thus page 2 seems to be the "least relevant" and pages 5 and 6 the "most important" with respect to the query from which this network was formed. This may, indeed, be so and we shall continue to use this, admittedly rather toy example, in the sequel. There are, however, at least two problems with this "scoring by sheer numbers" approach. The first of which is that it is very easy for unscrupulous users to inflate the importance of a chosen page which, in reality, is of little interest. How so? Let us suppose our putative dishonest user wishing to bolster the "significance" of page 2, creates a number of additional "dummy" pages all of which contained the search term of interest and configured these as shown in Figure 7.2.

On the scoring by "number of links to" measure now page two has a score of 9: three times higher than any rival page. Notice that a link has been added from page 2 to the new page 7. This is not strictly necessary, however, it guarantees that the connectivity structure of the original network is preserved: it is still possible to reach any page starting from any other page. In addition it is a reasonable assumption that the person seeking to boost the importance of

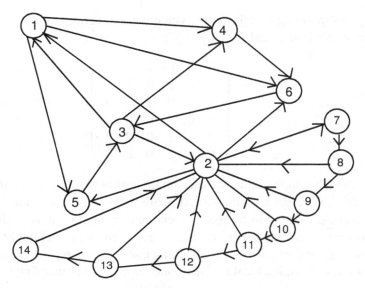

Figure 7.2: Inflating a page's importance

page 2 actually has control over its contents and so editing this to add a link to page 7 does not appear to be an undue requirement.

So we have one drawback to the "importance by number of links" measure: it is very easy to manipulate and although the device in Figure 7.2 is rather primitive there are more sophisticated ways of achieving the same outcome.

To get a sense of the second problem, consider the following question.

"Which is more important? A page pointed to by several thousand **distinct** users or a page pointed to by exactly two?"

The qualification "distinct" is intended to rule out of consideration devices such as those of Figure 7.2.

Once again, noting the attempt to rule out manipulation, the answer may seem "obvious": several thousand is, of course, better than two. It may well, indeed be so, but not **necessarily**. A typical academic may have links to their home page from previous and current students both undergraduate and research, from researchers in the same specialist field, various indices and databases collating scholarly activity and so on. This might total a few hundred different and "genuine" links. What, however, about someone who has only two links to their home page but one of these is from www.microsoft.com and the other from www.google.com? There is a good case for viewing the second scenario as reflecting an individual having a more important web presence. Even with of the order of several hundreds of links directed towards them it seems unlikely that this fact alone will lead to more "hits" on the personal page. By their very nature as large successful companies with significant size user communities so that often personal users will have the default browser page set to one of these two and will not bother to change the two commercial sites are likely to attract a huge number of visitors. It does not seem too much of a leap, that having landed on the Google (or Microsoft) home page users may be tempted to explore further i.e. to visit sites to which these point.

What we arrive at is the second insight underpinning the methods used in Google's search approach: it not how **many** backlinks a given page has that determines its significance; it is the **source** of these. One link from `www.microsoft.com` carries more weight than ten thousand links from relative obscurity.

And so if we do not use mere "counting" how do we assess the "importance" of a given page? By the "importance" of those pages that are its backlinks.

In the Google pagerank approach, having formed the local structure just described, suppose we are left with n pages ($n \in \mathbb{N}$), which we are denoting

$$\{w_1,\ w_2, \ldots,\ w_{n-1},\ w_n\}$$

We seek to determine a **score**, r_i, for each page w_i in such a way that the "most important" pages will be awarded the highest score.

Two parameters colour the determination of r_i:

PS1. The scores, r_j of pages for which w_j is a backlink of w_i, i.e for which $< w_j, w_i >\in L$.

PS2. The total **number** of pages for which w_j is a backlink, i.e.

$$|\{\ w_k\ :\ \ < w_j, w_k >\in L\}|^{-1}$$

The parameter (PS2) may look a little strange, however, the thinking underlying it is that if w_k is "important" and links to many other pages, then its score r_k should be "fairly distributed" among those to which it points rather than unevenly allocated amongst them. To take an extreme case, one would not expect a page pointed to from `www.google.com` to inherit the **entirety** of Google's importance score. While it is reasonable to expect a portion of this to contribute, other pages for which `www.google.com` is a backlink have a good argument for a portion of the score to be allocated to them.

In total. the score, r_i assigned to w_i is obtained as

$$r_i = \sum_{k \,:\, <w_k, w_i> \in L} \frac{r_k}{|\{\, w_j \,:\, <w_k, w_j> \in L\}|}$$

So that each page w_k linking to w_i contributes to r_i the fraction of its score given by the number of pages to which w_k links.

Now although this "compute the score for page i in terms of the scores of pages that link to page i" appears to involve a non-terminating regression e.g. page ... links to page 4 links to page 3 ... links to 2 then 1, there is a very straightforward method of encapsulating the relationship between scores needed for ranking and the number of backlinks: we just recast the problem as a matrix-vector product.

Suppose we define the **score matrix**, $\mathbf{W}$ to have order $n \times n$, n being the number of web pages in our set, as

$$w_{ij} = \begin{cases} |\{\, w_k \,:\, <w_i, w_k> \in L\}|^{-1} & \text{if} \quad <w_i, w_j> \in L \\ 0 & \text{if} \quad <w_i, w_j> \notin L \end{cases}$$

Our score computation is then
$$\mathbf{W}\mathbf{r}^\top$$

wherein
$$\mathbf{r} = <r_1; r_2, \ldots, r_n>$$

That is to say the n-vector of page scores we are attempting to find. This vector, however, needs to have a specific relationship with the matrix $\mathbf{W}$. What relationship? That
$$\mathbf{W}\mathbf{r}^\top = \mathbf{r}^\top$$

In other words, the score vector we seek must be an eigenvector with respect to an eigenvalue 1 of $\mathbf{W}$. Looking at $\mathbf{W}$ in our six page web example we get

$$\mathbf{W} = \begin{pmatrix} 0 & 1/3 & 1/4 & 0 & 0 & 0 \\ 0 & 0 & 1/4 & 0 & 0 & 0 \\ 0 & 0 & 0 & 0 & 1 & 1 \\ 1/3 & 0 & 1/4 & 0 & 0 & 0 \\ 1/3 & 1/3 & 1/4 & 0 & 0 & 0 \\ 1/3 & 1/3 & 0 & 1 & 0 & 0 \end{pmatrix}$$

In this particular instance our matrix $\mathbf{W}$ is **column stochastic**, viz. Property 18. So not only is 1 a largest eigenvalue in the sense that $|\lambda| \leq 1$ for all other eigenvalues of $\mathbf{W}$, but if 1 is **dominant** ($|\lambda| < 1$) then we can find an eigenvector via the power method or otherwise for **W**. Going further[34] if **W** is **irreducible** then we not only have such an eigenvector we have an eigenvector containing **only positive components** cf. (F2) of Property 17.

Now this is precisely what we need for the purpose of ranking pages: each page has a positive Real score assigned it via the eigenvector and ordering these individual scores gives the importance of each page.

The specific case used in our example we have seen to be column stochastic. This instance is also irreducible. This, however, is not because we have manipulated the underlying web graph to attain such an end. The property of "column stochastic" and irreducible will hold of any matrix constructed in the way we have just described provided that its underlying directed graph structure is **strongly connected**.

Overall the very elementary form of Google's page rank algortihm is,

1. Assuming the raw collection of pages has been identified. Given

$$W = \{w_1, w_2, \ldots, w_n\}$$

a collection of n pages.

Construct the matrix, **W** defined earlier, for which

$$w_{ij} = \begin{cases} |\{ w_k : \; <w_i, w_k> \in L \}|^{-1} & \text{if} \quad <w_i, w_j> \in L \\ 0 & \text{if} \quad <w_i, w_j> \notin L \end{cases}$$

2. Construct an eigenvector, **r** comprising only positive components satisfying

$$\mathbf{W}\mathbf{r}^\top = \mathbf{r}^\top$$

3. Report relevant pages using the convention that if within this score vector $r_i \geq r_j$, then page w_i is more important *vis-a-vis* the query concerned than page w_j.

At this level all that is needed is for the underlying graph to be strongly-connected.

---

[34]The property of row or column stochastic does not mean that the matrix exhibiting it is necessarily irreducible.

Turning to the six page example, we see that for

$$
\mathbf{W} = \begin{pmatrix}
0 & 1/3 & 1/4 & 0 & 0 & 0 \\
0 & 0 & 1/4 & 0 & 0 & 0 \\
0 & 0 & 0 & 0 & 1 & 1 \\
1/3 & 0 & 1/4 & 0 & 0 & 0 \\
1/3 & 1/3 & 1/4 & 0 & 0 & 0 \\
1/3 & 1/3 & 0 & 1 & 0 & 0
\end{pmatrix}
$$

The value 1 is the dominant eigenvalue (note definite article). An associated eigenvector comprising only positive components is

$$
\mathbf{r} = \; < 1, \, 3/4, \, 3, \, 13/12, \, 4/3, \, 5/3 >
$$

So that the corresponding ranking of pages is

$$
< w_3, \, w_6, \, w_5, \, w_4, \, w_1, \, w_2 >
$$

It is useful to compare this ordering with the directed graph from which it arose (Figure 7.1). As suggested page 2 is seen as least important: the computed ranking justifies our informal view. There is, however, one aspect which was not suspected: although pages 5 and 6 win out on the "most pointed to" metric, i.e. these have the largest number of backlinks, neither is ranked by the algorithm as most important. This accolade goes to page 3 which has "only" 2 backlinks: both of these, however, are from the "naive most important" pages, 5 and 6.

What of the owner of page 2? Finding this ranked lowest both by naive and Google scoring, suppose this owner decides to attempt inflating the ranking by mechanisms such as that shown in Figure 7.2?

Now, we have 14 pages to order including the eight freshly introduced "dummy" pages.

The reader may readily confirm that the resulting matrix, $\mathbf{W}$, is

$$
\begin{pmatrix}
0 & 1/4 & 1/3 & 0 & 0 & 0 & 0 & 0 & 0 & 0 & 0 & 0 & 0 & 0 \\
0 & 0 & 1/3 & 0 & 0 & 0 & 1/2 & 1/2 & 1/2 & 1/2 & 1/2 & 1/2 & 1/2 & 1 \\
0 & 0 & 0 & 0 & 1 & 1 & 0 & 0 & 0 & 0 & 0 & 0 & 0 & 0 \\
1/3 & 0 & 1/3 & 0 & 0 & 0 & 0 & 0 & 0 & 0 & 0 & 0 & 0 & 0 \\
1/3 & 1/4 & 0 & 0 & 0 & 0 & 0 & 0 & 0 & 0 & 0 & 0 & 0 & 0 \\
1/3 & 1/4 & 0 & 1 & 0 & 0 & 0 & 0 & 0 & 0 & 0 & 0 & 0 & 0 \\
0 & 1/4 & 0 & 0 & 0 & 0 & 0 & 0 & 0 & 0 & 0 & 0 & 0 & 0 \\
0 & 0 & 0 & 0 & 0 & 0 & 1/2 & 0 & 0 & 0 & 0 & 0 & 0 & 0 \\
0 & 0 & 0 & 0 & 0 & 0 & 0 & 1/2 & 0 & 0 & 0 & 0 & 0 & 0 \\
0 & 0 & 0 & 0 & 0 & 0 & 0 & 0 & 1/2 & 0 & 0 & 0 & 0 & 0 \\
0 & 0 & 0 & 0 & 0 & 0 & 0 & 0 & 0 & 1/2 & 0 & 0 & 0 & 0 \\
0 & 0 & 0 & 0 & 0 & 0 & 0 & 0 & 0 & 0 & 1/2 & 0 & 0 & 0 \\
0 & 0 & 0 & 0 & 0 & 0 & 0 & 0 & 0 & 0 & 0 & 1/2 & 0 & 0 \\
0 & 0 & 0 & 0 & 0 & 0 & 0 & 0 & 0 & 0 & 0 & 0 & 1/2 & 0
\end{pmatrix}
$$

Again we find that 1 is the dominant eigenvalue and a corresponding eigenvector is

$$
< 0.299, 0.293, 0.666, 0.318, 0.172, 0.493,
$$
$$
0.073, 0.037, 0.018, 0.009, 0.005, 0.002, 0.001, 0.001 >
$$

That is the pages are ordered

$$
< w_3, w_6, w_4, w_1, w_2, w_5, w_7, w_8, w_9, w_{10}, w_{11}, w_{12}, w_{13}, w_{14} >
$$

Now there are a number of interesting points to note about this particular example. The unscrupulous owner of page 2, through the machinations indulged in in order to bring about Figure 7.2, has not actually managed to accomplish much. Page 2 has improved by one position in the ranking at the expense of the previously highly regarded page 5.[35] In addition all of the "new" pages, whose only purpose was artificially to boost the score of page 2 ar ranked lowly: the lowest eight positions are taken by the eight pages added. After all of the attempts to manipulate the scoring page 3 remains the highest ranked.

In total rather more sophisticated techniques than the version of "link spamming" as such practices are dubbed, the method of Figure 7.2 being one such approach used here are needed in order to fool Google's ranking approach.

---

[35]It is possible that this has arisen as account of corrections from numerical errors: unable - in this instance - to use values $(1/3, 1/3, 1/3)$ it was necessary to correct to $(0.334, 0.333, 0.333)$ in order to preserve column stochasticity.

There is one issue which we have still to deal with. The methods we have just described, generally, work very successfully when we are dealing with a strongly-connected structure. If, however, we have some page that does not link to any other page then we will not have an underlying strongly-connected graph. In fact, worse from the perspective of computational activity, our basic matrix representation will have a row which consists entirely of the value 0.[36] Why would anyone be interested in looking at a page from which they cannot return? We have already given an example of an instance where such would arise in a natural manner: it is not invariably the case that a .pdf document will contain hyperlinks and even should it do so these may be to sections within the document itself rather than to external sites. In this event, particularly when collating data relating to a current research or pedagogical activity, it is likely that one will access information held in the form of an on-line .pdf file. One solution to "dangling pages" arising in this manner e.g. .pdf, images such as .jpg or gifs, sound or video files, such as .avi, .wmv, .mp3. would be not to include these in the resulting tranche of chosen pages identified within one's preliminary, that is prior to ranking, cull, and only to include "real web pages" i.e. .html or similar, with the precondition that a "real web page" links to somewhere else.[37]

Such mechanisms as limit consideration to only specific file extensions; throw out dead-end pages satisfying the extension criterion are rather brute-force. They are also unnecessary. Rather than artificially constrain the nature of the search and ranking process a better solution is to engineer the resulting network structure in such a way that the ranking order would be unchanged but that dead-ends are no longer present. This is what happens with Google's method and it is achieved not by dint of removing pages but through **adding links**.

While the exact mechanics used by Google are commercially sensitive, the general approach used is open and it is this we now discuss.

---

[36] All of which, of course, holds true if we have a page with no backlinks. These are, however, easily handled: if w has no backlinks then we cannot reach w by surfing over other pages in the system, and so w and the links emanating from w may be deleted with no loss of information.

[37] Taking the reading that the developer of a web page that does not go anywhere is either incompetent (does not know how to include relevant links) or arrogant (believes their page to be the final statement on an activity in question and so does not see any reasons why, having discovered their page, anyone would wish or need to go elsewhere), one might think such pages are redundant and simply not include in the pool being processed.

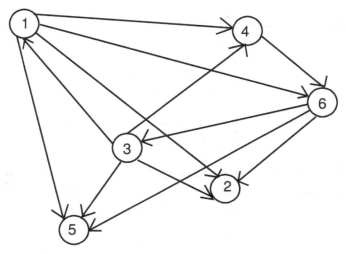

Figure 7.3: Dead-ends in the 6 page web world

Dead-ends & Dangling Pages

We have seen one consequence of a page having no outgoing links: when we form the matrix of the web-graph one of its rows will contain only zeros.

The method used is simply to modify W (the web-graph) in such a way that the corresponding matrix has at least one 1 in every row. Suppose that $\mathbf{W}$ describes the score matrix i.e. whose elements are Rationals as we introduced it earlier. Of course, since W has dead-ends, so too $\mathbf{W}$ will have **columns** containing only the value 0. Suppose that there are t such columns in $\mathbf{W}$ and these have indices

$$\{c_1, c_2, \ldots, c_t\}$$

For example, after noting the initial pre link spamming outcomes, the controllers of the six pages featured in the graph of Figure 7.1 may decide to edit their respective pages so that the structure of Figure 7.3 is the result,

There are now two dangling pages: page 2 and page 5 and the resulting matrix of links, L will become

$$\mathbf{L} \;=\; \begin{pmatrix} 0 & 0 & 0 & 1 & 1 & 1 \\ 0 & 0 & 0 & 0 & 0 & 0 \\ 1 & 1 & 0 & 1 & 1 & 0 \\ 0 & 0 & 0 & 0 & 0 & 1 \\ 0 & 0 & 0 & 0 & 0 & 0 \\ 0 & 1 & 1 & 0 & 0 & 0 \end{pmatrix}$$

With the score-matrix, $\mathbf{W}$ becoming

$$\mathbf{W} \;=\; \begin{pmatrix} 0 & 0 & 1/4 & 0 & 0 & 0 \\ 1/4 & 0 & 1/4 & 0 & 0 & 1/3 \\ 0 & 0 & 0 & 0 & 0 & 1/3 \\ 1/4 & 0 & 1/4 & 0 & 0 & 0 \\ 1/4 & 0 & 1/4 & 0 & 0 & 1/3 \\ 1/4 & 0 & 0 & 1 & 0 & 0 \end{pmatrix}$$

so that columns 2 and 5 of this matrix are the $\mathbf{0}^{\top}$ column vector. The columns we wish to change in this example are 2 and 5. In general the columns are $\{c_1, c_2, \ldots, c_t\}$. Consider the n-vector d defined through

$$d_k \;=\; \begin{cases} 0 & \text{if} \quad c_k \notin \{c_1, c_2, \ldots, c_t\} \\ 1 & \text{if} \quad c_k \in \{c_1, c_2, \ldots, c_t\} \end{cases}$$

So for our example $\mathbf{d} =< 0, 1, 0, 0, 1, 0 >$.

Furthermore, suppose that $\mathbf{b}$ is **any** n-vector that satisfies the two conditions

B1. The components of $\mathbf{b}$ are all **positive**.

B2. The components of $\mathbf{b}$ add up to 1, i.e.

$$\sum_{i=1}^{n} b_i \;=\; 1$$

The result of multiplying $\mathbf{b}^{\top}$ by d is an order $n \times n$ matrix, $\mathbf{D} = \mathbf{b}^{\top} \cdot \mathbf{d}$ so we can **add** this matrix to $\mathbf{W}$.

Returning to our example, we might choose $\mathbf{b} =< 1/6, 1/6, 1/6, 1/6, 1/6, 1/6 >$ giving

$$\mathbf{D} = \mathbf{b}^{\top} \cdot \mathbf{d} \;=\; \begin{pmatrix} 0 & 1/6 & 0 & 0 & 1/6 & 0 \\ 0 & 1/6 & 0 & 0 & 1/6 & 0 \\ 0 & 1/6 & 0 & 0 & 1/6 & 0 \\ 0 & 1/6 & 0 & 0 & 1/6 & 0 \\ 0 & 1/6 & 0 & 0 & 1/6 & 0 \\ 0 & 1/6 & 0 & 0 & 1/6 & 0 \end{pmatrix}$$

Adding this matrix to $\mathbf{W}$ would only change the elements in the second and fifth columns, leaving the rest unaltered **and** our new matrix would have no zero columns and be column stochastic: $\mathbf{W} + \mathbf{D}$ would be a suitable matrix to which we could apply our previous algorithm.

$$\mathbf{W} + \mathbf{D} = \begin{pmatrix} 0 & 1/6 & 1/4 & 0 & 1/6 & 0 \\ 1/4 & 1/6 & 1/4 & 0 & 1/6 & 1/3 \\ 0 & 1/6 & 0 & 0 & 1/6 & 1/3 \\ 1/4 & 1/6 & 1/4 & 0 & 1/6 & 0 \\ 1/4 & 1/6 & 1/4 & 0 & 1/6 & 1/3 \\ 1/4 & 1/6 & 0 & 1 & 1/6 & 0 \end{pmatrix}$$

So this approach – identify $\mathbf{0}^\top$ columns (d); form any $\mathbf{b}$ subject to the constraints (B1) and (B2); build the matrix $\mathbf{D} = \mathbf{b}^\top \mathbf{d}$ and add it to $\mathbf{W}$ – will, in general, result in a column stochastic matrix for which we have 1 as the dominant eigenvalue and, the most important aspect for ranking, an eigenvector consisting solely of positive components.

Now if we look at the ranking produced by our new column stochastic matrix we obtain the score vector

$$\mathbf{r} = \left\langle \frac{9461}{15552}, \frac{37787}{31104}, \frac{6617}{7776}, \frac{23803}{31104}, \frac{37787}{31104}, \frac{41857}{31104} \right\rangle$$

with ordering

$$< r_6, \{r_2, r_5\}, r_3, r_4, r_1 >$$

This may not look entirely satisfactory: both of the dangling pages are identically ranked as joint second highest and this may look as if it is the result of the implied change to L which can be interpreted as removing dead-ends through adding a link from each such page to every other page in the system. An approach which might suggest a rather more "creative" way of artificially boosting a page's score: to impove the score of page w_k, remove all references to other pages from its contents so turning w_k into a dead-end and await the results of $\mathbf{W} + \mathbf{D}$ in reporting an ordering.

The characteristic polynomial, $\chi_{\mathbf{W}+\mathbf{D}}$ of this matrix is,

$$\lambda^6 - \frac{\lambda^5}{3} - \frac{5\lambda^4}{18} - \frac{7\lambda^3}{24} - \frac{13\lambda^2}{144} - \frac{\lambda}{144}$$

While 1 is the dominant eigenvalue, we also find 0 to be an eigenvalue.

In fact, using $\mathbf{G}$ to denote the $n \times n$ mmatrix $\mathbf{W} + \mathbf{D}$, the Google ranking approach does not directly use G, but a "tuned" version defined from $\mathbf{G}$, a **damping** factor, $\delta \in \mathbb{R}$ and a **choice** n-vector, $\mathbf{c}$. Similarly to $\mathbf{b}$, the choice vector satisfies $c_i > 0$ for each i and that its individual components sum to 1. Using these the matrix analyzed to obtain a ranking is

$$\mathbf{R} = \delta\mathbf{G} + (1 - \delta)\mathbf{c}^\top\mathbf{1}$$

In order to protect against malicious manipulation of links and for reasons of commercial sensitivity, just as the exact choice of $\mathbf{b}$ is secret, so too are the choices of δ and $\mathbf{c}$. Empirical studies of the discoverers, Brin and Page reported in [32], suggest values for δ around 0.85 and, similarly to $\mathbf{b}$ a choice vector in which $c_i = 1/n$ for each i. Returning to our dead-end example using these choices, $\mathbf{R}$ becomes

$$0.85 \begin{pmatrix} 0 & 1/6 & 1/4 & 0 & 1/6 & 0 \\ 1/4 & 1/6 & 1/4 & 0 & 1/6 & 1/3 \\ 0 & 1/6 & 0 & 0 & 1/6 & 1/3 \\ 1/4 & 1/6 & 1/4 & 0 & 1/6 & 0 \\ 1/4 & 1/6 & 1/4 & 0 & 1/6 & 1/3 \\ 1/4 & 1/6 & 0 & 1 & 1/6 & 0 \end{pmatrix} + $$

$$0.15 \begin{pmatrix} 1/6 & 1/6 & 1/6 & 1/6 & 1/6 & 1/6 \\ 1/6 & 1/6 & 1/6 & 1/6 & 1/6 & 1/6 \\ 1/6 & 1/6 & 1/6 & 1/6 & 1/6 & 1/6 \\ 1/6 & 1/6 & 1/6 & 1/6 & 1/6 & 1/6 \\ 1/6 & 1/6 & 1/6 & 1/6 & 1/6 & 1/6 \\ 1/6 & 1/6 & 1/6 & 1/6 & 1/6 & 1/6 \end{pmatrix}$$

In other words,

$$\mathbf{R} = \begin{pmatrix} 0.025 & 0.167 & 0.238 & 0.025 & 0.167 & 0.025 \\ 0.238 & 0.167 & 0.238 & 0.025 & 0.167 & 0.308 \\ 0.025 & 0.167 & 0.025 & 0.025 & 0.167 & 0.308 \\ 0.238 & 0.167 & 0.238 & 0.025 & 0.167 & 0.025 \\ 0.238 & 0.167 & 0.238 & 0.025 & 0.167 & 0.308 \\ 0.238 & 0.167 & 0.025 & 0.875 & 0.167 & 0.025 \end{pmatrix}$$

Now we do not need to be too concerned about rounding inaccuracies: $\mathbf{R}$ contains only positive Real entries. Applying the power method and ordering results we get the ranking,

$$< 0.679, 1.193, 0.868, 0.813, 1.193, 1.272 >$$

This being exactly the same ranking without the adjustment for damping. Notice in both cases we have matrices, $\mathbf{W} + \mathbf{D}$, which have 0 as an eigenvalue since their determinants are both zero and this is a consequence of there being more than one dead-end.

Suppose we look at the case of there being **exactly one** such page. We have the two alternatives

Table 7.1: Single dead-ends in the 6 page web

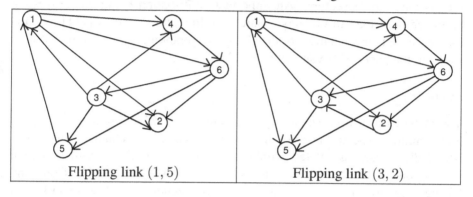

| Flipping link $(1, 5)$ | Flipping link $(3, 2)$ |

In the first of these we obtain, $\mathbf{G}_{1 \to 5}$ as

$$\begin{pmatrix} 0 & 1/6 & 1/4 & 0 & 1 & 0 \\ 1/3 & 1/6 & 1/4 & 0 & 0 & 1/3 \\ 0 & 1/6 & 0 & 0 & 0 & 1/3 \\ 1/3 & 1/6 & 1/4 & 0 & 0 & 0 \\ 0 & 1/6 & 1/4 & 0 & 0 & 1/3 \\ 1/3 & 1/6 & 0 & 1 & 0 & 0 \end{pmatrix}$$

and in the second, $\mathbf{G}_{3 \to 2}$ as

$$\begin{pmatrix} 0 & 0 & 1/3 & 0 & 1/6 & 0 \\ 1/4 & 0 & 0 & 0 & 1/6 & 1/3 \\ 0 & 1 & 0 & 0 & 1/6 & 1/3 \\ 1/4 & 0 & 1/3 & 0 & 1/6 & 0 \\ 1/4 & 0 & 1/3 & 0 & 1/6 & 1/3 \\ 1/4 & 0 & 0 & 1 & 1/6 & 0 \end{pmatrix}$$

Ignoring the damping factor, α, leads to after a few iterations of the power method

$$\mathbf{r}_{1 \to 5} = \ <1.182,\ 1.215,\ 0.646,\ 0.771, 0.808,\ 1.376>$$

So that the ranking is now,

$$<w_6,\ w_2,\ w_1,\ w_5,\ w_4,\ w_3>$$

In the second instance

$$\mathbf{r}_{3 \to 2} \;=\; < 0.646,\; 0.771,\; 1.376,\; 0.808,\; 1.215,\; 1.182 >$$

and the ranking $< w_3,\; w_5,\; w_6,\; w_4,\; w_2,\; w_1 >$.

Considerable study has gone into the issue of tamper resistant damping factors and choice vectors. An important contribution being the TrustRank approach described in Gyöngyi, Garcia-Molina and Pedersen [111]. A further, accessible presentation of the Google pageranking approach may also be found in the paper of Bryan and Leise [35].

Summary

The methods just discussed are still the subject of active research. As a general technique, spectral analysis has been studied as a mechanism for a number of divers ranking related problem from the superficially similar to page ranking problem of citation metric analysis, e.g. Kleinberg [142], Cohn and Chang [47]; to predictive ranking of sports leagues, e.g. Keener [139], to its application in the arena considered in the final section: argument ranking, cf. Butterworth and Dunne [39]. Many of these approaches work from the basis provided by the Perron-Frobenius Theorem, as the combination of Property 15 and Property 17 is called and the known spectral behaviour of stochastic matrices. Often, even techniques unsuited to the determination of all eigenvalue/vector pairs such as the Power Method, suffice to glean the information needed to offer a sensible rank ordering. The commercial dominance of Google as a preferred search engine offers ample evidence of this fact.

Matrices and their Singular Value Decomposition

The matrix forms we have considered so far have one common feature: these are **square**, their order being such that the number of rows is exactly equal to the number of columns. The spectral application considered now is a rare exception to this ubiquity of the square: it can be applied to **any** matrix[38] irrespective of the cardinality relation between n the number of rows and m the number of columns.

The representation of a matrix, M, through what is called its **singular value decomposition** (or, as we shall use subsequently, SVD) offers a useful means of identifying (and discarding) information about M without losing significant detail about its essential character. Thus we have a means by which image files may be compressed with, depending on the scale of compression sought, no unreasonable reduction in the quality of the reconstituted image. In analysing the relationship between data presented in a tabular form SVD thereby provides a mechanism for filtering away contributions that have little significant effect and to focus on the relationship between parameters of importance. In the field of Machine Learning within AI such processes form the heart of a computational technique known as Principal Components Analysis (PCA).

In [133], Kalman attributes the development of the SVD method to Gilbert Strang (from the 1980 edition of [225, p. 142], a later edition of this text being [227]). After describing its basic structure we consider one CS application of SVD: as a method of image compression.

Overall a wide range of practical approaches exploit this representational method, from Image Processing, e.g. Rufai *et al.* [198], through to Data Analysis e.g. Wall *et al.* [250], Mees *et al.* [162]. And the power of the technique itself? This derives from spectral analysis and treatments of eigenvalues and vectors.

Underlying form of Singular Value Decomposition

Suppose we have been given some matrix, M, having n rows and m columns wherein we assume that $n \geq m$ otherwise we look at $M^\top$ and with all of its elements drawn from $\mathbb{R}$. We know, already, these appurtenances of M.

M1. Both the matrix products, $M \cdot M^\top$ and $M^\top \cdot M$ are

---

[38]There is an underlying assumption that the number of rows is at least as large as the number of columns, however, in the event that this is false there is an easy transformation that can be applied: namely to work with the transpose matrix.

a. Well-defined, since, using $\mathbf{A} \cdot \mathbf{B}$ for the product concerned, the number of columns in $\mathbf{A}$ (m for $\mathbf{M}$; n for $\mathbf{M}^\top$) is equal to the number of rows in $\mathbf{B}$ (m for $\mathbf{M}^\top$; n for $\mathbf{M}$).

b. The order of $\mathbf{M} \cdot \mathbf{M}^\top$ is $n \times n$; that of $\mathbf{M}^\top \cdot \mathbf{M}$ is $m \times m$.

c. Both $\mathbf{M} \cdot \mathbf{M}^\top$ and $\mathbf{M}^\top \cdot \mathbf{M}$ are **symmetric**.

M2. By virtue of point M1(c), we also know courtesy of Property 13 that:

a. All n eigenvalues of $\mathbf{M} \cdot \mathbf{M}^\top$ and the m eigenvalues of $\mathbf{M}^\top \cdot \mathbf{M}$ are drawn from $\mathbb{R}$.

b. There are **orthogonal** bases of eigenvectors for both. That is to say, recalling Property 13(S2), sets of Real vectors,

$$\mathbf{Or}(\mathbf{M} \cdot \mathbf{M}^\top) \;=\; \{\mathbf{u}_1, \ldots, \mathbf{u}_n\}$$

and

$$\mathbf{Or}(\mathbf{M}^\top \cdot \mathbf{M}) \;=\; \{\mathbf{v}_1, \ldots, \mathbf{v}_m\}$$

each of which is an eigenvector for the corresponding eigenvalue and matrix product and with any pair of distinct, $\mathbf{y}_i$ and $\mathbf{y}_j$ drawn from the sets, satisfying

$$\mathbf{y}_i \cdot \mathbf{y}_j \;=\; \mathbf{y}_j \cdot \mathbf{y}_i = 0$$

We have one further point of importance from Property 13: we may write $\mathbf{M} \cdot \mathbf{M}^\top$ as
$$\mathbf{M} \cdot \mathbf{M}^\top \;=\; \mathbf{Q} \cdot \mathbf{L} \cdot \mathbf{Q}^\top$$
in which $\mathbf{L}$ is a diagonal matrix and $\mathbf{Q}$ constructed from $\mathbf{Or}(\mathbf{M} \cdot \mathbf{M}^\top)$.

Notice that, by virtue of
$$(\mathbf{M} \cdot \mathbf{M}^\top)^\top \;=\; \mathbf{M}^\top \cdot \mathbf{M}$$
and $\det \mathbf{A} \;=\; \det \mathbf{A}^\top$, $\sigma(\mathbf{M} \cdot \mathbf{M}^\top) = \sigma(\mathbf{M}^\top \cdot \mathbf{M})$.

In total we obtain,

Description 7. *For* $\mathbf{M}$ *an order* $n \times m$ *Real-valued matrix, with* $n \geq m$*, the* ***singular value decomposition*** *of* $\mathbf{M}$*, denoted* SVD$(\mathbf{M})$*, is given by writing,* $\mathbf{M}$ *as the product*
$$\mathbf{M} \;=\; \mathbf{U} \cdot \mathbf{S} \cdot \mathbf{V}^\top$$
In this $\mathbf{U}$ *has order* $n \times n$*;* $\mathbf{S}$ *has order* $n \times m$ *and* $\mathbf{V}^\top$ *order* $m \times m$*. Here,*

a. *The matrix* $\mathbf{S}$ *has order* $n \times m$ *recalling that* $m \leq n$ *and is a **diagonal** matrix.*[39]

$$\mathbf{S} = \begin{pmatrix} \sqrt{\lambda_1} & 0 & \cdots & 0 & 0 \\ 0 & \sqrt{\lambda_2} & \cdots & 0 & 0 \\ 0 & 0\cdots & 0 & 0 \\ \cdots \\ 0 & 0 & \cdots & \sqrt{\lambda_{m-1}} & 0 \\ 0 & 0 & \cdots & 0 & \sqrt{\lambda_m} \\ 0 & 0 & \cdots & 0 & 0 \\ 0 & 0 & \cdots & 0 & 0 \\ \vdots & \vdots & \ddots & \vdots & \vdots \\ 0 & 0 & \cdots & 0 & 0 \end{pmatrix}$$

where

$$\sigma(\mathbf{M} \cdot \mathbf{M}^\top) = (\lambda_1, \lambda_2, \cdots, \lambda_n)$$

are the non-negative eigenvalues of $\mathbf{M} \cdot \mathbf{M}^\top$ *given in non-decreasing order, i.e.* $\lambda_i \geq \lambda_{i+1}$.

b.

$$\mathbf{U} = \begin{bmatrix} u_{11} & u_{21} & \cdots & u_{i1} & \cdots & u_{n1} \\ u_{12} & u_{22} & \cdots & u_{i2} & \cdots & u_{n2} \\ \vdots & \vdots & \ddots & \vdots & \ddots & \vdots \\ u_{1n} & u_{2n} & \cdots & u_{in} & \cdots & u_{nn} \end{bmatrix}$$

In this,

$$\mathbf{u}_i = \; < u_{i1}, u_{i2}, \ldots, u_{in} >$$

is an eigenvector of the order $n \times n$ *matrix,* $\mathbf{MM}^\top$ *from* $\mathbf{Or}(\mathbf{M} \cdot \mathbf{M}^\top)$

c.

$$\mathbf{V}^\top = \begin{bmatrix} v_{11} & v_{21} & & v_{i1} & & v_{m1} \\ v_{12} & v_{22} & \cdots & v_{i2} & \cdots & v_{m2} \\ \vdots & \vdots & \cdots & \vdots & \cdots & \vdots \\ v_{1j} & v_{2j} & \ddots & v_{ij} & \ddots & v_{mj} \\ \vdots & \vdots & \cdots & \vdots & \cdots & \vdots \\ v_{1m} & v_{2m} & & v_{im} & & v_{mm} \end{bmatrix}$$

---

[39]Notice we are a little free with the term "diagonal": $\mathbf{S}$ could fail to be a square matrix, so our notion of "diagonal" is simply that: the only non-zero elements of $\mathbf{S}$ are s_{ii} when $1 \leq i \leq m$.

And, in this case,

$$\mathbf{v}_j \;=\; <v_{1j},\; v_{2j},\; \ldots,\; v_{mj}>$$

is an eigenvector of the order $m \times m$ matrix $\mathbf{M}^\top \mathbf{M}$ from $\mathbf{Or}(\mathbf{M}^\top \mathbf{M})$.

*So the **columns** of $\mathbf{U}$ are eigenvectors respecting $\lambda_i \in \sigma(\mathbf{M}\mathbf{M}^\top)$ and the **rows** of $\mathbf{V}^\top$ similarly so with regards to $\lambda_i \in \sigma(\mathbf{M}^\top \mathbf{M})$.*

And this is all very elegant and very pretty looking at the basis from Linear Algebra concerning which sufficient thereof has been given should a reader feel inclined to embark on formally proving the properties advertized in Description 7.

We, however, are interested in how this representation is used. So let us begin by looking at one such application: image compression.

Image Compression through SVD

As has been emphasized in a number of places earlier in this volume, e.g. in looking at one use of the DFT in Section 5.8, an image whether .gif or .jpg or other convention is simply a table of values, a **matrix**. In conventions such as RGB or as applied in the example discussed earlier the YC_bC_r form, we are dealing with tables of integers.[40] We looked at the motivating reasons for image compression when we presented our earlier DFT supported method. In both that technique and the one which we are now going to consider, the thinking is to exploit the limited nature of human visual perception: we are unable to distinguish **every** single colour that could be encoded in RGB; we are responsive only to a limited range[41] of light frequencies. Thus, should we be able to determine that large amounts of the data encoding an image are dedicated to presenting redundant detail in the sense that its removal would not make much difference to how the image is perceived then some savings in space would result simply by eliminating such redundancy. The question is, however, how do we model and discover that which can be thrown away? The DFT approach did so by translating into the "frequency domain" and discarding that image information corresponding to barely seen frequencies. In the SVD based compression method, we attack the redundant data directly not through stealth.

Figure 7.4 shows an example image.[42]

---

[40]In fact integers modulo a maximum value, that is $\mathbb{Z}_{256}$.

[41]Strictly speaking one should use "spectrum" however one is conscious of the dangers of overloading this particular terminology.

[42]See Endnote 4.

Figure 7.4: Greyscale Uncompressed Image

This is a `.jpg` image having dimensions 388×504 leading to a total space in its unrestricted form of $\sim 1.5Mb$ or equivalently $\sim 0.5M$ for each separate colour channel.

Suppose we form the transpose matrix of order 504×388. Looking at the SVD representation of the order 504×388 matrices, $\mathbf{M}_C$ for each of the colours $C \in \{R,G,B\}$, we find $\mathbf{U}_C$ has order 504×504, $\mathbf{S}_C$ has order 504×388 and $\mathbf{V}_C^\top$ order 388×388. This, of course, is no reduction in the number of bytes we were using originally. In order to obtain such the method of applying SVD for the purpose of image compression begins by looking at $\mathbf{S}_C$. This we have seen has 504 rows and 388 columns: the rows s_{389} through s_{504} are all zero: in computing the product $\mathbf{U}_C \mathbf{S}_C \mathbf{V}_C^\top$ these rows of will have no influence on the outcome $\mathbf{M}_C$. If we rendered $\mathbf{S}_C$ a **square** matrix (of order 388×388) not only would this make no difference to $\mathbf{S}_C \mathbf{V}_C^\top$ other than reporting a matrix of order 388×388 rather than 504×388 it also forces a change to $\mathbf{U}_C$: we cannot multiply a matrix having order 504×504 with one having order 388×388. So in order to reconcile the difference we need to eliminate some columns of $\mathbf{U}_C$. Deciding which of these should be removed is not too difficult: the columns are eigenvectors of some λ_i and, as we move along from

CHAPTER 7. MATRICES REVISITED
440   INTRODUCTION TO SPECTRAL METHODS

column 1 an eigenvector of λ_1 through column j an eigenvector of λ_j the related eigenvalues decrease[43] Given that we must eliminate some columns from $\mathbf{U_C}$ the sensible choice would seem to be those that make the "least" contribution to recovering $\mathbf{M_C}$, i.e. those associated with the eigenvalues λ_{389} through λ_{504}.

So far these changes to $\mathbf{U_C S_C V_C^\top}$ are not resulting in a significant saving certainly not of the order to overcome the fact that a single matrix, $\mathbf{M_C}$, is being described as the product of three matrices. Where we can start, however, to look at the outcome of further compression is by looking at $\mathbf{S_C}$ now assumed to be a square matrix in more detail. We have seen that $\mathbf{S_C}$ is a diagonal matrix whose diagonal is formed by $\sqrt{\lambda_i}$ with these eigenvalues arranged in non-increasing order. Reducing $\mathbf{S_C}$ from its original order (504×388) was just a matter of discarding rows equal to $\mathbf{0}$ and while this occassioned some alteration to $\mathbf{U_C}$ this was of no great significance in changing the matrix $\mathbf{M_C}$. What if we went further and decided to discard not only the redundant row in the original form of $\mathbf{S_C}$ but also those rows and columns whose $\sqrt{\lambda_{ii}}$ was considered to be "too small" to make any difference? For every row so removed from $\mathbf{S_C}$ we would need to remove a corresponding column from $\mathbf{U_C}$ **and** a corresponding **row** from $\mathbf{V_C^\top}$ otherwise the product of the three remaining matrices will be ill-defined. Taking this concept further if we have decided that we wish to reduce the image representation to some maximum number of bytes heedless, for the moment, of its quality in order to do so we just need to determine the value, K say, such that reducing $\mathbf{S_C}$ to just its **first** K rows and K columns will give the required size: in this scheme the image of interest will still be encoded as three matrices $\mathbf{U_C}$ now, for our example image, of order $504 \times K$, $\mathbf{S_C}$ now having order $K \times K$ and $\mathbf{V_C^\top}$ of order $K \times 388$: the product of the three will result in the same[44] dimensions (504×388) as our original but now each colour channel of the image is described in $504K + K^2 + 388K$, i.e. $K^2 + 892K$ bytes as opposed to the previous $\sim 0.5M$.

In Table 7.2 the result of five alternatives to the original $K = 388$ are presented, the "size" figure being the number of bytes used in a single colour channnel. In Endnote 5, similar views of the effect on the colour original are shown.

Judgements about image quality are, of course subjective, and while some degree of noise and foxing is apparent in all of the reduced versions, it is defensible that with all save the most compressed these do not render the outcome "unusable".

---

[43]Or rather do not increase.
[44]It should be remembered we have taken the transpose of the corresponding matrices.

Table 7.2: Six shades of Grey(scale) – Image Compression through SVD

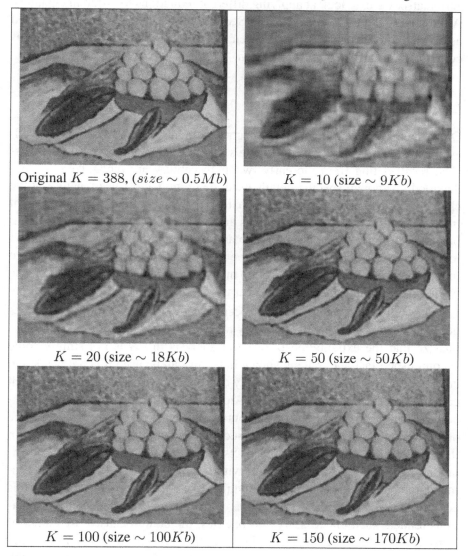

Original $K = 388$, ($size \sim 0.5Mb$)	$K = 10$ (size $\sim 9Kb$)
$K = 20$ (size $\sim 18Kb$)	$K = 50$ (size $\sim 50Kb$)
$K = 100$ (size $\sim 100Kb$)	$K = 150$ (size $\sim 170Kb$)

Summary

We have just given a very basic illustration of one application of SVD. In practical contexts one might well look at additional features. For example in the case presented the same scale has been adopted for all three colour channels, however in some images e.g. where the R channel is very near to the zero matrix we may look at applying different reductions to different channels. Alternatively the method outlined in Section 5.8 whereby an image is treated as divided into disparate blocks chosen to exploit large areas of homogenous colour can produce better compression.

Computational Argument

Our two preceding applications of spectral methods in CS are, now, quite well-established: the mechanics of Google's search engine and its basis in a classical result dating from the early twentieth century are recognized and understood. Although specific details exact damping factors used, nature of the choice vector remain commercially guarded that spectral methods give insight into the nature of ranking problems is an accepted fact. Similarly the decomposition of matrix forms through SVD and its use in allowing "redundant" or, more accurately, unimportant data to be ignored provides a strong approach to image compression and also leads into many analytic techniques of importance within Data Science and Machine Learning.

The application we consider of spectral methods that we now review does not have such established history. My main reason for presenting it is to emphasize that the exploitation of spectral analysis in CS is not simply some accomplished fact and, having shown how this can be used it is not needed to consider further. Spectral methodology continues to find fresh arenas in which computational problems are tackled. Alongside the traditional domains of machine learning, image analysis, computational game theory and data science new worlds to conquer emerge. One such is that subfield of AI specifically in its reasoning and representation aspects known as Computational Argumentation. In particular that specialism within this field dubbed Abstract Argumentation. Space does not permit anything like a thorough description of this activity. In any event the large number of recent and detailed such presentations renders such unnecessary. So one has, the comprehensive treatment of Baroni *et al.* [19] consisting of specialist contributions from every currently active leading researcher; a similar edited collection of Rahwan & Simari [192], and less wide-ranging but tightly focused presentations such as Besnard & Hunter [27]. Apart from dedicated research level texts a number of detailed expositions have appeared given as introductions to specialized issues of general research journals. In this context one of the most cited and used is that of Bench-Capon and Dunne [25] for a seminal special volume of the leading AI journal.

Argumentation in general and computational argument in particular continues to thrive and grow as a highly active research theme within AI and, consequently, CS as a whole. For the benefit of readers who may be unfamiliar with its activities, let us begin by summarizing very informally just what the field of argumentation concerns. In this regard there are worse choices than to quote from [25]:

"the study of argumentation may, informally, be considered as concerned with how assertions are proposed, discussed, and resolved in the context of issues upon which several diverging opinions may be held." [25, p. 619]

So in essence we have conflict and disagreement, we have proof that a viewpoint is justified not solely in the narrow "mathematical" sense of proof as a reasoned conclusion following accepted deductive processes but also in the sense of, for example, "proof" as interpreted in legal domains e.g. with respect to divers standards such as "beyond reasonable doubt" or "on the balance of probabilities" or again in the sense of "a proof is 'correct' if it achieves the ends sought". In this final instance "the ends sought" can range from "purchase a particular brand" to "vote for a particular policy or political party". So proof becomes more than an abstract, cold consideration and weighting of factual data: it turns upon all manner of "non-mathematical", emotive and irrational prejudices. This idea of "argument" provides yet another demonstration of the interconnected mendacity of politics and advertizing. Before computational argument became formalized as an academic discipline a number of classical texts had begun to chip away at the smug dishonesty of these practices. We do not have room to present a full account of these, but of landmark importance are Toulmin [235] (originally published 1958) with its formal model of argument structure via a "labelled **graph** structure"; Packard and Miller's exposé of unscrupulous techniques in advertizing [180] and, of course, Perelman's defence of argument as something more than simply "mathematical logic" [183]. Even before this, Greek scholars, pre-eminent among whom was Aristotle (ca. 384–322 BC), had considered and analyzed the forms, nature and rationales underpinning argument.[45]

The sheer mass of differing concerns, aspects and methods creates enormous problems if we wish to bring computational techniques into to play. We must simplify, abstract and strip away the accumulated coats of irrelevant[46] and redundant gloss: the divers Logics – classical and non-classical –; the

---

[45] Understanding of such among contemporary audiences was sufficiently strong that the comic playwright Aristophanes, (ca. 446–386, BC) could satirize Socratic method as dedicated to "proof via Inferior Arguments" ($N\epsilon\varphi\epsilon\lambda\alpha\iota$, *The Clouds*, orig. 423 BC).

[46] Irrelevant that is with respect to the immediate issue of **modelling** argument.

gamut of debate rules and procedures; the taxonomy of aims. In this respect, the achievement of groundbreaking importance is the abstract argumentation model discovered and presented by Phan Minh Dung [66]. The significance of this article has been recognized by the AI community in it being awarded the prestigious IJCAI Classic Paper award (2018). One can do no better than to reproduce the words of the award citation.

"This is the seminal paper on argumentation theory that laid the foundations for almost all subsequent work in the area. This rich and elegant argumentation framework is developed from a few simple abstract primitives and is used to establish a crisp and meaningful relation between argumentation and theories of non-monotonic reasoning, logic programming, social choice, and cooperative games."

In brief: argumentation can be described as a **graph** structure. And if it can be described as a graph, then it can be analyzed using graph-theoretic technology. And, as we have described in this Chapter, one such technology is **Spectral Analysis**.

First, let us look at Dung's abstract model of argument itself.

Description 8. *(from [66]) We use $\mathcal{X}$ to denote a* finite *set of arguments with $\mathcal{A} \subseteq \mathcal{X} \times \mathcal{X}$ the so-called* attack *relationship over these. An* argumentation framework *(AF) is a pair $\mathcal{H} = <\mathcal{X}, \mathcal{A}>$. A pair $< x, y > \in \mathcal{A}$ is referred to as 'y is attacked by x' or 'x attacks y'. Using S to denote an arbitrary subset of arguments for $S \subseteq \mathcal{X}$,*

$$
\begin{aligned}
S^- &=_{\text{def}} \{\, p \,:\, \exists\, q \in S \text{ such that } < p, q > \in \mathcal{A} \} \\
S^+ &=_{\text{def}} \{\, p \,:\, \exists\, q \in S \text{ such that } < q, p > \in \mathcal{A} \}
\end{aligned}
$$

Here we have the idea of "argument" reduced to its absolute minimum. We are not concerned with the internal viscera of argument **structure**, such as minutiae as premises, deductive rules, conclusions and so on. We **are** very much concerned with a far more important matter: how two arguments **relate** to one another. One argument $p \in \mathcal{X}$ may be "incompatible" with another $q \in \mathcal{X}$ so that a belief in the validity of p cannot be held "rationally" and simultaneously with a belief in the validity of q. There are two high-level reasons why this may be so: the matter proposed by p may **attack** that proposed by q; or the reverse could be the case. In the substance of Description 8 we have the whole process of argument and its interactivity described through a directed graph structure.

As a concrete instance we might have the very simple framework of Figure 7.5.

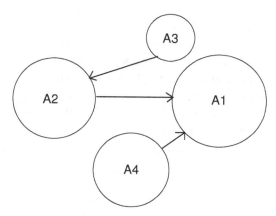

Figure 7.5: A very basic Argument Framework

In the structure depicted in Figure 7.5 we have four separate arguments. We are uninterested for the moment in **what** the claims represented by these actually are. All that we are concerned with is the **relationship** between these four. There are four arguments and three links: $A1$ and $A4$ are "incompatible" since the matter of $A4$ **attacks** that of $A1$. In the same way $A2$ and $A1$ and, also, $A3$ and $A2$ are incompatible since the former in each case attacks the latter. Notice we make no statement about what one may call "rationality of belief" in any one of these. Various concepts of what could be understood by "consistent collection of beliefs" were proposed in Dung's paper: so-called *argumentation semantics*. There is no consensus as regards what constitutes the "best" semantics. There would, after much debate, finally appear to be general agreement in the reality of there being no "one true argumentation semantics". If we take one widely accepted starting point for "consistent collection of arguments" the view of Figure 7.5 would give, under this, the set $\{A3, A4\}$. Or, alternatively, that the arguments $A2$ and $A1$ **cannot** be defended: $A4$ directly attacks $A1$ and we have in the framework no basis as yet for rejecting $A4$. In much the same way, $A3$ directly attacks $A2$ and, again, we have in this framework no rational basis for disputing $A3$. Suppose, however, we knew not of the argument $A4$? Then the form of Figure 7.5 would be reduced to just the three arguments $\{A1, A2, A3\}$, no longer would $A1$ be attacked by $A4$ since neither $A4$ nor its outgoing link would be present.

In this environment **exactly the same semantics** by which we concluded only subsets of $\{A3, A4\}$ were defensible would tell us that the only defensible positions are $\{\{\emptyset\}, \{A3\}, \{A1, A3\}\}$. We can accept nothing at all ($\{\emptyset\}$); we can defend $A3$ alone or we can accept **both** $A3$ and $A1$. Notice if we wish to propose a case for $A1$ we must rebut **all** attacks on $A1$ within this specific semantics. Much of the power of Dung's formalism arises through its provision for developing in a clear manner the ramifications of this interplay of "attack" and "reinstatement". We do not have space to elaborate in great detail upon this point, and refer the interested reader to any of the collections we mentioned earlier particularly Parts 1 and 2 of Baroni *et al.* [19] or Bench-Capon and Dunne [25, pp. 626–628].

We might instantiate the abstraction of Figure 7.5 as Figure 7.6.

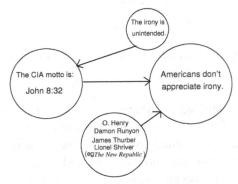

Figure 7.6: Possible instantiation of the framework in Figure 7.5

Here our argument $A1$ is an oft-expressed lazy opinion common to British alternative comedians[47] regarding appreciation of U.S. audiences. In attacking this claim one might put forward $A2$: for when an intelligence agency one of whose primary aims is the protection of secrecy adopts as an (unofficial) motto the text "For ye shall know the truth and the truth shall set you free" this must be with humourous and ironic intent.[48] This attack on $A1$ one might attempt to rebut with the claim expressed in $A3$: "whoever chose this motto was unaware of what they were doing". Now if one wishes to find a case for rejecting $A1$ one has two options: advance an argument that attacks $A3$ or advance a fresh attack on $A1$. In the scheme of Figure 7.6 the latter option is chosen.[49]

---

[47]Listening to the worst of these, legal niceties in the U.K. preventing names being named, one often has the impression that the "alternative" in "alternative comedy" is the radical innovation that "comedy" should be totally devoid of any humorous content.

[48]The official motto of this agency is the somewhat dreary slogan "The Work of a Nation. The Center of Intelligence".

[49]It is not difficult to construct an attacking argument on $A3$: it is unlikely that Allen Dulles the Director responsible for this being adopted was unaware of its connotations, c.f. www.cia.gov/about-cia/headquarters-tour/headquarters-photo-tour/.

The use of spectral methodology to analyze, as they are termed, abstract argumentation frameworks, is an approach as yet in its infancy, Nonetheless, here is one such application from [71]. The considerations addressed there are with regard to the manner in which individuals promote their own case even to the extent of this interfering with the right of others to promote their own viewpoint.

Consider a debating arena in which numerous different and conflicting opinions are being championed by several protagonists. There are a number of tactics sometimes adopted by participants that are not intended to progress their stance through rational discourse, but rather since those using such means, mistakenly and naïvely believe them to make their point of view more compelling. Thus one finds, for example in playground or nursery debate, techniques such as wearisome repetition of the same point over and over, this sometimes reduced to single word utterances. Repetition as an indicator of logically "weak" argument, has, of course, long been recognized and studied as one class of fallacious reasoning: e.g. the consequences of *eo ipse* moves in the dialogue protocol of Vreeswijk and Prakken [248], the review of "stone-walling" and other non-cooperative tactics from Gabbay and Woods [95, 94]. More generally, strategies whose aim is not to advance but rather to stifle or impede discussion underlie several studies, e.g. Dunne [69, 70], Sakama [202], Budzynska and Reed [37].

Participants contributing within supposedly more mature contexts will usually recognize the futility of constant repetition as an argumentative tool. To compensate, however, and often not consciously aware that such measures are being used they may have recourse to another technique: that of increasing the force with which their points are delivered. Thus in non-structured debates this will often take the form of increasing vocal volume in an attempt to drown out the arguments of opponents, so rendering them inaudible to neutral observers. This, in turn, may lead to those same opponents adopting identical tactics reiterating their stance at louder and louder volumes. To counteract the deleterious effect on reasoned debate that results from discussions sinking to the level of shambolic shouting contests, in many legislative assemblies a neutral member is recognized as having – among other responsibilities – some authority to intervene and impose a semblance of order. For example, in the U.K. House of Commons, the rôle of Speaker fulfils this function.[50]

Nevertheless, despite the presence of a mediator to oversee the conduct of discussions, it can happen particularly on sensitive issues that their authority

---

[50]In the UK, the Speaker although having represented one of the major parties as a member of parliament, on assuming this office, is non-partisan.

is ignored.[51] Given that, even within structured settings with a recognized moderator, there is the potential for debate to descend to acrimonious discord, the likelihood of *un-mediated* exchanges degenerating to similar levels is so much the greater.

Suppose we introduce a means of measuring how much "noise" a participant is making: a **volubility** function.

A *debate arena*, $\mathcal{D}$, is formed by a triple $< \mathcal{X}, \mathcal{A}, \nu >$ where $< \mathcal{X}, \mathcal{A} >$ is an AF and $\nu : \mathcal{A} \to \mathbb{R}^+$ is the *debate volubility* function, associating with each $< x, y > \in \mathcal{A}$ a *positive* Real value. The debate volubility function is viewed as describing the force with which its *promoter*, $\pi(< x, y >)$, asserts the argument to its **antagonist**, $\alpha(< x, y >)$. The scenarios of interest involve an aspect which the quantitive formulation of debate arena fails to describe: its treatment of volubility is **static**.

In practice, given the context modelled, one would expect the level at which a promoter directs the attack on an antagonist to vary. Such variation need not necessarily be a monotonic increase in $\nu(< x, y >)$: one instance of such is the often used rhetorical device of reducing the level at which a point is made for emphasis.[52]

In total,

we have n participants - $\mathcal{X} = \{x_1, x_2, \ldots, x_n\}$

an argument promoted by x_i may be opposed by that advanced by x_j.

$\mathcal{A}$ will be the set of all such opposition.

each attack $< x_j, x_i >$ has a **noise level** $\nu(< x_j, x_i >) \in \mathbb{R}^+$.

Overall $(< \mathcal{X}, \mathcal{A} >, \nu : \mathcal{A} \to \mathbb{R}^+)$ is a **weighted** graph.

The question of interest is, if the debate described by $(< \mathcal{X}, \mathcal{A} >, \nu)$ has an (external) moderator, M: how may M determine if $(< \mathcal{X}, \mathcal{A} >, \nu)$ is unstable by reason of $\nu(< x_i, x_j >)$ being overloud?

---

[51]Among many such examples in the UK, is the incident of the senior Conservative MP, Michael Heseltine, seizing and waving the symbolic mace at Labour members singing the *Red Flag* in the aftermath of a heated 1976 debate on state ownership (nationalization): the Speaker was forced to suspend the sitting.

[52]For example notice: the contrasting questioning styles in Maximilian Schell's cross-examination of Montgomery Clift and the underspoken manner in which its final observation is delivered (*Judgement at Nuremberg*, Kramer, 1961); the unvarying level of Olivier's repetition of the question "Is it safe?" with finality indicated by only a slight drop in tone. (*Marathon Man*, Schlesinger, 1976).

Each individual participant, P_i promoting the argument x_i will have a maximum level of noise, μ_i, they are prepared to tolerate.

Spectral methods to check instability

We have, as yet, not seen a link to spectral properties.

Let us define the "amount of shouting" participant P_i is doing to be some positive Real value s_i. The amount of interference P_i has from P_j (denoted F_{ij}) is $\nu(< x_j, x_i >)$ if x_j attacks x_i otherwise $F_{ij} = 0$.

The debate is unstable if **at least one** P_i has to suffer an amount of interference which exceeds the tolerance μ_i. In order words, stability requires

$$\left(\frac{s_i}{\sum_{j \neq i} F_{ij} s_j} \right) \leq \mu_i \text{ for each } 1 \leq i \leq n$$

That is to say, each participant (P_i) can make a given amount of noise (s_i) but should this be "too much in excess" of a weighted sum of the noise directed by other participants (P_j) **against it** $(F_{ij} s_j)$ as measured by the ratio stated then the situation has become unstable.

Overall, using the values P_i and the structure F_{ij} the moderator is faced with the task of deciding if "debate has got out of control". In addressing this we can introduce two further and final matrices.

$$\mathbf{F}_{ij} = \begin{cases} 0 & \text{if } i = j \\ F_{ij} & \text{otherwise} \end{cases} \quad ; \quad \mathbf{C}_{ij} = \begin{cases} \mu_i & \text{if } i = j \\ 0 & \text{otherwise} \end{cases}$$

In addition write $\mathbf{s} = < s_1, s_2, \ldots, s_n >$ and $\mathbf{B} = \mathbf{C} \times \mathbf{F}$. With these, we are now able to express conditions to be met in order for stability to be maintained.

The debate defined by the argument graph $< \mathcal{X}, \mathcal{A}, \nu >$ is stable for the tolerance levels $\mu = < \mu_1, \mu_2, \ldots, \mu_n >$ if $\mathbf{Bs}^\top \geq \mathbf{s}^\top$

In other words if $\mathbf{s}$ is an eigenvector of $\mathbf{B}$ for some eigenvalue $\lambda \geq 1$ of $\mathbf{B}$.

Conditions that guarantee "good behaviour"

Whether the current level of noise as given by the values of $\nu(x_i, x_j)$ is seen as reasonable with respect to the advertized tolerances μ_i of participants is dependant on the matrices $\mathbf{C}$ and $\mathbf{F}$ from which $\mathbf{B} = \mathbf{CF}$ arises. Using the Perron-Frobenius Theorem, that is to say, the combination of Property 15 and Property 17 we find a sufficient condition for $(< \mathcal{X}, \mathcal{A}, \nu >, \mu)$ to be stable.

Namely,

Moderation Condition I

If $\mathbf{B} = \mathbf{CF}$ is irreducible and $\lambda^{\mathbf{B}}_{pf} \geq 1$ then $\mathbf{s}$ can be set as $\mathbf{v}/\|\mathbf{v}\|$ for any eigenvector $\mathbf{v}$ of $\mathbf{B}$ with $\lambda^{\mathbf{B}}_{pf}$

Moderation Condition II

If the amount of noise from P_i i.e. s_i is defined as the sum over $\nu(< x_i, x_j >)$ then

M1. $s_i = \sum_{j \neq i} F_{ji}$

M2. The debate $(\mathcal{X}, \mathcal{A}, \nu)$ is stable for $< \mu_1, \ldots, \mu_n >$ if $\lambda \geq 1$ is an eigenvalue of $\mathbf{CF}$ and $\mathbf{F}^{\top}\mathbf{1}^{\top}$ an eigenvector of $\mathbf{CF}$ for λ.

Summary – Spectral methods and Argument

As we mentioned at the opening of this part, use of spectral analysis as a tool in studying argumentation is a quite recent innovation. In focussing on one particular aspect – that of determining whether a debate has become out of control – we have looked at only a fraction of potential work. Much current work in computational argument had considered the idea of separating the weak from the strong, of deciding an **ordering** of argument power, e.g. Bonzon *et al.* [30], Amgoud and Ben-Naim [9]. The notion of "strong" and "weak" are already implicit in the recognition that different participants in a debate may bring different orderings of which ethical and moral values they rate highly, see e.g. Bench-Capon *et al.* [24]. In total we have a rich source of possible future development. All from the fundamental insight, promoted in Dung's work [66]: an argumentation process is a directed graph.

7.7 Summary – Matrix and Spectral Methods in CS

Matrix methods and such operations as inspecting the determinant of a matrix with the aim of computing its inverse underpin many important computational activities. We have seen that this concept of "determinant" has several different but equivalent formulations: as the outcome of a recursive process, a sum of alternating in sign permutations, as the eventual result of a structured processing of the rows and columns of a matrix. A key significance is, however, the relationship between this idea of determinant and that of eigenvalue. In eigenvalues through the concept of the characteristic polynomial once again we see a basic computational form and a suite of operations on that form: polynomial structures and their roots.

In the use of spectral methods we light upon a range of techniques of enormous importance to Computer Science: in dealing with problems of ranking and ordering which we illustrated through a cursory examination of Google's approach; in image and more generally data analysis through the information provided by particular matrix decompositions. We have suggested, without elaboration, a broad range of active fields wherein spectral techniques are used: machine learning, computational game theory, and data science. From the powerful approaches that are brought to solving computational problems in these fields, it should be clearly apparent that an awareness of this technology is crucial to modern Computer Science.

7.8 Projects

1. Many programming formalisms such as MATLAB, PYTHON, and through the JAMA package, JAVA, provide as basic methods features to compute matrix determinants, inverses, and spectral aspects. Using such explore the effectiveness of SVD as an image reduction approach. Among other aspects of interest in this regard may be gleaning further image information to combine with the SVD form; assuming encoding schemes other than RGB, etc.

2. There is an implicit assumption of strong-connectivity in the argument graph modelling of unstable debate. It is often the case that the argument graphs in practice fail to satisfy such single component assumptions. Baroni *et al.* [20] examine approaches to processing argumentation frameworks in terms of their strongly-connected component representation. To what extent do these techniques aid in this specific application of spectral methods? If the dangling page solution were adopted what might the consequences for debate moderation be?

7.9 Endnotes

1. *"such devices may all be treated as **matrices**"*: Regarding viewing a "multiplication table" as applying a matrix operation, it suffices to take the following approach. Suppose one wishes to have a table describing multiplication by any Natural number, p between 1 and some maximum N. Form the $N \times N$ matrix, $\mathbf{M} = [m_{ij}]$ in which $m_{ij} = i \cdot j$. In order to look up the result of multiplying p and q simply form the vector-matrix-vector product $\mathbf{e}_p \mathbf{M} \mathbf{e}_q^\top$, recalling that $\mathbf{e}_k$ is the *standard basis N-vector* from $\mathbb{Z}^N$ described in Section 3.3 and defined as

$$\mathbf{e}_k \quad = \quad < \underbrace{0,\ 0,\ \ldots,\ 0}_{k-1 \text{ times}},\ 1,\ \underbrace{0,\ 0,\ \ldots,\ 0}_{n-k \text{ times}} >$$

Thus, $\mathbf{e}_p \mathbf{M}$ selects row $\mathbf{M}_p$ an order $1 \times N$ matrix whose product with the order $N \times 1$ matrix described by $\mathbf{e}_q^\top$ i.e. the dot product $(\mathbf{e}_p \mathbf{M}) \cdot \mathbf{e}_q$ is the scalar pq.

2. *"A university ... of light, of liberty, and of learning"*: The great Victorian statesman and last, truly distinguished peace time, Conservative Prime Minister, Benjamin Disraeli (1804–1881) speaking in the U.K. House of Commons respecting the 1872 Universities Act. The matter of this legislation is obscure and of no great importance. Disraeli's sentiments, on the other hand, were probably the last occasion on which a Conservative leader indicated the faintest understanding of the idea of a university. His successors have, piece by piece, expunged each of Disraeli's expressed desiderata from universities descending to the nadir of the present wherein Learning is considered to be a dispensable luxury. The scale of political interference in U.K. university processes has been bad enough but has been exacerbated by the gutless incompetence of those supposedly leading – from the deceased and unlamented spectacle of the CVCP through to the latter day and equally supine UUK.[53] Too engaged in infantile name-calling and oneupmanship truly to represent the interests of those they are supposed to serve, not a single item of political meddling from student fees, through to the playground games of "mine's bigger than yours" represented by "league tables" and "assessment regimes" to the racist persecution of those who choose to study in

---

[53] CVCP≡"Committee of Vice-Chancellors and Principals"; UUK≡"Universities U.K.". As commented earlier (fn. 20, Chap. 6) despite "luminaries" from this outfit (CVCP) being apprehended when found crawling around the red-light district of an inner city, "vice" continues to mean "in place of". There is, at any rate, little danger of confusing "Principal" with "Principle".

the UK in preference to alternative venues, has been opposed in word (other than token whimpering) or deed.[54] All is cravenly indulged and the response to the latest stupidity to start unfurling the white flag before the ink is dry on a Green Paper and to acclaim every fresh betrayal of "Light, of Liberty, and of Learning" with shouts of approbation: *"Fiat, Fiat, Fiat; claudere libro!"*.

3. *"I am much afraid ... the great gates of hell"*: The reformer, Martin Luther (1483–1546), lamenting the tendency of the great European universities of his time (The Sorbonne, Heidelberg, Padua, Marburg etc) in making insufficient efforts to preach the word of God (as Luther saw it). In much the same way, contemporary politicians blare that present-day Universities do too little in preaching the word of Mammon.

4. This still-life is in a private collection and the author has full permission from both owner and artist to depict it in this volume.

5. For completeness Table 7.3 shows the outcome of applying SVD to the colour original image. It should be noted that since we still use the RGB convention there is no additional saving resulting from greyscale: the same three colour channels are used. What is apparent, however, is the increased distortion in image quality comparing the greyscale images with colour.

---

[54]This is not, strictly, true, the sound of bleating and whining occasioned by government suggestions that steps should be taken to rein in the untrammeled greed of vice-chancellors still echoes: when commentators from opposite sides of the political spectrum remark on the obscene levels of vice-cancellarian pay (Mount [171], Liddle [155]), it is clear that this has reached unacceptable levels of avarice and contempt.

Table 7.3: Six shades of Colour – Image Compression through SVD

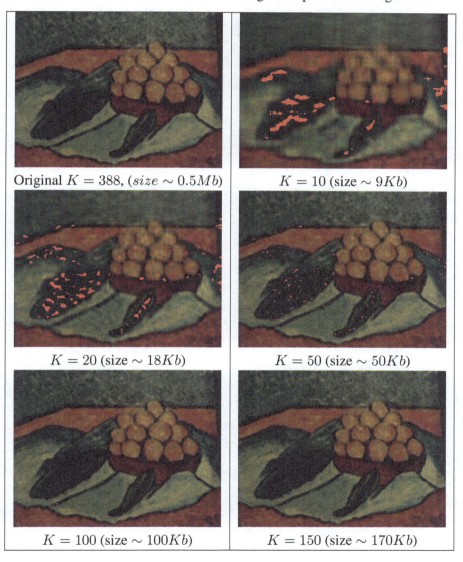

Chapter 8

Epilogue

Hier hinein? ... Man sieht den Weg nicht

Erwartung
MARIE PAPPENHEIM (libretto for Schönberg's monodrama)

8.1   Introductory Remarks

Emerging into the bright afternoon sunlight from the National Library of Dublin, Stephen Dedalus reflects on the effects, both personal and external, of the discourse which has occupied the previous hour of his time: "What have I learned? Of them? Of me?".[1]

It is, as with so much in *Ulysses*, an apparently casual thought but one which on deeper study reveals a wealth of meaning and insight. It is also, I think, an appropriate consideration for the author of any textbook or presenter of any course. The stereotypical "conclusion of taught module" question is, of course, "What have *they* learned?": "they" being the audience to whom content was addressed. This is the question asked implicitly in the current[2] obsessive packaging of all that is offered within the realms of degree level study into neat little bundles tagged "Learning Outcomes", "Transferrable Key Skills", "Aims and Objectives" or whatever pretentious management-speak gobblede-gook happens to be in vogue.   But in its very arrogance and presumption,

---

[1] James Joyce, *Ulysses*, Chapter 9 (Scylla and Charybdis).

[2] These observations refer to the UK system rather than the US which, to the best of my knowledge, has managed to avoid and resist such a pathetically inadequate "a place for every-thing and everything in its place" view of the idea of a university.

qualities not unknown among the Arakcheevshchina of the Gradgrinds and Morlocks considered fit to determine the directions of learning and scholarship, "What have *they* learned?" is the wrong question: at least as a primary concern (and, indeed, arguably even as a secondary or tertiary one).

Why so? Let us look at the subtext of "What have I learned?" in more depth. Its substantive import is that "*I*" am not omniscient: there may be lacunae which one only becomes aware of in the heat of delivery; there may be methods used in the course of presentation that *might* not have been as successful as envisaged when designed. It is such introspection, scrutiny and concomitant discovery that determine the nature of potential improvement. So much then for "What have I learned?", however Dedalus' musings raise two further related questions:[3] With this "Of them?" concerns one's perception of how the audience has reacted, and this is again a matter of introspection: was the inclusion of some topics too difficult (or too easy)? Finally with "Of me?" we return again to the need constantly to review and revise material, context, and delivery.

In this final Chapter, my main concern will be considering the content and topics presented earlier with respect to what is brought to Computer Science. Some of these are long-established tools applied in Computational settings e.g. the use of Differential Calculus in treating Optimization problems; others are more recent innovations e.g. the approaches to Algorithmic Composition based on properties of iterated functions over the Complex numbers. All, however, are, in my view, relevant and central to the study of Computer Science.

8.2 Significance and Prospects

We have over the six principal technical chapters of this volume considered the following topics.

T1. Number: its importance, representation, and evolution.

T2. Elementary properties of vectors and modelling of graphical processes by matrices.

T3. The nature and importance of Calculus in CS.

---

[3]There is a reading of these eight words as two rather than three questions, the final two merely qualifying and elaborating the first. Given the structure into three sentences rather than using a colon as separator between the introduction and following questions, I think there is also a defensible reading of this extract as three separate questions albeit with the final two linked to the first.

T4. The genesis and application of Complex Numbers to CS.

T5. Statistics, Data Analysis and the view of CS as an experimental discipline.

T6. General matrix properties with a particular emphasis on spectral methods.

The reader may have noted that as we have progressed space devoted to each topic has steadily increased culminating in the final technical chapter wherein applications of spectral methods in CS has had almost as many pages dedicated to its exegesis as our opening description of Number and its importance. This structure is no accident.[4]

The rationale for such an approach is, I hope, easily seen: partly it is occasioned as, for example in the case of Calculus and Complex Analysis by dint of the historical origins being of such importance that to launch immediately into technical exposition would be, in my view, to diminish their significance to an insultingly low level redolent of an action of intellectual dishonesty.

I have consistently for many years attempted to stress historical importance when presenting these subjects to undergraduate students. What we work with did not "just happen", let alone "just happen on the eve of the lectures in question", let alone "just happen for the sake of filling up a syllabus and imparting sufficient thereof to pass an exam". Much of what may seem, from the recent nature of its application, to be radically modern and innovative has, more often than not, been built on centuries (even millenia) of intellectual endeavour. We forget such efforts from the past at our peril: to ignore the past is not only to ignore the evolution of that which has survived but it is also to ignore the false steps and why they turned out to be so of those approaches long since discredited and discarded. To so forget is to risk repetition and hence discussion and presentation of technically sophisticated concepts cannot solely expound on success as if the point we have reached today were achieved effortlessly: we must mention the wrong directions, not with the aim of sneering at failures but with the object of respecting and acclaiming the honesty of facing challenge.

If I am to be completely candid there are many students possibly/probably even a majority who understand this conceit and respond positively to its recognition. There are, regrettably, still a sizable number who are only appreciative of the "straightforward bash on the nut" school of pedagogical method.

---

[4]Neither, I hasten to point out, is it especially original, Joyce using much the same device in his great works, reverting (in the single chapter *Ricorso* forming Part IV of *Finnegans Wake* and the free flowing soliloquy of *Penelope* concluding *Ulysses*) to rather more terse, in comparison with their predecessor chapters, finales.

I continue to present, however, as I feel appropriate: *"Hier stehe ich und kann nicht anders"*.[5]

Historical genesis and importance is one rationale, the fact that those technologies described require, in my view, an awareness of the whys and wherefores of their origin: these are essential accoutrements of any genuine Computer Scientist. It is not enough to know **what** is involved within a particular field, one has, also, to understand **why** things are as they (currently) are.

In summary my purpose in this conclusion is to attempt to offer, in some small regard, such potential directions of interest reviewing what we have seen in each technical chapter and highlighting issues that remain open and of some interest to the community of researchers in CS.

Numbers & Polynomials

We have, repeatedly, emphasized a view that the fundamental computational question is that of **measurement**. From this basis spring two central concepts: the class of entities which are manipulated i.e. the objects with which we express measures, from number types through to complex structural forms such as matrices and beyond. The second is that suite of operations which we use to **perform** such manipulations.

Here, immediately, we find three key notions pervading modern CS.

C1. Symbolic manipulation of expressions.

C2. Efficient algorithmic implementation of computational process.

C3. Classical numerical methods, analysis and approximation techniques.

Now the first of these is the aim of many of the polynomial processing methods we discussed in Section 2.4. In reporting, say the outcome of dividing a polynomial $s(x)$ by another $t(x)$ expressing the outcome as quotient, $q(x)$ and remainder, $r(x)$, i.e $s(x) = t(x) \cdot q(x) + r(x)$ we are less concerned with direct **physical evaluation** of the outcome itself, but very much concerned with the symbolic aspects, i.e. what are the coefficients of x^k in the respective quotient and remainder terms. At its deepest level such problems as "find the coefficients of" rather than "evaluate" lead to the many and varied concerns of the specialist discipline of Computer Algebra, ably presented in the standard text of von Zur Gathen and Gerhard [246]. In addressing the issues raised by

---

[5]Luther's defence of his position on Church Reformation: "Here I stand and can do none other."

symbolic manipulation, however, we also meet deep and historical problems from Logic and the intensely researched arena of automated theorem proving. Overall what may seem like a relatively straightforward activity has an intimate relationship with many trends in modern CS: Computer Algebra and Automated Theorem Proving being just two of these.

With respect to the second point, the CS specialism of Computational Complexity Theory is concerned with precisely such matters. While implementation of arithmetic processes is, of course, one issue this is but one subtopic. We have outlined in Section 5.8 when discussing the Discrete Fourier Transform how one particular problem, that of how to multiply two n-bit integers, gave rise to one exploratory method eventually reconciled by the discoveries of Schönhage and Strassen [207]. There are other areas, of a numerical taint, where a similar "how can I improve the 'obvious' means" issue, after some initial success, remains short of a definitive resolution. So we find the process of computing the product of two order $n \times n$ matrices after examining the initial "straightforward" divide-and-conquer technique: split each matrix into four quadrants and express the outcome of multiplying $n \times n$ matrices as that of a high-level 2×2 matrix multiplication leading to a process requiring n^3 operations. Then, Volker Strassen in [228] – a work of similar watershed importance as that in which Karatsuba's discoveries were presented ([138]) – demonstrated that the eight recursive calls to compute each $n/2 \times n/2$ product were not all needed: the same process could be achieved by seven leading to an algorithm requiring $n^{2.81}$ steps. At present, matrix multiplication is, however, still in the throes of constant shaving. I am unable to recall what the current record stands at and how many infinitesimally small points have been saved: these are important, in my view, only as stepping stones to something more final and more definite whose discovery is still awaited.

Efficient algorithms and complexity analysis, is as is well attested to by the sheer volume of textbooks covering everything from introductory levels through the most recent specialized directions, continues to be a thriving and important specialist field of CS.[6]

So we have computer algebra; we have computational complexity and theory of efficient algorithms, all extending and building on the basis provided by the fundamental idea of number and one very basic elaboration of this, that of polynomial forms.

The final class of studies, raised under C3 was of incalculable importance

---

[6]I have mentioned some of the former earlier, e.g. [51], however to give a basic idea of the breadth of the latter domain one has topics such as Parameterized Algorithms [65, 89]; Randomized Methods [170]; Parallel Algorithms, e.g. Gibbons & Rytter [102] etc etc.

in the development of CS. We mentioned earlier, in Section 4.6 the importance of numerical methods in one application of Calculus, that of unearthing the roots of a given function. In contrast to the symbolic concerns within (C1), under (C3) our sole interest is in evaluation.[7] With numerical techniques we wish to **compute** a result: the root of a function; the area spanned by a curve; a confidence level within some probability function; an eigenvalue and vector etc. Often, as we have seen, there is little prospect of doing so with 100% accuracy: the real world is irrational and those quantities we wish to compute are, in the main, inexpressible as a ratio of two Natural numbers. And thus we must **approximate**, we must find a value as close as possible to the true value. In this concept of "approximation" a whole gamut of possibilities arise: convergence of methods used as we have seen in the Power Method for determining a dominant eigenvector; the amount of error in the sense of a numerical difference between what we wish to find – but can never **know** – and what we have found so far. Numerical analysis and its attendant related studies continue to be pursued in depth. I do not think it is an overstatement to observe that CS, as a discipline, owes an enormous debt to Numerical Analysis both in terms of its origin cf. [253, 256, 257] and for its successes.

Vectors, Matrices and Graphics

The nature of vector and matrix processes we reviewed as a direction by which some concept of order and structure could be imposed. In terms of applications issues partly as a consequence of limiting matrices in this chapter to small – 2×2 and 3×3 – instances, the principal interest has been with respect to those fields of CS in which arise modelling of motion in 2 or 3 dimensional space. Chief among these are graphics especially "basic" games and primitive instructions respecting robot movement. In the latter instance, there are of course many additional factors: exploiting sensory data so that obstacles may be detected and avoided; planning and responding to changes independently of human intervention and control. There is, however, at the core of these more sophisticated concerns a basic modelling process in terms of matrices and matrix vector products. Such matters as responsiveness, planning and interpretation underpin many aspects of the theory of autonomous agent systems, see e.g. Wooldridge [259], So, for example, one has models such as "partially observable Markov decision processes" (POMDP) which are prescribed in terms of systems capturing changes of state and, one of whose standard representations, is via a matrix form. Much in the same way that we treated matrix-vector

---

[7]This, of course, does not preclude methods as a legitimate study within such concerns.

product as implementing a change encoded by the matrix to be applied to an existing state e.g the vector which might describe a coordinate, so too the concept of Markov process reflects changes in observation and state data again held in the form of a vector by applying a specific matrix.

The theory of autonomous agents is a comparatively recent innovation.[8] Long before this was mooted, however, basic matrix and vector manipulation had played an important rôle in recognizing the potential importance of computational methods. So much as the Indo-Arabic decimal representation system rendered the skills of Roman numeral magicians redundant as discussed in the opening of Chapter 2, so too the use of even very basic and, by contemporary standards, primitive vector graphics displays[9] was making the subject of "technical drawing" whereby highly-skilled and painstaking technicians could draft and copy templates such as architectural blueprints, exact specifications of machine components etc. obsolete. Increasingly sophisticated Computer-Aided Design packages and displays had two consequences: an increased tolerance of drafting errors (a mistake in transcription using a computer display can be easily corrected; a similar mistake in a technical drawing context could mean having to restart everything); secondly richer design visualizations become possible: one can actually **see** the effect on a surface mesh of some distortion; one can rotate the object being created through three dimensions. These are impossible in a static hard-copy environment and these are a result of applying the already known relationship between models in 2 and 3 dimensions with matrix and vector processes to an **implementation** in computational environments.

Calculus & Computer Science

Chapter 4 offered a very superficial overview of Differential and Integral Calculus. The latter we have viewed as a basic technique with which to treat one aspect of the central computational question of measurement: in this case that of area. In reviewing the nature of what Calculus brings to CS, I will concentrate on aspects of Differential Calculus. The nature of approximation techniques to which Integration affords in select cases exact solutions was one of the cornerstones of Numerical Analysis, a subject which, among other contributions, offered refinements of the Method of Exhaustion, e.g. such as the Trapezium Rule, Simpson's Rule etc. I have earlier highlighted some points concerning Numerical Methods and its critical historical importance to Com-

---

[8] See fn. 8 in Section 7.4.

[9] see, e.g. [233], Gareeboo [97], Waltz and McCarthy [251] among others.

puter Science, and for this reason, within this section I will concentrate on those fields within CS in which Differential Calculus plays an important rôle.

One such rôle we have emphasized is, of course, that of Optimization Theory. We have seen that mechanisms such as finding those points for which the first derivative of a function attains the value zero, provide important information about the behaviour of that function, about its **critical points**, Going further, examining the second derivative, we are, often able to elucidate the exact nature of such critical points, whether they are maxima or minima. Furthermore we can, admittedly with an increased level of analytic concern, leverage these ideas up to functions of two or more variables.

Even if the relevance to Optimization Theory were the only rationalization for discussing Differential Calculus within CS, its importance in this respect would suffice to justify even, arguably, necessitate its inclusion. Optimization is, however, **not** the only fruit. Applying derivatives to explore critical points we have to identify the zeros of such derivatives. As we have seen this is a considerable challenge even in the case of polynomial expressions. We may, however, produce as the outcome of differentiation, functions involving trigonometric, exponential and logarithmic expressions. Here, provided certain technical conditions are satisfied we are able to use the foundational form of differential calculus as the basis for iterative algorithms, e.g. as discussed in Section 4.6. Leaving aside the exact nature of such algorithms, the paradigm so illustrated is of considerable importance from a computing perspective. We are familar with the notion of recursion; we may even have seen some important examples of the power brought to algorithmic synthesis by recursive approaches e.g. in sorting, in the realization of arithmetic operations such as multiplication of large values, etc. In methods such as Halley's and Laguerre's which we described in Section 4.6 and methods such as Newton's (which we did not), we exploit the other major computational control structure: iteration. Furthermore we do so in a highly sophisticated and ordered style: by examining how close what we have found so far is to what we want/need to find. By this we reach important ideas of "convergence" and "rates of convergence", notions that we see again when considering the identification of eigenvalues and eigenvectors. While we did not elaborate in great detail on these aspects to the extent of intricate formal analysis, these are of crucial importance.

The use of Calculus is, therefore, fundamental to many processes in computing as both an analytic and evaluative device, and Chapter 4 has given some surface indication of these.

Complex Analysis and its Importance in CS

Within the idea of Complex Number Theory we may appear to have a **computational** dilemma. Much of what we had looked at in the preceding Chapters had been directed at what has been a central tenet of this book. What we can, perhaps somewhat glibly, summarize by the statement "Computation **counts**". In the concept of "a Complex Number" we may appear to lose this connection: unlike integer or technically even Rational values we cannot count or measure with Complex Numbers. In fact, other than through the device of modulus, we cannot really make sense of as basic an idea as "this Complex number w is "smaller" than this other Complex number z". Complex numbers we presented, initially, as a way out of a difficulty, namely that issue implicitly raised in Fact 1 of Section 2.4: if it is the case that polynomials of degree k have k roots then what are the two roots of $x^2 + 1$?

Introducing the concept of an object, which following tradition we denoted as $\imath$, having the behaviour that $\imath^2 = (-\imath)^2 = -1$ provided at least to the satisfaction of those who deal with formalism a way out of this dilemma. The two "roots" of $x^2 + 1$ are $\imath$ and $-\imath$.

Were the conceit of $\imath$ to be of no more interest than how it empowers various techniques and theories in the domain of Pure Mathematics then its rationale would be a matter of no moment to us, as Computer Scientists.

Thus this object and its associated theory must bring *something* to the computational table: it is not elegant disquisition on recherché mathematical concerns; it is not, alone, a device for helping out Laguerre's method should such be unfortunate enough to be invited to find the roots of $x^2 + 1$. The concept and ramifications of $\imath$ provide a means and a precedent for viewing the world of computation that is of inestimable significance. It would not be an exaggeration to assert that without $\imath$ we would not have the concept of quaternion algebra; and without quaternion algebra we would not have a practical, effective and powerful means of realizing all manner of sophisticated renderings in $3D$-graphics.[10]

From a computational perspective $\imath$ results in yet more: we have the technology afforded by its treatment in advanced calculus which leads to a detailed approach to the average-case analysis of combinatorial structures. We have, also, Primitive roots of unity and the Discrete Fourier Transform. The latter we have seen may be used in image compression. It may also, however, be directly

---

[10]Some readers may, with justice, reinterpret this statement as "without quaternions we would not have *Tomb Raider*". A statement which is, almost certainly, true, although as to whether such offers an argument for or (yet another) argument against $\imath$, I make no comment.

linked to algorithmic issues related to that most basic of **measurement** activities: multiplication. The achievement of Schönhage and Strassen presented in [207] bringing to a high-point the astonishing insight of Karatsuba [137] would not have been possible without the structure provided through the DFT.[11]

Effective and powerful realistic graphics; a computational tool via the Fourier Transform whose wider use we have hardly touched upon. As a final, I stress again **computational** gain, we have the iteration of Complex number functions and the interpretation of the outcome for aesthetic purposes: both graphical arts and music. Elaine Walker's work [249] in the last of these, brings together to striking effect the seemingly abstract irrelevance (it isn't) of Complex Analysis and computational technology.

Exploration of all of these successes – new uses of the Fourier Transform, new avenues to explore average-case properties, new ways to use complex (in both senses) function iteration – continues to be active. Complex Number Theory and an understanding of its basics is, thereby, an essential computational component.

Statistical Methods: Computing is Empirical

I have in Chapter 6 tried to defend the position that the study of computational process is a study that requires empirical methodologies to be adopted. If, as with all other fields of scientific investigation be they physical sciences or life sciences or social sciences, the study of computation is, indeed, an empirical study, then a knowledge of those means by which experimental outcomes are investigated is essential. Chief amongst such means is the discipline of Statistics. Overall in this chapter there is less of a concern with identifying new directions and more of an interest with bringing to light what existing methods there are: how to deal with issues in sampling data; measures by which empirical results are assessed and conclusions made; means by which such conclusions are defended as being something other than coincidence. As a side-effect of these questions we also find the problem of presenting analyses through particular means and the concomitant problem of justifying the interpretation lent. Here we meet such techniques as that of "finding the 'best' line" fitting our data.

In highlighting the importance of Statistical analysis and its rôle in computational study, we are only reiterating an aspect that has permeated computational study from its earliest days. As the theory of Operating system design

---

[11]and, of course, by the fast algorithm for DFT computation discovered by Cooley and Tukey [50].

developed and those of the other core components taken for granted in contemporary layouts such as compilers and database systems, one understanding became clear: gauging the worth of specific techniques could only be carried out by experimental investigation, For instance in addressing such questions as: which process scheduling method works "best"; which page replacement algorithm, how large an allocation should the working set of pages be allowed to be, do these optimization techniques really produce faster/more compact machine level code and so on.

I could easily continue to list fifty or more such questions all of importance to computer performance issues. It is, of course, true that while many such are now well understood at a theoretical level, equally so many of the assumptions that led to such understanding are not as valid as they once were. The spectacle of the monolithic single mainframe access to which is regulated to allow a collection of several hundred individuals an illusion of being the sole user, is long past as the standard computational environment. Now we have desktops, laptops, tablets, even mobile phone devices and a change of scale and emphasis. In the late 1960s through to the late 1990s and the death of the mainframe it would have been unimaginable that people could carry around with ease devices having a memory capacity of several terabytes. Memory was expensive and a resource to be monitored carefully.[12] As a result the rules of the game from 1960 – ca. 1998 have changed beyond recognition. And if the rules have changed the conclusions drawn under the "old rules" ought to have changed also: and yet computer science which was, already, an empirical discipline half a century ago is **still**, despite the changes, despite the advances, an empirical discipline **now**.

Hence we still need to consider performance assessment using experimental methodologies, we still need Statistics to do so.

This, however, is merely one rationale: we can identify at least three further reasons for Statistics being essential. Two of these are matters we have raised throughout this text, the third has been hinted at: the specialisms Machine Learning, Data Science and Algorithm Engineering. That Statistical methods are essential to the first is self-evident: how otherwise would one be in a position to make claims about a novel learning algorithm or justify conclusions proposed on the basis of studying a large volume of data? Algorithm Engineering concerns not so much a search for new "general" algorith-

---

[12]The nearest one remembers coming close a "single user" machine as an undergraduate student (1977–1981) was using various Digital Equipment Corporation machines, e.g. PDP-9. A number of programming exercises at the time turned on being able to accomodate solutions within limited space, e.g. a multiprogramming O/S within 1Kb: this is **not** a mistyping of 1Mb!

mic methods but rather more sophisticated approaches by which those already discovered may be realized. Thus one may be concerned less with asymptotic behaviour with respect to worst-case instances but more with improving constant factors qualifying theoretically efficient methods, e.g. usable realizations of the methods described in Ajtai, Komlós, and Szemerédi [5] or those from Khachiyan [141]. Failing worst-case guarantees one may look for effective *average case* techniques a very basic and naïve approach to such study was given in Section 6.10. Once again empirical methods come into force and an associated statistical treatment.

Matrices, Spectral Methods and CS

In our final technical Chapter we return to Matrix algebra and, in particular, the topic of Spectral Methods. In many ways the latter approach combines together all of the themes we have been considering: polynomial forms and their roots in the relevant treatment of matrix determinants; matrix algebra itself since the ideas we consider greatly extend the initial forms offered in Chapter 3. With respect to objects such as the Hessian, briefly presented at the end of Section 4.7, we see that an awareness of deeper and general ideas from the theory of matrices feeds into Calculus. Finally, given the form of eigenvalues as roots of a particular polynomial we again find Complex analysis arising.

All, of course, matters which appeal from the perspective of Pure Mathematics, however, as has consistently been emphasized our interest is **computational use**. Here, and especially so in the arena of Spectral Theory, we find such in abundance.

A classical result underpins the dominant[13] standing of one commercial enterprise: the Perron-Frobenius conditions and their variants (from Section 7.4) and the success of Google's web page ranking methods (discussed in Section 7.6). Views of matrices and their spectral properties support the highly versatile restructuring that is the Singular Value Decomposition, also presented in Section 7.6. This approach offers one technique for compressing the amount of data required to reproduce in "reasonable" quality a large image as well as offering a means, of importance in Data Science, by which "irrelevant" details can be ignored in significant size data pools. Although newer and more powerful methods have emerged in both of these areas, SVD offers an important and accessible tool.

---

[13]Apologies for the rather gruesome pun.

In presenting as our final example of spectral analysis its use in argumentation frameworks, we see that not only are such approaches of historical importance but also continue to find new and topical fields of action: in argument, in computational game theory and in data science.

As with Calculus and Complex Analysis, matrix and spectral properties have an influence and potential of great importance for all practical computational endeavours.

8.3 Lacunae

Looking back over the range of subjects discussed in this book, one might reasonably ask "why is nothing said about X?" where X may well be a field not only of some interest but, more importantly, an area that feeds into computational activity in a significant way. It is, of course, the case that one cannot satisfy all demands of the form "there **should** be something about ...". In part, as observed at the opening of the present chapter, this is due to the author's lack of omniscience. There are many relevant activities which one would like to have dealt with: in deciding not to do so this decision is largely motivated by the belief that a superficial limited coverage (necessarily superficial because of lack of confidence in one's grasp) is an even worse approach than an error strewn attempt at coverage in depth: again, necessarily error strewn because of lack of awareness.

In the Preface to this volume I remarked on the reasons for omission of what are usually referred to as "Discrete Methods" and while probability theory treads a thin line between "discrete" and "analytic" this exception aside, as the reader will have seen there has been no detailed presentation of combinatorics, set theory, relational structures and so on and so forth.

There are, however, some fields which while one would not claim to have great expertise in their deeper achievements, one admittedly with some considerable reluctance has not considered even though there is a strong argument for inclusion.

One of these is the whole vast arena of "Numerical Methods": I have stressed in several places the intimate link between Numerical analysis and the birth of Computer Science as an academic discipline. This, however, is a huge field. One could, of course, choose a selected specialist and relevant topic within this, e.g. treatment of numerical error, or convergence analysis, or approximation theory, or . . . I have some awareness of and considerable respect for this field: what I am not, however, is an expert in its achievement,

"*La chair est triste, hélas! et j'ai lu tous les livres* (but, regrettably, to little avail).

For rather different reasons, it is with some regret that after long consideration, I felt that the hugely significant topic of Information Theory was very narrowly outside the scope of this text. An awareness of Claude Shannon's 1948 article [210] is, I think, essential for any Computer Scientist. Shannon's contributions to the foundations of Computing are, without question, of inestimable importance. This is not only in the ambitious attempt to answer what some may see as the basic computational question "What is information?" but also in the consequences arising from investigating this issue.[14] So why is Information Theory missing? Ultimately, I felt its techniques fell rather uncomfortably between what is clearly within the domain of discrete methods: properties of alphabets of symbols, coding schemes, probabilistic models, etc. and not so directly within what has been the primary focus of this text. This, however, may well be a view that one will subsequently revisit.

---

[14]Not least among which I would include Shannon's article [211].

8.4 Conclusion – Some Personal Observations

I have, until this point, made no comment in respect of the text with which this final chapter opens. One does not choose such references in an arbitrary manner and the line adopted (the opening words of *Erwartung*) seems, to me, to have a bearing on what has gone before and, indeed, may reflect the views of many who have laboured through the preceding several hundred pages striving to glean some sense of why the methods presented are of signal importance to computational technology: *"Hier hinein? ... Man sieht den Weg nicht"*; "Is this the way? The path cannot be seen.".

In earlier drafts I had considered using the Virgilian tag, *"Forsan et haec olim meminisse iuvabit"*.[15] In rejecting this, part of the reason lies in its failure to communicate the right sense of doubt and uncertainty that a reader still un- convinced that the topics *are* essential Computer Science may be experiencing, creating rather a somewhat pompous "the author knows best" rationalization for the content. Partly, also, due to a strong antipathy towards the cringing imperialistic sycophancy that disfigures rather too much of the Aeneid.[16] And, indeed, partly because I have always regarded this tag as one of the crassest sentiments in the entire canon of classical literature: Aeneas, having guided his hapless followers from one calamity to another seeks to put an encourag- ing gloss on the latest disaster with the reassurance "Well maybe, this will look good later on.". And hence, *"Hier hinein? ... Man sieht den Weg nicht"*.

Charles Rosen, the eminent musicologist, distinguished pianist and able champion of Schönberg's achievement, has written of *Erwartung*:

> "In this work Schönberg did away with all the traditional means by which music was supposed to make itself intelligible $\cdots$ There is no sense of key anywhere in *Erwartung* and each motif that appears is abandoned after a few seconds $\cdots$ This apparently total freedom from the requirements of musical form has made *Erwartung* a well-attested miracle, inexplicable and incontrovert- ible." ([197, p. 47])

It is a work of undeniable importance in the evolution of Western music, cre- ating an ambience as instantly recognizable as the "impossibly wrong" Horn motif following the opening of the *Eroica* symphony or the shock of the *Tris-*

---

[15]"Perhaps, one day, even these things will be pleasant to remember" (*Aeneid*, I:203).
[16]cf. VIII:671–731.

tan chord in the prelude to *Tristan und Isolde*: sadly, its status is not reflected in frequency of performance.[17]

These atonal and athematic elements are integral to the dramatic context of the work itself: a single act monodrama wherein a lone figure (The Woman) wanders distraught and disorientated through a dense forest, apparently looking for her lover. The half-light, shadows and sounds are interpreted, as she progresses, sometimes positively but more often in a highly charged negative sense. Sometimes she imagines her lover has been murdered and she has stumbled over his mutilated corpse; at others that he has deserted her and berates his infidelity.[18]

Overall the atmosphere depicted is neurasthenic, deeply disturbing and disquieting: a waking nightmare. How much of the accompanying monologue is delusion, fantasy and false hope, and how much a true commentary on events is never clear, always shifting and fluid.

This, I think, provides an apt metaphor for much of academic activity whether research focused or pedagogical. In pursuing an original line of thought it is often hard to be completely certain that the approach adopted will be fruitful or, indeed, that the programme undertaken will be received with any interest. Self-doubt, delusion and false starts permeate the tracks of creative research just as much these elements colour the thoughts of the solitary figure in Schönberg's monodrama. Again (and here one feels there is some relevance to the perceptions of readers to whom the material of this book is unfamiliar), there are similar crises of confidence accompanying the study and struggle to comprehend the direction, focus and relevance of complex technical matter. In both spheres for every occasion that it is felt such-and-such an approach *is* the way forward, that such-and-such a reading *is* the correct one, there will be others where one despairs of making headway and doubts one's capabilities.

Reactions such as these are, I think, experienced by most perhaps even all individuals endeavouring to produce original work at one time or another. And, given the similarity, such qualms may be felt by those taking on the challenges raised in striving to come to terms with novel and complicated technical matter. The elements of the unknown, common to both research and study, create very

---

[17]The resource at `https://bachtrack.com/find-concerts/` lists 5 performances over 3 venues all in Europe between September 2018 and May 2019. The same site reports over 100 scheduled performances spanning 67 venues world-wide for Stravinsky's *Le Sacre du Printemps*. In over 40 years of attending orchestral concerts, I have only once heard this work of Schönberg's performed live (Edinburgh Festival, 25th August 1983, LSO, cond. Abbado; soloist Phyllis Bryn-Julson).

[18]cf. *"Du siehst wieder dort hin!... Wo ist sie denn... die Hexe, die Dirne..."* ("You were seen with her! Where is she then? ... the Witch, the Whore..."), (Scene IV).

similar problems for their practicioners. In total, it seems to me that what is most important is to engage with such challenges rather than surrendering in the likely mistaken belief that understanding and progress are impossible.

In the final passages of *Erwartung*, the scene has shifted to a locked and shuttered building, the solitary figure standing on a white stone balcony outside this. Looking eastwards a faint glow is visible in the sky but whether it is dawn or moonlight or candlelight is unclear. She thinks it to be the approaching dawn and just as she is on the verge of despairing in her search (*"Wo bist du? ... Es ist dunkel ..."*[19]) believes she has seen someone (or something). Whether this is reality or just another delusion is not indicated. The music gives no suggestion as it shifts its dynamics ambiguously from *ppp* to *fff*. This refusal to direct the spectator is only right: listeners must decide for themselves whether the quest is finally over or whether this is another false start. What matters is that she *believes* her lover has been found. What matters in research or study is to have that same level of conviction reflected with absolute certainty in her final words, *"Oh, bist du da ... ich suchte ..."*: "Oh, you **are** there ... I was looking ...".

---

[19]"Where are you? It is dark."

Bibliography

[1]   R. P. Agarwal, S. K. Sen, et al. *Creators of mathematical and computational sciences*. Springer, 2016.

[2]   A. V. Aho, J. E. Hopcroft, and J. D. Ullman. *The Design and Analysis of Computer Algorithms*. Addison–Wesley, 1974.

[3]   A. V. Aho and J. D. Ullman. *Principles of Compiler Design*. Addison–Wesley, 1979.

[4]   A. V. Aho and J. D. Ullman. *Data structures and algorithms*. Pearson, 1983.

[5]   M. Ajtai, J. Komlós, and E. Szemerédi. An $O(n \log n)$ sorting network. In *Proceedings of the 15th Annual ACM Symposium on Theory of computing*, pages 1–9. ACM, 1983.

[6]   V. Aksyonov. *Generations of Winter*. Vintage International, 1994.

[7]   B. W. Aldiss. *The Penguin science fiction omnibus: an anthology*. Penguin Books Ltd, 1973.

[8]   L. J. S. Allen, F. Brauer, P. van den Driessche, and J. Wu. *Mathematical epidemiology*, volume 1945. Springer, 2008.

[9]   L. Amgoud and J. Ben-Naim. Ranking-based semantics for argumentation frameworks. In *International Conference on Scalable Uncertainty Management*, pages 134–147. Springer, 2013.

[10] E. Amiot. Gammes bien réparties et transformée de Fourier discrète. *Mathématiques et sciences humaines. Mathematics and social sciences*, 178:95–118, 2007.

[11]   E. Amiot, T. Noll, M. Andreatta, and C. Agon.   Fourier oracles for computer-aided improvisation. In *ICMC 2006*, pages 1–1, 2006.

[12]   D. Angluin and L. G. Valiant. Fast probabilistic algorithms for hamiltonian circuits and matchings. *Journal of Computer and system Sciences*, 18(2):155–193, 1979.

[13]   J. R. Argand. *Essai sur une manière de représenter les quantités imaginaires dans les constructions géométriques*. Gauthier-Villars, 1874.

[14]   M. D. Atkinson and J-R Sack. Generating binary trees at random. *Information Processing Letters*, 41(1):21–23, 1992.

[15]   O. T. Avery, C. M. MacLeod, and M. McCarty. Studies on the chemical nature of the substance inducing transformation of pneumococcal types: induction of transformation by a desoxyribonucleic acid fraction isolated from pneumococcus type iii. *Journal of experimental medicine*, 79(2):137–158, 1944.

[16]   R. G. Ayoub. Paolo Ruffini's contributions to the quintic. *Archive for history of exact sciences*, 23(3):253–277, 1980.

[17]   C. Babbage. Difference Engine No. 1. In *Passages from the Life of a Philosopher*. 1864.

[18]   D. H. Bailey and J. M. Borwein. The greatest mathematical discovery?   Technical Report LBNL-3500E, Lawrence Berkeley National Lab.(LBNL), Berkeley, CA (United States), 2010.

[19]   P. Baroni, D. M. Gabbay, M. Giacomin, and L. van der Torre, editors. *Handbook of formal argumentation*. College Publications, 2018.

[20]   P. Baroni, M. Giacomin, and G. Guida. SCC-recursiveness: a general schema for argumentation semantics. *Artificial Intelligence*, 168(1–2):162–210, 2005.

[21]   D. W. Barron. *Computer Operating Systems*. Chapman and Hall, 1977.

[22]   M. Batty. Fractals: Geometry between dimensions. *New Scientist*, 105:31–35, 1985.

[23]   P. Beckmann. *A history of π*. St. Martin's Griffin, 1971.

[24] T. J. M. Bench-Capon, S. Doutre, and P. E. Dunne. Audiences in argumentation frameworks. *Artificial Intelligence*, 171:42–71, 2007.

[25] T. J. M. Bench-Capon and P. E. Dunne. Argumentation in artificial intelligence. *Artificial intelligence*, 171(10-15):619–641, 2007.

[26] B. Berger. The fourth moment method. *SIAM Journal on Computing*, 26(4):1188–1207, 1997.

[27] P. Besnard and A. Hunter. *Elements of argumentation*, volume 47. MIT Press Cambridge, 2008.

[28] A. D. Beyerchen. *Scientists under Hitler: Politics and the physics community in the Third Reich*. Yale University Press, 2018.

[29] F. Black and M. Scholes. The pricing of options and corporate liabilities. *Journal of political economy*, 81(3):637–654, 1973.

[30] E. Bonzon, J. Delobelle, S. Konieczny, and N. Maudet. A comparative study of ranking-based semantics for abstract argumentation. In *Proc. of the 30th AAAI Conference on Artificial Intelligence, February 12-17, 2016, Phoenix, Arizona, USA.*, pages 914–920, 2016.

[31] R. P. Brent. Recent progress and prospects for integer factorisation algorithms. In *International Computing and Combinatorics Conference*, pages 3–22. Springer, 2000.

[32] S. Brin and L. Page. The anatomy of a large-scale hypertextual web search engine. *Computer networks and ISDN systems*, 30(1-7):107–117, 1998.

[33] F. Brooks. Decimal and other arithmetical notations. *van Nostrand's Eclectic Engineering Magazine (1869-1879)*, 114(18):548, 1878.

[34] A. E. Brouwer and W. H. Haemers. *Spectra of graphs*. Springer Science & Business Media, 2011.

[35] K. Bryan and T. Leise. The $25,000,000,000 eigenvector: The linear algebra behind Google. *Siam Review*, 48(3):569–581, 2006.

[36] A. Buades, B. Coll, and J.-M. Morel. A review of image denoising algorithms, with a new one. *Multiscale Modeling & Simulation*, 4(2):490–530, 2005.

[37] K. Budzynska and C. Reed. The structure of *ad hominem* dialogues. In *Proc. 4th COMMA*, volume 245 of *FAIA*, pages 410–421. IOS Press, 2012.

[38] A. Bundy. *Artificial Intelligence: an introductory course.* Edinburgh University Press, 1978.

[39] J. Butterworth and P. E. Dunne. Spectral techniques in argumentation framework analysis. In *Proc. 6th COMMA*, volume 287 of *FAIA*, pages 167–178. IOS Press, 2016.

[40] K. Cabeen and P. Gent. Image compression and the discrete cosine transform. *College of the Redwoods*, 1998.

[41] F. Cajori. Horner's method of approximation anticipated by Ruffini. *Bulletin of the American Mathematical Society*, 17(8):409–414, 1911.

[42] G. Cardano. *Artis Magnae, Sive de Regulis Algebraicis.* 1545.

[43] A.S. Cavaretta. An elementary proof of Kolmogorov's theorem. *The American Mathematical Monthly*, 81(5):480–486, 1974.

[44] J. Chasseguet-Smirgel. Les Années Brunes. Psychoanalysis under the Third Reich. *Journal of the American Psychoanalytic Association*, 36(4):1059–1066, 1988.

[45] S. Chrisomalis. Trends and transitions in the history of written numerals. *The shape of script: How and why writing systems change*, pages 229–254, 2012.

[46] W. Cobbett and T. C. Hansard. *The Parliamentary History of England from the Earliest Period to the Year 1803: From which Last-mentioned Epoch it is Continued Downwards in the Work Entitled "The Parliamentary Debates".* Hansard, 1808.

[47] D. Cohn and H. Chang. Learning to probabilistically identify authoritative documents. In *ICML*, pages 167–174, 2000.

[48] T. M. Connolly and C. E. Begg. *Database systems. A practical approach to design implementation and management. global ed.* Harlow, Pearson Education, 2015.

[49]   S. A. Cook. The complexity of theorem-proving procedures. In *Proceedings of the third annual ACM symposium on Theory of computing*, pages 151–158. ACM, 1971.

[50]   J. W. Cooley and J. W. Tukey. An algorithm for the machine calculation of complex Fourier series. *Mathematics of computation*, 19(90):297–301, 1965.

[51]   T. H. Cormen, C. E Leiserson, R. L. Rivest, and C. Stein. *Introduction to algorithms*. MIT press, 2009.

[52]   J. M Cushing. *Integrodifferential equations and delay models in population dynamics*, volume 20. Springer Science & Business Media, 2013.

[53]   Y. Danisman, M. F. Yilmaz, A. Ozkaya, and I.T. Comlekciler. A comparison of eigenvalue methods for Principal Component Analysis. *Appl. Comput. Math*, 3(13):316–331, 2014.

[54]   J. Dauben. The universal history of numbers and the universal history of computing (i). *Notices of the American Math. Soc.*, 49(1):32–38, 2002. (review).

[55]   J. Dauben. The universal history of numbers and the universal history of computing (ii). *Notices of the American Math. Soc.*, 49(2):212–216, 2002. (review).

[56]   R. Dedekind. Was sind und was sollen die zahlen? In *Was sind und was sollen die Zahlen?. Stetigkeit und Irrationale Zahlen*, pages 1–47. Springer, 1965.

[57]   R. Dedekind and W. W. Beman. *Essays on the Theory of Numbers: I. Continuity and Irrational Numbers, II. The Nature and Meaning of Number*. Open court publishing Company, 1901.

[58]   S. Dehaene. Varieties of numerical abilities. *Cognition*, 44(1-2):1–42, 1992.

[59]   I. J. Depman. *Rasskazy o matematike*. Gosudarstvennoe izdatel'stvo detskoj literatury ministerstva prosveščenija SSSR, 1954.

[60]   R. Descartes. *La géométrie*. 1637.

[61]   R. Descartes. *Discourse on method, optics, geometry, and meteorology*. Hackett Publishing, 2001.

[62] D. Deutsch. Quantum theory, the Church–Turing principle and the universal quantum computer. *Proc. R. Soc. Lond. A*, 400(1818):97–117, 1985.

[63] L. Devroye. A note on the height of binary search trees. *Journal of the ACM (JACM)*, 33(3):489–498, 1986.

[64] J. C. Dixon. *The shock absorber handbook*. John Wiley & Sons, 2008.

[65] R. G. Downey and M. R. Fellows. *Fundamentals of parameterized complexity*, volume 4. Springer, 2013.

[66] P. M. Dung. On the acceptability of arguments and its fundamental role in nonmonotonic reasoning, logic programming, and N-person games. *Artificial Intelligence*, 77(2):321–357, 1995.

[67] P. E. Dunne. *The complexity of Boolean networks*. Academic Press, 1988.

[68] P. E. Dunne. *Computability Theory: concepts and applications*. Ellis Horwood, 1991.

[69] P. E. Dunne. Prevarication in dispute protocols. In *Proc. 9th ICAIL*, pages 12–21. ACM Press, 2003.

[70] P. E. Dunne. Suspicion of hidden agenda in persuasive argument. In *Proc. 1st COMMA*, volume 144 of *FAIA*, pages 329–340. IOS Press, 2006.

[71] P. E. Dunne. I heard you the first time: Debate in cacophonous surroundings. In *Proc. 6th COMMA*, volume 287 of *FAIA*, pages 287–298. IOS Press, 2016.

[72] P. E. Dunne. Unconscious patterns in argument: Fractal dimension in oratory. In *COMMA 2018*, volume 305 of *FAIA*, pages 301–312. IOS Press, 2018.

[73] P. E. Dunne and P. H. Leng. The average case performance of an algorithm for demand-driven evaluation of boolean formulae. *Journal of Universal Computer Science*, 5(5):288–306, 1999.

[74] P. E. Dunne and M. Zito. An improved upper bound on the non-3-colourability threshold. *Information Processing Letters*, 65(1):17–23, 1998.

[75] D. I. Duveen. Antoine Laurent Lavoisier and the French Revolution (I). *Journal of chemical education*, 31(2):60–65, 1954.

[76] A. Eftekhari. Fractal geometry of texts: An initial application to the works of Shakespeare. *Journal of Quantitative Linguistics*, 13(2-3):177–193, 2006.

[77] G. Eisenstein. Über die Irreductibilität und einige andere Eigenschaften der Gleichung, von welcher die Theilung der ganzen Lemniscate abhängt. *Journal für die reine und angewandte Mathematik*, 39:160–179, 1850.

[78] P. Erdös and A. Rényi. On the evolution of random graphs. *Publ. Math. Inst. Hung. Acad. Sci*, 5(1):17–60, 1960.

[79] E. Estrada. Spectral moments of the edge adjacency matrix in molecular graphs. 1. definition and applications to the prediction of physical properties of alkanes. *Journal of chemical information and computer sciences*, 36(4):844–849, 1996.

[80] E. Estrada. Spectral moments of the edge-adjacency matrix of molecular graphs. 2. molecules containing heteroatoms and qsar applications. *Journal of chemical information and computer sciences*, 37(2):320–328, 1997.

[81] E. Estrada. Spectral moments of the edge adjacency matrix in molecular graphs. 3. molecules containing cycles. *Journal of chemical information and computer sciences*, 38(1):23–27, 1998.

[82] L. Euler. *Introductio in analysin infinitorum*. MM Bousquet, 1748.

[83] P. Fatou. Sur les substitutions rationnelles. *Comptes Rendus de l'Académie des Sciences de Paris*, 164:806–808, 1917.

[84] W. Feller. *An introduction to probability theory and its applications*, volume 1. Wiley, New York, 1968.

[85] R. P. Feynman, R. B. Leighton, and M. Sands. *The Feynman lectures on physics*. Addison-Wesley, 1977.

[86] J. A. Fill and S. Janson. The number of bit comparisons used by Quicksort: an average-case analysis. In *Proceedings of the 15th Annual ACM-SIAM symposium on Discrete algorithms*, pages 300–307. Society for Industrial and Applied Mathematics, 2004.

[87] P. Flajolet and R. Sedgewick. *Analytic combinatorics*. Cambridge University press, 2009.

[88] J. Floyd and H. Putnam. A note on Wittgenstein's "notorious paragraph" about the Gödel theorem. *The Journal of Philosophy*, pages 624–632, 2000.

[89] J. Flum and M. Grohe. *Parameterized Complexity Theory*. EATCS Series in Theoretical Computer Science. Springer, 2006.

[90] J. D. Foley, A. van Dam, S. K. Feiner, J. F. Hughes, and R. L. Phillips. *Introduction to computer graphics*, volume 55. Addison-Wesley Reading, 1994.

[91] J. W. Freeman. Hard random 3-sat problems and the Davis-Putnam procedure. *Artificial intelligence*, 81(1-2):183–198, 1996.

[92] J. Friedman. On the second eigenvalue and random walks in random d-regular graphs. *Combinatorica*, 11(4):331–362, 1991.

[93] G. Frobenius. Über matrizen aus nicht negativen elementen. *Sitz. Königl. Preuss. Akad. Wiss.*, pages 456–477, 1912.

[94] D. Gabbay and J. Woods. More on non-cooperation in dialogue logic. *Logic Journal of IGPL*, 9(2):305–324, 2001.

[95] D. Gabbay and J. Woods. Non-cooperation in dialogue logic. *Synthese*, 127(1):161–186, 2001.

[96] M. Gardner. White and brown music, fractal curves and one-over-f fluctuations. *Scientific American*, 238(4):16–27, 1978.

[97] F Gareeboo. Hardware platforms for computer graphics visualization. *WIT Transactions on Information and Communication Technologies*, 5, 1970.

[98] M. R. Garey and D. S. Johnson. *Computers and Intractability*. W. H. Freeman New York, 2002.

[99] C. F. Gauss. Mutationen des Raumes. *Königlichen Gesellschaft der Wissenschaften*, pages 357–362, 1900.

[100] W. Gautschi. Interpolation before and after Lagrange. *Rend. Sem. Mat. Univ. Politec. Torino*, 70(4):347–368, 2012.

[101] S. A. Gershgorin. Uber die abgrenzung der eigenwerte einer matrix. *Iszv. Russ. Acad. Nauk, Ser. Matematika*, 6:749–754, 1931.

[102] A. M. Gibbons and W. Rytter. *Efficient parallel algorithms*. Cambridge University Press, 1989.

[103] K. Gödel. Über formal unentscheidbare sätze der *Principia Mathematica* und verwandter systeme I. *Monatshefte für mathematik und physik*, 38(1):173–198, 1931.

[104] J. A. Goldstein and M. Levy. Linear algebra and quantum chemistry. *The American mathematical monthly*, 98(8):710–718, 1991.

[105] G. H. Golub and H. A. van der Vorst. Eigenvalue computation in the 20th century. *Journal of Computational and Applied Mathematics*, 123(1):35–65, 2000.

[106] J. Goodare. The long hundred in medieval and early modern Scotland. *Proc. of the Society of Antiquaries of Scotland*, 123:395–418, 1993.

[107] P. Gordan. Transcendenz von e und π. *Math. Ann.*, 43:222–224, 1893.

[108] D. Gries. *Compiler Construction for Digital Computers*. John Wiley & Sons, 1971.

[109] V. Grossman. *Life and Fate*. Vintage Classics, 2006.

[110] J. Guillaume. Chronique des falsifications : à propos de Lavoisier et d'un mot légendaire. *Les Cahiers du Mouvement Ouvrier*, 49:199–206, 2011.

[111] Z. Gyöngyi, H. Garcia-Molina, and J. Pedersen. Combating web spam with trustrank. In *Proceedings of the Thirtieth international conference on Very large data bases*, pages 576–587. VLDB Endowment, 2004.

[112] E. Halley. A Synopsis of the Astronomy of Comets. *Miscellanea Curiosa*, 2, 1705.

[113] T. Halsey. *Compiler Design: Principles, Techniques and Tools*. Larsen and Keller Education, 2018.

[114] W. R. Hamilton. XI. on quaternions; or on a new system of imaginaries in algebra. *The London, Edinburgh, and Dublin Philosophical Magazine and Journal of Science*, 33(219):58–60, 1848.

[115] H. Hammarström. Rarities in numeral systems. In *Rethinking universals: How rarities affect linguistic theory*, volume 45, pages 11–53. Mouton de Gruyter Berlin, 2010.

[116] E. Hansen and M. Patrick. A family of root finding methods. *Numerische Mathematik*, 27(3):257–269, 1976.

[117] S. Havlin, S.V. Buldyrev, A.L. Goldberger, R.N. Mantegna, S.M. Ossadnik, C.-K. Peng, M. Simons, and H.E. Stanley. Fractals in biology and medicine. *Chaos, Solitons & Fractals*, 6(Supplement C):171 – 201, 1995. Complex Systems in Computational Physics.

[118] W. Heisenberg. Über den anschaulichen Inhalt der quantentheoretischen Kinematik und Mechanik. *Zeitschrift für Physik*, 43:172–198, 1927.

[119] C. A. R. Hoare. Quicksort. *The Computer Journal*, 5(1):10–16, 1962.

[120] H. Hollerith. The electrical tabulating machine. *Journal of the Royal Statistical Society*, 57(4):678–689, 1894.

[121] J. E. Hopcroft, R. Motwani, and J. D. Ullman. *Introduction to Automata Theory, Languages, and Computation*. Addison–Wesley, 2001.

[122] J. E. Hopcroft and J. D. Ullman. *Introduction to Automata Theory, Languages, and Computation*. Addison–Wesley, 1979.

[123] W. G. Horner. A new method of solving numerical equations of all orders by continuous approximation. *Phil. Trans. Roy. Soc.*, 109:308, 1819.

[124] D. Huff. *How to lie with statistics*. W. W. Norton & Company, 1993.

[125] G. Ifrah. *The universal history of numbers: From prehistory to the invention of the computer*. New York, NY: Wiley, 2000.

[126] E. Isaacson and H. B. Keller. *Analysis of numerical methods*. Courier Corporation, 2012.

[127] C. G. J. Jacobi. Über ein leichtes verfahren, die in der theorie der säkularstörungen vorkommenden gleichungen numerisch aufzulösen. *Journal für die reine und angewandte Mathematik*, 30(30):51–94, 1846.

[128] M. A. Jenkins. Algorithm 493: zeros of a real polynomial [c2]. *ACM Transactions on Mathematical Software (TOMS)*, 1(2):178–189, 1975.

[129] M. A. Jenkins and J. F. Traub. Algorithm 419: zeros of a complex polynomial [c2]. *Comm. of the ACM*, 15(2):97–99, 1972.

[130] G. Julia. Memoire sur l'iteration des fonctions rationnelles. *J. Math. Pures Appl.*, 8:47–245, 1918.

[131] B. Jüttler. Visualization of moving objects using dual quaternion curves. *Computers & Graphics*, 18(3):315–326, 1994.

[132] R. C. Kadosh and V. Walsh. Numerical representation in the parietal lobes: Abstract or not abstract? *Behavioral and brain sciences*, 32(3-4):313–328, 2009.

[133] D. Kalman. A singularly valuable decomposition: the SVD of a matrix. *The college mathematics journal*, 27(1):2–23, 1996.

[134] E. Kaltofen. Polynomial factorization. In *Computer Algebra*, pages 95–113. Springer, 1982.

[135] E. Kaltofen. Polynomial factorization 1982-1986. *Computers in mathematics*, 125:285–309, 1990.

[136] E. Kaltofen. Polynomial factorization 1987–1991. In *Latin American Symposium on Theoretical Informatics*, pages 294–313. Springer, 1992.

[137] A. A. Karatsuba and Y. P. Ofman. Multiplication of many digital numbers by automatic computers. *Doklady Akademii Nauk*, 145(2):293–294, 1962. (in Russian).

[138] A. A. Karatsuba and Y. P. Ofman. Multiplication of multidigit numbers on automata. *Soviet Physics Doklady*, 7:595, 1963.

[139] J. P. Keener. The Perron-Frobenius theorem and the ranking of football teams. *SIAM Review*, 35(1):80–93, 1993.

[140] M. G. Kendall. A new measure of rank correlation. *Biometrika*, 30(1/2):81–93, 1938.

[141] L. G. Khachiyan. A polynomial algorithm in linear programming. *Doklady Academii Nauk SSSR*, 244:1093–1096, 1979.

[142] J. M. Kleinberg. Authoritative sources in a hyperlinked environment. *JACM*, 46(5):604–632, 1999.

[143] M. Kline. *Mathematical Thought From Ancient to Modern Times*. OUP USA, 1990.

[144] D. Knuth. *The art of computer programming 1: Fundamental algorithms*. Addison-Wesley, 1968.

[145] D. Knuth. *The art of computer programming 2: Seminumerical algorithms*. Addison-Wesley, 1968.

[146] D. Knuth. *The art of computer programming 3: Sorting and searching*. Addison-Wesley, 1968.

[147] D. Kroenke. *Database Processing*. Science Research Associates, 1977.

[148] L. Kronecker. Grundzüge einer arithmetischen theorie der algebraischen grössen. *Journal für die reine und angewandte Mathematik*, 92:1–122, 1882.

[149] J. B. Kuipers. *Quaternions and rotation sequences*, volume 66. Princeton University Press, NJ, 1999.

[150] J. L. Lagrange. *Nouvelle méthode pour résoudre les équations littérales par le moyen des séries*. 1770.

[151] T. Larrabee. Evidence for a satisfiability threshold for random 3cnf formulas. In *Proc. AAAI Symp. on AI NP-Hard Problems, 1992*, 1992.

[152] K. Lengnink and D. Schlimm. Learning and understanding numeral systems: Semantic aspects of number representations from an educational perspective. *PhiMSAMP. Philosophy of Mathematics: Sociological Aspects and Mathematical Practice*, 11:235–264, 2010.

[153] A. K. Lenstra, H. W. Lenstra, and L. Lovász. Factoring polynomials with rational coefficients. *Mathematische Annalen*, 261(4):515–534, 1982.

[154] L. A. Levin. Universal sequential search problems. *Problemy Peredachi Informatsii*, 9(3):115–116, 1973.

[155] R. Liddle. *Selfish Whining Monkeys: How we Ended Up Greedy, Narcissistic and Unhappy*. Harper Collins UK, 2014.

[156] F. Lindemann. Über die Ludolph'sche Zahl. *Sitzungsberichte der Königlich Preussischen Akademie der Wissenschaften zu Berlin*, 2:679–82, 1882.

[157] F. Lindemann. Über die Zahl π. *Math. Ann.*, 20:213–225, 1882.

[158] A. M. Lister. *Fundamentals of operating systems*. Macmillan, 1975.

[159] T. D. Lysenko. Tekhnika i metodika selektsii tomatov na belot-serkovskoi selekstantsii. *Biulleten Sortovodno-semennogo Upravleniia*, 4:73–76, 1923.

[160] T. D. Lysenko and D. A. Dolgushin. On the essense of the winter nature of plants. In *Trudy Vsesoyuznogo c'ezda po genetike, selektsii, semenovodstvu i plemennomu zhivotnovodstvu*, pages 189–199, 1929.

[161] B. Mandelbrot. How long is the coast of Britain? statistical self-similarity and fractional dimension. *Science*, 156:636–638, 1967.

[162] A. I. Mees, P. E. Rapp, and L. S. Jennings. Singular-value decomposition and embedding dimension. *Physical Review A*, 36(1):340, 1987.

[163] A. A. Michelson. The relative motion of the earth and the luminiferous ether. *The American Journal of Science, Series 3*, 22(128):120–129, 1881.

[164] A. A. Michelson and E. W. Morley. On the relative motion of the earth and of the luminiferous ether. *The American Journal of Science, Series 3*, 34(203):333–345, 1887.

[165] S. Milgram. Behavioral study of obedience. *The Journal of abnormal and social psychology*, 67(4):371, 1963.

[166] S. L. Miller et al. A production of amino acids under possible primitive earth conditions. *Science*, 117(3046):528–529, 1953.

[167] S. L. Miller and H. C. Urey. Organic compound synthesis on the primitive earth. *Science*, 130(3370):245–251, 1959.

[168] M. L. Minsky. *Computation: finite and infinite machines*. Prentice-Hall, Inc., 1967.

[169] B. Mohar. Laplace eigenvalues of graphs – a survey. *Discrete mathematics*, 109(1-3):171–183, 1992.

[170] R. Motwani and P. Raghavan. *Randomized algorithms*. Cambridge university press, 1995.

[171] F. Mount. *The new few: or a very British oligarchy*. Simon and Schuster, 2012.

[172] S. H. Mueller, A. Färber, H. Prüss, N. Melzer, K. S. Golombeck, T. Kümpfel, F. Thaler, M. Elisak, J. Lewerenz, M. Kaufmann, et al. Genetic predisposition in anti-LGI1 and anti-NMDA receptor encephalitis. *Annals of neurology*, 83(4):863–869, 2018.

[173] J. Myhill. Criteria of constructibility for real numbers. *The Journal of Symbolic Logic*, 18(1):7–10, 1953.

[174] M. Newman, D. J. Watts, and S. H. Strogatz. Random graph models of social networks. *Proceedings of the National Academy of Sciences*, 99(suppl 1):2566–2572, 2002.

[175] I. Newton. *Quadratura curvarum*. 1704.

[176] I. Newton. *Method of Fluxions*. 1736.

[177] T. F. Nonnenmacher, G. A. Losa, and E. R. Weibel. *Fractals in biology and medicine*. Birkhäuser, 2013.

[178] W. O'Connor and R. I. Jacobs. Tomâs Torquemada and some orthopaedic CPT coding problems (God is a comedian, playing to an audience who is afraid to laugh!). *The Iowa orthopaedic journal*, 13:204, 1993.

[179] J. Oró and S.S. Kamat. Amino-acid synthesis from hydrogen cyanide under possible primitive earth conditions. *Nature*, 190(4774):442–443, 1961.

[180] V. Packard and M. C. Miller. *The hidden persuaders*. D. McKay Company New York, 1957.

[181] V. V. Patil and H. V. Kulkarni. Comparison of confidence intervals for the poisson mean: some new aspects. *REVSTAT–Statistical Journal*, 10(2):211–227, 2012.

[182] K. Pearson. Notes on the history of correlation. *Biometrika*, 13(1):25–45, 1920.

[183] C. Perelman and L. Olbrechts-Tyteca. *The New Rhetoric: A Treatise on Argumentation*. Univ. of Notre-Dame Press, 1969.

[184] O. Perron. Zur theorie der matrizen. *Mathematische Annalen*, 64(2):248–263, 1907.

[185] A. D. Petford and D. J. A. Welsh. A randomised 3-colouring algorithm. *Discrete Mathematics*, 74(1-2):253–261, 1989.

[186] G. Petit-Bois. *Tables of indefinite integrals*. Dover, 1961.

[187] S. T. Piantadosi. Zipf's word frequency law in natural language: A critical review and future directions. *Psychonomic Bulletin & Review*, 21(5):1112–1130, Oct 2014.

[188] D. Pletinckx. Quaternion calculus as a basic tool in computer graphics. *The Visual Computer*, 5(1-2):2–13, 1989.

[189] G. Pólya. Kombinatorische Anzahlbestimmungen für Gruppen, Graphen und chemische Verbindungen. *Acta Math.*, 68:145–254, 1937.

[190] G. Pólya and R. C. Read. *Combinatorial enumeration of groups, graphs, and chemical compounds*. Springer-Verlag, 1987.

[191] H. A. Priestley. *Introduction to Complex Analysis*. OUP Oxford, 2003.

[192] I. Rahwan and G. R. Simari, editors. *Argumentation in artificial intelligence*, volume 47. Springer, 2009.

[193] V. R. Remmert. Mathematical publishing in the Third Reich: Springer-Verlag and the Deutsche Mathematiker-Vereinigung. *The Mathematical Intelligencer*, 22(3):22–30, 2000.

[194] F. Richman. Is 0.999 . . . = 1? *Mathematics Magazine*, 72(5):396–400, 1999.

[195] J. M. Robson. The height of binary search trees. *Australian Computer Journal*, 11(4):151–153, 1979.

[196] O. Rodrigues. Des lois géométriques qui régissent les déplacements d'un système solide dans l'espace: et de la variation des cordonnées provenant de ces déplacements considérés indépendamment des causes qui peuvent les produire. *Journal de Mathématiques Pures et Appliquées*, 5:380–440, 1840.

[197] C. Rosen. *Schoenberg*. Fontana, 1976.

[198] A. M. Rufai, G. Anbarjafari, and H. Demirel. Lossy image compression using singular value decomposition and wavelet difference reduction. *Digital signal processing*, 24:117–123, 2014.

[199] B. Russell. *History of Western Philosophy, and its Connection with Political and Social Circumstances from the Earliest Times to the Present Day*. George Allen & Unwin, 1948.

[200] B. Russell. Logical Positivism. In *Logic and Knowledge: Essays 1901–1950*, pages 365–382. George Allen & Unwin, 1956.

[201] S. J. Russell and P. Norvig. *Artificial intelligence: a modern approach*. Pearson Education Limited,, 2016.

[202] C. Sakama. Dishonest arguments in debate games. In *Proc. 4th COMMA*, volume 245 of *FAIA*, pages 177–184. IOS Press, 2012.

[203] A. Salovin, J. Glanzman, K. Roslin, T. Armangue, D. R. Lynch, and J. A. Panzer. Anti-NMDA receptor encephalitis and nonencephalitic HSV-1 infection. *Neurology - Neuroimmunology Neuroinflammation*, 5(4):1–5, 2018.

[204] K. Sassa and M. D. Tokio. Observations on reflex responses to rhythmical stimulation in the frog. *Proc. R. Soc. Lond. B*, 92(648):328–341, 1921.

[205] J. Schillinger. *The Schillinger System of Musical Composition*. Carl Fischer, 1946.

[206] T. Schönemann. Von denjenigen Moduln, welche Potenzen von Primzahlen sind. *Journal für die reine und angewandte Mathematik*, 32:93–118, 1846.

[207] A. Schönhage and V. Strassen. Schnelle multiplikation grosser zahlen. *Computing*, 7(3–4):281–292, 1971.

[208] F. T. Schubert. De Iventione Divisorum. *Nova Acta Academiae Petropolitanae*, 11:172–182, 1793.

[209] K.-Y. Seng, C.-Y. Fun, Y.-L. Law, W.-M. Lim, W. Fan, , and C.-L. Lim. Population pharmacokinetics of caffeine in healthy male adults using mixed-effects models. *Jnl. of Clinical Pharmacy and Therapeutics*, 34:103–114, 2009.

[210] C. E. Shannon. A mathematical theory of communication. *Bell system technical journal*, 27(3):379–423, 1948.

[211] C. E. Shannon. The synthesis of two-terminal switching circuits. *Bell system technical journal*, 28(1):59–98, 1949.

[212] K. Shoemake. Animating rotation with quaternion curves. *Computer Graphics*, 19(3):245–254, 1985.

[213] P. W. Shor. Polynomial-time algorithms for prime factorization and discrete logarithms on a quantum computer. *SIAM review*, 41(2):303–332, 1999.

[214] A. Silberschatz, P. B. Galvin, and G. Gagne. *Operating System Concepts (8th Edition)*. John Wiley & Sons, 2010.

[215] D. E. Smith and J. Ginsburg. *Numbers and Numerals*. ERIC, 1937.

[216] R. C. Smith and P. Smith. *Mechanics*. John Wiley & Sons, 1971.

[217] V. N. Soyfer. The consequences of political dictatorship for Russian science. *Nature Reviews Genetics*, 2(9):723–729, 2001.

[218] C. Spearman. The proof and measurement of association between two things. *The American journal of psychology*, 15(1):72–101, 1904.

[219] M. Spivak. *Calculus*. Addison-Wesley, 1973.

[220] H. E. Stanley and N. Ostrowsky. *On growth and form: fractal and non-fractal patterns in physics*, volume 100. Springer Science & Business Media, 2012.

[221] J. Steinbeck. The short-short story of mankind. *Playboy Magazine*, 4(5):32–34, April 1958.

[222] J. Steiner, T. Clausen, and N. Abel. Aufgaben und lehrsätze, erstere aufzulösen, letztere zu beweisen. *Journal für die reine und angewandte Mathematik*, 2:286–7, 1827.

[223] J. Stirling. *Methodus differentialis*. Whiston and White, 1764.

[224] J. Stoer and R. Bulirsch. *Introduction to numerical analysis*, volume 12. Springer Science & Business Media, 2013.

[225] G. Strang. *Linear Algebra and its Applications.: Thomson Brooks*. Academic Press, NY, USA, 1980.

[226] G. Strang. The discrete cosine transform. *SIAM review*, 41(1):135–147, 1999.

[227] G. Strang. *Linear Algebra and its Applications.: Thomson Brooks*. Cole, Belmont, CA, USA, 2005.

[228] V. Strassen. Gaussian elimination is not optimal. *Numerische mathematik*, 13(4):354–356, 1969.

[229] Student. The probable error of a mean. *Biometrika*, 6(1):1–25, 1908. (Student was a pseudonym of W. S. Gosset).

[230] S. Sukumaran and D. Thiyagarajan. Generation of fractal music with Mandelbrot set. *Global Journal of Computer Science and Technology*, 9(4), 2009.

[231] E. A. Suominen. *An Examination of the Pearl*. 2012.

[232] E. Tal. Old and new problems in philosophy of measurement. *Philosophy Compass*, 8(12):1159–1173, 2013.

[233] UK Tektronix and Beaverton House. Graphics terminals. *Displays*, page 185, 1980.

[234] D. Tilman, C. L. Lehman, and P. Kareiva. Population dynamics in spatial habitats. *Spatial ecology: The role of space in population dynamics and interspecific interactions*, pages 3–20, 1997.

[235] S. E. Toulmin. *The uses of argument*. Cambridge university press, 2003.

[236] A. M. Turing. On computable numbers, with an application to the Entscheidungsproblem. *Proceedings of the London mathematical society*, 2(1):230–265, 1937.

[237] J. D. Ullman. *Principles of database systems*. Galgotia publications, 1984.

[238] J. van Den Heuvel. Hamilton cycles and eigenvalues of graphs. *Linear algebra and its applications*, 226:723–730, 1995.

[239] A. Veevers. Some issues in software reliability assessment. *Software Testing, Verification and Reliability*, 1(1):17–22, 1991.

[240] A. Veevers and A. C. Marshall. A relationship between software coverage metrics and reliability. *Software Testing, Verification and Reliability*, 4(1):3–8, 1994.

[241] T. Verguts and W. Fias. Representation of number in animals and humans: A neural model. *Journal of Cognitive Neuroscience*, 16(9):1493–1504, 2004.

[242] J. Vince. *Quaternions for computer graphics*. Springer Science & Business Media, 2011.

[243] J. S. Vitter and P. Flajolet. Average-case analysis of algorithms and data structures. In *Algorithms and Complexity – Volume A: Handbook of Theoretical Computer Science*, pages 431–524. Elsevier, 1990.

[244] L. von Bortkiewicz. *Das gesetz der kleinen zahlen*. BG Teubner, 1898.

[245] K. von Fritz. The discovery of incommensurability by Hippasus of Metapontum. *Annals of mathematics*, 46(2):242–264, April 1945.

[246] J. von Zur Gathen and J. Gerhard. *Modern computer algebra*. Cambridge university press, 2013.

[247] R. F. Voss and J. Clarke. '$1/f$ noise' in music and speech. *Nature*, 258(5533):317–318, 1975.

[248] G. Vreeswijk and H. Prakken. Credulous and sceptical argument games for preferred semantics. In *Proc. 7th JELIA*, volume 1919 of *LNAI*, pages 224–238. Springer-Verlag, 2000.

[249] E. Walker. Chaos melody theory. *Music in Music Technology New York University, Master's thesis*, 2001.

[250] M. E. Wall, A. Rechtsteiner, and L. M. Rocha. Singular value decomposition and principal component analysis. In *A practical approach to microarray data analysis*, pages 91–109. Springer, 2003.

[251] J. Waltz and J. McCarthy. Computer graphics in the 1980s. In *Proceedings of The Conference of the National Computer Graphics Association*, page 239. The Association, 1980.

[252] Y. Y. Wang. Probabilities of the type I errors of the Welch tests for the Behrens-Fisher problem. *Journal of the American Statistical Association*, 66(335):605–608, 1971.

[253] K Weekes and M. V. Wilkes. Atmospheric oscillations and the reso-
nance theory. *Proc. R. Soc. Lond. A*, 192(1028):80–99, 1947.

[254] B. L. Welch. The significance of the difference between two means
when the population variances are unequal. *Biometrika*, 29(3/4):350–
362, 1938.

[255] C. Wessel. Om directionens analytiske betegning, et forsog, anvendt
fornemmelig til plane og sphæriske polygoners oplosning. *Nye Samling
af det Kongelige Danske Videnskabernes Selskabs Skrifter*, 5:469–518,
1799.

[256] M. V. Wilkes. The design of a practical high-speed computing machine.
the EDSAC. *Proc. R. Soc. Lond. A*, 195(1042):274–279, 1948.

[257] M. V. Wilkes and W. Renwick. The EDSAC – an electronic calculating
machine. *Journal of Scientific Instruments*, 26(12):385, 1949.

[258] L. Wittgenstein. *Remarks on the Foundations of Mathemtics*. (Lecture
notes), 1937–1942.

[259] M. Wooldridge. *An introduction to multiagent systems*. John Wiley &
Sons, 2009.

[260] K. Wynn. Psychological foundations of number: Numerical competence in human infants. *Trends in cognitive sciences*, 2(8):296–303,
1998.

[261] P. G. Zimbardo, C. Haney, W. C. Banks, and D. Jaffe. *Stanford prison
experiment: A simulation study of the psychology of imprisonment*.
Philip G. Zimbardo, Incorporated, 1972.

[262] G. K. Zipf. The psychology of language. *NY Houghton-Mifflin*, 1935.

[263] G. K. Zipf. Human behavior and the principle of least effort. *Addison-
Wesley, Cambody Mus. Am. Arch. and Ethnol.(Harvard Univ.), Papers*,
19:1–125, 1949.

List of Symbols

Approximation
$\hat{y}_i$, 334

Calculus
$D(x, y)$, 165
$\frac{\partial^2 z}{\partial x^2}$, 165
$\frac{\partial^2 z}{\partial y \partial x}$, 165
$\frac{d^k x}{dy^k}$, 141
$\frac{dy}{dx}$, 134
$\int f(x)dx$, 179
$\int_a^b f(x)dx$, 179
$\mathbf{H}_m$, 169
$\lim_{\delta \to 0}$, 132
$\partial f / \partial x$, 164
$f'(x)$, 134
$f''(x)$, 142
$f^{(k)}$, 140
f_x, 164
f_{xx}, 165
f_{xy}, 165

Complex numbers
$\imath$, 194
$\Im$, 198
$\Re$, 198
$|z|$, 198
$\bar{z}$, 198
z^{-1}, 200
$\arg v$, 204
$\mathrm{e}^{\imath\theta}$, 206

α_i, 213

Fourier Transform
$\mathcal{F}(\mathbf{x})$, 225
$\mathcal{F}^{-1}(\mathbf{y})$, 229
$\mathbf{M}_{\mathcal{F}^{-1}}$, 229
$\mathbf{M}_{\mathcal{F}}$, 229
$\mathbf{u} \diamond \mathbf{v}$, 231
$\mathbf{u} \otimes \mathbf{v}$, 230
ω_k, 226
DFT, 224

Matrix
adj, 379
det, 375
$|\mathbf{A}|$, 377
$\mathbf{A}^{-1}$, 89, 375
$\mathbf{A}^{\top}$, 86
$\mathbf{A}_{ij}$, 377
$\mathbf{I}_2$, 89
$\mathbf{I}_n$, 375
rank, 383
sgn, 382
$n \times m$, 84

Number representation
$\textcircled{n}$, 52
Number Type
$\mathbb{C}$, 198
$\mathbb{T}$, 24

$\mathbb{Z}$, 18
$\mathbb{Z}_k$, 77
$\mathbb{N}$, 17
$\mathbb{Q}$, 18
$\mathbb{R}$, 22
$\mathbb{W}$, 17
Numerical Convention
   $(m)_{base}$, 14

Operations
   $|x|$, 67
   $frac(q)$, 19
   $int(q)$, 19

Polynomials
   $\mathbb{T}[X]$, 25
   $\deg(p)$, 24
   $p(x)$, 24
   $p_n(x)$, 25
   $p_{n,\underline{c}}(x)$, 25

Quaternions
   $[\alpha, \mathbf{v}]$, 217
   $\mathbb{H}$, 217
   $\|q\|$, 218
   $\bar{q}$, 219
   q_θ, 220

Spectral methods
   $\chi_{\mathbf{A}}(\lambda)$, 392
   λ, 387
   λ_{pf}, 398
   $\mathbf{x}_{pf}$, 398
   SVD$(\mathbf{M})$, 436
   $\rho(\mathbf{A})$, 395
   $\sigma(\mathbf{A})$, 393
Statistics
   $Var(X)$, 290
   $\mathbf{E}[X]$, 281
   $\mathcal{N}(\mu, \sigma^2)$, 298

Ω, 275
$\mathbf{P}[X(\omega) \leq x]$, 279
$\mathbf{P}[X]$, 276
$\mathbf{P}[Y|X]$, 286
s_N, 295
s_N^{B}, 295
μ_k, 303
σ, 291
τ_1, 313
τ_2, 313
$b(N, > k)$, 289
$b(N, k)$, 288
df_w, 313
m_k, 303
s_1^2, 313
s_2^2, 313
$t(\mathrm{D.F.}, C)$, 309
t_w, 313
t_{N-1}, 309
D.F., 309
N.H., 306

Vectors
   $< x_1, x_2, \ldots, x_n >$, 59
   E_n, 63
   $\mathbb{T}^k$, 62
   dim, 80
   $\|\mathbf{x}\|$, 66
   $\|\mathbf{x}\|_2$, 68
   $\mathbf{0}$, 62
   $\mathbf{e}_k$, 63
   $\mathbf{x}$, 59
   $\mathbf{x} < \mathbf{y}$, 62
   $\mathbf{x} = \mathbf{y}$, 62
   $\mathbf{x} > \mathbf{y}$, 62
   $\mathbf{x} \cdot \mathbf{y}$, 69
   $\mathbf{x} \times \mathbf{y}$, 72

Main Index

$1/f$-music, 252, 257, 260
1-tail test, 309, 313
2-tail test, 309, 310, 313

abacus, 272
algebraic number, 29
algorithmic composition, 246, 249
Altavista, 417
animation effect, 58, 83
anthropometry, 247
anti-derivative, 179, 181
apostrophus, 11
approximation model, 334
    exponential function, 336, 348
    linear function, 336
    linear rational function, 336, 349
    logarithmic function, 336, 348
    polynomial function, 336
    real power function, 336
    residual, 334
Archie, 417
Argand diagram, 207
argumentation, 442
argumentation framework, 444
Ask, 417
Ask Jeeves, 417
average-case, 222

backlink, 421
Bessel's correction, 295, 313, 360

best fit, 334
Bing, 417
binomial (factor), 33

Calculating Clock, 272
cancellation law, 72
central moment, 303
complex number, 198
    addition, 199
    Argand representation, 202
    complex conjugate, 198
    complex division, 200
    complex multiplication, 199, 206
    Complex plane, 202
    complex powers, 208
    exponent (Euler) form, 205
    Imaginary part, 198
    logarithm, 214
    matrix representation, 202
    modulus, 198
    phase, 204
    polar coordinate, 203
    principal value, 210
    Real part, 198
    scalar multiplication, 199
computer art, 247
computer graphics, 216
conditional probability, 286
confidence interval, 306
confidence level, 306

coordinate axes
    Left-handed, 73
    Right-handed, 73
correlation
    correlation coefficient, 355
    determination coefficient, 360
    Pearson correlation coefficient,
        358
    Spearman rank correlation, 360,
        362
    strong negative, 356
    strong positive, 356
    uncorrelated, 356
    weak negative, 356
    weak positive, 356
critical point, 139, 167

dangling page, 429
De Moivre's Formula, 207
degrees of freedom, 309
dependent event, 286
derivative
    kth derivative, 140
    chain rule, 136
    composition rule, 136
    first, 134
    partial, 163, 338
    product rule, 136
    quotient rule, 136
    second derivative test, 139, 142,
        171
Distributive Property, 71

Euler angle, 219
Euler's formula, 206
extrapolation, 331

Fourier Transform
    and image compression, 231
    and integer multiplication, 233

convolution, 230
    discrete, 224
    inverse, 228
    linearity, 228
fractal dimension, 247
fractal set, 247
fractional part, 19
function
    linear, 123
    logarithm, 123
    periodic, 123
    polynomial, 123
    trigonometric, 123

Gimbal lock, 219
Google, 417
    page rank algorithm, 425
    page score, 424
gradient, 124
graphical effect
    3-d rotation, 108
    X-shear, 103
    Y-shear, 103
    Move-Scale-Rotate model, 104
    reflection, 99, 102
    rotation, 102, 105
    scale, 101
    translation, 101

Halley's method, 155
Hamiltonian Cycle, 372
homogeneous coordinate, 98

IBM, 418
Imaginary number, 195
independent event, 286
integer part, 19
integral
    definite, 179
    indefinite, 179

Integral calculus, 174
interpolation, 331
    polynomial, 350
    trigonometric, 352
iterative method, 154

Jughead, 417
Julia-Fatou set, 249

Lagrange interpolation, 350
Laguerre's method, 156, 214
Law of Large Numbers, 282
least squares method, 335
line function, 125
line touching, 126
link spamming, 427
Lycos, 417

Mandelbrot set, 249
Markov's inequality, 303
matrix, 84
    addition, 85
    adjoint, 379
    characteristic polynomial, 392
    column, 84
    determinant, 89, 375, 381
    diagonal matrix, 84
    elementary row operation, 384
    Hessian, 169
    identity, 89, 375
    inverse, 89, 375
    irreducible, 399
    lower triangular, 380
    non-singular, 383
    of a linear transformation, 95
    order, 84
    product of matrices, 86
    rank, 383
    row, 84
    scalar multiplication, 85

similarity, 386
singular, 383
square, 84
symmetric, 84
transpose, 86
triangular, 380
upper triangular, 380
Method of exhaustion, 175
Microsoft, 417
moment, 304
    first moment method, 306
    second moment, 306

Null hypothesis, 306

optimization problem, 166
    multivariable, 161

Pascaline, 272
polynomial
    addition, 30
    awkward, 194
    cubic, 44
    discriminant, 44
    division, 33
    factorization, 37
    irreducible, 37
    multivariate, 45
      degree, 46
      zeros, 46
    primitive, 39
    product of polynomials, 30
    quadratic, 43
    quartic, 45
    quotient, 33
    Rational root test, 41
    remainder, 33
    root, 27
      multiplicity, 28
    root finding, 37

scalar multiplication, 30
primitive root, 211, 224
    n'th root of unity, 212
principal root of unity, 224
Probability distribution
    biased, 276
    binomial, 287, 299, 323
    geometric, 300, 322
    Normal, 298
    Poisson, 301, 324, 327
    unbiased, 276
    uniform, 278
probability distribution function, 279

quaternion, 216
    addition, 219
    conjugate, 219
    product, 219
    reciprocal, 219
    scalar multiplication, 219
    unit quaternion, 218
q-test, 292
Quicksort, 320

radian, 204
random variable, 279
    discrete, 280
    expected value, 281
    graph model, 304
    median, 283
    mode, 283
    Poisson, 301
    standard deviation, 291
    variance, 290
regression
    geometric, 344, 346
    linear, 339, 346
    quadratic, 353
RGB encoding, 59
Right-hand rule, 73

Roman Numeral, 9, 11, 51, 463

Sample standard deviation, 295
sampling, 294
scatter plot, 332, 355
significance level, 306
signmum, 382
slide rule, 272
soroban, 272
spectral analysis, 387
    deflation, 409
    dominant eigenvector, 398
    eigenspace, 397
    eigenvalue, 392
        dominant, 395
    eigenvector, 392
        left, 397
        right, 397
    inverse power method, 407
    irreducible matrix, 399
    orthogonal basis, 396
    power method, 403
    Rayleigh quotient, 406
    representative eigenvector, 398
    spectral radius, 395
    stochastic matrix, 401
Student's t-distribution, 309

t-value, 297, 310
tied ranks, 362
Total ordering, 62
transcendental number, 29
transformation
    affine, 97, 98
    linear, 92, 220
    perspective, 99
    projection, 99
Travelling salesperson, 216
turning point, 139
Type I error, 307

Type II error, 307

vector
    addition, 63, 85
    cross product, 72, 74, 218
    directed area product, 74
    direction, 60
    dot product, 69, 74
    length, 65
    linear combination, 79
    linear dependence, 80
    linear independence, 80
    normalization, 68
    orthogonal, 71
    scalar multiplication, 63
    scalar triple product, 75
    size, 60
    standard basis, 62, 82
    standard position, 64
    vector space, 77
    vector space basis, 78
    vector space dimension, 78
vinculum, 11

web graph, 420
Welch's test, 312, 328

Yahoo, 417
YC_bC_r encoding, 232

Zipf's Law, 366

Index of Names

Abbado, C., 472
Abel, N., 45, 214
Abelard, P., xxi
Agarwal, R. P., 55
Aho, A. V., 111, 221
Ajtai, M., 320, 468
Aksyonov, V., 255
al-Khowarizmi, 12
Aldiss, B., 258
Allen, L. J. S., 2
Alusi, S., xxvii
Amgoud, L., 450
Amiot, E., 246
Angluin, D., 372
Archimedes, 118, 175
Argand, J.-R., 202
Aristophanes, 443
Aristotle, 443
Atkinson, K., xxv
Atkinson, M. D., 277, 371
Avery, O., 269
Ayoub, R. G., 45

Babbage, C., 186, 267
Bailey, D. H., 11, 12, 49
Baroni, P., 442, 446, 452
Barron, D. W., 111
Batty, M., 248
Beckmann, P., 55
Begg, C. E., 112

Ben-Naim, J., 450
Bench-Capon, T. J. M., 442, 446, 450
Berger, B., 306
Berio, L., 247
Besnard, P., 442
Bessel, F., 295
Beyerchen, A. D., 259
Birch, B., xxvi
Birtall, J., xxvi
Black, F., 299
Bonzon, E., 450
Bortkiewicz, L., 301
Borwein, J. M., 11, 12, 49
Boulez, P., 247
Brent, R. P., 189
Brin, S., 432
Brodie, J., 70
Bronowski, J., 54
Bronzino, A., 186
Brooks, F., 49
Brouwer, A. E., 393, 397
Bruckner, A., 8
Bruno, G., 259
Bryan, K., 434
Bryn-Julson, P., 472
Buades, A., 233
Budzynska, K., 447
Bulirsch, R., 153, 352

Bundy, A., 111
Butterworth, J., 434

Cabeen, K., 233
Cage, J., 246
Cajori, F., 33
Cardano, G., 44, 45, 54
Cardono, G., 194
Catro, F., 114
Cavaretta, A. S., 193
Chadwick, L., xxvi
Chandler, R., 271
Chang, H., 434
Chassequet-Smirgel, J., 259
Chebyshev, P., 303
Chrisomalis, S., 49
Clarke, J., 248
Clausen, T., 214
Clift, M., 448
Cobbett, W., 221
Coffinhal, J.-B., 259, 419
Cohn, D., 434
Coll, B., 233
Collingwood, P., 327
Connolly, T. M., 112
Cook, S. A., 372
Cooley, J. W., 225, 241, 255, 466
Copernicus, N., 44, 54, 55
Cormen, T. H., 221
Corregio, A., 186
Cushing, J. M., 2

Danisman, Y., 413
Dauben, J., 49
Dedalus, S., 457
Dedekind, R., 190
Dehaene, S., 49
Depman, I., 54
Descartes, R., 58, 195
Deutsch, D., 189

Devroye, L., 278, 364
Dewey, T., 267
Dirac, P., 2
Disraeli, B., 267, 453
Dixon, J. C., 55
Doutre, S., 450
Dulles, A., 446
Dung, P. M., 444, 450
Dures, K., xxvi
Duveen, D. I., 259

Eastwood, C., 278
Eftekhari, A., 367
Einstein, A., 2, 114
Eisenstein, G., 42
Erdös, P., 371
Estrada, E., xxv, 2
Eudoxus of Cnidus, 118, 175
Euler, L., 205

Fatou, P., 249
Fearnely, J., xxvi
Feller, W., 264
Ferrari, L., 45, 54, 55
Feynman, R., 206
Fias, W., 49
Fibonacci, 11
Fields, W. C., 114
Fill, J. A., 320
Flajolet, P., 223, 224
Flanders, N., 114
Fleming, V., 260
Floyd, J., 260
Foley, J. D., 99
Freeman, J. W., 303
Friedman, J., 393
Frobenius, G., 398, 399

Gödel, K., 260
Gabbay, D., 447

Gagne, G., 111
Galilei, G., 54, 55
Gallup, G., 267, 278
Galsworthy, J., 373
Galton, R., 57
Galvin, P. B., 111
Garcia-Molina, H., 434
Gardener, M., 252
Gardner, M., 249, 256
Gareeboo, F., 463
Garey, M. R., 372
Gauss, C. F., 216
Gautschi, W., 350
Gent, P., 233
Gerbert of Aurillac, 49
Gerhard, J., 460
Gershgorin, S., 402
Gibbons, A. M., 461
Gide, A., xxvi
Ginsburg, J., 49
Goldstein, J. A., 2
Golub, G. H., 402
Goodare, J., 49
Gordan, P., 29
Gosset, W. S., 309
Grasso, F., xxvi, xxvii
Gries, D., 111
Grossman, V., 2, 271
Guillaume, J., 259
Gyöngi, Z., 434

Haemers, W. H., 393, 397
Haldane, J. B. S., 268
Halley, E., 153, 155
Halsey, T., 111
Hamilton, W. R., 216, 218
Hammarström, H., 49
Hancock, A., 57
Hansard, T. C., 221

Hansen, E., 153, 155, 156
Harding, J., xxvi
Hartley, L. P., 112
Havlin, S., 248
Heisenberg, W., 2, 260
Henry, O., 446
Herodotus, 11
Heseltine, M., 448
Hilbert, D., 2
Hippasus of Metapontum, 22, 258
Hoare, C. A. R., 320
Hollerith, H., 221
Hopcroft, J. E., 111, 221
Horner, W. G., 33
Huff, D., 314
Hunter, A., xxvi, 442

Ifrah, G., 12, 49
Isaacson, E., 352, 407

Jüttler, B., 217
Jackson, D., xxvi
Jacobi, C. G. J., 414
Jacobs, R. I., 55
James VI/I, 52
James, S., 57
Janson, S., 320
Jarvis, S., xxvii
Jenkins, M. A., 153
Johnson, D. S., 372
Joyce, J., 457, 459
Julia, G., 249

Kadosh, R. C., 49
Kalman, D., 435
Kaltofen, E., 39
Kamat, S. S., 269
Karatsuba, A., 236, 255, 461, 466
Karpechenko, G., 259
Keener, J. P., 434

Keller, H. B., 352, 407
Kendall, M. G., 364
Kermit (the Frog), 114
Khachiyan, L. G., 468
Klein, Y., 247
Kleinberg, J. M., 434
Kline, M., 258
Knuth, D., 221
Komlós, J., 320, 468
Konev, B., xxv, xxvii
Kramer, S., 448
Kroenke, D., 112
Kronecker, L., 39
Kuipers, J. B., 220
Kulkarni, H. V., 312, 328

Lagrange, J., 186
Laguerre, E., 153, 155, 156
Landon, A., 267, 278
Larrabee, T., 303
Lavoisier, A., 259, 419
Leibniz, G., 137, 186, 272
Leise, T., 434
Leiserson, C. E., 221
Leng, P. H., 278
Lengnink, K., 49
Lenstra, A. K., 42
Lenstra, H. W., 42
Levin, L., 372
Levitsky, G., 259
Levy, M., 2
Liddle, R., 454
Ligeti, G., 247
Lindemann, F., 29
Lister, A. M., 111
Losa, G. A., 248
Lovász, L., 42
Luther, M., 454, 460
Lysenko, T., 259

MacLeod, C., 269
Magritte, R., xxi, xxv
Mamoulian, R., 260
Mandelbrot, B., 247
Markov, A. A., 303
Marshall, A. C., 273
Martin, R., xxvi
Maxwell, J. C., 2
McCarthy, J., 463
McCarty, M., 269
Mees, A. I., 435
Michelson, A., 268, 269
Milgram, S., 269
Miller, M. C., 443
Miller, S., 268, 269
Minsky, M., 111
Moamina, D., xxvii
Mohar, B., 393
Montaigne, M. de, 12
Morel, J.-M., 233
Morley, E., 268, 269
Motwani, R., 111
Mount, F., 454
Mozart, W. A., 246
Mueller, S. H., 283
Myhill, J., 190

Napier, J., 52
Newman, M., 371
Newton, I., 2, 155, 186
Nonnenmacher, T. F., 248
Norvig, P., 111

O'Brien, F., 7, 8
O'Connor, W., 55
Olivier, L., 448
Oparin, A., 268
Oró, J., 269
Ostrowsky, N., 248

Pólya, G., 2
Packard, V., 443
Page, L., 432
Paine, T., 366
Pappenheim, M., 457
Pascal, B, 272
Patil, V. V., 312, 328
Patrick, M., 153, 155, 156
Paul III, 54
Payne, T., xxvi
Pearson, K., 358
Pedersen, J., 434
Perelman, C., 443
Perron, O., 398
Petford, A. D., 303
Petit-Bois, G., 138, 181
Piantadosi, S. T., 366
Pietkiewicz, W., xxvii
Pitiscus, B., 52
Pletinckx, D., 217, 220
Pollock, J., 246
Powell, A., 263
Prakken, H., 447
Priesley, H., 193
Proust, M., xxvi
Putnam, H., 260
Pythagoras, 22, 54, 66, 258

Rényi, A., 371
Rahwan, I., 442
Rana, O., xxvi
Read, R. C., 2
Reed, C., 447
Remmert, V. R., 259
Respighi, O., 246
Richman, F., 190
Robson, J. M., 278, 364
Rodrigues, B. O., 216
Rolle, J., 190

Roosevelt, F. D., 267, 278, 315
Rosen, C., 471
Rufai, A. M., 435
Ruffini, P., 33, 45
Runyon, D., 446
Russell, B., 188, 197
Russell, S. J., 111
Rytter, W., 461

Sachs, H., 191
Sack, J-R., 277
Sack, J.-R., 371
Sakama, C., 447
Salaun, P., xxvi
Salovin, A., 283
Sassa, K., 221
Satherley, J., xxvi
Schönberg, A., 457, 471
Schönemann, T., 42
Schönhage, A., 237, 255, 461, 466
Schell, M., 448
Schickard, W., 272
Schillinger, J., 248
Schlesinger, J., 448
Schlim, D., 49
Schmidt, F., 8
Scholes, M., 299
Schrödinger, E., 2
Schubert, F. T., 39
Sedgewick, R., 223
Seng, K.-Y., 138, 146, 150
Shannon, C. E., 470
Sheffield, L., xxvi
Shield, D., xxvii
Shoemake, K., 217
Shor, P., 189
Shriver, L., 446
Silberschatz, A., 111
Simari, G., 442

Simpson, A., 57
Simpson, B., 114
Smith, D. E., 49
Smith, P., 186
Smith, R. C., 186
Sofyer, V. N., 259
Soseki, N., 1
Spark, M., 70
Spearman, C., 361
Spirakis, P., xxvii
Spivak, M., 188, 190
Stalin, J., 54, 255, 259
Stanley, H. E., 248
Steinbeck, J., 258
Steiner, J., 214
Stevenson, R. L., 260
Stevinus, S., 52
Stirling, J., 288
Stockhausen, K., 8, 246
Stoer, J., 153, 352
Strang, G., 233, 435
Strassen, V., 237, 255, 461, 466
Stravinsky, I., 472
Stuart, M., 286
Sukumaran, S., 248
Suominen, E. A., 55
Sylvester II, 49
Szemerédi, E., 320, 468

Tal, E., 49
Tamma, V., xxvi
Thiyagarajan, D., 248
Thurber, J., 446
Tilman, D., 2
Titian, 186
Tokio, M. D., 221
Torquemada, T., 54, 55
Toulmin, S., 443
Traub, J. F., 153

Truman, H., 267
Tukey, J. W., 225, 241, 255, 466
Turing, A., 187, 260

Ullman, J. D., 111, 112, 221
Urey, H., 268

Valiant, L. G., 372
Valmes, P., 54, 258, 419
van Dam, A., 99
van den Heuvel, J., 393
van der Vorst, H. A., 402
Varese, E., 246
Vavilov, N., 259
Veevers, A., 273
Verguts, T., 49
Villa-Lobos, H., 246
Vince, J., 220
Virgil, P. M., 471
Vitter, J. S., 224
von Fritz, K., 22
von Zur Gathen, J., 460
Voss, R. F., 248, 252, 256
Vreeswijk, G., 447

Wagner, R. W., 191, 256
Walker, E., 248, 251, 466
Wall, M. E., 435
Walsh, V., 49
Walton, H., xxvii
Waltz, J., 463
Wang, Y. Y., 314
Warne, S., 327
Weiber, E. R., 248
Welch, B., 312
Wellesley, A., 267
Welsh, D. J. A., 303
Wessel, C., 202
Wilkes, M., 189
Wittgenstein, L., 260

Wolter, F., xxvi
Woods, J., 447
Wooldridge, M. J., 462
Wynn, K., 49

Xenakis, Y., 247

Yeats, W. B., 117

Zeno of Elea, 258
Zimbardo, P., 269
Zipf, G., 366
Zito, M., 306

9 781848 903104

Printed in March 2021
by Rotomail Italia S.p.A., Vignate (MI) - Italy